Sustainability, Circular Economy, and Transformation in Organizations

Mehtap Özşahin
Gebze Technical University, Turkey

Vladimir Simovic
Institute of Economic Sciences, Serbia & Australian University, Kuwait

Alper Ertürk
Australian University, Kuwait

IGI Global
Scientific Publishing
Publishing Tomorrow's Research Today

Vice President of Editorial	Melissa Wagner
Managing Editor of Acquisitions	Mikaela Felty
Managing Editor of Book Development	Jocelynn Hessler
Production Manager	Mike Brehm
Cover Design	Phillip Shickler

Published in the United States of America by
IGI Global Scientific Publishing
701 East Chocolate Avenue
Hershey, PA, 17033, USA
Tel: 717-533-8845
Fax: 717-533-8661
Website: https://www.igi-global.com E-mail: cust@igi-global.com

Library of Congress Cataloging-in-Publication Data

Names: Özsahin, Mehtap, 1978- editor. | Simović, Vladimir M., editor. | Ertürk, Alper, 1973- editor.
Title: Sustainability, circular economy, and transformation in organizations / [edited by] Mehtap Özsahin, Vladimir Simovic, Alper Ertürk.
Description: Hershey, PA : IGI Global Scientific Publishing, [2025] |
Includes bibliographical references and index. | Summary: "This book explores the concepts of digitalization, sustainability, resilience and human orientation from the business perspective in the Industry 5.0 era.
Ultimately, the book offers a comprehensive guide for business leaders, entrepreneurs, and policymakers seeking to explore the latest trends, academic insights, and business perspectives related to industry 5.0 and digitalization to be able to establish and maintain sustainable, human-centric, and resilient organizations that can thrive in the future"-- Provided by publisher.
Identifiers: LCCN 2025003751 (print) | LCCN 2025003752 (ebook) | ISBN 9798337325231 (hardcover) | ISBN 9798337325248 (paperback) | ISBN 9798337325255 (ebook)
Subjects: LCSH: Technological innovations--Management. | Sustainability. | Circular economy. | Artificial intelligence. | Organizational change.
Classification: LCC HD45 .S895 2025 (print) | LCC HD45 (ebook) | DDC 658.5/14--dc23/eng/20250331
LC record available at https://lccn.loc.gov/2025003751
LC ebook record available at https://lccn.loc.gov/2025003752

British Cataloguing in Publication Data
A Cataloguing in Publication record for this book is available from the British Library.

Table of Contents

Detailed Table of Contents

This paper emphasizes the challenges that green transformation triggers in the labor market about the necessity to distribute fairly benefits and costs among vulnerable and responsible, and to restore the harms generated with specific reference to the concept of Fair Transition having three main dimensions namely distributive justice, procedural justice, and restorative justice. It prioritizes human well-being and employability amid sanctions and challenges of green transformation. Twin transformation - digital one added to the green one, might cause the loss of some basic skills and decline of some traditional occupations, or diminishing the need or value for certain traditional skills. Therefore, we highlight the importance of continuously equipping current workers with necessary skills for a sustainable economy. We also provide a set of twin (green and digital) skills employees need to cope with these transformations.

This study examines the integration of artificial intelligence (AI) into organizational structures, focusing on the challenges and opportunities AI presents for modern businesses. AI technologies such as machine learning, natural language processing, and generative AI are being increasingly utilized to enhance decision-making processes, optimize workflows, and improve human-machine collaboration. The research explores AI's potential to revolutionize industry operations, while addressing employees' concerns and resistance to AI adoption. By analyzing organizational readiness for AI implementation, the study identifies key strategies for overcoming barriers and enhancing employee engagement. The findings suggest that a well-prepared organizational culture, alongside proper leadership and training, is essential for successful AI integration. Furthermore, this research contributes to the

This study ranks and discusses the 7 dimensions of the circular economy in the context of Industry 5.0 proposed by Payer et al. (2024): Energy Circularity, Circularity of Inputs, Investments in circularity, Establishment of new circular businesses, Circular and non-circular supply chain integration, Circularity of product components, and Compliance and governance for circularity. The Hierarchical ordering (ranking) between these dimensions is done using the Analytic Hierarchy Process (AHP) method based on the opinion of 7 experts consulted (one expert for each dimension). These experts also discussed the main issues in evidence within these 7 dimensions. Organizations that aim to move towards the circular economy in the context of Industry 5.0 often need to prioritize efforts and start by treating some aspects, so this ranking can be a proposal of which dimensions can be prioritized in this scenario

This paper evaluates Turkish manufacturing managers' perceptions regarding the impact of Industry 4.0 and the circular economy on seeking excellence in operational processes. A research framework was proposed to assess executives' attitudes towards these approaches to supply chain sustainability and corporate performance. Data collection was conducted through an online questionnaire, with 126 valid responses subjected to statistical analysis. The findings suggest that participants are not fully prepared for autonomous digital transformation and exhibit reluctance to invest in radical digital technology changes. Transformation projects such as cyber-physical systems seem potentially disruptive to existing operations as they observe a negative correlation with other factors. The research presents a model for evaluating Industry 4.0 and circular economy performance expectations to guide digital transformation in manufacturing for competitiveness. Limitations of the study include a small sample size and a focus on Turkish manufacturers, which may restrict its broad applicability.

policymakers and business leaders on addressing unemployment's multifaceted nature and fostering sustainable development.

Preface

The emergence of Industry 5.0 represents a transformative phase in organizational strategy, one that transcends traditional paradigms and places sustainability, digitalization, circular economy, and resilience at the heart of innovation. In this book, *Sustainability, Circular Economy, and Transformation in Organizations*, we explore these interconnected concepts from a business perspective, highlighting their importance in navigating the complexities of the Industry 5.0 era.

This book builds upon the foundational discussions presented at the 19th International Strategic Management Conference, which was themed "Planning for Industry 5.0: Human-Centric, Sustainable, and Resilient Organizations." In addition to selected papers from the conference, we have invited contributions from scholars and practitioners worldwide to provide a broader spectrum of insights. The resulting collection examines the theoretical underpinnings and practical implications of Industry 5.0 across diverse organizational settings, ranging from non-profits and government institutions to industries such as education, healthcare, aviation, tourism, and logistics.

Unlike its predecessor, Industry 4.0, which primarily emphasizes productivity-driven economic growth through automation and connectivity, Industry 5.0 advocates for a forward-looking agenda that prioritizes environmental sustainability, human values, and economic circularity. Industry 5.0 leverages the technological advancements of Industry 4.0 while expanding its scope to include long-term resilience and social responsibility. This evolution represents a fundamental shift in how organizations operate, innovate, and contribute to society.

The chapters in this book provide a comprehensive overview of Industry 5.0 and its implications for businesses and policymakers. They delve into strategies for fostering sustainability, circular economy and digital transformation in organizations. From theoretical frameworks to case studies and empirical research, this book offers actionable insights that aim to equip leaders, researchers, and decision-makers with the knowledge and tools necessary to thrive in the Industry 5.0 landscape.

As editors, our objective is to present a holistic understanding of Industry 5.0's transformative potential while encouraging further exploration and dialogue within the academic and professional communities. The insights offered here are particularly relevant to stakeholders in the Middle East, Europe, and Asia, where the interplay between digitalization and sustainable development is shaping new economic realities.

We hope this book serves as a valuable resource for academics, students, practitioners, and policymakers, inspiring innovation and guiding strategic decision-making in the digital age. By embracing the principles of Industry 5.0, we can build organizations that not only excel in competitive markets but also contribute meaningfully to the preservation of our environment and the betterment of society.

We express our gratitude to the contributors whose work forms the backbone of this publication, and to the institutions and individuals who supported this project. Together, let us envision and create a future where digital transformation harmonizes with sustainability and human well-being.

ORGANIZATION OF THE BOOK

Chapter 1: Fair Transition on the Eve of Green Transformation

In this chapter, the authors address the multifaceted challenges posed by green transformation in the labor market, emphasizing the critical need for a fair distribution of benefits and costs. Framed within the dimensions of distributive, procedural, and restorative justice, the discussion underscores the importance of prioritizing human well-being and employability amidst the dual pressures of green and digital transitions. With the potential loss of traditional skills and occupations, the chapter highlights the urgency of equipping workers with "twin" skills—those required for both green and digital economies—to ensure a sustainable future. This chapter provides actionable insights into fostering equity and resilience during this transformative period.

Chapter 2: Empowering Organizations with AI: Strategies, Challenges, and Future Directions

This chapter delves into the integration of artificial intelligence (AI) within organizational structures, exploring its transformative potential in decision-making, workflow optimization, and human-machine collaboration. The authors discuss the challenges and resistance faced by businesses during AI adoption and highlight strategies for overcoming these barriers, such as fostering organizational readiness, providing leadership, and enhancing employee engagement through targeted training. By examining AI's broader impact on organizational culture and structures, the chapter offers a roadmap for businesses to navigate the complexities of AI-driven transformations while addressing future research directions in this evolving domain.

Chapter 3: Exploring Digital Transformation in Turkiye: Barriers, Drivers, and Competencies

Focusing on the digital transformation journey in Turkiye, this chapter presents insights from interviews with 28 managers across diverse industries. It identifies leadership as the primary driver of digitalization and employee competence as the main barrier. The chapter connects digital transformation with key concepts such as productivity, innovation, and convenience, revealing that while managers recognize its significance, a lack of readiness among employees hinders progress. By shedding light on the managerial perspectives, this chapter contributes to understanding how organizations in Turkiye can foster the competencies needed to thrive in the digital age.

Chapter 4: Qualitative Outcomes of Digital Transformation for the Tourism Sector

This chapter examines the profound impact of digital transformation on the tourism industry, focusing on its role in reshaping organizational strategies, customer engagement, and marketing practices. Through qualitative analysis and expert interviews, the authors reveal how digitalization provides a competitive advantage by fostering systematic integration networks. Using advanced tools like Maxqda 21, the chapter identifies key features and best practices for leveraging digital transformation to meet evolving consumer expectations, offering critical insights for stakeholders in the tourism sector.

Chapter 5: ESG Performance and Financial Performance Relationship During the Covid-19 Pandemic: Evidence from Indonesia

Set against the backdrop of the Indonesian stock market, this chapter investigates the interplay between ESG (Environmental, Social, and Governance) performance and financial performance (FP) during the Covid-19 pandemic. Using panel data from 55 firms between 2018 and 2022, the research reveals that while environmental and social performance maintained a steady relationship with FP, corporate governance performance experienced significant negative impacts. The findings contribute to the understanding of ESG-FP dynamics during crises, offering empirical evidence and practical insights for investors and policymakers navigating the post-pandemic economic landscape.

Chapter 6: The Impact of Circular Ecological Transition Factors in the Industry 5.0 Era: Evidence from Furniture Sector Enterprises in Spain

Exploring the integration of circular economy principles within Industry 5.0, this chapter focuses on the Spanish furniture sector. Combining interviews and secondary data analysis, the research highlights the synergistic impact of circular policies and digital transformation on sustainability and innovation. Despite challenges like high costs and regulatory fragmentation, the findings emphasize the role of government policies and industry collaboration in fostering resilience. The chapter provides actionable recommendations for enhancing sustainable practices, addressing the specific needs of SMEs, and leveraging Industry 5.0's human-centric ethos.

Chapter 7: Dimensions to be Considered by an Organization That Wants to Achieve the Circular Economy in the Context of Industry 5.0

This chapter ranks seven dimensions of the circular economy within Industry 5.0—ranging from energy circularity to compliance and governance—using the Analytic Hierarchy Process (AHP). Drawing on expert consultations, the authors outline the critical issues and priorities for organizations aiming to transition to circular economy models. By offering a structured hierarchy, the chapter provides a practical framework for businesses to focus their efforts, ensuring an effective and sustainable integration of circular economy principles in an Industry 5.0 context.

Chapter 8: Evaluating Turkish Manufacturers' Perspectives on Industry 4.0, Circular Economy, and Corporate Performance

This chapter presents insights from Turkish manufacturers on the adoption of Industry 4.0 and circular economy principles. Based on survey data from 126 managers, the findings reveal a lack of preparedness for digital transformation and a reluctance to invest in disruptive technologies. The authors discuss the challenges of balancing innovation with operational continuity, proposing a framework for evaluating performance expectations in this domain. The chapter serves as a valuable guide for manufacturers navigating the complexities of digital transformation to enhance competitiveness and sustainability.

Chapter 9: The Impact of Store Deals on Consumer Satisfaction: The Mediating Role of Value Consciousness

This chapter explores the relationship between store deals, value consciousness, and consumer satisfaction using survey data from 500 Turkish grocery store consumers. The analysis reveals that store deals significantly enhance value consciousness, which in turn mediates consumer satisfaction. By highlighting the strategic importance of value-driven marketing, the chapter offers actionable recommendations for retailers to design effective store deals that foster long-term consumer loyalty.

Chapter 10: Investigation of Social Innovativeness and Product Involvement of Environmental Consumers

This chapter examines the demographic factors influencing environmentally conscious consumer behavior and their interest in socially innovative, eco-friendly products. Using ANOVA analysis, the study identifies significant differences in behavior based on demographic characteristics, providing insights into how social innovation and product involvement shape purchasing decisions. The chapter offers valuable guidance for businesses developing environmentally friendly products aimed at addressing societal challenges.

Chapter 11: Managing Risk in Real Estate Lending

This chapter investigates the risks associated with real estate lending in Bulgaria, emphasizing the role of credit risk management amid fluctuating property prices and borrower creditworthiness. Drawing on data from 2016 to 2024, the findings highlight the vulnerabilities of commercial banks to non-performing loans. The authors propose modern management tools to mitigate these risks, ensuring the financial health of banking institutions in dynamic real estate markets.

Chapter 12: Intellectual Structure of Unemployment Studies: A Bibliometric Analysis

Through a bibliometric analysis of 2,504 papers, this chapter explores the determinants of unemployment, with a particular focus on the overlooked impact of technological advancements such as automation. While acknowledging the role of macroeconomic factors and labor market institutions, the authors highlight the disruptive influence of emerging technologies on employment. This chapter serves as a critical resource for policymakers and researchers aiming to address unemployment in an era of rapid technological change.

CONCLUSION

As editors of this volume, we have strived to assemble a diverse array of scholarly contributions that delve into the intersections of sustainability, innovation, digital transformation, and socio-economic challenges in a rapidly evolving global landscape. The chapters presented in this book illuminate the multifaceted dimensions of pressing contemporary issues, ranging from the just transition amid green transformations to the integration of circular economy principles within Industry 5.0, and the critical role of artificial intelligence in organizational and societal shifts. By addressing these topics through both theoretical and empirical lenses, the authors have provided invaluable insights and actionable strategies for academics, policymakers, and industry practitioners.

It is our belief that the knowledge curated within these pages will not only spark meaningful dialogue but also inspire practical solutions to complex global challenges. By emphasizing the interconnectedness of economic, environmental, and social systems, this book underscores the urgent need for collaboration, innovation, and inclusivity as we navigate an era of unprecedented change. We hope this volume serves as both a source of knowledge and a call to action, encouraging readers to reimagine possibilities, foster sustainable practices, and champion equitable growth in all sectors of society.

This edited collection stands as a testament to the importance of interdisciplinary research and collective effort in addressing the challenges of our time. We extend our gratitude to the contributors for their rigor and dedication, and to our readers for engaging with these critical discussions. Together, we can move towards a future that harmonizes technological advancement with sustainability and equity for all.

Chapter 1
Fair Transition on the Eve of Green Transformation

Lutfihak Alpkan
https://orcid.org/0000-0002-7925-7102
Ministry of Labor and Social Security, Turkey

Nazmi Doğan
Türkiye's Ministry of Labor and Social Security, Turkey

ABSTRACT

This paper emphasizes the challenges that green transformation triggers in the labor market about the necessity to distribute fairly benefits and costs among vulnerable and responsible, and to restore the harms generated with specific reference to the concept of Fair Transition having three main dimensions namely distributive justice, procedural justice, and restorative justice. It prioritizes human well-being and employability amid sanctions and challenges of green transformation. Twin transformation - digital one added to the green one, might cause the loss of some basic skills and decline of some traditional occupations, or diminishing the need or value for certain traditional skills. Therefore, we highlight the importance of continuously equipping current workers with necessary skills for a sustainable economy. We also provide a set of twin (green and digital) skills employees need to cope with these transformations.

INTRODUCTION

A global rush for green transformation has become very popular among decision makers, practitioners, researchers, and the general public opinion with ever-increasing awareness on the climate crisis. Environmental harms caused by excessive

DOI: 10.4018/979-8-3373-2523-1.ch001

production with huge carbon emissions, unsustainable consumption habits with enormous wastefulness, and great reliance on fossil fuels to make transportation, produce energy, and manufacture products force nations and international organizations to opt for clean energy alternatives and eco-friendly practices in manufacturing, delivery, and consumption. However, most workers in those industries that depend heavily on traditional carbon-intensive sectors have just faced the emergent risk of becoming obsolete and/or unemployed in the era of green transformation, even though these workers' individual marginal responsibility for climate change is almost zero. At this point, the concept of **fair transition** as an attempt to keep employment safe and secure without leaving anybody behind during this long and challenging journey of green transformation has also become an interesting area of research and policy-making.

This study explores how to balance the environmental goals of green transformation with the imperative of global social justice in order to try to differentiate the rumors and myths from the root causes of the problem, to distribute fairly benefits and costs among vulnerable and responsible, and to restore the harms generated. In Section 1, we discuss the visible consequences of climate change, such as increasing temperatures, severe droughts, and the impact of industrial practices on our ecosystems. Section 1.1 delves into significant historical events that have shaped our awareness of environmental issues. Section 1.2 explores conflicting and/or confused perceptions of public opinion and media regarding climate news. By debunking myths related to population growth, we aim to provide a more nuanced understanding of the current situation. Then Section 1.3 analyzes the underlying causes of climate change, focusing on the role of greenhouse gas emissions from fossil fuels, manufacturing, deforestation, etc. In Section 1.4, we examine the harmful effects of greenhouse gases, detailing how emissions of carbon dioxide, methane, etc. are the primary drivers of climate change.

In Section 2, we argue for a fundamental shift in economic practices and societal values, promoting sustainable methods of growth and development. Section 2.1 introduces Society 5.0, a concept from Japan that emphasizes the integration of cyberspace and physical space to tackle societal challenges while advancing a more inclusive economy. Section 2.2 discusses the European Green Deal, a comprehensive climate action plan initiated by the European Union in 2019 that aims to transform Europe into the world's first climate-neutral continent. In Section 2.3, we explore the concept of Industry 5.0, as articulated by the European Commission's Directorate-General for Research and Innovation in 2021. In Section 2.4, we examine the challenges of green transformation, emphasizing that the attempts for a greener economy face several significant obstacles that must be overcome to ensure its success. In Section 2.5, we define green jobs as articulated by the International Labor Organization, highlighting their role in contributing to environmental sustainability.

Section 3 delves into the concept of **Fair Transition** that prioritizes human well-being and employability amid sanctions and challenges of green transformation. Section 3.1 describes the dimensions of transforming in a just way, i.e. distributive justice, procedural justice, and restorative justice. Section 3.2 mentions the digital transformation by addressing the loss of basic skills and occupational decline, highlighting how advancements in technology, particularly artificial intelligence are reshaping the job market and diminishing the need for certain skills. In Section 3.3, we emphasize the importance of transforming within each single organization by equipping current workers with necessary competencies for a sustainable economy.

1. CLIMATE CHANGE AND ENVIRONMENTAL CHALLENGES

Environmental problems affect all communities, societies, sectors, and companies simultaneously. Protecting the natural environment and offering a sustainable future to the next generations have become a common goal of humanity (Bekiroğlu, 2011). Climate change is becoming more and more apparent, especially as we see extreme weather events happening more frequently, such as hurricanes that cause massive destruction, wildfires that devastate forests and wildlife, and floods that inundate communities. Scientists have been sounding the alarm about the dangers of unchecked carbon emissions for many years. Today, it is clear that those warnings were not just idle threats; we are living through the consequences of inaction. Frequent news on natural disasters are fueling concerns about how we will sustain our food, resources, and life standards in the future. The current consumption patterns are unsustainable, pushing ecosystems to their limits, depleting natural resources, and threatening the stability of food supply systems. However, while some environmentally sensitive people fear a dystopian tomorrow where food shortages and environmental degradation will dominate, this bleak future is already a harsh reality for hundreds of millions of people already today -if not yesterday. Across many regions, especially in vulnerable parts of the world, hunger, poverty, and environmental collapse are immediate concerns, and the global response remains inadequate. These issues are not future predictions of separate catastrophic accidents; but they are present-day problems and crises that we often ignore. An inclusive and holistic approach that does not consider any superiority of a specific region or interest group over others is needed to assume ownership of global problems of fairness.

1.1. Awareness Building

Over the past three decades, several environmental disasters have shaken the world's consciousness. In the early 1980s, Africa began to face severe hunger and malnutrition, exacerbated by civil wars and droughts. During this period, approximately one million people lost their lives due to famine. In 1984, a pesticide factory leakage in Bhopal, India, caused the deaths of over 2,000 people and injured more than 200,000. Similarly, in the former USSR, the Chernobyl nuclear reactor exploded in 1986 that ended up with a radioactive wasteland in the surrounding areas and over 200,000 deaths in the long run due to cancer and other diseases (WCED, 1987). Environmental accidents have not been relegated only to the past. Several incidents have continued to highlight the ongoing dangers posed by industrial and environmental mismanagement. In 1999, a radioactive leak occurred at Japan's Tokaimura Nuclear Power Plant, raising fears of another large-scale nuclear disaster. One year later, in Romania, the collapse of a dam at a gold mine caused over 100,000 m^3 of cyanide water to spill into the Danube River, poisoning aquatic ecosystems and contaminating a vital water source. In recent years, the Deepwater Horizon explosion in 2010 caused the largest marine oil spill in history, with far-reaching effects on marine life and the economies of coastal communities. Similarly, in 2019, the collapse of an iron ore mine dam in Brazil released 60 million m^3 of toxic wastewater into villages and agricultural lands, once again showing how industrial activities can bring devastation to entire communities.

1.2. Facts and Figures

In the discourse around climate change and sustainability, several old-school myths and pretexts have taken root. Public opinion is shaped by many unrelated news and disinformation about what, why and how is changing. Especially policy makers have their own opinions and even their own theoretical lenses nourished by individual experiences, assumptions but also misevaluations that often oversimplify the complex problems of environmental degradation and propose misguided solutions. In fact, the true challenge lies not in population growth, but in wastefulness and unsustainable consumption patterns. In this section, we deal with common misconceptions, present facts and figures, and examine the negative impact of greenhouse gas emissions while exploring the available solutions.

One of the most prevalent myths is that the rapidly increasing world population is the primary cause of environmental problems. According to this view, reducing the global population would eliminate or drastically reduce the strain on natural resources. However, this assumption overlooks the complexities of population dynamics and resource distribution. In fact, population growth has slowed significantly over the past few decades while carbon emissions increased a lot. In the 1960s, the global total fertility rate—the average number of children born to each woman—was 5, but as of 2024, it has dropped to 2.4. In Türkiye, the fertility rate of early 1970s has fallen from 7 to 1.5 today (OECD, 2024). Moreover, the global population growth rate has declined from over 2% in the 1960s to just 0.87% in 2024 (Worldometers, 2024). Contrary to the myths surrounding population growth, the reality is that the world population is aging, and the rate of growth is slowing down. By 2050, the number of individuals aged 65 and older will be equal to the number of children under the age of 12 (UN, 2024). This demographic shift is expected to place new strains on economies and social systems, as aging populations require more healthcare and social support. Meanwhile population trends are not equal all over the world. Africa is projected to account for 38% of the world population, becoming the second most populous continent after Asia that is estimated to represent 45% of it towards the end of this century (Stanley, 2023). These figures highlight the need for sustainable development policies that address the unique challenges of different regions, rather than simply blaming world population growth for every problem.

Another common misconception is that livestock produce enormous amount of carbon dioxide, and also together with some wild animals consume the resources that humans need, leading to food and water shortages. Some proponents of this theory advocate for reducing or eliminating livestock to free up resources for human consumption. This myth fails to recognize that the food produced for livestock, such as feed crops, is often grown in areas unsuitable for direct human agriculture. Additionally, the share of all the agricultural activities in total greenhouse effect is less than 10% (see also Exhibit 1). In fact, the problem is not a shortage of food or carbon emission done by animals, but the wasteful practices surrounding food production and distribution and also water usage and irrigation. For example, approximately one billion tons of food—equivalent to one-fifth of all the food produced in the world—was wasted in 2022. This staggering amount of waste contributes to 10% of annual global greenhouse gas emissions, further exacerbating the climate crisis (UNEP, 2024). The issue is not that there is not enough food to feed the world, but rather that we are squandering the resources we already have. In this concern, some might also believe that the solution to environmental problems lies in feeding the global population with innovative synthetic materials and foods produced by multinational corporations, by arguing that synthetic foods can replace traditional agricultural practices and reduce their environmental harmful effects. However, this approach raises concerns about the healthiness of new foods and the concentration of power in the hands of a few global monopolies. Rather than relying on synthetic replacements, a more sustainable approach involves reducing unnecessary and wasteful consumption of food and water, promoting local organic food supply systems, and adopting more eco-friendly agricultural practices by empowering local communities and prioritizing natural and sustainable methods of production.

New industrial methods and materials since the second industrial revolution such as huge factories, fossil fuels, cement, plastics, etc. seem to take us down a pollution path of no return in some respects. For instance, in 1997, a 'microplastic continent' was discovered in the Pacific Ocean, covering an area of 1.6 million square kilometers and containing approximately 79,000 tons of plastic debris (UNEP, 2024). This floating mass of plastic waste poses a significant threat to marine life and ecosystems, as plastic particles are resistant to biodegradation and ingested by fish and other animals, ultimately affecting the food chain and human health, and penetrating even to the human brain and breast milk. Furthermore, even the digital world of the fourth and fifth industrial revolution, often seen as less environmentally impactful, plays a role in carbon emissions. Every page view on a website is estimated to generate between 1.2 and 3.6 grams of CO_2 (BBC, 2024). Although seemingly minor, the cumulative effect of billions of daily page views adds up, contributing to the overall carbon footprint of digital activities.

1.3. Main Causes

The main cause of climate change is the significant increase in greenhouse gas emissions (particularly carbon dioxide, methane, and nitrous oxide) that retain heat in the Earth's atmosphere, causing a steady rise in global temperatures. Graph 1 shows annual CO_2 emissions from 1900 to 2022 which highlights a troubling rise in global greenhouse gas levels, particularly driven by fossil fuels like oil, natural gas, and coal. A significant portion of these emissions can be traced to just 122 major carbon fuel and cement producers, emphasizing the outsized role that a few key industries play in climate change. Despite the 2015 Paris Agreement, which aimed to curb global temperature rise, emissions have continued to climb, particularly from oil and gas sectors. It also emphasizes the global dependency on fossil fuels and the slow transition to renewable energy. Even with increasing awareness of the climate crisis, energy demands have driven emissions to record levels. The persistence of coal, along with growing emissions from natural gas, further complicates efforts to reduce CO_2 levels. Achieving meaningful reductions will require not only policy changes but also significant shifts in industrial practices and energy consumption on a global scale.

Figure 1. Annual emissions, billion tonnes of CO_2

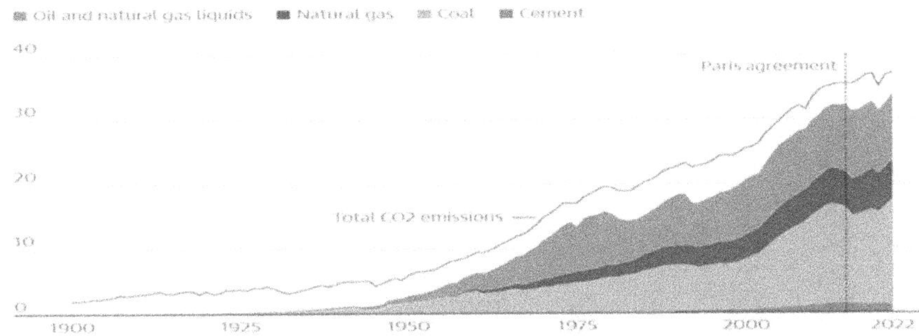

(https://www.theguardian.com/environment/2024/apr/04)

The majority of these emissions result from activities related to the production and consumption of goods and energy. Therefore, the roots cause of this climate crisis include usage of fossil fuels, processes of manufacturing and mining, and deforestation (UN, 2024):

Burning Fossil Fuels: Fossil fuels (coal, oil, natural gas, etc.) are used extensively to generate electricity, heat, and power transportation systems worldwide. Fossil fuels met 80% of global energy demand in 2023 by making the biggest contribution to total carbon emissions (IEA, 2024). Many countries continue to rely heavily on coal-fired power plants, which release large amounts of CO_2 and other harmful pollutants. Similarly, the transportation sector contributes significantly to greenhouse gas emissions, with cars, trucks, airplanes, and ships powered primarily by fossil fuels (UN, 2024).

Industrial Processes of Manufacturing and Mining: Industrial activities are another significant source of greenhouse gas emissions. The production of goods such as cement, iron, steel, electronics, plastics, and clothing all involve processes that release large quantities of CO_2 and other greenhouse gases. The mining of raw materials, the energy-intensive processing of metals, and the chemical reactions involved in manufacturing all add to the overall carbon footprint of industrial activities (UN, 2024).

Deforestation: Forests are vital in stabilizing the Earth's climate by acting as carbon sinks—absorbing CO_2 from the atmosphere through photosynthesis. However, deforestation rapidly reduces the size of these carbon sinks and results in soil degradation, habitat destruction, and changes in local climate patterns. The Amazon rainforest, which is Earth's vital carbon sink, has been severely affected by deforestation, contributing to rising CO_2 levels globally (UN, 2024).

In brief, the emission of gases such as carbon dioxide (CO_2), methane (CH_4), and nitrous oxide (N_2O) is accepted as the primary cause of greenhouse effect. Particularly the burning of fossil fuels, industrial processes, and deforestation, have increased the concentration of these gases in the atmosphere, trapping heat and causing a range of harmful effects. (Nunez, 2019)

Figure 2. Greenhouse gas emissions global and by sector

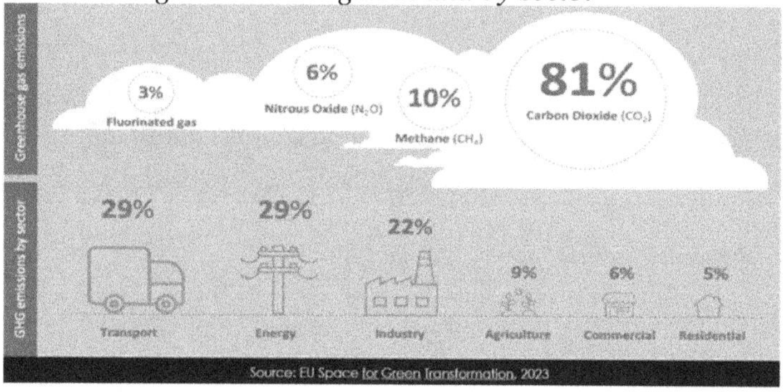

Figure 2 illustrates the distribution of greenhouse gas emissions by sector and type of gas. Carbon dioxide (CO_2) is the dominant greenhouse gas, accounting for 81% of emissions, methane (CH_4) follows at 10%, while nitrous oxide (N_2O) and fluorinated gases make up 6% and 3%, respectively. When we look at the sectors responsible for these emissions, the transportation and energy sectors are tied, each contributing 29% to the total. This is a significant amount and shows that our reliance on fossil fuels for moving people and goods, as well as generating electricity, plays a huge role in the climate crisis. Industry, which includes manufacturing and production processes, is responsible for 22% of emissions, while agriculture contributes 9%. Commercial activities (6%) and residential sectors (5%) make smaller but still notable contributions to global emissions.

Table 1. Top 5 countries producing 2/3 of CO_2

Countries	CO_2 Emissions (10^6 tons)	CO_2 Emissions per capita (tons)	GDP (trillion $)	Population (million)	Share of World CO_2 (%)	Share of World GDP
China	12.667	8,89	18	1.425	33	18
USA	4.853	14,21	25,5	341	13	25
India	2.693	1,89	3,5	1.425	7	3
Russia	1.909	13,11	2,2	145	5	2
Japan	1.082	8,66	4,2	125	3	4
			Total %:	*43%*	*61%*	*52%*

(https://www.worldometers.info/gdp/gdp-by-country, https://www.worldometers.info/co2-emissions/co2-emissions-per-capita)

Table 1 highlights the significant contribution of the top five countries to global CO_2 emissions, which together account for approximately two-thirds of the world's total. China emits an impressive 12.667 million tons of CO_2, which represents 33% of the global total. With a GDP of $18 trillion and a population of 1,4 billion, China's emissions are tied to its rapid industrialization and economic growth. However, China has relatively low emissions per capita (8,89 tons). Following China, the United States emits 4.853 million tons of CO_2, making up 13% of global emissions. The USA, despite having lower total emissions, has the highest per capita emissions at 14,21 tons among five countries listed in the table. With a GDP of $25,5 trillion and a population of 341 million, the U.S. also has a significant environmental footprint in relation to its economic output.

India ranks third with CO_2 emissions of 2.693 million tons, contributing 7% to the world's total. India hast the lowest per capita emissions (1,89 tons) among five countries listed in the table. Russia and Japan follow, emitting 1.909 million tons (5% of global emissions) and 1.082 million tons (3% of global emissions), respectively. Russia's GDP stands at $2,2 trillion, while Japan's GDP is $4,2 trillion, with populations of 145 million and 125 million, respectively. Russia (13,11 tons per capita) and Japan (8,66 tons per capita) also exhibit high individual emissions compared to global averages.

Together, these five countries account for 61% of global CO_2 emissions, while their combined GDP represents 52% of the world's total GDP. The data further reveals that the top 40 countries contribute about 90% of both global carbon emissions and GDP. Notably, there is a strong correlation (r=0,8) between the share of world CO_2 emissions and the share of world GDP among these countries, indicating that higher economic output often leads to increased carbon emissions.

As of 2023, Türkiye ranks as the 14th highest carbon emitter globally, contributing around 1,3% of the world's total carbon emissions. When we look at carbon emissions per capita, Türkiye ranks 56th globally (European Commission, 2024a). This suggests that Türkiye's emissions on a per-person basis are lower compared to more industrialized nations. For instance, annual carbon emissions per household in Türkiye, as well as in Mexico, are approximately 1 ton of CO_2, which is relatively low. However, this figure is considerably smaller when compared to countries in Europe, such as Poland, where the average household emits 6 tons of CO_2 per year, and France and Germany, where households produce between 8 and 9 tons annually (OECD, 2024).

1.4. Main Consequences

Global warming leads to more frequent and severe heatwaves, droughts, and extreme weather events such as hurricanes, floods, and wildfires that reduce crop yields, cause food shortages, disrupt ecosystems and displace communities. Moreover, these gas emissions contribute also to a range of public health problems, including respiratory diseases, heat-related illnesses, and the spread of malaria in the long run (Nunez, 2019). Figure 3illustrates the correlation between CO_2 emissions and global temperature rise. The graph reveals a clear upward trend in both CO_2 emissions and global temperature, suggesting a strong correlation between the two (IEA, 2024).

Figure 3. $C0_2$ emissions and global temperature rise

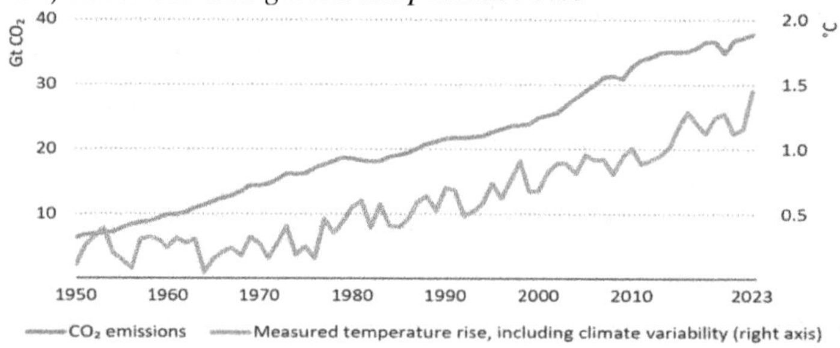

(IEA, 2024)

Hotter temperatures, drought, loss of biodiversity, and health risks are among of the most significant results of the climate crisis. Global temperatures have been rising steadily since the late 19th century, with recent years seeing record-breaking heat. The summer of 2024, for instance, was the hottest on record. This increase in temperature has far-reaching effects on ecosystems and weather patterns (UN, 2024). Also, energy use for residential cooling is expected to rise 280% by 2050 to accommodate the growing heat (IEA, 2024).

Climate change is also causing increasingly intense and widespread droughts in many parts of the world. Prolonged periods of dry weather reduce the availability of freshwater resources, leading to water shortages for agriculture, industry, and human consumption. Another consequence is the extinction of species at an alarming rate. It is feared that one million species are at risk of extinction within the next few decades due to habitat destruction, climate change, pollution, and over-exploitation. Finally, in the long run, malnutrition, heat-related illnesses, and respiratory diseases occur. Rising temperatures increase the prevalence of heatwaves, which can cause heatstroke and exacerbate cardiovascular and respiratory conditions. Air pollution, largely driven by the burning of fossil fuels, leads to respiratory diseases such as asthma and lung cancer. Hunger and malnutrition are also on the rise as climate change disrupts agricultural production. Around 13 million people die every year due to hunger and malnutrition, air pollution, extreme weather events, forced displacement, etc. (UN, 2024).

Fortunately, a range of green technologies is available to help reduce the negative impacts of greenhouse gases and slow the pace of climate change. Firstly, replacing fossil fuels with renewable energy sources such as solar, wind, and hydroelectric power is one of the most effective ways to reduce gas emissions. Renewable energy technologies are becoming increasingly affordable and efficient, making them a viable alternative to traditional sources. Carbon capture and storage technologies can remove CO_2 from the atmosphere and store it underground, preventing it from contributing to global warming. These technologies are particularly useful in sectors that are challenging to decarbonize, like cement and steel manufacturing. Enhancing energy efficiency in infrastructure, transportation, and industrial operations can significantly reduce gas emissions. For example, better insulation in buildings can reduce the need for heating and cooling, while more fuel-efficient vehicles can lower transportation-related emissions. Finally, planting trees and conserving existing forests and grasslands are essential for reducing atmospheric CO_2 levels. Forests function as natural carbon absorbers, capturing CO_2 from the atmosphere and storing it in biomass and soil. Protecting and restoring natural ecosystems is therefore a crucial component of climate change mitigation. (Nunez, 2019)

Figure 4 depicts the global energy breakdown from 1950 to 2050, illustrating the projected shift from fossil fuels to clean energy sources. Historically, fossil fuels, particularly oil and coal, have dominated global energy consumption. However, the graph indicates a significant trend towards cleaner energy sources. Clean energy is projected to experience a substantial increase in consumption over the next few decades. By 2050, it is expected to surpass all other energy sources, signifying a major transition away from fossil fuels.

Figure 4. Global energy breakdown

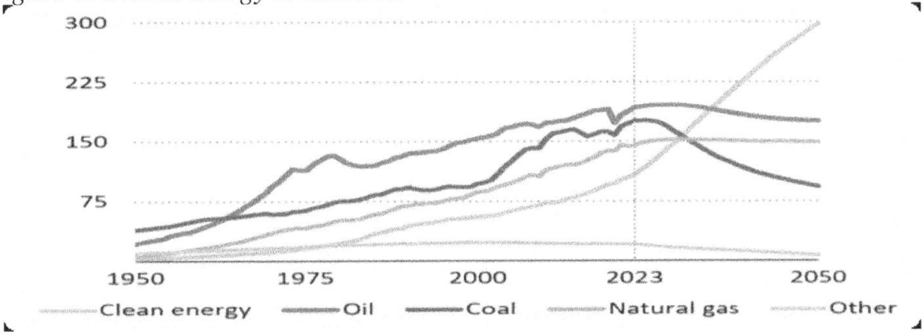

(IEA, 2024)

2. GREEN TRANSFORMATION

The classical model of economic development, which is built on excessive production and consumption, has long prioritized profit and growth at the expense of the natural world and the creatures that inhabit it. While this approach has driven industrialization and economic expansion, it has also led to severe environmental degradation. The consequences of this development model are becoming increasingly visible, most notably in the form of the climate crisis, which is now one of the greatest challenges humanity faces. As noted by Ecer et al. (2021), the environmental damage caused by unchecked economic activities has reached a point where we are all obligated to pursue a green transformation.

This transformation involves a fundamental change in our approach to growth and development, requiring us to move away from practices that harm the environment and embrace more sustainable methods. As emphasized by the EU Space for Green Transformation (2023), ecological mindfulness must replace the exploitative attitudes of the past. This means implementing strategies that focus on reducing greenhouse gas emissions, which are a primary driver of global warming. Along with cutting emissions, reducing the consumption of essential resources such as water, electricity, and raw materials is crucial. Overuse of these resources not only depletes them but also contributes to the destruction of ecosystems and loss of biodiversity. Additionally, improving waste management and promoting recycling are critical components of this green transformation. By effectively managing waste, we can minimize pollution, reduce the burden on landfills, and lower the demand for new raw materials. Recycling helps reduce the energy needed to produce goods and decreases the carbon footprint of industries. Organizations are also striving to reduce their environmental footprint, increase efficiency and profitability in their operations and routines, keep up with rapidly changing regulations, and stay competitive by adapting to changing technologies and responding to customer expectations.

Green transformation is also the twin sister of digital transformation. The former might balance the latter's side effects. Therefore, global attempts towards turning greener seems to be not only a reaction to the climate change but also a desire for more human-centric way of doing our jobs that were threatened by the rapid expansion of digital technologies that began to replace the human labor.

2.1. Society 5.0: Japan 2016

Society 5.0 is a concept introduced in 2016 that focuses on the merging of cyberspace and physical space to address societal challenges while promoting economic progress (Leng et al., 2022). It represents a shift toward a human-centric model, where technological advancements serve to improve the quality of life and solve social issues. Unlike previous industrial revolutions, which focused on production and efficiency, Society 5.0 aims to create a more inclusive and sustainable future by leveraging the latest innovations in technology. One of the key features of Society 5.0 is the merging of cyber-physical spaces. This integration allows for seamless interaction between the digital and physical worlds, where data and technology are used to enhance human capabilities and address complex problems. Whether in healthcare, education, or transportation, the aim is to create smarter and more responsive systems that cater to human needs. Additionally, Society 5.0 envisions a knowledge-intensive society where information is the most valuable asset. With the rapid growth of digital technology, data has become a crucial resource for innovation and decision-making. In this data-driven society, vast amounts of information are processed and analyzed to generate insights that can lead to more informed, effective policies and business strategies. This knowledge-driven approach enables societies to tackle challenges such as aging populations, environmental sustainability, and economic inequality, while still fostering growth and development.

2.2. European Green Deal: EU 2019

The European Union represents 6% of the world population and consumes approximately 10% of global energy introduced in 2019 The European Green Deal. It aims at making Europe world's first climate-neutral continent by reducing greenhouse gas emissions by 55% by 2030 and achieving net-zero emissions by 2050; it extends to countries that maintain commercial relationships with the EU, requiring them to adhere to its environmental standards. (European Commission, 2019, 2024a; Ecer et al., 2021; EU Agency for the Space Program, 2023; IEA, 2024)

In the context of the EU's Green Deal, the transportation sector is undergoing stringent CO_2 emissions regulations to meet climate goals. For cars, emissions must be reduced to 93,6 g CO_2/km (a 15% reduction compared to 2021) during the period 2025-2029, with a target of 49,5 g CO_2/km (a 55% reduction) set for 2030-2034. From 2035, all new cars must achieve a 100% CO_2 reduction, transitioning to fully zero-emission vehicles. For lorries and buses, reductions in CO_2 emissions compared to 2019 are set at 15% by 2025-2029, 45% by 2030-2034, and 65% by 2035-2039, reaching a 90% reduction by 2040 onwards. Urban bus manufacturers must ensure that 90% of new buses are zero-emission by 2030 and 100% by 2035. (Menner et al., 2024)

Figure 5. The European green deal

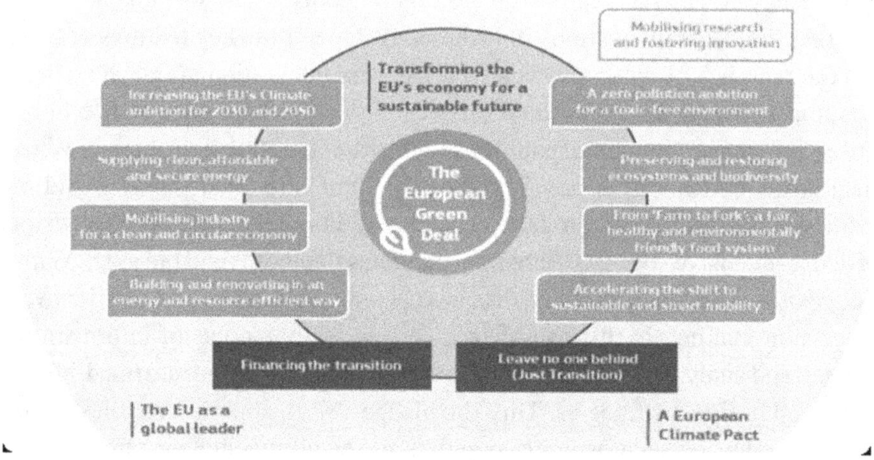

In parallel, the Carbon Border Adjustment Mechanism aims to tackle carbon leakage by applying a carbon cost to imported goods like steel, cement, and electricity, which is equivalent to EU production standards. This mechanism ensures that foreign manufacturers bear the same carbon costs, fostering fair competition and encouraging global shifts toward lower-emission production. (European Commission, 2023)

Amid these regulatory changes, the European automotive market, particularly in Germany, is undergoing a significant transformation towards greener technologies. Vehicle sales across the EU have been declining since their peak in 2019, with a sharp 26% drop in 2021. In August 2024, Germany saw a production increase with 313,700 cars manufactured, a 24% year-on-year rise. However, new registrations sharply fell to 197,300 vehicles, marking a 28% decline compared to the previous year. The electric vehicle sector followed this trend with 40,600 new registrations in August, down 60% from the previous year's inflated figures due to the expiration of government incentives. Despite these challenges, Germany is expected to produce around 1,3 million electric vehicles in 2024, a 4% increase over the previous year. This rise is driven predominantly by exports, which account for 80,3% of all electric vehicles. Although progress in electric vehicle adoption is evident, traditional vehicles still dominate the market as the industry faces growing regulatory pressure to reduce emissions. (ICCT, 2023; VDA, 2024)

2.3. Industry 5.0: EC's Directorate-General for R&D- 2021

Industry 5.0 emphasizes a shift in industrial practices by placing worker well-being and ecological responsibility at its core. Unlike previous industrial revolutions that prioritized economic growth and technological advancement often at the expense of the environment and workforce, Industry 5.0 aims for a more balanced and sustainable approach. It focuses on creating a harmonious relationship between humans and machines, ensuring that technological advancements complement rather than replace human skills and creativity (Leng et al., 2022).

One of the key aspects of Industry 5.0 is its human-centric approach, which prioritizes customer-oriented designs and fosters advanced interactions between humans and machines. This approach ensures that technology is developed in a way that enhances human creativity and skills, allowing for greater innovation and personalization in products and services. Rather than simply automating tasks, the goal is to enable machines to work alongside humans, creating a more dynamic and flexible working environment. Sustainability is another crucial pillar of Industry 5.0 that promotes environmentally friendly production processes, green innovation, and the development of new materials that contribute to carbon neutrality, paving the way for industries to thrive while respecting ecological boundaries. Resilience as the third pillar ensures that institutions, systems, industries and organizations are robust enough to withstand and survive future challenges, environmental problems, economic crises, or technological disruptions.

2.4. Challenges of Green Transformation

The transition to a greener economy faces numerous substantial obstacles that need to be overcome to ensure its success. One of the primary issues is its uncertainty, as many new green technologies, sectors, and professions are still in their early stages of development. This can hinder investment, produce immature, unsatisfactory, and even harmful solution proposals, and slow down the adoption of sustainable practices.

Risk of unemployment is another major challenge, particularly in carbon-emitting sectors that currently employ a large number of traditional workers. As industries shift toward greener alternatives, there is a risk of job losses without adequate support and retraining for affected ones. Additionally, vocational training programs for green professions are still evolving, and both theoretical and practical training curricula need further development to align with the needs of a rapidly changing workforce. Lastly, acquiring the critical skills necessary for green jobs requires also on-the-job experience and mentorship, which are not easy to provide.

The risk of not being able to balance twin transformations at the same time is another challenge since green transformation is not complete without digital transformation. The integration of the Industry 4.0 technologies i.e. data analytics, internet of things, robotics, etc. can contribute to sustainable economic growth and environmental sustainability by decreasing ecological footprints in the long term (Akın & Dinçer, 2024).

2.5. Green Jobs

International Labour Organization (ILO) defines a green job as a decent job that contributes to environmental sustainability by reducing the consumption of energy and raw materials, limiting greenhouse gas emissions, minimizing waste and pollution, protecting and restoring ecosystems, and enabling communities and enterprises to adapt to climate change (ILO, 2013). Environmental degradation and growing awareness of sustainability issues are fueling the expansion of the circular economy and creating more green jobs. This rising demand has led to new initiatives in various areas, including renewable energy, nature-based solutions, biotechnology, recycling, water security, high-tech agriculture, sustainable food production, green construction, ecotourism, and the sharing economy (or peer-to-peer economy) (UNDP, 2021). Some examples of green jobs include renewable energy engineers, energy efficiency experts, and carbon footprint advisors, all vital in supporting a sustainable future. Meanwhile, the shift towards greener practices may lead to the loss of brown jobs (traditionally more carbon emitting ones) especially in the oil, gas, coal, chemicals, etc., all of which contribute much more to environmental problems (Zurich Insurance Group, 2021).

3. FAIR TRANSITION

A fair transition seeks to distribute both the benefits and burdens of green transformation equitably, ensuring that no one (especially laborers) is left behind since in a fair world, labor policies should be evaluated not only by GDP growth but also by their impact on improving labor safety and conditions (Ramsarup, et al., 2023; Ding and Hirvilammi, 2024). This transition aims to enhance both human well-being and sustainability in the face of environmental challenges by implying a green model of "coopetition," which merges competition among firms for green innovations and cooperation among public and private stakeholders to provide joint solutions for vulnerable groups to promote global social justice and human development.

One key aspect of a fair transition is differentiating between those who are responsible for environmental harm and those who are vulnerable and innocent (Galanis et al., 2024). This differentiation is critical to ensure that vulnerable populations do not bear the burden of the changes needed to achieve sustainability. Additionally, policies must aim to distribute the economic and social costs of the green transition fairly among various societal groups (Marklund, 2023). Moreover, this transition must prioritize providing decent jobs for all, emphasizing social inclusion and the eradication of poverty (ILO, 2015). By focusing on these principles, a just transition can ensure that the shift toward a greener economy benefits everyone, fostering a sustainable future that uplifts communities while addressing the urgent challenges posed by climate change.

3.1. Dimensions of Justice

The dimensions of justice in the context of green transformation are essential to ensure that the shift toward a sustainable economy is equitable for all stakeholders involved (Galanis et al., 2024). The three primary dimensions are distributive justice, procedural justice, and restorative justice.

Distributive justice addresses the fair distribution of both the costs and benefits linked to the green transformation. The shift toward a sustainable economy will bring challenges particularly in carbon-intensive sectors, including job losses, capital investments, stranded assets, and economic disruptions. For example, coal demand is projected to fall by 80% from 2023 to 2035, resulting in the shutdown of coal-fired power plants (IEA, 2024). However, this transition also offers significant benefits, such as reduced pollution, enhanced climate resilience, increased productivity, and better public health. The key challenge is to be able to ensure that these impacts are distributed equitably across different regions, sectors, and social groups. (Sabato et al., 2024; Galanis et al., 2024).

Procedural justice emphasizes the need for inclusive and participatory decision-making processes regarding economic, environmental, and employment-related issues. Policies are more likely to gain legitimacy and effectiveness when all stakeholders, except the most vulnerable groups, have a voice in shaping them. Ensuring that marginalized communities are included in these discussions fosters trust and collaboration. (Sabato et al., 2024; Galanis et al., 2024)

Restorative justice addresses the challenges faced by workers in brown jobs, who may lose their positions in the transition to green jobs while bearing little responsibility for climate change. Policymakers and responsible entities must work together to restore inequalities by providing adequate job and retraining opportunities and financial support for these vulnerable groups, ensuring they can successfully benefit also from the green economy (Sabato et al., 2024; Galanis et al., 2024). Only by focusing on these dimensions of justice, societies can promote a more equitable transition toward a sustainable future.

3.2. Loss of Basic Skills and Occupational Decline

The rapid advancement of technology, particularly artificial intelligence, has significantly reshaped the job market and the skills required for various occupations. As we move further into an era dominated by automation and digital tools, certain skills have become less relevant, leading to a notable decline in their necessity. By 2030, 30% of current job activities is predicted to be automated, encompassing not only physical and routine tasks but also more complex and cognitive ones. By 2030, 27% of working hours in Europe and 30% in the United States will be automated. This clearly highlights that significant transformations in talent management will occur by 2030 (Demirel, 2023).

Some skills that are expected to be automated and no longer needed to learn by humans are (Marr, 2024):

1. **Writing:** While effective communication remains essential, AI tools can now generate written content, reducing the need for individuals to develop strong writing skills.
2. **Art Design:** AI-powered design software can create visually appealing content quickly and efficiently, diminishing the demand for traditional art design skills.
3. **Data Entry:** Automation and machine learning have streamlined data entry processes, making this skill less critical in today's workforce.
4. **Data Analysis:** Advanced AI algorithms can analyze vast datasets more accurately and swiftly more than humans, leading to a decline in the need for manual data analysis skills.
5. **Video Editing:** AI-driven editing software has simplified the video production process, reducing the necessity for individuals to possess traditional video editing skills.

As specific skills become less valuable, occupational decline manifests in three primary areas (Gaskell, 2019):

1. **Need for Current Skills:** Many jobs that relied on outdated skills are becoming obsolete, leading to fewer opportunities for those who possess them.

2. **Time Spent on Current Tasks:** The efficiency brought by AI means that tasks that once took significant time can now be completed more quickly, altering job descriptions and responsibilities.
3. **Monthly Salary for Current Tasks:** As the demand for traditional skills wanes, salaries for roles that primarily rely on them may also decline, affecting traditional workers' financial stability.

Conversely, the job market is also witnessing shifts in occupational mobility, characterized by (Gaskell, 2019):

1. **Need for Newer Skills:** workers must adapt to the evolving demands of the job market by acquiring skills relevant to newer technologies and practices.
2. **Time and Money Spent on Gaining Newer Skills:** as individuals seek to remain competitive, they may need to invest considerable time and financial resources into retraining and upskilling.
3. **Looking for Newer Jobs:** as occupational roles evolve; many individuals may find themselves in the position of searching for new job opportunities that align with the skills they possess or are in the process of acquiring.

Twin transformations are actually reshaping the landscape of skills and employment. As certain skills become obsolete and occupational decline occurs, traditional workers must remain agile and should spend the time they save from automation on acquiring new skills by continuously learning and adapting to stay relevant in an ever-changing job market. This may affect those traditional workers who have mid-level skills more severely than those with lower-level skills, since industrial transformations reduce mostly those jobs that necessitate mid-level skills by enforcing those who lost their jobs to upskill or even downskill (Karaçay and Alpkan, 2019). Downskilling is much easier and less costly for both employers and employees. Therefore, employers, vocational training institutions and policy makers should be aware of the downskilling trap that might happen also because of time and budget pressures to keep up with the pace of technological changes that limit the necessary time to learn from experience, tacit knowledge transfers from masters' to apprentices, or to follow long-term diploma programs.

3.3. Transition via New Skills

The ongoing shift toward environmentally friendly practices is significantly transforming various aspects of the job market, including investments, technologies, legislation, customer expectations, business models, work processes, and job contents. These changes are not only altering job descriptions and titles but also reshaping the skills required of current and future employees. As the demand for green jobs grows, higher education, vocational training, and on-the-job training programs will need to adapt their content and delivery methods in order to equip workers with the necessary competencies for a sustainable economy. According to ILO, it is projected that by 2030, approximately 18 million green jobs will be created globally, requiring a diverse range of new skills (ILO, 2024). This surge in green job opportunities highlights the urgency of re-skilling and up-skilling the existing workforce. Personalized training programs will be essential in this transition, ensuring that individuals are equipped to meet the evolving demands of their industries. However, it is important to note that while training can enhance skills, the individual attachment to specific jobs and professions, and the accumulation of work experience are irreplaceable aspects of career development (Denyer, 2023; Astarita, 2024).

The Chartered Institute of Personnel and Development that conducts studies in the field of Human Resources development, published a report titled "Resourcing and Talent Planning" in September 2024. In this report, 69% of survey participants expressed that competition for qualified talent has increased in the past year. While 84% of companies attempted to fill open positions, 64% of these companies struggled to find the right talent, with only 20% able to locate the desired candidates. Therefore, focusing on reskilling presents a more effective option for closing skill gaps. Companies that adopt reskilling strategies not only promote talent development by equipping their current employees with new skills but also enhance employee loyalty and engagement (Demirel, 2023). By 2030, in Türkiye the skill requirements for laborers will vary significantly, with a substantial portion of the workforce needing to adapt to changes in their current roles through reskilling. This process will involve approximately 58% of workers acquiring new skills to stay relevant in their positions (see Table 2). Additionally, around 15% of workers will focus on upskilling to enhance their qualifications for promotions within their existing fields. There will also be a smaller group, about 5%, transitioning into entirely new sectors. Finally, the labor market will welcome an estimated 21% of newcomers who will bring fresh skills and knowledge necessary for the green economy. (McKinsey Global Institute, 2020)

Table 2. New skills for laborers by 2030 in Türkiye

Skill Requirements	Restoration	Estimated Ratio
New skills within the same job	Reskilling	58%
New skills for promotion	Upskilling	15%
New skills for new sectors	Transition	5%
Fresh laborers with newer skills	New comers	21%

(Source: Future of Work- 2020- McKinsey Global Institute)

The intersection of digital and green transformations requires a comprehensive skill set across various domains. Table 3 provides a comprehensive overview of the essential skills required to navigate the twin transformations of digital and green technologies. It highlights key competencies in areas like big data analytics, machine learning, cybersecurity, green building, biodiversity conservation, and environmental policy. Table 3 demonstrates the need for a multidisciplinary skillset to address the challenges and opportunities presented by these interconnected transformations. As the twin transformations of technology and automation continue to reshape the workforce, many professions, including teaching, nursing, and elderly care, face significant threats to their traditional roles. Even fields that require technical expertise, such as human resource management, law, and retail, are not immune to the changes brought about by automation. While many routine and standardized jobs are increasingly being taken over by machines, there remains a critical demand for soft, social, and cognitive skills that are not easily automated. Skills such as communication, critical thinking, creativity, emotional intelligence, adaptation, and decision-making continue to be irreplaceable aspects of human labor (Shaukat et al., 2024; Raman, 2024).

As machines increasingly learn and replace routine tasks, employees must rely on their unique human capabilities, such as judgment, morals, creativity, and the ability to learn to learn—traits that machines have yet to master. In an evolving work environment characterized by heightened technical competition and cultural diversity, social and cognitive skills have become more essential than ever. Key skills in demand include self-awareness, self-efficacy, empathy, and compassion, which foster collaboration and understanding among diverse teams (OECD, 2019; World Economic Forum, 2020; UNDP, 2021). Moreover, skills like curiosity, perseverance, emotional stability, and responsibility are critical for navigating the complexities of modern workplaces. The ability to respect, communicate with, and influence others remains paramount, along with developing emotional intelligence and global awareness. Strategic, analytical, and critical thinking skills are essential for tackling complex problems arising in the contemporary landscape, while originality, initiative, and innovation are crucial for driving progress and adaptability. Proficiency in technology use and control has become an indispensable part of the skill set for the future workforce. This ongoing demand for social and cognitive skills highlights the importance of preparing current and future workers to thrive in an increasingly automated and interconnected world (OECD, 2019; World Economic Forum, 2020; UNDP, 2021).

In a 2023 study conducted by the Republic of Türkiye Institution of Providing Jobs and Employees (İŞKUR), employers were asked open-ended questions to predict which professions are likely to become prominent over the next decade. Several key professions emerged as potential future careers according to the feedback from employers. Table 4 illustrates the evolving landscape of careers across different sectors. In the realm of information and communication, roles such as software engineers, artificial intelligence experts, and data scientists are expected to be in high demand. The finance and insurance sector is also showing significant changes, with an increasing need for professionals like AI experts, investment advisors, and e-commerce specialists. On the other hand, the health and social services sector will see the rise of professions such as speech therapists, social workers, and gerontologists, reflecting the growing importance of addressing the needs of aging populations and mental health challenges.

Table 3. Twin skills for twin transformation

Domain	**Skills**
Digital Transformation Elements	
Big Data Analytics	- Proficiency in data analysis tools, Ability to interpret complex datasets - Knowledge of data visualization techniques
Machine Learning	- Understanding of algorithms and predictive modeling, - Ability to implement AI solutions for business optimization
Blockchain Technology	- Understanding of blockchain principles and applications - Ability to develop smart contracts, Knowledge of decentralized applications
Cybersecurity	- Understanding of security protocols and risk management - Skills in incident response and threat mitigation, compliance standards
Digital Marketing	- Expertise in SEO, PPC, and content marketing - Ability to analyze marketing data and optimize campaigns - Skills in social media management and engagement strategies
Green Transformation Elements	
Green Building	- Knowledge of eco-friendly materials and energy-efficient designs - Skills in sustainable construction practices - Proficiency in building energy modeling and certification
Biodiversity Conservation	- Expertise in habitat restoration and wildlife management - Skills in conducting biodiversity assessments - Understanding of ecological principles and conservation strategies
Eco-friendly Technology	- Proficiency in developing and implementing renewable energy solutions - Skills in sustainable software engineering and green IT practices - Knowledge of energy-efficient technologies and smart systems
Water Conservation	- Skills in water management techniques and sustainable use practices - Understanding of watershed protection strategies - Ability to assess and implement water-saving technologies

continued on following page

Table 3. Continued

Domain	Skills
Sustainable Supply Chain Management	- Understanding of sustainable sourcing practices - Skills in logistics optimization with a focus on minimizing environmental impact - Ability to assess and implement circular economy principles
Environmental Policy	- Knowledge of environmental regulations and compliance standards - Skills in advocacy for sustainable practices and policy development - Ability to analyze the impact of policies on environmental sustainability

(Sources: adapted and compiled from European Commission, 2024b; T4 Education, 2023; Sanga, 2023)

Table 4. Future professions by sector

Information and Communication	Finance and Insurance	Health and Social Services
Software Engineer	Software Engineer	Speech Therapist
Artificial Intelligence Expert	IT Specialist	Ergotherapist
Computer Engineer	AI Expert	Physiotherapist
Software Developer	Investment Advisor	Social Worker
IT Specialist	Actuary	Special Education Teacher
Data Analyst	E-Commerce Specialist	Special Education Teaching
Social Media Specialist	Insurance Technician	Psychologist
AI Engineer	Social Media Expert	Elderly Care Worker
Data Scientist	Software Developer	Aesthetician
Web Editor	Marketing Specialist	Gerontologist

(Source: Republic of Türkiye Institution of Providing Jobs and Employees (İŞKUR) - 2023 Labor Market Research Report for Türkiye)

CONCLUSION

The transition toward a greener economy is not just an environmental necessity; it also presents significant social challenges that require a fair approach. As highlighted throughout this paper, the concepts of green jobs and just transition emphasize the critical importance of creating sustainable employment opportunities while addressing the diverse needs of vulnerable populations affected by this transformation. As industries evolve and the demand for green jobs increases, it is essential to prioritize retraining and reskilling initiatives with local and tailor-made solutions.

These efforts are vital for equipping workers with the necessary competencies for emerging roles in renewable energy and sustainable technologies.

The dimensions of justice outlined in this paper—distributive, procedural, and restorative—offer a thorough framework for ensuring that the benefits and burdens of green transformation are fairly distributed among all stakeholders. Policymakers must recognize the responsibility of those contributing to environmental harm while implementing inclusive decision-making processes that actively engage underrepresented communities. This inclusive approach promotes trust, collaboration, and social cohesion as society navigates the complexities of a sustainable future. Moreover, addressing the challenges associated with the green transition requires proactive measures that extend beyond merely creating new jobs. There is an urgent need for policies and programs that focus on social safety nets, retraining opportunities, and pathways to employment for those displaced from carbon-intensive sectors. By recognizing the specific needs of these workers and providing adequate support, society can mitigate the adverse impacts of the transition and promote a more inclusive labor market.

The rapid advancement of technology, particularly artificial intelligence, adds another layer of complexity to this transition. As technology reshapes the job market, workers must adapt by acquiring new skills that align with the evolving demands of various industries. The emphasis on soft, cognitive, and technological skills will be crucial in building resilience and ensuring that workers remain competitive in an increasingly automated landscape. The ongoing shift toward green jobs necessitates that educational institutions, businesses, and governments collaborate to create effective training programs tailored to the needs of the future workforce.

Furthermore, cultivating a culture of lifelong learning and adaptability is essential in preparing individuals for the job market's dynamic nature. Workers should be encouraged to embrace continuous learning and skill development, enabling them to navigate the changing employment landscape effectively. This adaptability will not only benefit individual workers but also contribute to the broader goal of achieving a sustainable economy.

A just transition must prioritize decent work for all, emphasizing social inclusion and the eradication of poverty. By focusing on these principles, society can ensure that the shift toward a greener economy benefits everyone, enabling a sustainable future while addressing the urgent challenges posed by climate change. It is crucial to recognize that the fight against climate change and the pursuit of social justice are interconnected goals that must be pursued simultaneously. Therefore, the transition to a greener economy presents an opportunity to rethink our economic models and labor policies. By evaluating labor policies not solely on GDP growth but also on their impact on improving labor safety and conditions, we can promote a more just and inclusive society.

In conclusion, achieving a just transition is not merely a moral obligation but a strategic necessity to ensure that economic growth and environmental sustainability are aligned. By fostering inclusive policies, prioritizing decent work for all, and encouraging continuous learning and adaptation, society can lay the foundation for a sustainable future that uplifts communities and effectively addresses the pressing challenges posed by climate change without leaving anybody behind.

REFERENCES

T4 Education. (2023). Sustainable education for a sustainable future. Retrieved October 10, 2024, from https://t4.education/blog/sustainable-education-for-a-sustainable-future/

Agency, E. U., & the Space Programme. (2023). EU Space for Green Transformation: A new tool for companies to monitor their sustainability targets. Retrieved from https://www.euspa.europa.eu/sites/default/files/eu_space_for_green_transformation_a_new_tool_for_companies_to_monitor_their_sustainability_targets_2023_issue_1.pdf

Akin, F., & Dinçer, S. (2024). "Endüstri 4.0 ve Çevresel Sürdürülebilirlik Arasındaki İlişki: Avrupa Birliği Ülkeleri Üzerine Ampirik Bir Analiz." Yönetim Bilimleri Dergisi/Journal of Administrative Sciences, 22(54), 2449-2469. DOI: DOI: 10.20460/JGSM.2011515820

Astarita, C. (2024), 'Policy brief to enhance industrial relations and social dialogue on adult learning for an inclusive digital and climate-neutral economy', I SKILL Project – Industrial Relations and Social Dialogue to Kick-in Inclusive Adult Learning – Deliverable 4.2DOI: 10.20460/JGSM.2011515820

Bekiroğlu, Ç., Erdil, O., & Alpkan, L. (2011). Variables Perceived by Managers as Antecedents That Lead Firms to Environmental Management: An Empirical Research in the Turkish Construction Sector. *Journal of Global Strategic Management*, 9(2), 157–174. DOI: 10.20460/JGSM.2011515820

Demirel (2023), İş dünyasını değiştirecek 2030 yetkinlikleri, Harvard Business Review Türkiye, https://hbrturkiye.com/sponsorlu-icerik/is-dunyasini-degistirecek-2030-yetkinlikleri

Denyer, K.L.R (2023), A Just Transition for UK oil and gas workers? Re-employment after job lossDOI: 10.1080/21582041.2024.2316656

Ding, J., & Hirvilammi, T. (2024). Three pillars of just transition labor market policies. *Contemporary Social Science*, 19(1-3), 244–261. DOI: 10.1080/21582041.2024.2316656

Ecer, K., Güner, O., & Çetin, M. (2021), Avrupa yeşil mutabakatı ve Türkiye ekonomisinin uyum politikaları. İşletme ve İktisat Çalışmaları Dergisi, 9(2), 125-144. DOI: 10.1080/21582041.2024.2316656

European Commission. (2019), The European Green Deal. Retrieved from https://eur-lex.europa.eu/legal-content/EN/TXT/?uri=CELEX:52019DC0640

European Commission. (2023), Carbon Border Adjustment Mechanism, https://trade.ec.europa.eu/access-to-markets/en/news/carbon-border-adjustment-mechanism-cbam

European Commission. (2024a), The green transition: What implications for employment? Retrieved from https://ec.europa.eu/regional_policy/whats-new/panorama/2024/06/06-12-2024-the-green-transition-what-implications-for-employment_en

European Commission. (2024b), Digital skills and knowledge concepts. ESCO. https://esco.ec.europa.eu/cs/node/427#:~:text=It%20includes%20information%20and%20data,problem%20solving%20and%20critical%20thinking

Future, B. B. C. (2024). Visualizing the Great Pacific Garbage Patch. Retrieved from https://www.bbc.com/future/article/20240115-visualising-the-great-pacific-garbage-patch

Galanis, G., Napoletano, M., Popoyan, L., Sapio, A., & Vardakoulias, O. (2024). Defining just transition. *Ecological Economics*, 227, 108370. DOI: 10.1016/j.ecolecon.2024.108370

Gaskell, A. (2019). The Key To Solving Future Skills Challenges. Forbes. https://www.forbes.com/sites/adigaskell/2019/01/02/solving-future-skills-challenges/

ICCT. (2023), International Council on Clean Transportation (ICCT). (2023). European Vehicle Market Statistics 2023/24 Pocketbook. https://theicct.org/publication/european-vehicle-market-statistics-2023-24/

IEA, 2024, International Energy Agency-World Energy Outlook 2024.

ILO. (2013), ILO Report V: Sustainable development, decent work and green jobs. International Labour Conference, 102nd Session.

ILO (2015), International Labour Organization, Guidelines for a just transition towards environmentally sustainable economies and societies for all

ILO. (2024), Green jobs: Just transition towards environmentally sustainable economies and societies, https://www.ilo.org/topics-and-sectors/just-transition-towards-environmentally-sustainable-economies-and-societies#:~:text=ILO%20studies%20show%20that%20implementing,18%20million%20jobs%20by%202030

İŞKUR (2023), Institution of Providing Jobs and Employees' Labor Market Research Report for Türkiye

Karaçay, G., & Alpkan, L. (2019). Dijital dönüşümün işgücü piyasalarına etkileri: türkiye işgücü piyasası için sosyal politika önerileri (Effects of digital transformation on labor markets: social policy recommendations for the Turkish labor market). *Türk İdare Dergisi*, 91(488), 345–373.

Leng, J., Sha, W., Wang, B., Zheng, P., Zhuang, C., Liu, Q., Wuest, T., Mourtzis, D., & Wang, L. (2022) Industry 5.0: Prospect and retrospect, Journal of Manufacturing Systems, 65, 279-295, ISSN 0278-6125, DOI: 10.1016/j.jmsy.2022.09.017

Marklund, M. J. (2023), At the heart of the transition? Making sense of agency, policy, and post-politics within just transition in Scotland

Marr (2024), https://www.euronews.com/next/2024/09/28

McKinsey & Company. (2020). Future of Work: Turkey's Talent Transformation in the Digital Era.

Menner, M., Reichert, G., Voßwinkel, J. S., & Wolf, A. (2024). Towards decarbonised road transport driven by a globally competitive EU automotive industry: Further development of a resilient EU regulatory framework to safeguard the transformation.

Nunez, C. (2019). Carbon dioxide levels are at a record high. National Geographic. Retrieved from https://www.nationalgeographic.com/environment/article/greenhouse-gases

OECD (2019), OECD Future of Education and Skills 2030, OECD Learning Compass 2030, A Series of Concept Notes

OECD. (2024), Fertility rates, Retrieved from https://www.oecd.org/en/data/indicators/fertility-rates.html

Raman (2024), 6 Critical Human Skills for the Age of AI, https://www.linkedin.com/business/talent/blog/learning-and-development/human-skills-age-of-ai

Ramsarup, P., McGrath, S., & Lotz-Sisitka, H. (2023). Reframing skills ecosystems for sustainable and just futures. *International Journal of Educational Development*, 101, 102836. DOI: 10.1016/j.ijedudev.2023.102836

Sabato, S., & Mandelli, M. (2024). Towards an EU framework for a just transition: Welfare policies and politics for the socio-ecological transition. *European Political Science*, 23(1), 14–26. DOI: 10.1057/s41304-023-00458-1

Sanga, B. (2023), Top 10 green skills shaping the future, LinkedIn, https://www.linkedin.com/pulse/top-10-green-skills-shaping-future-beuuy-sanga-cfowf

Shaukat, K., Iqbal, F., Alam, T. M., Aujla, G. K., Devnath, L., Khan, A. G., Iqbal, R., Shahzadi, I., Rubab, A. (2024). The impact of artificial intelligence and robotics on the future employment opportunities.

Stanley, A. (2023), African Century, IMF, https://www.imf.org/en/Publications/fandd/issues/2023/09/PT-african-century

UNDP. (2021). *The Changing Nature of Work, 30 signals to consider for a sustainable future*. UNDP Accelerator Labs.

UNEP(2024), United Nations Environment Programme, Food Waste Index Report 2024

United Nations. (2024), Global issues: Ageing. Retrieved from https://www.un.org/en/global-issues/ageing

VDA. (2024), German Association of the Automotive Industry (VDA). (2024). August 2024 production and registration figures for the German automotive market. https://www.vda.de/en/press/press-releases/2024/240904_PM_National_PM_Production_and_market_in_August_2024

WCED. 1987, Our Common Future, Oxford University Press, 1987, https://sustainabledevelopment.un.org/content/documents/5987our-common-future.pdf

World Economic Forum. (2020), The Future of Jobs Report 2020

Worldometers (2024), World population by year. Retrieved from https://www.worldometers.info/world-population/world-population-by-year/

Zurich Insurance Group. (2021), 5 green jobs of the future. Retrieved from https://www.zurich.com/media/magazine/2021/5-green-jobs-of-the-future

Chapter 2 Empowering Organizations With AI: Strategies, Challenges, and Future Directions

Tolga Tacettin Tuncer
https://orcid.org/0009-0007-6667-981X
Başkent University, Turkey

A. Kadir Varoglu
https://orcid.org/0000-0001-7857-5013
Başkent University, Turkey

ABSTRACT

This study examines the integration of artificial intelligence (AI) into organizational structures, focusing on the challenges and opportunities AI presents for modern businesses. AI technologies such as machine learning, natural language processing, and generative AI are being increasingly utilized to enhance decision-making processes, optimize workflows, and improve human-machine collaboration. The research explores AI's potential to revolutionize industry operations, while addressing employees' concerns and resistance to AI adoption. By analyzing organizational readiness for AI implementation, the study identifies key strategies for overcoming barriers and enhancing employee engagement. The findings suggest that a well-prepared organizational culture, alongside proper leadership and training, is essential for successful AI integration. Furthermore, this research contributes to the understanding of AI's impact on organizational structures and offers recommendations for future research in managing AI-driven transformations.

DOI: 10.4018/979-8-3373-2523-1.ch002

1. INTRODUCTION

In the 1950s, experts who developed artificial intelligence (AI) envisioned a technology that could feel, think, and produce logical outcomes like humans. This vision remains relevant today. The simplest and most general definition of AI is technology that accomplishes tasks requiring human intelligence (Zhu et al., 2020). According to another definition, it is "technology that can solve problems requiring thinking and perform tasks humans need to do" (Walsh et al., 2019). Although AI is considered one of the most advanced technologies in the world, the number of businesses implementing this technology is still insufficient (Mao et al., 2019; Ellefsen et al., 2019). Businesses worldwide are in the midst of a technological revolution referred to as the fourth industrial revolution, the second machine age (Brynjolfsson & McAfee, 2014), or the algorithmic age (Danaher et al., 2017). This revolution is reshaping the nature of human work and organizations. The challenges of AI for the organizations are multifaceted like humancentric adaptation, having sustainable strategies and resilient organization structures. Therefore, it is crucial for organizations to accurately understand AI technologies to ensure the necessary change processes, cultural necessities, and adaptation to the change. AI technologies have subcomponents that can be deployed according to different needs. For example, machine learning, which can detect patterns in large data sets, natural language processing that can read written or spoken texts, image and visual recognition features, decision support systems, and deep learning can be used as a single module or together (Walsh et al., 2019). Currently, Generative AI, which is "a subset of artificial intelligence capable of generating new content based on textual commands," is actively used. Existing forms of AI designed for specific tasks are called Narrow AI. The power of AI to transform business models mainly comes from the technique of machine learning. Machine learning is defined by computational algorithms programmed to mimic human intelligence. The degree of complexity may vary according to processes, thus requiring machine-human interactions at different stages (El Naqa & Murphy, 2015). As machine learning techniques advance in the future, businesses will derive more benefits (Brynjolfsson & McAfee, 2017). AI is vital for businesses to remain competitive. Despite the rapid advancements in AI, Knickrehm (2018) expressed that predicting its future effects is difficult. The developments in recent years make it challenging to predict how fast and far AI can progress. However, it is certain that organizations need to understand, use, and take necessary precautions regarding this technology. Knickrehm (2018) emphasized that the views of managers and employees on AI might differ. It is crucial for leaders to understand these differences in opinion and the broad spectrum of ideas to shape the workforce of the future. Organizations need to find the right balance between maintaining their current status in a competitive environment and investing in new technologies. For this, managers need the help of their employees. The right decisions will enable businesses to compete today, tomorrow, and in the future (Knickrehm, 2018)

Research Aim

The purpose of this research is to study how artificial intelligence can be integrated into organizational structures, exploring its related challenges and suggesting recommendations for AI adoption between scalability such as limitations. This study aims to understand how AI can catalyze organizational transformation, improve human-AI collaboration and fuel innovation — all while overcoming the cultural and, structural challenges inhibiting end-to-end AI integration.

Research Questions

To achieve the aim, the study addresses the following research questions:

What are the key challenges organizations face when adopting AI technologies?
How can AI be integrated into existing organizational structures without disrupting workflow?
What strategies can be employed to mitigate employee resistance to AI?
How does organizational readiness impact the success of AI implementation?
What role do leadership and organizational culture play in facilitating AI adoption?

Methodology

This study employs a qualitative research design, utilizing extensive literature review and document analysis to evaluate the adoption of AI across various industries. The research draws upon a thorough examination of existing academic literature, industry reports, and relevant documentation to provide a comprehensive analysis of the human and organizational dynamics that shape AI integration. The literature review focuses on theoretical frameworks related to AI adoption, identifying key challenges, organizational readiness, and transformation processes. Additionally, document analysis based on case studies from published reports and industry sources offers valuable insights into real-world applications and the obstacles faced during AI implementation. By relying exclusively on secondary data sources, this study aims to develop a nuanced understanding of the human and organizational dimensions of AI adoption, contributing to the broader discourse on successful technological transformation.

Contribution of the Paper

This study contributes to AI integration in organizations literature. The identification of obstacles hindering the adoption of AI is provided including employee resistance and the lack of organizational readiness providing insights into how these barriers could be tackled. By showcasing effective human-AI collaboration in action, the paper successfully illustrates why a harmonious relationship between humans and AI is essential and how it can improve operational capabilities and decision-making. It also offers real-world strategy and advice for companies looking to implement AI, centered around building an organizational climate that both limits resistance and promotes innovative thinking. Moreover, it points out important shortcomings in the existing literature on human-machine interactions and provides ideas for future research that will help us to better understand how AI changes organizational landscapes and workforce.

2. INDUSTRIAL REVOLUTIONS AND ARTIFICIAL INTELLIGENCE

2.1 History of Industrial Revolutions

The Industrial Revolution represents the arrival of industrial society and a watershed in this process as an agrarian economy based on manual labor was replaced by one dominated by industry. Since the early days of industrialization, technological advances have always brought about seismic changes — what we now think of as transformations from the first to fourth Industrial Revolution. The use of steam and water power The mechanical inventions defined the first Industrial Revolution that began in the late 18th century, The following Industrial Revolution, on the other hand, occurred for most of the 19th century and brought along electrical energy which allowed mass production at a scale like never seen before. The third Industrial Revolution, which occurred throughout the 20th century added the automation of internet processes and communications technologies introduced how communication is made digitally performing process innovation on Industry (Lasi et al., 2014; Lele, 2019; Morgon, 2016). The boundary conditions between the physical and digital worlds were beyond human imagination falling in Fourth Industrial Revolution — but converge they did (Lele, 2019). As Lele (2019) puts it, these advancements have cones long way from the days of steam engines and railway system and then to steel industry which now are the foundation for electronic and computing revolution on which forth Industrial Revolution is proved. Not only that, but according to Lele (2019), this is a revolution beyond just updated technology and marks the change of industrial paradigms in a fundamental sense. In fact, Lasi and Kemper (2014) predict that new development of advanced digitalization & strategic integration of internet techs with another blossoming inventions to revolutionize this era since they force the landscape transfer into shape at most their opinion basic paradigm. Consequently, Industry 4.0 has been introduced to describe the rapid wave of change to an improved manner to conduct work in production (Lasi et al., 2014; Lele, 2019; Culot et al., 2020). Today, the idea is also used to refer to what is termed a "smart factory," which means that automation, digitization, machines, information systems and human interaction form an integrated system as part of one unified operational landscape (Ustundag & Cevikcan, 2017). Scholars and Industrialists, who envisaged Industry 4.0 as the next chapter in the evolution of Industries, also contributed significantly in popularising it worldwide thus making it global phenomenon during the early 2010s. AI is responsible for fast and wide-ranging changes in a large number of domains (Martin & Leurent, 2017). Industry 4.0, of which AI is a main component (Riberio 2021), provides significant promise for more autonomous and efficient production process improvement efforts. As companies are trying to cope with the fast-paced adoption of Industry 4.0, there is starting to be some attention placed on the coming age of Industry 5.0.

2.2 Industry 5.0 and the Role of Artificial Intelligence

The rapid development of Artificial Intelligence (AI) and the efficiency gains brought about by robotics and automation are paving the way for Industry 5.0. Industry 5.0, synonymous with the concept of "Human in the Loop," signifies the collaboration of humans and robots or humans and AI to enhance productivity. An essential aspect of Industry 5.0 is the use of green energy and environmentally friendly technologies. While information technology and other advanced technologies offer numerous benefits, they are also major consumers of energy. Therefore, developing a sustainable system powered by renewable energy is a crucial indicator of maturity for Industry 5.0. Lastly, the concept of the Digital Twin should be highlighted (Wagg et al., 2020). The primary goal in Industry 5.0 is to create a digital twin of the entire business, enabling quick adaptation to changes and maintaining competitive strength. For this to happen, end-to-end must be digitized across the organization — from robots and AI to IoT sensors and complete automation. Even if Industry 4.0 is expanding rapidly, automation continues to disappoint in terms of maturity. And, most enterprises are battling to move completely to automation, deplete the labour wage-bill and uplift productivity in a major way. The truth is that far fewer businesses have been successful in adapting to these shifts. The issue is also evolving, particularly with the development of Industry 5.0 and Human in The Loop becoming stronger as more advanced automation and artificial intelligence become integrated. That advantage in the global market is slipping as huge corporations like Tesla and Ford question what to do as they struggle with the buildout of so-called dark factories—factories that are fully automated, lights-out operations. The gulf between the global competitive advantages in large enterprises that have mastered AI and those that have not are widening, thereby creating billion-dollar companies (and billionaires) while increasing both global inequality and also geopolitical tensions. A Shift in Business, Worldwide But for businesses around the world this is a crucial moment. Adaptation as well as a proactive course of action will eventually become necessary due to the rapid pace of technological evolution. Enterprises need to realize automation along with use of AI are changing their field and they have to adapt quickly or risk falling behind competitors. This discrepancy are now underlined more than before: use these techs or face the possibility of being left behind. This engagement is leading to a fierce competition where high stakes are even more involved than before. Given these advancements, it is crucial for businesses to realize the importance of transitioning themselves towards Industry 5.0. They will need to commit to truly end-to-end digital transformation, and create a culture where innovation and change are accepted. Includes installing AI, robotics, IoTs, sensors and fully automating their operations. The successful implementation of these new technologies can greatly improve the overall efficiency, output and revenue, further strengthening your position on the market. Hence, not only should businesses keep up with these evolutions but also capitalize on them further to stay ahead and to remain competitive in the long run. Recognize how significant of a change this is happening, and what opportunities exist for any business who wants to excel in this new era of industrial 5.0. To answer this question, companies bridge the gap to level of competition but also create more opportunities for everyone down the line.

3. ARTIFICIAL INTELLIGENCE AND POTENTIAL IMPACTS

3.1 AI for Today

Canals and Heukamp (2020) pointed out that AI has been a thing since 1956 but 2022 will stand out as the year of leaps and bounds towards AI. It is a general consensus that if these accomplishments have been arrived at today, then we owe much rise to the magical hand of artificial neural networks as they were constructed with human brain structure in mind. These networks can be successfully used in emotion recognition and problem solving. For example, in medical diagnoses, optimization problems, weather forecasting, stock market predictions (Bostrom 2016). The recent advances in technologies like large language models and generative AI, as well as trends like ChatGPT, have produced three new broad categories of AI(edges). They are Artificial Narrow Intelligence (ANI), Artificial General Intelligence (AGI) and Super (Human-level) Intelligent. This is because narrow AI does not possess human-level general intelligence in all domains and can only yield positive results in some special cases (Russell & Norvig 2016.). This one is what we know and have in use nowadays (Carriço, 2018): Narrow AI It is used in medicine (and gets results that are more similar to a human diagnosis) to detect cancer and other diseases (O'Carroll 2017). Daily used Narrow AI applications are: Alexa, Google Assistant, Siri and autonomous vehicles and facial recognition systems (Davidson, 2019).

3.2 AI for Tomorrow

Artificial General Intelligence (AGI) is defined as a system that exhibits intelligent behaviors at least as advanced as a human's in all cognitive tasks. In recent years, researchers have predicted that such AI would emerge around 2050 and beyond (Russell & Norvig, 2016). However, recent developments suggest that the first versions may be released by 2025. AGI is noted for its ability to use its intelligence not only to solve problems but also to improve itself. Artificial Super Intelligence (ASI), the next step beyond AGI, represents AI significantly more intelligent than humans in every aspect (Barrett & Baum, 2016). Machines with ASI possess consciousness and self-awareness, outperforming human capabilities and intelligence. Theoretically, they would provide much better outputs in everything compared to humans. ASI has the capacity to process and analyze data faster, make better decisions, and solve problems flawlessly (O'Carroll, 2017). While some find the potential of such powerful algorithms appealing, others are concerned about the possible consequences. Some argue that the realization of ASI could lead to a global catastrophe, with AI potentially taking full control and even causing human extinction (Barrett & Baum, 2016). The idea of a world with AGI and ASI capabilities worries many people, including AI experts. Although the likelihood of ASI entering our lives in the near future is very low, Zhu et al. (2020) state that even the AI applied today causes concerns for many, leading to worries about ethics, data security, and unemployment. Employees fear losing power and their jobs, which can lead to a breakdown of trust between employers and employees, resulting in employee resistance.

4. HUMAN RESOURCES AND ARTIFICIAL INTELLIGENCE

4.1 Perception of Threat

The technological advancements we have experienced in recent years, the availability of large data sets, and the rapid automation of business processes are paving the way for AI technologies. Especially with the evolving capabilities in learning, problem-solving, emotion recognition, and autonomous management of business processes and supply chains, successful outcomes are increasingly being achieved (Daugherty & Wilson, 2018). For instance, machine learning algorithms can detect suspicious financial transactions and provide decision support to prevent fraud (Davenport, 2019). Current AI solutions have become capable of performing various human achievements, such as understanding spoken words, recognizing emotions, engaging in conversation, and even demonstrating creativity. Examples of intelligent voice assistants, industrial robots, and autonomous vehicles are increasing (Canals & Heukamp, 2020). The technological revolution, increasingly felt thanks to these examples, is transforming industries and organizations, pushing traditional companies out of the game and creating anxieties due to the social changes it imposes (Canals & Heukamp, 2020). While AI offers innovative opportunities for organizations, it can also lead to various challenges. When AI technologies are implemented in an organization, they can result in different outcomes in terms of limiting, complementing, and/or replacing employees. Daugherty and Wilson (2018) noted that organizations see intelligent machines as a force that will replace humans, thus creating a sense of threat for humanity. Although this perception of threat has been experienced in all past industrial revolutions and technological developments, intelligent machines have enhanced human skills, led to the emergence of new professions, and made it possible to achieve previously unattainable efficient outcomes through human-machine collaboration. For example, while typewriter operators may have lost their jobs with the advent of computers and the internet, there has been a much greater demand for computer operators, software engineers, and computer specialists. AI's new capabilities in areas specific to humans bring about concerns regarding their consequences. Particularly for organizations, while the number of areas where positive outcomes can be beneficial increases, the likelihood of undesirable outcomes for individuals also rises. Therefore, we can say that the benefits of AI have the potential to vary among stakeholders. This variability depends on the interaction between employees and AI, the nature of the work, and the structure of the organization. This results in a comparison between employees skills and performance with AI which would be discussed under successful AI outcomes (Schuetz & Venkatesh, 2020). The rapid dissemination of AI can make employees feel impotent and helpless, stress out, negative emotions and contrary behavior. This could be a barrier to their AI adoption and success (Zhu et al., 2020). Common reasons for these negative attitudes are also detailed by Kotter and Schlesinger (2008) some of which include the sense that power is being lost, structural inertia within the organization, limited focus of change in terms of needs and benefits, marginalization through poor involvement in planning decisions brought about during change phases, or simply general rudeness. The proliferation of AI technology will cause a public discussion on the effects that workers and organizational structure, and we already see very strong polarization. While some argue that this will eliminate many jobs (Frey & Osborne, 2017), others suggest that it will only enhance productivity and improve the quality of jobs (Jarrahi, 2018; Spencer, 2018). Artistic genre influence by science fiction films, news, and social media can lead to employees having perceptions of what AI is and what it capable of (Aleksander 2017; Borges et al. 2020; Johnson & Verdicchio 2017). It could also make things worse to mischaracterise the AI that is already in (Cave et al., 2018). One could predict that the interaction of these three may eliminate any positive constructive purpose for AI, and this collective experience would inevitably result in social identity threat leading to the negative attitudes, job affect, low job commitment, cynicism, and intention to leave (Brougham & Haar, 2018). This is a pattern that usually comes into play when the staff knows about the situation. Essentially, the biggest concern is about AI and smart technologies being able to take jobs away from employees or make them redundant, meaning they will not be able to do their current job anymore. Employees also worry that their skills will quickly become old with changing technology, and they will no longer be needed. Fear and threat-based attitudes are connected with low job engagement and commitment, increased turnover intentions, burnout of the job, along with resistance to change and external technologies. Employees often hold ambivalent attitudes, research finds but across the board, studies have mixed news for employees on AI. While they accept that AI can help them do their work, also think it may replace some of their jobs.

4.2 Behavioral Models and Attitudes of Human Resources

Zhu et al. (2020) found that the reactions of employees to AI (both positive and negative) are influenced by various attitudes, which encompass cognitive appraisals as well as affective responses. These orientations are mediated by the theory of cognitive appraisal (Lazarus & Folkman, 1984), which posits that individuals' cognitive, affective, and behavioral responses are externalities when under stressors. Therefore, organizations must understand that employees are not passive participants of AI implementations but an active voice influencing their success. In conclusion, managers need to account for employees' attitudes towards AI, as these attitudes can help predict how employees may behave towards AI in the future, making it an essential step towards adopting AI in an effective manner by originally creating an association between employees and AI. Zhu et al. (2020) note as well that employees often have a pre-attitude towards AI before they have any experience with how it actually works. These attitudes, covering rational and emotional dimensions alike, can be either positive or negative. Rational evaluations depend on calculating the potential costs and benefits of AI (Zhu et al., 2020). For instance, employees who believe that AI will enhance productivity or remove repetitive work are more likely to form positive beliefs. In contrast, others may be less positive about AI, (Davenport, 2019) if they believe that it threatens their performance or they routine. Unlike rational assessments, emotional attitudes arise from psychological reactions to perceived opportunities or threats. On the one hand, positive emotions like hope for genuine potential of AI future can add to more progressive attitudes, on the other hand anxiety and stress due to threat perception can give a negative emotional reaction (Zhu et al., 2020). During this appraisal process, cognitive attitudes are formed, and these are structured by the behaviors and resources employees perceive they have. High personal agency, in terms of skills, knowledge base and social skills makes people feel less threatened by emerging AI capabilities while individuals with limited resources may experience a loss of control and adopt a defensive posture (Fadal & Brown, 2010; Zhu et al., 2020). Zhu et al. (2020) have grouped employees into four distinct categories based on their attitude towards AI: Reluctants, Enthusiasts, Opponents, and Skeptics. Reluctants understand the logical advantages of AI yet might continue to have adverse emotional reactions such as fear or anxiety. Conversely, fans are generally favourable toward AI, both logically and sentimentally, expressing hopefulness and involvement in its potential. In contrast, the opponents who are the least positive of all about AI are more negatively rational and negatively emotional. Finally, Skeptics believe in AI emotionally but still they are rationally skeptical — doubtful of the practicality and benefits of AI, always asking whether the costs outweigh the benefits. Kotter and schlesinger (2008) underline that it is only natural for some people to be afraid of changes, but fear of innovation is a catalyst to negative behavior as long as people perceive themselves threatened by change.

5. ARTIFICIAL INTELLIGENCE IN ORGANIZATIONS

AI can be applied in organizations to enhance decision-making, transform processes, and improve products and services (Davenport, 2020). Indeed, Ng (2019) posits that AI has the potential to revolutionize every industry in much the same way that electricity did a century ago. The continuous advancement of AI, therefore, offers organizations and their leaders the opportunity to differentiate and safeguard their operations. It is estimated that by 2030, AI will contribute approximately 13 trillion dollars in additional global economic value (Ng, 2019; Bughin et al.,

2018). Consequently, the transformative potential of AI compels organizations to reconsider and redefine their foundational principles. Moreover, AI can provide new opportunities by simplifying and optimizing organizational structures (Canals & Heukamp, 2020). However, AI does not merely call for a transformation of business processes (Daugherty & Wilson, 2018). The successful integration of AI, indeed, requires careful planning (Jöhnk et al., 2020). In this regard, it is necessary to involve all stakeholder groups in the planning and preparation phases to guarantee a successful outcome (Wright & Schultz, 2018). In order to make AI able to perform such tasks, this preparation is necessary (Lokuge et al., 2019). Alsheiabni et al. As (2018) put it, the preparation phase encompasses the "changes that must be made" at the stage before the implementation of AI. Multiple studies have identified numerous conditions and factors that affect an organization's readiness for AI adoption. Some of the main factors are financial and technical resources, the support from the management, organizational culture and clear goals and objectives (Chwelos et al., 2001; Damanpour & Schneider, 2006; Iacovou et al., 1995; Lokuge et al., 2019; Robey et al., 2008). Organizational readiness is also influenced by psychological constructs such as resistance to change and support, commitment, and structural components like adaptability (Lokuge et al., 2019; Weiner, 2009). As Snyder-Halpern (2021) and Weiner (2009) highlight, a high readiness proves to be an enabler for successful AI adoption and as risk mitigator against adoption failures. As AI is a highly complex issue due to the fact that it is a hot technology in addition to requiring specialist knowledge, preparation becomes essential for any organisation that wants to deploy it (Gallivan, 2001). Thus, organizations unwilling to undergo AI - such organizations are very likely to go down. In order for an organization to make the jump to AI applications successfully, it will be up to the manager to not only do the required research but to also find ways to motivate change. In addition, the move to AI is a step-change, and managers need to carefully plan for such a transition. They can only effectively embrace AI and successfully manage the transformation by doing so (Knickrehm, 2018). Groopman (2018) argues that organisations should do more than claim the advantages of AI, they should also be ready to make significant changes, including those impacting human resources. Like all organizational change, employees will have mixed feelings about AI. Moreover, it has been recognized that maturity is correlated with organizational readiness (Ellefsen et al., 2019). To be sufficiently prepared to adopt AI, managers should conduct an assessment of the readiness and maturity levels of the organization based on suitable measurement scales (Pringle & Zoller, 2018). New research highlights the vital role of adequate knowledge to help individuals and organizations gear up for AI. Humans are capable at adapting to the change, hence in making learning easier by having knowledge is said to be the prerequisite of evolution. According to Gallivan (2001), the complexity of AI applications often results from missing information and technological variance. In this regard, Groopman (2018) notes that insufficient information can make organizations unsure of where or how to start the AI process, regardless, adversely impacting their AI readiness. Armenakis et al. (1993) argue that the relationships one has with attitude and previous experience with similar activities acts as a filter through which individuals process the need for change. Zhu et al. Fadal and Brown (2010) and Saqr et al. On the macro level, knowledge is a tool to wipe out prejudices, which means employees know almost everything about the changes coming up, and they respond positively to change. Employees who are most educated on AI, for example, feel the least threatened by it, while those with fewer resources and less information are also more prone to defensive or negative attitudes, motivated largely by a sense of lost control. While not a new concept, AI has seen significant momentum in recent years (Canals & Heukamp, 2020). Even though it is becoming popular, some people have no idea it even exists. Most people perceive AI based on the movies, television shows, news or social media. According to Zhu et al. (2020); the information obtained from these sources tends to be incomplete or erroneous. Consequently, employees who rely on these sources may be misinformed about AI, ideas which may cultivate oppositional behavior across the organization. Accordingly, Groopman (2018) argues that managers need to improve their own knowledge and educate and collaborate with their employees. Comprehensive information shows good faith, raises awareness and reduces fear, all of which help build a positive construction in the organization and ultimately the confidence to adopt AI.

5.1 Change Management for the Use of AI in Organizations

Change is undeniably challenging, with research indicating that approximately 70% of change initiatives ultimately fail, and only a minority of managers are able to navigate the complexities of the process successfully (Nohria & Beer, 2000). Often, during periods of change, managers fail to prioritize the crucial task of securing employee support. However, Kotter and Schlesinger (2008) propose six strategies to manage change effectively: education and communication, participation and involvement, facilitation and support, negotiation and agreement, manipulation and co-optation, as well as explicit and implicit coercion. Furthermore, it is essential to recognize that different types of change necessitate the application of varying strategies. Notwithstanding the inherent difficulties, organizations in the AI era cannot afford to delay change. It is imperative that all managers within an organization possess the capability to diagnose the need for change and attitudes toward it, as well as develop themselves to implement appropriate methods for overcoming these challenges. As with other forms of transformation, AI implementation is expected to elicit a range of employee reactions. It would be overly simplistic to expect employees to readily accept AI and its positive implications (Zhu et al., 2020). Therefore, it is vital for managers to ensure that all employees remain engaged and aligned with the organization's objectives. The leaders of the future will be those who are adept at fostering collaboration, leveraging collective intelligence, and transforming not only their businesses but also entire industries and workforces (Daugherty & Wilson, 2018). While some organizations have already begun to embrace AI, many remain in the initial stages of adoption, comprehension, and acceptance. As with any significant transformation, the adoption phase is crucial, as it sets the groundwork for future implementation efforts (Zhu et al., 2020). Consequently, readiness for change is a prerequisite for organizations aspiring to successfully navigate the AI adoption process. A widely accepted definition of readiness for change is provided by Armenakis et al. (1993, p. 681), who describe it as "beliefs, attitudes, and intentions regarding the extent to which changes are needed and the organization's capacity to successfully implement those changes." Nevertheless, numerous organizations face challenges in initiating the change process, often due to a lack of sufficient information (Groopman, 2018). Rafferty et al. (2012) contend that readiness for change differs across organizations, with distinct requirements emerging depending on the specific context. Also, readiness for change is isomorphic, such that individuals and groups, when placed in similar situations, will tend to perceive readiness in similar yet not identical ways. At an individual level, behaviours conducive to change, positive attitudes, job satisfaction and organizational commitment represent signs of readiness for change. Kim et al. (2011) characterize these indicators as the active participation, facilitation and contributions of employees in organization-driven change, or "behaviors that support change." Moreover, extensive research reveals that employees' change attitudes represent some of the most cited reasons for planned initiatives' failure (e.g., Miller et al., 1994; Rafferty et al., 2012). In addition, we need to remember that the success or failure of change initiatives is ultimately defined in the leadership. The way that leaders behave and approach their strategy has a huge impact (e.g., Berson & Avolio, 2004; Bommer et al., 2005; Eisenbach et al., 1999; Fiol et al., 1999; Higgs & Rowland, 2000; Higgs & Rowland, 2005; House et al., 1991; Howell & Higgins, 1990; Struckman & Yammarino, 2003; Waldman et al., 2004; Knickrehm, 2018). It means that leaders who are dealing with change need to sharpen their diagnostic skills to detect different attitudes in various stakeholders and address the challenges that follow. There are different approaches to change management, Kotter and Schlesinger (2008) suggested six principal tactics of change as education and communication, participation and involvement, facilitation and support, negotiation and agreement, manipulation and co-optation, and explicit and implicit coercion. According to Kotter and Schlesinger (2008), some simple but effective strategies, including employee education, allowing time to adjust to the change, listening to concerns, and providing support, can significantly diminish negative attitudes and help those involved in the change process. And finally, there are negotiations and agreements that can be an effective tool for resistance. For example, leveraging financial rewards with a change as a means to discount resistance can support a more productive organizational climate.

5.2 The Stages of Change Management Process

It is clear that organizations cannot just re-design the process over which AI will operate; we need to map the transformation of effective AI adoption, which must be a holistic preparation effort. According to Jöhnk et al. (2020) argue, involves the foundational tasks to enable certain actions being performed by AI systems, which Lokuge et al. (2019) as a key part of readiness. Indeed, Alsheiabni et al. (2018) define AI readiness as the organization-wide changes needed for AI implementation. Different studies suggest that there is a variety of determinants that impact the preparedness of an organization for adopting AI including financial and technical resources, management support, organizational culture and clearly defined goals and objectives that facilitate such preparations. Preparedness is not only determined by the structural aspects of change, in organizations such as the capacity of the organization to change but also the psychological aspects of change resistance and the support and level of commitment. As noted by Lokuge et al. (2005) and Weiner (2009), organizational readiness significantly improves the odds of successful AI adoption and lowers the risk of such adoption being a failure. Because AI is complex by nature, from its complex technology to the deeper technical knowledge needed to set it up, organizations that wish to successfully transition to AI need to double down on their preparation efforts. As such, organizations that don't prepare adequately risk lagging in their AI journey. Preparing is often associated with maturity and a good organizational process, however, we have to draw the line between preparing and maturity. While preparation is evaluated ahead of the maturation process, Ellefsen et al. (2019) specifically states that maturity assessments must be done during the development phase. Understanding and assessing organizational maturity on appropriate assessment models is imperative for organizations that want to stay ahead of the curve or catch up with emerging technologies. There are several such models, each with its own set of criteria and custom applications. Pringle and Zoller (2018) even described an AI maturity model and defined stages organizations go through, from those who have hardly started to those who are far ahead of their competitors. New organizations may still be in evaluation stage where they are limited by the lack of strategy and unusable data on their part, but advanced organizations must not allow themselves to become complacent and settle, relying on what had already been proven for the sake of not finding new strategies or technologies to move forward. In order to assess the AI maturity of an organization, however, various dimensions play a role: the presence of a clear strategy, a culture that is ready for AI, the state of available data and its quality, the applicability of AI technologies, as well as successful operational integration. Focusing on these areas will allow organizations to better position themselves for success in the AI era, ensuring competitiveness and full preparedness to harness the potential of this transformative technology.

5.3 Awareness and Collaboration

Integrated and systematic perspectives are needed to study the effects of AI on individuals and organizations (von Krogh, 2018). The impact of these technologies is too nuanced to be sufficiently captured by either the doomist or the techno-optimist narrative. Depending on the knowledge of individuals on what AI should be used for, their perspective on the results of AI might defer, and ultimately work results. Unfortunately, we have an insufficient amount of studies which focus on treating business processes and practical skills in times of AI (Meijer et al., 2021). Few studies have addressed how employees perceive and react to these changes (Bucher et al., 2021). In retrospect, some key points can be taken by looking down the path we walked. The first is that the beneficial outcomes and efficiencies promised from AI rely on the partnership and cohesion between humans and technology. This means that it is important to support the understanding that AI systems are used to augment rather than replace human capabilities. This awareness will stop the bias that there will be workers, who will be replaced by the AI. AI helping humans can take on many forms with applications, approaches and specific solutions. These examples include performance feedback and digital assistants (Malik et al., 2022), decision-making processes (Meijer et al., 2021), and customer interactions and service offerings (Kim et al., 2011). The factors contributing to each solution and the techno-economic advantages that can be obtained vary at both the individual and organizational levels. The joint effort between humans and AI will depend on how AI impacts tasks and job designs, and employees' perceptions of and attitudes toward AI. Thus, the generated technologies satisfaction is related to how responsive the results' or outputs', both in terms of needs, effectiveness of the outcomes (Nguyen & Malik, 2022a), employees' job satisfaction (Nguyen & Malik, 2022a), and productivity or performance (Marikyan et al., 2022). During AI evaluation, a collaborator needs to be mindful of an employee's state of awareness. The process of achieving intended successful outcomes is more reachable by having the knowledge that AI can handle monotonous tasks (Sowa et al., 2021), be tailored to specific task type (Sowa & Przegalinska, 2020), enhance decisions (Kawaguchi, 2021), and improve quality positively. In the study, involving hundreds of employees, it was shown that when employees trust AI, understand what AI is and its purpose, and how to work with it (Chowdhury et al., 2022), human-AI collaboration improves. In organizations that have high levels of awareness, successful AI applications have been shown to reduce workers' mental and physical fatigue, and foster positive emotions (Qiu et al., 2022). Such outcomes enable human-technology interactions and hybrid working practices across the organisation. The role of leadership and dynamic capability-building in successfully deploying AI in the organization.

5.4 Leadership and Dynamic Capabilities

Numerous organizational aspects of human ratification contribute to family and artificial intelligence. Stages: Organizational mechanisms and cultures that support innovation, facilitate the adoption of AI by employees, as these cultures stimulate innovative behaviour and expectation around replacement are managed (Verma & Singh, 2022). A focus on the strategic use of AI to improve productivity and drive positive organizational outcomes, aligned with active leadership, strong HR practices, substantial technology investments and higher organizational readiness, creates a fertile environment where AI adoption can succeed. With developments in AI on the rise, the business landscape is changing so rapidly that organizations must continuously question their basic tenets of operation. Far more than just automating and scaling activities, AI empowers individuals to assume entirely new roles, something that will significantly elevate the need for agile, dynamic leadership and organizational adaptability. Yet, the evolution of AI often requires organizational changes that are likely to engender negative attitudes in managers and employees (Frick et al., 2021). Thus, leaders must transition from their management styles to create dynamic capabilities to navigate their businesses and workforces through these complexities of change (Daugherty & Wilson, 2018). Indeed, one body of change management research highlights that these types of leadership behavior are effective in preventing negative attitudes toward organizational change (Prosci, 2018), cementing the appeal for managers to proactively align employee attitudes in the change process (Pharoah, 2018). In addition, considerable literature highlights the crucial importance of interaction of managers with employees in the workflows of the change processes needed for digital transformations (Ahmad et al., 2020; Stefanou, 2001; Baptista et al., 2020; Heavin & Power, 2018; Prince, 2017; Vial, 2019). Managers have the power to significantly impact employee perceptions in a favorable manner and consequently are a crucial element determining the success or failure of AI implementations (Alsheiabni et al., 2018; Lichtenthaler, 2020). Thus, leaders possess the unique power to facilitate organizational preparedness and reduce employee resistance to change. Bader and Kaiser (2019) go on to suggest that without the support of leadership the challenges surrounding human-AI interaction are likely to be formidable. Hence, organizational culture, employee alignment, and inspiring them to seek active participation that leads to a need to innovate must be seen as central to the strategy focused on the successful implementation of AI. But one of the biggest points to highlight is that technology in itself makes up only half of the innovation when it comes to digital transformation. Ransbotham et al. (Mohammed et al. 2017) find that While 85% of organizations claim they are willing to utilize on AI, but in fact many have not achieved this. Simply realizing the potential of AI is not enough for organizations to realize its benefits; they have to be properly prepared (Groopman, 2018). Although most people think data wins the day on AI investment, Groopman (2018) made the case that investing in people is more valuable than investing in data. Employee and manager expectations of AI can be profoundly disparate, with some employees taking a decidedly positive view of AI, ready to welcome automation with open arms, while others are skeptical or fearful. The very idea that AI could change the nature of their job or their performance may feel threatening to some employees (Groopman, 2018). Thus, supportive behaviors and positive attitudes are key indicators for readiness for change. At the organizational level, the products of readiness to change provide dynamic capabilities that are critical for the adaptation of low-skilled and often routine tasks (Salvato & Rerup, 2011). Organizations need to make expectations clear and build a common understanding to ensure the successful adoption of AI and that employees will accept it. This requires input from domain experts with different knowledge and perspectives in developing and designing AI in the large. Additionally, AI should not be seen as a linear goal but as a long, continuous road of learning and adaptation. This means that organizations need to promote wide contributions to AI creation with existing tools, training programs and cross-functional collaborations (Groopman 2018, p. 11). Training employees for AI, then, is not just about giving them the skills needed to work with new technologies; it's also about creating a mindset shift that engenders trust and reduces fears. Organizations should take care of the transition to AI by clearly articulating the areas where it is applicable, the new opportunities it is going to create, the scope of work for employees, the people who will be involved in the process, and the aspects of their world that are affected. Because AI threatens more conventional roles and paths than any other technology, whether the revolution succeeds depends on employees' willingness to embrace it. Despite this, a global research study from 3,000 employees found that only 58% of organizations have even begun to consider the impact of AI on HR more broadly (Bolden-Barrett 2018). Hence, it is the responsibility of organizational leaders to address the emotions, apprehension and concerns that their employees have with respect to AI implementation. These factors are a crucial consideration not just for seamless AI integration but creating an organizational culture conducive to AI adoption longevity.

5.5 Culture and Adaptation

Deloitte (2022) identifies Trust, Data, and Agility as key components for AI readiness in organizational culture. High-performing organizations exhibit more than twice the fear levels compared to low-performing ones, primarily due to job loss concerns. However, these high-performing organizations invest in employee training and change management rather than reducing headcount, indicating a bold AI vision. Actions supporting this vision, combined with cultural and change management strategies, foster success and build trust. Andrew Beers, CTO at Tableau, states, "For AI to succeed, people need to change their relationship with data." Increasing data literacy at all levels is crucial. Employees must ask the right questions and obtain the right data to solve work problems. When data literacy is improved, and teams trust AI, good things happen. AI-empowered organizations need to constantly monitor, learn and enhance. Agility, or the ability to take fast action, is key. "Getting comfortable that failing is a possibility and being able to respond quickly is critical," says Rajeev Ronanki, SVP Digital Services Officer at Anthem. AI investments are characterized by trial and error, learning from failures." In short, trust, data literacy, and agility will be the pillars on which organizations will be built to prepare for and successfully implement AI. Based on information from SpencerStuart (2024), important aspects of an AI-ready organizational culture include Disruption and Innovation: Organizations like Google and Microsoft cultivate a mindset of perpetual learning and experimentation. An environment where employees feel empowered to explore new ideas and learn from their mistakes fosters innovation and pushes the boundaries of creativity. Data-Driven Approach: There should be data supporting the innovation. They bring their ideas to AWS, where employees use data to back up their ideas, so ideas are critically evaluated and constantly improved. Ethical Sensitivity Organizations should tackle ethical issues associated with AI, including transparency, inclusivity and diversity. A proper equilibrium with entrepreneurial risks guarantees core values and public confidence are preserved. Risk Management: AI can help identify and mitigate risks using predictive tools and data design. AI and worker training programs improve employees' risk management capabilities and preparedness. Collaboration: Implementation of AI would require cooperation between departments. With this, it becomes a platform to share innovative ideas and design well-rounded solutions that resonate with business objectives. To conclude, nurturing a culture of learning, innovation, data-driven decision-making, ethical sensitivity, risk management, and collaboration is critical for organizations that are adopting AI.

6. CONCLUSIONS AND RECOMMENDATIONS

Mintzberg (1979), Galbraith (2014), and Morgan (2006) have considerably evolved our understanding of organizational structure, management, and operations, particularly with the advancement in technologies. Mintzberg describes an organization through identical structures namely, simple structure, machine bureaucracy, professional bureaucracy, divisionalized form, and adhocracy that helps the organizations adapt themselves as per the AI. Because simple structures are flexible and adhocracies value innovation, they lend themselves well to AI integration. Mintzberg's managerial roles such as the "monitor role" and the "entrepreneur role" nicely complement with AI's abilities in data analysis and strategic decision making. Star Model by Galbraith, which lays emphasis on strategy-structure-processes-rewards-people- can be beneficial for AI integration. He points out the need for organizational strategy to be in alignment with AI capabilities and that structural flexibility needs to be maintained. And structures must reward AI-led innovation, and the workforce must be trained to ensure effective AI-human collaboration, Galbraith adds. Morgan finds metaphors that describe organizational dynamics. The Good News: Bureaucracies Enabled By AI Adapt to Change The machine metaphor frames things well for bureaucracies, and the organism metaphor views AI as upgrading adaptability. Brain metaphor: Organization as a structure that processes information — AI centers will significantly improve the ability of an organization to make decisions. They have been able to adopt Ai technologies, which have created a huge impact on organizations, from increasing efficiency to saving costs and innovation. But there are challenges to implementing AI, and employees are concerned. Managing employee attitudes towards AI is important for success. This article reveals that cultural and structural transformations are needed to tackle the technical and human aspects with training, change management, and employee engagement. The impact of AI on the future labor market is significant, as some of the work people do today will disappear, but new jobs will also be created. Organizations have to build dynamic capabilities to prosper in this transformation.

6.1 Contributions to Future Research

This paper analyzes the effects of AI within organizations and provides avenues for future research. Studies would be required to assess the long-term implications of AI on organizational structure, design, processes, culture, business practices, and management strategies. Such research can uncover AI's potential for sustainable competitive advantages and transformational strategies. There's still a lot to learn about AI's impact on employees — on things such as job satisfaction, motivation, stress levels and overall well-being. Future research may look at how employees adapted to AI, development of training programs, and effectiveness of these programs. Societal and ethical aspects of AI are also important. More research is needed on data privacy, algorithmic fairness, transparency, and AI's societal impacts, such as in labor market changes and social inequalities. We need models to guide human-AI collaboration. Research should study how humans and machines collaborate effectively, how we leverage their contributions to achieve organizational efficiency, and the expectation of employee capabilities, across sectors and job roles. Two key areas are change management and organizational readiness. Research should look at how ready organizations are for AI, whether change management strategies are working, and what the challenges are. Recognising the critical steps in preparing for the successful integration of AI is imperative. Finally, there's a need for extensive research into the large-scale economic and social effects of A.I. We need to be able to mitigate against the societal negative and positive aspects that arise. Overall, future research will need to provide deep insights into AI implications within the context of organizations in general by offering strategies for optimal use of AI, as well as proactive solutions addressing leaking issues.

REFERENCES

Ahmad, F., Widén, G., & Huvila, I. (2020). The impact of workplace information literacy on organizational innovation: An empirical study. *International Journal of Information Management*, 51, 51. DOI: 10.1016/j.ijinfomgt.2019.102041

Aleksander, I. (2017). Partners of Humans: A Realistic Assessment of the Role of Robots in the Foreseeable Future. *Journal of Information Technology*, 32(1), 1–9. DOI: 10.1057/s41265-016-0032-4

Alsheiabni, S., Cheung, Y., & Messom, C. (2018). Artificial intelligence adoption: AI-readiness at firm-level. In: PACIS 2018 Proceedings.

Armenakis, A., Harris, S., & Mossholder, K. (1993). Creating readiness for organizational change. *Human Relations*, 46(6), 681–703. DOI: 10.1177/001872679304600601

Baptista, J., Stein, M.-K., Klein, S., Watson-Manheim, M., & Lee, J. (2020). Digital work and organisational transformation: Emergent digital/human work configurations in modern organisations. *The Journal of Strategic Information Systems*, 29(2), 101618. DOI: 10.1016/j.jsis.2020.101618

Barrett, A., & Baum, S. (2016). A Model of Pathways to Artificial Superintelligence Catastrophe for Risk and Decision Analysis. *Journal of Experimental & Theoretical Artificial Intelligence*, 29(2), 1–18.

Berson, Y., & Avolio, B. (2004). Transformational leadership and the dissemination of organizational goals: A case study of a telecommunication firm. *The Leadership Quarterly*, 15(5), 625–646. DOI: 10.1016/j.leaqua.2004.07.003

Bolden-Barrett, V. (2018, February 20). Employees think AI is good, but employers' silence creates fear. Retrieved April 2, 2020, from HRDive: https://www.hrdive.com/news/employees-think-ai-is-good-but-employers-silence-creates-fear/517361/

Bommer, W., Rich, G., & Rubin, R. (2005). Changing attitudes about change: Longitudinal effects of transformational leader behavior on employee cynicism about organizational change. *Journal of Organizational Behavior*, 26(7), 733–753. DOI: 10.1002/job.342

Borges, A., Laurindo, F., Spínola, M., Gonçalves, R., & Mattos, C. (2020). The strategic use of artificial intelligence in the digital era: Systematic literature review and future research directions. *International Journal of Information Management*.

Bostrom, N. (2016). *Superintelligence: Paths, Dangers, Strategies*. Oxford University.

Brynjolfsson, E., & McAfee, A. (2017). The Business of Artificial Intelligence: What it can — and cannot — do for your organization.

Bughin, J., Seong, J., Manyika, J., Chui, M., & Joshi, R. (2018). *Notes from the AI frontier: Modeling the impact of AI on the world economy*. McKinsey Global Institute.

Canals, J., & Heukamp, F. (2020). *The Future of Management in an AI World: Redefining Purpose and Strategy in the Forth Industrial Revolution*. IESE Business Collection. DOI: 10.1007/978-3-030-20680-2

Carriço, G. (2018). The EU and artificial intelligence: A human-centred perspective. *European View*, 17(1), 29–36. DOI: 10.1177/1781685818764821

Chowdhury, G., & Hu, S. (2022). Employee Perceptions of AI Integration in Workplaces. *Journal of Organizational Behavior*, 43(5), 987–1002.

Chwelos, P., Benbasat, I., & Dexter, A. (2001). Research Report: Empirical Test of an EDI Adoption Model. *Information Systems Research*, 12(3), 304–321. DOI: 10.1287/isre.12.3.304.9708

Culot, G., Nassimbeni, G., Orzes, G., & Sartor, M. (2020). Behind the definition of Industry 4.0: Analysis and open questions. *International Journal of Production Economics*, 226(107617), 107617. DOI: 10.1016/j.ijpe.2020.107617

Damanpour, F., & Schneider, M. (2006). Phases of the Adoption of Innovation in Organizations: Effects of Environment, Organization and Top Managers. *British Journal of Management*, 17(3), 215–236. DOI: 10.1111/j.1467-8551.2006.00498.x

Daugherty, P., & Wilson, H. (2018). *Human + Machine: Reimagining Work in the Age of AI*. Harvard Business Review Press.

Davenport, T. (2019). Can We Solve AI's′ Trust Problem'? *MIT Sloan Management Review*, 60(3), 1–5.

Davenport, T. (2020). The State of AI in Businesses. In T. Davenport, E. Brynjolfsson, A. McAfee, & H. Wilson, Artificial Intelligence: The Insights You Need from Harvard Business Review.

Davidson, L. (2019, August 12). Narrow vs. General AI: What's Next for Artificial Intelligence? Retrieved from Springboard: https://www.springboard.com/blog/narrow-vs-general-ai/

Deloitte. (2022). State of AI in the Enterprise, 4th Edition. Deloitte Insights. https://www2.deloitte.com/us/en/insights/focus/cognitive-technologies/enterprise-artificial-intelligence-4th-edition.html

Eisenbach, R., Watson, K., & Pillai, R. (1999). Transformational leadership in the context of organizational change. *Journal of Organizational Change Management*, 12(2), 80–88. DOI: 10.1108/09534819910263631

El Naqa, I., & Murphy, M. (2015). What is Machine Learning? In I. El Naqa, R. Li, & M. Murphy,Machine Learning in Radiation Oncology (pp. 3-11). Springer. DOI: 10.1007/978-3-319-18305-3_1

Ellefsen, A., Oleśków-Szłapka, J., Pawłowski, G., & Tobola, A. (2019). Striving for Excellence in AI Implementation: AI Maturity Model Framework and Preliminary Research Results. *Scientific Journal of Logistics*, 15(3), 363–376.

Fadal, K., & Brown, S. (2010). Information Systems Appraisal and Coping: The Role of User Perceptions. *Communications of the Association for Information Systems*, 26(1). Advance online publication. DOI: 10.17705/1CAIS.02606

Fiol, C., Harris, D., & House, R. (1999). Charismatic leadership: Strategies for effecting social change. *The Leadership Quarterly*, 10(3), 449–482. DOI: 10.1016/S1048-9843(99)00021-1

Frick, N., Mirbabaie, M., Stieglitz, S., & Salomon, J. (2021). Maneuvering through the stormy seas of digital transformation: The impact of empowering leadership on the AI readiness of enterprises. *Journal of Decision Systems*, 30(2-3), 235–258. DOI: 10.1080/12460125.2020.1870065

Galbraith, J. R. (2014). *Designing Organizations: Strategy, Structure, and Process at the Business Unit and Enterprise Levels*. Jossey-Bass.

Gallivan, M. (2001). Organizational adoption and assimilation of complex technological innovations: Development and application of a new framework. *The Data Base for Advances in Information Systems*, 32(3), 51–85. DOI: 10.1145/506724.506729

Groopman, J. (2018). *AI Readiness; Five Areas Businesses Must Prepare for Success in Artificial Intelligence*. Kaleido Insights.

Heavin, C., & Power, D. (2018). Challenges for digital transformation – Towards a conceptual decision support guide for managers. *Journal of Decision Systems*, 27(1), 38–45. DOI: 10.1080/12460125.2018.1468697

Higgs, M., & Rowland, D. (2000). Building change leadership capability: 'The quest for change competence'. *Journal of Change Management*, 1(2), 116–130. DOI: 10.1080/714042459

Higgs, M., & Rowland, D. (2005). All changes great and small: Exploring approaches to change and its leadership. *Journal of Change Management*, 5(2), 121–151. DOI: 10.1080/14697010500082902

House, R., Spangler, W., & Woycke, J. (1991). (1991). Personality and charisma in the US presidency: A psychological theory of leader effectiveness. *Administrative Science Quarterly*, 36(3), 364–396. DOI: 10.2307/2393201

Howell, J., & Higgins, C. (1990). Champions of technological innovation. *Administrative Science Quarterly*, 35(2), 317–341. DOI: 10.2307/2393393

Iacovou, C., Benbasat, I., & Dexter, A. (1995). Electronic Data Interchange and Small Organizations: Adoption and Impact of Technology. *Management Information Systems Quarterly*, 19(4), 465–485. DOI: 10.2307/249629

Jöhnk, J., Weißert, M., & Wyrtki, K. (2020). *Ready or Not.* AI Comes— An Interview Study of Organizational AI Readiness Factors.

Johnson, D., & Verdicchio, M. (2017). AI Anxiety. *Journal of the Association for Information Science and Technology*, 68(9), 2267–2270. DOI: 10.1002/asi.23867

Kawaguchi, K. (2021). Enhancing Decision-Making Processes with Artificial Intelligence: A Comprehensive Overview. *Journal of Decision Systems*, 30(4), 321–334.

Kim, T.-G., Hornung, S., & Rousseau, D. (2011). Change-supportive behavior: Antecedents and the moderating role of time. *Journal of Management*, 37(6), 1664–1693. DOI: 10.1177/0149206310364243

Knickrehm, M. (2018). *How will AI Change the Work*. Harvard Business Review Press.

Kotter, J., & Schlesinger, L. (2008). Choosing Strategies for Change. *Harvard Business Review*, •••, 106–114. PMID: 10240501

Lasi, H., Fettke, P., Kemper, H.-G., Feld, T., & Hoffman, M. (2014). Industry 4.0. *Business & Information Systems Engineering*, 4(4), 239–242. DOI: 10.1007/s12599-014-0334-4

Lazarus, R., & Folkman, S. (1984). *Stress, Appraisal and Coping*. Springer.

Lele, A. (2019). Industry 4.0. In A. Lele, Disruptive Technologies for the Militaries and Security (pp.205-215). Springer.

Lichtenthaler, U. (2020). Beyond artificial intelligence: Why companies need to go the extra step. Journal of Business Strategy. *The Journal of Business Strategy*, 41(1), 19–26. DOI: 10.1108/JBS-05-2018-0086

Lokuge, S., Sedera, D., Grover, V., & Dongming, X. (2019). Organizational readiness for digital innovation: Development and empirical calibration of a construct. *Information & Management*, 56(3), 445–461. DOI: 10.1016/j.im.2018.09.001

Malik, A., & Nguyen, N. (2022). The Impact of AI-Powered Digital Assistants on Workplace Productivity. *Journal of Artificial Intelligence Research*, 45(3), 123–145.

Mao, S., Wang, B., Tang, Y., & Qian, F. (2019). Opportunities and Challenges of Artificial Intelligence for Green Manufacturing in the Process Industry. *Engineering (Beijing)*, 6(6), 995–1002. DOI: 10.1016/j.eng.2019.08.013

Marikyan, D., Papagiannidis, S., & Alamanos, E. (2022). The Role of Digital Assistants in Enhancing Employee Productivity: An Empirical Study. *Journal of Business Research*, 144, 106–121.

Martin, C., & Leurent, H. (2017, March 31). White Paper: Technology and Innovation for the Future of Production: Accelerating Value Creation. Retrieved April 1, 2021, from World Economic Forum: https://www.weforum.org/whitepapers/technology-and-innovation-for-the-future-of- production-accelerating-value-creation

Meijer, A., Conradie, P., & Choenni, S. (2021). Improving Decision-Making through Data-Driven Policing: A Case Study of the Rotterdam Police Force. *Government Information Quarterly*, 38(1), 101534.

Miller, V., Johnson, J., & Grau, J. (1994). Antecedents to willingness to participate in a planned organizational change. *Journal of Applied Communication Research*, 22(1), 59–80. DOI: 10.1080/00909889409365387

Mintzberg, H. (1979). *The Structuring of Organizations: A Synthesis of the Research*. Prentice-Hall.

Morgan, G. (2006). *Images of Organization. Updated Edition*. SAGE Publications.

Morgon, J. (2016, February 19). What is the Forth Industrial Revolution? Retrieved April 1, 2021, from Forbes: https://www.forbes.com/sites/jacobmorgan/2016/02/19/what-is-the-4th- industrial-revolution/?sh=3dad0a72f392

Ng, A. (2019). *How to Choose Your First AI Project*. Harvard Business Review Press.

Nguyen, N., & Malik, A. (2022a). Job Satisfaction and Artificial Intelligence: A Study. *International Journal of Human-Computer Studies*, 68(2), 98–115.

Nohria, N., & Beer, M. (2000). Cracking the Code of Change. *Harvard Business Review*. PMID: 11183975

O'Carroll, B. (2017). What are the 3 types of AI? A guide to narrow, general, and super artificial intelligence.

Pharoah, M. (2018). Preparing for the inevitable resistance to Artificial Intelligence

Prince, K. (2017). Industrie 4.0 and Leadership. In: *International Conference on Electronic Business* (pp. 132-139). Association for Information System.

Pringle, T., & Zoller, E. (2018). *How to Achieve AI Maturity and Why It Matters*. Ovum.

Prosci. (2018). Best Practices in Change Management (11 ed.). Prosci Inc. Prosci. (n.d.). Definition of Change Management. Retrieved March 31, 2021, from Prosci: https://www.prosci.com/resources/articles/definition-of-change-management

Qiu, X., & Zhang, Y. (2022). Reducing Mental and Physical Fatigue of Workers with AI: A Comprehensive Study. *Journal of Human-Computer Interaction*, 38(4), 567–580.

Rafferty, A., Jimmieson, N., & Armenakis, A. (2012). Change Readiness: A Multilevel Review. *Journal of Management*, 39(1), 110–135. DOI: 10.1177/0149206312457417

Ransbotham, S., Kiron, D., Gerpert, P., & Reeves, M. (2017). Reshaping Business with Artificial Intelligence: Closing the Gap Between Ambition and Action. *MIT Sloan Management Review*.

Riberio, J. (2021, February 2). A (very) Brief Introduction to AI in the Industry 4.0. Retrieved April 1, 2021, from Towards Data Science: https://towardsdatascience.com/a-very-brief-introduction-to-ai-in-the-industry-4-0-14e6f4b46cd1

Robey, D., Ghiyoung, I., & Wareham, J. (2008). Theoretical Foundations of Empirical Research on Interorganizational Systems: Assessing Past Contributions and Guiding Future Directions. *Journal of the Association for Information Systems*, 9(9), 497–518. DOI: 10.17705/1jais.00171

Russell, S., & Norvig, P. (2016). Artificial Intelligence: A Modern Approach (3 ed.). Pearson.

Salvato, C., & Rerup, C. (2011). Beyond collective entities: Multilevel research on organizational routines and capabilities. *Journal of Management*, 37(2), 468–490. DOI: 10.1177/0149206310371691

Snyder-Halpern, R. (2021). Indicators of Organizational Readiness for Clinical Information Technology/Systems Innovation: A Delphi Study. *International Journal of Medical Informatics*, 63(3), 179–204. DOI: 10.1016/S1386-5056(01)00179-4 PMID: 11502432

Sowa, J. F., Hu, S., & Shapiro, R. (2021). The Impact of AI on Repetitive Task Management. *Journal of Organizational Behavior*, 42(5), 1025–1040.

Sowa, J. F., & Przegalinska, A. (2020). Enhancing Employee Productivity with AI: Case Studies and Insights. *Journal of Artificial Intelligence Research*, 44(3), 150–165.

SpencerStuart (2024) 5 Essential Elements of an AI-Ready Corporate Culture

Stefanou, C. (2001). Organizational key success factors for implementing SCM/ERP systems to support decision making. *Journal of Decision Systems*, 10(1), 49–64. DOI: 10.3166/jds.10.49-64

Struckman, C., & Yammarino, F. (2003). Managing through multiple change activities: A solution to the enigma of the 21st century. *Organizational Dynamics*, 32(3), 234–246. DOI: 10.1016/S0090-2616(03)00033-0

Ustundag, A., & Cevikcan, E. (2017). *Industry 4.0: managing the digital transformation*. Springer.

Verma, R., & Singh, P. (2022). Organizational Strategies for AI Adoption: Mitigating Displacement Fears and Enhancing Productivity. *Journal of Organizational Behavior*, 43(7), 789–810.

Vial, G. (2019). Understanding digital transformation: A review and a research agenda. *The Journal of Strategic Information Systems*, 28(2), 118–144. DOI: 10.1016/j.jsis.2019.01.003

Wagg, DJ, Worden, K, Barthorpe, RJ, & Gardner, P (2020) Digital twins: state-of-the-art and future directions for modeling and simulation in engineering dynamics applications. ASCE-ASME J Risk Uncert Engrg Sys Part B Mech Engrg 6(3) DOI: 10.1016/j.jsis.2019.01.003

Waldman, D., Javidan, M., & Varella, P. (2004). (2004). Charismatic leadership at the strategic level: A new application of upper echelons theory. *The Leadership Quarterly*, 15(3), 355–380. DOI: 10.1016/j.leaqua.2004.02.013

Weiner, B. (2009). A theory of organizational readiness to change. *Implementation Science : IS*, 4(1), 1–9. DOI: 10.1186/1748-5908-4-67 PMID: 19840381

Wright, P. M., & Schultz, L. (2018). Organizational Readiness for Change: Integrating Employee and Management Perspectives. *Journal of Organizational Change Management*, 31(3), 523–538.

Zhu, Y.-Q., Corbett, J., & Chiu, Y.-T. (2020). Understanding employees' responses to artificial intelligence. *Organizational Dynamics*, •••, 1–10.

Chapter 3
Exploring Digital Transformation in Turkiye:
Barries, Drivers, and Competencies

Ece Nur Polat
https://orcid.org/0000-0002-9904-4577
Gebze Technical University, Turkey

Mehtap Özşahin
https://orcid.org/0000-0003-2527-4166
Gebze Technical University, Turkey

ABSTRACT

This study aims to investigate the perceptions of the managers in Turkiye about the digitalization; drivers and barriers of digital transformation; and new employee and leader competencies which are required in the digital age in context of Turkiye. A semi-structured, in-depth interview study was conducted on 28 managers at different hierarchical level of the organizations, those have initiated digitalization process and operate in different industries. Analyses results revealed main driver of the digitalization as "leader or manager"; while main barrier as "lack of employee competence". According to analyses results of this study, managers participating the this survey pairs digitalization with the concepts of "productivity", "integration of new technologies", "the necessity of era", "convenience" and "innovation".

DOI: 10.4018/979-8-3373-2523-1.ch003

1. INTRODUCTION

On the one hand, with the rapid development of digital technologies, their use has become a necessity for every organization. While organizations that use technologies to their advantage are successful, those that do not participate in this process can collapse (Griggs et al. 2019). Due to the limited empirical and conceptual studies in the literature, it is recommended that more research be conducted on how organizations transform digitally (Ellström et al., 2021). Studies have focused on digital transformation in the context of business models and their social outcomes at a more macro level, but it has been seen that interest and understanding at the micro level need to be deepened (Chatterjee et al., 2023).

The study aims to ascertain the attitudes that Turkish organizations have regarding digitalization, as well as the variables that spur or impede digitalization. Moreover, the study aims to identify and understand the competencies that employees and leaders need to succeed in the digital age. Therefore, this research aims to provide practical suggestions to improve workforce development and rethink strategies to respond to digital challenges in the context of digital transformation. Also, this study aims to contribute to the theoretical framework of identifying the competencies found to be important in the workplace environment of today's organizations.

In order to achieve the objectives of this research, a qualitative study method was adopted, and interviews were conducted on 28 managers from different levels. After introducing the basic concepts of this research in the following section, the methodology is then outlined. Then, the findings of this study are reported. The last section provides an explanation of the contributions of the study.

2. REVIEW OF THE LITERATURE ON DIGITALIZATION AND DIGITAL COMPETENCIES

In recent years, the idea of digital transformation has gained attention from academics and business professionals. Digital transformation is a three-stage process. The first stage is the digitization stage, where information is transferred to the digital environment. The second stage is the digitalization stage, where digital technologies and information in the digital environment are used in business processes. Lastly, there is the digital transformation phase, which creates new business models by altering the organizational structure (Verhoef et al. 2021; Kane, 2019). In this context, digital transformation basically refers to the process of using new generation digital technologies in organizational life (Warner & Wager, 2019). Verhoef et al. (2021) stated that creating more value is the main goal in digital transformation. In this context, value creation includes objectives such as operational efficiency, cost advantage, improved customer experiences, strategic differentiation, and competitive advantage (Cichsoz et al 2020).

The use of new generation digital technologies in both daily and business life is changing consumer behavior, the way organizations are organized, and the role of actors in the market (Zaki, 2019). These technologies have differentiated customers' lifestyles, needs, service experience expectations, and preferences (Shrivastava, 2017). For this reason, to remain competitive, it has become critical to respond to changes in customer expectations and even to offer new services by predicting them (Vial, 2019). However, the adoption of digital technologies leads to a change not only in the customer perspective but also in markets (Mithas et al. 2013). Situations such as the reduction of entry barriers in existing markets, the emergence of digital markets (Tiwana et al., 2010), the shortening of the process of converting ideas into business (Nandkarai and Prügl, 2020), and the reduction of carbon emissions with digitalization (Shang et al. 2023) are reshaping the market (Tiwana et al., 2010). In addition, as business processes become digital, some monitoring and control costs within the enterprise decrease (George et al, 2022). Thus, it is important to adopt digital transformation both to meet market demands and for organizational effectiveness. For this reason, it is possible to say that digital transformation can be adopted due to internal factors such as leadership or senior management commitment or external factors such as legal obligations and stakeholder perspective (Tangi et al. 2020; Ko et al. 2018). Although the literature defines the adoption of transformation by enterprises in order to benefit from the opportunities provided by digital technologies, the fact that enterprises see the digital transformation process as a threat and define it as a reactive response process to an external disruptive change (Vial, 2019) supports this situation.

Organizations should make structural changes while using digital technologies and therefore determine the factors that hinder transformation efforts (Vial, 2019). In their study, Kane et al. (2019) identified these barriers as follows: assuming that previous achievements provide competencies that are sufficient; selecting suitable technology; managing change and uncertainty; and lack of organizational support. Nadkari and Prügl (2020) stated that the increasing skill gap between current and potential employees due to the complexity and speed of the transformation is a threat. Vogelsang et al. (2019) highlighted technology barriers, missing comptenecies, individual barriers including fear of losing one's job, and organizational-cultural barriers insufficient resources and resistance to change. Vial (2019) defined organizational resistance and inertia as obstacles in the process of creating value with digital transformation; and culture, structure, leadership, and employee competencies are also among the critical factors affecting the process. Toytari et al. (2017) mentioned lack of resources and internal barriers such as culture. Cichosz et al. (2020), like previous studies, identified lack of competence, the ability to choose the right technology and, resistance to change as barriers, and also identified data security as a new barrier.

The intensive adoption of information and communication technologies has initiated the digital transformation process (Moroz, 2018). In digital transformation, which is a process of change, not only technology but also the manpower and business processes of the organization are changing (McCarthy et al. 2022). Therefore, although technology is one of the requirements of digital transformation, people with talents and skills that allow organizations to respond to this change emerge as more important (Fonseca, 2020).

The transformation process required a new set of competencies to be used in cloud computing, next-generation technologies, social media, agile program management, cyber security, and internal and external communications. However, there is no commonly accepted definition of digital competencies in the literature regarding the whole set of knowledge and skills we call digital competencies. However, there are different views not only on terminology but also on the structure of the concept (Oberlander et al. 2020). Since the process constantly demands new competencies from employees and reshapes business and decision-making processes, it is recommended that future research on the axis of digitalization and competence be conducted (Ganz et al. 2018).

Before digital transformation, digital competencies were only expected to be present in people working in technical departments, but now it has become critical for employees in almost all departments to understand basic technology knowledge, digital competencies, and the potential benefits of digitalization (Blanka et al., 2022). In this context, Van Laar et al. (2019) stated that the content of digital competencies no longer consists only of technical knowledge and that many dimensions such as knowledge management, communication, collaboration, creativity, critical thinking, problem solving, ethical and cultural awareness, flexibility, self-direction, and lifelong learning are important. The competency contents addressed in this context also differ in the studies. The competencies obtained from studies on employee competencies are presented in Table 1.

Table 1. Research on employee competencies and identified competencies

Research	Competencies
Zhen and Ding, 2024	Three-dimensional employee empowerment: ability, motivation and opportunity
Shao et al. 2022	Digital knowledge
Ahmed et al. 2022	Self-efficacy, Technological self-efficacy
Ostmeier and Strobel, 2022	Realizing the opportunities offered by digitalization

continued on following page

Table 1. Continued

Research	Competencies
Blanka et al. 2022	General digital skills (knowledge, media and technology skills), intrapreneurial competence
Buonocore et al., 2021	Basic digital skills (using computers etc.) and specific digital skills (coding etc.)
Eller et al. 2020; Foerster-Pastor and Glowko, 2018	IT and computer skills
Çetindamar-Kozanoğlu and Abedin, 2020; Hunter, 2018; Greene et al. 2014	Digital literacy
Bradic-Martinovic and Banovic, 2018	Eurostat Digital Comptence Framework (communication, knowledge, information, software, problem-solving skills)
Lavrynenko et al. 2018	Standard software applications and increasing programming skills and expertise in data analysis in multiple formats
Ilomäki et al. 2016	Technical knowledge, ability to use technology, ability to understand the phenomenon of digital technology, motivation to participate in technological culture
OECD, 2016	Basic, general, specific and supplementary skills

In order to successfully realize digital transformation, organizations should develop combinations of employee competencies. This development process consists of 3 steps: developing new competencies, combining existing and new competencies, and leading with transformational leadership (Pihlajamaa et al., 2023). At this point, another critical element, leadership, is also highlighted. Effective management of digital transformation is vital for organizations to successfully complete digital transformation and get positive results from it (McCharty et al. 2022; Fitzgerald et al. 2014).

The characteristics or competencies of managers are associated with successful digital transformation (Yao et al., 2024). Leaders now play an important role in managing the transformation process and the organization, both in dealing with tensions and remaining competitive in the digital age (Klein, 2020). Emerging digital technologies mean new forms of communication and organization and pose new challenges for leaders/managers in different sectors (Zhu et al., 2022). For this reason, traditional leadership styles do not adequately address the opportunities and challenges of digitalization (Zhu et al., 2022) and many researchers are concerned about the management capabilities of managers/leaders in the digital environment. As a result, new manager/leadership styles with new skills are needed (Yao et al. 2024). Table 2 presents the competencies identified for leaders in the digital transformation process.

Table 2. Research on leadership competencies and identified competencies

Researchs	Competencies
Cortellazzo et al. (2019)	technical skills, managing change, decision-making, digital communication, managing network
Hensellek (2020)	digital mindset, digital skills, digital practitioner, digital vision
Imran et al. (2021)	digital vision, digital knowledge; learning from mistakes, empowerment, being able to manage different teams
Magesa and Jonathan (2021)	inspiring, visionary, able to manage uncertainty, innovative, adaptable
Weber et al. (2022)	digital transformation focused and people focused
Weber et al. (2022)	digital pioneer, innovator, facilitator, mentor, networker and manager
Schiuma et al. (2022)	mentor, pragmatic, honest, catalyst, communicator, facilitator
Abbu et al. (2022)	digital literacy, positive attitude, new skill acquisition, knowledge sharing, participatory style, performance monitoring
Schiuma et al. (2024)	sustainable, pragmatic, knowledgeable, catalyst, communicator, facilitator

Employing managers who can drive the transformation, use their knowledge and experience to influence the process, make quick decisions, promote change, analyze when and how to adopt new technologies, and recognize and address employees' fears of losing their jobs as a result of digitalization are essential (Sow and Aborbie, 2018; Tigre et al., 2023).

There is a limitation of study in the literature regarding understanding the concept of digital transformation. Therefore, it is recommended to conduct more research on how organizations are digitally transformed (Ellström et al., 2021). Since organizations need to have a human resource equipped with digital competencies in order to benefit from their investments in technologies and achieve organizational goals (Kane et al., 2019), the digital competencies of the workforce and the components within the business, such as new leadership roles, need to be further investigated (Çetindamar-Kozanoğlu & Abedin, 2021).

3. METHODOLOGY

The purpose of this study is to reveal the perceptions of the managers in Turkiye about the digitalization; drivers and barriers of digital transformation; and new employee and leader competencies which are required in the digital age in context of Turkiye. For this purpose, the following research questions are expected to be answered:

- What has changed with digitalization in Turkiye?

- What are the factors that make digitalization easier and more difficult?
- What are the competencies expected from employees and leaders in the digitalization process?

This research is qualitative in nature. Qualitative research is the one in which data is collected using open-ended surveys, interviews, or questionnaires. To broaden the concept of digital transformation in Turkey, this study required interviewees opinions and experiences without time limit; therefore, this method was chosen. Semi-structured interview questions were used in the research. Based on the gap in the literature, 8 questions were asked, 6 of which were open-ended and 2 of which were multiple choice questions where more than one option could be marked. In this context, interviews were conducted on 28 managers at different hierarchical level of the organizations, those have initiated digitalization process and operate in different industries. The interviews were subjected to content analysis.

Rather than validity and reliability, trustworthiness is crucial in qualitative research. Four fundamental criteria—"Credibility, Reliability, Verifiability, and Transferability"—are used to ensure credibility (Guba & Lincoln, 1982). Multiple researchers were involved in the review process to establish credibility; transferability was achieved by interviewing employees from various sectors and organizations; and verifiability was maintained by direct quotations and transparent explanations of the procedure.

Both in-person and online data collection methods were used in the research. The data were fully transcribed, and themes were identified by content analysis. To comprehend the perceptions, barriers, drivers, and competencies associated with digital transformation, researchers reviewed the results iteratively and collaboratively with the literature.

3.1. Sample and Analysis

The research sample consists of organizations in Turkiye that have started the digitalization process. For confidentiality reasons, the names of the organizations and respondents are veiled and general information about the organizations and respondents is provided in Table 3 and Table 4.

Table 3. Demographic characteristics of interviewers

Gender	
Female	**13**
Male	15
Education	
High School	3
Associate Degree	2
Bachelor's Degree	15
Master's Degree	8
Age	
25-34	8
35-44	9
45-54	10
Unidentified	1

Table 4. General information of organizations

Area of Business	
Service	**17**
Manufacture	11
Size of Business	
Small	6
Medium	7
Large	15

3.2. Findings

Interview questions were grouped under three main headings. The first three questions aim to reveal the perception of managers about digitalization. In this context, respondents were asked to state the concepts which define the digitalization and changes they have experienced in their work and business processes with the digitalization process and how they perceive digitalization, whether a necessity or an option for their work. In this way, it is aimed to understand the respondents' attitudes and perceptions towards digitalization. The second group of questions aim to reveal main drivers and barriers of the digitalization process that managers experienced. In this context, respondents responded the questions regarding the factors that initiate digitalization, the factors that hinder digitalization, the difficulties encountered in the digitalization process and the resistance of employees. The last part of the interview contains the questions aiming to reveal managers' and employees' competences, which are needed for a successful digital transformation.

Content analyses results revealed findings on the perception of managers about digitalization, drivers and barriers that managers experienced during the digitalization process and required competencies by managers and employees for a successful digital transformation, which are provided flowing sections.

3.2.1. Perceptions Towards Digitalization

The employment of digital technology in corporate processes has become unavoidable due to its widespread development and integration into various aspects of our lives. But since the pandemic, corporations have been using this technology far more frequently. Radical changes in firms and business processes have been noticed in light of all these advancements. According to all twelve of our interviews, they identified a change in the last years caused by the integration of digital technologies into business processes. According to their statement, they act in response to consumer requests by establishing digital applications and connecting with them via digital channels.

- *Y1: Our organization brings its users together with its products with an augmented reality add-on. We can say that with Covid-19, brands have been forced to offer their users a safe beauty experience.*
- *Y12: Before and with Covid-19, people turned to digital banking because they no longer felt the need to come to the branch. This situation pushed us to develop our digital banking application*

Furthermore, the interviewees stated that they use digital technologies to improve productivity at various stages in the organization.

- *Y8: We moved the handheld terminals we use in our warehouse to the field and increased their number. In this way, the workload of accounting staff was reduced and we encouraged them to work more efficiently in their actual jobs.*

These technologies, which integrate business processes, have also made a difference in the way of doing business. In the context of Turkiye, 17 of our interviewees emphasized that the working system has changed. They stated that digitalization processes mostly started with the pandemic and talked about the permanence of the change.

- *Y9: With the Covid 19 pandemic, we have started to use digital working methods more than we could have ever imagined. Now, even when we come to the office, we use digital meeting platforms, and sometimes even when we are sitting next to each other, so as not to occupy meeting rooms. Thanks to the platforms where employees plan the days they want to come to the office, etc., organizations can also make their plans for issues such as food and transportation more effectively.*

But these technologies haven't just changed how the business operates. Additionally, they changed the procedures for conducting business internationally and corresponding with international firms.

- *Y13: We had problems with not being able to meet face to face with customers and foreign investors. Online meetings have become a part of our lives. We continue to hold online meetings due to the high cost of traveling. Our customers also prefer online meetings. It is easier and less expensive for us.*

The digital transformation process can have different meanings for organizations and individuals. For this reason, we examined what the concept of digitalization means for our interviewees. It is possible to say that the answers given are gathered around 5 main headings.

Productivity: According to eight interviewees, the idea of digitization enhances corporate processes, boosts competitiveness, and enhances customer experience through data optimization in this digital world. It was also said that as systems get more digitalized, their decision-making processes operate more quickly and healthily.

- *Y3: Digitalization means optimizing business processes and operations, increasing efficiency and improving customer experience.*

Integration of new technologies: As part of the process of digitalization, six interviewers discussed and assessed the benefits of integrating new generation digital technologies into corporate operations.

- *Y10: We are talking about managing everything with programs or rather using software.*

The necessity of era: According to four interviewees, the idea of digitalization is essential to the circumstances of our era.

- *Y19: Digitalization has become indispensable for all organizations. We live in a time when technology is evolving every day and falling behind in technology significantly endangers the sustainability of organizations.*

Convenience: 4 interviewees explained the concept of digitalization as convenience.

- *Y21: Digitalization means convenience for me.*
- *Y13: Digitalization means convenience to me. It allows us to get our work done faster. It helps us provide a better experience to customers.*

Innovation: Finally, in defining the concept of digitalization, 3 interviewers indicated that they considered the concept to be an innovation.

- *Y28: The first concept that comes to my mind is innovation.*

The motivation for digital transformation may vary, just as the notion of digitalization holds different meanings for individuals and organizations. We questioned the interviewees about whether they perceived the digitalization process in their organizations as a necessity or a an option. In response to this question, 24 interviewees indicated that digitalization is a path that is unavoidable. They characterized the industry's intense competitiveness and consumer need as reasons why digitalization was essential for survival. They added that after a certain size or scale, organizations must digitally transform themselves.

- *Y24: Digitalization has become a necessity for both us and all organizations. We predict that organizations that do not digitalize will be excluded from the system over time.*

According to four interviewees, it is an option. They stated that their organizations started this transformation process due to their own preferences. They also mentioned how the epidemic caused the process to settle and accelerate. The interviewees add, though, that they would have to begin the digitalization process today if they had not started it earlier.

- *Y7: It wasn't actually mandatory, but we wanted to stay up-to-date and make our jobs easier. We followed the technological developments of our age. If we didn't do it now, we would have to do it in the near future. The digitalization steps we are taking today put us ahead of our competitors.*

3.2.2. Digitalization Drivers and Barriers

When the interviewees were asked about the factors that initiated the digitalization process in their organizations, their answers were as follows*: leader or manager, customers' demand or expectation, nature of the sector, Covid-19 and then sustainability and digital technology* with the other option as the next option. The frequency of these concepts which are repeated in interview reports are given in Figure 1.

Figure 1. Digitalization drivers

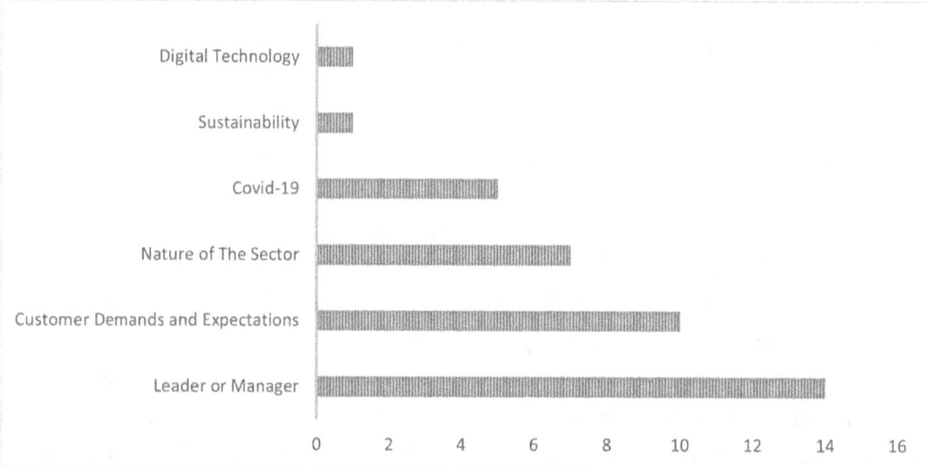

Content analysis results revealed the barriers such as *lack of employee competence, costs, organization culture, nature of the sector, manager or leader, customer, legal issues, digital security, and employee resistance*. Those barriers were indicated by different respondents frequently. The frequency of those concepts which are repeated as barriers in interview reports are given in Figure 2.

Figure 2. Digitalization barriers

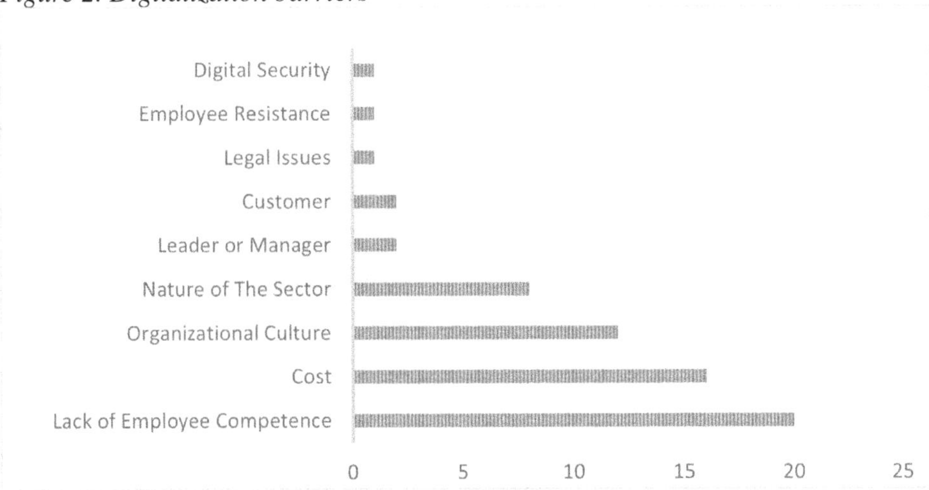

As digital technologies take hold in organizations, employees who are not knowledgeable about the use of this technology may react differently to the situation. We questioned our interviewees about any resistance they faced during the digitization process. Seven interviewees stated that there was no employee resistance but difficulty in accepting digital technology. They noted that employees were hesitant and underlined that they did not want to change their ways of working. They also emphasized that the existence of digital technologies alone is not sufficient for the business; therefore, it is important to adopt them in order to integrate them into business processes.

- *Y16: People do not want to give up the order they are used to. Even though they know it will be easier, they still say they are used to it. They do not want innovation...*
- *Y25: Of course, it took time for the familiar business practices to be adopted by both the staff and 3rd parties, and it is still ongoing. Digitalization is not a culture, it is not software that can be purchased and implemented at once, it is necessary to base all business processes on it, and this requires constant changes in the entire organization.*

Five interviewees emphasized that employees feel negatively about digitalization. These include beliefs that digitalization is unnecessary, digitalization will replace their jobs, they will make mistakes while learning, and that it is a monitoring mechanism. It was mentioned that training and transparent communication could help overcome the process.

- *Y6: Employees may think that the digitalization process is a for them, but this situation can be overcome. In fact, we have seen that we can overcome this problem by explaining the concept of digitalization to blue-collar workers in its simplest and most understandable form.*
- *Y20: Some of our employees resisted digitalization for fear of losing their jobs. To overcome this problem, we organized training and ensured that employees understood the advantages of digitalization.*

Three interviewees pointed out the challenge of utilizing technology. Because some employees lack the competencies they need to use digital technologies, it was challenging for them to learn how to use these technologies in their work processes. As a result, a variety of failures occurred in their work processes.

- *Y21: One of the challenges for us was for employees to actually learn and apply it. Changing people's behavior was our main problem.*

While two interviewees mentioned that the difficulties experienced due to technical infrastructures caused reluctance or tension, 10 interviewees stated that they did not encounter any difficulties or resistance.

3.2.3. Competencies Required for a Successful Digital Transformation

The literature review highlights the importance of leadership competencies to succeed in digital transformation process the study's focus was on what type of competencies managers as leaders need or will need because of the new roles that the changing environment has required. Analyses results revealed three primary categories—*digital technology knowledge, personal traits, and leadership style*—in context of competencies managers require for a successful digital transformation. Digital technology knowledge was the most repeated competency that interviewees addressed. According to the respondents, managers should be people who embrace technology (3 respondents), digital technology knowledge (3 respondents), and follow digital technologies (4 respondents).

- *Y4: From a management perspective, if there is a technological development, I think the most efficient method is to adapt to it. I also think there is no point in insisting too much. There is a developing technology, it offers different opportunities. Instead of opposing these, we should understand this and think about how we can make it most useful and most efficient for us*

Other competencies are formed by the manager's personal characteristics. The most frequently mentioned competency among these characteristics was openness to innovation (11 respondents). The interviewees also identified two more crucial traits: the capacity for adaptation (6 respondents) and being receptive to new information (2 respondents).

- *Y12: Managers need to be somewhat familiar with the digital world. If they don't know, they should make an effort to learn the things they don't know.*
- *Y19: Managers who cannot keep up with and adapt to the digital environment have no chance of becoming managers in this period.*

Digital technologies are changing business processes. It has been noted that managers need to broaden their business knowledge (1) in order to understand and evaluate these changes.

- *Y7: It is not enough for managers to just be technology-savvy people; they should know the business processes in their areas of responsibility as well as the business units in their areas of responsibility, so that they can integrate technology into the operation properly.*

Digitalization, as a new transformation process, also brings uncertainty. For this reason, it has been stated that managers should maintain a determined (2 respondents) and patient (1 respondent) attitude in the digitalization process.

- *Y17: It is difficult to find support for innovations in a traditional organization, so managers must be determined.*
- *Y28: For digital to become widespread, it is necessary to create an active area and transfer people there. Some patience may be required from managers because it is necessary to look at each person as uneducated in this field and teach everything from scratch.*

Furthermore, there are competencies associated with the manager's personal perception. In this regard, it has been stated that managers *need to be able to follow the agenda* and the sector (5 respondents), *act proactively* (4 respondents), and *think analytically* (2 respondents) in order to keep up with the digital age and even gain competitive advantage.

In terms of leadership styles, we have seen an emphasis on the manager-employee relationship. This is a new process for everyone in the organization. For this reason, it was highlighted that the *manager's communication skills* (6 respondents) are crucial in this process. It was even stated that the manager should give *healthy feedback* (2 respondents) to his/her subordinates about the process.

- *N27: It should be someone who can provide healthy feedback, question the reason for the mistake, report it, and explain it.*

The digitalization process also appears as a learning process. For this reason, it has been stated that the manager should include his/her subordinates in the process and *empower* them (2 respondents).

- *Y7: Managers are not expected to have these competencies only in themselves. I think they should also trigger this curiosity in gaining knowledge of business processes in their teams.*

As a result of the uncertainty that the process brings, the expected leadership competencies of the manager have also changed. In this context, it was stated that managers should be *flexible* (4 respondents), and be *equipped about change management* (5 respondents) and *crisis management* (3 respondents).

- *Y8: I think the most important feature of a manager today is ability to manage crises*
- *Y22: Recent times, there has been a need for leaders rather than managers. In recent times, a management style that leads, not gives orders, and can manage this process has been demanded.*

Employee competencies are critical to the success of digital transformation initiatives, as noted in the literature and our findings in the barriers to digitalization. Our interviewees indicate that knowledge of digital technology (12 respondents) and openness to learning (11 respondents) are the two key competencies that employers look for in their employees. The result emphasized the increasing importance of employees' technological knowledge to develop and to be able to use it. However, it might be that current staff's level of technological knowledge will be insufficient considering the adaptation of new technologies in organizations. Therefore, willingness to learn may tolerate the employees' current lack of technological knowledge.

- Y1: *Since it cannot be expected from every employee to be at the same technological level in terms of previous opportunities in their packages, their aptitude and suitability for training in these technologies will be essential.*
- Y19: *They must have at least a command of all digital channels at a level appropriate to the requirements of the age and be able to use them actively.*

Customer focus (5 respondents) and problem-solving skills (4 respondents) were also indicated as employee competences which are required for successful digitalization process in digital age. Digitalization is related to customer demand and is also carried out to increase customer satisfaction. The two competencies identified are close to each other, in line with the interviewees' responses. Customer focus also states ability to provide solutions that meet customer needs and problems.

- *Y2: It is important that customer needs are met quickly.*
- *Y10: They should analyze the needs of customers well.*

Other employee competencies, which have been revealed as a result of content analyses, are tendency *for teamwork (7* respondents*), openness to change (5* respondents*), analytical thinking (4* respondents*), flexibility (4* respondents*), communication skills (4* respondents*), innovation (3* respondents*), language knowledge (2* respondents*), and proactive behavior (1* respondents*).*

Briefly, the findings of this study is summarized in Table 5.

Table 5. Brief findings of study

Perceptions	Drivers	Barriers	Leadership Competencies	Employee Competencies
• Productivity • Integration of new technologies • The necessity of era • Convenience • Innovation	*• Leader or manager • Customers demand or expectation • Nature of the sector • Covid-19 • Sustainability • Digital technology*	*• Lack of employee competence • Costs • Organization culture • Nature of the sector • Manager or leader • Customer • Legal issues • Digital security • Employee resistance*	*• Embracing technology • Digital technology knowledge • Following digital technologies • Openness to innovation • Adaptability • Being receptive to new information • Business knowledge • Determined • patient • following the agenda and the sector • Act proactively • Analytical thinking • Communication skills • Healthy feedback • Empowering • Flexibilty • Change management • Crisis management*	• Digital technology knowledge • Openness to learning • Customer focus • Problem-solving skills • Teamwork • Openness to change • Analytical thinking • Flexibility Communication skills • Innovation • Language knowledge • proactive behavior

4. CONCLUSION

The findings of the study demonstrate that digital transformation is influenced by a variety of human-centered elements in addition to technology. Taking all these factors into consideration, it is possible to propose that the research findings enhance our understanding of the notion of digital transformation and its human component.

The concept of digitalization has generally been defined in the literature as the application of digital technologies to organizations, which is the most basic definition. Considering the digital transformation process, which is a multi-stage process, the fact that digitalization is also generally expressed with concepts such as the use of digital technology in our findings may indicate that most organizations in the Turkish context are in the second stage, the digitalization stage, which refers to the use of information in the digital environment in the decision-making process.

It is discovered that the drivers for implementing digital transformation are similar to the literature. According to Vogelsang et al. (2018), employing these technologies for digital transformation is unavoidable because competitors are either using them already or will do so soon. According to our findings, the majority of interviewees also stated the process of digitalization as a requirement, compulsory, and even those who did not agree with this statement acknowledged that they would eventually need to undertake it. To survive in the present market conditions, organizations at all sizes and in all industries must keep up with the digital world.

In the literature, the concepts of leadership (Tangi et al., 2020), changing customer expectations, a different market (Mithas et al., 2013), and cost efficiency (George et al., 2022) are prominent among the elements that initiate digitalization. The leader and the customer expectations that follow, which are significantly highlighted in our findings, reveal both the internal and external drivers of the process.

In our study, leadership was found to be the first element that initiates the digital transformation process. Considering the vital role of top management in innovation and change (Ibrahım and Benabdelhad, 2022), it is not surprising that digital transformation in Turkiye is initiated by the leaders or managers. Furthermore, one of the five success factors critical to digital transformation is described as having a leader with digital understanding (McCharty et. al. 2022; Fitzgerald et. al. 2014); therefore, the findings are assessed according to the literature.

The next initiating element or driver was found to be customers' demand or expectation. Digital technologies are being adapted because, in principle, they offer significant opportunities for organizations. Now, due to changes in customer preferences and expectations stemming from digitalization (Hanelt et al. 2021), organizations have had to adapt to this change to manage customer relationships. Therefore, it can be said that customer satisfaction is at the center of digital transformation.

Lack of competent employees, costs, and culture are the main obstacles to digital transformation. A review of the literature indicates that although studies define different barriers, the point of intersection is employee competence (Nadkari and Prügl, 2020; Vogelsang et al. 2019; Kane et al. 2018). For this reason, although each factor in our findings finds its place in literature, it can be said that the most critical element is the lack of competent employees. Digital transformation is not just about buying technology. It is important to have competent employees who can use the technology when it is brought into the business (Kane, 2019). In the process of digital transformation, many organizations have started to realize the importance of having competent employees, as digital strategies need to be supported by digital competencies and skills for their successful implementation (Teng et al. 2022). For this reason, it is possible to say that employees are the key element of digital transformation, and in line with literature, it could be stated that employee competencies are the most critical barrier.

Another element is costs. The purchase of new technologies, their integration into business processes, and sometimes, because no one in the organization knows them, the purchase of an external service to solve the transformation and problems in the digital transformation process create costs for organizations. (Shahi and Sinha, 2021). Finally, looking at culture, it is important to create a culture in the business that supports the process together with the technology (Kamalaldin et al. 2020). In fact, Kane (2019) defines culture as one of the key elements of digital transformation. In an inappropriate culture, change is likely to be resisted and therefore not achieve the desired effectiveness. Leaders have an important responsibility in creating an appropriate culture (Trenerry et al. 2021).

As a result of our study, the competencies expected from managers were identified as technical knowledge and skills (digital literacy, knowledge of using technology, technology acceptance), in line with the literature. Literature suggests, which is consistent with our findings, that managers should have technical abilities, including the ability to use digital technologies (Cortelazzo et al. 2019; Hensellek. 2020), be pioneers in adopting and implementing digital technologies (Weber et al. 2022) and be familiar with and able to implement these technologies (Kane, 2019). Furthermore, in line with the literature, our finding emphasized that today's managers should be open to innovation (Weber et al. 2022; Magesa and Jonathan, 2021). By sector and agenda, communication skills and empowerment are other common findings with the literature. Our respondents rated the ability to follow the sector and agenda as important in order not to fall behind competitors and to ensure customer satisfaction. In the literature, it is stated that the ability to analyze when and how to adopt new technologies (Kensbock and Stöckmann, 2021) and to effectively evaluate the process with knowledge and experience (Sow and Aborbie, 2018) are important competences.

However, another important issue is that the leader should not only be a manager but also a mentor in the change process (Weber et al. 2022; Schiuma et al. 2022), sharing information with employees and involving them in the process in a participatory way (Abbu et al. 2022). Encouraging employees about the change and ensuring their acceptance (Trenerry et al. 2021) emerges as a critical competency in the new order. Moreover, this competence is also critical for the part of our findings on 'employee resistance to the digitalization process'. The success of the process can be ensured by preventing the process from being interrupted by employees' failure to adopt digital technologies and their resistance.

We found that manager-employee relationships and communication play a critical role. As a result of the change, managers are now communicators (Schiuma et al., 2022). The use of digital technology has led to the development of new forms of communication, which have presented challenges (Zhu et al., 2022) as well as unfavorable attitudes and feelings among employees due to uncertainty (Kensbock and Stöckmann, 2021). Managers who are aware of these challenges and respond to them appropriately are therefore required for successful digital transformation. Our results indicate that fear of unemployment, fear of being followed, and fear of making mistakes are additional reasons why employees resist. With an open communication system, this resistance is likely to be overcome.

The requirement for managers who can handle change and crises was the final competency found in the interviews. Stated differently, managers are now required to guide staff members through this process. It is necessary to have leaders who can handle disruptive changes, manage employees' reactions during this process, and offer leadership and a vision for change (Kane, 2019; Onyeneke and Abe, 2021).

Among the competencies expected from employees, the use and adaptation of digital technology was found to be the first to confirm the need for digital literacy in each department. However, it is not possible for each current or even potential employee to master digital technology. Moreover, the competencies that each unit requires will vary (Buonocore et al., 2021). For this reason, another competency emerges that is at least as important as employees' technological knowledge, namely openness to learning. Butschan et al. (2019) state in their study that the employee profile needed in the digital transformation process is one with a high emotional and cognitive desire to learn, high problem-solving skills, and openness to change.

In conclusion, this study revealed the drivers of digitalization as leader or manager, customer demands or expectations and nature of the sector, and barriers hindering digitalization as lack of employee competence, costs and organizational culture in Turkiye specific to our sample. Moreover, it also highlighted the managers' and employees' competencies which are required for successful digital transformation in as digital age as: openness to innovation, adaptation, digital technology knowledge, follow the digital and sectoral agenda for managers and digital technology knowledge, openness to learning for employees. Those findings are expected to contribute to literature in expanding the understanding of drivers and barriers of digitalization and required competencies of managers and employees to handle the digitization process smoothly. Furthermore, analysis results of this study showed that Turkish managers match the digitalization with the concepts such as productivity, integration of new technologies, the necessity of era, convenience and innovation. This finding also opens a window on managers' digitalization perceptions that future researchers and practitioners may benefit.

4.1. Theoretical Implications

This study provides several theoretical contributions. Previous studies have demonstrated the importance of leadership in the digital age (Klein, 2020). As a pioneering study that examines competencies in the context of Turkiye, our study provides an in-depth understanding by providing a detailed list of competencies.

Although various studies have attempted to reveal the framework of competencies for employees (Blanka et al. 2022; Çetindamar-Kozanoğlu and Abedin, 2020) and leaders (Abbu et al. 2022; Hensellek, 2020) a common conceptual framework cannot be developed due to both developing technology and regional differences. For this reason, our study serves as a steppingstone.

Although digital transformation is the subject of many articles in information systems literature, there are very few studies in the context of competences. If researchers focus only on the technical aspects of digital transformation, it is not possible to achieve a comprehensive transformation. Therefore, the critical role of employees and managers should be understood. In this context, our study adds a human-centered perspective to digital transformation.

4.2. Practical Implications

The findings of this research have important practical implications for organizations considering undertaking a digital transformation journey. In this context, the enablers, barriers and competencies identified in our research provide important guidance. Therefore, it is important for organizations aiming for a successful digital transformation to be aware of the barriers and take initiatives to improve them.

Given the investment and growing importance of digital transformation, competencies play a critical role. The development and improvement of employee and manager competencies, which is a critical element, should be transformed into a prioritized policy. However, individuals should be voluntary and willing to develop these competencies. Employees may be encouraged to attend external training or trainings that will build competencies within the company can be arranged. Consequently, this will also enhance the process of personal development. Therefore, our findings show that digital transformation requires a development process at both individual and organizational levels.

In today's rapidly changing and digitized environment, having a competent workforce is becoming a challenge to gain competitive advantage. For this reason, it is of strategic importance to implement programs to develop these competencies and to seek to employ a workforce with these competencies. Organizations that prioritize this are likely to survive the challenges and complexities of digital transformation and make a successful transition to the digital world.

5. LIMITATIONS AND FUTURE RESEARCH

There are a few limitations of the study conducted. This study used cross-sectional data. Therefore, we suggest that future research may further obtain longitudinal data. We also suggest that longitudinal studies may be useful to reveal this change due to the rapid development of digital technologies, which also change the needed competencies.

This study is limited in the context of Turkiye. The business environment also differs from one country to another. This may cause perceptions, barriers, drivers, and competencies about digital transformation to differ. Therefore, cross-cultural study may broaden the notion of human-driven digital transformation.

The result of this study is limited to a sample of 28 respondents, which survey hinder the generalizability of the findings. Therefore, further researchers are suggested to conduct quantitative research with extended sample sizes to increase generalizability of the findings.

REFERENCES

Abbu, H., Mugge, P., Gudergan, G., Hoeborn, G., & Kwiatkowski, A. (2022). Measuring the Human Dimensions of Digital Leadership for Successful Digital Transformation: Digital leaders can use the authors' Digital Leadership Scale to assess their own readiness and ability to accelerate digital transformation. *Research Technology Management*, 65(3), 39–49. DOI: 10.1080/08956308.2022.2048588

Ahmed, W., Hizam, S. M., & Sentosa, I. (2022). Digital dexterity: Employee as consumer approach towards organizational success. *Human Resource Development International*, 25(5), 631–641. DOI: 10.1080/13678868.2020.1835107

Blanka, C., Krumay, B., & Rueckel, D. (2022). The interplay of digital transformation and employee competency: A design science approach. *Technological Forecasting and Social Change*, 178, 121575. DOI: 10.1016/j.techfore.2022.121575

Bradić-Martinović, A., & Banović, J. (2018). Assessment of digital skills in Serbia with focus on gender gap. *JWEE*, (1-2), 54–67. DOI: 10.28934/jwee18.12.pp54-67

Buonocore, F., Agrifoglio, R., & De Gennaro, D. 2021. "The role of digital competencies and creativity for job crafting in public administration". Digital Transformation and Human Behavior: Innovation for People and Organisations. Editörler: Metallo, C., Ferrara, M., Lazazzara, A., Za, S. Springer International Publishing. DOI: 10.1007/978-3-030-47539-0_7

Buonocore, F., Annosi, M. C., de Gennaro, D., & Riemma, F. (2024). Digital transformation and social change: Leadership strategies for responsible innovation. *Journal of Engineering and Technology Management*, 74, 101843. DOI: 10.1016/j.jengtecman.2024.101843

Butschan, J., Heidenreich, S., Weber, B., & Kraemer, T. (2019). Tackling hurdles to digital transformation—The role of competencies for successful industrial internet of things (IIoT) implementation. *International Journal of Innovation Management*, 23(04), 1950036. DOI: 10.1142/S1363919619500361

Çetindamar-Kozanoğlu, D., & Abedin, B. (2021). Understanding the role of employees in digital transformation: Conceptualization of digital literacy of employees as a multi-dimensional organizational affordance. *Journal of Enterprise Information Management*, 34(6), 1649–1672. DOI: 10.1108/JEIM-01-2020-0010

Chatterjee, S., Chaudhuri, R., Vrontis, D., & Giovando, G. (2023). Digital workplace and organization performance: Moderating role of digital leadership capability. *Journal of Innovation & Knowledge*, 8(1), 100334. DOI: 10.1016/j.jik.2023.100334

Cichosz, M., Wallenburg, C. M., & Knemeyer, A. M. (2020). Digital transformation at logistics service providers: Barriers, success factors and leading practices. *International Journal of Logistics Management*, 31(2), 209–238. DOI: 10.1108/IJLM-08-2019-0229

Cortellazzo, L., Bruni, E., & Zampieri, R. (2019). The role of leadership in a digitalized world: A review. *Frontiers in Psychology*, 10, 1938. DOI: 10.3389/fpsyg.2019.01938 PMID: 31507494

Eller, R., Alford, P., Kallmünzer, A., & Peters, M. (2020). Antecedents, consequences, and challenges of small and medium-sized enterprise digitalization. *Journal of Business Research*, 112, 119–127. DOI: 10.1016/j.jbusres.2020.03.004

Ellström, D., Holtström, J., Berg, E., & Josefsson, C. (2021). Dynamic capabilities for digital transformation. *Journal of Strategy and Management*, 15(2), 272–286. DOI: 10.1108/JSMA-04-2021-0089

Fitzgerald, M., Kruschwitz, N., Bonnet, D., & Welch, M. 2014. "Embracing Digital Technology: A New Strategic Imperative," MIT Sloan Management Review (55:2), pp. 1-12. DOI: 10.1108/JSMA-04-2021-0089

Foerster-Metz, U. S. F. P., & Golowko, N. (2018). The need for digital and soft skills in the Romanian business service industry. *Management & Marketing*, 13(1), 831–847. DOI: 10.2478/mmcks-2018-0008

Fonseca, P., & Picoto, W. N. (2020). The competencies needed for digital transformation. [OJAKM]. *Online Journal of Applied Knowledge Management*, 8(2), 53–70. DOI: 10.36965/OJAKM.2020.8(2)53-70

Ganz, W., Dworschak, B., & Schnalzer, K. (2018, June). Competences and competence development in a digitalized world of work. In *International Conference on Applied Human Factors and Ergonomics* (pp. 312-320). Cham: Springer International Publishing.

George, G., & Schillebeeckx, S. J. (2022). Digital transformation, sustainability, and purpose in the multinational enterprise. *Journal of World Business*, 57(3), 101326. DOI: 10.1016/j.jwb.2022.101326

Greene, J. A., Seung, B. Y., & Copeland, D. Z. (2014). Measuring critical components of digital literacy and their relationships with learning. *Computers & Education*, 76, 55–69. DOI: 10.1016/j.compedu.2014.03.008

Griggs, T., Griffiths, M., & Fletcher, G. (2019). Managing the digital transformation of an organisation. In *Strategic Digital Transformation* (pp. 48–54). Routledge. DOI: 10.4324/9780429020469-5

Guba, E. G., & Lincoln, Y. S. (1982). Epistemological and methodological bases of naturalistic inquiry. *Educational Communication and Technology*, 30(4), 233252. DOI: 10.1007/BF02765185

Hanelt, A., Bohnsack, R., Marz, D., & Antunes Marante, C. (2021). A systematic review of the literature on digital transformation: Insights and implications for strategy and organizational change. *Journal of Management Studies*, 58(5), 1159–1197. DOI: 10.1111/joms.12639

Hensellek, S. (2020). Digital leadership: A framework for successful leadership in the digital age [JMME]. *Journal of Media Management and Entrepreneurship*, 2(1), 1–15. DOI: 10.4018/JMME.2020010104

Hunter, I. (2018). Digital literacy in the workplace: A view from the legal sector. *Business Information Review*, 35(2), 56–59. DOI: 10.1177/0266382118772675

Ibrahim, A. K., & Benabdelhadi, A. (2022). Organizational change management of digital administration. International Journal of Accounting, Finance, Auditing, Management and Economics, 3(2-1), 339-353. DOI: 10.1177/0266382118772675

Ilomäki, L., Paavola, S., Lakkala, M., & Kantosalo, A. (2016). Digital competence–an emergent boundary concept for policy and educational research. *Education and Information Technologies*, 21(3), 655–679. DOI: 10.1007/s10639-014-9346-4

Imran, F., Shahzad, K., Butt, A., & Kantola, J. (2021). Digital transformation of industrial organizations: Toward an integrated framework. *Journal of Change Management*, 21(4), 451–479. DOI: 10.1080/14697017.2021.1929406

Kamalaldin, A., Linde, L., Sjödin, D., & Parida, V. (2020). Transforming Provider-Customer Relationships in Digital Servitization: A Relational View on Digitalization. *Industrial Marketing Management*, 89, 306–325. DOI: 10.1016/j.indmarman.2020.02.004

Kane, G. (2019). The technology fallacy: People are the real key to digital transformation. *Research Technology Management*, 62(6), 44–49. DOI: 10.1080/08956308.2019.1661079

Kensbock, J. M., & Stöckmann, C. (2021). "Big brother is watching you": Surveillance via technology undermines employees' learning and voice behavior during digital transformation. *Journal of Business Economics*, 91(4), 565–594. DOI: 10.1007/s11573-020-01012-x

Klein, M. (2020). Leadership characteristics in the era of digital transformation. DOI: 10.1177/0266382118772675

Ko, A., Fehér, P., Kovacs, T., Mitev, A., & Szabó, Z. (2022). Influencing factors of digital transformation: Management or IT is the driving force? *International Journal of Innovation Science*, 14(1), 1–20. DOI: 10.1108/IJIS-01-2021-0007

Lavrynenko, A., Shmatko, N., & Meissner, D. (2018). Managing skills for open innovation: The case of biotechnology. *Management Decision*, 56(6), 1336–1347. DOI: 10.1108/MD-04-2017-0301

Magesa, M. M., & Jonathan, J. (2022). Conceptualizing digital leadership characteristics for successful digital transformation: The case of Tanzania. *Information Technology for Development*, 28(4), 777–796. DOI: 10.1080/02681102.2021.1991872

McCarthy, P., Sammon, D., & Alhassan, I. (2022). Digital transformation leadership characteristics: A literature analysis. *Journal of Decision Systems*, 32(1), 1–31. DOI: 10.1080/12460125.2021.1908934

Mithas, S., Tafti, A., & Mitchell, W. (2013). How a firm's competitive environment and digital strategic posture influence digital business strategy. *Management Information Systems Quarterly*, 37(2), 511–536. DOI: 10.25300/MISQ/2013/37.2.09

Moroz, M. (2018). Acceleration of digital transformation as a result of launching programs financed from public funds: Assessment of the implementation of the operational program digital Poland. *Foundations of Management*, 10(1), 59–74. DOI: 10.2478/fman-2018-0006

Nadkarni, S., & Prügl, R. (2021). Digital transformation: A review, synthesis and opportunities for future research. *Management Review Quarterly*, 71(2), 233–341. DOI: 10.1007/s11301-020-00185-7

Oberländer, M., Beinicke, A., & Bipp, T. (2020). Digital competencies: A review of the literature and applications in the workplace. *Computers & Education*, 146, 103752. DOI: 10.1016/j.compedu.2019.103752

OECD. (2016). Skills for a Digital World. In *Policy Brief on The Future of Work*. OECD Publishing.

Onyeneke, G. B., & Abe, T. (2021). The effect of change leadership on employee attitudinal support for planned organizational change. *Journal of Organizational Change Management*, 34(2), 403–415. DOI: 10.1108/JOCM-08-2020-0244

Ostmeier, E., & Strobel, M. (2022). Building skills in the context of digital transformation: How industry digital maturity drives proactive skill development. *Journal of Business Research*, 139, 718–730. DOI: 10.1016/j.jbusres.2021.09.020

Pihlajamaa, M., Malmelin, N., & Wallin, A. (2023). Competence combination for digital transformation: A study of manufacturing companies in Finlan. *Technology Analysis and Strategic Management*, 35(10), 1355–1368. DOI: 10.1080/09537325.2021.2004111

Schiuma, G., Santarsiero, F., Carlucci, D., & Jarrar, Y. (2024). Transformative leadership competencies for organizational digital transformation. *Business Horizons*, 67(4), 425–437. DOI: 10.1016/j.bushor.2024.04.004

Schiuma, G., Schettini, E., Santarsiero, F., & Carlucci, D. (2022). The transformative leadership compass: Six competencies for digital transformation entrepreneurship. *International Journal of Entrepreneurial Behaviour & Research*, 28(5), 1273–1291. DOI: 10.1108/IJEBR-01-2021-0087

Shang, Y., Raza, S. A., Huo, Z., Shahzad, U., & Zhao, X. (2023). Does enterprise digital transformation contribute to the carbon emission reduction? Micro-level evidence from China. *International Review of Economics & Finance*, 86, 1–13. DOI: 10.1016/j.iref.2023.02.019

Shao, Z., Li, X., & Wang, Q. (2022). From ambidextrous learning to digital creativity: An integrative theoretical framework. *Information Systems Journal*, 32(3), 544–572. DOI: 10.1111/isj.12361

Shrivastava, S. (2017). Digital disruption is redefining the customer experience: The digital transformation approach of the communications service providers. *Telecom Business Review*, 10(1), 41.

Sow, M., & Aborbie, S. (2018). Impact of leadership on digital transformation. *Business and Economic Review*, 8(3), 139–148.

Tangi, L., Janssen, M., Benedetti, M., & Noci, G. (2020). Barriers and drivers of digital transformation in public organizations: Results from a survey in the Netherlands. In Electronic Government: 19th IFIP WG 8.5 International Conference, EGOV 2020, Linköping, Sweden, August 31–September 2, 2020 [Springer International Publishing.]. *Proceedings*, 19, 42–56.

Tigre, F. B., Curado, C., & Henriques, P. L. (2023). Digital leadership: A bibliometric analysis. *Journal of Leadership & Organizational Studies*, 30(1), 40–70. DOI: 10.1177/15480518221123132

Tiwana, A., Konsynski, B., & Bush, A. A. (2010). Research commentary—Platform evolution: Coevolution of platform architecture, governance, and environmental dynamics. *Information Systems Research*, 21(4), 675–687. DOI: 10.1287/isre.1100.0323

Töytäri, P., Turunen, T., Klein, M., Eloranta, V., Biehl, S., Rajala, R., & Hakanen, E. (2017), "Overcoming institutional and capability barriers to smart services", Proceedings of the 5oth Hawaii International Conference on System Sciences, pp. 1642-1651.

Trenerry, B., Chng, S., Wang, Y., Suhaila, Z. S., Lim, S. S., Lu, H. Y., & Oh, P. H. (2021). Preparing workplaces for digital transformation: An integrative review and framework of multi-level factors. *Frontiers in Psychology*, 12, 620766. DOI: 10.3389/fpsyg.2021.620766 PMID: 33833714

Van Laar, E., van Deursen, A. J., Van Dijk, J. A., & de Haan, J. (2019). Twenty-first century digital skills for the creative industries workforce: Perspectives from industry experts. *First Monday*. Advance online publication. DOI: 10.5210/fm.v24i1.9476

Verhoef, P. C., Broekhuizen, T., Bart, Y., Bhattacharya, A., Dong, J. Q., Fabian, N., & Haenlein, M. (2021). Digital transformation: A multidisciplinary reflection and research agenda. *Journal of Business Research*, 122, 889–901. DOI: 10.1016/j.jbusres.2019.09.022

Vial, G. (2019). Understanding digital transformation: A review and a research agenda. *The Journal of Strategic Information Systems*, 28(2), 118–144. DOI: 10.1016/j.jsis.2019.01.003

Vogelsang, K., Liere-Netheler, K., Packmohr, S., & Hoppe, U. (2019b), "Success factors for fostering a digital transformation in manufacturing companies", Journal of Enterprise Transformation, 1-22. DOI: 10.1016/j.jsis.2019.01.003

Warner, K. S., & Wäger, M. (2019). Building dynamic capabilities for digital transformation: An ongoing process of strategic renewal. *Long Range Planning*, 52(3), 326–349. DOI: 10.1016/j.lrp.2018.12.001

Weber, E., Büttgen, M., & Bartsch, S. (2022). How to take employees on the digital transformation journey: An experimental study on complementary leadership behaviors in managing organizational change. *Journal of Business Research*, 143, 225–238. DOI: 10.1016/j.jbusres.2022.01.036

Weber, E., Krehl, E. H., & Büttgen, M. (2022). The digital transformation leadership framework: Conceptual and empirical insights into leadership roles in technology-driven business environments. *Journal of Leadership Studies*, 16(1), 6–22. DOI: 10.1002/jls.21810

Yao, Q., Tang, H., Liu, Y., & Boadu, F. (2024). The penetration effect of digital leadership on digital transformation: The role of digital strategy consensus and diversity types. *Journal of Enterprise Information Management*, 37(3), 903–927. DOI: 10.1108/JEIM-09-2022-0350

Zaki, M. (2019). Digital transformation: Harnessing digital technologies for the next generation of services. *Journal of Services Marketing*, 33(4), 429–435. DOI: 10.1108/JSM-01-2019-0034

Zhen, M., & Ding, W. (2024). Empowering employees for digital transformation in manufacturing enterprises: A case study. *South African Journal of Business Management*, 55(1), 4207. DOI: 10.4102/sajbm.v55i1.4207

Zhu, J., Zhang, B., Xie, M., & Cao, Q. (2022). Digital leadership and employee creativity: The role of employee job crafting and person-organization fit. *Frontiers in Psychology*, 13, 827057. DOI: 10.3389/fpsyg.2022.827057 PMID: 35615170

Chapter 4
Qualitative Outcome of Digital Transformation Aspects for the Tourism Sector

Kerime Karataş
Bahçeşehir University, Turkey

Pelin Vardarlıer
https://orcid.org/0000-0002-5101-6841
Balıkesir University, Turkey

Abdullah Türk
Istanbul Bilgi University, Turkey

ABSTRACT

Digital transformation has caused a radical organizational change in the tourism industry in every sector, transforming and accelerating both business processes and strategies, customer interaction, and marketing of tourism products. At this point, it seems critical to answer questions such as which outputs the elements that will give organizations a competitive advantage and how to produce them, which practices are important, and why. The research aims to reveal the impact roles of digitalization on the tourism sector. For this purpose, in-depth interviews were conducted with experts in qualitative analysis management. The data obtained as a result of the interviews were conceptually coded for content analysis. After the coding, the data were analyzed using the Maxqda 21 program. According to the findings obtained from this analysis, the most important feature of the tourism sector in the digitalization process is that it creates a competitive advantage by providing

DOI: 10.4018/979-8-3373-2523-1.ch004

access to a systematic integration network.

1. INTRODUCTION

The tourism sector, offering the widest service network industrially, is deeply intertwined with innovation in business processes and customer interaction. While innovative product technologies drive gradual advancements, radical changes are more apparent in service marketing and delivery. Adapting digital innovations to the tourism sector has introduced various options regarding service quality, response speed, accessibility, reach, and flexibility. The integration of services and the opportunities offered through different destinations have significantly influenced the direction and intensity of demand.

As these developments become increasingly intelligent, a new perspective on innovation emerges. This perspective evolves cumulatively, leveraging measured knowledge, skills, and experience to enhance service production, distribution, and utilization. It is also essential to integrate know-how, create organizational roadmaps, determine success factors, and foster a human resource capacity to learn from failures and transform them into constructive behaviors. The future of the tourism industry appears to be closely tied to science and technology.

From this perspective, the main purpose of this study is to investigate the role of digital transformation in the tourism sector, focusing on customer preferences, competitive advantages, human resource considerations, and technology utilization. The tourism sector has become a significant competitive arena for leveraging innovation and advanced technological infrastructure. Innovation in tourism, employee competence, market monitoring, and customer expectations hold a critical role in service quality and differentiation.

This area of competence involves a rational and systematic process. Information technologies are highly valuable for service efficiency and destination management because tourism is a social development tool with the capacity and potential to deeply influence the economy and culture. This tool facilitates developing and implementing common strategies for transforming supply and demand processes and contributing to social progress. Organizational structures' interest in innovation enhances their management capabilities and agility in responding to customer demands (Yung & Khoo-Lattimore, 2019; Kurt, 2020; Antoniadis et al., 2020; Thees et al., 2020).

Strategic planning in enterprises supports the belief in delivering high-quality services and achieving meaningful change in the medium and long term. Technological advancements allow unlimited promotion and marketing of services and products, creating ample opportunities for tourism providers and related sub-sectors.

These advancements offer advantages in communication, cost reduction, access to up-to-date information, and the ability to gain competitive edge rapidly.

Today, the rapid pace of transformation driven by technological products makes digitalization a powerful tool. It provides opportunities to save time, effort, and costs while expanding reach, integrating systems, creating meaningful information packages from large datasets, and optimizing them for organizational needs. Technologies such as the Internet of Things (IoT), chatbots, Virtual Reality (VR), facial recognition, Blockchain, and big data analytics can support competition by enabling customer experience personalization, multi-channel recommendations, and real-world cognitive computing.

Addressing critical questions becomes essential in this context: What outputs do these competitive technologies produce? How are they generated? Which applications hold the most importance, and why? These questions are pivotal for understanding and leveraging the competitive potential of these technologies (Rejeb & Karim, 2019; Xie & He, 2022; Rawal et al., 2023; Lv et al., 2022).

2. RELATIONSHIP BETWEEN DIGITAL TRANSFORMATION AND TOURISM SECTOR

In tourism, digital transformation enhances business value creation and bridges the gap between customers and high-quality services. In this respect, digital transformation involves integrating digital technology into all areas of a business. It fundamentally reshapes business operations and value delivery, driven by its inherently disruptive nature. This process requires a cultural shift, compelling businesses to challenge the status quo, experiment, and embrace the possibility of failure (Libert et al., 2016).

While digital transformation has become a necessity for many businesses in today's world, its meaning remains unclear to many organizations (Herrmann et al., 2018). The benefits of Industry 4.0 include various digital tools that support highly effective and efficient processes with significant flexibility. These advanced technologies—such as the Internet of Things (IoT), Artificial Intelligence (AI), Virtualization, Big Data, Cloud Computing, and Blockchain—directly impact service quality. The increasing adoption of these technologies is transforming businesses into integrated "SMART" systems.

In an ever-evolving technological environment, organizations must invest in technological value-added solutions to sustain growth and gain a competitive edge in the market. To keep pace with these changes, businesses must encourage continuous employee training and development, promoting both personal and professional growth within the new ecosystem (Peres et al., 2020; Vardarlier, 2020). Effectively applying Industry 4.0 technologies can boost customer satisfaction, cut labor costs, improve profitability, drive innovation, and expand R&D capabilities. Consequently, an Industry 4.0 strategy can help organizations create smart business operations, ensuring sustained growth and increased stakeholder value (Banjanović-Mehmedović & Mehmedović, 2020).

Leveraging technological infrastructure to enable digital transformation can yield numerous positive outcomes for businesses. By embracing technologies that are central to modern life, businesses can improve service delivery, attract customers, and create a more comfortable experience for them (Rodrigues, 2022). This transformation optimizes organizational processes and market dynamics. However, implementing these changes is not straightforward; it represents a significant organizational responsibility. Digital transformation is a collective effort, requiring everyone within an organization to adapt to the substantial changes it entails.

At its core, digital transformation is a people-centric process. It often reshapes work groups, job titles, and long-term business processes. More importantly, it frequently involves discarding outdated processes and legacy technologies rather than simply adopting new technology. For large, well-established companies, digital transformation demands a major organizational initiative (Gomes et al., 2019). For small and medium-sized enterprises (SMEs), developing a strategic approach before implementing digital transformation is a critical factor (Libert et al., 2016). Like any fundamental change in business operations, digitalization must be approached strategically (Schallmo et al., 2020). This involves critically evaluating every aspect of the organization's activities and processes.

The first step in undertaking and internalizing digital transformation is understanding the available technologies and determining how they can be effectively applied to the business (Ebert & Duarte, 2018). Traditionally, the tourism industry has been one of the earliest adopters of technological advancements to benefit its operations (Stanojevic et al., 2022). Industry 4.0 technologies are now widely applied across all aspects of social life, including tourism. Consequently, tourism education institutions, which serve as the engines of the tourism industry, must undergo radical transformations to adapt to technological advancements (Ghobakhloo & Iranmanesh, 2021).

3. USES OF DIGITAL TRANSFORMATION ELEMENTS IN THE TOURISM SECTOR

Modern technology has reduced working hours by automating tasks. Digitalization offers tourism businesses numerous advantages, including cost reduction, customer satisfaction, improved accessibility, advertising and promotion, remote experiential service delivery, facilitation of cultural transmission, demand management and guidance, time management, information management and sharing, and coordination and optimization among service networks. Numerous studies in the literature provide insights into these advantages.

The primary focus of most studies highlights the significant reduction in business costs and the decreasing costs of tourism services (Stankov & Gretzel, 2020). One of the most critical outcomes of the digital transformation process in the sector is the ability to offer more affordable services by emphasizing convenience and accessibility (Hang, 2021). Online booking platforms, with user reviews and shared experiences, have created rational cost-comparison systems. For instance, obtaining positive reviews on platforms like TripAdvisor has become a strategic goal for many travel service providers (Korže, 2019).

Tourism 4.0 has enhanced the production of innovative and attractive tourism products. Virtual technology, in particular, enables the reproduction of historical events, ancient cultural sites, and natural landscapes. This provides customers with a unique experience, enhancing satisfaction by allowing guests to engage with these attractions on a sensory level through superior technological tools (Kurt, 2020). Using VR technology, businesses can present immersive, 3D digital environments, such as hotel locations or historical sites, to potential customers. This addresses common issues faced by remote customers, such as uncertainty about hotel ambiance or room quality, by providing virtual tours (Yung & Khoo-Lattimore, 2019).

The revival and digital presentation of historical places, cultures, and natural heritages through 3D or 4D videos enhance global accessibility. People worldwide can easily explore the tourism resources of different regions and countries, thereby encouraging tourism and influencing demand (Erdem & Şeker, 2022). Beyond offering attractions and prior experiences, digital technology significantly reduces time costs through the optimization of various processes.

For example, facial recognition technology has been widely adopted in the travel and tourism industry. Previously, travelers faced repetitive and complex procedures for document verification at customs, immigration, and airports, which consumed time and often led to dissatisfaction (Haynes, 2020). Today, AI-driven technologies save time and streamline security processes, providing cost savings during transitions for travel. Since tourism is inherently international, blockchain technology has emerged as a key solution for secure and traceable payments. For instance, Winding Tree offers an open-source distribution ecosystem that simplifies booking air and hotel tickets (Antoniadis et al., 2020). Airlines like Air New Zealand have integrated blockchain technology, streamlining ticket sales processes. Payments can now be completed quickly and securely using blockchain-based systems, enabling a seamless travel experience (Thees et al., 2020).

Blockchain-enabled digital identity platforms, such as ShoCard, facilitate secure identity verification and digital payments without requiring centralized databases prone to hacking (Rejeb & Karim, 2019). Artificial intelligence (AI) applications, which enhance both security and service quality, have also revolutionized Tourism 4.0. For example, pre-programmed chatbots offer personalized support for tasks like food ordering, taxi booking, and room services. (Amalia & Suprayogi, 2019; Bowen & Whalen, 2017).

Additionally, IoT technologies have transformed guest experiences by automating tasks like adjusting lighting, tracking luggage, or providing navigation. Robot receptionists and airport guides are now trending innovations that improve customer interaction and service efficiency (Xie & He, 2022).

AI further optimizes services through algorithms like Maximum Likelihood, which analyzes historical data to predict price trends. This enables customers to make informed decisions about booking hotels, flights, or cabins based on cost fluctuations (Rawal et al., 2023). Similarly, AI supports cross-selling strategies, offering complementary recommendations such as nearby entertainment options or bundled services, enhancing the overall travel experience (Lv et al., 2022).

These technological applications cumulatively contribute to timeliness, accessibility, cost efficiency, speed, and productivity, delivering significant benefits aligned with the Tourism 4.0 perspective of digital transformation. However, realizing these benefits is not without challenges. Implementing such advanced technologies requires substantial financial investment, and there is a shortage of trained human resources capable of utilizing and managing these systems, particularly in environments where digital transformation has not yet been fully embraced.

4. METHODOLOGY

This study used the qualitative method. The qualitative method allows the data collected through techniques such as observation, interview and document analysis to be presented together. Although conducting research with the qualitative method can be challenging, it is considered an important research technique in social sciences (Tanyas, 2014). The universe of this study consists of mid- and senior-level professionals working in managerial roles in tourism enterprises in Turkey for the sake of conciseness. For this reason, the purposeful sampling method was used in the study. Purposeful sampling is a sampling method generally used in qualitative research in which the researcher deliberately selects units in the universe for a specific purpose (Patton, 2002). Purposeful sampling is defined as a non-random sampling type in which the researcher deliberately selects participants with characteristics appropriate to the purpose of the study and is frequently preferred in qualitative research (Yıldırım & Şimşek, 2011). The study was conducted with 20 people working as managers, assistant managers and chiefs in the management teams of 15 enterprises in Turkey. The interviews were conducted one-on-one with the semi-structured question set conveyed in the subparagraph, and the one-on-one interviews were recorded by taking notes on the forms, and then transferred to Word format to be made suitable for analysis. In this technique, the data was coded and categorized according to themes. Coding in the program serves as a tool for systematically analyzing and classifying texts (Schönfelder, 2011). In the next stage, the codes that form a meaningful whole were divided into categories (themes) and the analysis process was initiated. As a result of the analysis, the findings were defined and interpreted using MAXQDA 2021. The data obtained through the interviews were compiled and analyzed using the content analysis technique of Strauss and Corbin (1990). The basic aspect of content analysis is to categorize a small number of critically important words in the answers given to open-ended questions (Miles and Huberman, 2015). The following questions were included in the questionnaire:

1. What do you think about the place and importance of digital transformation in your sector?
2. What do you think about the relationship between using digital opportunities and competitiveness?
3. What do you think about the contribution of digital technology to the sector?
4. Which digital technologies do you use in your work?
5. What do you think about the contribution of digital technology to your company?
6. What can you say about the digital services your company offers to customers?
7. What can you say about the contribution of the digital technologies your company offers to the company itself?
8. How do you perceive the challenges of using digital technology?

5. ANALYSIS AND FINDINGS

Purposeful sampling method was used in the selection of participants to participate in the study. Purposeful sampling is a sampling method generally used in qualitative research, in which the researcher deliberately selects units in the universe for a specific purpose (Patton, 2002). Purposeful sampling is defined as a non-random sampling type in which the researcher deliberately selects participants with characteristics appropriate to the purpose of the study and is often preferred in qualitative research (Yıldırım and Şimşek, 2011).

Figure 1. Code relationship scanner

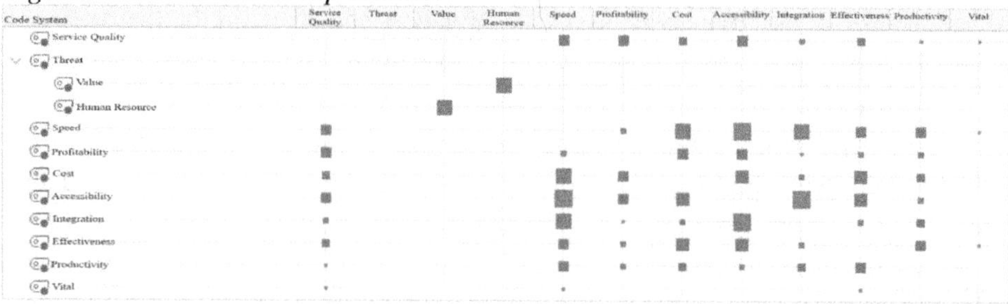

Another dataset generated using the MAXQDA 21 program is the code-based frequency analysis, presented in Figure 2. This analysis highlights the occurrence with which each code was highlighted in the responses given by the interview participants. The responses of the interviewed professionals were analyzed, and 12 codes were found to have varying levels of concentration. It was observed that 100% of the respondents emphasized the code "Integration," 60% highlighted "Accessibility," 60% noted "Value," 55% noted "Effectiveness," and 50% referred to "Human Resources."

Figure 2. Dataset generated using MAXQDA 21 program

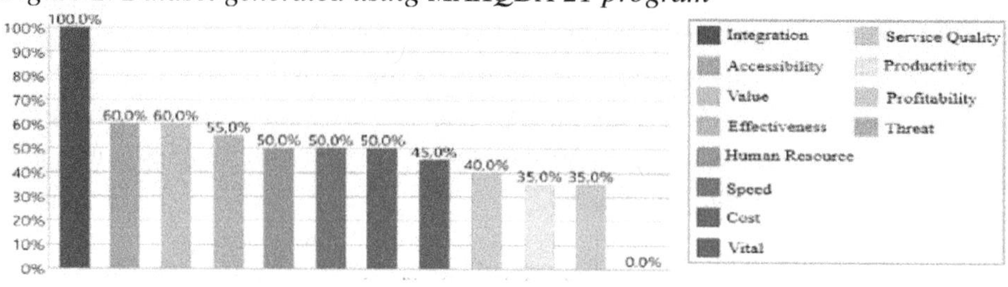

The most significant feature of this analysis is that it discloses the proportional frequency of the key roles in the research, based on the expertise and experiences of the interviewed professionals. Accordingly, while the professionals recognized integration as the key factor in the relationship between digitalization and the tourism sector, every participant emphasized integration and mentioned the improved accessibility of the sector due to digitalization. On the other hand, the professionals perceived the high cost of digitalization as an investment and the severe lack of trained human resources in the field as major threats.

Another dataset obtained using the MAXQDA 21 program is the single-case model. This model is based on assessing all the responses provided by the professionals during the interviews as if they came from a single individual. In other words, the texts are treated as a single source to reveal a unified code structure and relationship. In this context, the overall perspective of all professionals participating in the research was synthesized through the assigned codes.

While code-based frequency analysis typically treats each participant's responses as an individual data point, the single-case model aggregates all responses into a collective perspective. The single-case model is presented in Figure 3.

Figure 3. Single case model

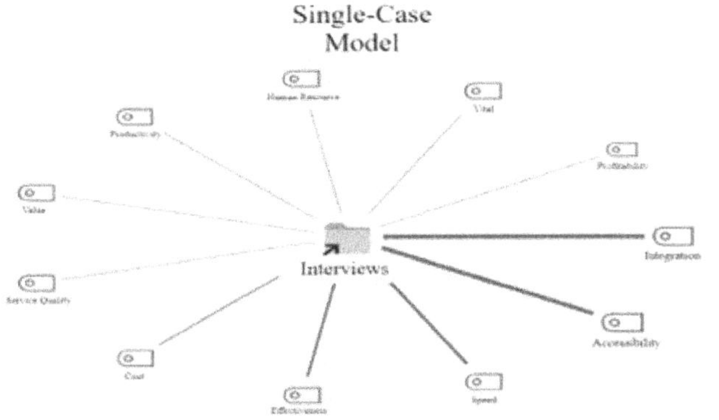

The single case model presented in the study emphasizes the common voice of the interviewees and the elements that play a key role in the relationship between digitalization and the tourism sector. The thickness of the lines connecting the single main source containing all the interview texts quoted in the model to the codes shows the intensity of the participants' relationship with the relevant codes. It is seen that the thickness of these lines shows the codes on which the participants concentrate and therefore shows the robustness of the model. In this stage, integration, accessibility and speed were determined as key codes.

Another data set obtained by the analysis performed with the MAXQDA 21 program is the word cloud model analysis. The word cloud analysis shows the key elements of all the concepts in the sentences presented as content by the participants. The word cloud was created after removing words such as "but", "however" and "maybe" that are not directly related to the conceptual structure of the study. The size and thickness of the words thematically represent the conceptual weight of the sentences created by the participants.

Figure 4. Word cloud

By creating a word cloud and analyzing the size and boldness of the words in Figure 4, it can be observed that concepts such as technology, contribution, service, integration, transformation, and competition are prominent in the relationship between digitalization and tourism. This suggests that the interview group reflects the anticipated level of expertise when conveying the relationship between digitalization and tourism.

6. DISCUSSION AND SUGGESTION

Digitalization has dramatically changed the travel and tourism sector, transforming it into a smart, innovative, and technologically advanced industry fully immersed in industrial digitalization. The most important feature of technologically driven development is mass customization and improved quality. This transformation has enabled companies to overcome challenges such as shorter time-to-market, faster service turnaround, and higher value creation. In this process, it seems inevitable that those unable to keep up with the new ecosystem will disappear and cease operations.

At this point, this study aims to reveal the roles and impacts of digitalization on the tourism sector. For this purpose, in-depth interviews were conducted with field experts using qualitative analysis methods. The data obtained from the interviews were coded conceptually for content analysis. After coding, the data were analyzed using the MAXQDA 21. According to the findings of this analysis, the most significant feature of the tourism sector's digitalization process is that it offers access to a systemic integration network. Indeed, as Pencarelli (2020) notes, the most prominent feature of digitalization in the tourism sector is that it facilitates internal collaboration, network-based horizontal integration, and flexible delivery systems integrated with engineering along the company, customer, and service value chain.

Moreover, as the systems offered by digitalization create a global network for businesses in the tourism sector by enabling the physical and digital worlds to come together, integration and interoperability have emerged. This refers to the ability of two systems to understand each other and utilize each other's functionality in exchanging data and sharing knowledge (Lu, 2017). The integration of digitalization into the tourism sector facilitates easy access to services, particularly through smart tourism applications, online booking systems, and payment methods (Prakosa, 2023). Specifically, this integration allows internal and external processes to communicate with each other in independent environments, enabling services to be provided across diverse platforms.

Additionally, blockchain technology enhances reservation process security, while data mining improves marketing strategies by analyzing tourist behaviors. Blockchain-based systems significantly reduce the risk of data breaches (Bekele & Raj, 2024). Another significant finding of the study is accessibility, which allows customers and companies to connect anytime, anywhere. In the code relationship analysis presented in Figure 1, which demonstrates the critical relationship between digital transformation and the tourism sector, the strongest link was found between integration and accessibility. The most appealing aspect of this relationship is its speed. In the digital age, where time costs directly affect economic costs, delays lead to serious issues such as decreased perceptions of service quality and increased expenses.

The goal is not only to enhance service quality but also to reduce bureaucratic business processes, increase efficiency, and consequently boost profitability through the speed provided by digitalization. Online platforms reduce costs for businesses by minimizing the need for intermediaries (Filipiak et al., 2020). For instance, cloud computing lowers data management costs while increasing operational flexibility. In another study, Vatan and Doğan (2021) found that digital applications in hotel management save time, reduce costs, lighten workloads, and increase efficiency. AI-supported chatbots, in particular, have enhanced customer satisfaction by providing instant responses to inquiries and offering multilingual support, enabling effective communication with international tourists (Akgün, 2023).

Digitalization serves as a lever in the tourism sector by optimizing services, enabling preference analysis through artificial intelligence and data analytics, supporting personalized service provision, and thus improving business efficiency (Lučić, 2022). The use of IoT devices in smart destinations has facilitated the analysis of tourist movements, improving service delivery. The study highlighted that IoT-based guidance systems personalize tourist experiences (Galvão, 2024). Jung et al. (2015) conducted a study on augmented reality experiences in a theme park in Korea, finding that participants were highly satisfied with the experience in terms of customer satisfaction and perceived service quality. Similarly, Ciliberti et al. (2023) noted that a metaverse platform developed in Bari, Italy, enhanced tourist experiences by using virtual reality technologies, allowing destinations to be explored without a physical visit.

These impacts of digitalization on tourism have led to the emergence of the concept of "smart tourism," which refers to the efficient and effective use of new technologies applied to tourism services. Smart tourism is based on a vision of sustainability, aiming to improve the quality of life for individuals, groups, citizens, and tourists in tourism destinations (Pencarelli, 2020). The wider range of options offered by digitalization compared to the pre-internet era has significantly increased the competitive impact of accessibility. From this perspective, companies must maintain up-to-date systems.

However, digitalization also presents challenges. Among the most significant results of this study are the high costs of digitalization, the necessity of constant updates, and the insufficient availability of trained human resources for software and hardware management, all of which are seen as serious disadvantages. Vatan and Doğan (2021) noted that the use of smart technology increases costs. Indeed, while artificial intelligence reduces human error and enables faster, more accurate operations, it also demands skilled professionals. According to Pencarelli (2020), there is a need for specialized roles in the digital ecosystem, such as cybersecurity experts, 3D printing designers, social media managers, Big Data scientists, and content marketing experts. In some European tourist destinations, such as Italy, skills shortages in trained human resources have been identified as one of the risks hindering the tourism sector's digital growth.

This study recommends that companies in the tourism sector recognize digitalization as a critical distinction and make strategic decisions to digitize their systems promptly. To ensure their sustainability, companies should adopt a scientific perspective, be open to academia-industry collaborations, and utilize research findings. They should also consider financing such studies to enhance their permanence in the sector.

Given the challenges of adapting to digitalization, such as high costs and the lack of trained human resources, it is recommended that real-sector organizations create a learning ecosystem rather than a competitive one. This can be achieved through sectoral summits, training seminars, and strategic collaborations. Furthermore, the study emphasizes the need for more research in this field. It is recommended to conduct studies with different methods, scopes, and samples to enrich the academic literature and deepen the understanding of digitalization's impacts on tourism.

7. CONCLUSION

Based on the qualitative outputs of digital transformation elements within the tourism sector, this study emphasizes the intensive integration of systems by examining the role of digitalization in the relevant profession in question. From this perspective, the main purpose of this study is to investigate the role of digital transformation in the tourism sector in terms of customer preferences, competitive advantages over competitors, human resource aspects, and technology use. At this point, innovation, employee competence, market monitoring, and customer expectations play an important role in both service quality and differentiation in tourism.

Digital transformation in tourism, a social development tool with the capacity and potential to deeply affect the economy and culture, has the power to integrate the transformation of supply and demand processes and the development of common strategies to contribute to social processes. This integration facilitates fast company-customer and company-market access points. The most critical aspect of smart technology enabled by digitalizatio is its time-saving effect, resulting in savings in cost, labor, and physical equipment. This enables companies to provide more effective services and is directly linked to profitability. When the results of the study are evaluated from this perspective, a network of relationships supporting speed, cost efficiency, profitability, and productivity comes to the forefront. Given the pace of technological advancement and the benefits of digitalization, the rapid evolution of existing systems is a foreseeable outcome.

However, digitalization has both advantages and disadvantages. When the disadvantages under the "Threat" code are examined, two obvious problems emerge: high investment costs and the need for constant updating, along with the lack of trained human resources to meet these demands. This caused the "Cost" and "Human Resources" relationship to appear nine times, making it the second most frequently referenced link. The most significant impact of digital transformation elements on tourism is integration. With system integration, physical barriers are eliminated, accessibility is provided, and these processes are carried out at high speed, thus increasing the connectivity and competitiveness of the digitalized tourism sector.

REFERENCES

Akgün, A. (2023). Otel faaliyetleri için yapay zekâ destekli uygulamalar. *Selçuk Turizm ve Bilişim Araştırmaları Dergisi*, (3), 1–21.

Amalia, A., & Suprayogi, M. (2019, October). Engaging millennials on using chatbot messenger for eco-tourism. *Third International Conference on Sustainable Innovation 2019–Humanity, Education and Social Sciences (IcoSIHESS 2019)* (pp. 484-487). Atlantis Press. DOI: 10.2991/icosihess-19.2019.84

Antoniadis, I., Spinthiropoulos, K., & Kontsas, S. (2020). Blockchain applications in tourism and tourism marketing: A short review. *Strategic innovative marketing and tourism*, 375-384.

Banjanović-Mehmedović, L., & Mehmedović, F. (2020). Intelligent manufacturing systems are driven by artificial intelligence in Industry 4.0. In *Handbook of Research on Integrating Industry 4.0 in Business and Manufacturing* (pp. 31–52). IGI Global. DOI: 10.4018/978-1-7998-2725-2.ch002

Bekele, H., & Raj, S. (2024). Digitalization and digital transformation in the tourism industry: a bibliometric review and research agenda. *Tourism Review*, (ahead-of-print).

Bowen, J., & Whalen, E. (2017). Trends that are changing travel and tourism. *Worldwide Hospitality and Tourism Themes*, 9(6), 592–602. DOI: 10.1108/WHATT-09-2017-0045

Ciliberti, E. C., Fiore, M., & Mongiello, M. (2023, June). Development of a metaverse platform for tourism promotion in Apulia. In *2023 IEEE International Conference on Metaverse Computing, Networking and Applications (MetaCom)* (pp. 680-681). IEEE. DOI: 10.1109/MetaCom57706.2023.00123

Ebert, C., & Duarte, C. H. C. (2018). Digital transformation. *IEEE Software*, 35(4), 16–21. DOI: 10.1109/MS.2018.2801537

Erdem, A., & Şeker, F. (2022). Tourist Experience and Digital Transformation. In *Handbook of Research on Digital Communications, Internet of Things, and the Future of Cultural Tourism* (pp. 103–120). IGI Global. DOI: 10.4018/978-1-7998-8528-3.ch006

Filipiak, B.. (2020). Economic development trends in the EU tourism industry. Towards the digitalization process and sustainability. *Quality & Quantity*. Advance online publication. DOI: 10.1007/s11135-020-01056-9 PMID: 33132445

Galvão, A., Brito, F., & de Melo, J. J. (2024). Towards a Consensual Definition for Smart Tourism and Smart Tourism Tools. DOI: 10.1007/s11135-020-01056-9 PMID: 33132445

Ghobakhloo, M., & Iranmanesh, M. (2021). Digital transformation success under Industry 4.0: A strategic guideline for manufacturing SMEs. *Journal of Manufacturing Technology Management*, 32(8), 1533–1556. DOI: 10.1108/JMTM-11-2020-0455

Gomes, J. G. C., Okano, M. T., Simões, E. A., & Otola, I. (2019). Management strategy and business models in the era of digital transformation. *South American Development Society Journal*, 5(14), 252. DOI: 10.24325/issn.2446-5763.v5i14p252-270

Hang, N. T. (2021). Universal education development to enhance the quality of human resources in the context of digital transformation and industrial revolution 4.0. *The USV Annals of Economics and Public Administration*, 21(1 (33)), 88–95.

Haynes, N.C.(2020).Robots, artificial intelligence, and service automation in travel, tourism, and hospitality. *Journal of Tourism Futures*. DOI: 10.1007/s11135-020-01056-9 PMID: 33132445

Herrmann, M., Boehme, P., Mondritzki, T., Ehlers, J. P., Kavadias, S., & Truebel, H. (2018). Digital transformation and disruption of the health care sector: Internet-based observational study. *Journal of Medical Internet Research*, 20(3), e9498. DOI: 10.2196/jmir.9498 PMID: 29588274

Jung, T., Chung, N., & Leue, M. C. (2015). The determinants of recommendations to use augmented reality technologies: The case of a Koreanthemepark. *Tourism Management*, 49, 75–86. DOI: 10.1016/j.tourman.2015.02.013

Korže, S.Z.(2019).From Industry 4.0 to Tourism 4.0. *Innovative issues and approaches in social sciences, 12*(3), 29-52. DOI: 10.1016/j.tourman.2015.02.013

Kurt, A. S. (2020). Dijital dönüşümün ekonomiye etkileri: Türkiye Ekonomisi'ne yansımaları. *OPUS Uluslararası Toplum Araştırmaları Dergisi*, 16(30), 3083–3109. DOI: 10.26466/opus.714393

Libert, B., Beck, M., & Wind, Y. (2016). How to navigate a digital transformation. *Harvard Business Review*, •••, 4.

Lu, Y. (2017). Industry 4.0: A survey on technologies, applications, and open research issues. *Journal of Industrial Information Integration*, 6, 1–10. DOI: 10.1016/j.jii.2017.04.005

Lučić, S. (2022). Digitalization And Artificial Intelligence: New Dimensions In Tourism. *Tourism and Hospitality Management Conference Proceedings*. DOI: DOI: 10.52370/TISC22564SL

Lv, H., Shi, S., & Gursoy, D. (2022). A look back and a leap forward: Are view and synthesis of big data and artificial intelligence literature in hospitality and tourism. *Journal of Hospitality Marketing & Management*, 31(2), 145–175. DOI: 10.1080/19368623.2021.1937434

Miles ve Huberman. M. B. (2015). Nitel Veri Analizi. Ankara: Pegem Akademi Yayıncılık.

Ozdemir, A. I., Ar, I. M., & Erol, I. (2020). Assessment of blockchain applications in the travel and tourism industry. *Quality & Quantity*, 54(5), 1549–1563. DOI: 10.1007/s11135-019-00901-w

Patton, M. Q. (2002). *Qualitative research and evaluation methods. Thousand Oaks*. Sage Publications.

Pencarelli, T. (2020). The digital revolution in the travel and tourism industry. *Information Technology & Tourism*, 22(3), 455–476. DOI: 10.1007/s40558-019-00160-3

Peres, R. S., Jia, X., Lee, J., Sun, K., Colombo, A. W., & Barata, J. (2020). Industrial artificial intelligence in Industry 4.0-systematic review, challenges and outlook. *IEEE Access : Practical Innovations, Open Solutions*, 8, 220121–220139. DOI: 10.1109/ACCESS.2020.3042874

Prakosa, R. M. (2023). Information Technology Implementation (Digitalization) on Booking and Payment Online System to Village's Tourism Product in Bali. *Journal of Tourism and Cultural Change*. Advance online publication. DOI: 10.19184/etc.v7i1.37868

Rawal, Y. S., Soni, H., Dani, R., & Bagchi, P. (2023). A Review on Service Delivery in Tourism and Hospitality Industry Through Artificial Intelligence. In *Proceedings ofThird InternationalConferenceonComputing, Communications, and Cyber-Security* (pp. 427–436). Springer. DOI: 10.1007/978-981-19-1142-2_34

Rejeb, A., & Karim, R. (2019). Blockchain technology in tourism: Applications and possibilities. *World Scientific News*, 137, 119–144.

Rodrigues, J. C. (2022). Business models for the digital transformation of audiovisual archives. *International Journal of Entrepreneurial Behaviour & Research*, 28(8), 1975–1999. DOI: 10.1108/IJEBR-01-2021-0073

Schallmo, D., Williams, C. A., & Boardman, L. (2020). Digital transformation of business models—best practice, enablers, and roadmap. In *Digital Disruptive Innovation* (pp. 119- 138).

Schönfelder, W. (2011). Caqdas and qualitative syllogism logic-nvivo 8 and maxqda 10 compared. Qualitative Social Research, 21. DOI: 10.1016/j.tourman.2015.02.013

Şimşek, H., & Yıldırım, A. (2011). Sosyal bilimlerde nitel araştırma yöntemleri. *Ankara. Seçkin Yayıncılık*, 432, 113–118.

Stankov, U., & Gretzel, U. (2020). Tourism 4.0 technologies and tourist experiences: A human-centered design perspective. *Information Technology & Tourism*, 22(3), 477–488. DOI: 10.1007/s40558-020-00186-y

Stanojevic, L., Vukotic, S., & Cvijanovic, D. (2022). Digital transformation of business processes in tourism. *Economics, Entrepreneurship and Management Research, 1*(1). DOI: 10.1016/j.tourman.2015.02.013

Strauss, A., & Corbin, J. (1990). *Basics of Qualitative Research: Grounded Theory Procedures and Techniques*. SAGE Publications.

Tanyaş, B. (2014, Nisan). Nitel Araştırma Yöntemlerine Giriş:Genel İlkeler ve Psikolojideki Uygulamalar. Eleştirel Psikoloji Bülteni. DOI: 10.1016/j.tourman.2015.02.013

Thees, H., Erschbamer, G., & Pechlaner, H. (2020). The application of blockchain in tourism: Use cases in the tourism value system. *European Journal of Tourism Research*, 26, 26. DOI: 10.54055/ejtr.v26i.1933

Vardarlier, P. (2020). Digital transformation of human resource management: digital applications and strategic tools in HRM. *Digital business strategies in blockchain ecosystems: Transformational design and future of global business*, 239-264. DOI: 10.54055/ejtr.v26i.1933

Vatan, A., & Dogan, S. (2021). What do hotel employees think about service robots? A qualitative study in Turkey. *Tourism Management Perspectives*, 37, 100775. DOI: 10.1016/j.tmp.2020.100775

Xie, D., & He, Y. (2022). Marketing Strategy of Rural Tourism Based on Big Data and Artificial Intelligence. *Mobile Information Systems*, 2022, 2022. DOI: 10.1155/2022/9154351

Yung, R., & Khoo-Lattimore, C. (2019). New realities: A systematic literature review on virtual reality and augmented reality in tourism research. *Current Issues in Tourism*, 22(17), 2056–2081. DOI: 10.1080/13683500.2017.1417359

Chapter 5
ESG Performance and Financial Performance Relationship During the COVID-19 Pandemic:
Evidence From Indonesia

Berto Usman
https://orcid.org/0000-0003-0210-3858
University of Bengkulu, Indonesia

Mine Aksoy
https://orcid.org/0000-0002-4773-1770
Yalova University, Turkey

ABSTRACT

The objective of this research is to explore the effect Covid-19 on the relationship between ESG and financial performance (FP) in the Indonesian stock market. By employing panel data analysis, this research aims to see if the crisis affected the relationship between ESG and FP across 55 firms in Indonesia from 2018 to 2022. The findings reveal that the relationship between FP and environmental performance and social performance was not significantly affected by the Covid-19 epidemic, while FP and corporate governance performance were negatively and significantly affected. Furthermore, it can also be elaborated that Covid-19 did not have a significant effect on FP. This research augments the existing understanding of the ESG-FP interplay by presenting contemporary empirical data set against the backdrop of the Indonesian stock market during the pandemic.

DOI: 10.4018/979-8-3373-2523-1.ch005

1. INTRODUCTION

A new coronavirus strain, widely known as Covid-19, has wreaked unsuccessful havoc in many parts of the world, leading to unprecedented lockdown of economic and social activities worldwide since early 2020 (Bose et al, 2022). While several pandemics spanning infectious diseases, such as Zika fever, Ebola, SARS, avian flu, swine flu, MERS have emerged from the late twentieth century to the early twenty-first century, Covid-19 proved to be more deadly and is much more widespread, primarily because of the present-day service-based economy (Baker et al., 2020; World Bank, 2020).

The Covid-19 pandemic has had a deleterious impact on progress towards the Sustainable Development Goals (SDGs) particularly in developing economies. Recovery efforts, while unprecedented in scale, have missed the mark on sustainable development (Jackie Hsu et al. 2024; Zhao et al. 2022). While many countries have faced these challenges, emerging markets have suffered particularly during the pandemic based on a lack of vaccines, greater vulnerability to commodity price fluctuations, and limited support for finances (Alberola et al, 2021). In many low-income and lower-middle-income countries, progress towards the Sustainable Development Goals has dramatically slowed and their health systems, infrastructure, markets, and regulation systems appear underprepared to handle emergencies like that posed by Covid-19. These governments frequently do not have the financial means necessary for a sufficiently responsive reaction to such crises (Barbier & Burgess, 2020).

Amid unprecedented challenges and uncertainty around the world, there is a growing link between Environmental, Social, and Governance (ESG) disclosures and the financial performance of companies. ESG disclosures have important downstream implications that go beyond satisfying regulatory requirements, as they reflect corporate transparency and accountability, which are fundamental principles in a society plagued by environmental degradation, social inequalities and governance irregularities. At the start of the Covid-19 pandemic, business operations suddenly faced very high levels of uncertainty, especially for businesses that stayed open in the first quarter of the pandemic were unprecedented by Kubiczek & Derej (2021) analysis. Due to the widespread economic and societal impacts of the pandemic, the importance of non-financial disclosures has increased significantly, prompting scholars and practitioners alike to study their empirical ramifications on corporate performance (Tandelilin & Usman, 2023). ESG practices during the Covid-19 pandemic, being perceived as an underlying stakeholder message of survivability, flexibility, and commitment to sustainable principles. This dynamic period offered a unique opportunity to assess how ESG disclosures affected corporate financial performance during a crisis, and the lessons concerning implications for ESG strategy on a scale. A plethora of empirical studies across myriad geographical contexts have enriched the understanding of this relationship during this pandemic. Through the collective analysis of multiple organizations, a study conducted in India, showcased a strong association between ESG performance and financial performance indicators of organizations, where governance and social factors seem to have a massive impact on the financial performance of an organization (Maji and Lohia, 2023). Based on a survey of 222 Indian firms, CRISIL ESG score determines the ESG performance of the Indian firms and uses the ACE Equity database for financial data. Corporate performance is measured in terms of both accounting and market-based metrics. They use ordinary least squares regression models for empirical analysis. According to the study, Corporate India stacks governance and social factors above environmental considerations. This is verified by plotting the ESG factors adjusted for two separate measures of financial performance that quite frequently correlate with ROA. The final components of environmental (E), social (S), and governance (G) statistically correlate with ROA, but only social (S) and governance (G) are statistically linked with Tobin's Q; thus, it is demonstrated that ESG performance and its components correlate positively with company performance.

On the contrary, European studies indicated a huge positive impact of ESG disclosure including stock returns and volatility on companies, especially focusing on the governance element (Climent et al., 2021). The research also emphasized the importance of having good governance, even in shifting and difficult times, as investors and stakeholders increasingly gravitate towards organizations who operate effective governance in periods of uncertainty. The results in the context of insights into the effect of ESG disclosures on Norwegian listed companies, provided an intriguing analysis of their financial impact over time, indicating a complex relationship based on a range of financial metrics (Giannopoulos et al., 2022). Their research examines how ESG activities affect the financial performance of publicly traded firms in Norway between 2010 and 2019. The Thomson Reuters Eikon ESG disclosure score is used for the evaluation of ESG while ROA and Tobin's Q are employed to assess financial performance.

Using data from S&P BSE 500 index, a study examined the complex impact of ESG disclosure during the pandemic and revealed the paradoxes and complexities regarding ESG reporting (Khandewal et al., 2023). The focus of this study is the influence of ESG disclosure on firm performance using an extensive dataset of companies in the S&P BSE 500 index that disclosed ESG parameters during the period of 2014 to 2021. The study found that ESG disclosure leads to a negative premium, which means that businesses with high transparency have lower returns than businesses with low transparency. The current findings differ from many earlier studies that showed a positive disclosure premium. Such results confirmed a nuanced link between disclosure and performance that challenged accepted notions and called for further investigation of the strategic role of ESG practices.

A study that datanized Chinese manufacturing enterprises extended the research scope by assessing whether ESG performance affected companies' value and identified finance constraints and R&D input intensity as key factors (Duan et al., 2023). This paper investigates the relationship between ESG performance and corporate values among publicly listed manufacturing firms in China from 2009 to 2021, paying attention to the mediating role of financial constraints, and the moderating effect of R&D investment intensity. According to research, the ESG performance of manufacturing companies plays a major role in realizing company value. The study broadened the empirical dimension and blurred the regional context of ESG disclosure impacts and offered critical information for organizations actively engaged or contestants interested in the Asian market.

More importantly, this empirical research combined provides robust and significant evidence of how CSR is related to ESG disclosures and organization financial performance across the Covid-19 pandemic. They underline the varying impacts of ESG practices, driven by regional elements, industry settings, and company-specific characteristics. Now that the world is moving towards a post-pandemic society, the information gleaned from these studies has far-reaching implications for future corporate planning, state growth, and academic study. The lessons learned from the Covid-19 epidemic highlight the need to adopt a holistic, integrated approach to ESG as part of business model transformation. It encourages the integration of ESG disclosures into the broader strategic lens of being essential to operating as a business needed to assess the risks of a rapidly changing global environment. With these takeaways, the conversation about what goes in and how to leverage ESG disclosures is changing, creating an updated vision for responsible corporate action and sustainability.

The ESG field is important for Indonesian listed companies since it is aligned with the global trend of sustainability and responsible corporate behavior (Harymawan et al., 2021). As the nation's commitment to transparency and accountability in the implementation of corporate activities concerned with the three aspects of ESG, sustainability reporting is regulated by the Indonesian Stock Exchange through regulation of the Financial Services Authority. Such regulations applied to financial service institutions, issuers, and public business entities (implemented for banks since 2019 and listed firms since 2020) (Tandelilin & Usman, 2023), so that financial institutions and issue partners uphold the principles of sustainability financing. Amidst the delay of these standards due to the outbreak of Covid-19, based on the data in 2022, approximately 73 percent of Indonesian publicly listed companies had produced and uploaded their Sustainability Reports, reflecting the increasing attention given to ESG reporting. These reports serve not only as a tool for compliance, but also as a tool that enables companies to improve their ESG performance while communicating their strategies and results to stakeholders including customers and investors (Harymawan et al., 2021).

On the new ESG reporting No. 51/POJK/03/2017 the Indonesian Financial Services Authority has issued comprehensive rules, which highlighted the need for listed companies to submit ESG-related information (Tandelilin, Usman, 2023). This reflects a growing trend where such disclosure will likely transition from a best practice into a requirement, an indication of a company's commitment to sustainability, which is under heightened scrutiny from global stakeholders. Under the cap-and-trade and/or cap-and-tax arrangements for carbon trading Indonesia aims to develop, companies in particular sectors will be subject to the government-imposed emissions ceiling (Purwienanti & Purwanto, 2023). These proposed rules and the infrastructure to be created for them hint that a navigated way through ESG isn't just a matter of compliance with the law but also a commercial need that affects how to compete in the market and the price franchises obtain to financing.

Given these trends, ESG studies can provide listed firms in Indonesia with guidance on how to approach models that keep up with these changing laws and how they can capitalize on opportunities generated by them (Nareswari et al. 2023). Furthermore, investors are now relying on ESG performance as an important factor in assessing the long-term sustainability of a company and the risk involved with their investment. For publicly listed companies looking to thrive in today's marketplace, a holistic understanding and thoughtful implementation of ESG principles is essential. The main contributions of this study are as follows: First, it examines the effect of ESG performance on financial performance in non-financial companies by utilizing multiperiod data from both the pre- and post-pandemic periods in Indonesia. Second, different from previous studies, this research uses ESG ratings to measure the sustainability performance of the business.

To systematically explore the topic, this chapter is organised into six main sections. Following this introduction, the next sub-section discusses the effect of the epidemic toward the Indonesian economy. Section three provides a comprehensive review of the literature, creating the theoretical background for the analysis and defining the hypotheses. The fourth section is dedicated to describing how the data and methods are presented, and lays out the empirical framework, including the variables involved, the characteristics of the data and the analytical approaches used. The fifth part discusses the empirical results of the study. It methodically shows the findings that were derived through the application of the theory, with relevant statistics and interpretations to confirm the assumptions that were mentioned before. The sixth part tackles the findings. The paper ends with a section that substantiates the findings in relation to the larger field. The final section is devoted to discussing implications of the results and evaluating some limitations of the study. Then it discusses potential avenues for future work, highlighting how subsequent research might build upon the current work to further understanding of the topic.

2. THE EFFECT OF PANDEMIC ON INDONESIAN ECONOMY

2.1. The Effect of Pandemics on the Indonesian Economy: Insights from SARS, H1N1, and Covid-19

Historically, pandemics have posed major challenges to the world health systems affecting the socio-economic layout of countries. Indonesia's economic landscape had already been deeply affected by previous outbreaks such as the Severe Acute Respiratory Syndrome (SARS) epidemic of 2002–2003, the H1N1 influenza pandemic of 2009, and the Covid-19 pandemic of 2020–2022. While each of the pandemics had distinct effects, they collectively highlight how vulnerable economies are to global health emergencies and the importance of preparedness, resilience and adaptability. This chapter examines the economic impacts of several pandemics in Indonesia, focusing on key sectors such tourism, manufacturing, employment, financial markets and government policy responses.

The SARS pandemic that originated in late 2002 escalated into a health crisis by 2003. Although Indonesia did not face a serious outbreak of the virus, compared with other Southeast Asian nations such as Singapore or Vietnam, the economic impacts were still felt across the region. The tourism industry, an essential pillar of Indonesia's economy, suffered heavily. In many countries, the implementation of travel restrictions resulted in the decline of international tourism, particularly to and from China and other East Asian nations (Keogh-Brown & Smith, 2008). Indonesia's reliance on tourism — particularly in places like Bali — means that even small disruptions in global travel cause massive economic damage. Hotels, restaurants and other travel-related businesses experienced reduced revenues, leading to layoffs and rising unemployment in the industry. While Indonesia's highly diversified economy cushioned the overall economic impact, the SARS pandemic exposed the underlying weakness of the country to external shocks in essential sectors.

The H1N1 (swine flu) pandemic of 2009–2010 had a global impact but varied in terms of severity by region. The impacts on health in Indonesia were not as dramatic as those in other countries — but the economic impact was still significant. As a global pandemic, H1N1 led to travel restrictions and global supply chain disruptions (Wang & Thi, 2006). Like with SARS, Indonesia's tourism sector faced significant disruption; however, H1N1 did not hinder the length and magnitude of our pandemic like the Covid-19 pandemic did. Besides tourism, the industrial and export sectors were forced to contend with the ripple effects of the disruptions to global supply chains. A reduced demand for Indonesian products, specifically in key markets such as China, the United States, and Europe, led to a temporary economic slowdown. The drop was most pronounced in sectors like electronics, textiles and automotive manufacture, which are heavily reliant on global supply chains in Indonesia, Vietnam and Thailand (Pongcharoensuk, 2012).

As very mild relative to the great effort during Covid-19 epidemic, Indonesian government response to H1N1 pandemic was found. Public health measures were taken to increase awareness of the infection; however, there were no statewide lock-downs, nor were there tight controls on movement. The economic crisis was not long lasting, and Indonesia quickly began to return to its original growth trajectory after the abatement of the epidemic (Adnan, 2023). Compared to SARS or Covid-19, the capital market impact of the H1N1 pandemic was much more muted. By 2009, Indonesia's capital market had matured and shown greater resilience to external shocks, driven by improvements in regulatory oversight and market infrastructure made after the 1997–1998 Asian Financial Crisis.

Initiated in 2020, the Covid-19 pandemic was, for the most part, the most severe and prolonged global public health emergency in modern times. The economic impact on Indonesia is far worse than the impact of SARS or H1N1, causing major disruptions in several industries, rising unemployment, and the country's first recession in nearly two decades (OECD, 2021). Indonesia's GDP contracted by 2.1% in 2020 amid a drop in consumption, investment and exports. The tourism and hospitality industries, an integral part of Indonesia's gross domestic product (GDP), bore the brunt of travel restrictions and falling international tourists (World Bank, 2020). Responding to the economic turmoil, the Indonesian government implemented a series of fiscal and monetary policies aimed at easing the impacts of the pandemic. These included stimulus packages, tax incentives and social safety nets designed to protect at-risk populations and businesses. Interest rates were lowered and liquidity support for banks and financial institutions was introduced by the Bank of Indonesia to stabilize the financial industry (OECD, 2021).

2.2. Lessons from the Pandemics: Strengthening Economic and Market Resilience

Pandemics have presented considerable problems to global health systems, significantly affecting the social and economic structure of nations. The Severe Acute Respiratory Syndrome (SARS) epidemic of 2002–2003, the H1N1 influenza pandemic of 2009, and the Covid-19 pandemic of 2020–2022 have each significantly impacted Indonesia's economic landscape. Although these pandemics yielded unique outcomes, they collectively emphasize the susceptibility of economies to global health emergencies and show the necessity of preparedness, resilience, and flexibility. This chapter analyses the economic impacts of various pandemics in Indonesia, emphasizing critical sectors such tourism, manufacturing, employment, financial markets, and governmental policy responses.

The tourism sector, a vital element of Indonesia's economy, was significantly impacted. The implementation of travel restrictions resulted in a significant decrease in international tourism, especially from China and other East Asian nations (Keogh-Brown & Smith, 2008). Indonesia's dependence on tourism, particularly in areas like Bali, means that even slight disruptions in worldwide travel led to substantial economic losses. Hotels, restaurants, and other tourism-related enterprises had diminished income, resulting in layoffs and heightened unemployment within the sector. Despite Indonesia's somewhat diversified economy mitigating the broader economic impact, the SARS pandemic revealed the nation's vulnerability to external shocks in critical sectors.

The Indonesian government's reaction to the SARS outbreak was marked by a prudent, wait-and-see strategy. Due to the restricted transmission of the virus in Indonesia, the authorities abstained from enforcing stringent domestic measures. Rather, it concentrated on preserving consumer confidence and guaranteeing economic stability (Hanna & Huang, 2004). Investor sentiment in the financial markets deteriorated due to uncertainties regarding the epidemic, obscuring the economic outlook throughout Southeast Asia. The Jakarta Composite Index (JCI) encountered a brief decline as foreign investors exited riskier emerging economies (Nippani & Washer, 2004). Nevertheless, the market swiftly recovered after the virus was contained, supported by governmental actions designed to restore investor confidence and enhance financial stability. As a result, long-term economic harm was mitigated, and the economy rapidly rebounded following the resolution of the SARS outbreak.

The H1N1 (swine flu) pandemic of 2009–2010 exerted a worldwide influence, although its intensity differed by location. In Indonesia, the health impacts were less significant than in other nations, however the economic consequences remained considerable. The World Health Organization (WHO) classified H1N1 as a global pandemic, resulting in travel restrictions and disruptions in international supply chains (Wang & Thi, 2006). Like SARS, Indonesia's tourism industry experienced considerable disruption; however, the duration and intensity of the H1N1 pandemic were less pronounced than that of Covid-19. In addition to tourism, the industrial and export sectors experienced repercussions from interruptions in global supply chains. A decline in demand for Indonesian products, especially in major markets like China, the United States, and Europe, resulted in a temporary economic downturn. The decline was especially evident in sectors such as electronics, textiles, and automobile manufacture, which depend significantly on international supply chains in Indonesia, Vietnam, and Thailand (Pongcharoensuk, 2012).

2.3 Theoretical Background

2.3.1. Theoretical Framework

The relationship between ESG performance and corporate profitability has been the subject of much academic research. According to research, firms with strong procedures in ESG typically have better risk profiles and are associated with better financial performance (Kubiczek & Derej, 2021). Moreover, corporate sustainability and ethics can lead to long-term profits (Dhaliwal et al., 2011) as they address operational (Benlemlih et al., 2016), reputational (Bebbington et al., 2008), and regulatory (Tandelilin & Usman, 2023) problems. While overall ESG has exhibited a positive correlation to profitability, the understanding is that this will largely underline why ESG integration performs better over the long-term than negative screening techniques.

The linkage between ESG disclosure and corporate profitability can be astutely assessed through the lenses of Legitimacy Theory and Stakeholder Theory. According to Legitimacy Theory, firms disclose ESG data to legitimize their practices and align with societal norms and expectations to enhance their image and financial performance (Suchman, 1995). According to Stakeholder Theory, satisfying various stakeholders' demands and addressing their interests (not just shareholders), through exhaustive ESG disclosure, can improve trust, consumer loyalty, and investment, serving profitability (Freeman, 1984). The theories emphasize the power of ESG disclosure in building firms' legitimacy as well as their connection to stakeholders, which are a precondition of firms' financial performance.

2.3.2. The ESG Performance and Firm Profitability

The debate around the connections (or lack thereof) between ESG performance and corporate profit is a complex and evolving body of research. In doing so, it is important to combine the foundational work of Friede, Busch, and Bassen (2015) which suggests a positive relationship between ESG and financial performance with more up to date research which better situates and elaborates on those findings. One of the important advancements made by Khan, Serafeim, and Yoon (2016) was to focus on the materiality of some specific ESG issues. They argue that not all ESG investments are the same; rather, their effect on firm value is determined by the strategic relevance of each ESG dimension to the firm's core activities. This matter is critical because it challenges the notion of a homogeneous ESG performance and compels a closer look at the ESG components.

According to Eccles et al. (2014), integrating ESG into a firm's strategy architecture leads to stronger financial performance. In this unified spirit, compliance becomes an enabler of cutting-edge creativity and efficiency, rather than merely a box-ticking exercise. Recent studies, including those by Edmans (2020) and Gibson, Krueger, and Schmidt (2021), have sought to build upon these findings. According to Edmans (2020), an emphasis on employee satisfaction amongst best social practices may lead to greater long-run profits, reaffirming the relevance of the social dimension. Gibson et al. (2021) offer a geographical perspective and show that the positive relationship between ESG and profitability is particularly strong in countries where institutional conditions are very solid, implying that the governance context beyond the firm itself matters for the success of ESG.

However, the debate is contentious, as the discussion is unfixed. However, the popular wisdom about a positive correlation isn't necessarily true as Jhanji & Connor (2021) demonstrate that the relationship between ESG and profitability yielded positive results is confounding by methodological biases and that the overall positive correlation is weaker than existing literature suggests when methodological poor practices are accounted for. These studies converged on the conclusion that the link between ESG, and profitability is complex and contextually dependent. They argue that while engaging in ESG can increase profits, the strength and nature of this relationship is strongly influenced by firm-specific strategies, the relevance of particular ESG issues, and the prevailing institutional framework. We thus proposed the following hypothesis:

H1: ESG performance has a positive effect on firm profitability.

2.3.3. The Covid-19 Pandemic and Firm Profitability

The Covid-19 pandemic has highlighted the significance of strong Environmental, Social, and Governance (ESG) policies, with increasing evidence indicating that superior ESG performance is associated with improved firm resilience and profitability, especially during crises. Lins, Servaes, and Tamayo's (2017) pivotal research indicates that companies with high ESG ratings are more proficient at enduring financial crises, sustaining performance throughout downturns more effectively than their lower-rated counterparts. The resilience concept is corroborated by Albuquerque, Koskinen, Yang, and Zhang (2020), who demonstrate that enterprises with robust ESG records were insulated from the pandemic's initial impact, as indicated by less negative stock returns. Furthermore, after the catastrophic earthquake in Türkiye on February 6, 2023, Aksoy & Yilmaz (2024) analysed the immediate stock price responses of firms listed on Borsa Istanbul (BIST). The study employed a sample of

450 enterprises to calculate abnormal returns (ARs) through event study methods. The results indicated that financial sector enterprises exhibiting superior sustainability performance showed enhanced resilience in the aftermath.

The case for ESG's advantageous impact during crises is bolstered by Cheema-Fox et al. (2021), who provide evidence of substantial capital inflows into high-ESG-rated financial products during the pandemic. This trend indicates an increasing belief among investors that companies with an ESG focus provide more security during market volatility. The synthesis of these viewpoints reveals that ESG investment functions both as a risk reduction instrument and as a strategic asset that enhances corporate value amid global problems. The trend of capital flows during the pandemic, preferring companies with strong ESG profiles, indicates a market perception that regards sustainability as essential to a company's fundamental value proposition and long-term performance, rather being merely a compliance or reputational concern.

Due to heightened investor emphasis on ESG considerations, companies may need to reassess and maybe adjust their plans to guarantee that their ESG activities are both substantial and seamlessly incorporated into their fundamental business processes. This transition may enhance their appeal to investors who are increasingly aiming to reduce risk by directing capital towards enterprises with sustainable and socially responsible operations. Based on these arguments, we suggest the subsequent hypothesis:

H2: The Covid-19 pandemic has a negative effect on firm profitability.

2.3.4. The Relationship Between the ESG and Firm Profitability During Covid-19 Pandemic

To further support the argument for a moderating effect of ESG during the Covid-19 pandemic, it is important to include studies that address this relationship in a variety of sectors and geographical settings. The pandemic has been a stress test of the durability that ESG integration is thought to provide to corporate profitability. Eccles, Ioannou, and Serafeim (2014) laid the groundwork by suggesting that ESG practices are positively associated with financial performance, yet the complexities of the current global crisis call for deeper exploration. The subject has garnered increasing attention, and recent evidence shows that ESG performance may act as a resilience factor and a driver of investment decisions during the pandemic. Ding, Levine, Lin, and Xie (2021) found that firms with strong ESG ratings were less likely to lose value and attract investment during the first quarter of 2020, at a period of extreme volatility. This is consistent with the findings by Cheema-Fox et al. (2021) at the same time when ESG funds received significant inflows in the period.

Additionally, the work of Giese, Lee, Melas, Nagy, and Nishikawa (2019) is consistent with the idea that ESG investing can serve as a risk management tool, which seems increasingly pertinent in light of recent pandemic developments. They argued that ESG indicators — such as management of the supply chain and approach to labour practices — might help drive a company's capacity to address supply chain challenges and labour challenges triggered by Covid-19. Further investigation confirms that the effectiveness of ESG is not uniform across industries and geographies. Whelan and Fink (2016) also pointed out that businesses are especially impacted by consumer behaviour and regulatory changes, such as energy, utilities, and consumer goods, and thus, there may be a stronger link between ESG performance and pandemic resilience among these types of companies. This is even more relevant as the crisis has fundamentally changed consumer behaviour as well as heightened awareness around corporate accountability. Although hundreds of previous studies have shown that ESG initiatives usually improve firm sustainability, research by Kim et al. which shows that this effect is muted during times of unavoidable market risks, like during the Covid-19 pandemic (2022). Their data suggest no substantive differences in sustainability outcomes between organizations with high and low ESG scores throughout the pandemic. In addition, they learnt that the individual components of ESG did not influence sustainability since the same results were obtained from both quarterly and semi-annual data sets.

Fatemi et al. (2018) argue that the link of ESG to performance may be weaker in emerging markets, where legal regimes for ESG are more nascent, than in more developed markets. These findings suggest the institutional context plays a crucial role in the relationship between ESG and performance in the epidemic. The prior research lays the groundwork for claiming that while ESG outcome might be associated with enhanced business profitability, particularly in times of crises, the relationship is complex and heterogeneous. Thus, we derive the below hypotheses:

H3: ESG performance positively moderates the relationship between the Covid-19 pandemic and firm profitability.

3. METHODOLOGY

We use data of non-financial firms that were listed on the Indonesian stock exchange. The data consist of panel data from 2018 to 2022. Data were obtained from the Thomson Reuters EIKON database. The sample consists of 213 observations from 55 firms. Financial performance (FP) is used here as a dependent variable in line with previous studies (Bayindir & Aksoy, 2024). Net income to total assets was used to calculate FP. At the same time, the Covid-19 epidemic serves as an explanatory variable. Covid-19 was quantified using a dummy variable taking a value of '1' for the years 2020 and 2021, and '0' for all other years. We used the ESG scores of the company, with a total of three components: the Environmental score (EScore), the Social score (SScore), and the Corporate governance score (CGScore), which we obtained from the Refinitiv database as a proxy for the ESG performance (Yilmaz et al., 2023). The variable Firm size (Size) is the log of total assets. Lev: ratio of short-term and long-term debt to total assets. Sector (Sec) works as a categorical variable. It takes the value "1" for the service sector and "0" for the production sector.

We applied a panel data analysis method (cross-sectional data and longitudinal data) in our study. This included observations from 55 organizations, which spanned 213 company-year cases across multiple years. The observations spanned five years — 2018 through 2022. Following the perspectives of Pedhazur (1997) and Baltagi (2008) our analysis combined cross-sectional data of 55 publicly traded firms with cross-temporal data over the specified five years in our panel-data estimates. The ordinary least squares (OLS) regression model was implemented indicating heteroscedasticity, as evidenced by the variance of errors across a number of cross-sectional units. Accordingly, we could deem the SE estimates (or the OLS model here) as a misplaced statement. Statistical procedures identified the decision to use panel corrected standard error methods as individual cross-sectional entities are assumed to be homoscedastic (Usman, 2019); consequently, the methodology was defined as appropriate to address this. We then tested our theoretical propositions by calculating the models as described in Equation 1.

$$FP_{i,t} = \alpha + X_1 ESG_{i,t} + X_2 Covid19_{i,t} + X_3 ESG_{i,t} * Covid19_{i,t} + X_4 Size_{i,t} + X_5 Le$$
$$X_6 Sec_{i,t} + e_{i,t}$$

The above econometrical model is applied to our panel data analysis, where the index 'i' represents the different companies and 't' reflects the moment in time within the window of observation. The model is, FP as a response variable FP (net income / total assets) The effect of the Covid-19 pandemic is included as an explanatory variable, defined by a dichotomous indicator taking the value '1' for the years 2020 and 2021, and '0' for the remaining years. To assess ESG Performance, our study employs ESG scores — which represent the environmental (EScore), social (SScore) and corporate governance (CGScore) aspects of corporate behaviour — obtained from the Refinitiv database. Furthermore, it uses the logarithm of total assets as Firm Size (Size), and Financial Leverage (Lev) is the ratio of the sum of short-term and long-term liabilities to total assets. In added, the sectoral classification is based on a binary variable.

4. ANALYSIS AND FINDINGS

In this section, we offer a detailed examination of the data collected from Indonesian sample firms.

Table 1. Descriptive statistics and correlation matrix

Variables		Mean	S.D.	1	2	3	4	5	6	7	8
1.FP	Financial Performance	0.079	0.103	1.000							
2.EScore	Environment Score	41.132	23.258	0.247*	1.000						
3.SScore	Social Score	53.287	21.424	0.146*	0.718*	1.000					
4.CGScore	Corporate Governance Score	47.895	23.211	0.198*	0.536*	0.618*	1.000				
5.Covid19	Covid-19 Pandemic	0.437	0.497	-0.080	0.039	-0.008	0.015	1.000			
6.Size	Firm Size	24.309	1.149	-0.103	0.246*	0.237*	0.108	-0.068	1.000		
7.Lev	Financial Leverage	0.477	0.211	-0.266*	-0.078	0.064	0.001	0.023	0.073	1.000	
8.Sec	Sector	0.188	0.391	-0.131	-0.266*	0.001	-0.066	-0.011	-0.053	0.268*	1.000

Notes: *p<0.05 N=213

Table 1 presents the Pearson correlation matrix, illustrating several variables alongside their descriptive data, including means and standard deviations, as well as the Pearson correlation coefficients among them. The average score of Financial Performance (FP) is 0.079, with a standard deviation of 0.103. These factors demonstrate substantial positive relationships with Environment Score (EScore), Social Score (SScore), and Corporate Governance Score (CGScore), as evidenced by coefficients of 0.247*, 0.146*, and 0.198* respectively. The asterisks denote statistical significance at the 0.05 level, indicating a likelihood of under 5% that these relationships arise from random chance. Furthermore, the EScore has a mean of 41.132 and a standard deviation of 23.258. A strong positive association with SScore is evident, indicated by a coefficient of 0.718*, suggesting that enterprises with elevated environmental scores tend to possess higher social scores as well. The SScore has a mean of 53.287 and a standard deviation of 21.424. It exhibits a moderately high correlation with CGScore, indicated by a coefficient of 0.618*. The CGScore has a mean of 47.895 and a standard deviation of 23.211. Notable positive relationships are observed with both EScore and SScore, whereas no significant associations are evident with the Covid-19 Pandemic, Firm Size, Financial

Leverage, or Sector. The variable denoting the Covid-19 Pandemic exhibits a mean of 0.437 and a standard deviation of 0.497, showing no significant connections with other examined variables.

The Firm Size (Size), with a mean of 24.309 and a standard deviation of 1.149, demonstrates a strong positive correlation with EScore and SScore, while showing a negative correlation with Financial Performance. Financial Leverage (Lev), with a mean of 0.477 and a standard deviation of 0.211, shows a notable negative association with Financial Performance and a positive correlation with Sector. Finally, Sector (Sec), a categorical variable, exhibits a mean of 0.188 and a standard deviation of 0.391. It exhibits a substantial negative correlation with EScore and a positive correlation with Financial Leverage. These correlations suggest potential linkages among different aspects of business performance and characteristics, necessitating further examination to clarify the nature and implications of these relationships.

Table 2. Regression results

Variables	**Variable Name**	**Model 1**	**Model 2**	**Model 3**
EScore	Environment Score	0.000		
		(0.000)		
SScore	Social Score		-0.001*	
			(0.000)	
CGScore	Corporate Governance Score			0.001*
				(0.000)
Covid-19 Pandemic	*Covid19*	0.005	0.010	0.007
		(0.019)	(0.015)	(0.016)
Interaction Term	*Covid19**EScore	-0.000		
		(0.000)		
Interaction Term	*Covid19**SScore		-0.000*	
			(0.000)	
Interaction Term	*Covid19**CGScore			-0.000**
				(0.000)
Firm Size	*Size*	0.001	0.034	0.000
		(0.014)	(0.039)	(0.013)
Financial Leverage	*Lev*	-0.183***	-0.235***	-0.180***
		(0.045)	(0.059)	(0.045)
Sector Dummies	*Sec*	-0.036	-	-0.035

continued on following page

Table 2. Continued

Variables	Variable Name	Model 1	Model 2	Model 3
		(0.044)		(0.043)
Constant		0.132	-0.576	0.133
		(0.328)	(0.932)	(0.310)
Observations		213	213	213
Number of firms		55	55	55
R^2		0.095	0.015	0.115
Wald chi2 (p value)		54.94 (0.000) ***		54.42(0.00) ***
F-test (p value)			5.10 (0.000) ***	

Notes: Robust standard errors in parentheses *** p<0.01, ** p<0.05, * p<0.1

Table 2 presents the findings of the panel data analyses. Model 1 has the independent variables Environment Score (EScore), Covid-19 Pandemic (Covid19), Firm Size (Size), Financial Leverage (Lev), Sector Dummies (Sec), and a constant term. In this model, only Financial Leverage has a significant negative correlation with the dependent variable, evidenced by a coefficient of -0.183 and a p-value denoted by three asterisks, normally indicating $p < 0.01$. Covid-19 demonstrates a favorable albeit statistically insignificant correlation. Model 2 substitutes EScore with Social Score (SScore) and incorporates the interaction term Covid19*SScore. In this model, SScore exerts a substantial negative effect on the dependent variable (coefficient of -0.001, $p < 0.1$), and the interaction term Covid19*SScore is likewise significant, indicating a negative correlation. Financial leverage exhibits a markedly negative correlation with the dependent variable. The R^2 value is inferior than that of Model 1, indicating this model accounts for less variability in the dependent variable. Model 3 incorporates the Corporate Governance Score (CGScore) and the interaction term Covid19*CGScore in lieu of EScore or SScore. In this context, CGScore exerts a modest yet noteworthy beneficial effect (coefficient of 0.001, $p < 0.05$). The interaction term Covid19*CGScore is strongly negative, shown by a double asterisk, which usually signifies $p < 0.05$. Financial leverage continues to be markedly unfavorable. This model possesses the highest R2 value among the three, indicating it offers the optimal fit.

Covid19 is positively but not significantly associated in Model 1, Model 2, and Model 3. The interaction terms show that the relationship between ESG and FP is negative for the Covid-19 period. The results suggest that Covid-19 had a non-trivial impact on the relationship between financial performance and the environmental and social facets of the triple line — the triad used for measuring sustainability — albeit the association between both financial performance and corporate governance turned negative and significant because of Covid-19. These elevated social scores suggest consistent excellence in a number of dimensions, such as benefits for employees, involvement in the community, charitable contributions, and the handling of social issues. Some businesses were forced to keep employees employed rather than lay them off during the pandemic. As a result, they have underperformed financially by failing to offset the cost pressures stemming from Covid-19 and fulfill their social responsibilities during the pandemic (Broadstock et al., 2021). The inverse correlation between the social score and FP refers to the labour conditions during the Covid-19 pandemic.

Additionally, company size did not matter in any models except Sector Dummies in Model 1. The constant is also not significant in all models. Statistical significance for all models (including the Wald chi-squared test and F-test) associated with a p-value < 0.001 indicates that models display statical significance, suggesting that the associations identified are unlikely to be due to chance alone. The models seem to be consistently applied on a dataset of 213 observations and 55 business. As reflected in the peculiar R2 values, different models demonstrate different explanatory power: about 11.5% extractable variability explains the dependent variable via Model 3.

5. DISCUSSION OF THE RESULTS

During the Covid-19 pandemic, many firms in developing countries, such as firms in Indonesia and Malaysia experience significant financial troubles. As a result, many companies might face the need to tighten CG in times when they need cash the most, which finds support in research that shows that CG proves to be beneficial in normal times but poses additional constraints during economic downturns. According to a poll conducted by EY (2020), in Malaysia; the economic downturn, aggravated by corporate governance specifications, intensified the financial burden on many companies. However, the bureaucratic restrictions and work from home phenomena due to the Movement Control Order (MCO) that were imposed to slow the virus's spread have inflicted delays on corporate operations and increased compliance and governance costs, denting companies' already bleak cash flows and financial results (EY, 2020).

According to a study conducted by Tanjung (2023), organizations with a high corporate governance score may focus more on following the rules of governance instead of enhancing operational efficiency and building financial resilience. When survival was all that mattered during the pandemic, those companies that chose to put governance ahead had less room to maneuver in what was a fast-evolving economic environment. As stated by Indonesia Financial Service Authority (OJK,

2014) during crisis, the complexity and inertia in corporate governance structure prevents timely decisions. Firms that adhered to strict governance procedures faced bureaucratic inertia in responding to sudden market volatility, which had a negative impact on their financial results. This shows the challenge of reconciling governance commitments with the need for agility and adaptability in the face of economic uncertainty.

The empirical findings provide a rich description of how business characteristics influenced business performance during the Covid-19 epidemic, compared to the existing literature. These observations are consistent with and, in some ways, contrary to fundamental paradigms. The persistent ghost of financial leverage among all models parallels earlier findings that high leverage can reflect increased risk and reduce business value in times of economic downturn (Frank & Goyal, 2009; Myers, 1977). The negative relationship between the level of leverage and the performance of a firm holds true, particularly in the midst of a crisis, lending to the risk-averse perspective articulated by Modigliani and Miller (1958) on the cost of debt. On the contrary, the role of Social Score (SScore) displayed in Model 2 not only challenges the overwhelmingly positive image of corporate social responsibility (CSR) existing in the literature (McWilliams & Siegel, 2001) but also adds another layer of complexity to the similar debates on the short-term impact of it during the queried pandemic. While firms with superior social performances are often recognized as being at reduced risk (Lins et al., 2017), this damaging interaction with the impact of Covid-19 reflects a complex short-term trade-off which might arise when firms prioritize social behaviour in times of crises. This result encourages a reconsideration of the temporal nature of CSR benefits, which have generally been assumed to be positive (Servaes & Tamayo, 2013). Broadstock et al. (2021) finds that organizations with superior social performance scores empirically under-perform in financial returns most of the time, suggests that good social metrics often come with higher ideals, including employee retention during crises instead of mass layoffs to balance the books.

Model 3 adds further complexity with the Corporate Governance Score (CG-Score). While governance is generally associated positively with organizational performance (Gompers, Ishii, & Metrick, 2003), the negative interaction effect that emerges in the wake of the pandemic is particularly enlightening. It implies that governance structures that are typically robust, such as corporate governance, may not possess the agility to respond effectively to the unprecedented face of the pandemic, which brings to mind a recent debate on the elasticity of governance frameworks to crisis periods (Tricker & Tricker, 2020). This finding differs significantly from the literature, which tends to argue in favor of larger organizations, where firms have access to more resources and resilience to withstand shocks (Amihud & Lev, 1981), indicating that firm size was not a statistically significant predictor in this study and requires further exploration. Despite expected sector variations to drive firm performance during the pandemic, where certain sectors were more affected than others (Alfaro & Chari, 2020), the importance of Sector Dummies in isolation in Model 1 may suggest that financial leverage plays the more significant role. This shows that financial structuring is more decisive than industry characteristics in driving business outcomes during the pandemic, supportive of Opler and Titman (1994) an argument that capital structure is crucial in economic fluctuations.

As a measure of explanatory power, the differences in R^2 values across models denote model-specific sensitivity to different dimensions of firm characteristics. Finally, the strength of the models, shown via the Wald chi^2 and F-test results, supports the validity of the examined relationships and suggests that the models successfully capture key aspects of firm behaviour during the Covid-19 pandemic. The diminished impacts of Covid-19 on ESG scores represent fertile ground to re-assess the evidence presented by Friede et al. (2015) that shows the long-term value creation associated with ESG. This study adds to the conversation by highlighting the complexity of the immediate impacts of these practices during a worldwide crisis. The panel data analysis conducted in this study sheds light on the complexity of financial and non-financial synergies and how they affect company performance across the duration of the epidemic.

Financial leverage consistently emerged as an important predictor of business performance across all of the models we tested, consistent with standard financial theory, which often points to the negative ramifications of increased leverage especially during periods of economic uncertainty. In contrast, business size, which is often viewed in the literature as a buffer against economic shocks, does not significantly impact performance; this suggests that its protective power may have been overstated or outweighed by other factors during the plague. The roles of Environmental, Social, and Governance (ESG) scores were complex. While high ESG scores were interpreted as a signal of resilience, there was no unambiguous effect of social and environmental scores on financial performance during the Covid-19 period. It was found that Corporate Governance Scores (CGScore) had a positive, but modest, effect on firm performance, but this effect disappeared when considering the interaction with Covid-19, indicating that even the best governance frameworks are susceptible to the destructive effects of global catastrophes. In periods of uncertainty, ESG or sustainable performance appears to add a measure of calm. Bayindir and Aksoy (2024) in their research prove that corporate sustainability performance (KSP) of non-financial firms listed in the Borsa Istanbul 100 (BIST 100) index could lead to lower overall risk.

These findings have all sorts of implications. One of the most crucial lessons concerning managing financial leverage, especially in a crisis, we offer for practitioners. Policymakers should therefore focus any support mechanisms on more indebted firms, rather than assuming larger businesses are inherently more at risk. The findings invite experts to explore further the complex relationships between ESG factors, resilience, and performance in a crisis. Indeed, whereas financial structure explains substantially a firm's vulnerability to an economic downturn, the various Covid-19 pandemic impact dimensions, accounted through ESG pillars, suggest a more complex interplay of factors influencing firm performance. This work adds seasoning to the academic discussion but also conversely demonstrates that the shield effect of ESG may not be particularly strong in an unpredictable shock/post-attack tail risk event, and therefore the potential for further research is extended. However, the study is not without limitations. The R^2 values are high, but they still indicate that the models explain only a moderate part of variance in business performance, even though there are probably more relevant unobserved variables. Omitted variable bias (i.e. not controlling for relevant variables) may also be an issue with these findings. However, the data are limited in that they are categorical, which restricts the ability to make any causative conclusions about any of the presented associations. The analysis is also limited to a short time risking the omission of any long-tern impact that both the Covid-19 Pandemic or ESG initiatives have on company performance. Another complicating factor, the use of aggregated ESG scores can obscure specific drivers of company performance. Furthermore, organizations vary in quality and consistency in ESG reporting, subsequently affecting the credibility of such numbers.

Future research should seek to address these limitations. Also, a longitudinal study design would be advantageous for analyzing the progression of the effects of financial leverage and ESG scores on company performance over time, especially to comprehend post-pandemic recovery trends. The explanatory power of the models might be improved by incorporating a more extensive range of control variables. Prices may also need further explanation, especially in the context of market dynamics, changes in consumer behaviour due to the pandemic, disruptions in supply chains, and digital transformation initiatives. An analysis of the disaggregated components of ESG scores would help to identify which aspects of ESG are most beneficial or harmful during times of crisis. Understanding better exactly how ESG initiatives impact firm performance would be particularly helpful. A comparative study of multiple geographical areas would help in a better understanding of how regional regulatory regimes and cultural differences may influence research.

6. CONCLUSION

Using data from 55 listed companies in Indonesia, this research provides new evidence on the Covid-19 pandemic effects on corporate profitability, measure by financial leverage, and ESG (Environmental, Social, and Governance) performance.

These findings suggest that financial leverage had an uninterrupted impact on firm performance during the pandemic period, which are consistent with existing financial theories on the risks associated with high leverage in economic downturns. Importantly, business size, which is often deemed a protective factor, similarly did not impact performance in this case. The research uncovered nuanced relationships between ESG scores and corporate performance during the pandemic. While high ESG scores are often associated with resilience, the results suggest that their buffering effects may be limited during a global crisis. Conversely, the Social and Governance aspects were more nuanced, with the Social Score showing a negative relationship to financial outcome on several occasions, challenging the strong prevailing view of corporate social responsibility as beneficial in a crisis.

Despite the limitations of the study, including potential missed factors and a short time frame, the results have important implications. This study finds a need for practitioners to contain financial leverage in crises. It suggests that authorities may be able to focus support efforts more efficiently on firms with high leverage. The study calls for more research on the effect of ESG factors on crisis resilience, suggesting future research work should adopt a longitudinal approach but also a wider view on what constitutes ESG factors, and that future performance comparisons between ESG and non-ESG firms take a broader set of ESG risk dimensions into account. Overall, the study elucidates the predominant role of financial structure in ensuring business resilience during economic downturns and challenges the perception that ESG characteristics provide a universally effective buffer during times of crisis. This is foundational knowledge that sets the stage for further research on how companies might be better prepared to deal with future global disruptions.

REFERENCES

Adnan, A. T. M. (2023). Asian perspective of capital market performance amin the Covid-19 pandemic. *Asian Journal of Accounting Research*, 8(3), 210–235. DOI: 10.1108/AJAR-10-2021-0223

Aksoy, M., & Yilmaz, M. K. (2024). Stock market response to natural disasters: Does corporate sustainability performance make difference? *Journal of Cleaner Production*, 454, 142294. DOI: 10.1016/j.jclepro.2024.142294

Alberola, E., Arslan, Y., Cheng, G., & Moessner, R. (2021). Fiscal response to the COVID-19 crisis in advanced and emerging market economies. *Pacific Economic Review*, 26(4), 459–468. DOI: 10.1111/1468-0106.12370

Albuquerque, R., Koskinen, Y., Yang, S., & Zhang, C. (2020, November). Resiliency of Environmental and Social Stocks: An Analysis of the Exogenous COVID-19 Market Crash. *The Review of Corporate Finance Studies*, 9(3), 593–621. DOI: 10.1093/rcfs/cfaa011

Amihud, Y., & Lev, B. (1999). Risk reduction as a managerial motive for conglomerate mergers. *The Bell Journal of Economics*, 12(2), 605–617. DOI: 10.2307/3003575

Baker, S. R., Bloom, N., Davis, S. J., Kost, K. J., Sammon, M. C., & Viratyosin, T. (2020). The unprecedented stock market impact of COVID-19 (No. w26945). National Bureau of economic research. DOI: 10.2307/3003575

Baltagi, B. H. (2008). Econometric analysis of panel data. *Econometric Theory*, 13(05), 351.

Barbier, E. B., & Burgess, J. C. (2020). Sustainability and development after COVID-19. *World Development*, 135, 105082. DOI: 10.1016/j.worlddev.2020.105082 PMID: 32834381

Bayindir, A. B., & Aksoy, M. (2024). The Relationship Between Corporate Sustainability Performance And Financial Performance During The Covid-19 Pandemic Period. *Anadolu University Journal of Economics and Administrative Sciences*, 25(1), 453–478.

Bebbington, J., Larrinaga, C., & Moneva, J. M. (2008). Corporate social reporting and reputation risk management. *Accounting, Auditing & Accountability Journal*, 21(3), 337–361. DOI: 10.1108/09513570810863932

Benlemlih, M., Shaukat, A., Qiu, Y., & Trojanowski, G. (2016). Environmental and social disclosures and firm risk. *Journal of Business Ethics*, 152(3), 613–626. DOI: 10.1007/s10551-016-3285-5

Bose, S., Shams, S., Ali, M. J., & Mihret, D. (2022). COVID-19 impact, sustainability performance and firm value: International evidence. *Accounting and Finance*, 62(1), 597–643. DOI: 10.1111/acfi.12801

Broadstock, D. C., Chan, K., Cheng, L. T., & Wang, X. (2021). The role of ESG performance during times of financial crisis: Evidence from COVID-19 in China. *Finance Research Letters*, 38, 101716. DOI: 10.1016/j.frl.2020.101716 PMID: 32837385

Cheema-Fox, A., LaPerla, B. R., & Serafeim, G. (2021). Corporate Resilience and Response to COVID-19. *The Bank of America Journal of Applied Corporate Finance*, 33(2), 24–40. DOI: 10.1111/jacf.12457

Climent, R, B., Garrigues IF-F, Paraskevopoulos I, Santos A. (2021). ESG Disclosure and Portfolio Performance. *Risks*. Vol (10):172. DOI: 10.1111/jacf.12457

Dhaliwal, D. S., Li, O. Z., Tsang, A., & Yang, Y. G. (2011). Voluntary nonfinancial disclosure and the cost of equity capital: The initiation of corporate social responsibility reporting. *The Accounting Review*, 86(1), 59–100. DOI: 10.2308/accr.00000005

Ding, W., Levine, R., Lin, C., & Xie, W. (2021). Corporate immunity to the COVID-19 pandemic. *Journal of Financial Economics*, 141(2), 802–830. DOI: 10.1016/j.jfineco.2021.03.005 PMID: 34580557

Duan, Y., Yang, F., & Xiong, L. (2023). Environmental, Social, and Governance (ESG) Performance and Firm Value: Evidence from Chinese Manufacturing Firms. *Sustainability (Basel)*, 15(17), 12858. DOI: 10.3390/su151712858

Eccles, R. G., Ioannou, I., & Serafeim, G. (2014). The Impact of Corporate Sustainability on Organizational Processes and Performance. *Management Science*, 60(11), 2835–2857. DOI: 10.1287/mnsc.2014.1984

Edmans, A. (2020). *Grow the pie: How great companies deliver both purpose and profit*. Cambridge University Press. DOI: 10.1017/9781108860093

EY (Ernst and Young). (2020). *COVID-19: Impact on Malaysian businesses*. EY Malaysia. https://www.ey.com/en_my/take-5-business-alert/covid-19-impact-on-malaysian-businesses

Fatemi, A., Glaum, M., & Kaiser, S. (2018). ESG performance and firm value: The moderating role of disclosure. *Global Finance Journal*, 38, 45–64. DOI: 10.1016/j.gfj.2017.03.001

Freeman, R. E. (1984). *Strategic Management: A Stakeholder Perspective*. Pitman.

Friede, G., Busch, T., & Bassen, A. (2015). ESG and financial performance: Aggregated evidence from more than 2000 empirical studies. *Journal of Sustainable Finance & Investment*, 5(4), 210–233. DOI: 10.1080/20430795.2015.1118917

Giannopoulos, G., Kihle Fagernes, R. V., Elmarzouky, M., & Afzal Hossain, K. A. B. M. (2022). The ESG Disclosure and the Financial Performance of Norwegian Listed Firms. *Journal of Risk and Financial Management*, 15(6), 237. DOI: 10.3390/jrfm15060237

Gibson, R., Krueger, P., & Schmidt, P. S. (2021). ESG Rating Disagreement and Stock Returns. *Financial Analysts Journal*, 77(4), 104–127. DOI: 10.1080/0015198X.2021.1963186

Giese, G., Lee, L.-E., Melas, D., Nagy, Z., & Nishikawa, L. (2019). Foundations of ESG Investing: How ESG Affects Equity Valuation, Risk, and Performance. *Journal of Portfolio Management*, 45(5), 69–83. DOI: 10.3905/jpm.2019.45.5.069

Gompers, P., Ishii, J., & Metrick, A. (2003). Corporate governance and equity prices. *The Quarterly Journal of Economics*, 118(1), 107–155. DOI: 10.1162/00335530360535162

Hanna, D., & Huang, Y. (2004). The impact of SARS on Asian economies. *Asian Economic Papers*, 3(1), 102–112. DOI: 10.1162/1535351041747978

Harymawan, I., Putra, F. K. G., Fianto, B. A., & Wan Ismail, W. A. (2021). Financially Distressed Firms: Environmental, Social, and Governance Reporting in Indonesia. *Sustainability (Basel)*, 13(18), 10156. DOI: 10.3390/su131810156

Jackie Hsu, W.-C., Lin, K.-Y., Lo, H.-W., & Yang, J.-J. (2024). Assessing corporation sustainability performance towards achieving sustainable development goals using a novel trapezoidal fuzzy ITARA-RIM approach. *Annals of Operations Research*. Advance online publication. DOI: 10.1007/s10479-024-05987-6

Jhanji, A., & Connor, Y. (2021). ESG resilience: A true measure of success Activating ESG through the risk lens in GrantThornton. Availabe on: https://www.grantthornton.com/content/dam/grantthornton/website/assets/content-page-files/advisory/pdfs/2021/esg-resilience-true-measure-success/esg-resilience-true-measure-success.pdf.coredownload.pdf

Keogh-Brown, M. C., & Smith, R. D. (2008). The Economic Impact of SARS: How Does the reality match the predictions? *Health Policy (Amsterdam)*, 88(1), 110–120. DOI: 10.1016/j.healthpol.2008.03.003 PMID: 18436332

Khan, M., Serafeim, G., & Yoon, A. (2016). Corporate Sustainability: First Evidence on Materiality. *The Accounting Review*, 91(6), 1697–1724. DOI: 10.2308/accr-51383

Khandelwal, V., Sharma, P., & Chotia, V. (2023). ESG Disclosure and Firm Performance: An Asset-Pricing Approach. *Risks*, 11(6), 112. DOI: 10.3390/risks11060112

Kim, J., Choi, D., Cho, E., Okafor, C. E., & Park, B. I. (2022). Corporate Sustainability in the Wake of the COVID-19 Global Pandemic: Does CSR Enhance Corporate Survival during a Market Crisis? *Sustainability (Basel)*, 14(21), 14438. DOI: 10.3390/su142114438

Kubiczek, J., & Derej, W . (2021). Financial performance of businesses in the COVID-19 pandemic conditions - comparative study. *Polish Journal of Management Studies*. Vol 24 (1). DOI: 10.3390/su142114438

Lins, K. V., Servaes, H., & Tamayo, A. (2017). Social Capital, Trust, and Firm Performance: The Value of Corporate Social Responsibility during the Financial Crisis. *The Journal of Finance*, 72(4), 1785–1824. DOI: 10.1111/jofi.12505

Lins, K. V., Servaes, H., & Tamayo, A. (2017). Social capital, trust, and firm performance: The value of corporate social responsibility during the financial crisis. *The Journal of Finance*, 72(4), 1785–1824. DOI: 10.1111/jofi.12505

Maji, S. G., & Lohia, P. (2023). Environmental, social and governance (ESG) performance and firm performance in India. *Society and Business Review*, 18(1), 175–194. DOI: 10.1108/SBR-06-2022-0162

McWilliams, A., & Siegel, D. S. (2001). Corporate social responsibility: A theory of the firm perspective. *Academy of Management Review*, 26(1), 117–127. DOI: 10.2307/259398

Modigliani, F., & Miller, M. H. (1958). The cost of capital, corporation finance and the theory of investment. *The American Economic Review*, 48(3), 261–297.

Myers, S. C. (1977). Determinants of corporate borrowing. *Journal of Financial Economics*, 5(2), 147–175. DOI: 10.1016/0304-405X(77)90015-0

Nareswari, N., Tarczyńska-Łuniewska, M., & Hashfi, R. U. A. (2023). Analysis of Environmental, Social, and Governance Performance in Indonesia: Role of ESG on Corporate Performance, *Procedia Computer Science*, Nippani, S., & Washer, K. M. (2004). SARS: a non-event for affected countries' stock markets? *Applied Financial Economics*, 14(15), 1105–1110.

OECD. (2021). Indonesia: Public deficit and effects of Covid indicators. *OECD Economic Outlook.*: Vol. 2021. *Issue 2*. OECD Publishing.

OJK. (Indonesian Financial Service Authority (2014). *The Indonesia Corporate Governance Manual. OJK and IFC advisory service in Indonesia*. Jakarta. https://www.ojk.go.id/Files/box/The-Indonesia-Corporate-Governance-Manual-First-Edition.pdf

Pedhazur, E. J. (1997). *Multiple regression in behavioral research*. Retrieved from https://www.amazon.com/J-Pedhazur-Multiple-Regression-Behavioral/dp/B008VR4WMG

Pongcharoensuk, P., Adisasmito, W., Sat, L. M., Silkavute, P., Muchlisoh, L., Cong Hoat, P., & Coker, R. (2012, August). Adisasmito, w., Sat, L, M., Silkavute, P., Muchlisoh, L., Hoat, P, C., Coker, R., Avian and pandemic human influenza policy in South-East Asia: The interface between economic and public health imperatives. *Health Policy and Planning*, 27(5), 374–383. DOI: 10.1093/heapol/czr056 PMID: 21859775

Priscilla, S., Hatane, S, E., & Tarigan, J. (2023). *Covid-19 catastrophes and stock market liquidity: evidence from technology industry of four biggest ASEAN capital market*. DOI: 10.1093/heapol/czr056 PMID: 21859775

Purwienanti, E N.F., & Purwanto, P. (2023). Carbon Tax Policy Toward Net Zero Emission. *E3S Web of Conferences*, 01022 ICENIS 2023 448. DOI: 10.1093/heapol/czr056 PMID: 21859775

Suchman, M. C. (1995). Managing legitimacy: Strategic and institutional approaches. *Academy of Management Journal*, 20(3), 571–610.

Tandelilin, E., & Usman, B. (2023). Toward a better understanding of social impact, CSR reporting and firm performance: A look at the ASEAN banking industry. *Social Responsibility Journal*, 19(3), 579–600. DOI: 10.1108/SRJ-04-2021-0167

Tanjung, M. (2023). Determinants of corporate governance compliance: what matters and what does not? *Journal of business and socio-economic development*. Vol 3 (3) pp 237-252. DOI: 10.1108/SRJ-04-2021-0167

Usman, B. (2019). Ownership structures, control mechanism and related party transaction: An empirical study of the Indonesian public listed companies. *International Journal of Economics and Management*, 13(1), 1–20.

Usman, B., Bernardes, O. T. F., & Kananlua, P. S. (2020). On the nexus between CSR practices, ESG performance, and asymmetric information. *Gadjah Mada International Journal of Business*, 22(2), 151–177. DOI: 10.22146/gamaijb.54053

Wang, K. (2006). M., & Thi, T.-B. N. (2006). Does Contagion Effect Exist Between Stock Markets of Thailand and Chinese Economic Area (CEA) during the "Asian Flu?". *Asian Journal of Management and Humanity Sciences*, 1(1), 16–36.

Whelan, T., & Fink, C. (2016). The Comprehensive Business Case for Sustainability. *Harvard Business Review*. Retrieved from https://hbr.org/2016/10/the-comprehensive-business-case-for-sustainability

World Bank. (2020). *Indonesia economic prospects: Towards a secure and fast recovery*. World Bank.

World Bank. (2020). COVID-19 to plunge global economy into worst recession since World War II. Available at: https://www.worldbank.org/en/news/press-release/2020/06/08/covid-19-to-plunge-global-economy-into-worst-recession-since-world-war-ii

Yilmaz, M. K., Hacioglu, U., Tatoglu, E., Aksoy, M., & Duran, S. (2023). Measuring the impact of board gender and cultural diversity on corporate governance and social performance: Evidence from emerging markets. *Economic research-. Ekonomska Istrazivanja*, 36(2), 2106503. DOI: 10.1080/1331677X.2022.2106503

Zhao, W., Yin, C., Hua, T., Meadows, M. E., Li, Y., Liu, Y., Liu, Y., Cherubini, F., Pereira, P., & Fu, B. (2022). Achieving the Sustainable Development Goals in the post-pandemic era. *Humanities & Social Sciences Communications*, 9(1), 1–7. DOI: 10.1057/s41599-022-01283-5 PMID: 35967482

Chapter 6
The Impact of Circular Ecological Transition Factor in the Industry 5.0 Era:
Evidence From Furniture Sector Enterprises in Spain

Almudena Muñoz Puche
https://orcid.org/0000-0002-7647-0311
Universitat Oberta de Catalunya, Spain

Ana Jiménez-Zarco
https://orcid.org/0000-0002-8980-6814
Open University of Catalunya, Spain

Alicia Izquierdo-Yusta
https://orcid.org/0000-0001-5894-6577
Burgos University, Spain

ABSTRACT

This study examines the integration of Circular Economy principles and digital transformation in the Spanish furniture sector, highlighting their combined impact on sustainability, resource efficiency, and technological innovation amid global challenges. The research focuses on how these principles and digital technologies like IoT can foster sustainable industrial practices in the Industry 5.0 era, characterized by human-centricity and environmental sustainability. Through semi-structured interviews and secondary data analysis, the study finds that circular policies drive

DOI: 10.4018/979-8-3373-2523-1.ch006

technological innovation and resilience but face obstacles like high costs, technical expertise gaps, and regulatory fragmentation, particularly for SMEs. It emphasizes the importance of government policies and industry collaboration in overcoming these barriers. The research provides recommendations for policymakers and industry leaders to enhance regulatory frameworks, support SMEs and promote innovation, contributing valuable insights into sustainable industrial practices in a dynamic global market.

INTRODUCTION

In an era characterized by rapid and accelerating changes, both society and business environments are experiencing unprecedented transformations (Mochón Morcillo & Cardona, 2021). Factors such as climate change, the COVID-19 pandemic, geopolitical tensions including the Ukraine and Gaza conflicts, and the escalation of fuel and raw material prices are contributing to a volatile global landscape (Allam et al., 2022). Enterprises are compelled to initiate investment and behavioural changes to minimize the impact of these disruptions on their daily operations and to enhance their resilience against future shocks (Building Back Better, 2020). This resilience is expected to be driven primarily by a technological revolution, marked by the accelerated adoption of digital technologies which transform business models and generate new revenue streams (Galvin et al., 2021).

The shift towards a digital world is accelerating every year. According to the International Data Corporation (IDC), global spending on digital transformation is expected to grow at an annual rate of 16.4% between 2021 and 2025. This growth is driven by companies adopting comprehensive digital strategies that integrate people, processes, technology, data, and governance. By 2025, global spending on the digital transformation of business practices, products, and organizations is expected to reach USD 2.8 trillion, more than double the figure of 2020 (Shirer, 2022).

Industry 5.0 builds upon the principles of Industry 4.0, advancing towards a more human-centric, sustainable, and resilient industrial paradigm. This new approach shifts the focus from purely economic gains to a broader perspective that values environmental sustainability and social well-being (European Commission. Directorate General for Research and Innovation., 2021). Integral to Industry 5.0 are Circular Economy principles, which advocate for efficient resource use, waste reduction, and recycling (Van Erp et al., 2024). These principles promote a shift from a linear economy, characterized by a 'take-make-dispose' model, to a circular one where resources are continuously cycled back into the production process (Van Erp et al., 2024).

The furniture sector, long reliant on manual labour and traditional manufacturing methods, encounters distinct challenges in adopting digital transformation. Companies in the furniture sector must address high material costs, strict environmental regulations, and increasing consumer demand for sustainable products (Masood & Sonntag, 2020; Rame et al., 2023). In this context, digital transformation involves integrating technologies like IoT, AI, and blockchain to enhance production efficiency, reduce waste, and improve supply chain transparency (Martínez-Peláez et al., 2023). Existing studies emphasize the opportunities and challenges of this transition, offering context for our research (Cathles et al., 2023; Rame et al., 2023; Sgaravatti, 2021).

This chapter examines how circular ecological transitions influence the adoption of digital technologies in Spain's furniture sector. Motivated by the rapid societal and environmental changes—including climate change, the COVID-19 pandemic, geopolitical tensions, and resource availability and cost fluctuations—this research aims to understand how these factors influence the adoption of advanced technologies in manufacturing, particularly in traditional sectors like furniture. This understanding is crucial for fostering sustainable and resilient business practices.

The primary mission of this chapter is to provide empirical evidence on the role of circular ecological transition in facilitating or hindering the adoption of digital technologies by furniture enterprises in Spain. This chapter is based on comprehensive research conducted with Spanish furniture companies since mid-2020, employing a qualitative approach that includes in-depth interviews with stakeholders and experts in the furniture sector. This method allows for a detailed understanding of the factors influencing technology adoption, with a particular focus on circular ecological transition. The qualitative data is supplemented by secondary sources such as industry reports, policy documents, and existing literature on digital transformation and sustainability.

LITERATURE REVIEW

Overview of Industry 5.0 and its Principles

Industry 4.0, often referred to as the Fourth Industrial Revolution, marked a significant leap forward in manufacturing and industrial processes through the integration of digital technologies (Schwab, 2016). Characterized by the adoption of cyber-physical systems, the Internet of Things (IoT), big data analytics, and cloud computing, Industry 4.0 aimed to create "smart factories" where machinery and equipment are interconnected, capable of autonomously exchanging information and optimizing production processes in real-time (Dalenogare et al., 2018). This technological shift resulted in unprecedented efficiency gains, reduced operational costs, and enhanced production flexibility (Moran, s. f.).

However, as Industry 4.0 evolved, it became apparent that the emphasis on automation and technological efficiency needed to be balanced with broader socio-environmental considerations. This realization paved the way for the emergence of Industry 5.0, which extends beyond the technological advancements of its predecessor by incorporating human-centricity, sustainability, and resilience into the core framework of industrial development (European Commission. Directorate General for Research and Innovation., 2021).

A core principle of Industry 5.0 is its commitment to sustainability. This involves integrating environmentally responsible practices into industrial processes to minimize ecological footprints and ensure long-term ecological balance (Ghobakhloo et al., 2022).

Sustainability in Industry 5.0 is achieved through several strategies (Ghobakhloo et al., 2022; Van Erp et al., 2024):

- Use advanced manufacturing technologies to reduce waste, optimize material consumption, and improve energy efficiency.
- Incorporate renewable energy sources, such as solar and wind power, into the manufacturing process to reduce dependence on fossil fuels.
- Assessing the environmental impact of products throughout their life cycle, from raw material extraction to disposal, and implementing measures to mitigate negative impacts.
- Encouraging suppliers and partners to adopt sustainable practices that ensure that the entire supply chain operates in an environmentally friendly manner.

Digital Transformation in the Manufacturing Sector

Digital transformation in the manufacturing sector is fundamentally reshaping how products are designed, produced, and delivered (Praxie, s. f.-a; Rishabh Software, 2023). Digital transformation is about integrating digital technologies into all aspects of production to improve processes, increase efficiency and create new value for customers. These changes are driven by the need to remain competitive in a rapidly changing market environment and to respond to changing customer demands (Dini et al., 2021; Kraus et al., 2021).

One of the primary drivers of digital transformation is the pursuit of greater efficiency and cost reduction (Verhoef et al., 2021). By leveraging advanced digital tools, manufacturers can streamline operations, minimize waste, and optimize the use of resources. This results in significant cost savings, which are crucial for maintaining profitability in a competitive global market. Automation of repetitive tasks and the use of data analytics to inform decision-making enable manufacturers to enhance productivity while maintaining high quality standards (Momani, 2024).

Enhanced productivity is another critical outcome of digital transformation. Digital tools and systems enable manufacturers to increase production speed and accuracy. Automation reduces the time required for manual tasks, freeing up human workers to focus on more complex and value-added activities. This not only improves overall output but also contributes to higher job satisfaction as employees engage in more intellectually stimulating and rewarding work (Du & Jiang, 2022; Jovevski et al., 2023).

In addition to efficiency and productivity gains, digital transformation enhances market competitiveness (Sui et al., 2024). Manufacturers with digital technology can lead to a faster response to market changes, such as changes in consumer preferences or new trends. This dexterity allows you to meet the needs of customers and thus increase customer satisfaction and loyalty. Digital technologies also facilitate the development of new business models and revenue streams, further strengthening the competitive position of manufacturers (Agustian et al., 2023; Sui et al., 2024).

Finally, sustainability is a key aspect of digital transformation in manufacturing (Joshi, 2024). As environmental concerns grow and regulations become more stringent, manufacturers are increasingly adopting sustainable practices. Digital technologies play a vital role in this transition by optimizing energy use, reducing waste, and promoting resource efficiency (Moghrabi et al., 2023). For instance, advanced data analytics can identify opportunities to improve energy efficiency, while digital tools can help monitor and minimize waste throughout the production process. These sustainable practices not only reduce environmental impact but also align with the growing consumer demand for eco-friendly products (Ortega-Gras et al., 2021).

Despite these compelling drivers, several barriers impede the widespread adoption of digital transformation in manufacturing (Jones et al., 2021; Lola & Bakeev, 2020). One of the most significant challenges is the high initial investment required (Jones et al., 2021; Shoplogix, 2024). Implementing advanced digital technologies can be costly, particularly for Small and Medium-sized Enterprises (SMEs) with limited financial resources (Lola & Bakeev, 2020; Shoplogix, 2024). These costs include not only the purchase of new technologies but also the expenses associated with training employees and integrating new systems with existing infrastructure.

The skills gap is another critical barrier (Lola & Bakeev, 2020; Shoplogix, 2024). There is a shortage of skilled workers who are proficient in operating and maintaining digital technologies. This skills gap poses a significant challenge as manufacturers struggle to find and retain talent capable of driving digital transformation initiatives. Investing in education and training programs is essential to bridge this gap and ensure a workforce that is equipped to leverage digital tools effectively.

Resistance to change within organizations is another barrier that can impede digital transformation efforts (Jones et al., 2021; Shoplogix, 2024). Organizational culture and employee attitudes toward change can significantly impact the success of digitalization initiatives. Employees and management may be hesitant to embrace new technologies due to fear of the unknown or concerns about job security. Overcoming this resistance requires effective change management strategies, clear communication about the benefits of digital transformation, and employee engagement in the transformation process.

In the specific case of furniture sector, among other traditional sectors, they want to evolve and develop in an optimal way like other industrial sectors such as pharmaceuticals or the automotive industry, digital transformation must be given its rightful place (Subdirección General de Estudios, Análisis y Planes de Actuación, 2024; World Furniture online, 2024). These kinds of sectors tend to be characterised by low investment in innovation, limited internationalisation and high competition from other markets such as Asia (AREMA, 2019). They also tend to be low- to medium-tech industries, very labour-intensive and with little investment in innovation or Research & Development (R&D) (Aggity, 2018; Madrid-Guijarro et al., 2009).

Different studies have been carried out to try to estimate the level of digitalisation of the furniture sector (Madrid-Guijarro et al., 2009; Rame et al., 2023). One of the most relevant study, the Habitat 4.0 project, diagnosed the state of digitalisation of companies in the furniture sector in addition to define a roadmap strategy to enhance their transformation. The following conclusions were obtained from the "Habitat 4.0" project (AIDIMME et al., 2018):

- Companies obtain a level of digitalisation of around 35% for the areas of strategy and business model, processes, organisation and people and infrastructure, while the products and services dimension obtain only 13%.
- Only 7% of the companies are dynamic, i.e., they are in an intermediate state of advanced development and digital maturity; 23% are competent, i.e., they have a slightly advanced state of development, but the remaining 70% of the companies are at the level of aware, i.e., they are in a very basic state of introduction of I4.0.

But, while most companies have not taken this step, it is considered essential to analyse the factors that determine the integration of digital technologies in the furniture sector, either encouraging or inhibiting such implementation, since the theoretical framework analysed shows a very limited integration of I4.0 in the furniture sector and subsequently, the 5.0 industry is far of the reality yet.

The Impact of External Factors Such as Circular Ecological Transition on Technological Adoption

In the context of technological adoption within the manufacturing sector, external factors play a crucial role in shaping the pace and nature of digital transformation (Abdallah et al., 2021).

Climate change has emerged as a major driving force behind technological adoption, particularly in industries with significant environmental footprints. The growing urgency to address climate change has compelled businesses to adopt more sustainable practices, which often involves integrating advanced technologies (Martínez-Peláez et al., 2023).

For manufacturers, this shift is driven by increasing regulatory pressures and societal expectations regarding environmental responsibility (Shui et al., 2024). Governments worldwide are implementing stricter environmental regulations to curb greenhouse gas emissions and reduce pollution (Council on Foreign Relations, 2023; European Environment Agency, 2024). These regulations often require companies to invest in technologies that enhance energy efficiency, reduce waste, and promote the use of renewable resources. For example, technologies such as energy management systems, waste recycling solutions, and low-emission production processes are becoming essential for compliance with environmental standards (Ortega-Gras et al., 2021; Sánchez-García et al., 2024).

Additionally, consumer demand for eco-friendly products is rising, pushing manufacturers to innovate and adopt technologies that align with sustainable practices (White et al., 2019). This includes the integration of Circular Economy principles, where technologies are used to optimize resource use, extend product life cycles, and minimize waste (Le Moigne, 2021). The drive towards sustainability, therefore, not only influences regulatory compliance but also creates market opportunities for businesses that can demonstrate environmental stewardship through technological advancements (Nascimento et al., 2019).

METHODOLOGY

Research Methodology

There is growing concern among authorities, business and society about climate change and environmental degradation. At the business level, the main objectives are to modernise and decarbonise energy-intensive industries, to promote the use of smart and sustainable mobility within them, as well as the responsible use of raw materials (Benito, 2019). Many companies started with very simple measures for a greener ecological transition such as decreasing paper waste, switching lighting to LED, etc. However, companies are aware of the need to use 4.0 technologies to make major changes concerning the reduction of waste, raw materials, etc. in their entire value chain and business (Ortega-Gras et al., 2021).

Until now, the academic literature has not reported on the importance of this environmental factor in explaining the adoption of technological innovations, but due to the increasing prominence of environmental issues, it has been considered key to address this factor.

Focusing on the furniture sector, it is a sector that has been taking an interest in the environment for years and trying to be as sustainable as possible by applying eco-design practices or obtaining Zero Waste Certification (Carrillo González et al., 2020; Fama living, 2022; Stasiškienė, 2008). In recent times, companies want to focus more on sustainability and circular ecological transition to be able to respect market trends that are becoming greener, as well as the requirements for public tenders (McCabe et al., 2009; Öhgren et al., 2019). All this makes the ecological transition a key factor in the adoption of technology in the furniture sector (WOW Web Magazine, 2021) and, on this basis, the hypothesis of the present research has been formulated:

H1: The circular ecological transition positively influences the adoption of digital technologies in the furniture sector.

Research Design

This research primarily uses semi-structured interviews, offering flexibility to explore themes and gather detailed insights (DiCicco-Bloom & Crabtree, 2006). Interviews were conducted with key stakeholders from the Spanish furniture sector, including:

- **Industry Executives:** Senior managers and executives who are involved in strategic decision-making and technology adoption.
- **Operational Managers:** Managers responsible for day-to-day operations and implementation of Circular Economy practices.
- **Technology Providers:** Representatives from companies that provide digital technologies and solutions relevant to the furniture sector.
- **Regulatory Experts:** Experts who understand the regulatory landscape and its impact on Circular Economy and technology adoption.

Although the interviews included different topics and factors influencing the adoption of 4.0 technologies in furniture sector, the specific information for this article is marked in bold.

Table 1. Questions that the author asked in interviews at various stages of the research

Issue	Sample Question
General advantages of adopting 4.0 technologies	What are the benefits of adopting 4.0 technologies compared to traditional production? To what extent are companies aware of these advantages?
Disadvantages of adopting 4.0 technologies	What are the disadvantages compared to traditional production and to what extent do these negative factors influence the adoption of 4.0 technologies?
Circular Ecological Transition Factor	**Does the circular ecological transition have a positive influence on the implementation of 4.0 technologies in the furniture sector?**
Conclusions	How do you see the future of both 4.0 and non-4.0 companies, and to what extent do you see a complete digital transformation of industry being achieved?

Source: Own elaboration

Secondary data complements the primary data collected through interviews by providing broader context and validating qualitative insights. While interviews capture detailed perspectives from individuals, secondary data—such as statistics, reports, and prior studies—illustrates larger trends and patterns. These sources also enhance research credibility by triangulating findings and cross-verifying information. Additionally, secondary data saves time and resources by offering readily available information to enrich analysis, supporting a more comprehensive understanding of the topic (Greenhoot & Dowsett, 2012; Johnston, 2014).

In these resources, the secondary data used come from these sources:

- **Industry Reports:** Reports from industry organizations and market research companies that provide insights into trends, challenges, and practices in the furniture sector.
- **Policy Documents:** Documents related to environmental regulations and policies affecting the adoption of Circular Economy principles and digital technologies.
- **Academic Literature:** Existing research on the intersection of Circular Economy and digital transformation, including case studies and theoretical frameworks.
- Secondary data provides context and background information, supporting the interpretation of primary data and enhancing the overall analysis.

Data Collection and Analysis Process

The interviews started on July 2022 up to mid- September 2022. Nine in-depth interviews were conducted (Table 2). With participants' permission, interviews were audio-recorded to ensure accurate data capture.

Table 2. Information of the organisations interviewed

Int.	Research Date	Organisation	Position of the interviewee in the organisation	Location	Gender
#1	01/07/2022	LDK Living Outdoors	Key Account Retail	Alcoy (Alicante)	Male
#2	15/07/2022	DGH Group	Director of Corporate Innovation and Technology	Valladolid	Male
#3	26/07/2022	Mobile World Capital Barcelona; Universitat Oberta de Catalunya; 5G Barcelona; Col·legi Oficial d'Enginyeria Informàtica de Catalunya; Intelligent Conectviity AMETIC	CIO and Director of Intelligent Connectivity; Member of the Advisory Board; CEO 5G Barcelona; Dean; Chairman of the Commission	Barcelona	Male
#4	02/08/2022	Department of Business Administration, Haaga-Helia University + Universitat Oberta de Catalunya	Lecteur	Barcelona	Male
#5	03/08/2022	The Innovative Business Grouping of Furniture and Related Industries of the Region of Murcia (AMUEBLA); Deputy Director of the Technological Centre for Furniture and Wood of the Region of Murcia (CETEM)	Secretary General + Deputy Director	Murcia	Male
#6	05/08/2022	The Technological Centre for Furniture and Wood of the Region of Murcia (CETEM)	Process Technology Manager	Yecla (Murcia)	Male
#7	08/09/2022	Home & Contract furnishings cluster and innovation hub; Itinere Industrial	Project Manager for Industrial Processes; Project Manager	La Sénia (Tarragona)	Male
#8	09/09/2022	Metalworking, Furniture, Wood, Packaging and Related Technological Institute	Industrial Development, Technology and Processes Manager	Paterna (Valencia)	Male
#9	23/09/2022	Improvent	Operations Consultant	Valencia	Male

Source: Own elaboration

After those interviews, secondary data sources were utilised to complement and contextualise the primary data collected from interviews.

FINDINGS

1. What are the Benefits of Adopting 4.0 Technologies Compared to Traditional Production? To What Extent are Companies Aware of These Advantages?

The adoption of 4.0 technologies offers several key benefits over traditional production methods, particularly in the furniture sector. These benefits include increased operational efficiency, higher competitiveness, enhanced product quality, and better ergonomics for workers. As Interviewees 1 and 8 emphasized, Industry 4.0 technologies allow companies to automate processes, monitor operations in real-time, and customize products more effectively, leading to faster production times and reduced errors. Additionally, these technologies contribute to sustainable practices by optimizing resource use and reducing waste.

While many companies are aware of these advantages, the level of awareness varies. Larger companies, like those mentioned by Interviewee 1, tend to be more aware of the benefits of 4.0 technologies due to their proactive leadership and access to resources. However, smaller enterprises, particularly in the furniture sector, are still in the early stages of understanding the potential benefits. As Interviewee 5 highlighted, some companies may hesitate to invest in these technologies due to a lack of technical knowledge or understanding of how these benefits translate into tangible outcomes.

2. What are the Disadvantages Compared to Traditional Production and to What Extent do These Negative Factors Influence the Adoption of 4.0 Technologies?

The main disadvantages of adopting 4.0 technologies compared to traditional production methods include high initial investment costs, the complexity of implementation, and the need for specialized skills. Interviewees 1 and 2 noted that these technologies often require significant upfront investments, which can be a barrier for SMEs. Additionally, the complexity of integrating new technologies into existing systems and the need for specialized training were cited by Interviewees 3 and 6 as key challenges.

These negative factors have a substantial impact on the adoption of 4.0 technologies. As Interviewee 4 pointed out, companies often perceive the technologies as complex and hard to integrate, especially when transitioning from manual, traditional methods. The fear of losing control over production processes, as noted by Interviewee 5, and the perceived difficulty of the implementation process are additional factors that hinder adoption. These barriers, particularly in terms of cost and complexity, make companies cautious about fully embracing Industry 4.0.

3. Does the Circular Ecological Transition Have a Positive Influence on the Implementation of 4.0 Technologies in the Furniture Sector?

Currently, the circular ecological transition has limited direct influence on the implementation of 4.0 technologies in the furniture sector. While there is a growing awareness of the importance of sustainability, as Interviewee 7 highlighted, many companies are still in the early stages of adopting Circular Economy practices. The lack of specific regulations and standards, as noted by Interviewee 2, further limits the direct impact of the circular transition on technological adoption.

However, Interviewees 4 and 5 suggested that this influence is expected to grow in the future, particularly as mandatory regulations around sustainability and circularity are introduced. The shift towards greener practices will likely encourage the adoption of 4.0 technologies that support sustainability goals, such as energy efficiency and waste reduction. While the circular ecological transition is not currently a driving force for technology adoption, it will likely become a more influential factor as regulations tighten and new generations of environmentally conscious leaders enter the industry.

Experts also confirmed that the Twin Transition, encompassing both green and digital advancements, will profoundly impact the furniture sector in the coming years and decades. This transition will be driven by various EU and national strategies and policies, including the European Industrial Strategy (European Commission. Directorate General for Communication., 2020), the European Green Deal (Siddi, 2020), and the new Circular Economy Action Plan (COM/2020/98 final, 2020).

Interviewees 4 and 7 emphasized that aligning with Circular Economy principles will not only ensure regulatory compliance but also open new market opportunities.

The interviewees pointed out that elements such as suppliers, customers, and competitors exert pressure on companies to integrate these technologies into their production processes. However, they noted that the circular ecological transition does not currently have a direct impact. This aspect is expected to become crucial in the future, contingent upon mandatory compliance with existing regulations and the influence of new generations who are increasingly environmentally conscious and aim to incorporate sustainability into all areas of life.

4. How Do You See the Future of Both 4.0 and non-4.0 Companies, and to What Extent Do You See a Complete Digital Transformation of Industry Being Achieved?

The future of the furniture industry will likely be divided between those that embrace Industry 4.0 technologies and those that continue with traditional production methods. Larger companies with more resources, like those mentioned by Interviewee 1, are expected to fully adopt 4.0 technologies, gaining competitive advantages through increased efficiency and customization. Interviewees 3 and 7 pointed out that these companies will likely lead the way in digital transformation, leveraging automation and data analytics to stay ahead in the market.

However, many SMEs in the furniture sector may struggle to keep pace with the digital transformation. As Interviewee 8 noted, smaller companies face challenges in adopting new technologies due to resource limitations and lack of expertise. Interviewee 5 emphasized that for these businesses, the transition may be gradual, as they focus on more immediate operational needs rather than large-scale digital investments.

A complete digital transformation of the industry is expected but will take time. As Interviewee 2 observed, smaller companies may adopt 4.0 technologies incrementally, driven by external pressures from customers and suppliers. The speed of this transformation will depend on overcoming several barriers, such as high initial costs, lack of technical skills, and organizational resistance to change. Despite these challenges, Interviewees 6 and 9 suggested that the increasing importance of data and digital tools will eventually lead to widespread adoption, especially as younger, more tech-savvy generations enter the workforce.

Based on the extracted results, it is essential to understand in detail the legislation and other instruments that can influence the circular green transition factor in the digital transformation of companies in the furniture sector before drawing any conclusions. Additionally, an analysis is needed to identify which digital technologies are most suitable for the furniture sector with circular and sustainable objectives. This analysis will provide insights into how the furniture sector, currently lagging in this dual transition, can progress.

Analysis of Legislation and Other Instruments Impacting the Circular Ecological Transition in the Adoption of Digital Technologies in Furniture Companies

Given that legislation and related instruments represent significant challenges for the implementation of the circular ecological transition, it is necessary to analyse the deployment of these policies at the EU and national level. This analysis aims to understand and forecast the green evolution of the furniture sector.

Circular Economy Package of the European Commission

The European Commission adopted the New Circular Economy Action Plan (CEAP) in March 2020 (COM/2020/98 final, 2020). It is one of the main building blocks of the European Green Deal, Europe's new agenda for sustainable growth (COM/2019/640 final, 2019). The EU's transition to a Circular Economy will reduce pressure on natural resources and create sustainable growth and jobs. It is also a prerequisite for achieving the EU's 2050 climate neutrality target and halting biodiversity loss (European Environment Agency, 2024).

This new and updated action plan communicates initiatives across the product lifecycle. It focuses on how products are developed, promotes Circular Economy processes, encourages sustainable consumption and aims to ensure that waste is avoided and that used resources are kept in the EU economy for as long as possible (COM/2020/98 final, 2020).

In order to promote the transition towards a more Circular Economy model in Spain, the Government prepared the Spanish Circular Economy Strategy 2030, under the coordination and leadership of the Ministry of Agriculture and Fisheries, Food and Environment and the Ministry of Economy, Industry and Competitiveness, in collaboration with the other ministries involved, the Autonomous Communities and the Spanish Federation of Municipalities and Provinces (MITECO, 2020a).

Five priority sectors of activity are identified: the construction, agri-food, industry, consumer goods, and tourism sectors (MITECO, 2020a).

On the other hand, the Spanish waste plan for 2016-2022 sets the goal that 50% of waste must be recycled or prepared for recycling. As part of this, 2% of all furniture, textiles, appliances and other eligible items must be diverted from recycling or landfill and sent for repair and resale (MAPA, 2017).

The government is also working on a new state plan (PEMAR) with a time frame until 2035 (Pérez, 2023).

Waste Electrical and Electronic Equipment

The WEEE Directive, initially implemented in 2003 (Directive 2002/96/EC) and revised in 2012 (Directive 2012/19/EU), mandates the establishment of collection schemes, free of charge for consumers, to enhance the re-use and recycling of WEEE (European Commission, s. f.-c; Manickam, s. f.).

There is a debate on the scope of Article 2 of the WEEE Directive regarding furniture products containing electrical or electronic components. This article requires that from 15 August 2018 all electrical and electronic equipment must be classified according to the categories set out in Annex III to the Directive (open scope) (Forrest et al., 2017).

In Spain, the WEEE Directive was incorporated into national law through Royal Decree 110/2015 of February 20 (Ministerio de Industria y Turismo, s. f.).

Regarding the current situation in Spain, the Ministry for Ecological Transition published the selective collection targets for WEEE for 2019 (Eco RAEE, 2019). These targets are:

- Minimum quantity of separately collected waste electrical and electronic equipment: 436,941,261 kg (based on at least 65% of the weight of waste electrical and electronic equipment placed on the market in the previous three years), of which at least 373,946,238 kg is household waste electrical and electronic equipment and 62,995,022 kg is professional waste electrical and electronic equipment.
- A minimum of 9.35 kg of WEEE per inhabitant at the national level.

Restrictions of Use of Hazardous Substances in Electrical and Electronic Equipment (ROHS)

The Directive restricting the use of certain hazardous substances in electrical and electronic equipment, initially implemented in 2003 (Directive 2002/95/EC) and revised in 2011 (Directive 2011/65/EU), was further amended by Directive (EU) 2017/2102 (European Commission, s. f.-a). The amendment aims to promote the development of the Circular Economy in the European Union by amending the scope of certain product groups and supporting the operation of secondary markets for EEE, including repair, spare part exchange, refurbishment, reuse and modernisation (European Commission, s. f.-b; Ho, 2023).

This legislation mandates the use of safer alternatives for certain hazardous materials and substances, including flame retardants like PolyBrominated Diphenyl Ethers (PBDE) and PolyBrominated Biphenyls (PBB), as well as heavy metals such as lead, mercury, cadmium, and hexavalent chromium (European Commission, s. f.-b; Ho, 2023).

The Directive 2011/65/EU was incorporated to the Spanish law by the Royal Decree 219/2013 of 22 March (BOE, 2013).

Energy Related Products Directive

The directive published in 2009 (2009/125/EC) serves as the framework for defining Ecodesign requirements for products that use energy or are energy-related (i.e., they do not consume energy directly but can lead to additional energy use, such as windows). These Ecodesign requirements are detailed in specific Regulations for each product family (Intertek, s. f.).

Companies must ensure that the products they place on the EU market comply with these regulations (declaration of conformity) in order to be eligible for CE marking. Currently, the Ecodesign Directive does not have any regulations that directly affect furniture products. However, some furniture components such as LEDs, displays and motors may be affected (EU Monitor, s. f.; IMQ, s. f.).

Starting from July 18, 2024, the ESPR has replaced the Ecodesign Directive. The new regulation continues to guarantee compliance with environmental standards for product design, but will also introduce broader measures, such as the prohibition on the destruction of unsold products, in order to further increase the stability of the European Union. This new rule has furniture as one of the priority products (Nickel, 2024).

The eco-design Directive 2009/125/EC was transposed to Spanish law through the Royal Decree 187/2011 of 18 February (Global Regulation, s. f.).

There is little information available about the level of implementation of this directive in Spain. Some public administrations developed specific websites for this issue, for example IHOBE (public society of the Basque Government; https://www.ihobe.eus/inicio) and the Basque Ecodesign Center (http://www.basqueecodesigncenter.net).

Extended Producers Responsibility

Extended Producer Responsibility (EPR) is an approach to environmental policy in which producers' responsibility for their products extends to the post-consumer stage of their life cycle. EPR typically involves transferring responsibility (administrative, financial or physical) from national or local governments to manufacturers, and encouraging them to consider environmental aspects during the design and production of their products (OECD, 2024).

The principle of EPR has been applied to furniture items since January 1, 2013 (EcoMaison, s. f.). This scheme mandates recycling of furniture components and has gradually expanded to include new products such as comforters and pillows. As of January 1, 2023, it also covers textile decorative items like carpets and curtains (European Commission, 2023).

There is no specific EPR scheme for furniture waste in Spain, although it is expected by 2025 (Landbell Group, 2022). Similar to other countries, the selective collection of this type of waste is managed by municipal services or specialized organizations (Non-Governmental Organisations, NGOs, or similar) that focus on re-selling or recycling furniture (Ahlers et al., 2021). Often, these organizations are involved in social activities or donations.

Some examples include:

- Fundación Valora (https://www.fundacionvalora.org/)
- Dona Muebles (http://www.donamuebles.com/)
- Rastro Betel (https://www.rastrobetel.org/)
- Pont Solidari (http://pontsolidari.org/)
- Asociación Reto (http://www.asociacionreto.com/)

Hazards Substances/ REACH Regulation

The most relevant regulation related to hazardous substances at the European level is the REACH Regulation (EC 1907/2006). Its objective is to enhance both human health and environmental protection by identifying hazardous properties of chemical substances used in the EU at an earlier stage (Siam, s. f.). Manufacturers and importers must collect information on the specific and critical properties of the chemicals they use, with the aim of gradually replacing the most hazardous chemicals (known as "substances of very high concern") as soon as suitable alternatives are identified (Tickner & Jacobs, 2016).

The European Chemicals Agency (ECHA) coordinates these processes by managing the databases necessary for the operation of the system, coordinating the detailed analysis of critical and suspect chemicals, and maintaining a publicly accessible database. This database, accessible to professionals and consumers, provides information on hazardous substances (Assent, s. f.).

Regarding national legislation, the Law 8/2010 establishes the sanction regime provided in the REACH and CLP Regulations (Health Spanish Ministry, s. f.). The Ministry of Ecological Transition has a dedicated website to support the different agents in the application of REACH and CLP regulation (https://www.miteco.gob.es/es/calidad-yevaluacion-ambiental/temas/productos-quimicos/portal-reach-clp/).

Formaldehyde Emissions

Manufacturing resins, which account for around 60% of usage, are essential for producing a variety of consumer articles (Dizman & KaçakgîL, 2023). The primary application of these resins is as bonding agents in the production of wood-based panels, including plywood, particleboard, Oriented Strand Board (OSB), Medium Density Fibreboard (MDF), and other types of fibreboard like hardboard and soft-board (Hussin et al., 2022).

Formaldehyde-based resins are also utilized in producing other wood-based products such as furniture, flooring, and both indoor and outdoor building elements (Uchiyama et al., 2007). The EN 13986 is the harmonized European standard for measuring formaldehyde emissions from wood-based panels, defining the E1 and E2 product classes (ANSES & Bureau REACH, 2019). The reference test method is the EN 717-1 standard. These standards classify products but do not restrict the market availability of the higher-emission E2 class (formaldehyde release >0.124 mg/m^3) (Meyer, 2023).

At European level, there is no uniform legal requirement for these classes. However, since 2007, members of the European Panel Federation (EPF) have voluntarily agreed to produce only E1 wood-based panels, which emit lower emissions than E2 panels (European Panel Federation, 2019).

Spain does not have specific legislation regarding formaldehyde emissions from wood-based panels. However, concerning occupational exposure, the National Institute for Safety and Hygiene at Work (Instituto Nacional de Seguridad e Higiene en el Trabajo – INSHT, https://www.insst.es/) published a guide in December 2016 on the use of formaldehyde in wood-based boards (INSHT, 2016). Since 1999, Spain's occupational exposure limit for formaldehyde in short periods (VLA-EC®) has been 0.3 ppm (0.37 mg/m^3) (Santolaya & Blanxart, 2001).

EU's Rules on End-of-Life Waste Criteria

The objective of end-of-waste criteria is to alleviate the administrative burdens of waste legislation for safe and high-quality waste materials, thereby facilitating their recycling (ERA, s. f.). This is performed by guaranteeing high -quality material processing, promoting the normalization of products and quality, and improving harmony and legal trust in the market used (EPA, s. f.).

According to Article 6 (1) and (2) of the Waste Framework Directive 2008/98/EC, certain waste materials will no longer be classified as waste if they have undergone a recovery process, including recycling, and meet specific criteria established under legal conditions (Falkenberg, 2012). In relation to the furniture sector, wood waste, partially originating from furniture, has been examined in the JRC's initial study and several reports by the European Environmental Bureau (Forrest et al., 2017). These sources consider the wood waste stream to be potentially compatible with these principles. However, it is not always clear whether current management practices in the EU prioritise recycling over controlled energy recovery or institutional landfill.

The Waste Framework Directive 2008/98/EC has been incorporated into Spanish legislation via Law 22/2011 of July 28, which was derogated in 2022 by the Law 7/2022 of April 8. The new regulation, which transposes various EU directives into Spanish law, establishes the principles of a circular and low-carbon economy by means of a thorough revision of the basic state legislation on the subject (Envira, 2023). The new regulation calls for the establishment of an extended liability regime for manufacturers of furniture and interior items by April 2025. As a result, manufacturers, distributors and importers in the domestic market will have to take responsibility for the management of products at the end of their life cycle (AMBIT, 2024).

Flame Retardants

On June 25, 2019, the EU published Regulation (EU) 2019/1021, which updated the Persistent Organic Pollutants (POPs) Regulation (H. Tsang, 2019). This new law introduced several significant changes, including completely new entries for decabromodiphenyl ether (Deca-BDE) and PentaChloroPhenol (PCP) and its salts and esters in Part A of Annex I.

Some furniture products use flame retardants to meet various flammability standards, some of which require open flame testing, necessitating the use of flame retardants despite the lack of a legal requirement (de Witte & Hagen, 2022). There is no specific legislation regulating the use of flame retardants in the furniture sector. The use of such chemicals is guided by the requirements of the REACH Regulation and the POPs Regulation.

At the European level, environmental and health NGOs, industry groups, cancer organizations, firefighters, and labour unions have formed The Alliance for Flame Retardant Free Furniture in Europe. This coalition aims to eliminate the use of flame retardants in furniture products, advocating for safer alternatives to minimize fire risks (The Alliance for Flame Retardants Free Furniture, 2019).

In Spain, fire safety requirements for loose furnishings have been introduced, primarily covering public areas such as hospitals, prisons, hotels, and theatres (Hogar Sin Tóxicos, s. f.).

Renewable Energy Directive

The original Renewable Energy Directive establishes an overarching policy for the production and promotion of energy from renewable sources in the EU. Building on the 2009 (2009/28/EC) and 2018 (2018/2001/EU) directives, the revised directive of 2023 introduces stronger measures to fully utilize the potential for the further development and uptake of renewables (European Commission, s. f.-a). This is crucial for achieving the EU's objective of climate neutrality by 2050 and strengthening Europe's energy security (Mammonas, 2023).

In addition to the new flagship goal of doubling the current share of renewable energy, a strong policy framework will boost electrification across a range of sectors, including new increased sectoral targets for renewable energy in heating and cooling, transport, industry, buildings and district heating and cooling. The framework programme also promotes the development of electric vehicles and smart charging (European Commission, s. f.-a).

The revised directive incorporates into EU law some concepts from the 2020 energy system integration and hydrogen strategies (Franke, 2023). These concepts are aimed at creating efficient, circular and renewable energies, which maintains electrification based on renewable energy sources and the use of renewable fuel, including hydrogen, in sectors such as transport or industry, where electrification is not yet possible (Franke, 2023). For these hard-to-electrify sectors, the directive sets new binding targets for renewable fuels of non-biological origin (ICCT, 2018).

To address a major bottleneck in deploying renewables, permitting procedures will be simplified and expedited for renewable energy projects and necessary infrastructure projects. This includes shorter approval periods and the creation of "Renewables acceleration areas" (Store, 2022).

The revised command will enhance the standard of bio -fuel stability. This is increasing the demand for biofuels in combination with the pressure on the bio - fuel industry on the various flow of waste, agricultural residues, and forest bio -mas based second -generation bio -fuel research (Suzan & Smailagic, 2024). Wood-based panels and furniture exemplify the Circular Economy, as they can become inputs for renewable energy production at the end of their material life (Hague et al., 2023).

The Renewable Energy Directive (RED) of 2023 and Spain's Plan Nacional Integrado de Energía y Clima (PNIEC) 2021-2030 are closely aligned in their focus on advancing renewable energy and achieving climate goals within the framework of the European Union's broader green energy strategy (MITECO, 2020).

Suitable Digital Technologies for the Furniture Sector With Circular and Sustainable Objectives

According to experts, to overcome the current blockage and align with circular and sustainable objectives, the furniture sector should prioritize the adoption of the following digital technologies. Those technologies are closely linked to sustainability concerns, because they could modernize the manufacturing process of furniture sector while having direct impact on the adoption of sustainable practices, enabling the green and digital transition **[Figure 1].** They can enable several functionalities, from data collection and integration.

Figure 1. Technologies influencing circular practices

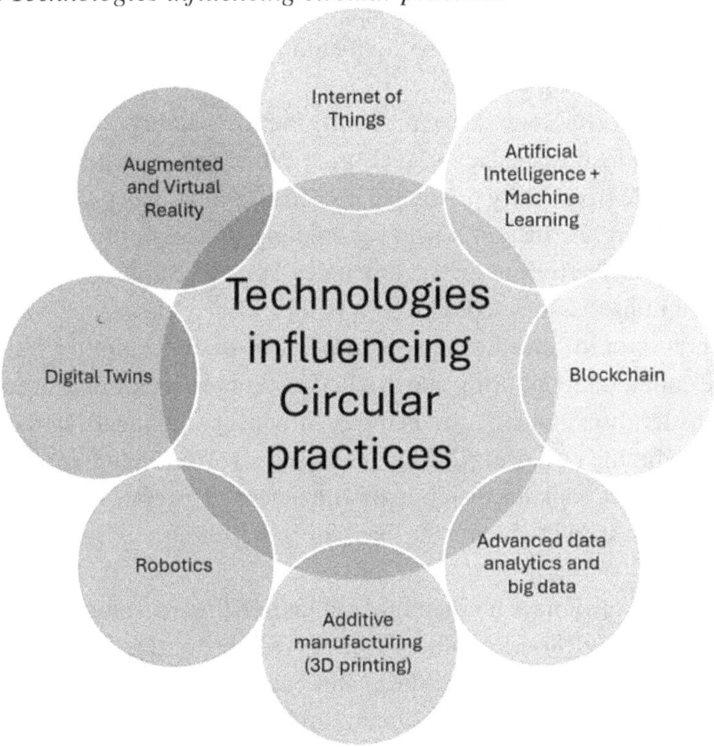

Internet of Things (IoT)

IoT technology is instrumental throughout the entire lifecycle of furniture products, from production to final use (European Subcontracting Network, s. f.). By embedding sensors and connectivity into manufacturing equipment and the furniture itself, companies can gather real-time data to optimize processes and enhance product performance (Ali et al., 2024; Praxie, s. f.-c). This data enables a range of capabilities that support both operational efficiency and sustainability.

During the manufacturing phase, IoT devices can track equipment performance, energy consumption, and material usage, ensuring efficient and sustainable production processes (Soori et al., 2023; Zhao, 2024). Continuous monitoring of these metrics enables companies to identify inefficiencies, reduce energy consumption, and minimize waste. This real-time production monitoring allows for immediate adjustments, improving efficiency throughout the process and contributing to more sustainable manufacturing practices.

Leveraging IoT technology can significantly improve quality control: sensors can detect defects and inconsistencies in real time, allowing for immediate correction and reducing waste from faulty products. This ensures that only products that meet high standards reach the market, further promoting sustainability. By minimizing the production of defective products, companies can save resources and reduce the environmental impact associated with rework and waste (Vidwans, 2024).

The integration of IoT into the final product creates smart furniture with advanced features like condition monitoring and predictive maintenance. For example, smart furniture can alert users when it needs repair or when components are nearing the end of their useful life (Ali et al., 2024; Praxie, s. f.-c). This proactive approach not only extends the product's lifespan but also enhances its overall value by ensuring optimal performance and reducing the need for premature replacements (Vidwans, 2024).

IoT technology also plays a crucial role in end-of-life management by tracking the product's lifecycle (Soori et al., 2023). Providing detailed information about the materials and components used promotes recycling and reuse. This tracking allows for a more efficient use of resources and improves dismantling processes. By recording the flow of products from the point of production to the point of disposal, the Internet of Things helps manage waste and optimize recycling processes, supporting the principles of a Circular Economy (Murugan, 2024).

Furthermore, IoT enables the implementation of circular business models, such as product-as-a-service models, where consumers pay per use or share products. This approach encourages the reuse and sharing of products, aligning with Circular Economy principles and reducing overall consumption (Rejeb et al., 2022). By promoting such innovative business models, IoT technology contributes to a more sustainable and efficient use of resources, driving the transition towards a Circular Economy in the furniture sector.

Artificial Intelligence (AI) and Machine Learning (ML)

AI and ML are powerful tools for analysing large datasets generated by IoT devices and other sources (Brock & Von Wangenheim, 2019; Holmström, 2022). These technologies can significantly enhance various aspects of the furniture sector, driving efficiency, sustainability, and innovation (Praxie, s. f.-c).

Optimizing supply chains is one of the primary benefits of AI in the furniture industry (InStyle, 2024; Praxie, s. f.-b). AI algorithms analyse supply chains to identify inefficient and improve. This allows reserve control, waste reduction, and more effective resources. AI, which predicts the demand and optimization of logistics, can help companies minimize surplus reserves and reduce the impact on over -production and transportation (RTS labs, 2024).

AI also plays a crucial role in enhancing the design of furniture products (Hestya, 2024). Using machine learning models, companies can predict the effectiveness of different materials and design options, guiding the development of products with a lower environmental impact. AI can help design more sustainable and recyclable furniture, taking into account factors such as material durability, ease of disassembly and recyclability (Hestya, 2024; Zahra, 2023). This data-driven approach ensures that sustainability is embedded in the design process from the outset.

Predictive maintenance is another critical application of machine learning in the furniture sector (Tr n et al., 2021). ML models can forecast when equipment is likely to fail or require maintenance, minimizing downtime and extending the lifespan of manufacturing machinery. By analysing historical data and identifying patterns, these models can predict potential problems before they occur, allowing for timely maintenance and reducing operational disruptions. This proactive approach not only improves production efficiency, but also reduces the need for costly repairs and equipment replacements. (Na et al., 2022; Tr n et al., 2021).

Iterative design steps are greatly improved by machine learning, driving innovation through rapid prototyping and testing. Designing with machine learning enables designers to rapidly iterate design concepts, test different configurations, and improve products more efficiently. This iterative process accelerates innovation and ensures designs are optimized for both performance and sustainability. By continuously learning from each iteration, AI enables designers to more quickly and effectively create furniture that meets the highest standards of quality and sustainability (Cong et al., 2022).

Blockchain

Blockchain technology provides transparency and traceability across the entire supply chain (Sunny et al., 2020), offering substantial benefits for the furniture sector by enhancing ethical sourcing, product lifecycle management, and consumer trust (Liu et al., 2022).

One of the primary advantages of blockchain technology in the furniture sector is ensuring ethical sourcing (Deloitte, s. f.-b; Gaur & Gaiha, 2020). By tracking the origin of materials, blockchain can verify that resources are sourced sustainably and ethically. Every step of the supply chain, from raw material extraction to the final product, can be recorded in an immutable ledger, providing a transparent and verifiable history of the materials used. This capability helps companies meet ethical and environmental standards by ensuring their products do not contribute to deforestation, exploitation or other unethical practices (Gaur & Gaiha, 2020).

Blockchain also significantly enhances product lifecycle management by maintaining detailed records of a product's journey from raw material extraction to end-of-life disposal (Bułkowska et al., 2023). This comprehensive traceability system facilitates recycling and reuse because the history and composition of each component is documented and easily accessible. When a product reaches the end of its life, this information can guide efficient disassembly and recycling processes, ensuring that materials are reused or disposed of in an environmentally friendly manner. By promoting a Circular Economy, blockchain technology helps reduce waste and improve resource efficiency (Bułkowska et al., 2023; Nuryanto et al., 2024).

Building consumer trust is another crucial benefit of blockchain in the furniture sector (Arangiaro et al., 2022). Consumers are increasingly requiring transparency regarding sustainability and ethical standards of the products they buy. Blockchain provides a reliable way to offer this information, because it allows companies to share verifiable data on the origins of their products, manufacturing processes and sustainability practices of their products (Arangiaro et al., 2022; Zhou et al., 2023). By scanning a QR code or accessing a digital ledger, consumers can confirm the authenticity and ethical standards of a product. This transparency not only enhances brand reputation but also strengthens customer loyalty by aligning with consumer values and expectations (Deloitte, s. f.-a).

Advanced Data Analytics and Big Data

Advanced Data Analytics and Big Data involve using complex algorithms and statistical methods to analyse vast amounts of data collected from various sources, including IoT devices and production systems. For the furniture sector, these technologies offer significant benefits that enhance efficiency, sustainability, and customer satisfaction (Badi, 2024).

Resource optimization is a key advantage provided by advanced data analytics in the furniture industry. By analysing large datasets on resource consumption and waste generation, companies can identify patterns and inefficiencies in their operations (Oliveira et al., 2016). This analysis enables the implementation of more effective resource management practices, leading to reduced waste and more sustainable production processes. By pinpointing areas where resources are underutilized or wasted, companies can make data-driven decisions to improve their overall resource efficiency (Y. P. Tsang et al., 2022).

Big data analytics also helps companies better understand their customers' expectations. By analysing data on customer preferences, behaviours, and trends, companies can better understand what they want. This information is invaluable for designing products that better meet market demands while aligning with sustainability goals. With detailed customer insights, companies can tailor their product offerings to match consumer expectations, increasing customer satisfaction and loyalty (Bretzfield, 2024; Seseni & Mbohwa, 2018).

Predictive analytics, powered by big data, allows companies to forecast demand, optimize inventory levels, and improve supply chain management (Kaplan, s. f.-c). Using history data and prediction models, furniture manufacturers can provide more accurate market needs. This ensures that the probability of excessive production is reduced, and resources are used more effectively. Optimized inventory management minimizes excess stock and associated costs, helping to create a leaner, more resilient supply chain (Tellius, 2024).

Improved process efficiency is another crucial advantage of advanced data analytics. By monitoring and analysing various aspects of the production process, from machine performance to energy usage, companies can make more informed decisions (Y. P. Tsang et al., 2022). Continuous analysis of production data identifies bottlenecks, inefficiencies and areas of improvement, resulting in continuous improvements in production efficiency, reducing energy consumption and operational costs, and increasing overall productivity.

Supporting Circular Economy initiatives is also facilitated by advanced data analytics and big data. By analysing data on product lifecycle and end-of-life processes, companies can develop more effective strategies for recycling and repurposing materials (Hariyani et al., 2024). This supports the creation of circular business models, where products and materials are continually reused, refurbished, and recycled. By integrating data-driven insights into their Circular Economy efforts, companies can enhance their sustainability performance and contribute to a more sustainable future (Klubnikin, 2023).

Additive Manufacturing (3D Printing)

Additive Manufacturing (AM), or 3D printing, offers transformative advantages for the furniture sector, particularly in the context of circular and sustainable objectives (Yang & Du, 2022). This technology brings a range of benefits that significantly enhance efficiency, sustainability, and customization in furniture production.

Waste reduction is a primary advantage of additive manufacturing. By producing items layer by layer from digital models, AM significantly minimizes excess material usage compared to traditional subtractive manufacturing methods. This precise manufacturing process ensures that only the necessary amount of material is used, significantly reducing waste and promoting more sustainable production methods. This waste reduction is essential to support the principles of a Circular Economy, where minimizing resource consumption and waste is paramount (Haleem et al., 2023; Javaid, Haleem, Singh, Suman, et al., 2021).

Energy efficiency is another notable benefit of additive manufacturing (May & Psarommatis, 2023). AM often consumes less energy compared to conventional manufacturing processes due to its ability to reduce the need for complex machining and transportation. Traditional manufacturing methods can involve multiple steps, each consuming energy, whereas AM streamlines production by creating parts directly from digital designs. This reduction in energy usage not only lowers operational costs but also reduces the overall environmental impact of the manufacturing process (May & Psarommatis, 2023).

Mass customization is facilitated by additive manufacturing, allowing to produce personalized and locally produced furniture. AM enables designers and manufacturers to create customized furniture pieces tailored to individual customer preferences without the need for large inventories. This capability aligns with Circular Economy principles by reducing overproduction and waste, supporting local manufacturing, and promoting efficient use of resources. Customers benefit from unique, made-to-order products that meet their specific needs and preferences (Kaplan, s. f.-a).

The production of spare parts on-demand is another significant advantage of additive manufacturing. AM enables the rapid and cost-effective production of spare parts for repairs, extending the lifespan of furniture products. This capability is particularly valuable in improving the design stage, as it allows for the quick creation of replacement components that fit precisely with existing products. By facilitating repairs and maintenance, AM helps reduce the need for complete product replacements, supporting sustainability and resource conservation (Javaid, Haleem, Singh, Suman, et al., 2021; Rommel & Fischer, 2013).

Robotics

Robotics adoption makes it simpler to change the manufacturing process and enhances operational efficiency in the furniture sector, offering several key benefits that significantly improve production capabilities and sustainability (Javaid, Haleem, Singh, & Suman, 2021).

Flexible manufacturing is one of the primary advantages of robotics in the furniture industry. Robots can be easily reprogrammed and adapted to different manufacturing tasks, enabling more flexible and efficient production processes (Kaplan, s. f.-b). This adaptability allows manufacturers to rapidly implement new designs and manufacturing techniques without extensive downtime or reconfiguration. By facilitating quick transitions between different production runs, robotics supports innovation and responsiveness to market demands (Emperor Brains, 2024).

Robotics also plays a crucial role in waste management within the furniture sector. Automated systems can streamline operations for classifying, disassembling, and remanufacturing waste, significantly reducing the need for manual labour and improving the accuracy of recycling processes. Robots can sort materials more efficiently, ensuring that recyclable components are accurately identified and processed. This enhanced efficiency in waste management contributes to the principles of a Circular Economy by minimizing waste and promoting the reuse of materials (Satav et al., 2023; Sohailkhan2k22, 2024).

Precision and efficiency are enhanced using robotics in tasks such as assembly, cutting, and finishing. Robots offer high precision, reducing waste and ensuring better quality control in the manufacturing process. Their efficiency leads to improved production rates, allowing for faster turnaround times and consistent product quality. By maintaining tight tolerances and precise execution, robotics helps reduce material wastage and enhances the overall sustainability of production operations (Emam, 2023; Rahman, 2024).

Enhanced safety is another significant benefit of robotics adoption in the furniture manufacturing sector. Robots can perform hazardous or repetitive tasks, reducing the risk of workplace injuries and improving overall safety in manufacturing environments. By taking over dangerous or monotonous jobs, robotics ensures that human workers are less exposed to harmful conditions and can focus on more complex and less risky tasks. This improvement in workplace safety not only protects employees but also enhances productivity by minimizing injury-related downtime (Kaplan, s. f.-b).

Digital Twins

Digital twins create virtual replicas of physical products and processes, which can be used for simulation and optimization (Batty, 2018). This technology offers numerous benefits for furniture companies, significantly enhancing design, production, and lifecycle management (Attaran & Celik, 2023).

Optimizing design is one of the foremost advantages of digital twins. By simulating different design scenarios, furniture companies can identify the most efficient and sustainable options before physical production begins (CGIFURNITURE, 2023). This virtual testing allows designers to explore a wide range of possibilities and assess their impacts on performance, cost, and sustainability. By selecting the best design based on comprehensive simulations, companies can ensure that their products meet high standards of efficiency and environmental responsibility, reducing the need for costly and time-consuming physical prototypes (Soori et al., 2023).

Streamlining production processes is another key benefit of digital twin technology. By creating virtual models of the manufacturing process, companies can test and optimize production workflows before implementing them on the factory floor. This pre-emptive optimization helps in identifying potential bottlenecks, inefficiencies, and waste points, allowing for adjustments that lead to smoother, more efficient production. The ability to virtually test and refine processes reduces material waste and energy consumption, contributing to more sustainable manufacturing practices and improved overall efficiency (Kannan, s. f.; Miura & Okabe, 2024).

Lifecycle management is greatly enhanced using digital twins. By monitoring products throughout their lifecycle, from design and production to end-of-life, companies can ensure that they meet sustainability standards at every stage. Digital twins provide valuable data on how products are used, maintained, and eventually disposed of, highlighting opportunities for recycling and reuse. This comprehensive monitoring enables companies to develop strategies that extend product lifespans, promote Circular Economy practices, and minimize environmental impact (Attaran & Celik, 2023; Pronost et al., 2024).

Augmented and Virtual Reality

Augmented Reality (AR) and Virtual Reality (VR) serve as powerful virtualization tools in the furniture sector, offering a range of applications that significantly enhance design, prototyping, consumer experience, and employee training (Ma et al., 2011).

Design optimization is one of the primary advantages of AR and VR in the furniture industry. These technologies allow designers to visualize and modify furniture designs in a virtual environment, making it easier to create modular and repairable products. By using AR and VR, designers can interact with their creations in a detailed and immersive way, identifying design improvements and assessing the impact of changes on product functionality and sustainability. This visualization capability ensures that design iterations are more informed and effective, leading to better-performing and more sustainable products (Pavlov, 2023).

Enhanced prototyping is another significant benefit facilitated by VR. VR enables designers to create and test virtual models of furniture before committing to physical production. This capability reduces the time and cost associated with traditional prototyping methods, which often involve multiple iterations of physical models. By using VR for rapid prototyping, designers can experiment with different design concepts and configurations more efficiently, supporting an iterative design process that accelerates innovation and ensures optimal product development (MoldStud, 2024).

The consumer experience is greatly enriched by using AR. AR can offer customers immersive experiences, such as visualizing how furniture will look in their own homes before making a purchase. This feature not only enhances customer satisfaction by providing a clear and accurate representation of the product in the intended space but also reduces the likelihood of returns. By helping customers make more informed purchasing decisions, AR supports more sustainable consumption patterns and reduces the environmental impact associated with product returns and exchanges (Jensen, 2024).

Training and education are also significantly improved through the application of AR and VR (Holuša et al., 2023). These technologies can be employed for training purposes, helping employees understand complex manufacturing processes and maintenance procedures. AR and VR offer immersive and interactive training experiences that enhance workforce skills and support more efficient operations. By simulating real-world scenarios, employees can practice and perfect their tasks in a risk-free virtual environment, leading to better preparedness and productivity in actual manufacturing settings.

CONCLUSION

The principles of the Circular Economy align closely with the goals of Industry 5.0, particularly in terms of sustainability and resource efficiency. By integrating Circular Economy practices, industries can achieve several benefits: reduced environmental impact, cost savings, innovation opportunities, enhanced resilience, etc.

In Industry 5.0, the adoption of Circular Economy principles is essential for achieving sustainable and resilient industrial systems. This integration supports environmental goals and drives economic and social benefits, creating a more holistic approach to industrial development in the modern era. By embracing the human-centric, sustainable, and resilient ethos of Industry 5.0, industries can navigate the complexities of the 21st century while contributing to a more sustainable and equitable world.

Digital transformation in the manufacturing sector is a multifaceted process offering numerous benefits, including increased efficiency, enhanced productivity, greater market competitiveness, improved sustainability, and innovation. However, significant barriers such as high costs, skills gaps, cybersecurity risks, legacy systems, and resistance to change must be addressed to fully realize these benefits. This chapter delve deeper into these aspects, examining expert interview and empirical evidence from the Spanish furniture sector to illustrate the impact and potential of digital transformation in this traditional industry.

The empirical evidence gathered from interviews with industry stakeholders and analysis of secondary data underscores the varying degrees of adoption and the contextual factors influencing this process. Companies that have successfully integrated Circular Economy principles with digital technologies report improved operational efficiencies, reduced environmental impact, and increased competitiveness. However, the extent of adoption varies widely, with larger companies being more proactive compared to SMEs.

Circular Economy policies and instruments are driving the furniture sector towards significant digital transformation. Compliance with these regulations necessitates adopting Industry 4.0 technologies, including IoT, AI, blockchain, and advanced data analytics. These tools enable furniture companies to optimize their operations, enhance sustainability, and remain competitive in an evolving regulatory landscape. Thus, Circular Economy policies not only push for ecological transitions but also necessitate the digital transformation of the furniture industry.

The long-term impact of circular instruments and policies extends beyond immediate operational benefits. By embedding sustainability into the core of business operations, companies build resilience against future economic and environmental shocks. The research indicates that firms adopting circular and digital practices are better prepared to navigate disruptions, such as supply chain volatility and regulatory changes, ensuring long-term viability and success.

- **Compliance and Monitoring:** The integration of IoT and AI in furniture manufacturing is crucial for compliance with stringent environmental regulations such as the Waste Framework Directive and the Renewable Energy Directive. These technologies allow for real-time monitoring of emissions and waste production, ensuring that companies adhere to legal standards. IoT sensors embedded in manufacturing equipment can track and report data on energy consumption and waste output, while AI algorithms can analyse this data to predict potential compliance issues and suggest corrective actions.

- **Enhanced Product Lifecycle Management:** Circular Economy policies emphasize the importance of sustainable product design and extended product lifecycles. Digital technologies, such as digital twins and advanced data analytics, facilitate enhanced product lifecycle management. Digital twins create virtual models of furniture products, allowing designers to simulate and optimize their performance and durability before physical production. This not only reduces material waste but also ensures that products are designed for longevity and recyclability.
- **Supply Chain Optimization:** Blockchain technology plays a pivotal role in ensuring transparency and traceability in the supply chain. Circular Economy policies require companies to provide detailed information about the origin and lifecycle of their materials. By leveraging blockchain, furniture manufacturers can create immutable records of their supply chain activities, from raw material sourcing to end-of-life disposal. This transparency not only helps in complying with regulations but also builds trust with consumers who are increasingly demanding sustainable and ethically sourced products.
- **Efficient Waste Management:** Effective waste management is a cornerstone of the Circular Economy. Advanced data analytics and AI can optimize waste management processes within furniture companies. These technologies can identify patterns in waste generation, enabling companies to implement targeted waste reduction strategies. For instance, AI-driven sorting systems can automatically segregate recyclable materials from waste streams, improving the efficiency of recycling operations. Moreover, predictive analytics can forecast waste generation trends, allowing companies to proactively address potential issues and minimize waste.
- **Sustainable Manufacturing Practices**: The adoption of Industry 4.0 technologies supports the implementation of sustainable manufacturing practices mandated by Circular Economy policies. For example, additive manufacturing, or 3D printing, can reduce material waste by creating products layer by layer with precision, using only the necessary amount of material. Additionally, IoT-enabled machinery can be programmed to operate at optimal efficiency, reducing energy consumption and minimizing environmental impact.
- **Consumer Engagement and Market Competitiveness:** Digital transformation driven by Circular Economy policies also enhances consumer engagement and market competitiveness. With the aid of advanced analytics, furniture companies can gain insights into consumer preferences and market trends. This data-driven approach allows for the development of products that

meet the evolving demands of eco-conscious consumers. Furthermore, digital platforms and e-commerce solutions enable companies to reach a broader audience and provide personalized shopping experiences, thereby increasing market reach and customer satisfaction.

- **Collaboration and Innovation:** Circular Economy policies encourage collaboration and innovation within the furniture sector. The integration of digital technologies facilitates better communication and coordination among stakeholders, including suppliers, manufacturers, and customers. Collaborative platforms powered by AI and blockchain can streamline information sharing and joint problem-solving efforts, fostering innovation and accelerating the transition to a Circular Economy.

FUTURE OUTLOOK

The ongoing digital transformation driven by Circular Economy policies positions the furniture industry for a sustainable and resilient future. As regulations continue to evolve, the adoption of Industry 4.0 technologies will remain critical for compliance and competitive advantage. The furniture sector's commitment to sustainability, supported by digital tools, will not only contribute to environmental preservation but also drive economic growth and job creation in the green economy.

To maximize the impact of circular instruments and policies on the digital transformation of the furniture sector, the following recommendations are proposed for policy makers and industry leaders:

- **Strengthening Regulatory Frameworks:** Develop and enforce robust regulatory frameworks that set clear targets for circularity and sustainability, providing a consistent and predictable environment for businesses to invest in green technologies.
- **Supporting SMEs:** Implement targeted support measures for SMEs, including financial incentives, technical assistance, and training programs, to overcome barriers to technology adoption and ensure inclusive growth.
- **Promoting Innovation and Collaboration:** Foster innovation through funding and support for research and development in sustainable technologies. Encourage industry-wide collaboration and knowledge sharing through initiatives such as industry consortia and public-private partnerships.
- **Enhancing Consumer Awareness:** Increase consumer awareness and demand for sustainable products through education campaigns and labelling schemes that highlight the environmental benefits of circular practices.

Finally, based on the findings of this study, which provide valuable qualitative insights into the adoption of Industry 4.0 technologies within the European furniture sector, there is a clear need for future research that can provide more concrete, quantitative data. A detailed quantitative analysis is essential to better understand the extent of Industry 4.0 adoption across different segments of the industry, the factors driving or hindering this adoption, and the actual economic and operational impacts on companies.

To achieve this, future research should focus on surveying a broad sample of companies across the European furniture sector. This survey would aim to collect numerical data on key factors such as the adoption rates of Industry 4.0 technologies, the challenges companies face in integrating these technologies, and the benefits they realize, particularly in terms of production efficiency, cost reduction, and product quality improvement. The data could also reveal how factors like company size, leadership support, and external pressures from suppliers, customers, and regulatory frameworks influence the decision-making process surrounding digital transformation.

The proposed research should use a stratified sampling method to ensure that companies of all sizes—from SMEs to large enterprises—are adequately represented. This would allow for a comprehensive analysis of how different types of companies approach Industry 4.0 adoption and the barriers they encounter. The survey would cover aspects such as the specific technologies implemented (e.g., automation, robotics, Internet of Things, big data, artificial intelligence), the perceived benefits of these technologies, and the financial and operational impacts they have had on companies.

The study would also investigate how external factors, particularly environmental and regulatory pressures, influence the adoption of 4.0 technologies. For instance, the research could explore how the growing emphasis on sustainability and the Circular Economy is shaping the way companies view technological investments. While the current study found that the circular ecological transition has a limited direct influence on technology adoption in the furniture sector, future research could track how regulatory changes and sustainability initiatives might drive further technological transformation, especially as new policies and frameworks are implemented.

The insights from this quantitative research would provide valuable data for both industry leaders and policymakers. Industry leaders would benefit from understanding the financial and operational advantages of adopting Industry 4.0 technologies, as well as the specific challenges that may be hindering adoption. Policymakers, on the other hand, could use this data to design more effective support mechanisms, such as funding programs, training initiatives, and regulations that encourage digital transformation and align it with sustainability goals.

REFERENCES

Abdallah, Y. O., Shehab, E., & Al-Ashaab, A. (2021). Digital Transformation Challenges in the Manufacturing Industry. In Shafik, M., & Case, K. (Eds.), *Advances in Transdisciplinary Engineering*. IOS Press., DOI: 10.3233/ATDE210004

Aggity. (2018). Industria 4.0 en el sector madera y mueble. *Industria y Producción*. https://aggity.com/industria-4-0-en-el-sector-madera-y-mueble/

Agustian, K., Mubarok, E. S., Zen, A., Wiwin, W., & Malik, A. J. (2023). The Impact of Digital Transformation on Business Models and Competitive Advantage. [TACIT]. *Technology and Society Perspectives*, 1(2), 79–93. DOI: 10.61100/tacit.v1i2.55

Ahlers, J., Hemkhaus, M., Hibler, S., & Hannak, J. (2021, junio). *Analysis of Extended Producer Responsibility Schemes*. adelphi consult GmbH. https://erp-recycling.org/wp-content/uploads/2021/07/adelphi_study_Analysis_of_EPR_Schemes_July_2021.pdf

AIDIMME. AMUEBLA, CENFIM, & CETEM. (2018). *Análisis de la viabilidad para la implantación de la Industria 4.0 en el sector del hábitat* (AEI-010600-2017-141, p. 99). HABITAT 4.0. https://www.cenfim.org/images/Noticias/Documents/PUBLICACION-HABITAT-4-0-REV-08.pdf

Ali, M. N., Senthil, T. S., Ilakkiya, T., Hasan, D. S., Ganapathy, N. B. S., & Boopathi, S. (2024). IoT's Role in Smart Manufacturing Transformation for Enhanced Household Product Quality. In Revathy, G. (Ed.), (pp. 252–289). Advances in Systems Analysis, Software Engineering, and High Performance Computing. IGI Global., DOI: 10.4018/979-8-3693-1694-8.ch014

Allam, Z., Bibri, S. E., & Sharpe, S. A. (2022). The Rising Impacts of the COVID-19 Pandemic and the Russia–Ukraine War: Energy Transition, Climate Justice, Global Inequality, and Supply Chain Disruption. *Resources*, 11(11), 99. DOI: 10.3390/resources11110099

AMBIT. (2024, junio 28). AMBIT presenta a sus asociados la nueva legislación sobre final de vida de muebles y enseres. *Ambit actualidad*. https://ambitcluster.org/es/actualidad/noticias/3097-ambit-presenta-a-sus-asociados-la-nueva-legislacion-sobre-final-de-vida-de-muebles-y-enseres

ANSES & Bureau REACH. (2019, junio 7). *SUBSTANCE EVALUATION CONCLUSION as required by REACH Article 48 and EVALUATION REPORT for Formaldehyde EC No 200-001-8 CAS No 50-00-0*. https://echa.europa.eu/documents/10162/cc0acabf-6e82-f2ed-5dbe-8058f48ce6c4

Arangiaro, V., Vishkaei, B. M., & De Giovanni, P. (2022). Blockchain for Circular Economy in the Furniture Sector: The Case of Cubo Design S.r.l. In De Giovanni, P. (Ed.), *Cases on Circular Economy in Practice* (pp. 238–275). IGI Global., DOI: 10.4018/978-1-6684-5001-7.ch011

AREMA. (2019). *Informe de tendencias en el comercio internacional de muebles*. AREMA.

Assent. (s. f.). *What Is the ECHA?* Recuperado 8 de septiembre de 2024, de https://www.assent.com/resources/knowledge-article/what-is-the-echa/

Attaran, M., & Celik, B. G. (2023). Digital Twin: Benefits, use cases, challenges, and opportunities. *Decision Analytics Journal*, 6, 100165. DOI: 10.1016/j.dajour.2023.100165

Badi, S. (2024). IoT and Big Data Analytics: Revolutionizing Business and Society with Advanced Insights. *International Journal of Applied Mathematics and Computer Science*, •••, 42–56.

Batty, M. (2018). Digital twins. *Environment and Planning. B, Urban Analytics and City Science*, 45(5), 817–820. DOI: 10.1177/2399808318796416

Benito, N. (2019). El papel de las empresas en la transición ecológica. *El Periódico-Valores*. https://www.elperiodico.com/es/activos/valores/20190118/empresas-transicion-ecologica-7253078

Brains, E. (2024, junio 13). Robotics in Manufacturing: Increasing Productivity and Safety. *Medium*. https://medium.com/@emperorbrains/robotics-in-manufacturing-increasing-productivity-and-safety-c44fd62916d7

Bretzfield, M. (2024, abril 4). Harnessing Data Analytics for Enhanced Customer Insight and Personalized Marketing. *Linkedin*. https://www.linkedin.com/pulse/harnessing-data-analytics-enhanced-customer-insight-bretzfield-lhsqc/

Brock, J. K.-U., & Von Wangenheim, F. (2019). Demystifying AI: What Digital Transformation Leaders Can Teach You about Realistic Artificial Intelligence. *California Management Review*, 61(4), 110–134. DOI: 10.1177/1536504219865226

Building back better: A sustainable, resilient recovery after COVID-19 (OECD Policy Responses to Coronavirus (COVID-19)). (2020). [OECD Policy Responses to Coronavirus (COVID-19)]. DOI: 10.1177/1536504219865226

Bułkowska, K., Zielińska, M., & Bułkowski, M. (2023). Implementation of Blockchain Technology in Waste Management. *Energies*, 16(23), 7742. DOI: 10.3390/en16237742

Carrillo González, G., Vázquez García, Á. W., & Solís Tepexpa, S. (2020). Ecodiseño: Estrategia Clave para la economía circular empresas del sector mueblero. En *Economía circular y ecodiseño en la industria del mueble* (1.ª ed., Vol. 4, p. 134). Universidad Autónoma de Querétano, México.

Cathles, A., Cardenas, G., & Henriquez Leblanc, P. (2023). *Opportunities and Challenges for the Twin Transition in Latin America and the Caribbean*. Inter-American Development Bank, Washington, D.C. USA. https://sdgs.un.org/sites/default/files/2023-05/A15%20-%20Cathles%20-%20Twin%20Transition%20in%20Latin%20America%20and%20the%20Caribbean.pdf

CGIFURNITURE. (2023, junio 1). *Digital Twins in Product Development:*https://cgifurniture.com/digital-twins-in-product-development-a-short-guide/
COM/2019/640 final. (2019). *The European Green Deal*. European Commission. https://eur-lex.europa.eu/legal-content/EN/TXT/?uri=COM%3A2019%3A640%3AFIN COM/2020/98 final. (2020). *A new Circular Economy Action Plan For a cleaner and more competitive Europe*. European Commission. https://eur-lex.europa.eu/legal-content/EN/TXT/?qid=1583933814386&uri=COM:2020:98:FIN

Cong, J., Zheng, P., Bian, Y., Chen, C.-H., Li, J., & Li, X. (2022). A machine learning-based iterative design approach to automate user satisfaction degree prediction in smart product-service system. *Computers & Industrial Engineering*, 165, 107939. DOI: 10.1016/j.cie.2022.107939

Council on Foreign Relations. (2023, julio 25). How Do Governments Combat Climate Change? *Climate & Change*. https://education.cfr.org/learn/reading/how-do-governments-combat-climate-change

Dalenogare, L. S., Benitez, G. B., Ayala, N. F., & Frank, A. G. (2018). The expected contribution of Industry 4.0 technologies for industrial performance. *International Journal of Production Economics*, 204, 383–394. DOI: 10.1016/j.ijpe.2018.08.019

de Witte, L., & Hagen, R. (2022, julio 13). The urgent need for fire safe upholstered furniture and mattresses in homes. *EURACTIV*. https://www.europeanfiresafetyalliance.org/news/need-for-fire-safe-upholstered-furniture-and-mattresses/

Deloitte. (s. f.-a). *Making blockchain real for customer loyalty rewards programs*. Recuperado 8 de agosto de 2024, de https://www2.deloitte.com/us/en/pages/financial-services/articles/making-blockchain-real-customer-loyalty-rewards-programs.html

Deloitte. (s. f.-b). *Using blockchain to drive supply chain transparency*. Recuperado 8 de agosto de 2024, de https://www2.deloitte.com/us/en/pages/operations/articles/blockchain-supply-chain-innovation.html

DiCicco-Bloom, B., & Crabtree, B. F. (2006). The qualitative research interview. *Medical Education*, 40(4), 314–321. DOI: 10.1111/j.1365-2929.2006.02418.x PMID: 16573666

Dini, M., Gligo, N., & Patiño, A. (2021). *Transformación digital de las mipymes. Elementos para el diseño de políticas*. División de Desarrollo Productivo y Empresarial de la Comisión Económica para América Latina y el Caribe.

Dizman, C., & Kaçakgi, L. E. C. (2023). Alkyd resins produced from bio-based resources for more sustainable and environmentally friendly coating applications. *Turkish Journal of Chemistry*, 47(1), 1–23. DOI: 10.55730/1300-0527.3511 PMID: 37731964

Du, X., & Jiang, K. (2022). Promoting enterprise productivity: The role of digital transformation. *Borsa Istanbul Review*, 22(6), 1165–1181. DOI: 10.1016/j.bir.2022.08.005

Eco, R. A. E. E. (2019, marzo 12). *El Ministerio para la Transición Ecológica publica los objetivos de recogida selectiva de RAEE para 2019*. https://www.eco-raee.com/resolucion-y-objetivos-minimos-recogida-de-raee-estatales-y-autonomicos-2019/

EcoMaison. (s. f.). *Furniture industry- A reuse and recycling network to give objects a second life*. Recuperado 6 de septiembre de 2024, de https://ecomaison.com/en/filiere-ameublement/

Emam, A. (2023). Robot-aided manufacturing and its impact on the future of the furniture industry in Egypt. *International Design Journal*, 13(2), 389–406. DOI: 10.21608/idj.2023.288432

Envira. (2023, diciembre 19). Puntos clave de la Ley de Residuos y Suelos contaminados para una Economía Circular. *Envira*. https://envira.es/es/ley-de-residuos-y-suelos-contaminados/

EPA. (s. f.). *End of Waste (Art. 28)*. Recuperado 8 de septiembre de 2024, de https://www.epa.ie/our-services/licensing/waste/end-of-waste-art-28/

ERA. (s. f.). *End-of-Waste Criteria*. Recuperado 8 de septiembre de 2024, de https://era.org.mt/topic/end-of-waste-criteria/

European Commission. Directorate General for Communication. (2020). *A European industrial strategy: Unleashing the full potential of European SMEs*. Publications Office. https://data.europa.eu/doi/10.2775/296379

European Commission. Directorate General for Research and Innovation. (2021). *Industry 5.0: Towards a sustainable, human centric and resilient European industry.* Publications Office. https://data.europa.eu/doi/10.2777/308407

European Commission. (2023, julio 5). *Circular economy for textiles: Taking responsibility to reduce, reuse and recycle textile waste and boosting markets for used textiles*. https://ec.europa.eu/commission/presscorner/detail/en/ip_23_3635

European Commission. (s. f.-a). Renewable Energy Directive. *European Commission*. Recuperado 8 de septiembre de 2024, de https://energy.ec.europa.eu/topics/renewable-energy/renewable-energy-directive-targets-and-rules/renewable-energy-directive_en#:~:text=The%20revised%20Directive,-%C2%A9AdobeStock%20Rafa&text=Given%20the%20need%20to%20speed,force%20on%2020%20November%202023

European Commission. (s. f.-b). *Restriction of Hazardous Substances in Electrical and Electronic Equipment (RoHS)*. Recuperado 6 de agosto de 2024, de https://environment.ec.europa.eu/topics/waste-and-recycling/rohs-directive_en

European Commission. (s. f.-c). *Waste from Electrical and Electronic Equipment (WEEE)*. Recuperado 6 de agosto de 2024, de https://environment.ec.europa.eu/topics/waste-and-recycling/waste-electrical-and-electronic-equipment-weee_en

European Environment Agency. (2024, marzo 25). Climate change mitigation: Reducing emissions. *In-Depth Topics*. https://www.eea.europa.eu/en/topics/in-depth/climate-change-mitigation-reducing-emissions

European Panel Federation. (2019, mayo 8). EPF strongly supports the Single Market. *European Panel Federation News Archive*. https://europanels.org/epf-strongly-supports-the-single-market/

European Subcontracting Network. (s. f.). *How the Internet ofThings is Driving Growth in Furniture Manufacturing?* Recuperado 8 de agosto de 2024, de https://subcontracteu.com/en/blog/internet-of-things-driving-growth-furniture-manufacturing

Falkenberg, K. (2012, junio). *Guidance on the interpretation of key provisions of Directive 2008/98/EC on waste*. https://ens.dk/sites/ens.dk/files/Affald/guidance_on_the_interpretation_of_key_provisions_on_waste.pdf

Fama living. (2022). Fama obtiene la certificación de Residuo Cero. *Noticias Fama*. https://www.fama.es/noticias/fama-obtiene-la-certificacion-de-residuo-cero

Forrest, A., Hilton, M., Ballinger, A., & Whittaker, D. (2017, septiembre). *CIRCULAR ECONOMY OPPORTUNITIES IN THE FURNITURE SECTOR*. European Environmental Bureau (EEB). https://eeb.org/wp-content/uploads/2019/05/Report-on-the-Circular-Economy-in-the-Furniture-Sector.pdf

Franke, A. (2023, octubre 9). EU adopts renewable energy directive targeting 42.5% share in 2030. *S&P Global*. https://www.spglobal.com/commodityinsights/en/market-insights/latest-news/electric-power/100923-eu-adopts-renewable-energy-directive-targeting-425-share-in-2030

Galvin, J., LaBerge, L., & Williams, E. (2021, mayo 26). The new digital edge: Rethinking strategy for the postpandemic era. *MC Kinsey Digital*, 17.

Gaur, V., & Gaiha, A. (2020, junio). Building a Transparent Supply Chain. *Harvard Business Review*. https://hbr.org/2020/05/building-a-transparent-supply-chain

General de Estudios, S. Análisis y Planes de Actuación. (2024). *Índice de fichas sectoriales* (p. 46). Ministerio de Industria y Turismo. https://www.mintur.gob.es/es-es/IndicadoresyEstadisticas/Sectores/sectores%20industria.pdf

Ghobakhloo, M., Iranmanesh, M., Vilkas, M., Grybauskas, A., & Amran, A. (2022). Drivers and barriers of Industry 4.0 technology adoption among manufacturing SMEs: A systematic review and transformation roadmap. *Journal of Manufacturing Technology Management*, 33(6), 1029–1058. DOI: 10.1108/JMTM-12-2021-0505

Global Regulation. (s. f.). *Royal Decree 187/2011,18February, Concerning The Establishment Of Eco-Design Requirements For Energy-Related Products*. Recuperado 6 de septiembre de 2024, de https://www.global-regulation.com/translation/spain/1437999/royal-decree-187-2011%252c-18-february%252c-concerning-the-establishment-of-eco-design-requirements-for-energy-related-products.html

Greenhoot, A. F., & Dowsett, C. J. (2012). Secondary Data Analysis: An Important Tool for Addressing Developmental Questions. *Journal of Cognition and Development*, 13(1), 2–18. DOI: 10.1080/15248372.2012.646613

Hague, B., Kozáková, J., & Veselá, A. (2023, julio). *Closing the loop on wood: Circular Bioeconomy Opportunities in the Value Chain for Forest Products and Wood in Czechia*. Institute of Circular Economy (INCIEN). https://circulareconomy.europa.eu/platform/sites/default/files/2023-07/Closing-the-loop-on-wood.pdf

Haleem, A., Javaid, M., Rab, S., Singh, R. P., Suman, R., & Kumar, L. (2023). Significant potential and materials used in additive manufacturing technologies towards sustainability. *Sustainable Operations and Computers*, 4, 172–182. DOI: 10.1016/j.susoc.2023.11.004

Hariyani, D., Hariyani, P., Mishra, S., & Kumar Sharma, M. (2024). Leveraging digital technologies for advancing circular economy practices and enhancing life cycle analysis: A systematic literature review. *Waste Management Bulletin*, 2(3), 69–83. DOI: 10.1016/j.wmb.2024.06.007

Health Spanish Ministry. (s. f.). Normativa relativa a los Reglamentos REACH y CLP. *Ministerio de Sanidad.* Recuperado 8 de septiembre de 2024, de https://www.sanidad.gob.es/ciudadanos/saludAmbLaboral/prodQuimicos/sustPreparatorias/reach/normativa.htm

Hestya. (2024, enero 25). *AI-Driven Furniture and Appliance Design: Shaping the Future of Home Interiors.* https://www.hestyadesign.com/post/ai-driven-furniture-and-appliance-design-shaping-the-future-of-home-interiors

Ho, K. (2023, septiembre 21). Understanding RoHS Compliance: A Comprehensive Guide. *Nemko.* https://www.nemko.com/blog/rohs-explained-a-comprehensive-guide-to-hazardous-substance-restrictions#:~:text=Requirements%3A%20RoHS%20restricts%20the%20presence,comply%20with%20these%20substance%20restrictions

Holmström, J. (2022). From AI to digital transformation: The AI readiness framework. *Business Horizons*, 65(3), 329–339. DOI: 10.1016/j.bushor.2021.03.006

Holuša, V., Vaněk, M., Beneš, F., Švub, J., & Staša, P. (2023). Virtual Reality as a Tool for Sustainable Training and Education of Employees in Industrial Enterprises. *Sustainability (Basel)*, 15(17), 12886. DOI: 10.3390/su151712886

Hussin, M. H., Abd Latif, N. H., Hamidon, T. S., Idris, N. N., Hashim, R., Appaturi, J. N., Brosse, N., Ziegler-Devin, I., Chrusiel, L., Fatriasari, W., Syamani, F. A., Iswanto, A. H., Hua, L. S., Al Edrus, S. S. A. O., Lum, W. C., Antov, P., Savov, V., Rahandi Lubis, M. A., Kristak, L., & Sedliačik, J. (2022). Latest advancements in high-performance bio-based wood adhesives: A critical review. *Journal of Materials Research and Technology*, 21, 3909–3946. DOI: 10.1016/j.jmrt.2022.10.156

ICCT. (2018, julio). *FINAL RECAST RENEWABLE ENERGY DIRECTIVE FOR 2021-2030 IN THE EUROPEAN UNION.* ICCT. https://theicct.org/wp-content/uploads/2021/06/EU_Fuels_Policy_Update_20180719.pdf

IMQ. (s. f.). *Directive2009/125/EC, Energy-Related Products (Ecodesign—ErP): Third-party verification of energy efficiency and performance, as a guarantee of transparency on the market.* Recuperado 6 de septiembre de 2024, de https://www.imq.it/en/eu-directives/ecodesign-directive-2009-125-ec

INSHT. (2016, diciembre). *Formaldehído en la industria de fabricación de tableros.* Instituto Nacional de Seguridad e Higiene en el Trabajo (INSH. https://www.insst.es/documents/94886/96076/Formaldehido.pdf/9d0297a4-8e99-4362-870a-ce15a92c18af?t=1527163280572

InStyle. (2024, enero 16). *The Impact of AI in the Furniture Industry and Home Decor*. https://www.instyledirect.com/blog/news/ai-in-furniture-industry/#:~:text=AI%20in%20Furniture%20Design%20Industry&text=AI%20algorithms%20can%20analyse%20vast,pleasing%20but%20also%20highly%20functional

Intertek. (s. f.). *Energy-related Products (ErP) Directive2009/125/EC (Formerly EuP)*. Recuperado 6 de septiembre de 2024, de https://www.intertek.com/electrical/erp-directive/

Javaid, M., Haleem, A., Singh, R. P., & Suman, R. (2021). Substantial capabilities of robotics in enhancing industry 4.0 implementation. *Cognitive Robotics*, 1, 58–75. DOI: 10.1016/j.cogr.2021.06.001

Javaid, M., Haleem, A., Singh, R. P., Suman, R., & Rab, S. (2021). Role of additive manufacturing applications towards environmental sustainability. *Advanced Industrial and Engineering Polymer Research*, 4(4), 312–322. DOI: 10.1016/j.aiepr.2021.07.005

Jensen, B. C. (2024, febrero 7). The Role of Augmented Reality in Enhancing Customer Experience. *Medium*. https://medium.com/@briancjensen1/the-role-of-augmented-reality-in-enhancing-customer-experience-4abb786fd38e

Johnston, M. P. (2014). *Secondary Data Analysis: A Method of which the Time Has Come. Qualitative and Quantitative Methods in Libraries, 3(3)*. Issue.

Jones, M. D., Hutcheson, S., & Camba, J. D. (2021). Past, present, and future barriers to digital transformation in manufacturing: A review. *Journal of Manufacturing Systems*, 60, 936–948. DOI: 10.1016/j.jmsy.2021.03.006

Joshi, N. (2024, julio 14). The Role of Digital Transformation in Achieving Sustainable Manufacturing Operations. *Snic Solutions*. https://snicsolutions.com/blog/the-role-of-digital-transformation-in-achieving-sustainable-manufacturing-operations#:~:text=Digital%20transformation%20plays%20a%20crucial,waste%2C%20and%20improve%20resource%20efficiency

Jovevski, D., Drakulevski, L., & Firfov, O. (2023). DIGITAL TRANSFORMATION AND PRODUCTIVITY. *KNOWLEDGE -. International Journal (Toronto, Ont.)*, 59(1), 15–21.

Kannan, R. (s. f.). The future of manufacturing: Self-optimizing factories powered by IIoT and digital twins. *UST*. Recuperado 2 de septiembre de 2024, de https://www.ust.com/en/insights/the-future-of-manufacturing-self-optimizing-factories-powered-by-iiot-and-digital-twins

Kaplan, S. (s. f.-a). Driving Innovation: Mass Customization in Manufacturing Unleashed. *Praxie*. Recuperado 2 de septiembre de 2024, de https://praxie.com/mass-customization-in-manufacturing/

Kaplan, S. (s. f.-b). Revolutionizing Home Furnishings: The Power of Robotics in Manufacturing. *Praxie*. Recuperado 2 de septiembre de 2024, de https://praxie.com/robotics-in-home-furnishings-manufacturing/

Kaplan, S. (s. f.-c). Transforming the Furniture Industry: The Impact of Data Analytics. *Praxie*. Recuperado 2 de septiembre de 2024, de https://praxie.com/data-analytics-in-furniture-industry/

Klubnikin, A. (2023, febrero 14). The Surprising Benefits of Data Analytics for Furniture Stores. *Smart Data Collective*. https://www.smartdatacollective.com/benefits-data-analytics-for-furniture-stores/

Kraus, S., Jones, P., Kailer, N., Weinmann, A., Chaparro-Banegas, N., & Roig-Tierno, N. (2021). Digital Transformation: An Overview of the Current State of the Art of Research. *SAGE Open*, 11(3), 215824402110475. DOI: 10.1177/21582440211047576

Landbell Group. (2022, mayo 9). *A step forward for EPR in Spain*. https://landbell-group.com/news/a-step-forward-for-epr-in-spain/

Le Moigne, R. (2021). The power of digital technologies to enable the circular economy. *Medium*. h

Liu, J., Liu, Z., Yang, Q., Osmani, M., & Demian, P. (2022). A Conceptual Blockchain Enhanced Information Model of Product Service Systems Framework for Sustainable Furniture. *Buildings (Basel, Switzerland)*, 13(1), 85. DOI: 10.3390/buildings13010085

Lola, I., & Bakeev, M. (2020). Digital Transformation In Manufacturing: Drivers, Barriers, And Benefits. SSRN *Electronic Journal*. DOI: 10.2139/ssrn.3570342

Ma, D., Fan, X., Gausemeier, J., & Grafe, M. (Eds.). (2011). *Virtual Reality & Augmented Reality in Industry*. Springer Berlin Heidelberg., DOI: 10.1007/978-3-642-17376-9

Madrid-Guijarro, A., Garcia, D., & Van Auken, H. (2009). Barriers to Innovation among Spanish Manufacturing SMEs. *Journal of Small Business Management*, 47(4), 465–488. DOI: 10.1111/j.1540-627X.2009.00279.x

Mammonas, D. (2023, octubre 9). Renewable energy: Council adopts new rules. *Council of the EU*. https://www.consilium.europa.eu/en/press/press-releases/2023/10/09/renewable-energy-council-adopts-new-rules/#:~:text=The%20Council%20today%20adopted%20the,contribute%20to%20this%20common%20target

Manickam, P. (s. f.). WEEE Directives: Managing E-Waste in the EU. *Talema Group*. Recuperado 8 de septiembre de 2024, de https://talema.com/weee-directives-managing-e-waste-in-the-eu/# MAPA. (2017). *Plan estatal marco de gestión de residuos (PEMAR) 2016-2022* (p. 192). MAPA. https://www.miteco.gob.es/content/dam/miteco/es/calidad-y-evaluacion-ambiental/planes-y-estrategias/pemaraprobado6noviembrecondae_tcm30-170428.pdf

Martínez-Peláez, R., Ochoa-Brust, A., Rivera, S., Félix, V. G., Ostos, R., Brito, H., Félix, R. A., & Mena, L. J. (2023). Role of Digital Transformation for Achieving Sustainability: Mediated Role of Stakeholders, Key Capabilities, and Technology. *Sustainability (Basel)*, 15(14), 11221. DOI: 10.3390/su151411221

Masood, T., & Sonntag, P. (2020). Industry 4.0: Adoption challenges and benefits for SMEs. *Computers in Industry*, 121, 103261. DOI: 10.1016/j.compind.2020.103261

May, G., & Psarommatis, F. (2023). Maximizing Energy Efficiency in Additive Manufacturing: A Review and Framework for Future Research. *Energies*, 16(10), 4179. DOI: 10.3390/en16104179

McCabe, S., Clement, S., & Ochoa, A. (2009). *Sustainable Procurement Guidelines for Office Furniture. Background report*. Local Goverment for Sustainability., https://sustainableprocurement.eu.com/documents/Category_Mangt/Furniture/United_Nations/UN_tech_report_furniture.pdf

Meyer, B. (2023, julio 20). EU-wide regulation of formaldehyde limits from August 6, 2026: Fraunhofer WKI offers "REAC-H-CHO" certification. *Fraunhofer WKI*. https://www.wki.fraunhofer.de/en/departments/qa/profile/news/certification-reach.html

Ministerio de Industria y Turismo. (s. f.). Aparatos eléctricos y electrónicos y la gestión de sus residuos. *Ministerio de Industria y Turismo*. Recuperado 8 de septiembre de 2024, de https://industria.gob.es/Calidad-Industrial/legislaciongeneral/Paginas/aparatos-electricos-gestion-residuos-rd-110-2015.aspx

MITECO. (2020a). *España Circular 2030. Estrategia Española de Economía Circular* (p. 65). MITECO. https://www.miteco.gob.es/es/calidad-y-evaluacion-ambiental/temas/economia-circular/espanacircular2030_def1_tcm30-509532.PDF

MITECO. (2020b, enero 20). *Plan Nacional integrado de energía y clima 2021-2030*. MITECO. https://www.miteco.gob.es/content/dam/miteco/es/ministerio/planes-estrategias/plan-nacional-integrado-energia-clima/plannacionalintegradodeenergiayclima2021-2030_tcm30-546623.pdf

Miura, T., & Okabe, H. (2024, julio 16). Leveraging the Industrial Metaverse for Digital Transformation in Manufacturing. *EY*. https://www.ey.com/en_jp/technology/industrial-metaverse-unlocks-the-future-realizing-next-generation-factories-through-digital-transformation

Mochón Morcillo, F., & Cardona, P. (2021). *Transformación digital de la empresa: Casos de éxito*. Marcombo.

Moghrabi, I. A. R., Bhat, S. A., Szczuko, P., AlKhaled, R. A., & Dar, M. A. (2023). Digital Transformation and Its Influence on Sustainable Manufacturing and Business Practices. *Sustainability (Basel)*, 15(4), 3010. DOI: 10.3390/su15043010

MoldStud. (2024, febrero 2). Applying Virtual Reality in Prototype Development for Product Engineers. *MoldStud*. https://moldstud.com/articles/p-applying-virtual-reality-in-prototype-development-for-product-engineers

Momani, S. (2024, enero 23). Cost Savings Through Automation: Unlocking Efficiency with AI Technologies Across Business Departments. *Linkedin*. https://www.linkedin.com/pulse/cost-savings-through-automation-unlocking-efficiency-ai-sam-momani-zxb3c/

Monitor, E. U. (s. f.). *Directive2009/125—Framework for the setting of ecodesign requirements for energy-related products (recast)*. Recuperado 6 de septiembre de 2024, de https://www.eumonitor.eu/9353000/1/j9vvik7m1c3gyxp/vitgbgiu1owm

Moran, K. (s. f.). Benefits of Industry 4.0. *SL Controls*. Recuperado 25 de enero de 2022, de https://slcontrols.com/benefits-of-industry-4-0/

Murugan, T. (2024, marzo 17). *Enhancing Sustainability in the Manufacturing Industry through IoT* [LinkedIN]. https://www.linkedin.com/pulse/enhancing-sustainability-manufacturing-industry-through-murugan-h1lac/

Na, S., Heo, S., Han, S., Shin, Y., & Roh, Y. (2022). Acceptance Model of Artificial Intelligence (AI)-Based Technologies in Construction Firms: Applying the Technology Acceptance Model (TAM) in Combination with the Technology–Organisation–Environment (TOE) Framework. *Buildings (Basel, Switzerland)*, 12(2), 90. DOI: 10.3390/buildings12020090

Nascimento, D. L. M., Alencastro, V., Quelhas, O. L. G., Caiado, R. G. G., Garza-Reyes, J. A., Rocha-Lona, L., & Tortorella, G. (2019). Exploring Industry 4.0 technologies to enable circular economy practices in a manufacturing context: A business model proposal. *Journal of Manufacturing Technology Management*, 30(3), 607–627. DOI: 10.1108/JMTM-03-2018-0071

Nickel, L. (2024). *Ecodesign for Sustainable Products Regulation (ESPR) – 2024 Overview*. https://ecochain.com/blog/espr-2024-overview/

Nuryanto, U. W., Basrowi, , Quraysin, I., & Pratiwi, I. (2024). Environmental management control system, blockchain adoption, cleaner production, and product efficiency on environmental reputation and performance: Empirical evidence from Indonesia. *Sustainable Futures : An Applied Journal of Technology, Environment and Society*, 7, 100190. DOI: 10.1016/j.sftr.2024.100190

OECD. (2024, abril 17). Extended Producer Responsibility: Basic facts and key principles. *OECD Publishing Paris, 41*. https://www.oecd.org/content/dam/oecd/en/publications/reports/2024/04/extended-producer-responsibility_4274765d/67587b0b-en.pdf

Öhgren, M., Milios, L., Dalhammar, C., & Lindahl, M. (2019). Public Procurement of reconditioned furniture and the potential transition to product service systems solutions. *Procedia CIRP*, 83, 151–156. https://www.diva-portal.org/smash/get/diva2:1465151/FULLTEXT01.pdf. DOI: 10.1016/j.procir.2019.02.134

Oliveira, O., Gamboa, D., & Fernandes, P. (2016). An Information System for the Furniture Industry to Optimize the Cutting Process and the Waste Generated. *Procedia Computer Science*, 100, 711–716. DOI: 10.1016/j.procs.2016.09.215

Ortega-Gras, J.-J., Bueno-Delgado, M.-V., Cañavate-Cruzado, G., & Garrido-Lova, J. (2021). Twin Transition through the Implementation of Industry 4.0 Technologies: Desk-Research Analysis and Practical Use Cases in Europe. *Sustainability (Basel)*, 13(24), 13601. DOI: 10.3390/su132413601

Pavlov, D. (2023, septiembre 22). Augmented Reality in Furniture Industry: How Can Brands Use It? *SmarTek*. https://smarttek.solutions/blog/augmented-reality-in-furniture-industry

Pérez, A. (2023, julio 5). El Gobierno saca a información pública el Plan de Residuos para 2035. *El Economista*. https://www.eleconomista.es/energia/noticias/12354348/07/23/el-gobierno-saca-a-informacion-publica-el-plan-de-residuos-para-2035.html

Praxie. (s. f.-a). Breaking Boundaries: How Digital Transformation is Revolutionizing Manufacturing. *Praxie*. https://praxie.com/manufacturing-industry-digital-transformation/#:~:text=In%20the%20context%20of%20the,and%20improve%20overall%20operational%20efficiency

Praxie. (s. f.-b). *From Traditional to Technological: AI in Furniture Manufacturing*. Recuperado 8 de agosto de 2024, de https://praxie.com/ai-in-furniture-manufacturing/

Praxie. (s. f.-c). *Streamlining the Future: How IoT Transforms Furniture Manufacturing*. Recuperado 8 de agosto de 2024, de https://praxie.com/iot-in-furniture-manufacturing/

Pronost, G., Mayer, F., Camargo, M., & Dupont, L. (2024). Digital Twins along the product lifecycle: A systematic literature review of applications in manufacturing. *Digital Twin*, 3, 3. DOI: 10.12688/digitaltwin.17807.2

Rahman, S. (2024, febrero 19). How Robotics and AI Will Transform Furniture Manufacturing: HATIL Case Study. *Linkedin*. https://www.linkedin.com/pulse/how-robotics-ai-transform-furniture-manufacturing-hatil-rahman-rxz3c/

Rame, R., Purwanto, P., & Sudarno, S. (2023). Transforming The Furniture Industry in The Digital Age. *Jurnal Riset Teknologi Pencegahan Pencemaran Industri, 14*(3), 53-69. Real Decreto 219/2013, de 22 de marzo, sobre restricciones a la utilización de determinadas sustancias peligrosas en aparatos eléctricos y electrónicos., BOE-A-2013-3210, Ministerio de la Presidencia 22935-11, BOE-A-2013-3210 (2213). 06/08/2024DOI: 10.21771/jrtppi.2023.v14.no3.p53-69

Rejeb, A., Suhaiza, Z., Rejeb, K., Seuring, S., & Treiblmaier, H. (2022). The Internet of Things and the circular economy: A systematic literature review and research agenda. *Journal of Cleaner Production*, 350, 131439. DOI: 10.1016/j.jclepro.2022.131439

Rishabh Software. (2023, noviembre 17). How Digital Transformation in Manufacturing is A Game-Changer for Industry 4.0. *Rishabh Software*. https://www.rishabhsoft.com/blog/digital-transformation-in-manufacturing-industry

Rommel, S., & Fischer, A. (2013). Additive Manufacturing – A Growing Possibility to Lighten the Burden of Spare Parts Supply. In Kovács, G. L., & Kochan, D. (Eds.), *Digital Product and Process Development Systems* (Vol. 411, pp. 112–123). Springer Berlin Heidelberg., DOI: 10.1007/978-3-642-41329-2_13

RTS labs. (2024, marzo 15). *The Environmental Imperative: How AI is Reshaping Sustainable Logistics*. https://rtslabs.com/green-logistics-ai

Sánchez-García, E., Martínez-Falcó, J., Marco-Lajara, B., & Manresa-Marhuenda, E. (2024). Revolutionizing the circular economy through new technologies: A new era of sustainable progress. *Environmental Technology & Innovation*, 33, 103509. DOI: 10.1016/j.eti.2023.103509

Santolaya, C., & Blanxart, A. F. (2001). *NTP 590: Prevención de la exposición a formaldehído*. INSST. https://www.insst.es/documents/94886/327064/ntp_590.pdf/0d2e6ea7-16a1-4bd7-9100-2db6c9c197a6

Satav, A. G., Kubade, S., Amrutkar, C., Arya, G., & Pawar, A. (2023). A state-of-the-art review on robotics in waste sorting: Scope and challenges. [IJIDeM]. *International Journal on Interactive Design and Manufacturing*, 17(6), 2789–2806. DOI: 10.1007/s12008-023-01320-w

Schwab, K. (2016). The Fourth Industrial Revolution: What it means and how to respond. *World Economic Forum*. The Fourth Industrial Revolution: what it means and how to respond

Seseni, L., & Mbohwa, C. (2018). The effects of using Big Data in Furniture Manufacturing SMEs. *Proceedings of the International Conference on Industrial Engineering and Operations Management, September 27-29*, 9. https://ieomsociety.org/dc2018/papers/385.pdf

Sgaravatti, G. (2021, junio 22). The Twin Transition Challenges [Web]. *Jeune Europe*. https://jeuneurope.com/the-twin-transition-challenges/

Shirer, M. (2022, octubre 26). IDC Spending Guide Sees Worldwide Digital Transformation Investments Reaching $3.4 Trillion in 2026. *IDC Media Center*. https://www.idc.com/getdoc.jsp?containerId=prUS49797222

Shoplogix. (2024, abril 30). 6 Key Challenges of Digital Transformation in Manufacturing. *Shoplogix*. https://shoplogix.com/challenges-of-digital-transformation/#:~:text=One%20of%20the%20major%20challenges,requires%20a%20significant%20financial%20investment

Shui, X., Zhang, M., Wang, Y., & Smart, P. (2024). Do Climate Change Regulatory Pressures Increase Corporate Environmental Sustainability Performance? The Moderating Roles of Foreign Market Exposure and Industry Carbon Intensity. *British Journal of Management*, 1467-8551.12841. DOI: 10.1111/1467-8551.12841

Siam. (s. f.). *Everything you need to know about the Regulation (EC) No1907/2006—REACH*. Recuperado 8 de septiembre de 2024, de https://www.siam-it.com/en/legislation/reach

Siddi, M. (2020). *The European Green Deal. Assessing its current state and future implementation* (114; FIIA Working Paper, p. 15). Finnish Institute of International Affairs.

Sohailkhan2k22. (2024, febrero 18). The Role of Robotics in Waste Sorting and Recycling. *Green.Org*. https://green.org/2024/01/30/the-role-of-robotics-in-waste-sorting-and-recycling/

Soori, M., Arezoo, B., & Dastres, R. (2023). Internet of things for smart factories in industry 4.0, a review. *Internet of Things and Cyber-Physical Systems*, 3, 192–204. DOI: 10.1016/j.iotcps.2023.04.006

Stasiškienė, Ž. (2008). Corporate Decision-Making in Furniture Industry: Weight of EMA and a Sustainability Balanced Scoreboard. *Environmental Research, Engineering and Management*, 1(43), 69–79.

Store, J. (2022, noviembre 24). EU to speed up permitting process for renewable energy projects. *Council of the EU*. https://www.consilium.europa.eu/en/press/press-releases/2022/11/24/eu-to-speed-up-permitting-process-for-renewable-energy-projects/

Sui, X., Jiao, S., Wang, Y., & Wang, H. (2024). Digital transformation and manufacturing company competitiveness. *Finance Research Letters*, 59, 104683. DOI: 10.1016/j.frl.2023.104683

Sunny, J., Undralla, N., & Madhusudanan Pillai, V. (2020). Supply chain transparency through blockchain-based traceability: An overview with demonstration. *Computers & Industrial Engineering*, 150, 106895. DOI: 10.1016/j.cie.2020.106895

Suzan, S., & Smailagic, B. (2024, julio). *The advanced and waste biofuels paradox: Availability and sustainability of advanced and waste biofuels*. T&E. https://www.transportenvironment.org/uploads/files/202407_TE_advanced_biofuels_report-1.pdf

Tellius, I. (2024, enero 18). Leveraging the Power of Inventory Management Predictive Analytics. *Medium*. https://medium.com/@telliusua12/leveraging-the-power-of-inventory-management-predictive-analytics-c9d89f55117b

The Alliance for Flame Retardants Free Furniture. (2019). *Policy paper Safe fire safety for everyone Avoid toxic flame retardants in our furniture*. https://zerowasteeurope.eu/wp-content/uploads/2019/11/FRFFalliance_policy_paper_en.pdf

Tickner, J., & Jacobs, M. (2016, agosto). *Improving the Identification, Evaluation, Adoption and Development of Safer Alternatives: Needs and Opportunities to Enhance Substitution Efforts within the Context of REACH*. https://www.actu-environnement.com/media/pdf/news-27483-substitution-chimique.pdf

Tóxicos, H. S. (s. f.). Retardantes de llama. *Hogar Sin Tóxicos*. Recuperado 8 de septiembre de 2024, de https://www.hogarsintoxicos.org/es/riesgos/retardantes-llama/

Tr n, N. T., Tri u, H. T., Tr n, V. T., Ngô, H. H., & Đào, Q. K. (2021). An overview of the application of machine learning in predictive maintenance. *Petrovietnam Journal*, 10, 47–61. DOI: 10.47800/PVJ.2021.10-05

Tsang, H. (2019, julio 3). EU Publishes POPs Recast Regulation. *SGS*. https://www.sgs.com/en/news/2019/07/safeguards-09519-eu-publishes-pops-recast-regulation

Tsang, Y. P., Wu, C. H., Lin, K.-Y., Tse, Y. K., Ho, G. T. S., & Lee, C. K. M. (2022). Unlocking the power of big data analytics in new product development: An intelligent product design framework in the furniture industry. *Journal of Manufacturing Systems*, 62, 777–791. DOI: 10.1016/j.jmsy.2021.02.003

Uchiyama, S., Matsushima, E., Kitao, N., Tokunaga, H., Ando, M., & Otsubo, Y. (2007). Effect of natural compounds on reducing formaldehyde emission from plywood. *Atmospheric Environment*, 41(38), 8825–8830. DOI: 10.1016/j.atmosenv.2007.09.046

Van Erp, T., Carvalho, N. G. P., Gerolamo, M. C., Gonçalves, R., Rytter, N. G. M., & Gladysz, B. (2024). Industry 5.0: A new strategy framework for sustainability management and beyond. *Journal of Cleaner Production*, 461, 142271. DOI: 10.1016/j.jclepro.2024.142271

Verhoef, P. C., Broekhuizen, T., Bart, Y., Bhattacharya, A., Qi Dong, J., Fabian, N., & Haenlein, M. (2021). Digital transformation: A multidisciplinary reflection and research agenda. *Journal of Business Research*, 122, 889–901. DOI: 10.1016/j.jbusres.2019.09.022

Vidwans, A. (2024, julio 29). *IoT and Quality Control: Ensuring Precision and Reducing Defects* [LinkedIN]. https://www.linkedin.com/pulse/iot-quality-control-ensuring-precision-reducing-defects-amol-vidwans-dj2yf/

Web Magazine, W. O. W. (2021). SUSTAINABILITY IS CHANGING THE FURNITURE INDUSTRY, LET'S FIND OUT HOW. *Ways of Working WOW!*https://wow-webmagazine.com/sustainability-is-changing-the-furniture-industry-lets-find-out-how

White, K., Hardisty, D. J., & Habib, R. (2019, julio). The Elusive Green Consumer. *Harvard Business Review*. https://hbr.org/2019/07/the-elusive-green-consumer

World Furniture online. (2024, octubre). Priorities and Perspectives of Digital Solutions in the Furniture Industry. *World Furniture Online*. https://www.worldfurnitureonline.com/trends/priorities-and-perspectives-of-digital-solutions-in-the-furniture-industry/

Yang, S., & Du, P. (2022). The Application of 3D Printing Technology in Furniture Design. *Scientific Programming*, 2022, 1–7. DOI: 10.1155/2022/1960038

Zahra, N. (2023). Role of artificial intelligence technology in the development of furniture design Process. *International Design Journal*, 13(6), 503–520. DOI: 10.21608/idj.2023.320147

Zhao, Y. (2024). Internet of Things Technology in Smart Furniture: An Overview. *Journal of Electrotechnology. Electrical Engineering and Management*, 7(1). Advance online publication. DOI: 10.23977/jeeem.2024.070114

Zhou, Y., Yan, S., Li, G., Xiong, Y., & Lin, Z. (2023). The impact of consumer skepticism on blockchain-enabled sustainability disclosure in a supply chain. *Transportation Research Part E, Logistics and Transportation Review*, 179, 103323. DOI: 10.1016/j.tre.2023.103323

KEY TERMS AND DEFINITIONS

Furniture Sector: Industry dedicated to the manufacture, marketing and supply of furniture items (chairs, tables, beds, cabinets, etc. from different spaces and applications such as home, workplace, hotels, etc.). Manufacturers, distributors, retailers, and other similar companies are included in this.

Digital Transformation: Process by which an organisation attempts to integrate digital technology into all the areas of the business in a way that completely changes the way it delivers value to customers.

Innovation: Process of developing something new or enhancing an existing product, service or process to better serve clients or address a challenge. For that purposes, ideas, resources or technology could be brought.

Circular Economy (CE): An economic model aimed at minimizing waste and making the most of resources by extending product lifecycles, promoting recycling, and reusing materials to create a closed-loop system.

Industry 5.0: An evolution of Industry 4.0, emphasizing human-centricity, sustainability, and resilience by integrating advanced technologies with a focus on enhancing social and environmental well-being.

Technological Adoption: The process by which businesses integrate new technologies into their operations, including the factors influencing the rate and extent of adoption.

Sustainability: The practice of meeting current needs without compromising the ability of future generations to meet their own needs, encompassing environmental, social, and economic dimensions.

Resilience: The ability of a system or organization to withstand and recover from disruptions, ensuring continuity and stability in the face of external shocks and stresses.

Chapter 7

Dimensions to Be Considered by an Organization That Wants to Achieve the Circular Economy in the Context of Industry 5.0:

How to Prioritize These Dimensions in the Management of the Circular Economy

Renan Carriço Payer
https://orcid.org/0000-0002-0417-082X
Universidade Federal Fluminense, Brazil

Pedro Gall Fernandes
https://orcid.org/0000-0003-3861-182X
Universidade Federal Fluminense, Brazil

Osvaldo Luiz Gonçalves Quelhas
https://orcid.org/0000-0001-6816-1677
Universidade Federal Fluminense, Brazil

Níssia Carvalho Rosa Bergiante
https://orcid.org/0000-0001-5131-1253
Universidade Federal Fluminense, Brazil

DOI: 10.4018/979-8-3373-2523-1.ch007

Ricardo Luiz Fernandes Bella
https://orcid.org/0000-0003-2212-1789
Universidade Federal Fluminense, Brazil

ABSTRACT

This study ranks and discusses the 7 dimensions of the circular economy in the context of Industry 5.0 proposed by Payer et al. (2024): Energy Circularity, Circularity of Inputs, Investments in circularity, Establishment of new circular businesses, Circular and non-circular supply chain integration, Circularity of product components, and Compliance and governance for circularity. The Hierarchical ordering (ranking) between these dimensions is done using the Analytic Hierarchy Process (AHP) method based on the opinion of 7 experts consulted (one expert for each dimension). These experts also discussed the main issues in evidence within these 7 dimensions. Organizations that aim to move towards the circular economy in the context of Industry 5.0 often need to prioritize efforts and start by treating some aspects, so this ranking can be a proposal of which dimensions can be prioritized in this scenario

1. INTRODUCTION

Given the current transformations in society and the scarcity of resources, it is necessary to increase sustainability in organizations in the manufacturing sector, making them more competitive (Kannan et al., 2024) through processes that can recover the value of the resources used (Hristova, 2024) by transforming production systems into circular chains (Assante et al., 2023). The achievement of sustainability and the circular model can be catalyzed using digital transformation technologies (Voulgaridis, Lagkas, & Sarigiannidis, 2022) that support resource optimization, monitoring, control, and mapping mechanisms (Banjanovi-Mehmedovic & Dželilović, 2024). It may act in the implementation of mechanisms that enable the circularity of materials, energy, and inputs (Gibbin et al., 2023).

Emerging digital technologies have revolutionized how organizations worldwide develop business models, contributing to improved efficiency, cost minimization, increased reliability, effective design, and better management control (Fraga-Lamas et al., 2021). Digital transformation can be understood as a process of fundamental change, enabled by the innovative use of digital technologies with the strategic leveraging of resources and capabilities, aiming to radically improve an entity and redefine its value proposition to its stakeholders (Garrido et al., 2024). This integration of digital technologies into business processes, therefore, can be referred to as digital transformation (Lytvynenko et al., 2024). The advent of technological resources has generated a higher level of automation through the connection of the virtual and physical worlds, culminating in the fourth industrial revolution or industry 4.0 (Ma et al., 2024) underpinned by coordinated communication and data sharing between components of a value network (Narula et al., 2024).

Despite its many benefits, industry 4.0 has not responded satisfactorily to increased personalization (Mesjasz-Lech et al., 2024). In other words, organizations have realized the need for agility to engage technology in fulfilling customer aspirations (Venturi et al., 2024). In addition to this issue of personalization and customer experience, industry 4.0, while supporting sustainable development at the organizational level (e.g., energy and resource efficiency consumed), has ignored some sustainability issues such as the digital divide, autonomy in the workplace and, consumption (Dhayal et al., 2023). This gap triggered the emergence of the new industrial paradigm 5.0, which emerged as the extension of Industry 4.0 with a social and environmental dimension (Mesjasz-Lech et al., 2024). On the one hand, industry 5.0 is focused on skills, knowledge, and abilities to cooperate with machines and robots, and on the other hand, on flexibility in production processes and environmental impact (Garrido et al., 2024). Therefore, industry 5.0 has three pillars: sustainability, resilience, and human-centricity (Voulgaridis, Lagkas, Angelopoulos, et al., 2022).

These transformations have brought challenges in technological, human, logistical, organizational, social, and environmental aspects (Thomas et al., 2024). Applying new technologies significantly impacts people, work, and everyday life (Dwivedi et al., 2023). Given this, it became necessary to establish processes that contemplated aspects of sustainability, resilience, and human-centered systems (Narula et al., 2024) aiming at collaboration between machines, humans, and technological resources (Lytvynenko et al., 2024). The industry 5.0 paradigm seeks to optimize smart factory processes through technology for sustainability (Voulgaridis, Lagkas, Angelopoulos, et al., 2022).

Technological resources have versatile applications to meet different goals of the circular economy. The technological components of Industry 5.0 are the technologies already present in Industry 4.0 (Thomas et al., 2024). The main difference is that digital transformation in Industry 5.0 has a strong connection with three criteria: resilience, human experience, and sustainability, which are key factors in the circular economy. The evolution of the model from Industry 4.0 to Industry 5.0 reflects the importance of the three criteria. Industry 5.0 expands the scope of Industry 4.0 by emphasizing not only efficiency, automation, and technologies, but also the consideration of broader values, such as environmental and social sustainability, in addition to adapting to the demands of stakeholders and a society in constant transformation.

This results in a more holistic and comprehensive approach, and more aligned with the principles of the circular economy (Gibbin et al., 2023).

Given the above scenario and given the complexity of the problem analyzed, Payer et al. (2024) applied the methodology SODA (Strategic Options Development and Analysis) to answer the question: "What is the path that an organization needs to take to achieve circularity in business in Industry 5.0 context?" having as its scope the manufacturing sector. The SODA mapping pointed out seven dimensions of the circular economy that explore operational and strategic aspects: Energy Circularity, Circularity of Inputs, Investments in circularity, Establishment of new circular businesses, Circular and non-circular supply chain integration, Circularity of product components, and Compliance and governance for circularity. These dimensions are pathways and requirements necessary to achieve circularity.

SODA, in turn, is a method of structuring problems used for group decision-making in situations characterized by uncertainties, non-trivial issues, and complexities that cannot be subject to formal algorithmic modeling. The construction of cognitive maps is how the problem structuring is done in the SODA method, bringing bipolar concepts, that is, with an assertion and a contrast. The concepts are written in logically connected constructs, providing information about the analyzed situation (Payer et al., 2024).

Seven experts (one expert for each dimension) were consulted to perform a hierarchical ordering (classification) of these seven dimensions using the Analytic Hierarchy Process (AHP) method. Propose measuring the intensity of each dimension according to the multicriteria decision-making approach analytic hierarchy process (AHP) presented by Saaty (1987). The utilization of MCDM approaches, as the AHP method, is shown by Appolloni et al. (2021) to evaluate the indicators of e-waste risk management based on interviews with consultants of companies, and Balwada et al. (2021) in the identification of the best recycling process for plastics. Then, the AHP method is proposed to define the weights for each dimension based on the paired comparisons from interviewees of seven companies.

After applying the AHP method, we could evaluate the judgment for each dimension according to the specialists' view to check if it follows the consistency ratio proposed by the method. The multicriteria decision-making methods support ranking the alternatives, however, in this case, we focused on the weight vector proposed by AHP to define the level of importance for each dimension to evaluate the consistency of the judgments of each specialist interviewed.

In addition, these same experts, versed in the subject, were able to discuss the main synergies between these 7 dimensions and the context of Industry 5.0 marked by sustainability, resilience and human experience. Organizations that aim to increase circularity in this context may need to prioritize efforts and resources, so this ranking can be useful to point out which dimensions can be prioritized in this context.

2. THE SEVEN DIMENSIONS OF THE CIRCULAR ECONOMY

Payer et al. (2024) applied the Strategic Options Development and Analysis (SODA) methodology. The outcomes obtained through SODA mapping led to the inference that organizations in the manufacturing sector aspiring to attain circular business practices face numerous requirements. These requirements can be distilled into seven dimensions: Energy Circularity, Circularity of Inputs, Investments in circularity, Establishment of new circular businesses, Circular and non-circular supply chain integration, Circularity of product components, and Compliance and governance for circularity.

Governance and compliance are strategic factors to meet the growing demands for social and environmental responsibility. Currently, several social transformations, investor expectations and other demands have required consolidation of objectives, ethical conduct, value addition and resilience. Thus, these two factors are key to long-term value creation and compliance with circularity requirements. Compliance and governance mechanisms can be aided by blockchain technology to ensure the authenticity of sustainability reports, trace the origin of raw materials, and monitor suppliers' adherence to sustainable practices.

It is worth mentioning the importance of controlling the use of inputs and how much waste is generated because this is used to measure the efficiency of the process aiming at cleaner and more sustainable production. Thus, it is important to integrate processes and equipment for the reuse of water and other inputs, reducing the production of waste and pollution

It is necessary for the organization to be aware, for example, of the possible environmental impacts generated by items supplied in its supply chain for a more sustainable production, as well as the existence of exploitation of workers in the production of these items. So, the supply chain must also be part of the ESG responsibility policy.

Sustainability needs to be included in the organization's strategic planning aiming at more investments in circular economy for sustainable, more resilient production and, therefore, more adherent to the Industry 5.0 paradigm. New technologies can facilitate the shift to the circular paradigm, as they provide tools capable of reducing costs, automating tasks, reducing waste, integrating processes, and adding value.

To achieve cleaner production, an industry can establish a decarbonization plan through a change in the energy matrix or carbon offsetting, when it is no longer possible to reduce emissions only with changes in its processes. The change in the energy matrix aims to renounce highly carbon-intensive energy resources, such as coal and petroleum products, and seek cleaner and renewable energies. Carbon offsetting, on the other hand, is a reduction or removal of emissions of carbon dioxide or other greenhouse gases made in one place to offset the emissions of others and may make use of carbon credits. This gradually translates into advantages and in adequacy and resilience in the face of growing stakeholder demands for renewable energies in the Industry 5.0 scenario.

The design for circularity method is very important for the industry that wants to achieve circularity. This method includes the creation of guidelines to assist the process of developing circular products (design for recycling) and the development of a methodology that can evaluate whether the material is convenient to be used again (design from recycling). Thus, less waste can be generated, and more resources can be reused in the value chain.

Remanufacturing and reconditioning processes are potential new business opportunities that can be obtained by organizations that apply circularity in their processes. In summary, remanufacturing consists of making a product work again at the end of its life cycle, while reconditioning helps to reduce waste and waste by restoring a new condition to products at the end of life. Both are important when it comes to achieving circular production, as they generate greater use of waste, rather than discarding it. In addition, reconditioning and remanufacturing can help reduce the amount of virgin raw materials in the supply chain.

Industry 5.0 does not necessarily operate as another industrial revolution but as an evolutionary addition to Industry 4.0 technologies to ensure a sustainable, human. The 7 dimensions obtained are important pillars of the circular economy and items to be considered for more sustainable production. From each of these dimensions, it is concluded that governance and compliance measures are essential to meet the demands of various stakeholders, the circularity of inputs is more efficient through process integrations, investments in circularity must start from the inclusion of sustainability in strategic planning, circular and non-circular supply chains need integration to ensure the supply of circular materials, the improvement of energy efficiency must involve procedures from the analysis of the energy matrix to the replacement by renewable technologies, the circularity of the product components needs a prior feasibility study, and, finally, the implementation of new circular businesses can be one of the consequences of the implementation of the circularity of processes.-experience-centric, and resilient industry (Hetmanczyk, 2024a).

Finally, according to Payer et al. (2024) it is worth highlighting some issues about the impacts of circular economy in the context of Industry 5.0:

- Resilience based on compliance and governance practices, adaptation to circularity involving inputs composed of toxic substances and the establishment of transparent supply chains.
- Human experience combined with technological resources to improve energy efficiency, increase the capacity of circular process and capture customer experiences (personalization) to reveal new opportunities of circular business.

- Sustainability through the design of efficient, responsive, and intelligent supply chains and through investments in technological innovation to increase economic, social, and environmental sustainability.

3. WEIGHTING OF DIMENSIONS ACCORDING TO THE MULTICRITERIA DECISION-MAKING APPROACH ANALYTIC HIERARCHY PROCESS (AHP)

Saaty (1987) define that pairwise comparisons are fundamental in using the AHP, and the seven interviewees must establish priorities for the main criteria by judging them in pairs for their relative importance to generate a pairwise comparison matrix. Table 1 presents the profile of these seven expert professionals Interviewed.

The green cells are filled out by interviewees based on the scale proposed by Saaty and adjusted for this research according to Table 2. The white cells should not fill out by interviewees because the values are reciprocals. If activity *i* has one of the intensities of importance assigned to it when with activity *j*, then j has the reciprocal value when compared with *j*.

Following the steps of normalization described by Saaty (1987), we applied the AHP method to find the weight vector based on each response provided by the interviews. After normalizations, we checked the consistency ratio (CR) proposed by Saaty to evaluate if there were inconsistencies in the judgments, which happens if the CR is greater than 10%. During the application of the AHP, we proposed to name the dimensions as criteria, from C1 to C7, as shown in Table 3. After the application of the AHP method, we found seven weight vectors based on the information provided by each specialist (table 4).

According to the CR smaller than 10%, the judgments provided by specialists 4 and 7 meet the requirement proposed by Saaty. Then, both scenarios show that "energy circularity" has the biggest weight in the vector created. In the case of specialist 7, the dimensions "circularity of product components," investments in circularity," and "circular and non-circular supply chain integration" have the same weight despite having different positions in the ordination. Specialist 4 believes that the "circularity of inputs" has bigger weight than "compliance and governance for circularity," in contrast to specialist 7.

Table 1. Profile of the expert professionals interviewed.

Specialist	Education and position currently held	Company
1	Chemical Engineer. Ph.D in Clean Energy Director	Multinational in the petrochemical sector
2	Industrial Engineer. Ph.D in Process Engineering Coordinator	Multinational in the food industry
3	Mechanical Engineer. Ph.D in Financial Audit CEO	Multinational pulp and paper company
4	Mechanical Engineer. Ph.D in Sustainable Businesses	Multinational beverage company
5	Production Engineer. Ph.D in Logistics.	Multinational car assembly company
6	Mechanical Engineer. Ph.D in Mechanical Engineer.	Multinational in information technology and computers
7	Chemical Engineer. Ph.D in Compliance	Multinational in paints and varnishes

Source: Authors (2024)

Table 2. Saaty scale adjusted for the interviews

Definition	Intensity of importance
Extremely unpreferred	1/9
Very strongly unpreferred	1/7
Strongly unpreferred	1/5
Moderately unpreferred	1/3
Equally important	1
Moderately more important	3
Strongly more important	5
Very strongly more important	7
Extremely more important	9

Source: Authors (2024)

Table 3. Criteria definition

Dimension	Criteria
Energy Circularity	C1
Circularity of inputs	C2
Circularity of product components	C3
Investments in circularity	C4
Circular and non-circular supply chain integration	C5
Compliance and governance for circularity	C6
Establishment of new circular businesses	C7

Source: Authors (2024)

Table 4. Weight vector

	Specialist 1	Specialist 2	Specialist 3	Specialist 4	Specialist 5	Specialist 6	Specialist 7
1st	C3 (0.342)	C3 (0.272)	C3 (0.302)	C1 (0.236)	C3 (0.318)	C3 (0.297)	C1 (0.207)
2nd	C5 (0.184)	C5 (0.188)	C1 (0.214)	C3 (0.219)	C1 (0.287)	C1 (0.270)	C3 (0.193)
3rd	C4 (0.166)	C1 (0.183)	C4 (0.160)	C4 (0.181)	C5 (0.127)	C5 (0.140)	C4 (0.193)
4th	C1 (0.164)	C4 (0.172)	C5 (0.143)	C5 (0.173)	C4 (0.117)	C4 (0.129)	C5 (0.193)
5th	C6 (0.063)	C6 (0.083)	C6 (0.095)	C7 (0.078)	C7 (0.062)	C7 (0.070)	C7 (0.095)
6th	C2 (0.049)	C2 (0.062)	C7 (0.049)	C2 (0.057)	C6 (0.049)	C6 (0.053)	C6 (0.071)
7th	C7 (0.031)	C7 (0.039)	C2 (0.037)	C6 (0.055)	C2 (0.040)	C2 (0.040)	C2 (0.048)
CR	15.2%	19.5%	13.2%	9.9%	21.4%	19.5%	5,4%

Source: Authors (2024)

However, the judgments provided by specialists 1, 2, 3, 5, and 6 presented a CR greater than 10%, which Saaty highlights a possibility of inconsistency in the set of values informed by interviews. Despite Saaty's recommendation to have a new judgment of the interviewees, we propose to keep the original results shown to compare with the results smaller than 10%. All specialists with CR greater than 10% defined "circularity of product components" as the biggest weight in the vector proposed; nonetheless, specialists 3, 5, and 6 did not consider the "circular and non-circular supply chain integration" as the second biggest weight, which is linked to have circularity of product components.

The relationship between the circularity of product components and the integration of the circular and non-circular supply chain, evident in the weights obtained, can be explained according to Payer et al. (2024), who defended the idea that the circular supply chain should provide enough circular materials and components to feed circular processes, so that the production chain is viable.

Here it is also worth highlighting the importance of the dimension energy circularity obtained with relatively high values in the weights obtained. With the current extreme weather events, there is growing concern about circularity and energy sustainability (Mesjasz-Lech et al., 2024). Energy circularity requires efforts to improve processes aimed at reusing energy and making it more efficient. Energy sustainability, on the other hand, requires energy generated from renewable sources, which are not exhausted like fossil fuels, and which do not cause pollution, being related to the use of clean and renewable sources, which are naturally replenished (Voulgaridis, Lagkas, & Sarigiannidis, 2022).

Based on this research's findings, two specialists are following the consistency ratio limit defined by Saaty. It is not possible to define the exact reason for inconsistent information from the other specialists, but one of the explanations is related to the real comprehension of the pairwise matrix shared with them. Additionally, we are working with seven dimensions of the matrix, which means it is close to the maximum number of elements proposed by Saaty for the AHP, considering seven elements plus or minus two. Then, when the magnitude of a matrix is high, inconsistency problems may happen.

Finally, it is important to highlight that energy circularity and circularity of product components are themes researched and disseminated in the industries currently, and then the level of importance defined by specialists is aligned with papers and projects about circularity. In addition, this research has been applied in a restricted group of industry segments, and this level of importance may have an impact if those dimensions are applied in other industries where circularity is not emphasized or where other dimensions of the circular economy are more important.

4. SYNERGIES BETWEEN EACH DIMENSION ACCORDING TO THE EXPERT'S OPINION

Below, some connections between each of the 7 dimensions of the circular economy and the paradigms of Industry 5.0 are explored, according to the vision of professionals. Each professional analyzed 1 dimension in which they are versed and specialized (Table 5).

Table 5. Dimensions analyzed by each specialist

Specialist	Dimension analyzed
1	Energy Circularity
2	Circularity of Inputs
3	Investments in circularity
4	Establishment of new circular businesses
5	Circular and non-circular supply chain integration
6	Circularity of product components
7	Compliance and governance for circularity.

Source: Authors (2024)

4.1 Energy Circularity

According to expert 1, the choice of energy consumption process can have a significant impact on the sustainability of an organization. By opting for a process that allows raw materials to be reused and consumes less energy, the organization will be able to reduce its carbon footprint, contributing to the preservation of the environment.

In addition, the possibility of using waste for energy generation should be observed, encouraging the development of new technologies and energy solutions. There are countless examples of technologies available for the use of gaseous waste or organic material. The use of these solutions contributes to boosting the energy transition, promoting the reduction of environmental waste and using resources until they are exhausted (Assante et al., 2023).

Another important factor is the implementation of energy efficiency programs, to reduce the company's energy consumption, whether electricity, gas or other fuels. Reducing energy consumption also contributes to environmental sustainability, as it requires fewer resources to produce the same goods or services. Companies and consumers, increasingly aware and concerned about environmental issues, adopt sustainable practices to have a competitive advantage, gaining the trust and loyalty of customers (Voulgaridis, Lagkas, & Sarigiannidis, 2022).

The generation of energy for own consumption is an interesting alternative to adopt more sustainable practices and contribute to a circular economy. Various energy sources and technologies can be used for this purpose. For industries that use steam in their processes, cogeneration – that is, the production of steam at higher pressure to generate energy in a turbine and feed its process – is a solution that has been expanding. In others, the waste process gases can be used to generate power in engines and the remaining heat can be used for heating (Banjanovi-Mehmedovic & Dželilović, 2024).

The use of waste for energy production, which meets even part of the consumption, is an interesting action of the circular economy. Retail businesses can use their organic or biomass waste to produce their energy. By investing in power generation, companies can reduce their dependence on external suppliers and secure a renewable energy source. In addition, the surplus energy produced can be directed to the electricity grid, contributing to the supply of other companies and homes (Gibbin et al., 2023).

Energy generation in organizations also promotes the decentralization of energy generation, making the electrical system more robust and resilient. This means that companies that adopt this practice can continue operating autonomously in cases of failures or interruptions in the supply of the interconnected system. Next, choosing the appropriate equipment and size the system according to the company's energy demand is necessary. In addition, it is essential to consider regulatory aspects and technical requirements related to the implementation of energy generation projects, to obtain the necessary registrations, licenses, and authorizations. Again, having professionals specialized in this process can facilitate compliance with legal requirements (Thomas et al., 2024).

In summary, energy generation emerges as a viable and promising solution for companies that want to adopt more sustainable practices and contribute to a circular economy. By investing in energy, companies reduce their dependence on external suppliers and become protagonists in renewable energy generation (Dwivedi et al., 2023).

4.2 Circularity of Inputs

According to expert 2, the crux of the matter about the advances of the circular approach to inputs (water, vapors, utilities, etc.), in relation to the linear approach, is that, while the linear model involves the extraction, use, and disposal of inputs, the circular model refers to a closed cycle where inputs are reused, which is particularly more adherent to the Industry 5.0 paradigm. The closed cycle considers inputs as finite resources with associated value, in addition to suggesting a reduction in extraction, efficiency in use, reduction of losses in production and distribution, and restoration and recovery of inputs.

In view of the more in-depth knowledge on the topic of "circularity of inputs", the relationship between it and "ESG" is of fundamental importance for the direction of corporate sustainability. In relation to the "environmental" theme (E), the actions should be to reduce the volume of water collected, use of sustainable water sources, minimize the impact of water stress and seek quality and efficiency in the use of various inputs (Voulgaridis et al., 2023).

In the case of the "social" (S), to involve the environment inside and outside the walls of the corporation, the objective should be: the increase in water availability both for the company and for society in general; the promotion of regional socioeconomic development; the contribution to the improvement of sanitation and public health indices in the surroundings; the encouragement of education and training programs for employees and society; in addition to ensuring access to water and consequently water and food security (Narula et al., 2024).

Finally, "governance" (G) is directly related to general guidelines and policies (public and private), management and results, performance goals and real commitments to achieve them, involvement of both employees in general and the corporation's top management, guarantee of strategies and investments as bases for decision-making, and the relationship with reputation and compliance (Lytvynenko et al., 2024).

Given the premise that the company's value is based on profits, growth capacity, and risks, its performance in ESG practices and adoption of the circular approach to inputs are capable of positively affecting this value, as they reduce internal costs, innovate in processes and products, generate new business opportunities, They create an environment of competitiveness, cause and expose a positive social impact, value the brand and reputation, reduce liabilities and consequently minimize the risks of environmental accidents, generate effects of less vulnerability to the risk of water shortage, guarantee environmental operating licenses, and necessarily generate more investments, engagement and trust. For some sectors, the management of inputs is a material issue with a financial impact and in these cases, the concern should be greater (Kumar et al., 2023).

Although the general theme is not exactly new, climate change and the COVID-19 pandemic were catalysts for these actions, that is, these events required organizational resilience, an attribute of Industry 5.0. In the case of climate change, droughts and floods have become more frequent and more intense, threatening water security, the production of goods and food production globally. The COVID-19 pandemic has exposed both the fragility of human beings in the face of nature, as well as social inequalities between regions and the impact of organizations on the environment and society (Turner & Oyekan, 2023b).

4.3 Investments in Circularity

According to expert 3, circular economy investment opportunities can be found in almost every industry. This strong growth spans a range of financial products and services, including public equity funds, bonds, private market funds, and banks. The circular economy is a key model to address the main issues linked to the global challenge of climate change, as it provides for the reuse of waste from operations for the manufacture of new raw materials and new products.

The growing concern with the environment and sustainability has brought a leading role to the circular economy, which thinks about the continuity of the process, and not about disposal. The focus is to think about how to use, recycle and reuse, that is, how to implement the circular economy. Many tons of virgin raw material are needed to produce and part of this total could be replaced by reused material (Voulgaridis, Lagkas, Angelopoulos, et al., 2022). There is an opportunity and a need. More and more organizations need to adapt, thinking about the environment, but also to serve consumers who are more demanding and signal a more conscious consumption (Suarez-Fernandez De Miranda et al., 2021).

In addition to addressing environmental issues, ESG practices are well regarded by the financial market, as companies gain credibility when they focus on these pillars, precisely because they protect themselves from risk factors that the lack of governance and social and environmental responsibility can lead to. By being part of the ESG agenda, the investor understands that the company is thinking about the long term and that it has processes and governance, and that it is committed to the rules and results not only in the short and medium term. There is an increasing movement of investors who value the reliability and responsibility of these companies (Sulich, 2024).

Thus, it is necessary to consider that the concept of circular economy, therefore, is not just recycling, it is a regenerative and restorative economy. In other words, the organization needs to act in a sustainable way from its origin to retail, throughout its value chain. The organization needs to make investments to add value (Turner & Oyekan, 2023a).

4.4 Establishment of New Circular Businesses

According to expert 4, when proposing to operationalize new circular businesses, an important implication is the interaction between external and internal factors to the organization. The real evaluation of the potentiality, such as installed infrastructure, organizational, managerial and human resources structure, is necessary for the organization to successfully implement its new circular businesses. The lack of knowledge of an organization's resources, such as facilities, personnel and motivational state, as well as the little exercise of the strategic vision of the future and the competition, will result in inefficiency, technological backwardness and the loss of competitive status.

In this sense, it is necessary for the organization to develop a continuous process of improving relationships with its customers, and start questioning aspects of the organization, aimed at establishing new businesses, to beat the competition and gain competitive advantage. To achieve success, organizations must coordinate all their efforts in anticipating customer needs, properly using their internal potential, as well as the efficient exploitation of external potential, and for this, they must see beyond their current business horizon, and even influence external environmental factors and beyond their direct reach (Panza et al., 2023).

Within this objective, it is important that managers develop a behavior that favors the establishment of new business opportunities, promoting interaction with the environment and the modification of the configuration and internal dynamic aspects (Ruiz-de-la-Torre-Acha et al., 2023). The development of a keen instinct to detect opportunities and make them a reality within the organization will strengthen its competitive strategies. Not forgetting that every strategy is formulated through the relationship with the environment and the way opportunities are planned and oriented to achieve objectives and goals. It should also not be forgotten that the strategy should not only respond to the environment, but also contribute to shaping the environment in favor of the organization (Marić et al., 2023).

It is also important to remember that given the speed with which changes occur and the way in which organizations imitate each other, they must anticipate the future by creating competitive spaces and new forms of competitive advantage (Turner et al., 2022). Another aspect to be observed lies in the perception of the differentiation between the perceived environment and the real environment, based on the analysis of the general and operational environment. The perceived environment does not always correspond to reality and can lead to the detection of non-advantageous market niches. There is then the problem of capturing, verifying and interpreting information from the external and internal environment aimed at enabling the establishment of new businesses and the condition of their effectiveness in the organization. The importance of recognizing how the organization reacts to its environment is emphasized (Khan & Abonyi, 2022).

The process of globalization and information technology has been causing changes in the way of planning and doing business, making it necessary to redo the total integration of the organization's value chain with customers and suppliers. There is also a need for interaction, conceiving that organizations operate within the environmental context, relevant so that they can survive, maintain, grow, and develop (Kopeinig et al., 2024). The examination of the relationship between the organization and the environment is of essential interest when it comes to defining objectives. These goals or purposes must be based on what society wants and what it can be persuaded to support, and therefore cannot be seen as static or arbitrarily established but result from interaction both within the organization and between it and the environment. The success of the organization thus depends on its sensitivity and adaptive capacity, a relevant factor in Industry 5.0 (Ruiz-de-la-Torre-Acha et al., 2023).

4.5 Circular and Non-Circular Supply Chain Integration

According to expert 5, the concept of Circular Supply Chain is linked to the industrial economy to the extent that it aims at greater resource productivity from the development of ways to acquire and reintroduce, continuously, discarded assets in life cycles. Thus, the value of products and materials is maintained for as long as possible, resource use and waste are minimized, and resources circulated within the system again and again generating value. Circular supply chains use materials and goods for as long as possible, rather than disposing of them immediately. Manufacturers reuse raw materials such as plastic, metal, cardboard, paper, steel, and glass. Used products are renewed and resold.

In a circular supply chain, manufacturers think about the environment at every stage of production. Recyclable materials are used in product and packaging design. This also ensures that the product is easy to disassemble and repair. Manufacturers work together with stakeholders, such as retailers, local authorities, and non-profit ecological organizations, to educate consumers on how to dispose of waste properly, making it easier to collect and recycle a wide variety of materials (Ma et al., 2024).

In addition to environmental benefits, circular supply chains offer business benefits such as:

- **Cost Reduction:** Through recycling programs, manufacturers can reduce costs by spending less on new materials, such as lithium used in electric vehicle batteries, which are in high demand and subject to price volatility, thereby reducing costs (Martini et al., 2024).
- **Supply Chain Resilience:** Recycling can also help manufacturers react to supply disruptions (Fraga-Lamas et al., 2021).
- **Increased Sales:** Skeptics point to higher costs for manufacturers in collecting, transporting and reprocessing waste. But even they recognize that a circular approach helps manufacturers win over eco-conscious customers (Delbari & Hof, 2024).
- **Improved Employee Relations:** This approach can be welcomed by environmentally conscious employees and shareholders, who examine the environmental, social, and governance performance of companies (Moller et al., 2022).

To establish a circular supply chain, manufacturers must rethink all aspects of their operations, including product design, material sourcing, and tracking of goods in transit, to minimize waste. The following strategies can help: create products that are easy to recycle and repair; reuse and renew products for resale; use recycled materials whenever possible; reducing waste by using recycled materials and designing products that consumers can safely dispose of; focus on transparency between suppliers and customers and; work together with suppliers to obtain recyclable materials (Hadi et al., 2023).

A circular supply chain can be created based on three strategies. The first is to design specifically for recycling using recyclable materials and ensuring that products can be easily repaired or restored. The second is to collaborate with suppliers by obtaining their input on the sourcing or development of sustainable materials. The third is to leverage technology like blockchain to track and trace products throughout the supply chain, as well as IoT solutions to evaluate returns, send usable products to inventory, and reduce waste (Nikseresht et al., 2024).

4.6 Circularity of Product Components

According to expert 6, it is necessary to think about the circularity of product components from different perspectives of business models. One of them is the product-as-a-service perspective. This type of business model is the most complete, requiring greater changes in the organization's processes. It often combines characteristics of other types of business models, such as extending the product's useful life. Relationships with customers become closer and add more value to the business. Better customer service and preventive maintenance become key processes and directly impact the profitability of the business model.

Thus, the customer can enjoy more the use of the product (experience), and issues such as maintenance, for example, are solved by the organization that can get closer to the customer and better understand their needs and expectations. In the industry 5.0 human experience landscape, this is particularly relevant. In addition, by increasing the durability of the product, it increases the profitability of the business and reduces the consumption of natural resources. The end of the product's life becomes the responsibility of the organization, allowing parts to be reused (Siakas et al., 2023).

Another perspective is the sharing business model, which has the user experience as its centerpiece, an important attribute of Industry 5.0. As with the product-as-a-service model, the focus here is that a product meets the needs of more than one person. This means intensifying the use of the product, reducing the need to produce more – which does not mean making less profit. There is then a dissociation between production and profit. One difference between this type of model and the product-as-a-service model is that the product is available to a group of people, who can use it at any time. Sharing business models can be monetized and non-monetized. In this second type, the main purpose is to solve some problem of the user or society (Voulgaridis et al., 2024).

It is also worth mentioning the business model based on resource recovery, which aims to recover value from resources through strategies such as recycling and cascading use in a closed or open cycle. In this model, reverse logistics processes and recycling partners are key to success. However, the recovered resource cannot always be reinserted into the same value chain. In addition, in value chains that involve end consumers, customers play a key role in returning products (Ramírez-Peña et al., 2023).

Finally, extending the product's lifespan is also a relevant perspective. The value proposition for circular economy in this type of model is to recover value by extending the product's lifespan. Product life can be extended through remanufacturing, reconditioning, maintenance and upgrade, reuse. For products with higher added value, for example, strategies such as upgrade, remanufacturing, reconditioning and maintenance are recommended. For products with lower added value, reuse may make more sense, as is the case with plastic packaging (Santiago et al., 2024).

4.7 Compliance and Governance for Circularity

Collaboration between humans and machines not only drives efficiency and productivity, but also strengthens corporate governance. Humans bring with them ethical values and a deep understanding of stakeholder needs. This interaction fosters an organizational culture based on transparency, accountability, and compliance. Human creativity is key to finding innovative and adaptable solutions, while decision-making based on ethical values ensures the integrity and reputation of the organization. With the support of technology, humans can make more informed and strategic decisions, optimizing processes and maximizing value for all stakeholders along the value chain.

In addition, human beings bring with them a social and ethical conscience that is essential for the sustainable development of organizations. By integrating emerging technologies, such as data analytics and artificial intelligence, with human ethics, companies can ensure that their operations are aligned with society's values and that they contribute positively to the well-being of the communities in which they operate. The active inclusion of humans in industry 5.0 results in significant gains across the value chain. From the conception of products and services to the final delivery to customers, human-machine collaboration drives innovation, improves quality, and increases efficiency, leading to a sustainable competitive advantage and strengthening relationships with customers and other stakeholders (Mesjasz-Lech et al., 2024).

Despite the evident benefits of technology in Industry 5.0, it is important to recognize the risks associated with excessive attachment to automation and artificial intelligence at the expense of the role of the human being. An exclusive focus on efficiency and productivity can lead to the devaluation of unique human skills, such as creativity, intuition, and the ability to adapt. In addition, over-reliance on technology can increase vulnerability to technical failures and cyber threats, putting the security and stability of organizations at risk. Therefore, it is essential to strike an appropriate balance between the use of technology and the recognition of the inestimable value of the human being in industry 5.0 (Venturi et al., 2024).

The need to comply with current regulations, prevent illegalities and mitigate risks has a positive impact on companies of any size. In addition to the most obvious advantage of complying with the laws, avoiding punishments and losses, it is also possible to list strategic reasons that make compliance a competitive advantage in the context of the circular economy. Among them, for example, the improvement in the chances of getting new business opportunities and increased access to credit, with the offer of more advantageous conditions and contracts (Dhayal et al., 2023).

Corporate governance and sustainability are concepts that go hand in hand, as both aim at responsibility and maintaining the well-being of the shared environment, including issues related to nature, society, and the economy. Corporate governance is a bridge that contributes to the development and ensuring the continuity of the best-case scenario in the long term at all these levels. It works as a safeguard of sustainability, requiring postures, actions, and choices aligned with the entire environment in which the organization is inserted (Atif, 2023).

In turn, sustainability requires action, both in a preventive and corrective and proactive nature, aiming to apply strategies to promote social, natural and economic improvements. It is necessary to conduct organizational activities in a less predatory and more ethical way, so that no one directly or indirectly affected by the corporation suffers negative effects of abusive or irresponsible decisions. Corporate governance and sustainability go hand in hand, as both seek actions in the financial, social, and environmental layers that create a better shared environment. By being guided by these two concepts, in addition to profits, a company starts to have intangible gains that lead it to stand out (Dabo & Hosseinian-Far, 2023).

Governance, sustainability, and social responsibility form a triad that depends on business ethics to be put into practice. In this context, the best way to avoid negative effects of decisions is to consider the impacts of actions at all levels. After all, from wages or prices to the use of resources or the choice of suppliers are corporate activities that impact the shared natural, economic and community environment. In this way, businesses that understand their role in the scenario can follow more sustainable, ethical, ecological, and fair paths (Hetmanczyk, 2024b).

4.8 Challenges, Limitations and Proposed Solutions

Despite the benefits and advantages discussed in the literature, several authors have pointed out limitations and challenges in the path of digital transformation in favor of the establishment of the circular economy. It was identified, for example, that the lack of information about the life cycle of a product, as well as the scarcity of advanced technologies for cleaner production decreased the reach of the circular economy by an organization. In addition, perceived uncertainties regarding costs, return on investments, and implementation timeline often result in an initial reluctance by companies to adopt these goals.

Other challenges also discussed: lack of stakeholder perception of the characteristics of discarded products and procedural non-compliance of those responsible for the life cycle of the products; the need for changes in the design philosophy using unconventional materials based on criteria of degradability and not always of quality or durability; and the complexity of the waste generated.

In several scenarios, the disassembly of products, aiming at reuse processes, is expensive and time-consuming due to the complex nature of the products. The products lack a circular design, which is why production and repurposing, disassembly, remanufacturing, etc. are difficult. The complexity of the supply chain is challenging, as an increase in the number of components of different natures with complex assembly procedures generates costs. Additionally, coordination between organizations is a barrier, as multiple businesses are required to adjust their day-to-day operations.

The complexity of the supply chain and coordination between organizations is a challenge. The implementation of technological potential requires a high degree of cooperation, coordination and integration of all parties from the manufacturer and supplier to the customer and between the pre-user and the re-user, which most of the time does not happen in the industry today.

In addition, there is the challenge of resource targeting, as organizations struggle to identify which organizational resources should be directed and how they should be leveraged to achieve an enterprise-wide business analytics capability for the circular economy.

A challenging issue that also draws attention is the lack of adequate flow of information. Adequate information and technological support are fundamental resources for sustainable organizations, as they allow the development of operating models and infrastructure to keep materials in circulation. So, data discrepancies, gaps, and lack of confidence about the confidentiality of data are issues that make it difficult to identify and implement circular models.

It is worth highlighting 3 challenges in the process of implementing circular models based on digital transformation. The first of these challenges is to convince stakeholders that the adoption of a circular model will bring benefits and organizational sustainability, and that investment in technology will be a driver of this process. The second challenge is to harmoniously aggregate the supply chain and all the organization's logistics for the implementation of the circular economy. The third challenge is the various industrial requirements that may require knowledge, experience, and technologies in the most diverse sectors of the organization.

To overcome these challenges and limitations, one can start with the organization, which needs to go through stages from discerning the most appropriate business model for its production processes to the integration of technologies in the digital transformation process. It is necessary to pay attention to a conception based on cost and benefit, adding technological resources to processes with a focus on the scope of the value chain, also seeking to increase organizational sustainability. The key to overcoming these challenges lies in the fact that the organization and its stakeholders must be aware of each other's interests and expectations about digital transformation, while integrating into a circular model for value addition.

An important contribution to overcoming these challenges is to reformulate traditional manufacturing configurations, that is, to carry out a transformation that contemplated an intelligent manufacturing model to achieve flexibility with high quality and low-cost production. Finally, to overcome such challenges, organizations need to build on previous and successful experiences and also consider the principles of sustainability and circular economy in their most diverse processes. Specifically, it is necessary to promote several improvements necessary to integrate cutting-edge technologies to make processes and services efficient in energy and economical. If necessary, it is recommended to promote greater collaboration between organizations and research centers.

5. FINAL CONSIDERATIONS

Industry 5.0 emphasizes collaboration between humans and machines, recognizing that while automation increases efficiency, certain tasks that require creativity and complex decisions must be led by humans. Focused on responsible environmental practices and the ability of companies to adapt quickly to changes, industry 5.0 promotes the use of renewable energy and the creation of sustainable products, aiming to reduce carbon emissions and limit global warming. Industry 5.0 values the importance of workers, promoting safe, welcoming work environments that offer opportunities for professional growth while prioritizing employee well-being and social inclusion.

In addition to favoring the implementation of new technologies, and continuing the changes initiated by Industry 4.0, industry 5.0 recognizes that people are the most valuable resource for the success of industrial operations. Thus, collaboration between humans and machines is encouraged. The idea is that technologies are put at the service of human beings, to favor more strategic decision-making, the resolution of complex problems and innovation. The focus on people also reverberates in the promotion of safer and more welcoming work environments, where workers are valued, respected, and have opportunities for professional and personal growth.

The adoption of environmentally responsible industrial practices is also gaining strength in Industry 5.0, being especially driven by the Paris Agreement and the UN Sustainable Development Goals. The development of production through systems based on renewable energies, to reduce carbon emissions and limit global warming, is one of the points that stand out. In addition, Industry 5.0 also promotes the creation of sustainable products and services, which meet present needs without compromising future generations.

Sustainability as a characteristic of Industry 5.0 advocates the efficient use of resources and the reduction of waste. Advanced technologies make it possible to monitor and optimize the use of energy, water, and raw materials, minimizing environmental impact. In addition, Industry 5.0 promotes the circular economy, where products are designed to be reused, recycled, or composted, reducing the need for new raw materials and decreasing waste disposal. This approach not only reduces environmental impact but can also result in significant savings for businesses.

Sustainability is a key pillar of Industry 5.0. Advanced technologies can be implemented to reduce environmental impact and promote more responsible industrial practices. Optimizing the use of resources, reducing waste, and implementing circular processes are some of the strategies adopted. Renewable energy and intelligent resource management are also integrated into production systems, aiming for a smaller ecological footprint.

Technologies such as IoT and AI are used to monitor and optimize energy consumption. Intelligent systems automatically adjust processes to consume less energy, contributing to sustainability and reduced operating costs. Production closer to the end consumer, facilitated by technologies such as 3D printing, reduces the need for transport and, consequently, carbon emissions. Such potential contributes to a faster response to changes in market demand.

Resilience in Industry 5.0 basically refers to the ability of companies to adapt and recover quickly in the face of challenges. This pillar involves implementing technologies and practices that make industrial operations more flexible, agile, and able to handle sudden changes in market demands. Resilience has become a key factor in fighting the COVID-19 pandemic. The European Commission's report reveals that geopolitical changes and natural crises, such as the COVID-19 pandemic, highlight the fragility of industries. Consequently, having the ability to adapt to adverse situations with positive results is a must in the new industry 5.0.

Industry 5.0 recognizes and values the irreplaceable role of human beings in corporate and technological governance. By integrating technology and human ethics, companies can reach new heights of performance and responsibility, ensuring a positive impact on all dimensions of the value chain. However, it is crucial to maintain a critical approach towards the use of technology, avoiding excessive attachment that can compromise human potential in industry 5.0. Corporate governance and sustainability are not only confused, but also mixed in companies that understand the importance of these concepts for their competitiveness.

Essentially, the seven dimensions of the circular economy considered in this chapter relate to Industry 5.0 as follows: The role of compliance and governance in Industry 5.0 to promote sustainability and have resilience in the face of emerging social changes and demands; the importance of technological resources in the circularity of inputs and compliance with standards about toxic substances. This can be useful in sustainability and resilience issues of Industry 5.0; the need to establish a transparent circular supply chain in the context of Industry 5.0 to provide more resilience to stakeholders' expectations and to identify opportunities for improvements in terms of sustainability in real time; the need for efficient, responsive, and intelligent supply chains to better adapt to the Industry 5.0 paradigm; Industry 5.0 values investments in innovation and efficiency, but in a broader way aiming to create value considering social and environmental sustainability; cooperation between technologies and human skills, as recommended by Industry 5.0, as a fundamental part of supporting energy efficiency measures; the relevance of synergy between human interaction and the functionality of intelligent systems, within the scope of Industry 5.0, to support production capacity in processes for the circularity of components; human experience combined with technological resources can capture customer experiences and reveal new circular business opportunities.

Although this chapter has focused on the seven dimensions of the circular economy proposed by Payer et al. (2024), future studies may develop other dimensions according to the context of application and establish models or frameworks in various circumstances. In addition, this work was limited to seven specialists to deal with each dimension, so future studies can consult a greater number of specialists, delving into aspects in these seven dimensions or in others that will be developed.

REFERENCES

Appolloni, A., D'Adamo, I., Gastaldi, M., Santibanez-Gonzalez, E. D. R., & Settembre-Blundo, D. (2021). Growing e-waste management risk awareness points towards new recycling scenarios: The view of the Big Four's youngest consultants. *Environmental Technology & Innovation*, 23, 101716. DOI: 10.1016/j.eti.2021.101716

Assante, D., Flamini, M., & Trinca, E. (2023). Towards Industry 5.0: Fostering a Circular Human Resources Management in the Foundry Sector. *2023 6th Experiment@ International Conference (exp.at'23)*, 232–236. DOI: 10.1109/exp.at2358782.2023.10545670

Atif, S. (2023). Analysing the alignment between circular economy and industry 4.0 nexus with industry 5.0 era: An integrative systematic literature review. *Sustainable Development (Bradford)*, 31(4), 2155–2175. DOI: 10.1002/sd.2542

Balwada, J., Samaiya, S., & Mishra, R. P. (2021). Packaging Plastic Waste Management for a Circular Economy and Identifying a better Waste Collection System using Analytical Hierarchy Process (AHP). *Procedia CIRP*, 98, 270–275. DOI: 10.1016/j.procir.2021.01.102

Banjanovi-Mehmedovic, L., & Dželilović, N. (2024). Towards a Greener Future: Sensor-Based Material Characterization in Waste Sorting for a Sustainable Recycling Model. Em I. Karabegovic, A. Kovačević, & S. Mandzuka (Orgs.), *New Technologies, Development and Application VII* (Vol. 1070, p. 3–11). Springer Nature Switzerland. DOI: 10.1007/978-3-031-66271-3_1

Dabo, A.-A. A., & Hosseinian-Far, A. (2023). An Integrated Methodology for Enhancing Reverse Logistics Flows and Networks in Industry 5.0. *Logistics (Basel)*, 7(4), 97. DOI: 10.3390/logistics7040097

Delbari, S. A., & Hof, L. A. (2024). Glass waste circular economy—Advancing to high-value glass sheets recovery using industry 4.0 and 5.0 technologies. *Journal of Cleaner Production*, 462, 142629. DOI: 10.1016/j.jclepro.2024.142629

Dhayal, K. S., Giri, A. K., Kumar, A., Samadhiya, A., Agrawal, S., & Agrawal, R. (2023). Can green finance facilitate Industry 5.0 transition to achieve sustainability? A systematic review with future research directions. *Environmental Science and Pollution Research International*, 30(46), 102158–102180. DOI: 10.1007/s11356-023-29539-w PMID: 37695480

Dwivedi, A., Agrawal, D., Jha, A., & Mathiyazhagan, K. (2023). Studying the interactions among Industry 5.0 and circular supply chain: Towards attaining sustainable development. *Computers & Industrial Engineering*, 176, 108927. DOI: 10.1016/j.cie.2022.108927

Fraga-Lamas, P., Lopes, S. I., & Fernández-Caramés, T. M. (2021). Green IoT and Edge AI as Key Technological Enablers for a Sustainable Digital Transition towards a Smart Circular Economy: An Industry 5.0 Use Case. *Sensors (Basel)*, 21(17), 5745. DOI: 10.3390/s21175745 PMID: 34502637

Garrido, S., Muniz, J.Jr, & Batista Ribeiro, V. (2024). Operations Management, Sustainability & Industry 5.0: A critical analysis and future agenda. *Cleaner Logistics and Supply Chain*, 10, 100141. DOI: 10.1016/j.clscn.2024.100141

Ghobakhloo, M., Iranmanesh, M., Foroughi, B., Babaee Tirkolaee, E., Asadi, S., & Amran, A. (2023). Industry 5.0 implications for inclusive sustainable manufacturing: An evidence-knowledge-based strategic roadmap. *Journal of Cleaner Production*, 417, 138023. DOI: 10.1016/j.jclepro.2023.138023

Gibbin, R. V., Sigahi, T. F. A. C., Pinto, J. D. S., Rampasso, I. S., & Anholon, R. (2023). Thematic evolution and trends linking sustainability and project management: Scientific mapping using SciMAT. *Journal of Cleaner Production*, 414, 137753. DOI: 10.1016/j.jclepro.2023.137753

Hadi, A., Cheung, F., Adjei, S., & Dulaimi, A. (2023). Evaluation of Lean Off-Site Construction Literature through the Lens of Industry 4.0 and 5.0. *Journal of Construction Engineering and Management*, 149(12), 03123007. DOI: 10.1061/JCEMD4.COENG-13622

Hetmanczyk, M. P. (2024a). A Method for Evaluating the Maturity Level of Production Process Automation in the Context of Digital Transformation—Polish Case Study. *Applied Sciences (Basel, Switzerland)*, 14(11), 4380. DOI: 10.3390/app14114380

Hetmanczyk, M. P. (2024b). A Method to Evaluate the Maturity Level of Robotization of Production Processes in the Context of Digital Transformation—Polish Case Study. *Applied Sciences (Basel, Switzerland)*, 14(13), 5401. DOI: 10.3390/app14135401

Hristova, T. (2024). Tracking mining company electric vehicles for sustainable development optimization using Distributed Ledger Technologies. *Journal of Sustainable Mining*, 23(3), 299–314. DOI: 10.46873/2300-3960.1425

Kannan, D., Amiri, A. S., Shaayesteh, M. T., Nasr, A. K., & Mina, H. (2024). Unveiling barriers to the integration of blockchain-based circular economy and Industry 5.0 in manufacturing industries: A strategic prioritization approach. *Business Strategy and the Environment*, bse.3886. DOI: 10.46873/2300-3960.1425

Khan, A. A., & Abonyi, J. (2022). Information sharing in supply chains – Interoperability in an era of circular economy. *Cleaner Logistics and Supply Chain*, 5, 100074. DOI: 10.1016/j.clscn.2022.100074

Kopeinig, J., Woschank, M., & Olipp, N. (2024). Industry 4.0 Technologies and their Implications for Environmental Sustainability in the Manufacturing Industry. *Procedia Computer Science*, 232, 2777–2789. DOI: 10.1016/j.procs.2024.02.095

Kumar, R., Kariminejad, A., Antonov, M., Goljandin, D., Klimczyk, P., & Hussainova, I. (2023). Progress in Sustainable Recycling and Circular Economy of Tungsten Carbide Hard Metal Scraps for Industry 5.0 and Onwards. *Sustainability (Basel)*, 15(16), 12249. DOI: 10.3390/su151612249

Lytvynenko, S., Vasylenko, I., Voitsehovskiy, V., Viniukov-Proshchenko, A., Gabrielova, T., & Lytvynenko, L. (2024). Providing energy efficiency and ecological compatibility in organising special cargo delivery. *E3S Web of Conferences, 559*, 03002. DOI: 10.3390/su151612249

Ma, S., Ding, W., Liu, Y., Zhang, Y., Ren, S., Kong, X., & Leng, J. (2024). Industry 4.0 and cleaner production: A comprehensive review of sustainable and intelligent manufacturing for energy-intensive manufacturing industries. *Journal of Cleaner Production*, 467, 142879. DOI: 10.1016/j.jclepro.2024.142879

Marić, J., Opazo-Basáez, M., Vlačić, B., & Dabić, M. (2023). Innovation management of three-dimensional printing (3DP) technology: Disclosing insights from existing literature and determining future research streams. *Technological Forecasting and Social Change*, 193, 122605. DOI: 10.1016/j.techfore.2023.122605

Martini, B., Bellisario, D., & Coletti, P. (2024). Human-Centered and Sustainable Artificial Intelligence in Industry 5.0: Challenges and Perspectives. *Sustainability (Basel)*, 16(13), 5448. DOI: 10.3390/su16135448

Mesjasz-Lech, A., Kemendi, Á., & Michelberger, P. (2024). Circular manufacturing and Industry 5.0. Assessing material flows in the manufacturing process in relation to e-waste streams. *Engineering Management in Production and Services*, 16(1), 114–133. DOI: 10.2478/emj-2024-0009

Moller, D. P. F., Vakilzadian, H., & Haas, R. E. (2022). From Industry 4.0 towards Industry 5.0. *2022 IEEE International Conference on Electro Information Technology (eIT)*, 61–68. DOI: 10.1109/eIT53891.2022.9813831

Montagnani, E. (2022). Le pubbliche amministrazioni nell'era delle tecnologie cloud ed edge computing tra opportunità e rischi: Il Piano Nazionale di Ripresa e Resilienza e le comunità digitali. *Rivista italiana di informatica e diritto, 4*(1), 12. DOI: 10.3390/su151612249

Narula, S., Tamvada, J. P., Kumar, A., Puppala, H., & Gupta, N. (2024). Putting Digital Technologies at the Forefront of Industry 5.0 for the Implementation of a Circular Economy in Manufacturing Industries. *IEEE Transactions on Engineering Management*, 71, 3363–3374. DOI: 10.1109/TEM.2023.3344373

Nikseresht, A., Golmohammadi, D., & Zandieh, M. (2024). Empirical modeling approaches in sustainable supply chain management: A review with bibliometric and network analyses. *Business Strategy and the Environment*, bse.3937. DOI: 10.3390/su151612249

Panza, L., Bruno, G., & Lombardi, F. (2023). Integrating Absolute Sustainability and Social Sustainability in the Digital Product Passport to Promote Industry 5.0. *Sustainability (Basel)*, 15(16), 12552. DOI: 10.3390/su151612552

Payer, R. C., Quelhas, O. L. G., & Bergiante, N. C. R. (2024). Framework to supporting monitoring the circular economy in the context of industry 5.0: A proposal considering circularity indicators, digital transformation, and sustainability. *Journal of Cleaner Production*, 466, 142850. DOI: 10.1016/j.jclepro.2024.142850

Ramírez-Peña, M., Cerezo-Narváez, A., Pastor-Fernández, A., Otero-Mateo, M., & Ballesteros-Pérez, P. (2023). Determination of Requirements for the Improvement of Occupational Safety in the Cleaning of Vertical Tanks of Petroleum Products. *Safety (Basel, Switzerland)*, 9(1), 6. DOI: 10.3390/safety9010006

Ruiz-de-la-Torre-Acha, A., Guevara-Ramirez, W., Río-Belver, R. M., & Borregan-Alvarado, J. (2023). Industry 5.0. The Road to Sustainability. Em Y. Borgianni, D. T. Matt, M. Molinaro, & G. Orzes (Orgs.), *Towards a Smart, Resilient and Sustainable Industry* (Vol. 745, p. 247–257). Springer Nature Switzerland. DOI: 10.1007/978-3-031-38274-1_21

Saaty, R. W. (1987). The analytic hierarchy process—What it is and how it is used. *Mathematical Modelling*, 9(3–5), 161–176. DOI: 10.1016/0270-0255(87)90473-8

Santiago, B. D. S., Scavarda, L. F., Gusmão Caiado, R. G., Santos, R. S., & Mattos Nascimento, D. L. D. (2024). Corporate social responsibility and circular economy integration framework within sustainable supply chain management: Building blocks for industry 5.0. *Corporate Social Responsibility and Environmental Management*, csr.2949. DOI: 10.1016/0270-0255(87)90473-8

Siakas, D., Lampropoulos, G., Rahanu, H., Georgiadou, E., & Siakas, K. (2023). Emerging Technologies Enabling the Transition Toward a Sustainable and Circular Economy: The 4R Sustainability Framework. Em M. Yilmaz, P. Clarke, A. Riel, & R. Messnarz (Orgs.), *Systems, Software and Services Process Improvement* (Vol. 1891, p. 166–181). Springer Nature Switzerland. DOI: 10.1007/978-3-031-42310-9_12

Suarez-Fernandez De Miranda, S., Aguayo-González, F., Ávila-Gutiérrez, M. J., & Córdoba-Roldán, A. (2021). Neuro-Competence Approach for Sustainable Engineering. *Sustainability (Basel)*, 13(8), 4389. DOI: 10.3390/su13084389

Sulich, A. (2024). Model of Relationship Between Circular Economy and Industry 5.0. Em E. Mercier-Laurent, G. Kayakutlu, M. L. Owoc, A. Wahid, & K. Mason (Orgs.), *Artificial Intelligence for Knowledge Management, Energy and Sustainability* (Vol. 693, p. 220–236). Springer Nature Switzerland. DOI: 10.1007/978-3-031-61069-1_16

Thomas, A., Chawla, Y., Varma, A., & Szleter, P. (2024). The Role of Business Leaders in Industry 5.0. Em A. Visvizi, O. Troisi, & V. Corvello (Orgs.), *Research and Innovation Forum 2023* (p. 629–640). Springer International Publishing. DOI: 10.1007/978-3-031-44721-1_47

Turner, C., & Oyekan, J. (2023a). Manufacturing in the Age of Human-Centric and Sustainable Industry 5.0: Application to Holonic, Flexible, Reconfigurable and Smart Manufacturing Systems. *Sustainability (Basel)*, 15(13), 10169. DOI: 10.3390/su151310169

Turner, C., & Oyekan, J. (2023b). Personalised Production in the Age of Circular Additive Manufacturing. *Applied Sciences (Basel, Switzerland)*, 13(8), 4912. DOI: 10.3390/app13084912

Turner, C., Oyekan, J., Garn, W., Duggan, C., & Abdou, K. (2022). Industry 5.0 and the Circular Economy: Utilizing LCA with Intelligent Products. *Sustainability (Basel)*, 14(22), 14847. DOI: 10.3390/su142214847

Venturi, F., Tonacci, A., Ascrizzi, R., Sansone, F., Conte, R., Pala, A. P., Tarabella, A., Sanmartin, C., Taglieri, I., Marangoni, R., Bietresato, M., Comuzzo, P., Zironi, R., Zironi, A., Ciotti, G., & Gubiani, R. (2024). "CANTINA 5.0"—A Novel, Industry 5.0-Based Paradigm Applied to the Winemaking Industry in Italy. *Applied Sciences (Basel, Switzerland)*, 14(11), 4777. DOI: 10.3390/app14114777

Voulgaridis, K., Lagkas, T., Angelopoulos, C. M., Boulogeorgos, A.-A. A., Argyriou, V., & Sarigiannidis, P. (2024). Digital product passports as enablers of digital circular economy: A framework based on technological perspective. *Telecommunication Systems*, 85(4), 699–715. DOI: 10.1007/s11235-024-01104-x

Voulgaridis, K., Lagkas, T., Angelopoulos, C. M., & Nikoletseas, S. E. (2022). IoT and digital circular economy: Principles, applications, and challenges. *Computer Networks*, 219, 109456. DOI: 10.1016/j.comnet.2022.109456

Voulgaridis, K., Lagkas, T., Karampatzakis, D., Argyriou, V., & Sarigiannidis, P. (2023). Realizing Digital Product Passports with Crowdsourcing Principles: The Case of Sustainable Smart Grids. *2023 19th International Conference on Distributed Computing in Smart Systems and the Internet of Things (DCOSS-IoT)*, 381–388. DOI: 10.1109/DCOSS-IoT58021.2023.00068

Voulgaridis, K., Lagkas, T., & Sarigiannidis, P. (2022). Towards Industry 5.0 and Digital Circular Economy: Current Research and Application Trends. *2022 18th International Conference on Distributed Computing in Sensor Systems (DCOSS)*, 153–158. DOI: 10.1109/DCOSS54816.2022.00037

ADDITIONAL READING

Marconnet, B., Gaha, R., Assuad, C., Martinsen, K., & Eynard, B. (2024). Selecting sustainability indicators for smart product design based on industry 4.0/5.0 technologies: Analysis and proposal of a methodological framework. *Proceedings of the Design Society*, 4, 1369–1378. DOI: 10.1017/pds.2024.139

Mejía-Moncayo, C., Kenné, J.-P., & Hof, L. A. (2023). On the development of a smart architecture for a sustainable manufacturing-remanufacturing system: A literature review approach. *Computers & Industrial Engineering*, 180, 109282. DOI: 10.1016/j.cie.2023.109282

Priyadarshini, J., Singh, R. K., Mishra, R., He, Q., & Braganza, A. (2024). Implementation of Additive Manufacturing in the Healthcare Supply Chain for Circular Economy Goals: Paradoxical Tensions and Solutions from an Industry 5.0 Perspective. *Information Systems Frontiers*. Advance online publication. DOI: 10.1007/s10796-024-10482-1

KEY TERMS AND DEFINITIONS

Analytic Hierarchy Process (AHP): Multicriteria method based on pairwise comparisons to rank options.

Circular Economy: Economic concept that seeks to reduce waste and pollution and maximize the use of resources. The goal is to create a more sustainable and efficient economic system, which reconciles economic growth, the well-being of society and the conscious management of natural resources

Industry 5.0: It is a new industrial phase that is characterized by the union between human beings and automated technologies. The goal is for the creative and questioning potential of the human being to be harnessed to create personalized products that meet the needs of customers. In addition to the human factor, in this industrial phase the pillars of sustainability and resilience gain special relevance.

Strategic Options Development and Analysis (SODA): Problem Structuring Method used in complex and challenging situations when algorithms or equations are not sufficient to model the problem studied. This method explores the gathering of different points of view on a subject through cognitive mapping of interviews.

Chapter 8
Evaluating Turkish Manufacturers' Perspectives on Industry 4.0, Circular Economy, and Corporate Performance

İbrahim Sarper Karakadılar
https://orcid.org/0000-0002-1785-5756
Kahramanmaraş İstiklal University, Turkey

ABSTRACT

This paper evaluates Turkish manufacturing managers' perceptions regarding the impact of Industry 4.0 and the circular economy on seeking excellence in operational processes. A research framework was proposed to assess executives' attitudes towards these approaches to supply chain sustainability and corporate performance. Data collection was conducted through an online questionnaire, with 126 valid responses subjected to statistical analysis. The findings suggest that participants are not fully prepared for autonomous digital transformation and exhibit reluctance to invest in radical digital technology changes. Transformation projects such as cyber-physical systems seem potentially disruptive to existing operations as they observe a negative correlation with other factors. The research presents a model for evaluating Industry 4.0 and circular economy performance expectations to guide digital transformation in manufacturing for competitiveness. Limitations of the study include a small sample size and a focus on Turkish manufacturers, which may restrict its broad applicability.

DOI: 10.4018/979-8-3373-2523-1.ch008

INTRODUCTION

A major trend in today's business world is the belief that companies can gain a competitive advantage by managing production and logistics processes using digital autonomous technologies. This contemporary approach suggests that adopting digital technology systems and implementing organizational transformation will make companies more competitive (Nguyen and Luu, 2020). Companies can increase their market share and competitive edge using Industry 4.0 innovative technologies. Conversely, delaying the adoption of Industry 4.0 technologies can result in falling behind the competition. Industry 4.0 and circular economy concepts aim to improve operational efficiency and performance through organizational and technological advances (Khan et al., 2021).

This study evaluates how managers of Turkish manufacturing companies view Industry 4.0 technologies and circular economy principles' impact on performance. An original research model is designed for Turkish business conditions, combining Industry 4.0 and the circular economy in supply chain management, this model executives' and operational managers' attitudes toward exporting firms. The study assesses expectations about how these approaches affect perceived performance and competitiveness in emerging markets like Turkey.

Existing literature has limited empirical research on the interaction between Industry 4.0 technologies and circular economy principles. The relationship between these two variables and their related variables is not comprehensively studied. This research subject presents a fruitful avenue for researchers. The primary research question is to investigate how the relationships between Industry 4.0 technologies and circular economy principles can influence manufacturers' performance across multiple dimensions (operational, supply chain, sustainability, and corporate).

This study distinguishes itself from existing literature by addressing this primary research question. For instance, Ghaithan et al. (2023) focused exclusively on sustainability performance, without considering other performance types. In contrast, Al-Swidi et al. (2023) investigated the combined effect of regulatory pressure, competitive pressure, and Industry 4.0 technologies implementing the circular economy by Indian companies to explain the motivations for adopting these approaches. A recent study by Rehman et al. (2024) examined the impact of Industry 4.0 on organizational performance, specifically financial and environmental performance, through the mediation effect of circular economy principles implementation.

This study also addresses the secondary research question of examining the effects of the research data obtained within this generic model based on the internationalization levels of Turkish manufacturing companies. By interpreting the managerial attitudes of production enterprises operating under different conditions and goals, with foreign capital partnerships and export-oriented, useful insights can be drawn for practical application.

Numerous publications have addressed Industry 4.0 and circular economy concepts. However, there is almost no comprehensive field research on how organizations, particularly in emerging markets, should adopt these approaches (e.g., Götz, 2020; Mishra et al., 2022). Conducting such scholarly studies is critically important. It becomes a strategically significant process for organizations with limited resources to undertake a radical digital transformation and reform their business models. This gap in the literature calls for field surveys to evaluate the topic from an academic perspective, enabling organizations to interact holistically with change. An index measuring an emerging country's competitiveness is needed.

Turkish exporters need rapid structural transformation to enhance efficiency and sustainability. This study provides managers with a survey that assesses their perspectives on adopting contemporary approaches to fill a research gap. Unlike previous studies, such as de Mattos Nascimento et al. (2024), which focused on Industry 4.0 and circular economy integration, this research compares theoretical insights with industry representatives' opinions. In Mattos Nascimento et al. (2024), the focus was on literature-based sources, aiming to measure the maturity of sustainable supply chain practices in the context of Industry 4.0 technologies and circular economy principles. Unlike the study of Karakadilar (2023), this paper focuses on regional and company sizes rather than small- to medium-sized enterprises (SMEs). This paper evaluates the broader views of Turkish manufacturing managers' perspectives on the impacts of Industry 4.0 and circular economy principles.

BACKGROUND

In today's global economy and trade structure, optimizing operations has become a top priority for firms as a competitive advantage (Naik et al., 2024). Firms must conduct operational activities in a cost-reducing, timely, and environmentally friendly manner (Pasupuleti et al., 2024; Wong et al., 2024). This requires the effective utilization of autonomous digital technologies and the transformation of companies' operational systems (Nguyen & Luu, 2020). Improving the operational performance of production, logistics, and supply chain networks will reduce carbon emissions and positively impact the company's marketing and financial performance (de Jesus Pacheco & Schougaard, 2024; Khan et al., 2021; Nascimento et al., 2019).

The literature regularly examines the countries' competitive position based on macroeconomic parameters (e.g., Alexandro & Basrowi, 2024; Benítez-Márquez et al., 2022; Kristjánsdóttir, 2017), but such research focuses on countries past performance rather than evaluating future potential. Concurrently there is also a need to develop a micro-based firm-level competitiveness index model that considers technological advancement and the imperative of achieving environmentally sustainable production (Ustun & Akkartal, 2024). Thus, it would be advantageous to develop such an index model that will lighten the hesitations of decision-making company owners or executives in developing countries regarding high-cost investments in Industry 4.0 technological tools and environmentally friendly production practices and provide guidance (Dalenogare et al., 2018; Karakadilar, 2023; Nascimento et al., 2019). In this context, it is argued that securing production enterprises' global competitiveness enhances future national competitiveness (Dogangun et al., 2023). This study focuses on developing a competitive index model to address how production enterprises can evaluate themselves to attain world-class level competitiveness, which differs from countries' economic parameters based on existing models in the literature.

Industry 4.0 Technologies

Manufacturing organizations must implement circular economy principles for Industry 4.0 technology to address environmental issues (Sun & Wang, 2022). If companies continue the conventional linear economic approach, investing in digital technologies will be ineffective (Dalenogare et al., 2018). The literature covers these concepts to describe interaction effects. This paper determines a research framework by reviewing empirical and theoretical studies and suggests model building.

Industry 4.0 technology tools enable digital information processing and autonomous task execution with minimal human intervention (Lopes de Sousa Jabbour et al., 2018). Thus, the benefits it provides, such as increased control of top management over operational activities and enabling real-time performance measurement (Horváth and Szabó, 2019), are persistently emphasized in the literature as the impacts of Industry 4.0 technologies on organizational performance.

This paper examines scholarly studies on how Industry 4.0 technologies impact operational excellence in manufacturing. These studies focus on operational performance criteria like reducing defective output rates (Awan et al., 2021; Khan et al., 2021; Lopes de Sousa Jabbour et al., 2018) and improving environmental waste performance (Cousins et al., 2019; Jain et al., 2020). Another important effect of Industry 4.0 is its contribution to enhancing environmental performance by reducing energy consumption and waste generation through increased production quality and efficiency with digital technologies (Moktadir et al., 2018).

The key challenge in reaping the benefits of digital transformation and Industry 4.0 technologies is to implement them radically by disrupting the status quo. To achieve this, top management must be convinced of the necessity of these transformation investments. Thus, the difficulties of employing a qualified workforce for the reformed business model or retraining existing personnel to adapt must be overcome (Bag & Pretorius, 2020).

A prerequisite for a successful digital transformation strategy is its implementation by other enterprises in the chain (Liu et al., 2023). Businesses must have financial and human resources to acquire the technology to effectively organize digital networks among chain participants. Investing in the necessary resources can establish a unique supply chain structure.

Circular Economy Principles

The circular economy principles have emerged as a response to rising pollution, greenhouse gas emissions, and resource depletion (Agyabeng-Mensah et al., 2020). In the manufacturing sector, the circular economy emphasizes sustainable operations for production facilities (Sun & Wang, 2022) to enhance environmental performance, improve quality, reduce costs, and reduce carbon footprint to gain a competitive edge. Its goal is to decrease natural resource use, employ renewable materials, and reuse waste in manufacturing processes (Lopes de Sousa Jabbour et al., 2018). Unlike the linear economy approach, it reduces negative environmental impacts through reuse, remanufacturing, and recycling (Awan, 2021).

The concept of a circular economy has multiple facets and broad coverage. Kirchherr et al. (2017) mentioned related subdimensions: sustainable development (balances social, environmental, and economic objectives for sustainable growth) and environmental quality (better natural environments and resource efficiency). This study primarily examined the circular economy concept in these subdimensions.

Nevertheless, green supply chain implementation is crucial for circular economy principles and system balance (Agyabeng-Mensah et al. 2020). Communication between stakeholder institutions and waste recycling is crucial for implementing the circular economy. Designing a structure for recent information sharing requires a smart system based on digital technologies. Hence, circular economy applications are associated with the Industry 4.0 approach (Atif, 2023; Lei et al., 2023). The environmental performance of a supply chain network is largely dependent on the reduction of waste, which harms the environment and benefits reverse logistics effectively (Nascimento et al., 2019).

Performance Evaluation Approaches

In the contemporary competitive business environment, achieving operational excellence is crucial. At this point, it is imperative to determine the criteria and methodologies for excellence. Organizations use performance evaluation systems to establish key performance indicators for operational performance and monitor compliance. This approach enhances operational efficiency and develops sustainable solutions, ensuring the system is updated to maintain excellence. The performance evaluation system should be fully implemented in accordance with the Kaizen philosophy (Sichinsambwe et al., 2023).

This study examines the impact of digital transformation and autonomous technologies on operations, focusing on organizational effectiveness and reducing carbon footprints from operational and managerial perspectives. Establishing logistics and production systems is essential for performance evaluation. Logistics operations should be time-efficient, meet customer expectations, and reduce costs. The production process should adhere to key performance indicators, minimize idle time, comply with production plans, and ensure preventive maintenance. Digital technology and efficient utilization of information and communication technologies within the supply chain are also crucial. An effective supply chain eliminates waste, creates value, reduces costs, and enhances environmental performance (Cannas et al., 2024). However, innovative investments that support environmentally friendly practices and prioritize environmental awareness in supply chain performance are equally vital.

The European Union's Green Deal policy emphasizes the importance of reducing and monitoring carbon footprints, which significantly impact current business models. Evolving practices to cut carbon emissions from logistics and production and tracking their effectiveness are essential. Adopting the principles of a circular economy with an environmentally conscious approach and obtaining independent carbon compliance certifications is key (Sheng et al., 2023). Beyond environmental concerns, respect for employees' social rights under the sustainability umbrella is important, and adopting a management philosophy aligned with corporate governance is also crucial (Ajmal et al., 2018). In today's competitive marketplace, assessing sustainability performance is also becoming increasingly vital.

Theoretical Framework

When developing a comprehensive research model that includes socio-economic and environmental management, it is insufficient to base the research on a single theory. This requires a broader study. The natural resource-based view emphasizes environmental sustainability and resource management, whereas the traditional resource-based view focuses on using resources for a sustainable competitive advantage. Both approaches improve organizational performance (Cousins et al., 2019).

The study's theoretical framework focuses on performance improvement and supply chain redesign using Industry 4.0 and circular economy capabilities, as well as environmental concerns like carbon emissions and waste pollution prevention. Scholars have focused on optimizing operational efficiency and reducing negative outputs based on ecological modernization and practice-based view theories (Khan et al., 2021). The green supply chain network, redesigned with technology, improves resource efficiency, leading to better environmental and economic performance. The application-based theory emphasizes companies' collective impact within the supply chain, which provides a competitive advantage (Sun & Wang, 2022).

The technology acceptance model, which posits that organizations' adoption of technology leads to transformation and competitiveness, further enhances the other theoretical foundation of the study. This theoretical framework explains the extent of corporate and employee adoption and use of novel technologies (Gögus & Özer, 2014). The theory proposes that perceived usefulness and perceived ease of use are critical factors that influence an individual's intention to use technology. Perceived usefulness refers to the degree to which a decision-maker allocating the budget for this technological investment and users of the technology believe that implementing the technology will enhance corporate performance, while perceived ease of use refers to the extent to which the decision-maker or practitioners believe the technology will require minimal effort to increase productivity (Sakkthivel & Ramu, 2018). Factors such as high-performance expectancy, low effort expectancy, and facilitating conditions are key determinants of technology adoption.

All these approaches view a company's entry into the transformation process by embracing current technology as dependent on factors like business conditions (competitive pressure, managerial requirements, and government incentives). These opinions are used to measure the key factors influencing companies' adoption of Industry 4.0 technologies.

METHOD

Research Model

This study builds on Karakadilar's (2023) research model. The updated scale items and modified model include new subdimensions like sustainability performance and carbon footprint, along with an original testing model. This study examines how Turkish manufacturers perceive circular economy principles and Industry 4.0 tools to boost export markets' competitiveness. This study explores achieving operational efficiency and its impact on corporate performance and the role of digital transformation in reforming operational processes. Figure 1 shows the research model.

The model highlights key variables as the antecedent factors affecting organizational performance: perceived operational issues like logistics, production, and carbon footprint, as well as positive expectations of Industry 4.0 technology implementation. These expectations involve the effects of creating cyber-physical systems, taking advantage of Industry 4.0 technology opportunities, and tackling digital transformation challenges. With all these antecedent factors, the performance evaluation system will operate effectively and continuously improve, thereby creating operational excellence and enabling the achievement of organizational performance goals through competitiveness. The performance evaluation system is a key factor that connects supply chain improvements and operational excellence to the system's efficiency and overall corporate performance. The model also links a firm's carbon footprint with sustainability performance, emphasizing its vital role in boosting corporate performance in today's environmentally conscious business world.

Figure 1. Proposed research framework

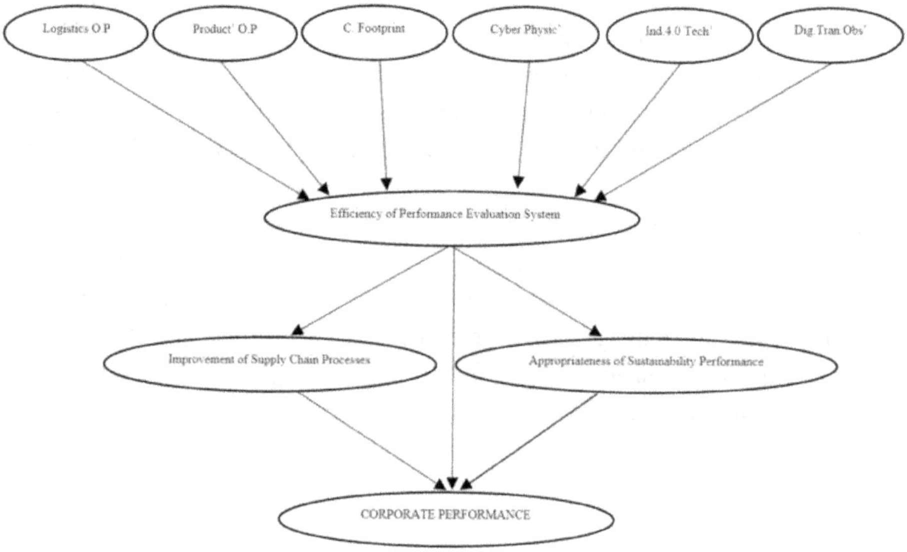

(generated by the author)

Research Design

This study collected data using an online questionnaire focused on Turkish exporter manufacturers' views of the benefits of the circular economy and Industry 4.0 technology. The survey targeted executive decision-makers or managers responsible for operations to reach a diverse group from various industries across Turkey. The unit of analysis is 'Anatolian Tigers', referring to export-oriented manufacturers in Turkey with different company sizes and business-trade volumes. The survey data were collected using simple random sampling, assuming a homogeneous group (based on management culture and attitudes) in which each individual had an equal chance of selection (Singh, 2003).

An online questionnaire was distributed via email to the companies' corporate email addresses. The researcher also uses a survey participant database from previous research to distribute the survey directly to industry experts. A total of 153 participants engaged in the survey. However, some participants indicated a lack of interest at the outset, while others did not respond to all the questions and were subsequently excluded. To keep the survey data relevant and current, the response collection period ended after one year, resulting in 126 usable questionnaire forms. Unfortunately, this did not reach the target of analysing over 200 responses. The survey questionnaire was distributed to 400 Turkish manufacturers across the country and received 126 responses, yielding a 31.5% response rate. The margin of error, which represents the maximum expected difference between the sample statistic and the true population parameter, was also examined to assess reliability. The margin of error for this survey is $\pm$4.08% (as calculated in Table 1).

Given the similarities in management styles and strategic objectives of the companies referred to as Anatolian Tigers, from which the data were collected within the scope of this study, it is posited that the results are sufficient to represent the research population despite the low response rate. Consequently, the relatively low number of observations, which would typically indicate a significant limitation for a research dataset, should not be considered problematic given the scope of this study. This is because it is posited that the Anatolian Tigers can provide valuable insights into their managerial attitudes and perspectives. Therefore, within the parameters of this research, Turkish manufacturers (Anatolian Tigers) can draw inferences regarding appropriate strategies and factors that export market-oriented producers with similar company characteristics in emerging countries should prioritize to enhance their global competitive position.

RESULTS

Respondents and Participating Companies

In Table 1, the survey's participant proportion was: 63% of the questionnaires were filled in by males, and the densest age group was over 50 years old at 29%. The majority of respondents were department managers (production, logistics, and supply) at 27%. In addition, Table 2 shows the distribution of survey companies. 19% were in the textile and related raw material production industry, and 22% were located in Istanbul. Furthermore, the majority of participating firms, comprising

71%, were wholly domestic capital enterprises without foreign partnerships or management collaborations.

Table 1. Respondents' profiles

Age of respondents	**Frequency**	**Per cent**	**Department of respondents**	**Frequency**	**Per cent**
Below 30	29	22.9	Department Managers (such as: logistics, supply chain etc.)	34	27.0
30-39	28	22.3	Top Level Managers (board member, coordinator, general manager etc.)	20	15.9
40-49	33	26.2	Factory Manager	12	9.5
50 and above	36	28.6	Sustainability (Environmental, Social, and Governance) Officer/Analyst	11	8.7
TOTAL	126	100	Company Founder Owner or Shareholder	8	6.4
Gender of respondents	**Frequency**	**Per cent**	Key Account Manager or Director of Operations	4	3.2
Male	79	62,7	Others	4	3.2
Female	47	37,3	Not Responded	33	26.1
TOTAL	126	100	TOTAL	126	100

Notes: n=126

Response Rate: 126/400 = 0.315 (Divide the total number of valid survey replies by the total number of surveys distributed to get the effective response rate).

The margin of Error: 1.96 * √[(0.315 * (1 – 0.315)] / 20.000 = 0.0408 (z * √[(p * (1 - p)] / N ; where z is the confidence level "desired confidence level is %95 and its z-score is typically assumed as 1.96", p is the proportion of the population that responded "as 0.315", and N is the population size "approximately 20,000 exporting manufacturers".

The analysis indicates that approximately 54% of firms in the sample have an export proportion of less than fifty percent of their production sold to foreign markets. When comparing organizations based on the number of employees, those with 250–2500 employees were the most represented, accounting for 42% of the total. On the other hand, nearly half of the respondents wished to remain silent when asked how much turnover they make during a given period of the year. This table shows once again that Turkish survey participants do not want to provide information about their company's financials and do not want to share their positions in the company to keep it secret.

Nonetheless, Table 1 illustrates that respondents possessed substantial experience and occupied significant positions within their organizations, enabling them to provide comprehensive information when responding to the questionnaire. Conversely, Table 2 demonstrates that the survey sampling adequately represents Turkish manufacturing firms in general, as evidenced by the diversity of industries and locations represented. The study's target audience aligned with the research sample profile, thereby ensuring representation validity through the sampling selection of the main population.

Table 2. Profiles of participating companies

Industry	**Frequency**	**Per cent**	**Location**	**Frequency**	**Per cent**
Textile and related raw material production	24	19.1	Istanbul	28	22.2
Automotive producers, subsidiaries and part suppliers	22	17.5	Kocaeli	19	15.1
Electric equipment producers	15	11.9	Bursa	13	10.3
Machinery parts manufacturers	13	10.3	Kahramanmaras	12	9.6
Chemical substances, derivative products (Plastic, PVC, etc.)	12	9.5	Izmir	11	8.7
Furniture, paper and forest products	9	7.1	Ankara	10	7.9
Industrial agriculture or packaged food and beverages	7	5.6	Gaziantep	10	7.9
Others	16	12.7	Denizli	6	4.8
Not Responded	8	6.3	Others	17	13.5
TOTAL	126	100	TOTAL	126	100
Foreign Shareholder Partnership	**Frequency**	**Per cent**	**Exporting Volume Proportion**	**Frequency**	**Per cent**
Completely local capital investment	89	70.6	More than 50%	58	46.1
Foreign capital investment partnership	37	29.4	Less than 50%	68	53.9
TOTAL	126	100	TOTAL	126	100

Research Items Development and Construct Validity

In the extant literature, there exists no comprehensive scale that adequately defines the concepts of Industry 4.0 and the circular economy while maintaining consistency with the scope of the research. Given the objective of measuring the behavioural attitudes of company owners or executives in decision-making positions regarding technology investments, a scale tailored to the research objective was necessary. This study's motivation was to transform issues previously addressed theoretically in a broad range of literature into a measurement instrument and validate this scale.

For this reason, the measurement instruments used in this study were originally developed for the first time, as there are no large-scale research items in this context.

The number of studies examining the research subject from the perspective of production and logistics operations is negligible (Dalenogare et al., 2018), and the research models presented in existing studies address the topic from a very narrow framework (Khan et al., 2021; Sun & Wang, 2022). In developing the scale, the focus is identifying common operational issues in industrial enterprises' production and logistics. Bag and Pretorius (2020) provided logistics and production performance criteria, which were used as survey measurement tools.

On the other hand, a literature review was conducted to examine how performance evaluation, Industry 4.0, and circular economy approaches can improve supply chains and corporate performance and develop scale items (Awan et al., 2021; Benešová et al., 2021; Castelo-Branco et al., 2022; Horváth & Szabó, 2019; Jain et al., 2020; Masood & Sonntag, 2020). Although these ideas are theoretically accepted, their systematic grouping in sectoral applications has not yet been explored. Examining these approaches through a survey scale and understanding their categorization into factor groups would greatly contribute to the existing body of literature.

The survey questionnaire was measured on a 5-point Likert scale ranging from "strongly disagree" (1 point) to "strongly agree" (5 points), with a middle point indicating "neither agree nor disagree" (3 points). Owing to the exploratory nature of this research, it is important to conduct step-by-step validity tests on the measurement instruments. The first step in these processes was to prove that the research items were distributed normally. The skewness and kurtosis values define the value interval between respectively +2.0 and -2.00 and +5.0 and -5.00, research items (George & Mallery, 2019). All research model constructs and items are shown with their exploratory factor analysis (EFA) loadings, means, standard deviations, and Cronbach's values in Table 3.

Table 3. Research items and construct validity

Factor components and questionnaire items	**EFA***	**Mean Std'Dv'**
Logistics Operational Performance	$\alpha = .83$	
Logistics operations can be completed quickly in our company.	.871	3.92 .796
Our logistics operations fully meet our customers' expectations.	.837	3.75 .920
Logistics operations are carried out at the appropriate level and a low cost.	.798	3.31 .862
Production Operational Performance	$\alpha = .89$	
The production process meets the key performance indicators (KPI).	.733	3.73 1.176
The production process is operated efficiently in high-tech machinery parks.	.785	3.66 1.272

continued on following page

Table 3. Continued

Factor components and questionnaire items	EFA*	Mean Std'Dv'
In facilities, preventive and protective maintenance is executed regularly.[a]	excl'	--- ---
Ensure proper flow according to the production program.	.703	4.17 1.265
Carbon Footprint Performance	α = .93	
The carbon footprint performance is satisfactory during manufacturing operations.	.819	3.89 .684
The carbon footprint performance is satisfactory during logistics operations.	.820	3.67 .780
The performance in implementing circular economy principles is satisfactory.	.842	3.90 .725
Benefits of Establishing Cyber-Physical Systems	α = .85	
Internet of Things (IoT) technology is expected to improve the company's performance.	.701	3.83 .919
Big data analysis technology is expected to improve the company's performance.	.707	3.48 .986
Cloud technology is expected to improve the company's performance.	.771	3.96 .871
Artificial intelligence-supported learning machine technology is expected to improve the company's performance.	.749	3.94 1.033
Facilities for Gaining Industry 4.0 Technologies	α = .86	
Our company can supply and use Industry 4.0 technologies at our location.[a]	excl'	--- ---
Our company has sufficient financial resources to acquire Industry 4.0 technologies.	.556	4.19 .836
Our company could hire qualified employees to work with Industry 4.0 technologies.	.676	4.09 .921
Our company can persuade other interested parties to invest in Industry 4.0 technologies.	.824	3.39 1.138
Obstacles to the Digital Transformation System Design	α = .90	
I fear that the company's top management will lose control of its operation processes.[a]	excl'	--- ---
I am concerned that the digital transformation process may cause chaos.[a]	excl'	--- ---
Because of the digital transformation process, the workforce's sense of belonging to the organization and motivation to work may decrease because of the risk of personnel being laid off.	.737	3.83 1.094
Organizations may encounter financial difficulties due to the salary expenses associated hiring high-quality personnel in the novel business model following digital transformation.	.822	3.88 1.107
Financial resources may be adversely affected because of the significant budget allocated to digital transformation.	.748	3.82 1.134
Individually, a firm's digital transformation design might negatively affect supply chain integration.	.795	3.49 1.002
Efficiency of Performance Evaluation System	α = .83	
To ensure operational excellence, the performance evaluation system is constantly updated.	.745	3.77 .887
The performance evaluation system could generate solutions to overcome problems.	.670	3.99 .916
The performance evaluation system increases productivity across the organization.	.656	3.79 .803
Improving Supply Chain Performance	α = .76	
Restructuring digital systems may provide the company with a competitive advantage.	.588	3.98 .698
By implementing digital systems, all parties in the supply chain could effectively communicate and gather information.	.663	4.52 .547
Investing in costly green innovation technologies will improve supply chain performance.	.637	4.37 .711
Re-designing the supply chain using digital technologies might improve the chain's performance.	.651	4.06 .708

continued on following page

Table 3. Continued

Factor components and questionnaire items	EFA*	Mean Std'Dv'
Environmental considerations must be a crucial factor when designing supply chain networks.	.717	4.14 .678
Appropriateness of Sustainability Performance	α = .91	
Environmental awareness should be one of the most important criteria for performance evaluation.	.845	3.86 .892
Carbon emissions should be assessed and certified by reputed international organizations.	.853	3.37 1.184
Organizations should pay attention to employee social rights.	.850	3.71 1.003
Organizations should pay attention to implementing and improving corporate governance principles.	.856	3.61 .955
Expected Corporate Performance	α = .85	
I am confident that organizations' marketing performance will improve.	.784	3.00 .955
I am confident that organizations' financial performance will improve.	.783	3.56 .664
I am confident that organizations' environmental performance will improve.	.771	3.49 .654
I am confident that organizations' overall performance will improve.	.853	3.75 .653

Notes: n=126

Kaiser-Meyer-Olkin measure of sampling adequacy = .827; Total variance explained = 70.982

*EFA: Exploratory factor analyses (Principal component analysis with Varimax rotation) >0.50

[a] According to the exploratory factor analysis results, the factor loading was found insignificant or unsuitable therefore bold-type measurement items were excluded from the scale.

The KMO value was found to be 0.83, which is higher than the threshold value of 0.70, and Bartlett's sphericity test was 0.00, indicating significance, deeming the items suitable for exploratory factor analysis. Factors affecting the adoption of digital transformation, focusing on circular economy principles of expectations and perceptions of the performance of manufacturers' businesses, have been dealt with through exploratory factor analysis. After eliminating insignificant and single items, suitable items in the groups were placed individually under factors. As a result, 36 items and 10 factors remained in the dataset (presented in Table 3). All constructs in the model have Cronbach's alphas above the threshold value of 0.70.

Findings

Before beginning the statistical analysis, all measurement items for each latent variable were aggregated and transformed into composite variables based on their mean values. Then, correlation analysis was performed using these composite variables to assess the relationships among the various components of the proposed research model. Table 4 illustrates that certain variables (particularly antecedent factors) are not correlated with corporate and sustainability performance. Based on the interpretation of the correlation coefficient scores, the proposed model was modified, as illustrated in Figure 2, to investigate the direct and indirect interaction effects of the variables.

Table 4. Correlation coefficients

	Produc'	CFP	CPS	Ind'4.0	Digital	PES	SC Pr'	Sustain'	Coop'
Logistics Opr. Pr'	.273**	.157 ^{NS}	.104 ^{NS}	.198*	.298**	.331**	.255**	-.073 ^{NS}	.092 ^{NS}
Production Operational Pr'		.376**	.457**	.556**	.617**	.601**	.138 ^{NS}	-.059 ^{NS}	-.15 ^{NS}
Carbon Footprint Performance			.477**	.368**	.318**	.565**	.285**	.316**	-.05 ^{NS}
Establishing of Cyber-Physical Systems				.605**	.461**	.498**	.269**	.155 ^{NS}	.129 ^{NS}
Facilities for Gaining Industry 4.0 Technologies					.533**	.721**	.324**	.213*	.120 ^{NS}
Obstacles to the Digital Transformation System Design						.488**	.337**	.089 ^{NS}	.088 ^{NS}
Efficiency of Performance Evaluation System							.324**	.167 ^{NS}	-.02 ^{NS}
Improving Supply Chain Process Performance								.303**	.375**
Appropriateness of Sustainability Performance									.329**

Notes: ** Correlation is significant at the 0.01 (2-tailed Pearson correlation), * Correlation is significant at the 0.05 (2-tailed Pearson correlation), ^{NS} Not Significant.

The research model considers perceived operational performance variables and potential performance expectations from Industry 4.0 technologies as antecedent factors. The model employs the efficiency of a firm's performance evaluation system as a consecutive factor due to its current, problem-solving-oriented, and productivity-enhancing characteristics. The correlation analysis results support this assertion, with coefficients significantly ranging from .331 to .721 between the antecedent factors and the efficiency of the performance evaluation system variable.

In conclusion, this research model addresses firms' performance efficiency improvements resulting from antecedent and consecutive factors. The correlation coefficient values indicate that the effectiveness of the performance evaluation system is only substantially correlated with improvements in supply chain performance, and not with sustainable or overall corporate performance. Moreover, improving supply chain implementation and increasing sustainability performance demonstrate strong correlations with the expected corporate performance variable.

Figure 2 shows that establishing a holistic structure significantly changes the interaction between variables. For instance, cyber-physical systems and obstacles to digital transformation are negatively linked to a firm's performance evaluation system, despite the positive and significant relationship observed in the correlation analysis.

Figure 2. Path analysis of the significant levels of the modified research model

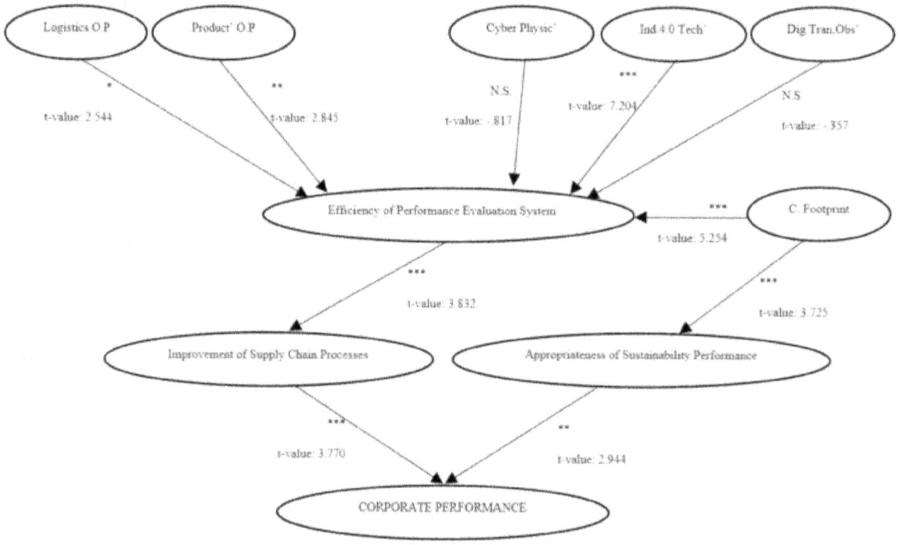

Additionally, there was a significant relationship between perceived operational performance, such as logistics ($p<0.05$ level; Beta=0.14), production ($p<0.01$ level; Beta=0.14), carbon footprint ($p<0.001$ level; Beta=0.35), and gaining Industry 4.0 technologies ($p<0.001$ level; Beta=0.49) on the firm's performance evaluation system. The gain of Industry 4.0 technologies, has the strongest interaction effect on a firm's performance evaluation system, where a one-unit increase in this factor can improve the performance system efficiency by half a unit.

Correspondingly, the efficiency of a firm's performance system ($p<0.001$ level; Beta=0.21) positively relates to the improvement in the supply chain process. Moreover, the second strongest effect observed in this model was between carbon footprint performance and sustainability performance. The results of the path analysis indicate that a unit change in carbon footprint performance ($p<0.001$ level; Beta=0.42) may increase the link between an organization's sustainability performance by approximately half a unit.

In the last phase of the proposed generic model, both factors are strongly related to corporate performance: improvement in supply chain performance ($p<0.001$ level; Beta=0.39) and appropriateness of sustainability performance ($p<0.01$ level; Beta=0.17). In conclusion, within the framework of this research model, improving supply chain performance in collaboration with supply chain partners by leveraging circular economy principles and digital transformation strategies is the most effective factor for improving corporate performance.

As corporate performance is the dependent variable, this study also investigates the indirect effects of antecedents and consecutive factors. This study found that the carbon footprint (approximately Beta=0.11) has a far stronger impact on corporate performance than the performance system (approximately Beta=0.10) if considering the indirect effects of antecedent factors.

This study also aims to address two secondary research questions: First, is there a difference in firms' level of internationalization in Turkey, in terms of foreign partnerships or export intensity, when compared with findings from the proposed generic research model? Second, if such a difference exists, how should these differences be interpreted? To explore these questions, companies in the dataset are divided into two groups based on their fully domestic capital status, despite having foreign capital partnerships or management collaborations with foreign firms. Additionally, the study investigates whether the degree of internationalization varies for companies with export intensity above or below 50%, compared to the results of the generic research model. The comparative results matrix is presented in Table 5.

Table 5 demonstrates that firms operating with full domestic capital ownership (n = 89) and firms with export shares exceeding 50% (n = 58) achieve results comparable to those of the generic research model. However, it is noteworthy that, in contrast to the generic model, the levels of statistical significance yield somewhat lower results.

In the dataset of foreign investment companies (n = 37), the relationship between the effectiveness of the performance evaluation system and the expectation of improving supply chain processes was statistically significant at $P < 0.10$. Similarly, in the dataset with an export rate of less than 50% (n = 68), the relationship between the expected benefits of establishing cyber-physical systems and the improvement of the performance evaluation system also yielded valid results at the $P < 0.10$ level.

The key finding from the perspective of internationalization is that the ability to acquire Industry 4.0 technologies is a critical factor in ensuring the effectiveness of the performance evaluation system of domestic capital production enterprises ($p<0.01$ level; Beta = 0.53). In light of this result, managers of Turkish manufacturing enterprises who participated in the survey appear to have high expectations for the integration of AI-supported autonomous technology into their business processes. Additionally, the performance of supply chain processes is strongly supported statistically ($p<0.01$ level; Beta = 0.21).

Table 5. Matrix for comparing participants' internationalization levels

Factors Paths	Foreign Shareholder Partnership				Exporting Volume Proportion			
	Having foreign investments (n=37)		Fully local capital owned (n=89)		More than 50% (n=58)		Less than 50% (n=68)	
	t-value	P level	t-value	P level	t-value	P level	t-value	P level
Logistics O.P. → P.E.S.	1,360	N.S.	2,047	**	2,614	**	1,460	N.S.
Production O.P. → P.E.S.	1,501	N.S.	2,380	**	,862	N.S.	3,062	***
CFP performance → P.E.S.	2,932	***	4,153	***	4,071	***	3,643	***
Cyber-Physical Systems → P.E.S.	-,808	N.S.	**-,276**	N.S.	,696	N.S.	*-1,699*	*
Industry 4.0 Techs' → P.E.S.	2,243	**	6,894	***	2,717	***	7,593	***
Obstacle Digital Transf' → P.E.S.	-,249	N.S.	**-,086**	N.S.	,424	N.S.	-,503	N.S.
P.E.S. → Improvement SC	1,875	*	3,259	***	2,334	**	3,101	***
CFP perf' → Sustainability	3,117	***	2,670	***	4,302	***	1,503	N.S.
Improvement SC → Corporate P.	3,079	***	2,651	***	2,890	***	2,501	**
Sustainability → Corporate P.	,633	N.S.	2,289	**	2,134	**	2,093	**

Notes: *** Path factors relations are significant at the $P < 0.01$ level, **P value is significant at the $P < 0.05$ level, *P value is significant at the $P < 0.10$ level, and N.S. means is Not Significant at the $P > 0.10$ level.

Another factor for which locally owned-capital production companies have high expectations is their carbon footprint performance. It is anticipated that both the effectiveness of the overall performance evaluation system (p<0.01 level; Beta=0.32) and sustainability performance (p<0.01 level; Beta=0.35) will have a positive impact. A similar trend is observed in businesses with export shares exceeding 50%. The effectiveness of the overall performance evaluation system (p<0.01 level; Beta=0.42) and sustainability performance (p<0.01 level; Beta=0.73) are expected to have a positive impact. A significant factor contributing to this notable result could be the increased awareness of the carbon footprints generated by persistent demand from the markets of developed countries.

A significant finding emerges from the analysis of export rates among manufacturers with export rates below 50% (n = 68). The primary observation from this dataset indicates that no statistically significant differences have been identified between the perception of logistical operational performance and the effectiveness of the performance evaluation system. This outcome is consistent with the understanding that export-oriented firms place greater emphasis on logistics performance perceptions. Consequently, it is logical to conclude that no statistically significant relationship is observed in Table 5 between the effectiveness of the performance evaluation system and logistics operations performance from the perspective of firms that operate with a more local market orientation.

A statistical relationship has been identified in the dataset of firms with lower export rates that operate with a local market focus regarding the expectation of influencing the performance evaluation system through investment in cyber-physical systems, notwithstanding a low significance level. However, there exists a negative relationship ($p<0.10$ level; Beta = -0.13), which aligns with the findings of the generic model. This suggests that production enterprises in Turkey have not yet fully recognized the necessity of cyber-physical systems and have maintained the perception that such substantial digital transformation would disrupt their operational processes.

Despite the limited sample size ($n = 37$), foreign-shareholder enterprises demonstrate results that contradict the generic model. The key finding is that no significant relationship has been identified between the effectiveness of the performance evaluation system and the operational performance of logistics and production in these companies, nor between sustainability performance and corporate performance. Although taking a broad view, these results may not be feasible, it is essential to consider that differences in management experience and approaches might be the underlying cause of this outcome.

DISCUSSION

Initial observations suggest that firms from emerging markets face challenges when managing the risks and expectations associated with integrating Industry 4.0 technologies into their businesses. To understand managers' perspectives on radical transformations, this study employed a scientific methodology to explain these perspectives. The complex research model of this investigation aims to clarify and simplify the understanding of the interrelationships between circular economy principles and the adoption of Industry 4.0 technologies on the performance factors of manufacturers.

Previous studies have indicated that companies in emerging markets are reluctant to invest in radically transformative digital technologies (Dalenogare et al. 2018). The study's path analysis verifies this interpretation by revealing the absence of a statistically significant relationship between cyber-physical systems and performance factors, as considered in the research model. This is a notable finding of the present study. This result represents the perspectives of strategic decision-makers, executives, or managers responsible for operational processes in Turkish manufacturing companies.

Another significant outcome of this research is the absence of a correlation between logistics operational performance and environmental criteria, such as carbon footprint and sustainability performance. This reflects the perspective of Turkish manufacturing executives on logistics operations, perceiving them as outbound activities outsourced to third-party logistics service providers.

However, Turkish manufacturers' managers must consider the corporate logistics operations associated with their production and distribution processes and assume responsibility for their improvement. According to this study, Turkish manufacturing firms prioritize supply chain operations through digitalization, environmental concerns, and comprehensive performance evaluations. As a result, an executive's ability to increase a company's success through the performance of its operational carbon footprint and the appropriateness of its sustainability practices is critical.

The results also indicate no relationship between corporate performance and performance evaluation systems, suggesting the need for reform. Turkish production companies must give importance to resolving operational process problems by strategically managing their performance evaluation systems. Companies address customer order issues on a case-by-case basis to avoid consumer dissatisfaction or decrease profit margins rather than offering long-term solutions. The performance evaluation system should be implemented in full accordance with the Kaizen philosophy, which focuses on ensuring efficiency, producing permanent solutions to problems, and updating performance criteria.

In emerging countries, TQM Kaizen activities are often fragmented and separated from operations (Sichinsambwe et al., 2023). Companies in these markets frequently fail to integrate continuous operational excellence into their evaluation processes. This research shows a negative link between implementing costly reform projects, like digital transformations involving autonomous cyber-physical systems, and performance evaluation systems. It is obvious that the performance evaluation system needs to undergo strategic reform to offer a sustainable solution to operational challenges.

In addition to the generic research model analysis, further analyses conducted on a group basis also support this perspective. Research indicates that fully domestically funded manufacturers tend to adopt Industry 4.0 technologies more intensely than foreign-partnered ones. This suggests that their technological investments are primarily focused on improving their efficiency. However, the acquisition of solely the Industry 4.0 technologies is insufficient. The critical factor is ensuring that technological investment has a significant impact on business models. Consequently, it is imperative to strategically address the barriers to digital transformation and manage change comprehensively while establishing autonomously operating cyber-physical systems. In this context, executives should be familiar with the fact that managing change within a holistic framework is inherently both a striving-intensive process and substantially more resource-intensive in terms of investment.

Another interesting finding is the statistically significant relationship between the perceived performance of logistics and production operations and the performance evaluation system. This is based on respondents' opinions when comparing firms with export rates above 50% with those with lower rates. For manufacturers with a more export-oriented approach, evaluating the performance of production operations becomes less significant because they focus more on assessing logistics performance. While this outcome aligns with the individual conditions of these companies, it is also necessary that their production operational performance is not overlooked. A lack of a systemic approach results in a lack of integrity. This finding indicates that manufacturers in Turkey limit themselves to a narrow perspective, instead of holistically adopting a broader vision in their management approach.

One of the interesting and notable findings from the group analyses is the absence of a statistically significant correlation between the sustainability performance of foreign capital and joint management firms and their corporate performance. This unexpected outcome suggests that sustainability performance may exert a more indirect influence on corporate performance than mentioned in previous studies. An alternative interpretation is that foreign clients have imposed sustainability performance requirements on Turkish capital firms; consequently, this may be perceived by managers of Turkish capital-owned companies as directly impacting market share and profitability.

However, for firms that are more focused on the domestic market and have an export share of less than 50%, no significant relationship was found between their carbon footprint performance and sustainability performance. The main reason that comes to mind for this surprising outcome is that the carbon footprint issue is primarily a concern for firms exporting to the European Union market, so respondents may not be familiar with this concept. Therefore, their responses may not reflect the statistical relationships between the two variables.

Eventually, this study finds that Turkish manufacturers believe that enhancing corporate performance requires focusing on environmentally oriented performance criteria aligned with global competition and improving supply chain performance and communication through modern technology. It is important to note that although previous studies (Lei et al., 2023) strongly suggest that integrating cyber-physical systems can significantly support the implementation of the circular economy, this study does not demonstrate a statistically significant relationship between these variables. These differing results may stem from differences in the content of the studies. Therefore, future empirical studies should carefully evaluate the variables and measurement instruments by comparing experiences from surveys of relevant subjects.

CONCLUSION AND IMPLICATIONS

This study examines how Turkish manufacturing firms integrate circular economy principles with Industry 4.0. Based on these concepts, this study seeks to create a Turkish competitiveness index model. The main contributions of this study are summarized below. First, it identifies managers' perceptions and expectations in manufacturing firms aimed at world-class competitiveness. To achieve this, it is crucial to gather insights from relevant individuals to understand how digital transformation can reform operational processes and help Turkish manufacturers enhance their competitive strength in the export markets. The literature highlights how Industry 4.0 can benefit operational excellence through cyber-physical systems and performance evaluation systems (de Mattos Nascimento et al., 2024). However, research indicates that Turkish manufacturing enterprises have not yet fully developed this awareness.

This empirical study also fills a critical gap in the literature by conducting field surveys that evaluate the interrelationships between Industry 4.0 and circular economy principles, which are underrepresented in current studies. By including various industries and exporting manufacturers in Turkey, this research model incorporates broader factor dimensions and measurement scale items than previous research, to improve its comprehensiveness.

A review of the literature reveals that studies conducted with large sample sizes (Dalenogare et al., 2018; Khan et al., 2021) examine these two main themes concerning firms' organizational performance (operational, financial, or environmental) or their potential expectations. In more comprehensive recent empirical studies, for instance, Ghaithan et al. (n = 486 and 6 items for each main theme) and Rehman et al. (n = 232 and 10 items for each main theme) also addressed the impact of these two concepts on sustainability performance. Therefore, following the studies mentioned earlier, this study focuses on how firms can adapt these approaches to the existing operational system rather than directly examining the relationships between the two concepts. Consequently, a comprehensive and complex structure was developed to evaluate manufacturing companies' effectiveness and competitiveness, resulting in a relatively low survey response rate.

The findings of this study provide valuable insights into how managers perceive the impact of these technologies on corporate performance, which can guide organizations' future strategic decisions. This research highlights the challenges faced by manufacturers in emerging markets in managing risks and expectations related to digital transformation, providing a framework for navigating these changes effectively. This paper contributes significantly to understanding how Turkish manufacturers can leverage Industry 4.0 and circular economy principles to enhance their operational efficiency and corporate performance in a competitive global market. The findings provide a foundation for both academic investigations and practical applications in the manufacturing sector.

This manuscript proposes and implements a research model that illustrates the interrelationships between the aforementioned theories and concepts. The model explores executives' attitudes toward the circular economy and Industry 4.0, and evaluates their expectations regarding the impact on corporate competitiveness. This framework serves as a foundation for assessing how digital transformation, supply chain network redesign, and sustainability can significantly improve corporate performance. In conclusion, the findings indicate a cautious yet potentially evolving attitude toward Industry 4.0 among Turkish manufacturers, which highlights both challenges and avenues for further investigation.

Limitations and Further Research Directions

Future research should address limitations in the current study, such as the small sample size and the lack of representation of Industry 4.0 technology tools and circular economy principles. Thus, researchers should investigate the maturity levels of Industry 4.0 and incorporate circular economy principles as a separate variable, following Ghaithan et al.'s (2023). Data collection should be conducted using computer-aided telephone interviews to increase participation rates. It is also recommended that the scale instruments be more precise and clearer so as not to confuse the participants when responding to the questionnaire.

During the study's design, actively exporting Turkish manufacturing companies were chosen as the unit of analysis, and managers who made decisions or experts in charge of these firms' operational procedures were chosen as participants. Therefore, scale questions and research models were created to measure respondents' expectations or views of pertinent aspects. It is important to remember that the conclusions of this research are based on the opinions and thoughts of the participants rather than on tangible data. If actual performance data can be acquired, then the development of a research design for future studies based on this data may be useful.

This study investigates the impact of Industry 4.0 technologies on firm performance in emerging markets such as Turkey. This research used composite variables to represent scale items and investigate the interactions between elements. Future studies should use latent variables, and at least 200 observations are required for confirmatory factor analysis.

This study examined the effects of links between antecedent and consecutive factors within the framework of pathway interactions. Testing this link for mediating effects, as in Al-Swidi et al. (2023) and Rehman et al. (2024), might be more advantageous. In this regard, scientific evidence should be used in further studies to support research hypotheses that show how variables relate to one another.

REFERENCES

Agyabeng-Mensah, Y., Afum, E., & Ahenkorah, E. (2020). Exploring financial performance and green logistics management practices: Examining the mediating influences of market, environmental and social performances. *Journal of Cleaner Production*, 258, XX–XX. DOI: 10.1016/j.jclepro.2020.120613

Ajmal, M. M., Khan, M., Hussain, M., & Helo, P. (2018). Conceptualizing and incorporating social sustainability in the business world. *International Journal of Sustainable Development and World Ecology*, 25(4), 327–339. DOI: 10.1080/13504509.2017.1408714

Al-Swidi, A. K., Hair, J. F., & Al-Hakimi, M. A. (2023). Sustainable development-oriented regulatory and competitive pressures to shift toward a circular economy: The role of environmental orientation and Industry 4.0 technologies. *Business Strategy and the Environment*, 32(7), 4782–4797. DOI: 10.1002/bse.3393

Alexandro, R., & Basrowi, B. (2024). The influence of macroeconomic infrastructure on supply chain smoothness and national competitiveness and its implications on a country's economic growth: Evidence from BRICS countries. *Uncertain Supply Chain Management*, 12(1), 167–180. DOI: 10.5267/j.uscm.2023.10.007

Atif, S. (2023). Analysing the alignment between circular economy and Industry 4.0 nexus with Industry 5.0 era: An integrative systematic literature review. *Sustainable Development (Bradford)*, 31(4), 2155–2175. DOI: 10.1002/sd.2542

Awan, U., Sroufe, R., Godinho Filho, M., & Shahbaz, M. (2021). Industry 4.0 and the circular economy: A literature review and recommendations for future research. *Business Strategy and the Environment*, 30(1), 2038–2060. DOI: 10.1002/bse.2731

Bag, S., & Pretorius, J. H. C. (2022). Relationships between Industry 4.0, sustainable manufacturing and circular economy: Proposal of a research framework. *The International Journal of Organizational Analysis*, 30(4), 864-898.

Behl, A., Singh, R., Pereira, V., & Laker, B. (2023). Analysis of Industry 4.0 and circular economy enablers: A step towards resilient sustainable operations management. *Technological Forecasting and Social Change*, 189. DOI: 10.1016/j.techfore.2023.122363

Benešová, A., Baslb, J., Tupa, J., & Steiner, F. (2021). Design of a business readiness model to realise a green Industry 4.0 company. *International Journal of Computer Integrated Manufacturing*, 34(9), 920–932. DOI: 10.1080/0951192X.2021.1946858

Benítez-Márquez, M. D., Sánchez-Teba, E. M., & Coronado-Maldonado, I. (2022). An alternative index to the global competitiveness index. *PLoS One*, 17(3), XX–XX. DOI: 10.1371/journal.pone.0265045 PMID: 35312691

Cannas, V. G., Ciano, M. P., Saltalamacchia, M., & Secchi, R. (2024). Artificial intelligence in supply chain and operations management: A multiple case study research. *International Journal of Production Research*, 62(9), 3333–3360. DOI: 10.1080/00207543.2023.2232050

Cousins, P. D., Lawson, B., Petersen, K. J., & Fugate, B. (2019). Investigating green supply chain management practices and performance: The moderating roles of supply chain ecocentricity and traceability. *International Journal of Operations & Production Management*, 39(5), 767–786. DOI: 10.1108/IJOPM-11-2018-0676

Dalenogare, L. S., Benitez, G. B., Ayala, N. F., & Frank, A. G. (2018). The expected contribution of Industry 4.0 technologies for industrial performance. *International Journal of Production Economics*, 204, 383–394. DOI: 10.1016/j.ijpe.2018.08.019

de Jesus Pacheco, D. A., & Schougaard, T. (2024). Operational performance improvement in manual assembly lines: A case study in Denmark and conceptual model for quick and long-term wins. *International Journal of Productivity and Performance Management*, 73(6), 1689–1718. DOI: 10.1108/IJPPM-11-2022-0566

de Mattos Nascimento, D. L., de Oliveira-Dias, D., Moyano-Fuentes, J., Maqueira Marín, J. M., & Garza-Reyes, J. A. (2024). Interrelationships between circular economy and Industry 4.0: A research agenda for sustainable supply chains. *Business Strategy and the Environment*, 33(2), 575–596. DOI: 10.1002/bse.3502

Dogangun, I., Oral, E., Akkartal, E., & Turegun, N. (2023). Exploring the multifractality in the precious metal market. *Fluctuation and Noise Letters*, 22(4), XX–XX. DOI: 10.1142/S0219477523400096

George, D., & Mallery, P. (2019). *IBM SPSS Statistics 26 Step by Step: A simple guide and reference*. Routledge. DOI: 10.4324/9780429056765

Ghaithan, A. M., Alshammakhi, Y., Mohammed, A., & Mazher, K. M. (2023). Integrated impact of circular economy, Industry 4.0, and lean manufacturing on sustainability performance of manufacturing firms. *International Journal of Environmental Research and Public Health*, 20(6), XX–XX. DOI: 10.3390/ijerph20065119 PMID: 36982026

Gögus, C. G., & Özer, G. (2014). The roles of technology acceptance model antecedents and switching cost on accounting software use. *Academy of Information and Management Sciences Journal*, 17(1), 1–24.

Götz, M. (2020). Cluster role in Industry 4.0 – a pilot study from Germany. *Competitiveness Review*, 31(1), 54–82. DOI: 10.1108/CR-10-2019-0091

Horváth, D., & Szabó, R. Z. (2019). Driving forces and barriers of Industry 4.0: Do multinational and small and medium-sized companies have equal opportunities? *Technological Forecasting and Social Change*, 146, 119–132. DOI: 10.1016/j.techfore.2019.05.021

Jain, N. K., Panda, A., & Choudhary, P. (2020). Institutional pressures and circular economy performance: The role of environmental management system and organizational flexibility in oil and gas sector. *Business Strategy and the Environment*, 29(8), 3509–3525. DOI: 10.1002/bse.2593

Karakadilar, I. S. (2023). A scale development study for Turkish exporting industries oriented to the Industry 4.0 and circular economy implementations. *Journal of Economics Business and Political Researches*, 21(8), 403–420.

Khan, S. A. R., Razzaq, A., Yu, Z., & Miller, S. (2021). Industry 4.0 and circular economy practices: A new era business strategies for environmental sustainability. *Business Strategy and the Environment*, 30(8), 4001–4014. DOI: 10.1002/bse.2853

Kirchherr, J., Reike, D., & Hekkert, M. (2017). Conceptualizing the circular economy: An analysis of 114 definitions. *Resources, Conservation and Recycling*, 127, 221–232. DOI: 10.1016/j.resconrec.2017.09.005

Kristjánsdóttir, H. (2017). National and regional competitiveness: Country competitiveness an empirical study. *Baltic Region*, 9(2), 31–44. DOI: 10.5922/2079-8555-2017-2-3

Lei, Z., Cai, S., Cui, L., Wu, L., & Liu, Y. (2023). How do different Industry 4.0 technologies support certain circular economy practices? *Industrial Management & Data Systems*, 123(4), 1220–1251. DOI: 10.1108/IMDS-05-2022-0270

Lindenmeier, J., & Tscheulin, D. K. (2008). The effects of inventory control and denied boarding on customer satisfaction: The case of capacity-based airline revenue management. *Tourism Management*, 29(1), 32–43. DOI: 10.1016/j.tourman.2007.04.004

Liu, L., Song, W., & Liu, Y. (2023). Leveraging digital capabilities toward a circular economy: Reinforcing sustainable supply chain management with Industry 4.0 technologies. *Computers & Industrial Engineering*, 178, XX–XX. DOI: 10.1016/j.cie.2023.109113

Lopes de Sousa Jabbour, A. B., Jabbour, C. J. C., Godinho Filho, M., & Roubaud, D. (2018). Industry 4.0 and the circular economy: A proposed research agenda and original roadmap for sustainable operations. *Annals of Operations Research*, 270(1), 273–286. DOI: 10.1007/s10479-018-2772-8

Masood, T., & Sonntag, P. (2020). Industry 4.0: Adoption challenges and benefits for SMEs. *Computers in Industry*, 121, XX–XX. DOI: 10.1016/j.compind.2020.103261

Mishra, R., Singh, R. K., & Govindan, K. (2022). Barriers to the adoption of circular economy practices in micro, small and medium enterprises: Instrument development, measurement and validation. *Journal of Cleaner Production*, 351, XX–XX. DOI: 10.1016/j.jclepro.2022.131389

Moktadir, M. A., Ali, S. M., Kusi-Sarpong, S., & Shaikh, M. A. A. (2018). Assessing challenges for implementing Industry 4.0: Implications for process safety and environmental protection. *Process Safety and Environmental Protection*, 117, 730–741. DOI: 10.1016/j.psep.2018.04.020

Naik, S., Sony, M., Antony, J., McDermott, O., Tortorella, G. L., & Jayaraman, R. (2024). Operational excellence framework for sustainability in the organisation: A design science approach. *Production Planning and Control*, 35(11), 1215–1231. DOI: 10.1080/09537287.2023.2165188

Nascimento, D. L. M., Alencastro, V., Quelhas, O. L. G., Caiado, R. G. G., Garza-Reyes, J. A., Rocha-Lona, L., & Tortorella, G. (2019). Exploring Industry 4.0 technologies to enable circular economy practices in a manufacturing context: A business model proposal. *Journal of Manufacturing Technology Management*, 30(3), 607–627. DOI: 10.1108/JMTM-03-2018-0071

Nguyen, X. T., & Luu, Q. K. (2020). Factors affecting adoption of Industry 4.0 by small and medium-sized enterprises: A case in Ho Chi Minh City, Vietnam. *The Journal of Asian Finance, Economics and Business*, 7(6), 255–264. DOI: 10.13106/jafeb.2020.vol7.no6.255

Pasupuleti, V., Thuraka, B., Kodete, C. S., & Malisetty, S. (2024). Enhancing supply chain agility and sustainability through machine learning: Optimization techniques for logistics and inventory management. *Logistics (Basel)*, 8(3), XX–XX. DOI: 10.3390/logistics8030073

Rehman, S., Hamdan, Y. H., & Sindhu, M. (2024). Impact of Industry 4.0 on firms' sustainable development in the GCC economies: A mediation and moderation approach. *Brazilian Journal of Operations & Production Management*, 21(4), XX–XX. DOI: 10.14488/BJOPM.2166.2024

Sakkthivel, A. M., & Ramu, N. J. (2018). Investigating the gender influence on technology adoption model towards smart phones-evidences from emerging economies. *International Journal of Business Excellence*, 16(1), 35–46. DOI: 10.1504/IJBEX.2018.094570

Sheng, H., Feng, T., & Liu, L. (2023). The influence of digital transformation on low-carbon operations management practices and performance: Does CEO ambivalence matter? *International Journal of Production Research*, 61(18), 6215–6229. DOI: 10.1080/00207543.2022.2088426

Sichinsambwe, C., Simasiku, P. L., Sikombe, S., & Nyimbili, H. (2023). Kaizen practices and performance improvement in Zambian manufacturing companies. *Cogent Engineering*, 10(1), XX–XX. DOI: 10.1080/23311916.2023.2183590

Singh, S. (2003). Simple Random Sampling. In *Advanced Sampling Theory with Applications*. Springer. DOI: 10.1007/978-94-007-0789-4_2

Sun, X., & Wang, X. (2022). Modeling and analyzing the impact of the internet of things-based Industry 4.0 on circular economy practices for sustainable development: Evidence from the food processing industry of China. *Frontiers in Psychology*, 13, XX–XX. DOI: 10.3389/fpsyg.2022.866361 PMID: 35548486

Ustun, K., & Akkartal, E. (2024). The Role of Logistics in Decent Work and Economic Growth. In *Effective Logistics for Sustainable Development Goals* (pp. 48–78). IGI Global. DOI: 10.4018/979-8-3693-7071-1.ch003

Wong, L. W., Tan, G. W. H., Ooi, K. B., Lin, B., & Dwivedi, Y. K. (2024). Artificial intelligence-driven risk management for enhancing supply chain agility: A deep-learning based dual-stage PLS-SEM-ANN analysis. *International Journal of Production Research*, 62(15), 5535–5555. DOI: 10.1080/00207543.2022.2063089

KEY TERMS AND DEFINITIONS

Carbon Footprints Performance: Low-carbon emissions operations involve integrating carbon efficiency into business processes through planning, implementation, and control. This approach is crucial for businesses struggling to reduce carbon emissions and address climate change. To manage emissions effectively, companies should leverage advanced technologies and redesign their operations for optimization. Procuring equipment with low-carbon emission machinery is essential for reducing emissions across life cycles. Improving operational processes enhances the efficiency of low-carbon activities. In logistics, transportation, and distribution, effective route planning and the establishment of green warehouses powered by environmentally friendly energy are necessary to cut emissions. By conducting low-carbon operations, organizations can comply with legal regulations and meet environmental standards while continuing their activities.

Circular Economy Principles: This concept focuses on minimizing the use of all the resources that Mother Nature gave to humanity, increasing efficiency, and reducing waste. The fundamental principles that need to be adopted for its implementation are: keeping resources within a closed loop (i.e., reducing the use of raw materials from nature), lessening waste through recycling and reuse, and developing sustainable and innovative business models. The six actions that must be taken to implement these principles are regenerate, share, optimize, loop, virtualize, and exchange. Thus, preventing waste allows us to achieve the goals of resource efficiency, operational cost reduction, and environmental pollution reduction. The circular economy is a promising framework that seeks to establish sustainable business practices.

Corporate Performance: Encompasses the evaluation of an organization's success through financial and non-financial measures, which is influenced by internal and external factors. Key indicators include financial metrics, corporate reputation from the perspective of society, economic-environmental-social sustainability, and customer satisfaction in the marketplace. Financial metrics include revenue, expenses, profitability, and ratios such as return on equity. Performance can be examined at national and organizational levels, with national indicators including value addition to the national eco-system and employment and organizational indicators comprising profit margins and competitive position in the marketplace. Internal factors affecting performance include organizational leadership, strategy, and efficiency, while external factors encompass market conditions and regulations. Effective management of these factors is essential for long-term success.

Cyber-Physical System Technologies: With cyber-physical systems, it is possible to acquire and process large data flows in real-time, both from internal organizational stakeholders and the global data pool. This data is then prepared for managers to use or integrated into operational processes via autonomous machines in routine tasks. Essentially, this digital management approach learns, self-improves, and operates with agility, particularly in production and business processes. In implementing these technologies, the Internet of Things (IoT) acts as an intelligent network, connecting objects through sensors in equipment like machines to facilitate information sharing. Cloud technology enables communication between machines and information sharing.

Big data technology extracts and analyses the necessary information from a data pool using various algorithms. As forms of artificial intelligence, machine learning and deep learning increase the efficiency of business processes through applications such as real-time detection and intelligent decision-making. The integration and support of all these technologies create what is known as cyber-physical systems.

Industry 4.0 Technology Tools: This concept refers to experiencing the fourth wave of the Industrial Revolution, which is characterized by the complete digitization of business processes. This approach aims to ensure that all elements, including objective units (things) used in all stages of business processes within the organization, are in communication with each other, that real-time data flow is established, and thus outputs are obtained most efficiently. At the focal point are machines and a production system engaged in autonomous activities, enabling technology to facilitate tasks and minimize human intervention. The Industry 4.0 technological tools generally defined in the literature are mentioned below. Internet of Things (IoT) / Sensors / Wireless Networks / Embedded Systems; Big Data Analytics; Cloud Computing / Fog Technologies; Artificial Intelligence / Automated Robots / Machine Learning / Deep Learning; Autonomous Technology for Predictive-Maintenance Applications of Machines; Digital Twins / Simulation; Augmented Reality / Virtual Reality; Wearable Smart Equipment Technologies / RFID Radio Frequency Readers; Blockchain Technology; “ERP or MRP” Computer Software Enterprise Resource Planning Systems; Devices Process Control with Smart Grid / Digital Energy Tracking; Layered Manufacturing with “3D Printing”. The ability of an organization to effectively integrate and use more than 10 of these listed tools in its operations is defined as the Industry 4.0 maturity level.

Operational Excellence: This concept involves the systematic and continuous improvement of processes, practices, and capabilities to achieve superior performance. It is crucial to create a robust value chain and provide a competitive edge to organizations. By regularly updating and refining processes, organizations can adapt to changing market conditions and achieve long-term success. Operational excellence helps create value chains by optimizing resources, reducing defects, eliminating waste, speeding up market response with faster cycle times, and improving performance through the effective implementation of a Kaizen culture. It strengthens an organization's market position by enabling the creation and tracking of performance indicators. Increased operational efficiency provides a competitive advantage, allowing organizations to compete effectively in terms of quality and price without compromising the pricing of products and services. As a result, organizations can gain significant market share and maintain leadership positions, because consistent, high-quality, and reliable work fosters customer loyalty.

Operational Performance: This notion expresses the effectiveness and efficiency of an organization's operations in achieving its goals. The ability to effectively sustain a business model by meeting quality standards, managing costs, and responding to customer needs. It involves skills such as reducing the costs of operational processes to create efficiency, ensuring a quick response to customer needs under appropriate cost conditions, measuring and evaluating the effectiveness of equipment usage, and making revisions if necessary. Furthermore, the optimization of operational performance needs to be supported by the company's individual efforts and all relevant critical supply chain stakeholders. Robust operational performance is a critical element of seamless supply chain management, as it impacts inventory management and delivery systems. For this, regular evaluations should be conducted in an integrated manner, and stakeholder institutions must identify areas for improvement and implement action plans accordingly.

Sustainability Performance: Sustainability is the ability of an organization to meet today's needs without borrowing future generations' natural resources. It has three key dimensions: economic, social, and environmental. Economic sustainability ensures that the organization remains profitable to continue its existence. Social sustainability involves respecting stakeholders' rights, particularly employees, and contributing positively to social development. Environmental sustainability focuses on maintaining and protecting ecological balances. Sustainability performance requires adopting circular economy principles, optimizing resource use, and using advanced autonomous AI to enhance operational efficiency. This approach creates value at every stage of operations and aims to eliminate waste. As a result, it reduces costs, improves employee working conditions and morale, positively impacts the environment by lowering emissions, and enhances the organization's reputation in the community. Ultimately, an organization can achieve long-term viability and competitiveness by improving its sustainability performance.

Chapter 9
The Impact of Store Deals on Consumer Satisfaction:
The Mediating Role of Value Consciousness

Aysun Sahin
https://orcid.org/0000-0003-3285-1232
Duzce University, Turkey

Meral Elci
Gebze Technical University, Turkey

Azize Sahin
Istanbul University, Turkey

ABSTRACT

This study aimed to examine the direct impact of store deal proneness on value consciousness and consumer satisfaction, alongside the mediating effect of value consciousness within these dynamics. Data were collected with an online survey from grocery store consumers in Turkey, and the proposed relationships were analyzed via partial least squares structural equation modeling (PLS-SEM) utilizing a sample comprising 500 Turkish consumers who demonstrate deal proneness and a preference for private labels. The findings reveal that store deal proneness positively affects consumers' value consciousness and satisfaction. Moreover, value consciousness has a positive effect on consumer satisfaction and has a mediating role in the relationship between store deal proneness and satisfaction. The present research provides valuable managerial insights for enhancing consumer satisfaction.

DOI: 10.4018/979-8-3373-2523-1.ch009

The study findings will contribute to retailers developing effective, value-driven strategies by emphasizing store deals that shape consumers' value consciousness and overall satisfaction.

1.INTRODUCTION

Globally, private labels have the highest market penetration in Europe, followed by North America. Although it varies by country, the private label segment generally accounts for 21% to 52% of supermarket sales in Europe (Statista, 2024). The PL market in Turkey is estimated to grow by 8% annually from 2021 to 2025, reflecting a positive outlook for these brands (Euromonitor International, 2021). Consumers are increasingly looking for both higher quality and more affordable alternatives without compromising on quality. Accordingly, private labels in Turkey are gaining strength in the market with innovation and product differentiation strategies.

Private labels are products manufactured, marketed, and sold under the retailer's brand name. They are utilized in a diverse range of consumer goods and are most commonly used in the grocery sector. Consumers are comparing private labels to national brands they have previously purchased or have realized that they may offer superior quality and value, and have therefore turned to private label products.

The economic climate that has inflationary pressures and rising living costs have led consumers to reduce their spending on national brands and instead opt for private label products, in line with their overall cost of living goals. Grocery store deals or discounts play an important role in consumers' grocery store choices, product and brand preferences. Percentage discounts offered by grocery stores to their customers, campaigns such as buy one get one free deals, or various discounts on special days are extremely attractive options for today's consumers. For this reason, grocery stores prioritize sales promotions to increase both their profitability and competitiveness.

Consumers are more price and value-oriented during economic recession (Gordon et al., 2013). Today's grocery stores have realized consumers' changing preferences, behaviors, and attitudes in an extremely competitive landscape (Van Heeerde, Gijbrechts, and Pauwels, 2008). More specifically, during economic downturns or recessions, retailers can prioritize pricing strategies through heavy sales promotions. They prioritize attracting consumers with a diverse sales promotion. As a result, the impact of sale promotions as a store deal on consumers' value consciousness and satisfaction remains unclear.

Within the marketing mix, sales promotion serves as one of the most impactful drivers of short-term consumption behavior (Laroche et al., 2003). The preceding literature has shown that sales promotion can encourage behavioral responses such as brand switching, stocking, expediting purchases, product trials, and spending larger amounts (i.e., Chandon, Wansink, and Laurent, 2000).

Our objective is to address the following research question: How do consumers' deal proneness and value consciousness relate to consumer satisfaction in an emerging market domain, and what managerial implications does this relationship have? Research data (n=500) were collected at the beginning of 2024. Partial least squares structural equation modeling (PLS-SEM) techniques were applied in this research to predict and evaluate the theoretical model, developed based on previous studies and validated through measurement models. This research adds valuable insights to the existing body of literature by exploring how consumers' deal proneness and value consciousness influence their overall satisfaction.

Grocery stores mainly aim to increase consumer satisfaction by improving the perceived value of their private labels. Because, due to the impact of today's economic conditions, consumers' value consciousness is at the forefront. Gaining the satisfaction of consumers as a result of their consumption experiences shaped by their value-conscious behaviors and attitudes is the main priority of grocery stores (Oliver, 1997).

From a managerial perspective, developing and strengthening consumer satisfaction through deal propensity can increase sales in the short term and enhance customer loyalty in the long term. Satisfied consumers are more inclined to return and participate in future sales promotions, creating a virtuous cycle of repeat purchases and deepening store loyalty. This effect is particularly pronounced in competitive grocery markets, where differentiation through price and deals is critical.

This research primarily aims to examine the impact of store deal proneness on value consciousness and consumer satisfaction. Store deal proneness of consumers that we explore shapes consumer behavior, as a result, fostering retailer profitability. This study fills a gap in the existing literature by offering a deeper understanding of consumer satisfaction in the context of private label products. By employing partial least squares structural equation modeling (PLS-SEM) and integrating importance-performance map analysis (IPMA), this research investigates these dynamics.

2. CONCEPTUAL FRAMEWORK

2.1. Store Deal Proneness and Consumer Satisfaction

Store deals play a critical role in shaping consumer behavior and increasing retailers' efficiency. Especially during economic turmoil, price-sensitive consumers seek out the best deals, which presents retailers with strategic opportunities. Promotions both attract value-conscious consumers and increase sales. Retailers provide consumers with economic benefits and a sense of satisfaction by increasing perceived value through discounts, loyalty incentives, and free product offers (Ailawadi et al., 2007).

Store deal proneness is described as the inclination of consumers to respond positively to discounts, sales, and coupons (Lichtenstein, Netemeyer, and Burton, 1990). This phenomenon is motivated by consumers' desire to seize deals and their search for both monetary and psychological rewards. Deal-prone consumers are proactive about promotions and discounts, and this segment is particularly likely to take advantage of sales (Lichtenstein et al., 1995; Ailawadi et al., 2001). Sales promotions are a powerful tool in influencing consumer behavior and are divided into two categories: price-driven and non-price-driven. Price-focused promotions focus on discounts, while non-price promotions include coupons and freebies (Laroche et al., 2003).

Consumer satisfaction is linked to the degree to which a product or service fulfills expectations. High customer satisfaction is important to retailers because it increases economic returns and reduces price sensitivity (Oliver, 1997).

The relationship between store deal propensity and consumer satisfaction can be explained by cognitive dissonance and expectation confirmation theories. Consumers are more satisfied when they receive a favorable deal; however, this satisfaction may decrease if the product quality does not meet their expectations (Lichtenstein et al., 1995). Perceived savings and excitement from seizing the opportunity contribute positively to consumer satisfaction (Grewal et al., 1998). Drawing from this rationale, we propose the following hypothesis.

H1: Consumers' store deal proneness has a positive influence on their satisfaction.

2.2. Store Deal Proneness and Value Consciousness

Value consciousness is a crucial factor influencing consumer decision-making within the grocery retail sector, where consumers aim to optimize their purchases according to their expenses, and where private label products are especially important (Ailawadi, Pauwels, and Steenkamp, 2008). Understanding consumers' value conscious attitudes and behaviors is of great importance in producing effective strategies for rapidly changing consumer preferences in markets where competition is intense.

The concepts of consumers' value consciousness and store deal proneness are deeply related to each other. In this direction, they serve each other with behavioral expressions. Since value-conscious consumers aim to obtain maximum benefit in all their purchasing behaviors, they follow and are affected by store deals offerings (Luo, Cheah, Hollebeek, and Lim 2024). Store deal proneness makes consumers care about visiting markets, searching and comparing product prices. This is the driving force of their value consciousness. Approaching store discounts and promotions cognitively makes value-conscious consumers experience a sense of success and winning. Therefore, this process is also a cognitive process (Martinez and Montener, 2006).

Deal-prone consumers engage in a cognitive processing process when evaluating store deals and promotions, because they need to evaluate not only monetary savings but also product quality. In this case, the consumer experiences a cognitive process in which he simultaneously considers both dimensions, price and quality, that shape consumer’s value consciousness (Martínez and Montaner, 2006). Therefore, deal-prone consumers closely examine the product's features and benefits in detail when evaluating the attractiveness of a deal and strengthen their value-seeking behavior (Flacandji and Vlad, 2022; Yazdanparast and Kukar-Kinney 2023).

The theoretical implications of store deal proneness can be associated with the tendency of value-conscious consumers to minimize costs and access attractive product offers. This situation is based on the consumer's general value-conscious mindset. Empirical research suggests that value-conscious consumers feel less pressure to evaluate deals and therefore may be tempted by store promotions and sales (Lichtenstein et al., 1995).

Store deal proneness and value consciousness are related to the consumer's desire to maintain quality at all costs; however, value consciousness is driven by the individual's personal values. Although the two factors have different characteristics, their interaction in the context of consumer behavior highlights how added value can be achieved through various deal mechanisms. Drawing from this rationale, we propose the following hypothesis.

H2: Consumers’ store deal proneness is positively related to value consciousness.

2.3. Consumers’ Value Consciousness and Consumer Satisfaction

Consumers with an increased level of value consciousness are generally more price sensitive. They also focus on overall high quality and benefits that justify the price they pay (Lichtenstein et al., 1990). The satisfaction of these consumers is not only about getting the lowest price, but also about obtaining the optimal balance between cost and value. Therefore, it is likely that value-conscious consumers experience greater satisfaction when they perceive that they are purchasing a quality product at an optimal price, and their overall consumption experience is shaped accordingly (Sahin, 2022). The preceding research shows that perceived value plays a key role in fostering satisfaction (Moriuchi and Takahashi, 2022).

When perceived value meets or exceeds consumers’ expectations, satisfaction is likely to increase, reinforcing the positive relationship between value-consciousness and satisfaction. Drawing from this rationale, we propose the following hypothesis.

H3: Consumers' value consciousness is positively related to their satisfaction.

Figure 1. The proposed model

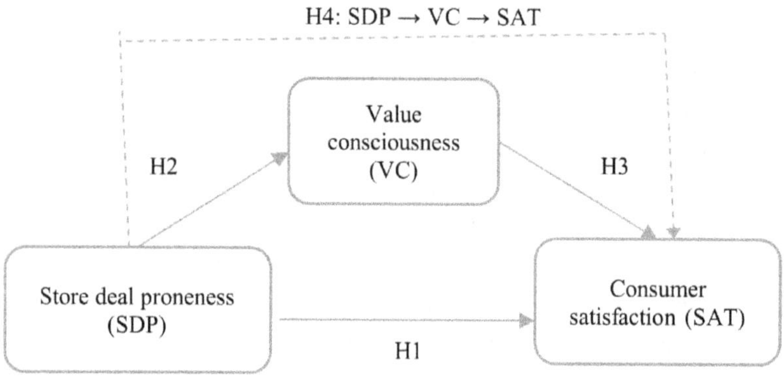

3. METHODOLOGY

3.1. Data Collection

The research data was gathered from supermarket consumers who live in major cities in Turkey. An online survey was used to gather data from 500 participants in this study. The data was collected from customers who prefer private labels of major supermarkets and sales promotions and store deals.

The research participant profile includes 500 supermarket consumers, with 60% of them being shoppers at Migros, 30% at CarrefourSA, and the remaining 10%. The study sample has a diverse mix of consumers across different age categories, educational backgrounds, and cities, with a strong presence in major residential cities, such as Istanbul and Ankara. The details about the sample profile are demonstrated in Table 2.

Table 1. Respondents profile (n=500)

	No.	%		No.	%
Supermarket chain			**Marital**		
Migros	300	60%	Single	300	60%
CarrefourSA	150	30%	Married	200	40%

continued on following page

Table 1. Continued

	No.	%		No.	%
Other	50	10%	**Occupation**		
Age			Student	150	30%
less than 20 years old	50	10%	Primary sector employee	150	30%
20-29 years old	200	40%	Government employee	100	20%
30-39 years old	50	10%	Business owner	25	5%
40-49 years old	50	10%	Retired	25	5%
50-59 years old	50	10%	House wife-not working	50	10%
more than 60 years old	0	0%	**Residencial City**		
Gender			Istanbul	300	60%
Female	300	60%	Ankara	100	20%
Male	200	40%	Izmir	75	15%
Education			Other	25	5%
Primary-secondary edu	55	15%			
High school	125	25%			
University	200	40%			
Graduate	50	10%			

3.2. Measures

All measurement items were taken from previously well-established scales to assure reliability and validity of the research (Hair et al., 2019). The research utilized a five-point Likert scale from 1 (totally disagree) to 5 (totally agree). All measurement items were shown in Table 2.

Table 2. Constructs and indicators

Construct*	**Indicators**	
Value consciousness (Lichtenstein, et.al. 1990)	VC1	Low prices concern me, but product quality is just as important.
	VC2	When I shop for groceries, I compare prices across brands and stores to get the best value.
	VC3	When I buy a product, I look for the highest quality for my money.
	VC4	I want to make sure that the product I buy is worth my money.

continued on following page

Table 2. Continued

Construct*	Indicators	
	VC5	I want to make sure that the product I buy is worth my money.
	VC6	I usually look for a low price, but the product must meet a certain quality.
	VC7	When shopping, I compare unit prices of brands I use frequently. I check the prices to see if they are worth the money I spend.
Store deal proness (Putrevu and Ratchford, 1997; Lichtenstein, Ridgway, and Netemeyer 1993)	SDP1	I follow newspapers, internet, social media or market brochures for discounts and opportunities.
	SDP2	I shop at some markets for their discounts.
	SDP3	I usually shop to catch discounted prices and opportunities.
Satisfaction (Fornell, 1992).	SAT1	How satisfied are you with your favorite? (Very dissatisfied–very satisfied)
	SAT2	How well does your favorite store meet your expectations? (not at all–completely)
	SAT3	Imagine a perfect store. How close is your favorite store close to this ideal? (Not at all close–very close)

a. All items were measured using five-point Likert scales. anchored by "strongly disagree" (1) and "strongly agree" (5) and "very unsatisfied" (1) and "very satisfied" (5).

3.3. Data Analysis

Partial least squares structural equation modelling (PLS-SEM) technique was utilized for data analysis (Chin, 1998; Chin and Newsted 1999). PLS-SEM technique that incorporates factor analysis and linear regressions, facilitates theoretical links between latent constructs to be analyzed via observed data (Hair et al., 2014). conceptual SmartPLS 4.0 software (Ringle et al., 2022) was used to analyze the hypothesized relationship in the model. Data analysis was performed in two stages; (1) a measurement model that connects the observed items to their latent constructs, and (2) a structural model that analyze the relationships among the latent constructs (Ramirez-Correa et al., 2019). Additionally, two advanced techniques were performed for deeper analysis, such as PLSpredict and IPMA procedures.

3.4. Common Method Bias (CMB)

For the possibility of common method bias, we employ an a priori strategy at the research design phase to prevent the effects of CMB. We implemented the procedural remedies recommended by Mackenzie and Podsakoff (2012). Additionally, we implement a posteriori approach. Thus, we have utilized the full lateral collinearity test recommended by Kock and Lynn (2012) to identify the possible sources of CMB. The findings in Table 3 show that the proposed model (Figure 1) is not affected by the CMB problem.

Table 3. Common method bias test. full collinearity VIFs

Store deal proneness	Satisfaction	Value consciousness
1.258	1.138	1.224

4. RESULTS

4.1. Measurement Model

The assessment of measurement model pursues Hair et al. (2019, 2022) and Sarstedt et al. (2021). The research model in this study includes reflective measurement items. The evaluation of reflective measurement models consists of item-level reliability, internal consistency (composite reliability), convergent validity (average variance extracted; AVE), and discriminant validity (heterotrait-monotrait ratio of correlations; HTMT).

Table 4. Measurement model

Construct/Item	γ	CA	rho_A	CR	AVE	VIF
Store deal proneness (SDP)		0.721	0.739	0.841	0.638	
SDP1	0.825					1.382
SDP2	0.818					1.434
SDP3	0.751					1.432
Satisfaction (SAT)		0.815	0.852	0.889	0.729	
SAT1	0.879					1.950
SAT2	0.905					2.154

continued on following page

Table 4. Continued

Construct/Item	γ	CA	rho_A	CR	AVE	VIF
SAT3	0.770					1.587
Value consciousness (VC)		0.855	0.859	0.889	0.535	
VC1	0.707					1.629
VC2	0.740					1.638
VC3	0.785					2.116
VC4	0.749					1.911
VC5	0.734					1.673
VC6	0.662					1.643
VC7	0.739					1.786

"**Notes:** γ are the individual indicator standardized loadings.α represents the Cronbach's alpha values of the constructs. CR indicate the composite reliability of the construct. Constructs reliability is achieved if α and CR are above 0.70. AVE represents the average variance extracted of each construct indicating the shared variance between a construct and its individual indicators. Convergent validity is achieved if AVE values are higher than 0.5."

As presented in Table 4, all constructs satisfy the suggested cut-off value of 0.7 for both Cronbach's alpha and composite reliability (CR) and 0.5 for average variance extracted (AVE) (Hair et al., 2014a), demonstrating that the measures are internally consistent and show convergent validity. Furthermore, all item loadings are above the suggested threshold value of 0.70 (Table 4). Then, the model discriminant validity was evaluated with the HTMT criterion (Henseler et al., 2015). As indicated in Table 5, all HTMT values are less than one (Franke and Sarstedt, 2019), which exhibits establishing discriminant validity. According to Table 4, the model includes valid and reliable constructs.

Table 5. Discriminant validity (HTMT criteria)

Constructs	SAT	SDP	VC
Satisfaction (SAT)			
Store deal proneness (SDP)	0.397		
Value consciousness (VC)	0.433	0.542	

Notes: SDP: Store deal proneness, SAT: Satisfaction, VC: Value consciousness

4.2. Structural Model

Structural model analysis begins with the prediction of the path model. The path model analysis was performed with 5,000-sample 95% bias-corrected bootstrap procedures to evaluate the direct and indirect paths with their significance levels (Hair et al., 2011). Structural model evaluation includes: collinearity (VIF); the significance of pat coefficients β; in-sample explanatory power with R^2 values; and out-of-sample predictive power with Q^2 and PLSpredict procedures. Additionally, the global fit measure with the standardized root mean square residual (SRMR) values was evaluated (Henseler, Ringle, and Sarstedt, 2015).

Initially, it is necessary to check collinearity problems in the study. Firstly, we examined the values of the Variance Inflation Factor (VIF) for every item within the construct. All VIF values of items (see Table 4) are below the recommended cut-off value of 3 (Hair et al., 2019). Thus, the model has no collinearity issues.

Table 6. Structural model

Direct effects	β	T	P	95% CI LL-UL	f^2	VIF	Sig.
H1: SDP -> SAT	0.175	3.078	0.002	[0.064; 0.284]	0.030	1.241	Yes
H2: SDP -> VC	0.441	11.257	0.000	[0.355; 0.510]	0.241	1.000	Yes
H3: VC -> SAT	0.306	5.358	0.000	[0.189; 0.411]	0.091	1.241	Yes
Indirect effects	**β**	**T**	**P**	**95% CI LL-UL**			
SDP -> VC -> SAT	0.135	4.492	0.000	[0.078; 0.195]			
Model Fit	SRMR= 0.080, d_{-ULS} = 0.578, d_{-G} =0.166, NFI = 0.796						
	$R^2(SAT) = 0.195$, $R^2(SAT)_{adj} = 0.198$, $R^2(VC) = 0.200$, $R^2(VC)_{adj} = 0.202$						

Notes: SDP: Store deal proneness, SAT: Satisfaction, VC: Value consciousness

Secondly, the path coefficients (β), which demonstrate the strength of the path between variables, were analyzed (Ramirez-Correa et al., 2019). As indicated in Table 6, all direct and indirect relationships in the path model are significant. The path model results (Table 6) show that store deal proneness is positively related to satisfaction (H1: SDP → SAT: $\beta = 0.175$, $T = 3.078$, $P<0.001$. $f^2 = 0.030$) and value consciousness (H2: SDP → VC: $\beta = 0.441$, $T = 11.257$, $P<0.001$, $f^2 = 0.241$). The 95% bias corrected confidence interval for H1 (BA: 0.064; 0.284) and H2 (BA: 0.355; 0.510) does not include zero. Thus, H1 and H2 hypotheses are confirmed. These findings indicate that consumers who are deal-prone tend to exhibit a higher level of satisfaction and value consciousness. The results are in line with the literature that shows promotional deals and discounts can foster consumer satisfaction by strengthening perceived value (Grewal et al., 1998). Also, promotional deals develop consumers perceptions of getting good value for money (Lichtenstein et al., 1990). The effect size in H1 refers to that small but meaningful impact on satisfaction, as suggested by Cohen's (1988) guidelines for the effect size. The effect size (f^2 = 0.241) in H2 demonstrates a moderate level impact, highlighting the substantial influence of store deals on value consciousness. The relationship between value consciousness and satisfaction is positive and significant (H3: VC → SAT: β = 0.306, T = 5.358, p <.0.001, f^2 = 0.091), thus the H3 hypothesis is confirmed. This finding aligns with prior research indicating that consumers who are more value conscious are more likely to be satisfied with their purchases (Sweney and Soutar, 2001). The effect size (f^2 = 0.091) shows a moderate impact, further indicating that value-conscious consumers develop greater satisfaction from their shopping and consumption experiences.

The indirect impact of consumers' store deal proneness on consumer satisfaction via consumer value consciousness is significant (H4: SDP → VC → SAT: β = 0.135, T = 4.492, p < 0.001) and partially mediates the relationship between consumers' store deal proneness and satisfaction. Therefore, H4 is supported, and this finding is aligned with the previous research (Lichtenstein et al., 1990). Consumers value consciousness fosters the effectiveness of promotional efforts, leading to a higher level of satisfaction. This mediating effect suggests that a significant portion of the effect of store deal propensity on satisfaction is mediated through its effect on value consciousness, deepening our understanding of how store deals affect consumer satisfaction.

Thirdly, the in-sample predictive power of the model was evaluated with the explained variance (R^2) values. The explained variance for satisfaction (R^2 = 0.195) and value consciousness (R^2 = 0.200) indicates weak in-sample predictive power (Hair et al., 2014).

Lastly, the out-of-sample predictive power of the model that enables its generalizability to other research populations was evaluated with PLSpredict and CVPAT procedures (Shmueli et al., 2016). In the PLSpredict procedure, RMSE (R mean square error), MAE (mean absolute error), and $Q^2_{predict}$. $Q^2_{predict}$ values have to be greater than zero. In this analysis, all Q^2 values are higher than zero (see Table 7). Also, positive values for RMSE and MAE show good predictability. Thus, this study indicated the predictive validity of the research framework or out-of-sample predictability (Woodside, 2013).

Table 7. PLS predictions

Indicators	Q^2predict	RMSE	
		PLS	LM
SAT1	0.067	0.964	0.963
SAT2	0.069	0.873	0.873
SAT3	0.062	0.990	0.990
VC1	0.094	0.920	0.920
VC2	0.140	0.866	0.866
VC3	0.059	0.875	0.870
VC4	0.039	0.880	0.874
VC5	0.122	0.899	0.900
VC6	0.082	0.951	0.956
VC7	0.142	0.870	0.873

An additional test for out-of-sample predictive power was performed with the Cross-Validated Predictive Ability Test (CVPAT). The results of CVPAT confirm that the PLS model has superior predictive accuracy compared to the indicator-adjusted (IA) model (see Table 8). For both satisfaction (SAT) and value consciousness (VC), the PLS loss values (0.891 and 0.801, respectively) are lower than the IA losses, with significant differences (SAT: $t = 2.997$, $p = 0.003$; VC: $t = 4.603$, $p = 0.000$). As demonstrated in Table 7, the PLS model outperforms the IA model ($t = 4.973$, $p = 0.000$), supporting its suitability for predicting consumer behavior, consistent with the preceding research (Hair, Ringle, and Sarstedt, 2011). The findings in Tables 7-8 indicate that this study indicated the predictive validity of the proposed model.

Table 8. Cross Validated Performance Test (CVPAT)

Construct	PLS loss	IA loss	Av. loss dif.	t value	p value
SAT	0.891	0.954	-0.063	2.997	0.003
VC	0.801	0.888	-0.087	4.603	0.000
Overall	0.828	0.907	-0.080	4.973	0.000

The global model fit was examined with the saturated root mean square residual (SRMR) values. As shown in Table 6, the model has an acceptable model fit. SRMR value is below the recommended threshold value of 0.08 (Henseler et al., 2014). In our analysis, SRMR shows a value of 0.08. NFI value is below the 0.80 threshold that indicates a modest fit.

Importance-performance map analysis (IPMA) was performed (Table 9 and Fig. 3). The findings of IPMA, as demonstrated in Table 8, show the importance and performance of the key variables in the conceptual model, focusing on satisfaction. The main goal of IPMA is to evaluate which constructs are more critical (importance) and how well they perform (performance) in impacting key outcomes, such as consumer satisfaction. The vertical axis shows attribute performance, ranging from poor to good performance. The horizontal axis shows the perceived importance of the attributes, from unimportant to very important (García-Fern´andez et al.,2020).

Table 9 exhibits IPMA results for satisfaction. According to Table 9, the importance of SDP is 0.310 that shows it has slightly higher influence on satisfaction compared to VC. The performance of SDP is 60.132 that indicates a moderate level of performance; thus, it needs to be improved in how store deals develop consumer satisfaction.

In table 9, the importance of VC is 0.306 and almost the same level with the importance of SDP, that means VC is as important in estimating consumer satisfaction. Its performance is 69.343 that is better than SDP performance, referring that VC performs well in effecting consumer satisfaction, but it needs to be improved.

Table 9. Importance performance map analysis (IPMA) for satisfaction

	Total effect (importance)	Index value (performance)
Store deal proneness (SDP)	0.310	60.132
Value consciousness (VC)	0.306	69.343

Figure 2. Importance performance map analysis chart (constructs)

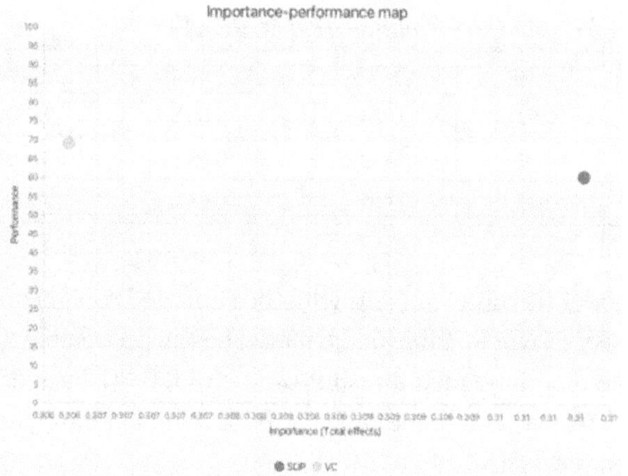

Figure 3. Importance performance map analysis chart (indicators)

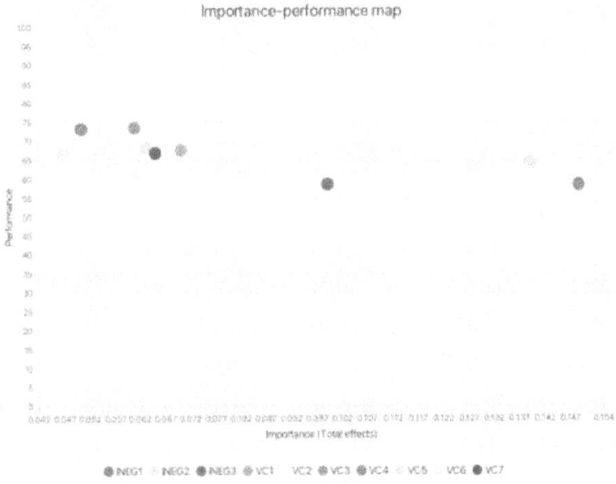

Figure 2 visually indicates the relative importance (x-axis) and performance (y-axis) of two variables, such as store deal proneness (SDP) and value consciousness (VC), in estimating an outcome construct (satisfaction).

The Importance-Performance Map Analysis (IPMA) for indicators chart is shown in Figure 3. That indicates the performance of each indicator (y-axis) and its importance (x-axis) in impacting the target construct. According to Figure 4, SDP1 (SDP1: I follow newspapers, the internet, social media, or market brochures for discounts and opportunities) and SDP2 (SDP2: I shop at some markets for their discounts) are the most important indicators for developing consumer satisfaction. But their performance could be strengthened, particularly for SDP1, which has the highest importance but moderate level of performance. VC3 and VC5 and other indicators of value consciousness are less important but contribute more positively. The performance of value consciousness indicators is moderate, but they improve consumer satisfaction more strongly. INEG3 and VC6-VC7 indicators are less important and have much lower performance in developing consumer satisfaction.

5. DISCUSSION OF FINDINGS

Hypothesis H1 in this research presented that there is a direct positive and significant relationship between store deal proneness and satisfaction (SAT) of consumers (H1: SDP → SAT: $\beta = 0.441$, $T = 11.257$, $P<0.001$, $f^2 = 0.241$). Consumers have a strong tendency to get the best value for the products they buy. In this direction, they feel higher level of satisfaction when they make economically smart purchases, and this result has been consistent with previous research in the marketing literature (Sweeney and Soutar, 2001). Private labels in grocery sector in Turkey are getting more popular. Value-conscious consumers are likely to be more satisfied with their purchases due to the perceived optimal balance between price and quality. This finding emphasizes that grocery stores should continue to encourage value-oriented strategies, especially in promoting private-label brands as affordable but high-quality alternatives to national brands (Diallo, 2012).

This study revealed that store deal proneness has a statistically significant positive impact on value consciousness (H2: SDP → VC: $\beta = 0.175$, $T = 3.078$, $P<0.001$. $f^2 = 0.030$), which aligns with the preceding studies (i.e., Bhatnagar and Ratchford, 2004; Lichtenstein et al., 1990). This finding shows that consumers who actively search for value-maximizing opportunities, such as discounts and promotions from grocery retailers, tend to reach a higher level of satisfaction when they get better store deal opportunities (Lichtenstein et al., 1993). Particularly in emerging markets such as Turkey, where economic conditions are getting more difficult day by day and consumers are highly price- and value-sensitive. While store deals create a significant effect in meeting the expectations of value-conscious consumers, they are also an important strategic tool for retailers (Grewal et al., 1998).

The research findings supported H3, which is the relationship between value consciousness and satisfaction. Value consciousness has a statistically significant positive impact on consumer satisfaction (H3: VC → SAT: $\beta = 0.306$, $T = 5.358$, $p <.0.001$, $f^2 = 0.091$). When value-conscious consumers perceive value meets or exceeds their expectations, their satisfaction level will increase. This finding is aligned with the preceding studies (Lichtenstein et al., 1990).

Hypothesis H4 in this research examined the mediating role of value consciousness in the relationship between store deal propensity and satisfaction. The study findings demonstrated that the mediating role of value consciousness has a positive and significant impact on the relationship between store deal proneness and satisfaction, thus hypothesis H4 was supported (H4: SDP → VC → SAT: $\beta = 0.135$, $T = 4.492$, $p < 0.001$). This result shows that the positive effect of store deals on satisfaction is partially explained by consumers' value consciousness. When consumers encounter store deals, those with more value consciousness tend to experience higher satisfaction because they perceive the deals to offer better value (Lichtenstein et al., 1993). This mediation impact shows the interactions between retailers' sale promotion strategies and consumers' value perceptions, presenting that retailers should focus not only on the frequency and visibility of deals but also on how these deals enhance the perceived value for the consumer.

The IPMA results of constructs, as shown in Table 9 and Figure 3, show that grocery retailers should focus more on developing store deals. Store deal proneness has slightly greater importance in impacting consumer satisfaction, but it has less performance. Grocery retailers should strengthen the effectiveness of their promotional deals and discount strategies by improving how consumers perceive store deals could boost satisfaction. Moreover, value consciousness plays a key role in developing consumer satisfaction.

The IPMA results of indicators, as shown in Figure 4, show the performance and importance of each indicator. Fig. 4 indicates that SDP1 and SDP2 are the most important indicators that influence the other constructs. Thus, retailers should pay attention to store deal programs that influence value-conscious consumers. Particularly, grocery retailers should include promotions and discounts that will affect their target audience, especially when preparing their marketing communication programs, and they should implement this with a correct strategic program. Also, it is fundamental to maintain product quality and to implement store deals so that they can attract consumers with the store deal programs and increase their satisfaction at the same time.

6. CONCLUSION

The present research investigated the associations between consumers' tendency to seek store deals and their impacts on their value consciousness and satisfaction toward private labels in the grocery retail market. The findings demonstrate that deal-prone consumers perceive higher value for their money. Because they think that they get the better optimal balance between price and quality. Moreover, those consumers have a higher level of satisfaction, caused by both the cost savings and sense of accomplishment from getting a deal.

The study findings provide important insights for retailers that operate in competitive markets with their private labels. By offering successful promotions, retailers can foster their consumer's perceptions of value and satisfaction. Thus, sales promotions are very important strategic tools for retailers to increase sales and strengthen relationships with their value-focused consumers.

The current study also contributes to a comprehensive understanding of how promotions influence consumer loyalty, emphasizing the mediating effects of value consciousness and satisfaction. It encourages retailers to approach promotional strategies not just as sales tools but as opportunities to build stronger customer connections. Retailers who effectively leverage this behavior are likely to improve customer satisfaction and, ultimately, support sustained business growth. Future studies could explore how these dynamics differ across various retail environments and consumer groups.

6.1. Managerial Implications

This research was conducted in Turkey on people who prefer private-label products from supermarkets. In the face of the difficult conditions of the economy, consumers constantly prefer whichever market offers more discounts and discount promotions, while in return, they prefer to get the best value for their money. This study aims to measure the effects of discount promotions or different promotional practices of markets on their value awareness and satisfaction. The information presented by this research has revealed important indicators and insights for both the academic world and the retail application world. Beneficial results have been presented for grocery retailers operating in the grocery retail sector, where competition is intense in an emerging market like Turkey.

The findings show that promotional deals of the stores foster consumer satisfaction by enhancing perceived value. Furthermore, consumer value consciousness strengthens the effectiveness of store promotional deals that foster consumer satisfaction. Thus, grocery stores should focus on developing effective store deal strategies that attract their target audience. Grocery retailers should strengthen the effectiveness of their promotional deals and discount strategies by improving how consumers perceive store deals could boost satisfaction. Moreover, value consciousness plays a key role in developing consumer satisfaction.

Grocery retailers should continuously develop and implement value-driven strategies, such as offering high-quality private labels at competitive prices, to maintain and improve consumer satisfaction. Thus, grocery retailers can develop consumer satisfaction by optimizing store deals and perceived value which leads to increased loyalty and superior competitive positioning.

6.2. Limitations and Future Research Directions

The current research, like all other studies, has some limitations and restrictions. The first limitation of this research is that this current research was conducted in only one developing market, Turkey, and the generalizability of the research results to other geographical regions or markets is limited. Consumer attitudes, behaviors and perceptions vary according to different cultural and economic conditions. Therefore, research to be conducted in this area can be conducted in developing and developed markets with different cultural and economic characteristics.

The second constraint of the current study is that the research focus is only on the examination of private label products of supermarkets and the focus is on the consumer segment that is inclined to store discounts. This research approach includes a limitation that excludes consumer segments that prefer national brands or are not inclined to store discounts from the scope of the findings. In future studies, private and national brands can be examined together with different consumer segments.

The third constraint of the current study stems from the structure of the research design. The data obtained in line with the research purpose measures the effects of store discounts on consumer satisfaction in a single time period, but it does not measure these effects in the long term. Longitudinal studies can be conducted to measure consumers' behaviors in this direction at different times.

The fourth constraint of the current study is that this research uses self-reported data that may be biased or biased due to reasons such as social desirability or recall errors. Future research in this area can use natural and real data consisting of consumers' actual purchase information.

The fifth constraint of the current study is that it can be investigated how technological innovations such as digital coupons or personalized promotions that attract consumers affect consumers' attitudes in this direction. In this context, the effects of promotional practices carried out by digital tools of consumers' preferred retailers and competitors on consumers' value awareness and satisfaction can be examined.

Finally, this research was conducted with a focus on private brands in markets. Future research can examine how these relationships occur in other retail sectors such as fashion, electronics, or home goods. This research model will reveal whether similar dynamics exist in different product groups, provide more comprehensive information about the applicability of the research results, and offer more comprehensive and detailed managerial implications for retailers in different sectors.

REFERENCES

Ailawadi, K. L., Lehmann, D. R., & Neslin, S. A. (2003). Revenue premium as an outcome measure of brand equity. *Journal of Marketing*, 67(4), 1–17. DOI: 10.1509/jmkg.67.4.1.18688

Ailawadi, K. L., Neslin, S. A., & Gedenk, K. (2001). Pursuing the value-conscious consumer: Store brands versus national brand promotions. *Journal of Marketing*, 65(1), 71–89. DOI: 10.1509/jmkg.65.1.71.18132

Ailawadi, K. L., Pauwels, K., & Steenkamp, J. B. E. (2008). Private-label use and store loyalty. *Journal of Marketing*, 72(6), 19–30. DOI: 10.1509/jmkg.72.6.019

Anderson, E. W., Fornell, C., & Lehmann, D. R. (1994). Customer satisfaction, market share, and profitability: Findings from Sweden. *Journal of Marketing*, 58(3), 53–66. DOI: 10.1177/002224299405800304

Chandon, P., Wansink, B., & Laurent, G. (2000). A benefit congruency framework of sales promotion effectiveness. *Journal of Marketing*, 64(4), 65–81. DOI: 10.1509/jmkg.64.4.65.18071

Chin, W. W. (1998). Issues and opinion on structural equation modeling management. *Management Information Systems Quarterly*, 22(1), 19–24.

Chin, W. W., & Newsted, P. R. (1999). Structural equation modeling analysis with small samples using partial least squares. *Statistical Strategies for Small Sample Research*, 1(1), 307–341.

Chin, W. W., & Todd, P. A. (1995). On the use, usefulness, and ease of use of structural equation modeling in mis research: A note of caution. *Management Information Systems Quarterly*, 19(2), 237–246. DOI: 10.2307/249690

Darke, P. R., & Dahl, D. W. (2003). Fairness and discounts: The subjective value of a bargain. *Journal of Consumer Psychology*, 13(3), 328–338. DOI: 10.1207/S15327663JCP1303_13

Diallo, M. F. (2012). Effects of store image and store brand price-image on store brand purchase intention: Application to an emerging market. *Journal of Retailing and Consumer Services*, 19(3), 360–367. DOI: 10.1016/j.jretconser.2012.03.010

Festinger, L. (1957). *A theory of cognitive dissonance*. Stanford University Press. DOI: 10.1515/9781503620766

Flacandji, M., & Vlad, M. (2022). The relationship between retailer app use, perceived shopping value and loyalty: The moderating role of deal proneness. *International Journal of Retail & Distribution Management*, 50(8/9), 981–995. DOI: 10.1108/IJRDM-10-2021-0484

Fornell, C. (1992). A national customer satisfaction barometer: The Swedish experience. *Journal of Marketing*, 56(1), 6–21. DOI: 10.1177/002224299205600103

Gordon, B. R., Goldfarb, A., & Li, Y. (2013). Does price elasticity vary with economic growth? A cross-category analysis. *JMR, Journal of Marketing Research*, 50(1), 4–23. DOI: 10.1509/jmr.11.0162

Grewal, D., Monroe, K. B., & Krishnan, R. (1998). The effects of price-comparison advertising on buyers' perceptions of acquisition value, transaction value, and behavioral intentions. *Journal of Marketing*, 62(2), 46–59. DOI: 10.2307/1252160

Hair, J. F.Jr. (2021). Next-generation prediction metrics for composite-based PLS-SEM. *Industrial Management & Data Systems*, 121(1), 5–11. DOI: 10.1108/IMDS-08-2020-0505

Hair, J. F.Jr, Black, W. C., Babin, B. J., & Anderson, R. E. (2014). *Multivariate data analysis (Pearson new internat* (Jersey, N., Ed.). Pearson.

Hair, J. F.Jr, Ringle, C. M., & Sarstedt, M. (2011). PLS-SEM: Indeed a silver bullet. *Journal of Marketing Theory and Practice*, 19(2), 139–151. DOI: 10.2753/MTP1069-6679190202

Hair, J. F., Risher, J. J., Sarstedt, M., & Ringle, C. M. (2019). When to use and how to report the results of PLS-SEM. *European Business Review*, 31(1), 2–24. DOI: 10.1108/EBR-11-2018-0203

Hair, J. F.Jr, Sarstedt, M., Hopkins, L., & Kuppelwieser, V. G. (2014). Partial least squares structural equation modeling (PLS-SEM). *European Business Review*, 26(2), 106–121. DOI: 10.1108/EBR-10-2013-0128

Handarkho, Y. D., & Harjoseputro, Y. (2019). Intention to adopt mobile payment in physical stores. *Journal of Enterprise Information Management*, 33(1), 53–67. DOI: 10.1108/JEIM-06-2019-0179

Henseler, J., Ringle, C. M., & Sarstedt, M. (2015). A new criterion for assessing discriminant validity in variance-based structural equation modeling. *Journal of the Academy of Marketing Science*, 43(1), 115–135. DOI: 10.1007/s11747-014-0403-8

Krishna, A., Briesch, R., Lehmann, D. R., & Yuan, H. (2002). A meta-analysis of the impact of price presentation on perceived savings. *Journal of Retailing*, 78(2), 101–118. DOI: 10.1016/S0022-4359(02)00072-6

Lamey, L., Deleersnyder, B., Dekimpe, M. G., & Steenkamp, J. B. E. (2007). How business cycles contribute to private-label success: Evidence from the United States and Europe. *Journal of Marketing*, 71(1), 1–15. DOI: 10.1509/jmkg.71.1.001

Lamey, L., Deleersnyder, B., Steenkamp, J. B. E., & Dekimpe, M. G. (2012). The effect of business-cycle fluctuations on private-label share: What has marketing conduct got to do with it? *Journal of Marketing*, 76(1), 1–19. DOI: 10.1509/jm.09.0320

Lichtenstein, D. R., Netemeyer, R. G., & Burton, S. (1990). Distinguishing coupon proneness from value consciousness: An acquisition-transaction utility theory perspective. *Journal of Marketing*, 54(3), 54–67. DOI: 10.1177/002224299005400305

Lichtenstein, D. R., Ridgway, N. M., & Netemeyer, R. G. (1993). Price perceptions and consumer shopping behavior: A field study. *JMR, Journal of Marketing Research*, 30(2), 234–245. DOI: 10.1177/002224379303000208

Liu-Thompkins, Y., Khoshghadam, L., Shoushtari, A. A., & Zal, S. (2022). What drives retailer loyalty? A meta-analysis of the role of cognitive, affective, and social factors across five decades. *Journal of Retailing*, 98(1), 92–110. DOI: 10.1016/j.jretai.2022.02.005

Luo, X., Cheah, J. H., Hollebeek, L. D., & Lim, X. J. (2024). Boosting customers' impulsive buying tendency in live-streaming commerce: The role of customer engagement and deal proneness. *Journal of Retailing and Consumer Services*, 77, 103644. DOI: 10.1016/j.jretconser.2023.103644

Martínez, E., & Montaner, T. (2006). The effect of consumer's psychographic variables upon deal-proneness. *Journal of Retailing and Consumer Services*, 13(3), 157–168. DOI: 10.1016/j.jretconser.2005.08.001

McCabe, S., & Illodo, I. B. (2018). Thrilled to have "bagged a bargain" or "bitter" and "very frustrating"? Exploring consumer attitudes to value and deals in tourism. *Journal of Travel Research*, 58(4), 575–593. DOI: 10.1177/0047287518790403

Oliver, R. L. (1980). A cognitive model of the antecedents and consequences of satisfaction decisions. *JMR, Journal of Marketing Research*, 17(4), 460–469. DOI: 10.1177/002224378001700405

Oliver, R. L., Rust, R. T., & Varki, S. (1997). Customer delight: Foundations, findings, and managerial insight. *Journal of Retailing*, 73(3), 311–336. DOI: 10.1016/S0022-4359(97)90021-X

Ramírez-Correa, P., Rond'an-Catalu˜na, F. J., Arenas-Gait'an, J., & Martín-Velicia, F. (2019). Analysing the acceptation of online games in mobile devices: An application of UTAUT2. *Journal of Retailing and Consumer Services*, 50(May), 85–93. DOI: 10.1016/j.jretconser.2019.04.018

Ringle, C. M., Wende, S., & Becker, J. M. (2015). *SmartPLS 3. Boenningstedt: SmartPLS GmbH*DOI: 10.1016/j.jretconser.2019.04.018

Shmueli, G., Ray, S., Manuel, J., Estrada, V., & Chatla, S. B. (2016). The elephant in the room: Predictive performance of PLS models. *Journal of Business Research*, 69(10), 4552–4564. DOI: 10.1016/j.jbusres.2016.03.049

Van Heerde, H. J., Gijsenberg, M. J., Dekimpe, M. G., & Steenkamp, J. B. E. (2013). Price and advertising effectiveness over the business cycle. *JMR, Journal of Marketing Research*, 50(2), 177–193. DOI: 10.1509/jmr.10.0414

Yazdanparast, A., & Kukar-Kinney, M. (2023). The effect of product touch information and sale proneness on consumers' responses to price discounts. *Psychology and Marketing*, 40(1), 146–168. DOI: 10.1002/mar.21755

Chapter 10
Investigation of Social Innovativeness and Product Involvement of Environmental Consumers:
Environmental Consumer Behaviors and Demographics

Tayfun Güven
https://orcid.org/0000-0002-2493-6909
İstanbul Topkapı University, Turkey

Fazilet Burcu Çam
https://orcid.org/0000-0003-4913-9065
Kocaeli University, Turkey

Bilsen Bilgili
https://orcid.org/0000-0002-8454-8318
Kocaeli University, Turkey

Aysel Erciş
https://orcid.org/0000-0002-9835-8574
Atatürk University, Turkey

ABSTRACT

Demographic characteristics, such as age, gender income are important that determine consumers' behaviors. These are determinants of physical, social and

DOI: 10.4018/979-8-3373-2523-1.ch010

economic resources that determine an individual and explain their position in the social environment. In explaining consumer behavior, the degree to which consumers attribute importance to events, objects, and products when perceiving them and how they relate to these products are important factors. And, the increasing importance of the social benefit of products in consumers' purchasing decisions has brought attention to the concept of social innovation aimed at developing new products to address societal issues such as environmentally friendly products. This study examines the demographic characteristics of environmentally conscious consumers and their interest in environmentally friendly products. An ANOVA test was performed. The study found significant differences in consumers' demographic characteristics and their environmentally friendly purchasing behavior in terms of product interest and social innovation levels.

1. INTRODUCTION

In primary research examining consumer purchasing behavior, the focus is primarily on the demographic characteristics of consumers. This is because it has been determined that demographic characteristics play an important role in defining individuals at a basic level and as influential factors in purchasing behavior. Demographic characteristics such as gender, age, income level, and education level are also expressed as individual factors in purchasing behavior (Solomon, et al., 2006; Kotler&Armstrong, 2008; Mucuk, 2010). Individual factors often explain changes in consumer preferences based on situations related to products or services. Consumer decisions regarding consumption and product preferences are also influenced by demographic characteristics, which are expressed as individual factors for each consumer (Rani, 2014).

Research examining the relationships between consumer purchasing behaviors and demographic characteristics related to consumption and product preferences reveals different findings for each characteristic. Many studies have examined demographic factors such as age, gender, education, income level, and occupation to identify the characteristics of environmentally sensitive consumers (Zimmer, et al., 1994; Yüksel & Okumuş, 2001). Research on the demographic characteristics that distinguish environmentally sensitive consumers from other consumers has resulted in conflicting findings (Roberts, 1996). Some studies on this topic have found that environmentally sensitive consumers are relatively younger, more educated, have higher incomes, and are more likely to be women (Straughan & Roberts, 1999). However, other research has shown contradictory results to the previous findings regarding the demographic characteristics of environmentally conscious consumers (Schwartz & Bilsky, 1990). The inconsistency in the relationship between consumers' demographic characteristics and environmentally friendly consumption behaviors in these studies highlights the importance of the topic and the significance of the findings that can be obtained. Therefore, it suggests that the purchasing behaviors of environmentally conscious consumers should be evaluated in conjunction with other variables, in addition to their demographic characteristics.

In recent years, the increasing number of environmentally sensitive and socially innovative consumers has led to a growing interest in eco-friendly products. Social innovation behavior can be expressed as a planned behavior (Ajzen, 1991). Consumers' behaviors are planned and realized in line with a certain purpose, which is explained by the Theory of Planned Behavior. This theory was first put forward by Fishbein & Ajzen (1975) and later revised by Ajzen. The theory of planned behavior suggests that three factors trigger behavior: "personal attitude, subjective norm, and perceived behavioral control." According to the theory, if a behavior is perceived positively (personal attitude), the probability of that behavior being performed is higher. Again, according to the theory, if the attitude of the people the individual considers important towards a behavior (subjective norm) is positive, this attitude will push the individual to perform that behavior. Finally, if individual perceptions are that the person has control over the behavior (perceived behavioral control), this will further encourage the behavior to be performed (Nunko & Ramkissoon, 2010:529).

On the other hand, it is possible to base the innovation dimension of the subject on the theory of diffusion of innovations. According to Rogers, innovation is "an idea, practice or object that is perceived as new by individuals or other units that adopt it" (Rogers, 1983). Technological innovation concretizes knowledge and thus reduces the uncertainty about cause-effect relationships in problem solving. In his book "The Diffusion of Innovations", Rogers defines diffusion as a process in which innovation is transmitted over time among the members of a social system through certain channels. The diffusion of innovation is based on four basic elements. These are; innovation, communication channels, time and social system Social system; refers to a structure that deals with the solution of problems that arise to achieve a certain purpose and is related to each other. The members of this social system are individuals, groups, organizations and subsystems. The constant sharing of new ideas and messages among members leads to a social change (Rogers, 1983). The development of attitudes towards environmentally friendly products within the scope of social innovation can be explained within the framework of this theory.

The concept of **social innovation**, which is generally defined as innovative activities and services developed and disseminated by social action institutions to meet social needs, is related to addressing economic and social problems faced by individuals and society through the implementation and development of new or improved activities, initiatives, services, processes, or products (Mulgan, 2006) (Tanimoto & Doi, 2007; Guzman, et al., 2021). Social innovation is a type of innovation that is often associated with various different concepts such as social entrepreneurship, social impact, public benefit, and management. It emphasizes the need for an innovative approach to solving social problems and suggests that it cannot be just a solution (Conger, 2002). Therefore, it can be interpreted as the eradication of poverty and disease for a more livable world, the development of civil society, the growth of local businesses, the fight for human rights compliance, the promotion of health and sustainable growth, the promotion of education, and the professional development of various social groups (Tatar & Arslan, 2017: 328; Stocker, et al., 2022).

The concept emphasizes that it is possible to find concrete ways to develop new services, processes, initiatives, or products that include efforts not only by businesses but also by consumers to find solutions to problems through social innovation. It is observed that consumers establish connections with products aiming to find more effective, efficient, sustainable, and fair innovative solutions to social issues. There is a growing interest in products that cause less harm to the environment, are recyclable, save energy, and efficiently use natural resources to provide societal benefits. The significance that environmentally conscious consumers attach to these products defined as environmentally friendly attracts the attention of marketers and leads innovative initiatives to focus on this area (Güven, et al., 2024).

Product involvement is related to the relationship established by the consumer with the product. Essentially, it is the personal value attributed to a specific product by the consumer (Lyons and Henderson, 2005: 320). Consumer involvement, also defined as the relative and changing need, value, and interest in an object or item (Zaichowsky, 1985), is expressed as the state of interest, adaptation, and motivation that a consumer feels towards a product (Baker & Lutz, 2000). Therefore, the motivation created by products in consumers affects their levels of interest in the products. The Consumer Involvement Profile-CP has been developed as a result of efforts to dimensionalize and measure involvement (Ozansoy, 2009:33). According to this, the five dimensions of product involvement are shown in Table 1.

Table 1. Dimensions of product involvement

Dimensions	Description
Interest	The consumer's personal interest in a particular product category, the meaning and importance of that product category for the consumer
Pleasure	The hedonic value of the product, the tendency to create pleasure and entertainment for the consumer
Symbol	The symbolic value of the product, the degree to which it reflects the consumer's personality

continued on following page

Table 1. Continued

Dimensions	Description
Risk Important	The relative importance of the negative consequences of choosing the wrong product
Risk Probability	Perceived probability of making a wrong choice

Reference: Kapferer, J.N. ve Laurent, G. (1985), Consumer İnvolvement Profiles: A New Practical Approach to Consumer İnvolvement, Journal of Advertising Research, Vol.25, No 6.

The interest of consumers in products is realized within these dimensions, and the importance of these dimensions varies for each product category. Assessing consumer interest levels and determining the dimensions within which this interest occurs for environmentally friendly products, which are evaluated within the scope of social innovations and are increasingly growing in the market, has become quite important. Considering the differences in consumer behaviors in terms of demographic characteristics, it is thought that the interest of consumers in environmentally friendly products and their levels of social innovation will also vary.

Based on this, in this study, the dimensions of environmental concern for environmentally friendly products, social innovation levels, demographic characteristics, and differences in environmentally friendly purchasing behavior of consumers have been examined.

Based on this, the aim of this study is to determine the dimensions of environmental concern and social innovativeness of environmentally conscious consumers, as well as the differences in their demographic characteristics and environmentally friendly purchasing behavior. Based on the results obtained, recommendations for the green market are intended to be developed. On the other hand, it is aimed to present research suggestions for future researchers regarding this growing market.

2. RESEARCH METHODOLOGY

2.1. Subject and Importance of the Research

A good or service is sold not only with its functional benefits but also with all the components that provide those benefits additional monetary or non-monetary worth. By considering their feelings and own living standards when making a purchasing decision, a consumer wants the product to have components that will enrich their lives in addition to the functional value it will offer. Therefore, the congruence between consumer characteristics and product qualities is genuinely necessary for the purchasing process. The level of customer interest in products is anticipated to rise as this concord between product features and consumer characteristics increases (Ozansoy, 2009). Customers might not always give everything similar weight, pay equal attention, or think it's important to them in the same way. When evaluating how consumers perceive events, objects, or products and how important these products are to them, the notion of involvement is applied (Koç, 2007). Accepted as a personal variable, involvement is described as an internal state variable that indicates the level of interest, arousal, and motivation sparked by a certain stimulus or circumstance. It is also expressed as "interest" and "importance" towards a product, subject, or problem. (Çakır, 2007;164). Based on the demands, values, and interests of the consumer, involvement is defined as the perceived connection between the product and the individual. To put it another way, involvement has to do with how much consumers care about things when they perceive them or how much they identify with them (Ozansoy, 2009;26).

The contribution of the products offered in the market to consumer welfare significantly affects the level of interest of consumers in the purchasing decision process. With the developments in economic, social, and especially information technologies, the factors affecting the level of interest in products have also changed in the perception processes of consumers whose awareness level has increased. In this context, the importance of products that not only offer innovation to the market with their technical features, but also offer social innovation with their technical features, is increasing. The social side of innovation is indicated by the definition of innovation as the creation and use of new techniques, modifications, and activities that will benefit all facets of society (Elçi, 2006;1). According to Mulgan (2006), innovative services and activities created and promoted by social institutions to address social needs constitute the concept of social innovation. In another definition, social innovation is expressed as an approach that offers new applications and solutions to various global-scale problems such as economic crises and climate change, which is becoming a bigger problem day by day, energy and resource depletion, health services and demographic problems (Edwards- Schahter et al., 2012;672). Social innovations are defined as new ways used to achieve goals. One of the important reasons for social innovation is that it creates solutions to meet the social needs of the society rather than individual needs by raising awareness on social issues, and it gives importance to the development of such products. At this point, the idea of environmental awareness starts to emerge as a crucial topic for making a difference in customers' lives, particularly in a context where the public interest in pollution and global warming is growing. On the other hand, environmentalist activities aimed at reducing environmental pollution through the creation of ecologically friendly products, using natural resources more wisely, and acting against global warming can be viewed as social innovation. By including such environmentalist comments on the goods, businesses genuinely hope to improve consumers' impressions of social innovation and, ultimately, product interest.

When the marketing literature is examined, no study has been found that examines the concepts in this study together. From this point of view, this research, which is thought to make significant contributions to both marketing science and its practitioners, examines the demographic characteristics of environmental consumers and the status of environmental product purchasing behavior according to social innovation levels and environmentally friendly product involvement. The study's target population is made up of environmentalist consumers, who are sensitive to the environment and act with environmental awareness at every stage of their purchasing behavior, who use their purchasing power and consumer rights to ensure sustainable environmental conditions, and who also feel a sense of responsibility for the society they live in as well as the environment in which future generations will live. It aims to determine the differences in social innovations and environmentally friendly product involvement levels according to environmental consumer groups. For this purpose, the survey data collected from the members of the Institutions of Greenpeace, DOĞADER (Nature and Environment Protection Association), DOĞÇEV (Nature and Environment Protection, Sustainability Association) and TÜRÇEK (Turkey Environmental Protection and Greening Association), particularly TEMA (Turkish Foundation for Combating Erosion, Afforestation and Conservation of Natural Assets) were subjected to statistical analysis and with regard to findings obtained, various comments and suggestions were presented to shed light on the subject.

2.2. Objective, Scope, and Limitations of the Research

Involvement, or the relationship between the consumer and the product, is a crucial idea since it shows the value people place on things and has a direct impact on their purchase behavior. As can be seen, the research done on the degree of involvement offer significant information to producers, sellers, and advertisers, as well as their contributions to the marketing literature.

This study focuses on social innovation and product involvement in relation to green customers and green products. It is crucial to investigate social innovation from an environmentalist point of view since it deals with the idea of innovation in the context of seeking solutions to social problems. On the other hand, because they are free of dangerous substances, environmentally friendly products can be seen as products that support this part of social innovation. This is because they are designed to discover solutions to environmental concerns. Since a large number of items on the market are harmful to the environment, it has been observed that consumers gradually alter their product preferences over time in order to protect the environment, and their involvement in environmentally friendly products rises. Environmental customers are predicted to be more interested in environmentally friendly innovative items that can be a solution to social problems, especially given their sensitivity to environmentalism. Environmentally friendly products were taken into consideration as a product group in the research to ascertain the level of product involvement among environmentalist consumers. Here, rather than focusing on a single product, it has been attempted to gauge the level of involvement in environmentally friendly products in general.

2.3. Research Model

The model showing the relationships between social innovation and product involvement in terms of environmental consumer groups is presented below.

Figure 1. Research model

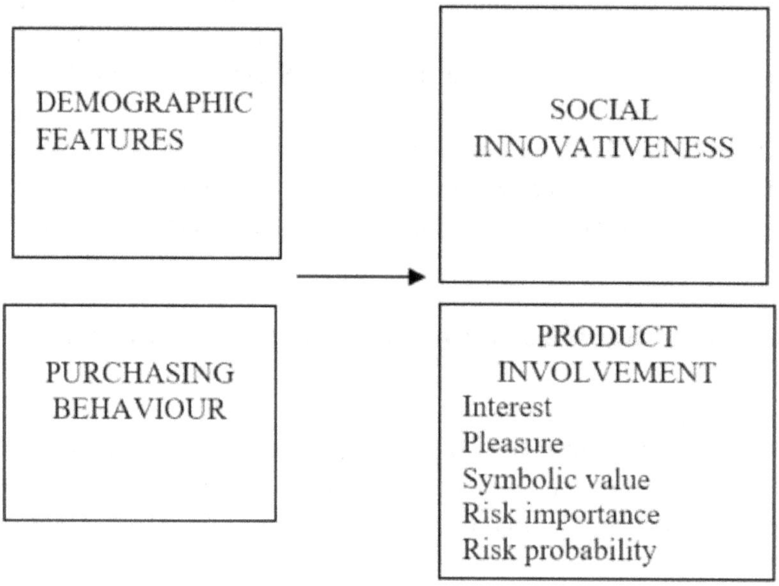

2.4. Research Hypotheses

The fast population growth, global warming, urbanization, and conflicts, among other social and ecological factors, have raised consumer awareness of the environment and the value they place on it. Environmental pollution, whose effects were less noticeable in the past, is now clearly visible. Companies and customers alike are starting to demonstrate sensitivity in an effort to solve this issue. Technological innovation has been shown to be insufficient in this setting, and it has become clear that social innovation needs to be prioritized and developed in at least equal measure to technological innovation (Eren, 2010). Environmentalist consumers stand out among the consumer profiles that show interest (Nakıboğlu, 2003;55) the concept of social innovation, which refers to the application and development of new or improved activities, initiatives, services, processes or products to find solutions to the economic and social problems faced by individuals and societies, to find concrete ways to bring about change in people's lives (Goldenberg, 2004a; Tanimoto & Doi, 2007; Neamtan, 2003; Goldenberg, 2004b;3). Environmentalist efforts to lessen environmental pollution by creating environmentally friendly products, to use natural resources more efficiently, and to take action against global warming might actually be seen from this perspective as social innovations.

Involvement refers to the personal interest between a product and the consumer. Basically, involvement is related to the extent to which consumers perceive events, objects or products, or how much they can associate them with themselves (Ozansoy, 2009;26). Involvement can also be defined as an internal state variable that expresses the amount of interest, arousal and motivation triggered by a certain stimulus or situation (Çakır, 2007;164).

Green consumers are anticipated to display social innovation tendencies and increase their interest in environmentally friendly items in order to make a difference. However, it is equally important to consider how environmentally conscious these consumers are. As it can be understood from these definitions, it is expected that consumers who are defined as environmentalists differ from each other according to their demographic characteristics and environmentally friendly product purchasing behaviors, according to their environmentally friendly product involvement and social innovation. Therefore, the following hypotheses for the research were formed in accordance with the theoretical model of the research as follows.

H_1: Social innovativeness of consumers differs according to the demographic characteristics of consumers.

H_2: The involvement of consumers in environmentally friendly products differs according to the demographic characteristics of the consumers.

H_3: Consumers' Attention Levels for Buying Environmentally Friendly Products and Consumers' social innovativeness are related.

H_4: Consumers' Attention Levels Towards Buying Environmentally Friendly Products and Consumers' involvement in environmentally friendly products are related.

2.5. Sampling Process

The population of the study is made up of environmentalist consumers since it looks at environmentalist consumers as a unit of analysis. Consumers who are members of these organizations and environmental volunteers were chosen as samples under the presumption that involvement in these organizations on a volunteer basis is a sign of a person's environmentalism. The sample includes environmentalist organizations that are active in our nation and have a significant number of engaged members. Members of environmental organizations including TEMA, Greenpeace, DODER, DOAEV, and TÜREK, as well as TEMA volunteers, make up the sample in this situation.

The convenience sampling method was utilized to make it simple to access the sample. In order to reach the members listed in the database of their organizations through their managers, official meetings with the managers of environmental organizations were organized for this reason. Permissions were also secured. The management of these organizations forwarded the link to the electronic questionnaire they had created to each member's email address. The questionnaires distributed in 2018-July received a total of 405 responses within 15 days from members. After removing incorrect and incomplete surveys, the study was conducted on 392 questionnaires. The number of participants is believed to be adequate to represent the homogeneous population. Another significant component of the data acquired is demonstrated by the fact that respondents to the questionnaire did it voluntarily.

2.6. Data Collection Method and Tool

The survey approach was used to collect the research's data electronically. The variables chosen in accordance with the study's goal were considered when creating the questionnaire. To attempt to uncover the distribution of respondents according to their membership in these organizations, consumers were first asked to identify which environmental organizations they were a part of. First, it was attempted to gauge the respondents' purchasing patterns for environmental products along with their demographic structure. Four questions—age, gender, education, and income—were utilized to ascertain the demographic factors. One question was posed, and a 5-point Likert-type scale was used to attempt to determine how much the respondents' attention was paid to the environmental friendliness of these products when making purchases.

The social innovativeness scale, which consists of 9 assertions and was first created by Halaç, Eren & Bulut (2014), was used to figure out how socially innovative consumers are. On a 5-point Likert scale, these statements were rated. The Consumer Involvement Profile: TYPE scale, which consists of 16 expressions used by Laurent and Kapferer (1985) to measure consumers' interest in the product, was used to determine the respondents' interest in environmentally friendly products. Çakır, who adapted the original version of this scale into Turkish, was also used in her study titled "Measuring Consumer Involvement" (2007), and the scale was reviewed and checked, and after necessary corrections were made, it was included in the questionnaire. A 5-point Likert-type scale was used in the expressions of this scale.

2.7. Analysis and Interpretation of Data

The data collected in accordance with the purpose of the research were analyzed in SPSS 25 package programs. First, frequency, percentage, mean and standard deviation distributions of the data were made. Then, the validity and reliability tests of the scales created for social innovation, product involvement and environmental consumption were conducted. For this purpose, confirmatory and exploratory factor analyzes were used. LISREL 8.7 program was used for Confirmatory Factor Analysis. t test, Anova test, and Kendall tau-b correlation analysis were used to show the relationships between purchasing behavior and other variables to determine the differences in terms of social innovativeness and product involvement according to the demographic characteristics of consumers.

Most of the respondents are TEMA members (62%). Others are members of Greenpeace, Doğçev (Nature and Environment Protection, Survival Association), Doğader (Nature and Environment Protection Association), Türçek (Turkish Environmental Protection and Greening Institution) and environmental volunteer participants.

The research sample consists of men and 64% of women. The respondents' ages were as follows: 25.8% were between the ages of 18 and 27; 29.3% were between the ages of 28 and 37; 23% were between the ages of 38 and 47; 15.1% were between the ages of 48 and 57; 5% were between the ages of 58 and 67; and 1.5% were between the ages of 68 and older. The research's findings indicate that customers between the ages of 28 and 37 make up the bulk of the study's participants. There aren't many replies who are older than a certain age. From this, it was discovered that the responses were predominantly young people. When the results of education, a different variable, are evaluated, 2.3% of the respondents graduated from primary school, 16.1% from secondary school, 50% from higher education, 23.7% completed their postgraduate degrees, and 7.9% earned their doctorates. It may be claimed that the majority of the study participants have a university degree or above. When the income level of the study is examined, it is seen that 7.9% of the respondents are $750 or less, 27.3% are $751-1500, 33.7% are &1501-2250, 17.3% are $2251-3000 and 13.8% of $3001 or more.

Analysis are show the distribution of environmentalist consumers participating in the research according to their level of attention to whether the products they purchase are environmentally friendly or not. To ascertain how much the respondents gave attention to a product's environmental friendliness when making a purchase, the distribution of attention levels was analyzed. It is evident from this that 27.8% of respondents checked the option that said, "I always pay attention," followed by 40.5% who said, "I often pay attention," 25.3% who said, "I sometimes pay attention," and 6.4% who said, "I rarely pay attention." Therefore, it can be said that the majority of the respondents have a very high level of attention towards purchasing environmentally friendly products. This situation can be explained as the research sample being a member of environmental organizations and as an indicator of environmental sensitivity.

2.7.1. Reliability and Validity Analysis of the Scales Used in the Research

One of the most important topics that needs to be stressed is the reliability and validity examination of the measurement tools used in research. Important details regarding what is being monitored and how precisely are contained in these analyses. The tools to be used for measurement must meet specific requirements for the research to be considered scientific (Kurtuluş, 2006;303). From this vantage point, in this study, exploratory and confirmatory factor analyses were utilized to test the validity of the scales while Cronbach Alpha analysis was employed to gauge the validity of the research. The Cronbach Alpha, standard deviation and variance values obtained because of the reliability analysis applied for the scales are shown in Table 2.

Table 2. Reliability analysis results for scales (cronbach alpha, mean, standard deviation and variance values

Scales	Cronbach Alpha Coefficient	Mean	St. Deviation	Variance	Number of Variables
Product Involvement Dimensions	0, 744	3, 3549	0, 46723	0, 218	16
Interest/ Importance	0, 895	3, 4413	0, 47256	0, 223	3
Pleasure	0, 841	4, 0723	0, 82007	0, 673	3
Symbolic Value	0, 795	3, 5587	0, 92545	0, 856	3

continued on following page

Table 2. Continued

Scales	Cronbach Alpha Coefficient	Mean	St. Deviation	Variance	Number of Variables
Risk Importance	0, 864	3, 5191	0, 94220	0, 888	3
Risk Probability	0, 764	2, 6752	0, 89832	0, 807	4
Social Innovativeness	0, 904	4, 0376	0, 67313	0, 453	9

The Cronbach Alpha test was used to reveal the internal consistency of the product involvement, social innovativeness and environmental behavior scales used in the research. As can be seen from the table, the product involvement scale has a near high reliability with a coefficient of 0.744. When the dimensions of product involvement are examined, it has been determined that they are highly reliable with a coefficient of 0.895 for the dimension of relevance/importance, a coefficient of 0.864 for the dimension of risk importance, and 0.841 for the dimension of pleasure. The symbolic value dimension was found to be reliable with a coefficient of 0.795 and the risk probability dimension with a coefficient of 0.764. Social innovativeness (α= 0.904) and environmental behavior (α= 0.859) variables also seem to have higher reliability.

2.7.1.1. Validity Analysis for Social Innovativeness

The social innovativeness scale's ten variables were subjected to factor analysis. A value of 91.0% was discovered during the reliability study for these variables. This is a very high value for a study's reliability. One variable ("I would like to develop new products and services with social content to improve the quality of life of the society") was omitted from the study as a result of the reliability analysis. Before applying factor analysis, KMO sampling fit measurement and Barlett's test were performed to test whether factor analysis is the correct statistical technique and to determine the significance of factor analysis, which allows summing up those with high correlation values among many variables and summarizing them under certain factors (Hair et al., 2006;99).

Barlett's test was used to determine the relationships between the variables, and a value of 1796,718 was found, it was determined that this value was significant at the $p<0.01$ level and there was a strong relationship between the variables. As a result of the KMO test performed to measure the sample adequacy of the social innovativeness variable, the KMO value was determined as 0.915. Accordingly, according to the KMO value of the social innovativeness variable, it was concluded that the sample adequacy in our study was suitable for the use of factor analysis. The social innovativeness variable was reduced to a single component as a consequence of the factor analysis. These factors were found using factors with eigenvalues larger than 1. This factor was found to have 4,932 eigenvalues and 61,654% variance overall. This scale is adequate for measuring the desired information, as evidenced by the social innovativeness variable's total variance of 61%, 154 (Güven, et al., 2024).

2.7.1.2. Validity Analysis for Product Involvement Scale

The independence test was performed for 16 expressions under 5 dimensions, namely interest/importance, pleasure, symbolic value, risk importance and risk probability of the original scale of product involvement used in the research, and it was determined that the expressions differed from each other at the $p<0.05$ significance level. Confirmatory factor analysis was conducted to test the suitability of the variables under the dimensions of the product innovativeness scale in terms of 5 factors in the original scale. Variables with negative variance, exceeding standard coefficients (very close to 1.0), or giving very large standard errors were controlled (Hair et al., 2006). As a result of the analysis, it was seen that the fit values were not at an acceptable level in terms of conformity. Variables were eliminated in line with the modification suggestions for the inconsistent variables. As a result of the modifications, it was observed that at least two factors were eliminated. For the product involvement scale, firstly Barlett's test was used to determine the relationships between variables and a value of 2626.025 was found, and it was determined that this value showed significance at the $p<0.01$ level). The KMO value was determined as 0.789. As can be seen from the table, the value found (0.789) is quite high and quite significant in terms of factor analysis. As a result of the Factor analysis for the product involvement variable, 4 factors were obtained for the product involvement variable. Factors with an eigenvalue greater than 1 were used to determine these factors. Confirmatory factor analysis was applied to the 4-dimensional product involvement model formed because of exploratory factor analysis, and the results are shown in Table 3. (Güven, et al., 2024).

Table 3. Values table of product involvement dimensions

Variables	Standard value	R^2	Standard Error	t-value
INTEREST/IMPORTANCE and PLEASURE Cronbach's Alfa: 0, 855	**0, 63**	**0, 40**	**0, 60**	**6, 74**
fit indices	**Chi-Square** = 171, 49; **Sd**=50 **Chi-Square /Sd**=3, 42; **RMSA** = 0.079 **GFI** = 0, 93; **CFI** = 0, 95 **AGFI** = 0, 89; **RMSR** = 0, 077			
1) Purchasing environmentally friendly products is extremely important to me.	0, 69	-0, 48	0, 29	12, 51
2) I am really interested in environmentally friendly product.	**Removed**			
3) It is a kind of pleasure for me to buy myself an environmentally friendly product	0, 88	0, 78	0, 22	15, 41
4)Purchasing an environmentally friendly product is like giving myself a gift.	0, 83	0, 69	0, 30	14, 77
5) Purchasing an environmentally friendly product gives me happiness	0, 80	0.64	0, 21	14, 26
SYMBOLIC VALUE Cronbach's Alfa: 0, 795	**0, 87**	**0, 76**	**0, 24**	**7, 51**
6)I can tell something about someone by looking at the environmentally friendly product they have chosen.	0, 76	0, 58	0, 35	10, 95
7) The brand of the environmentally friendly product someone gives clues about their personality.	0, 91	0, 82	0, 22	16, 77
8) The brand of the environmentally friendly product someone chooses reflects their personality.	0, 77	0, 59	0, 53	15, 27
RISK IMPORTANCE Cronbach's Alfa: 0, 864	**0, 42**	**0, 07**	**0, 91**	**2, 78**
9)It's not a big deal if I make the wrong decision when choosing an environmentally friendly product.	**Removed**			
10) It's really annoying to purchase an environmentally friendly product that doesn't meet my needs.	0, 36	0, 13	0, 91	9, 16
11) If I find out that I made a bad choice after purchasing an environmentally friendly product, I get very angry with myself.	0, 91	0, 89	0, 63	2, 02
RISK PROBABILITY Cronbach's Alfa: 0, 764	**0, 35**	**0, 01**	**0, 92**	**2, 01**
12) I'm always indecisive about which one to choose while window dressing in eco-friendly product stores.	0, 65	0, 42	0, 87	9, 45
13) When I purchase an environmentally friendly product, I don't know if I really should have purchased it (or something else)	0, 69	0, 48	0, 61	8, 31

continued on following page

Table 3. Continued

Variables	Standard value	R^2	Standard Error	t-value
14) Choosing an environmentally friendly product to purchase is quite a difficult decision.	Removed			
15) You can never be completely sure that you have made the right choice when purchasing an environmentally friendly product.	0, 66	0, 44	0, 65	8, 37

When the confirmatory factor analysis results are examined, it is seen that the 4 factors obtained in the exploratory factor analysis results were obtained and confirmed in the same way. As it can be understood from here, it is revealed that environmentalist consumers who participated in the research perceive environmentally friendly products around the titles of interest/importance-pleasure, symbolic value, risk importance and risk probability.

2.7.2. Social Innovativeness Differences by Demographic Characteristics

Whether the social innovativeness of the respondents differ in terms of demographic characteristics is explained in tables in the light of the analyzes below.

Table 4. Analysis of social innovativeness differences by gender of respondents

Variables	Gender	N	Mean	Std. Deviation	t	Df
Social Innovativeness	Female	251	4, 0752	, 64634	390	, 141
	Male	141	3, 9707	, 71583		

According to the results of the test conducted to determine the difference of social innovativeness in terms of gender, it was determined that there was no significant difference at the $p<0.01$ level in terms of gender.

Table 5(a). Analysis of social innovativeness differences by age of respondents

Variables		18-27		28-37		38-47	
		mean	LSD significance	Ort.	LSD significance	mean	LSD significance
Social innovativenss	18-27	3, 7302		3, 9620	, 008	4, 2222	, 000
	28-37		, 008				, 004
	38-47		, 000		, 004		
	48-57		, 000		, 002		, 578
	58-67		, 000		, 003		, 224
	68≥		, 089		, 399		, 897

Table 5(b). Analysis of social innovativeness differences by age of respondents

48-57		58-67		68≥		F	P
mean	LSD significance	Mean	LSD significance	mean	LSD significance		
4, 2818	, 000	4, 4107	, 000	4, 1875	, 089	9, 739	, 000
	, 002		, 003		, 399		
	, 578		, 224		, 897		
			, 427		, 731		
	, 427				, 451		
	, 731		, 451				

Variance analysis was conducted to determine whether the social innovativeness of the respondents within the scope of the research differed in terms of age groups. According to the results of the analysis, it was determined that there was a significant difference at $p<0.01$ level in terms of age groups of social innovativeness. The LSD test was conducted to determine from which age groups the difference in social innovativeness among age groups originated. According to the LSD test, it was determined that there were significant differences in terms of social innovativeness between the 18-27 age group, 28-37 age group, 38-47 age group, 48-57 age group, 58-67 age group ($p<0.01$). No significant difference was found for the age group over 67. There was a significant difference between the 28-37 age group with all except the 67-age group. It was determined that there was a significant difference between 38-47 age groups, 18-27 age groups and 28-37 age groups, but no significant difference was found between other age groups. It was determined that there was a significant difference between the 48-57 age group, 18-27 age group and 28-37 age group, but no significant difference could be determined between the other age groups. It was found that there was a significant difference between the age groups of 58-67, 18-27 and 28-37 years, but there was no significant difference between the other age groups.

No significant difference was found between the 68 and over age group and the other age groups. According to the test results, it is seen that the difference in social innovativeness in terms of age groups is mostly caused by the 18-27 and 28-37 age groups. From this point of view, it can be said that consumers in this age range are less socially innovative. It is understood that the social innovativeness levels of the elderly respondents are higher.

Table 6(a). Analysis of social innovativeness differences by respondents' income

Variables		≤2000 TL		2001-4000TL		4001-6000TL	
		Mean	LSD	Mean	LSD	Mean	LSD
Social innovativeness	≤$750	4, 0685		3, 9393	, 347	4, 0890	, 879
	75-1500		, 347				, 088
	$1501-2250		, 879		, 088		
	$2251-3000		, 867		, 316		, 656
	$3001≥		, 935		, 208		, 941

Table 6(b). Analysis of social innovativeness differences by respondents' income

6001-8000TL		8001≥ TL		F	P
Mean	LSD significance	Mean.	LSD significance		
4, 0441	, 867	4, 0810	, 935	, 836	, 503
	, 316		, 208		
	, 656		, 941		
			, 764		
	, 764				

Variance analysis was conducted to determine whether the social innovativeness levels of the respondents within the scope of the research differ according to their income status. According to the results of the analysis, no significant difference was found.

Table 7(a). Analysis of social innovativeness differences by education status of respondents

Variables		Primary education		Secondary education		Undergraduate	
		Mean	LSD significance	Mean	LSD significance	mean	LSD significance
Social innovativeness	Primary education	4, 3333		3, 9940	, 155	4, 0963	, 298
	Secondary education		, 155				, 291
	undergraduate		, 298		, 291		
	Graduate		, 047		, 254		, 007
	Doctorate		, 527		, 221		, 550

Table 7(b). Analysis of social innovativeness differences by education status of respondents

Graduate		Doctorate		F	P
mean	LSD significance	mean	LSD significance		
3, 8696	, 047	4, 1734	, 527	2, 681	, 031
	, 254		, 221		
	, 007		, 550		
			, 029		
	, 029				

The variance analysis result revealed that there was a significant difference in the respondents' social innovativeness at the p0.05 level depending on their education level, supporting the hypothesis that the social innovativeness of environmentalist consumers varies according to their education level. The LSD test was used to identify the educational level from which the respondents' social innovativeness varied depending on their degree of education. According to the results of the LSD test, there was a significant difference between the respondents who had a master's degree and those who had received their primary, undergraduate, or doctoral degrees at the 0.05 significance level. There was not a significant difference between other education levels. From this standpoint, respondents with graduate degrees exhibit a different level of social innovativeness than respondents with other educational backgrounds. It is clear from Table 7. that respondents with this level of education tend to be less socially innovative on average than respondents from other groups.

As a result, respondents with master's degrees are perceived as being less socially innovative than respondents with other levels of education.

2.7.3. Differences in Product Engagement by Demographic Characteristics

Whether the respondents differ in terms of environmentally friendly product involvement demographics is explained in tables in the light of the analyzes below.

Table 8. Analysis of product involvements by genders of respondents

Variables	Gender	N	Mean	St. Deviation	t	df
Interest-Importance/ pleasure	female	251	4, 2191	, 70519	390	, 003
	male	141	3, 9840	, 81076		
Symbolic Value	female	251	3, 6388	, 90412	390	, 022
	male	141	3, 4161	, 94881		
Risk Importance	female	251	3, 4761	, 96303	390	, 228
	male	141	3, 5957	, 90221		
Risk Probability	female	251	2, 5936	, 90159	390	, 016
	male	141	2, 8203	, 87697		

A t-test was conducted to determine whether the respondents' involvements in environmentally friendly products differed in terms of their genders. According to the test results, it was determined that the product involvement showed a significant difference at $p<0.05$ level according to gender. When the differences between women and men in terms of product involvement dimensions are examined, it is seen that they differ in the sub-dimensions of interest-importance/pleasure, symbolic value and risk probability. In other words, men's and women's involvement in environmentally friendly products differs in terms of the significance they place on them, their interest in them, the pleasure they derive from purchasing them, and the symbolic importance they attach to them. According to the table, it was concluded that women attach more importance to the dimension of interest-importance/pleasure and symbolic value than men, whereas men attach more importance to the possibility of risk than women. Considering that women develop more emotional bonds in their relations with products, it is considered normal for women to care about the symbolic meaning of environmentally friendly products and to be more interested in environmentally friendly products in terms of environmental awareness, the importance they attach to the subject and the pleasure they get from purchasing these products more than men.

Table 9(a). Analysis of product involvements by age of respondentsa

Variables		18-27		28-37		38-47	
		Mean	LSD significance	Mean	LSD significance	mean	LSD significance
Interest-Importance/ Pleasure	**18-27**	3, 8218		4, 0957	, 006	4, 2833	, 000
	28-37		, 006				, 067
	38-47		, 000		, 067		
	48-57		, 000		, 004		, 221
	58-67		, 010		, 301		, 957
	68≥		, 027		, 184		, 479
Symbolic value	**18-27**	3, 2211		3, 5449	, 009	3, 7296	, 000
	28-37		, 009				, 148
	38-47		, 000		, 148		
	48-57		, 000		, 049		, 506
	58-67		, 024		, 431		, 944
	68≥		, 188		, 640		, 985
Risk Importance	**18-27**	3, 3762		3, 5174	, 269	3, 4500	, 587
	28-37		, 269				, 609
	38-47		, 587		, 609		
	48-57		, 002		, 024		, 010
	58-67		, 511		, 977		, 745
	68≥		, 460		, 703		, 583
Risk Probability	**18-27**	2, 7690		2, 7014	, 582	2, 7037	, 616
	28-37		, 582				, 986
	38-47		, 616		, 986		

continued on following page

Table 9(a). Continued

Variables		18-27		28-37		38-47	
		Mean	LSD significance	Mean	LSD significance	mean	LSD significance
	48-57		, 115		, 253		, 268
	58-67		, 085		, 154		, 159
	68≥		, 477		, 593		, 591

Table 9(b). Analysis of product involvements by age of respondentsa

48-57		58-67		68≥		F	P
mean	LSD significance	mean	LSD significance	Mean	LSD significance		
4, 4322	, 000	4, 2738	, 010	4, 5000	, 027	7, 034	, 000
	, 004		, 301		, 184		
	, 221		, 957		, 479		
			, 390		, 827		
	, 390				, 501		
	, 827		, 501				
3, 8305	, 000	3, 7143	, 024	3, 7222	, 188	4, 693	, 000
	, 049		, 431		, 640		
	, 506		, 944		, 985		
			, 613		, 780		
	, 613				, 985		
	, 780		, 985				
3, 8559	, 002	3, 5238	, 511	3, 6667	, 460	2, 129	, 061
	, 024		, 977		, 703		
	, 010		, 745		, 583		
			, 163		, 637		
	, 163				, 742		
	, 637		, 742				
2, 5367	, 115	2, 3968	, 085	2, 5000	, 477	, 987	, 425
	, 253		, 154		, 593		
	, 268		, 159		, 591		
			, 540		, 924		

continued on following page

Table 9(b). Continued

48-57		58-67		68≥		F	P
mean	LSD significance	mean	LSD significance	Mean	LSD significance		
	, 540				, 804		
	, 924		, 804				

The product-importance/pleasure and symbolic value dimensions, which are sub-dimensions of product involvement, differed significantly at p 0.01 level according to age groups, according to the results of the analysis of variance, which was conducted to determine whether environmentally friendly product involvement differs according to the age groups of the respondents.

However, the risk importance and risk probability dimensions did not differ. In other words, it was found that, depending on the respondents' ages, consumers' perceptions of a product's interest, importance, pleasure, and symbolic value in their eyes differ depending on the product's involvement in an environmentally friendly product. The LSD test was used to identify which age groups were responsible for the respondents' varying levels of involvement in environmentally friendly products. The LSD test revealed that the 18–27 age group substantially varied from all other age groups in terms of the product-importance/pleasure dimension (p 0.05). It was understood that the differences disappeared with age. In the involvement of environmentally friendly products, the interest in the product, the importance of the product and the pleasure taken from the environmentally friendly product are evident in the older age groups. When the averages of the answers given by the age groups to this dimension were examined, it was seen that the 18-27 age group had the lowest average. It was determined that the respondents over the age of 58 gave much more importance to this dimension, distinguishing them significantly from other groups younger than themselves. From this point of view, we can say that the elderly is more interested in environmentally friendly products, they care more, and they enjoy these products more.

The symbolic value sub-dimension, one of the product involvement dimensions, was found to differ by age group as well. In particular, the 18-27 age group differed from the other age groups at the p0.05 significant level, except for the 68-year-old and older group. Table 9. In general, it was found that as the years went by, the symbolic importance of environmentally friendly products increased.

Table 10(a). Analysis of product involvements by incomes of respondents

Variables		≤2000 TL		2001-4000TL		4001-6000TL	
		mean	LSD significance	mean	LSD significance	mean	LSD significance
Interest-Importance/ Pleasure	**≤$750**	4, 2903		4, 0724	, 156	4, 0795	, 161
	751- 1500		, 156				, 942
	$1501- 2250		, 161		, 942		
	$2251- 3000		, 686		, 194		, 198
	$3001≥		, 554		, 351		, 365
Symbolic value	**≤$750**	3, 6882		3, 6044	, 656	3, 4268	, 156
	751- 1500		, 656				, 139
	$1501- 2250		, 156		, 139		
	$2251- 3000		, 310		, 405		, 670
	$3001≥		, 562		, 185		, 011
Risk Importance	**≤$750**	3, 5645		3, 5421	, 907	3, 3902	, 354
	75- 1500		, 907				, 216
	$1501- 2250		, 354		, 216		
	$2251- 3000		, 823		, 641		, 118
	$3001≥		, 694		, 500		, 091
Risk Probability	**≤$750**	3, 2473		2, 8380	, 022	2, 6263	, 000
	75- 1500		, 022				, 063
	$1501- 2250		, 000		, 063		
	$2251- 3000		, 000		, 001		, 080
	$3001≥		, 000		, 019		, 348

Table 10(b). Analysis of product involvements by incomes of respondents

6001-8000TL		8001≥ TL		F	P
mean	**LSD significance**	**mean**	**LSD significance**		
4, 2243	, 686	4, 1898	, 554	1, 006	, 404
	, 194		, 351		
	, 198		, 365		
			, 802		
	, 802				
3, 4853	, 310	3, 8086	, 562	1, 999	, 094
	, 405		, 185		
	, 670		, 011		
			, 055		
	, 055				
3, 6103	, 823	3, 6481	, 694	1, 065	, 373
	, 641		, 500		
	, 118		, 091		
			, 826		
	, 826				
2, 3971	, 000	2, 4938	, 000	6, 665	, 000
	, 001		, 019		
	, 080		, 348		
			, 544		
	, 544				

To see if the respondents' income distribution had an impact on their involvement with environmentally friendly products, variance analysis was done. Results of the analysis showed that only the risk probability dimension, at the p0.01 level, showed a significant difference between the product involvement sub-dimensions according to the respondents' income distribution; the other dimensions did not show a significant difference. To ascertain whether income distribution groups are responsible for the variance in risk probability dimension in respondents' involvement in environmentally friendly products, an LSD test was performed. According to the LSD test, it was concluded that the respondents in the income group of $750 and below differed from the respondents in all other income groups, the income group of $751-1500 differed from those in other income groups except $1501-2250, those in the $2251-3000 income group differed from those in the income groups of $750 and below and those in the $751-1500 income groups and respondents with $3001

TL and above differed from those in the income groups of only $750 and below and $751-1500. This suggests that respondents with the lowest income group—those making $750 or less—perceive the probability of danger in environmentally friendly products differently from respondents in the other income groups. The respondents' concern for the risk probability dimension appears to decrease as their money rises; in other words, they do not perceive environmentally friendly products to be risky. It can occasionally give the impression that environmentally friendly products are of poorer quality because they are less eye-catching than other product categories. Because of this, low-income respondents—even those who identify as environmentalists—may see a risk probability in environmentally friendly products.

Table 11(a). Analysis of product involvements by the education levels of the respondents

Variables		**Primary Education**		**Secondary Education**		**Undergraduate**	
		Mean	**LSD significance**	**Mean**	**LSD Sİgnificance**	**Mean**	**LSD Significance**
Interest-Importance/ Pleasure	Primary Education	4, 2778		4, 1389	, 604	4, 1990	, 758
	Secondary Education		, 604				, 581
	Undergraduate		, 758		, 581		
	Graduate		, 272		, 223		, 027
	Doctorate		, 562		, 875		, 554
Symbolic Value	Primary Education	4, 3704		3, 4550	, 005	3, 5272	, 007
	Secondary Education		, 005				, 588
	Undergraduate		, 007		, 588		
	Graduate		, 028		, 166		, 241
	Doctorate		, 007		, 860		, 544
Risk Importance	Primary Education	3, 8333		3, 3175	, 123	3, 5000	, 297
	Secondary Education		, 123				, 179
	Undergraduate		, 297		, 179		
	Graduate		, 694		, 012		, 084
	Doctorate		, 226		, 677		, 594
Risk Probability	Primary Education	3, 2593		2, 8519	, 202	2, 6071	, 033

continued on following page

Table 11(a). Continued

Variables		Primary Education		Secondary Education		Undergraduate	
		Mean	**LSD significance**	**Mean**	**LSD Significance**	**Mean**	**LSD Significance**
	Secondary Education		, 202				, 060
	Undergraduate		, 033		, 060		
	Graduate		, 058		, 205		, 597

Table 11(b). Analysis of product involvements by the education levels of the respondents

Graduate		Doctorate		F	P
mean	**LSD Significance**	**Mean**	**LSD Significance**		
3, 9892	, 272	4, 1129	, 562	1, 319	, 262
	, 223		, 875		
	, 027		, 554		
			, 428		
	, 428				
3, 6631	, 028	3, 4194	, 007	2, 494	, 043
	, 166		, 860		
	, 241		, 544		
			, 201		
	, 201				
3, 7043	, 694	3, 4032	, 226	2, 028	, 090
	, 012		, 677		
	, 084		, 594		
			, 122		
	, 122				
2, 6667	, 058	2, 6022	, 053	1, 912	, 108
	, 205		, 204		
	, 597		, 977		
			, 728		

Variance analysis was conducted to determine whether the environmentally friendly product involvement differs according to the educational status of the respondents. According to the results of the analysis, it was determined that the sub-dimensions of product involvement differed significantly only at the $p<0.05$ level with the symbolic value dimension and did not differ significantly with the other dimensions according to the educational status of the respondents. The LSD test was conducted to determine which income groups differed in the symbolic value dimension of the respondents' involvement in environmentally friendly products. The results of the LSD test showed that, at the 0.05 significance level, there was a significant difference between the groups of respondents from primary school and those from all other educational levels in terms of symbolic value sub-dimension. The average of the respondents who completed their primary school, as shown in the table, is higher than that of the other groups. In other words, a consumer's involvement in environmentally friendly products is more symbolic for those with lower levels of education. This condition becomes meaningless as education levels rise. In this situation, it is possible to assume that consumers with low levels of education view using environmentally friendly items as a status symbol.

2.7.4. Analysis of the Relationship Between Consumers' Attention Levels for Purchasing Environmentally Friendly Products and Social Innovativeness and Product Involvement

The relationship between the extent to which respondents pay attention to the environmental friendliness of a product while purchasing a product and the variables of product involvement and social innovativeness were sought. This relationship was tried to be determined by Kendall Tau-b Correlation analysis. According to the results of the analysis, it was seen that there was a $p<0.01$ significance level relationship between the attention levels of the respondents towards purchasing environmentally friendly products, and social innovativeness and product involvement. When the results were examined, a positive correlation was found between the attention level of the respondents for purchasing environmentally friendly products and the interest-importance/pleasure, symbolic value of the product involvement dimensions, at $p<0.01$ significance level, and a negative correlation between the risk probability dimension and $p<0.01$ significance level. Accordingly, as the importance given by the respondents to being environmentally friendly while purchasing a product increases, the importance they attach to the environmental-friendly product's interest-importance/pleasure and the symbolic value of the product also increases. On the other hand, it is seen that the respondents do not attach importance to the risk probability dimension as the importance they attach to the environmental friendliness of the product while purchasing a product. In other words, respondents who do not find any risk factor in environmentally friendly products give more importance to the environmental friendliness of the product when purchasing a product.

Table 12. Analysis of the relationship between respondents' attention levels for purchasing environmentally friendly products and social innovativeness and product interest

		Interest-Importance/ Pleasure	Symbolic Value	Risk Importance	Risk Probability	Social Innovativeness
Attention Levels for Purchasing Environmentally Friendly Products	Correlation Coefficient	, 425**	, 152**	, 029	-, 114**	, 356**
	Duplex significance)	, 000	, 000	, 478	, 005	, 000
	N	392	392	392	392	392

A positive and strong relationship was found at $p<0.01$ importance level between the extent to which respondents pay attention to the environmental friendliness of a product when purchasing a product and their social innovativeness levels. Accordingly, as the social innovativeness levels of the respondents increase, the importance they attach to the environmental friendliness of the product while purchasing a product also increases. From this point of view, it is thought that social innovation cares about innovative products and ideas that increase the life quality of the society and create social value, causing social innovative respondents to turn to environmentally friendly products that benefit the environment and therefore society.

3. CONCLUSION AND RECOMMENDATIONS

The concept of involvement, which is expressed as "interest" and "importance" for a product, a subject, or a problem, entered the marketing literature after Krugman's (1965) research on the learning styles of television advertisements and has been the subject of study that has long been used to understand and explain consumer behavior. Involvement is an internal state and a personal variable that expresses the amount of interest, arousal, and motivation evoked by a particular stimulus or situation.

Consumers do not care equally about every product or service, and they do not develop relationships with them in the same intensity, according to an analysis of consumer behaviors. Therefore, involvement can be viewed as a measure of the importance that consumers give them when evaluating events, things, or products, as well as how relevant they believe these things are to them (Koç, 2007). Consumers consider other factors in their purchasing decisions in addition to the items' practical advantages, and they create behavior by creating a connection between the product and themselves. With an increase in consumer consciousness over the past few years, consumers have begun to make this connection with goods that bring about social innovation and the welfare of society. As a result, this connection significantly influences how interested consumers are in purchasing goods that have a positive social impact. The importance of environmentally friendly items for consumers has been clear in this situation. On the other hand, businesses present innovative products to the market in an effort to expand the potential for the use of already-existing resources or to create wealth through the creation of new resources. In this regard, the idea of social innovativeness has gained prominence to develop services, plan events, and take initiatives while also finding solutions to the issues that both individuals and societies confront. A concept called "social innovativeness" refers to the creation of goods that advance society in a variety of ways and go beyond technological innovation. Social innovations thus serve as a complement to innovations in technology. Social innovativeness focuses on the creation of new or improved goods and services to find solutions to the economic and social problems faced by individuals and society. At this point, environmentally friendly products have become an important market for social innovativeness. Recently, the increase in environmentalist tendency and the more active environmentalist consumers force marketers to focus on these issues and cause them to focus their innovative activities on this field. Businesses that produce environmentally friendly products gain a competitive advantage in the market.

The population of this research consists of environmentalist consumers. For this reason, the research sample was selected from consumers who are members of environmental organizations and volunteer in these organizations, with the assumption that it is an indicator of environmentalism.

To as certain how much attention, the respondents gave to the environmental friendliness of a product when making a purchase, the attention levels of the respondents were examined. It was found that many of the respondents (68.3%) had a very high level of attention towards making a purchase of environmentally friendly products. This circumstance is explained by the research sample's membership in environmental organizations, which is a sign of environmental sensitivity.

Reliability analyzes were performed on the scales used in the research, and the Cronbach Alpha value for product involvement was found to be 0.744, and the Cronbach Alpha value for social innovativeness was found to be 0.904. It was determined that the scales used in the research had a very high reliability. Another result obtained from the research is that the total variance is 61%, the explanation rate of 154 is that social innovativeness is gathered under a single factor.

Reliability and validity analyses were carried out on the scale, which originally consisted of 16 statements and 5 dimensions, which was used to measure the involvement of environmental consumers in environmentally friendly products. As a result of the confirmatory factor analysis performed for this purpose, there was a need to perform exploratory factor analysis because two factors were eliminated. A total of 4 factors were retrieved with a very high explained variance rate of 69.897% because of the exploratory factor analysis, which revealed that 2 dimensions in the original scale were grouped under a single component. To validate these variables, a reconfirmatory factor analysis was carried out. Four elements were observed to have been acquired and validated in the same manner. The results of the exploratory and confirmatory factor analyses showed that the environmentalist consumers who took part in the research tended to value the titles of interest/importance pleasure, symbolic value, risk importance, and risk probability when judging how environmentally friendly products were perceived (Güven, et al., 2024). Therefore, the analyzes in this research were conducted based on these 4 confirmed factors.

According to the results of the research, it has been revealed that the difference in social innovativeness in terms of age groups is mostly caused by the 18-27 and 28-37 age groups. From this point of view, it has been understood that consumers in this age range are less socially innovative, while the social innovativeness levels of older respondents are higher. On the other hand, it has been determined that the difference in the social innovativeness of environmentalist consumers in terms of education level is mostly caused by those who have a master's degree. Therefore, it was revealed that respondents with a master's degree were less socially innovative than respondents at other educational levels.

Within the scope of the research, it was tried to determine whether the respondents' interest in environmentally friendly products differed in terms of demographic characteristics, and it was determined that some dimensions of product involvement differed according to demographic characteristics.

It was determined that the environmentally friendly product involvement of the respondents participating in the research showed a significant difference at the $p<0.05$ level according to gender. When the differences between women and men in terms of product involvement dimensions are examined, it is seen that they differ in the sub-dimensions of interest-importance/pleasure, symbolic value, and risk probability. Therefore, it was determined that men attached greater priority to the risk probability than women, but women attached greater importance to the dimensions of interest- importance/pleasure and symbolic value. Women cared about the symbolic meaning of environmentally friendly products and were more interested in them than men in terms of environmental sensitivity, the importance they attached to the subject, and the pleasure they derived from purchasing these products. This is because women develop stronger emotional bonds with the products they use. This finding does not support the conclusion in the study by Sun & Wang (2020) that despite men's positive attitudes towards environmentally friendly products, women's price sensitivity is higher. However, other research results showing that women have more positive attitudes towards environmentally friendly products than men support this finding (Winsente-Moline, et al., 2018; Wei, et al., 2018; Mohiuddin, et al., 2018;).

It was determined that the product-importance/pleasure and symbolic value dimensions, which are sub-dimensions of environmentally friendly product involvement, differed significantly at the $p<0.01$ level according to age groups, but the risk importance and risk probability dimensions did not differ. In other words, it was found that the evaluation of an environmentally friendly product varied depending on the respondents' ages in terms of their involvement with, interest in, and perceptions of its importance, pleasure, and symbolic value. The product-importance/pleasure dimension revealed a significant (p0.05) difference between the 18–27 age group and all other age groups. Environmentally friendly product involvement, interest in the product, the importance of the product and the pleasure taken from the environmentally friendly product became evident in the older age groups. It was concluded that the elderly was more interested in the environmentally friendly product, they cared more and they enjoyed these products more. Likewise, it was observed that the symbolic value sub-dimension, which is one of the product involvement dimensions, also differed by age groups, and especially the 18-27 age group differed significantly between the other age groups ($p<0.05$), except for the 68-year-old and older group. It was determined that as the age progressed, more importance was attached to the symbolic value of environmentally friendly products. A study found that younger consumers have more positive attitudes towards green products. It has been determined that purchasing intentions for these products are higher. It has been determined that the group in generation X is more sensitive to price consciousness, and this sensitivity negatively affects their intention to purchase green products (Heo & Muralidharan, 2019; Sun & Wang, 2020). The results of this research are similar to the findings obtained.

In accordance with the respondents' income distribution, it was found that the involvement of environmentally friendly products differed significantly ($p<0.01$) from the sub-dimensions of product involvement only with the dimension of risk probability. It did not differ significantly from the other dimensions. This finding showed that respondents in the income group of $750 and lower were different from those in all other income groups and that these respondents assessed the probability of risk in environmentally friendly products differently than respondents in all other income groups. It was shown that when respondents' wealth levels rose, they showed less interest in the risk probability dimension, or put another way, they did not perceive environmentally friendly products as dangerous. This was interpreted as the fact that environmentally friendly products were less appealing than other product categories, which could give the impression that these products were of lower quality. In a study by Sun & Wang (2020), they determined that high-income consumers have more positive attitudes about green products and have higher intentions to purchase these products. The results of this research support the findings. As a result, respondents with low incomes might view environmentally friendly products as potentially risky, even though they were risk-free. According to the respondents' levels of education, it was found that involvement of environmentally friendly products varied significantly (p0.05) from the sub-dimensions of product involvement only with the symbolic value dimension and did not differ significantly from other dimensions. The symbolic value dimension of the respondents' involvement in environmentally friendly products was found to differ significantly (p 0.05) depending on the respondents' level of primary education. It was observed that involvement in environmentally friendly products had greater symbolic value for consumers with lower levels of education and that this situation became less significant as education levels grew. It was hypothesized that consumers with low levels of knowledge viewed environmentally friendly items as a status symbol in this situation. A relationship was sought between the extent to which respondents pay attention to the environmental friendliness of a product when purchasing a product and the variables of product involvement and social innovation and it was seen that there were significant ($p<0.01$) relationships between the attention levels of the respondents towards purchasing environmentally friendly products, and social innovativeness and product involvement.

The findings revealed a positive correlation at a p0.01 significance level between the respondents' attention level for purchasing environmentally friendly products and the interest-importance/pleasure, a symbolic value from the product involvement dimensions, and a negative correlation with the risk probability dimension. Accordingly, it was observed that as the importance given by the respondents to being environmentally friendly while purchasing a product increased, the importance they attached to the environmental-friendly product's interest-importance/pleasure and the symbolic value dimension of the product increased. It was concluded that the respondents who did not have any risk factor in environmentally friendly products gave more importance to the environmental friendliness of the product when purchasing a product.

A positive and strong relationship ($p<0.01$) was found between the extent to which respondents paid attention to the environmental friendliness of a product while purchasing it and their social innovativeness levels. Accordingly, it was observed that as the social innovativeness levels of the respondents increased, the importance they attached to the environmental friendliness of the product while purchasing a product also increased. In line with the results obtained from the research, the following recommendations were developed.

- In recent years, the increase in the environmentalist tendency and the power of environmental groups in the public has forced businesses to focus on these issues. For this reason, it is estimated that in the coming days, the competition of enterprises in the market will be based on environmentally friendly products. For this reason, it is extremely important for businesses to develop products that bring practical solutions to environmental problems. It is thought that it would be beneficial for businesses to concentrate their innovative activities on this area.

- Environmentally friendly products currently have a significant market due to the focus on social innovativeness and social issues. Demand for environmentally friendly goods will rise as socially conscious consumers become increasingly prevalent. This perspective suggests that enterprises should concentrate on the market for environmentally friendly products. Businesses are advised to focus on this sector because it would be advantageous for them.
- The fact that environmentally friendly products are products that avoid harming the nature and are compatible with nature causes consumers to see these products as risk-free. Therefore, businesses should pay attention to highlight their environmental aspects while designing new products and carrying out promotional activities of these products.
- For new products to be successful in the market, the level of involvement of consumers in these products must also be high. The more consumers associate themselves with a certain product group, the easier their purchasing decisions are. Considering that social innovativeness is mostly related to the dimensions of interest-importance/pleasure and symbolic value in environmentally friendly product involvement, it would be appropriate for businesses producing environmentally friendly products to give the messages that these products fulfill an important responsibility. On the other hand, because socially innovative consumers place a high symbolic value on environmentally friendly products, it is advised that they provide this idea with connotations that will add value and can be turned into appealing slogans.
- Another important finding from the research is that young consumers are less socially innovative and less interested in products. Considering this information, the elderly environmentalists are more sensitive to social facts and their purchasing decisions are in the direction of environmentalist product preference. The population potential of young people is well acknowledged to be substantial, particularly for our nation. In their awareness research and training initiatives for various institutions, environmental organizations should now concentrate on reaching young people. Additionally, it is advised that firms develop marketing messages that will catch the attention of young people, arouse their interest in the environment, and encourage them to purchase environmentally friendly products.
- It would be acceptable to conduct the positioning studies in a way that emphasizes this, given that environmentally friendly items are also thought to be a sign of status.

- Researchers who are interested in this study can examine the subject of product involvement and social innovativeness on other product groups and different examples in their future studies. On the other hand, studies can be conducted on other types of innovativeness.

REFERENCES

Ajzen, I. (1991). The theory at planned behavior. *Organizational Behavior and Human Decision Processes*, 50(2), 179–211. DOI: 10.1016/0749-5978(91)90020-T

Baker, W. E., & Lutz, R. J. (2000). An empirical test of an updated relevance accessibility model of advertising effectiveness. *Journal of Advertising*, 29(1), 1–14. DOI: 10.1080/00913367.2000.10673599

Çakır, V. (2007). Tüketici ilgilenimini ölçmek. *Selçuk Üniversitesi İletişim Fakültesi Dergisi*, 4(4), 167–180.

Conger, D. S. (2002). "Social inventions". *The Innovation Journal*. http: //www .innovation.cc/books/social-inventions-isbn

Edwards-Schachter, M. E., Matti, C. E., & Alcántara, E.Edwards--Schachter. (2012). Fostering quality of life through social innovation: A living lab methodology study case. *The Review of Policy Research*, 29(6), 672–692. DOI: 10.1111/j.1541-1338.2012.00588.x

Elçi, Ş. (2006). *İnovasyon Kalkınmanın ve Rekabetin Anahtarı*. Pelin Ofset.

Eren, H. (2010). *Üniversite Öğrencilerinin Sosyal Yenilikçilik Kapasitelerinin Teknolojik Yenilikçilik Eğilimlerine Etkisini Ölçmeye Yönelik Bir Model Önerisi* (Vol. 37). KHO Savunma Bilimleri Enstitüsü.

Fishbeın, M., & Ajzen, I. (1975). *Bellefatlitude, Intention And Behavior: An Inlrod. Uc.Lion Theory And Research*. Addison-Wesley.

Goldenberg, M. (2004a), *Social Innovation in Canada How the Non-profit Sector Serves Canadians and How It Can Serve Them Beter*. Ottowa: Canadian Policy Research Networks Inc. Project (CPRN) Research Report W/25.

Goldenberg, M. (2004b), *The Future of Social Innovation in Canada*. Ottowa: Canadian Policy Research Networks Inc. Project (CPRN), Research Report W/26.

Güven, T., Çam, F. B., Bilgili, B., & Erciş, A. (2024). The impact of social innovation on environmentally friendly product involvement. *Innovation & Management Review*, 21(2), 94–109. DOI: 10.1108/INMR-10-2021-0191

Guzman, A. C., Francisco, M., & Rodrıguez, S. (2021). Do consumers value environmental innovation in product? *Administrative Sciences*, 11(33), 33. DOI: 10.3390/admsci11010033

Hair, J. F., Black, B., Babin, B., Anderson, R. E., & Tatham, R. L. (2006). *Multivariate Data Analysis* (6th ed.). Prentice Hall.

Halaç, D. S., Eren, H., & Bulut, Ç. (2014). Sosyal yenilikçilik: Bir ölçek geliştirme çalışması. *Hacettepe Üniversitesi İktisadi ve İdari Bilimler Fakültesi Dergisi*, 32(1), 165–190.

Heo, J., & Muralidharan, S. (2019). What triggers young Millennials to purchase eco-friendly products?: The interrelationships among knowledge, perceived consumer effectiveness, and environmental concern. *Journal of Marketing Communications*, 25(4), 421–437. DOI: 10.1080/13527266.2017.1303623

Koç, E. (2007). *Tüketici Davranısları ve Pazarlama Stratejileri: Global ve Yerel Yaklaşım*. Seçkin Yayınları.

Kotler, P., & Armstrong, G. (2008). *Principles of Marketing* (Vol. 12). Pearson Prentice Hall.

Krugman, H. E. (1965). The impact of television advertising: Learning without involvement. *Public Opinion Quarterly*, 29(3), 349–356. DOI: 10.1086/267335

Kurtuluş, K. (2004). *Pazarlama Araştırmaları*. Literatür Yayıncılık.

Laurent, G., & Kapferer, J. N. (1985a). Measuring consumer involvement profiles. *JMR, Journal of Marketing Research*, 22(1), 41–53. DOI: 10.1177/002224378502200104

Lyons, B., & Henderson, K. (2005). Opinion leadership in a computer-mediated environment. *Journal of Consumer Behaviour*, 4(5), 319–329. DOI: 10.1002/cb.22

Mohiuddin, M., Al Mamun, A., Syed, F. A., Mehedi Masud, M., & Su, Z. (2018). Environmental knowledge, awareness, and business school students' intentions to purchase green vehicles in emerging countries. *Sustainability (Basel)*, 10(5), 1534. DOI: 10.3390/su10051534

Mucuk, İ. (2010). *Pazarlama İlkeleri*, Gözden Geçirilmiş 18. Basım, İstanbul, Türkmen Kitabevi. DOI: 10.3390/su10051534

Mulgan, G. (2006). *Social Silicon Valleys-A Manifesto for Social Innovation*. The Young Foundation.

Nakıboğlu, M. A. (2003), *Çevreci Pazarlama Anlayışı ve Tüketicilerin Çevreci Tutumlarının Tüketici Davranışları Üzerindeki Etkisi ile İlgili Bir Uygulama.* (Yayımlanmamış Yüksek Lisans Tezi). Adana: Çukurova Üniversitesi, SBE. DOI: 10.3390/su10051534

Neamtan, N. (2003), *Non-profit Sector and Evaluation: The State of Play in Quebec (OEDC ed.). The Non-Profit Sector in a Changing Economy*, 221-238.

Nunkoo, R., & Ramkissoon, H. (2010). Gendered theory of planned behaviour and residents' support for tourism. *Current Issues in Tourism*, 13(6), 525–540. DOI: 10.1080/13683500903173967

Ozansoy, T. (2009), *Moda Ürünlerinin Pazarlanmasında Sosyo-Psikolojik Faktörlerin Tüketici Tercihleri İle İlişkisi Üzerine Bir Pilot Araştırma*, (Doktora Tezi). İstanbul Üniversitesi, Sosyal Bilimler Enstitüsü. DOI: 10.3390/su10051534

Rani, P. (2014). Factors influencing consumer behaviour. *International Journal of Current Research and Academic Review*, 2(9), 52–61.

Roberts, J. A. (1996). Green consumers in the 1990s: Profile and implications for advertising. *Journal of Business Research*, 36(3), 217–231. DOI: 10.1016/0148-2963(95)00150-6

Rogers, E. M. (1983). *Diffusion of Innovations* (3rd ed.). The Free Press.

Schwartz, S. H., & Bilsky, W. (1990). Toward a theory of universal content and structure of values: Extensions and cross-cultural replications. *Journal of Personality and Social Psychology*, 58(5), 878–891. DOI: 10.1037/0022-3514.58.5.878

Solomon, M., Bamossy, G., & Askegaard, S. (2006). *Consumer Behaviour: A European Perspective* (3rd ed.). Pearson Education.

Stocker, F., Sajjad, A., Raziq, M. M., & Pacheco, L. M. (2022). Editorial: Innovation and business strategy for sustainability. *Innovation & Management Review*, 19(3), 174–179. DOI: 10.1108/INMR-07-2022-183

Straughan, R. D., & Roberts, J. A. (1999). Environmental segmentation alternatives: A look at green consumer behavior in the New Millennium. *Journal of Consumer Marketing*, 16(6), 558–575. DOI: 10.1108/07363769910297506

Sun, Y., & Wang, S. (2020). Understanding consumers' intentions to purchase green products in the social media marketing context. *Asia Pacific Journal of Marketing and Logistics*, 32(4), 860–878. DOI: 10.1108/APJML-03-2019-0178

Tanimoto, K., & Doi, M. (2007). Social innovation cluster in action: A case study of the San Francisco Bay Area. *Hitotsubashi Journal of Commerce and Management*, 41(1), 1–17.

Tatar, Ş. B., & Arslan, M. (2017). Sosyal inovasyon kavramı: Bir literatür taraması. *International Journal of Academic Value Studies*, 3(12), 321–338.

Vicente-Molina, M. A., Fernández-Sainz, A., & Izagirre-Olaizola, J. (2018). Does gender make a difference in pro-environmental behavior? The case of the Basque Country University students. *Journal of Cleaner Production*, 176, 89–98. DOI: 10.1016/j.jclepro.2017.12.079

Wei, S., Ang, T., & Jancenelle, V. E. (2018). Willingness to pay more for green products: The interplay of consumer characteristics and customer participation. *Journal of Retailing and Consumer Services*, 45, 230–238. DOI: 10.1016/j.jretconser.2018.08.015

Wells, W. D. ve Prensky, D. (1996). *Consumer Behavior*. Kanada: John Wiley & Sons, Inc

Yüksel, C. A., & Okumuş, A. (2001). Çevre Dostu Ürün Satınalma İle İlgisi Bulunan Değişkenlerin Belirlenmesine Yönelik Araştırma. *Yönetim Dergisi:İstanbulÜniversitesi İşletme Fakültesi İşletme İktisadi Enstitüsü*, 12(40), 29–38.

Zaichkowsky, J. L. (1985). Measuring the Involvement Construct. *The Journal of Consumer Research*, 12(3), 341–352. DOI: 10.1086/208520

Zimmer, M. R., Stafford, T. F., & Stafford, M. R. (1994). Green issues: Dimensions ofenvironmental concern. *Journal of Business Research*, 30(1), 63–74. DOI: 10.1016/0148-2963(94)90069-8

Chapter 11
Managing Risk in Real Estate Lending

Kamelia Assenova
https://orcid.org/0000-0001-8726-0654
University of National and World Economy, Bulgaria

ABSTRACT

Real estate lending is a risky activity. Bulgaria is currently experiencing a boom in real estate market prices. The vast majority of purchases are financed with bank credit. This type of credit represents a major component of the asset side of banks' balance sheets. For 2016-2024, mortgage loans accounted for 42.66% of total household loans at the beginning of the period and 52.23% at the end. This bank activity creates asset management risk for commercial banks. Evidence from many countries shows severe bank losses or even failures caused by non-performing real estate loans. That is why credit risk must be managed. On the one hand, it is linked to the real estate market and the change in property prices there, and on the other, there is an indirect risk linked to the creditworthiness of borrowers, collateral, and depreciation and price risk. This research examines the changes in real estate lending in Bulgaria that are leading to an increase in the risk of managing it. The new management tools need to be used in order not to keep the financial health of the commercial banks.

1. INTRODUCTION

Real estate lending is inherently a high-risk activity. Bulgaria is currently experiencing a significant boom in real estate market prices, with the majority of property purchases financed through bank credit. This type of credit constitutes a substantial portion of the asset side of banks' balance sheets. During the period 2016–2024, at

DOI: 10.4018/979-8-3373-2523-1.ch011

the beginning of the period, mortgage loans accounted for 42.66% of total household loans increasing to 52.23% by the end. This trend has led to heightened asset management risks for commercial banks.

The empirical evidence from various countries highlights the financial losses or even failures of banks caused by non-performing real estate loans. In particular, during periods of economic crisis, losses from mortgage loans tend to increase sharply, posing systemic risks to the banking sector. Consequently, effective credit risk management is essential. Such risks are directly linked to fluctuations in the real estate market and property price dynamics, as well as indirectly associated with borrower creditworthiness, collateral valuation, and the risks of asset depreciation and price volatility.

The primary *aim of this research* is to examine how the continued expansion of mortgage lending in Bulgaria increases systemic risks for the banking sector. This aim is addressed by achieving the following specific research tasks:

- Identifying the key risks associated with mortgage lending
- Analyzing changes in the volume of mortgage loans
- Examining the role of shadow mortgage loans as a critical risk factor
- Proposing recommendations for effective risk management in mortgage lending

The study posits the following *main hypothesis*: the expansion of mortgage loans increases the risks faced by banks and the banking system as a whole. To ensure financial stability, it is therefore necessary to implement measures aimed at mitigating the risks associated with the rapid growth of mortgage lending.

2. STATEMENT OF THE PROBLEM

The role of real estate in financial crises has been well-documented, dating back to the South Sea bubble (Kindleberger, 2001). The "Asian Crisis" of the late 1990s provided further evidence of the interconnectedness of credit booms and real estate price bubbles during periods of economic growth, followed by the adverse effects of prolonged real estate price declines on bank capital adequacy, credit availability, and overall economic growth. Over the past two decades, the interplay between real estate cycles and financial systems has been extensively studied (Renaud, 1995; Herring & Wachter, 1999; Quigley, 2001; Mera & Renaud, 2000). The correlation between real estate markets and bank lending underscores systemic risks, which can be exacerbated by governance failures and lapses in financial regulation.

In extreme cases, real estate has played a central role in prolonged financial crises, such as the economic stagnation in Japan during the 1990s (Mera, 2000). Recognizing the critical impact of mortgage lending expansion on the crises necessitates a comprehensive investigation into the various risks associated with such loans.

2.1. Risks of Real Estate Loans

The Risk, as defined by Holberton et al. (2012), encompasses any factor that adversely affects a bank. DeLisle (2010) characterizes risk as the discrepancy between expectations and reality, encompassing both optimistic and pessimistic scenarios. The real estate, as a tangible asset, introduces additional layers of complexity in risk assessment.

The example is the significant decline in property prices, which reduces the value of collateral during foreclosure proceedings. The Banks often fail to account for such shocks when issuing loans. To manage these risks effectively, banks must assess the extent of their portfolio exposure and understand the tail risks associated with potential property market downturns. Awareness of these risks is a critical step toward effective risk mitigation.

Types of Risks

The Risk management in real estate lending involves the assessment of several factors, including credit risk, asset risk, market risk, interest rate risk, liquidity risk, and cash flow risk. Among these, asset risk is particularly significant because real estate loans are secured by the properties. The cyclical nature of the real estate market introduces uncertainties at different stages of a property's development, compounded by asymmetrical information between stakeholders.

- *Interest rate risk* is a prominent concern; as real estate loans are typically interest-bearing. The Fixed-rate loans expose banks to interest rate volatility, limiting their ability to adjust rates over time. While floating-rate loans have become more common to mitigate this risk (Anderson, 2016), fluctuations in interest rates remain a challenge for lenders.
- The Real estate is an *illiquid asset*, and transactions are infrequent, resulting in inconsistent and non-linear pricing. Unlike securities, real estate assets cannot be valued on a regular basis due to their long lifespan and limited market activity. The Properties are typically held as long as they generate income, making frequent valuation impractical. The Banks rely on market appraisals

to determine a property's "fair market value" for risk assessment purposes (Muller et al., 2010; Jonson et al., 2007).

- *The Cash flow risk* is another critical factor that has contributed to numerous bank failures. While banks may offload portions of their real estate holdings, they often retain significant exposure on their balance sheets. The size and irregular cash flow cycles of real estate loans make risk assessment particularly challenging. As these loans rely mainly on property-generated cash flows for repayment, maintaining consistent credit repayment is crucial for managing associated risks (Antoniades, 2015).
- The *concentration risk* further complicates the management of real estate loans. Banks cannot evaluate individual transactions in isolation; instead, they must assess portfolio-level exposure. The overvaluation of properties exacerbates this risk (Berhout et al., 2014). The Banks should adopt market benchmarks, loan loss provisioning, and securitization to mitigate these vulnerabilities.

Due to the inherent nature of real estate as an asset class, the banks cannot entirely eliminate risks associated with real estate lending. Even the most well-managed banks remain vulnerable to market unpredictability and systemic shocks. This underscores the necessity for robust risk management policies that identify and address key risk exposures.

The *effective risk management should prioritize the evaluation of credit risk, asset concentration, liquidity, and interest rate fluctuations*. Given the multifaceted nature of real estate risks, banks must adopt comprehensive strategies to manage these complexities. Awareness of inherent vulnerabilities, coupled with proactive measures, will ensure greater resilience in the face of market volatility.

2.2. Benefits for Commercial banks from mortgages loans

The Commercial banks play a crucial role as a source of funding for the real estate sector. In turn, the dynamics of the real estate market significantly influence commercial bank behavior through three distinct channels.

- Real Estate Lending

The first channel pertains to the direct lending activities of commercial banks in the real estate sector. As of early 2024, loans to the real estate sector account for approximately 20.93% of total bank lending. When considering all real estate-related loans, such as those for construction, the exposure rises to roughly 25%.

This concentration of lending towards the real estate sector is particularly attractive for banks due to the higher profit margins compared to prime corporate loans. In the case of prime corporate loans, borrowers often possess greater bargaining power, which limits profit margins. For real estate loans, however, most banks charge interest rates in Bulgaria closer to those in the interbank market. It due to also, mortgage loans are considered lower-risk instruments, as they are secured by collateral, which adds an extra layer of financial security for lenders.

- Real Estate Assets Owned by Banks

The second channel involves the real estate assets held by commercial banks. These assets include land and buildings owned as operational premises, as well as repossessed properties. Such holdings contribute to the overall value of the bank's assets and provide opportunities for banks to capitalize on property value appreciation or monetize these assets through resale.

- Collateral and Asymmetric Information

The third channel stems from the role of properties as collateral in lending. To mitigate risks arising from asymmetric information between banks and borrowers, commercial banks typically require collateral for loans. Approximately 80% of collateral provided for loans is in the form of real estate. Consequently, fluctuations in property prices directly influence the value of collateral and, in turn, the behavior of banks as lenders.

For example, rising property prices increase the net value of collateral, which encourages banks to lend more. This phenomenon was notably observed during the pre-crisis period, where rising property values fueled increased lending activity.

- Real Estate Cycles and Bank Lending Behavior

The interconnected cycles of property prices and bank lending are evident in the feedback loop they create. During periods of rising real estate prices, the perceived lifetime wealth of households and corporations owning property increases. This leads to higher levels of consumption and investment, which stimulate aggregate demand and further encourage lending. Simultaneously, rising property prices enhance the net asset value of banks, enabling them to expand their lending capacity.

This increase in lending perpetuates a cycle of rising demand and asset prices, creating a positive feedback loop in economic activity. However, the opposite occurs when property prices decline. The falling property values reduce the worth of collateral, eroding the net worth of both commercial banks and borrowers. As a result, banks become more cautious in their lending, leading to a contraction in aggregate demand and further declines in property prices.

Figure 1 illustrates these cyclical relationships between property prices, bank lending, and economic activity.

Figure 1. Way of lending boom

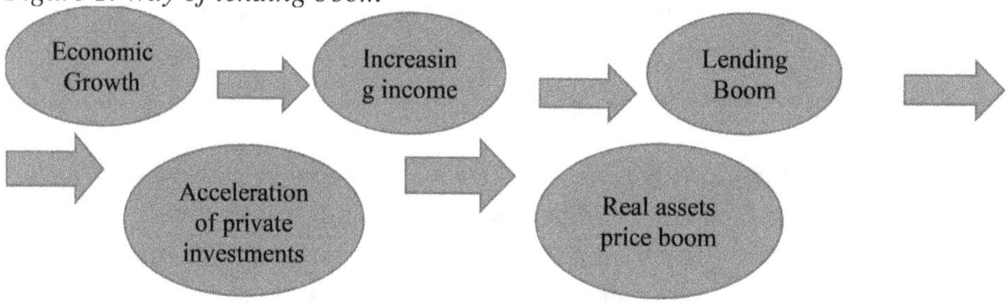

(Own Design)

The link between the real estate market and commercial banks makes the latter susceptible to real estate market risk. The banks with high exposure to the real estate sector will be more sensitive to fluctuations in the real estate market and property prices.

2.3. Bank Intermediation Through Mortgages Loans

The close link between the real estate market and commercial banks renders banks particularly vulnerable to real estate market fluctuations. The Banks with significant exposure to the real estate sector are more sensitive to changes in property prices and overall market dynamics.

In the context of asset pricing, mortgages are structured as contracts that allocate various types of risk between lenders and borrowers. The long-term mortgages provide borrowers with protection against potential declines in their own credit-worthiness or adverse changes in credit market conditions. For example, borrowers with existing mortgages are not required to provide additional collateral in the event of financial distress or stricter underwriting standards for new loans. Such protections, commonly taken for granted by mortgage and retail borrowers, are not typically available in other types of secured loans. This differentiation is primarily attributable to the limited access of mortgage borrowers to unsecured credit markets and the significant costs associated with foreclosure processes.

Despite lenders absorbing certain risks related to borrower circumstances and credit markets, other risks persist. These include risks associated with interest rates, inflation, and fluctuations in property prices. A closer examination of a fixed-rate mortgage (FRM) illustrates how risk allocation operates in practice.

A standard FRM involves a nominal payment schedule designed to amortize the principal and interest over the loan's term. The borrowers benefit from a constant stream of payments, which shields them from changes in interest rates. However, uncertainty remains concerning inflation during the mortgage term. If inflation accelerates, the real value of mortgage payments decreases, benefiting borrowers at the expense of lenders. This phenomenon was observed following the COVID-19 crisis. Conversely, in periods of declining inflation, the outcome depends on factors such as prepayment penalties and nominal house prices.

In Bulgaria, borrowers may refinance loans under the original terms if nominal house prices remain sufficiently high. In contrast, in countries like Germany, where prepayment penalties are common, or when house prices fall below levels that allow refinancing, borrowers face higher real payment burdens. Lenders, in turn, compensate for such risks through the initial interest rates charged on mortgage loans.

The issue of asymmetric information regarding household mobility also influences mortgage market dynamics. Lenders may attempt to segment borrowers based on their likelihood to relocate by offering lower interest rates in exchange for upfront fees. However, such segmentation can lead to illiquidity in mortgage-backed securities markets, as investors fear transacting with better-informed counterparties.

2.4. Different Systems for Financing Real Estate Loans and Their Impact on Risk

The mortgage lending requires funding mechanisms that involve financial intermediaries to originate loans and either hold them or repackage them for sale to investors. Other intermediaries may mitigate certain risks by providing guarantees. The risks not borne by borrowers are typically distributed among originators, end investors, and guarantors. The specific allocation of risks is critical, as it not only determines profit and loss distribution and mortgage pricing but also affects the incentives of financial intermediaries.

A successful mortgage system should incentivize intermediaries to assess borrower creditworthiness accurately, set appropriate mortgage rates, and, when necessary, modify mortgages in ways that serve both borrower and lender interests. There are three primary systems for financing mortgages, each with distinct approaches to risk allocation and intermediary incentives:

- Deposit-Financed Lending

The oldest system involves deposit-funded lending, where originators issue loans backed by deposits. This model has several advantages:

- ✓ Solvent originators have strong incentives to underwrite mortgages carefully and modify them when necessary.
- ✓ The alignment of incentives between originators and borrowers encourages prudent lending practices.

However, deposit-funded lending has notable drawbacks:

- ✓ The availability of mortgage loans is constrained by local deposit volumes.
- ✓ Liquidity transformation issues arise, as deposits can be withdrawn on demand, while mortgage loans are long-term commitments.
- ✓ Maturity transformation, particularly with fixed-rate mortgages, exposes lenders to interest rate risks.

In Bulgaria, where deposit-funded lending dominates and government insurance is absent, these risks are particularly pronounced. The economic downturns or rising interest rates exacerbate the financial challenges faced by deposit-funded intermediaries.

- Securitized Mortgages

In the aftermath of the 2008 financial crisis, many countries, such as the United States, transitioned to a securitized mortgage model. Under this system, originators package mortgages into pools for sale to end investors. The Credit guarantees, often provided by government-sponsored entities, address the information asymmetry between originators and investors.

While securitization spreads risks across a broader base of investors, it has inherent weaknesses:

- ✓ Originators may lack incentives to properly underwrite loans, particularly if credit guarantees are mispriced.
- ✓ Excessive reliance on guarantees can lead to riskier lending practices, shifting losses to taxpayers.

Research by Keys et al. (2010, 2012) highlights these concerns, demonstrating how misaligned incentives contributed to the global financial crisis.

- Covered Bonds

A third model, prevalent in Europe, uses covered bonds to mitigate some of the issues associated with securitization and deposit-funded lending. The Covered bonds are claims on banks, backed by pools of mortgages that remain on the banks' balance sheets. This structure ensures that banks retain strong incentives to underwrite and modify mortgages prudently.

The Covered bond systems also allow for maturity rescheduling, where the maturity of bonds differs from that of the underlying mortgages. However, excessive maturity transformation can introduce risks similar to those in deposit-funded lending. In countries with limited maturity transformation, covered bond systems have demonstrated impressive resilience.

For both securitized and covered bond systems, maintaining liquidity in mortgage-backed financial instruments is essential. Strategies to enhance liquidity include:

- Designing mortgages to minimize exposure to borrower-specific risks and behavioral uncertainty.
- Tranching mortgage pools to create instruments with varying levels of protection against prepayment or default.
- Providing public credit guarantees to reduce information asymmetry and enhance investor confidence.

Each financing system has unique strengths and vulnerabilities, and the choice of system significantly influences risk exposure, market stability, and overall economic resilience.

2.5. Stages of Credit Cycle and Real Estate

In countries like Bulgaria, a significant part of real estate investments is financed with bank loans. This requires tracing the relationship between the stages of the credit cycle and changes in the real estate market:

Table 1. Stages of credit cycle and real estate

Stages of the credit cycle	Banks	Market of real estate
Initial upswing	• Low interest rates	• Rising demand • Rising real estate prices • Rents are increasing • Real estate investment yields fall
Continuing upswing	• Lending continues at an increasing pace • Interest rates are low • Weak credit control • Regulatory and supervisory failures	• Supply shortages • A boom in construction starts • Rent hikes
Accelerating the rise	• Lending continues at an increasing pace • The value of bank assets and of collateral on existing loans is improving	• Rapid increase in demand • Rising property prices • Rising inflation
Economic peak	• The value of assets and collateral falls • Non- performing credits increase • Credit contraction. • Foreclosures and closures. • Property sales by distressed borrowers and banks.	• High inflation • Rising interest rates • Demand contracts • A sharp jump in the number of completed buildings • Rents are falling and yields are rising

Source: own design

In most economies, the real estate sector accounts for up to 15% of GDP, making it a critical component of national economic growth. Consequently, changes in the real estate market, as well as risks stemming from such changes, can significantly impact overall economic performance.

The Real estate investments are subject to two primary types of risk: specific risks and systematic risks, the latter often referred to as real estate market risk. While banks have traditionally focused on managing specific risks and have developed a variety of tools to do so, real estate market risk remains widely overlooked.

The significance of real estate market risk becomes particularly evident during downturns in the real estate cycle. During these periods, falling property prices often result in higher loan defaults and even bank failures. From the perspective of modern portfolio theory, market risk is that portion of total risk that cannot be eliminated through diversification, as it arises from economic changes that broadly affect all investments. Similarly, in the context of real estate, market risk refers to the non-diversifiable risk attributable to fluctuations in the real estate market.

While specific risks, such as those associated with individual borrowers, are often evaluated by banks based on the creditworthiness of the lender, market risk is driven by broader economic trends. As such, its impact is systemic, extending beyond individual loans or investments and influencing the stability of financial institutions and the economy as a whole.

Figure 2. Real estate risk by lending

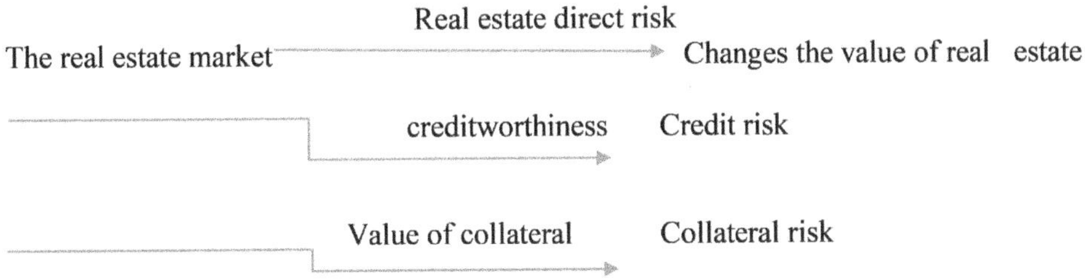

(Own design)

Risk in the real estate market can defer also as direct and indirect risks:

- Direct Real Estate Market Risk

The Direct risk arises when the value of an asset is fully and directly dependent on the real estate market, with no external factors capable of mitigating or influencing this relationship.

- Indirect Real Estate Market Risk

The Indirect risk occurs when the value of an asset is influenced not only by the real estate market but also by other contributing factors. Indirect risks can manifest in several forms:

✓ **Credit Risk:** This risk arises from fluctuations in the real estate market that negatively affect a borrower's creditworthiness, potentially leading to defaults on loans.

✓ **Collateral Risk:** Collateral risk occurs when adverse market trends reduce the value of secured properties, diminishing the adequacy of collateral against loans.

✓ **Profitability Risk:** Profitability risk refers to the threat that market fluctuations may compromise the expected returns of an investment in real estate.

✓ **Price Risk:** Price risk materializes when volatility in the real estate market adversely affects other market prices, such as share prices, resulting in broader financial instability.

These interconnected risks emphasize the multifaceted nature of real estate market exposure and underscore the importance of robust risk assessment and management practices to safeguard financial stability.

3. METHODOLOGY

This research investigates the correlation between the real estate market in Bulgaria and mortgage lending for the period 2016- 2024. In Bulgaria the main part of real estate is financed with credits from the Commercial banks due to the undeveloped financial market. If credit risk is not valued, the continued increase of loans could create liquidity problems for banks, and sometimes it could lead to insolvency. In the same time local market of collateral is weak and banks will find it difficult to sell real estate and cover their receivables.

The credit control in the country already realizes not only the Bulgarian National Bank, also by European Central Bank due to accession to the Eurozone in next two-three years. ECB supervisors are therefore closely monitoring level of mortgage loans in all banks. They also check that banks are adequately managing the riskiness of their loans and have appropriate strategies, governance structures and procedures in place. Non-Performing Loans (NPLs) can have a strong impact on a bank's stability.

The achievement of key targets and accomplishment of the main aim of the study is done by a systematic theoretical - empirical approach. In particular, this approach is realized as follows:

- Induction and deduction in the research of the facts characterizing bank lending of real estate
- Empirical study of the situation with NPLs of real estate
- Comparative analysis of all main variables with other countries

The chosen instruments for achieving the main objectives of the study use extensive statistical data. The data are illustrated by means of graphics and text application.

4. FINDINGS

4.1. Evidence on the Importance of Real Estate Market Risk for Banks

The Systematic risk in the real estate market is relatively lower than comparable risks, such as stock market risk. Since Keynes on the correlation between systematic risk in the financial services sector and the real estate market, it has been clear that crises in the real estate sector often precipitate significant banking crises. The past two decades demonstrate that many major banking crises originated in real estate market failures. This underscores the macroeconomic importance of real estate market risk.

At the micro level, there is substantial evidence of a strong correlation between the real estate market and mortgage loan performance for individual banks.

4.2 Analyze the Data for Mortgage Loans and Non-Performing Loans (NPLs) in Bulgaria

The Data spanning 2005–2024 reveal a steady increase in loans used to finance real estate purchases in Bulgaria, with the exception of 2015, when one of the structurally significant banks failed. While the period from 2005–2016 saw relatively stable levels of real estate lending, a marked expansion began in 2016 and has continued to date.

Figure 3. Mortgage loans for period 2005- 2024 in Bulgaria

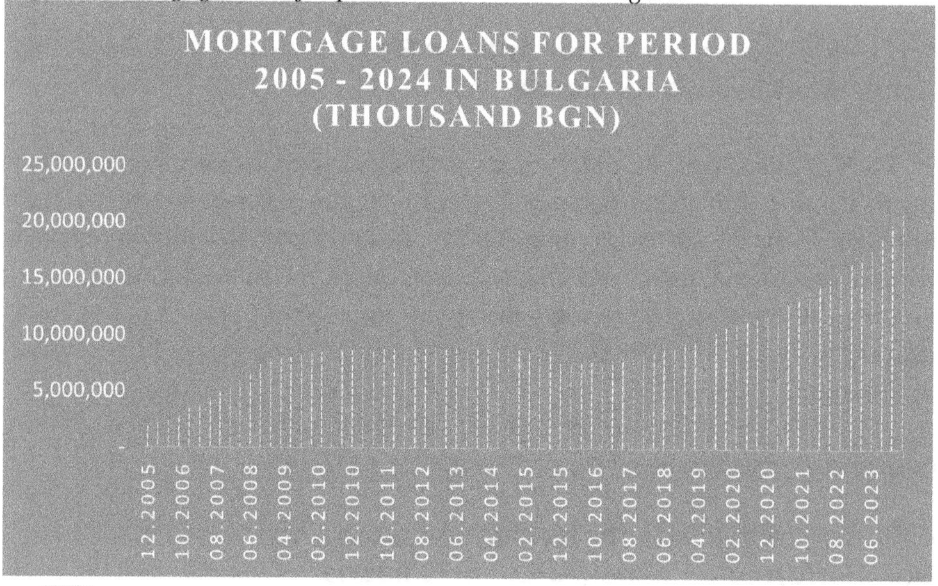

(BNB)

The average mortgages per quartier for period 2016 – 2024 is 11 962 million BGN, the increasing for this period is 175%. Every quarter the real estate lending rises with sustainable rate.

In spite of steadily increasing real estate loans, shadow loans for the period 2016 - 2024 are decreasing. This means that credit risk is properly accounted for by banks and well managed.

Figure 4. Non – performing mortgage loans for period 2015- 2024 in Bulgaria

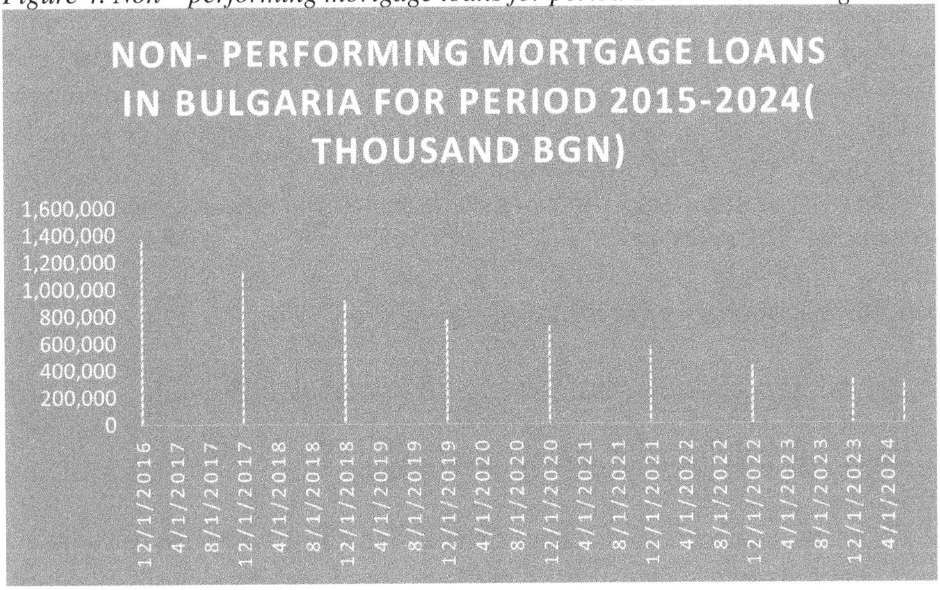

(BNB)

4.3 Risk Management in the Real Estate Market

4.3.1. Existing Situation

The Risk management in real estate encompasses a broad spectrum of risks related to diverse real estate businesses. The current practices primarily address risks associated with real estate lending, while direct investments are often excluded from formal risk management systems.

The standard elements of risk management—(1) risk identification and measurement and (2) risk control and hedging—are inconsistently applied:

- Quantitative approaches to measuring real estate risk, essential for controlling market risk, are underdeveloped. Hedging mechanisms, although theoretically available, are complex and infrequently utilized.
- Risk measurement in real estate could theoretically employ tools akin to those used for stock market risk, but practical applications remain rare. The Real estate markets face additional challenges due to non-normal risk distributions and the difficulty of constructing market prices.

In practice, banks often adapt tools from commercial lending, such as financial statement analysis, credit ratings, property valuation models, sensitivity analyses, and early warning systems. However, these tools primarily target specific risks and fail to account for systemic risk. Diversification of portfolios remains the primary method for controlling real estate market risk, although portfolio-level risk management practices are only beginning to gain traction.

Currently, most financial institutions lack the tools to measure or control real estate market risk effectively.

4.3.2 Implications for Risk Management

The critical importance of real estate market risk and the inadequacies of existing tools highlight the need for a comprehensive real estate risk management framework.

Key recommendations for improvement include:

- Developing advanced risk measurement tools: Risk and return parameters must be redefined for real estate portfolios, requiring new methods of market valuation and modeling real estate risk.
- Improving data infrastructure: In Bulgaria, the absence of reliable real estate databases hampers risk measurement. A robust database with historical and qualitative data is essential for analyzing returns, forecasting market trends, and understanding real estate cycles.
- Creating derivatives for risk hedging: Like equity and bond markets, real estate markets must adopt financial derivatives to hedge against market fluctuations effectively.
- Integrating bank-wide risk management: The Real estate market risks should be incorporated into a unified framework alongside other bank risks. Innovative approaches, such as asset-backed securities and capital market instruments, should play a greater role.

Ultimately, risk management tools must be actionable, and integrated into a risk-aware corporate culture. The success of risk management depends on the practical usability of these tools and the institution's awareness of their capabilities and limitations.

4.3.3. Challenges in Real Estate Risk Management

- Market Valuation and Liquidity Issues:

- ✓ The Property valuations are often inaccurate due to infrequent transactions, appraisal biases, and reliance on retrospective data. This leads to artificial stability and mispricing.
- ✓ The illiquidity of real estate extends to both physical assets and loans, complicating liquidation during crises. The Banks must develop strategies such as loan sales and securitization to manage liquidity risks.

- Price Fluctuations and Credit Risk:
  - ✓ The Real estate credit risks are highly sensitive to market risk factors such as interest rates, rents, and unemployment.
  - ✓ In economic downturns, the correlation between market risks and credit factors intensifies, exacerbating defaults and losses.
- Real Estate Concentration Risks:
  - ✓ Geographic concentrations particularly in regions like Bulgaria's Black Sea coast and Rila mountain area and asset-type concentrations expose banks to significant risks,
  - ✓ Concentrations can lead to asset bubbles and heightened vulnerabilities to market fluctuations.
- Regulatory and Operational Challenges:
  - ✓ Risks associated with property-level factors (e.g., management, financing, and tenant solvency) are often overlooked.
  - ✓ Regulatory oversight, including zoning and tax laws, adds complexity to risk management. Additionally, fraud in property valuations and transactions poses significant risks.
- Volatility and Risk Measurement:
  - ✓ Traditional volatility metrics, often used for liquid securities, are ill-suited for real estate due to its unique characteristics (e.g., infrequent trading, non-normal return distributions).
  - ✓ A broader set of indicators, beyond volatility, is required to accurately capture real estate risks.
- Diversification and Risk Mitigation:
  - ✓ High leverage and concentrated exposure to real estate increase systemic stress on banks. The Diversification across asset types, geographic areas is critical.
  - ✓ Effective contingency plans are essential to manage concentration risks and ensure resilience during market downturns.

5. THE FUTURE. THE ROLE OF FinTech IN MORTATES LENDING

The Technological innovation is reshaping the mortgage application and loan origination process. FinTech lenders leverage technology to improve efficiency (Syverson, 2011: Collard-Wexler et al, 2015) across key dimensions such as processing time, supply elasticity, and credit risk management (Philippon, 2016; Syverson, 2011). This results in a more streamlined and user-centric lending.

5.1. Key Innovations in FinTech Lending

- **Online Applications:** Borrowers can apply for a mortgage entirely online without interacting with loan officers or visiting physical branches.
- **Automated Data Collection:** Online platforms can access borrowers' financial data (e.g., bank statements, tax returns) electronically, reducing manual processes and enhancing accuracy (Housing Wire, 2015).
- **Customizable Mortgages:** The Borrowers can tailor their mortgage terms based on lenders' real-time underwriting standards and pricing.
- **Advanced Creditworthiness Assessment:**
    - ✓ Data collected during the application is automatically analyzed using algorithms.
    - ✓ Borrowers' information is verified against employment databases, ownership records, and other external data sources.
    - ✓ Fraud detection systems flag inconsistencies, such as mismatched pay stubs or irregular bank deposits.
- **Document Processing Automation:** Software tools review and process borrower-uploaded documents, identifying errors or missing information.

These advancements make the mortgage underwriting process more standardized, repeatable, and less prone to human error or subjectivity, while also reducing the potential for fraud (Goodman, 2016).

5.2. The Advantages of FinTech in Property Lending

The FinTech business model introduces several benefits for both lenders and borrowers:

- **Faster Processing:** Applications are processed more quickly than traditional mortgage processes, significantly reducing the lengthy timelines associated with conventional lending.

- **Convenience:** Borrowers can complete the entire process online, from application to approval, enhancing customer satisfaction.
- **Objectivity in Creditworthiness Assessment:** FinTech algorithms reduce subjective bias in decision-making, providing a more consistent evaluation of credit risk.
- **Fraud Detection:** Automated systems identify inconsistencies in borrower data and flag potential fraud.
- **Attraction for Higher-Income Borrowers:** FinTech borrowers tend to have higher incomes and education levels, reflecting the appeal of faster, tech-driven solutions.
- **Increased Refinancing:** The convenience and speed of FinTech platforms have led to a higher proportion of refinances compared to traditional lenders.

5.3. Challenges and Risks in FinTech Lending

Despite its advantages, FinTech property lending faces notable drawbacks and risks:

- **Higher Interest Rates:** FinTech lenders often charge higher interest rates than traditional commercial banks, offsetting the benefits of convenience and speed.
- **Regulatory Gaps:** FinTech companies remain less regulated by central banks compared to commercial banks, raising concerns about oversight and systemic risk.
- **Potential Over-Reliance on Automation:** While algorithms standardize processes, they may fail to capture nuanced, case-specific risks that human judgment could address.
- **Limited Accessibility:** Borrowers with lower income or education levels may struggle to access FinTech services due to the digital nature of the process.

5.4. Implications for Risk Management

FinTech lenders' reliance on automation introduces new opportunities and challenges in risk management:

- **Efficiency in Risk Assessment:** Automation enables faster and more accurate analysis of borrower data, improving risk assessment capabilities.
- **Fraud Mitigation:** Advanced algorithms and data-matching systems enhance the detection of inconsistencies, reducing fraud risks.

- **Regulatory Oversight Needs:** The growing influence of FinTech lending necessitates updated regulatory frameworks to ensure stability and protect consumers.
- **Economic Vulnerability:** High interest rates and partial regulation could expose FinTech lenders to greater risks during economic downturns.

FinTech is poised to redefine property lending, offering transformative improvements in efficiency, convenience, and fraud detection. However, its success will depend on addressing regulatory challenges, managing higher interest rates, and ensuring accessibility for diverse borrower profiles. Balancing innovation with risk management and oversight will be critical for the sustainable growth of FinTech in real estate lending.

6. DISCUSSION. WHAT IT NECESSARY TO CHANGE IN COMING YEARS TO REDUCE THE RISK?

For the last few years Bulgaria realized good economic growth and continued increase of income. These facts increase the creditworthiness of debtors.

Changes could also be made in the regulation:

- Credit maturity to be reduced to a maximum of 20 years
- Participation of the loan in the financing of the real estate to reduce not more than 75% of the price
- More accurate assessment of creditworthiness using additional sources of information such as tax declarations
- Monitoring of employment stability of debtor

CONCLUSION

Real estate lending is a risky activity. Bulgaria is currently experiencing a boom of real estate market prices. The vast majority of purchases are financed with bank credit. This type of credit represents a major component of the asset side of banks' balance sheets. For the period 2016-2024, mortgage loans accounted for 42.66% of total household loans at the beginning of the period and 52.23% at the end.

The interdependence between real estate cycles and financial systems has been widely documented in the real estate literature. The inversely proportional links of real estate markets and bank lending give rise to systemic risks and how these risks can be exacerbated by failures in bank governance or financial regulation.

In countries like Bulgaria, a significant part of real estate investments is financed with bank loans. This requires tracing the relationship between the stages of the credit cycle and changes in the real estate market. Specific issues for Bulgaria, NPLs are not in correlation with the continued increasing of credits for real estate.

The quantitative approach to real estate risk management, which is a prerequisite for measuring and controlling market risk, is relatively new to most banks; hedging uses complex instruments and is therefore not readily available. For real estate, things are more complicated as default risk is not normally distributed and the market and market prices are even more difficult to construct. The banks therefore often use tools from commercial lending that are adapted to real estate lending, for example: financial statement analysis, ratings or valuation tools, sensitivity analysis and early warning systems. It will be important for the future development of real estate risk management that the tools produce results are meaningful and can be easily interpreted and used by bank staff. Ultimately, the success of risk management does not depend on the level of sophistication of its tools, but on a culture in which risk is considered consciously and the opportunities and limitations of risk management are understood.

REFERENCES

Anderson, B. (2016). "Banks Pick Up Greater Share of Multifamily Lending Business". *National Real Estate Investor.*https://newslink.mba.org/mba-newslinks/2016/october/mba-newslink-wednesday-10-19-16/banks-pick-up-greater-share-of-multifamily-lending-business/

Antoniades, A. (2015). "Commercial Bank Failures During the Great Recession: The Real (Estate) Story." *European Central Bank Macroprudential Research Network, No. 1779.*https://www.ecb.europa.eu › ecbwp1779.en.pdf

Berkhout, T., Kil, J., Post, J., & Schrader, J. (2014). *Identifying Risk Perceptions by Real Estate Investors and Banks.* ING Real Estate Finance.

Collard-Wexler, A., & De Loecker, J. (2015). Reallocation and Technology: Evidence from the US Steel Industry. *The American Economic Review*, 105(1), 131–171. DOI: 10.1257/aer.20130090

DeLisle, J. R. (2010). "Chapter 4. Real Estate Risk Management." Fundamentals of Real Estate: A Behavioral Approach. 97-124.

Goodman, W.(2016). The promises and pitfalls of Benford's law. *Significance journal*, 13(3), 38-41. DOI:DOI: 10.1111/j.1740-9713.2016.00919.x

Herring, R. J., & Wachter, S. M. (1999). Real Estate Booms and Banking Busts: An International Perspective. *The Wharton School Research Paper No. 99-27.* https://ssrn.com/abstract=2546407

Holberton, R., Hallissey, A., Chang, D., & Chirgwin, B. (2012). *Risk Management in Corporate Real Estate within the Global Banking and Finance Sector.* CBRE Global Viewpoint.

Housing Wire. (2015): "Guaranteed Rate Purchases Remains of Discover Home Loans". https://www.housingwire.com/articles/34986-guaranteed-rate-purchases-remains-of-discover-home-loans/

Johnson, S., Sheely, M., Fitzgerald, T., & Foster, C. (2007). *Managing commercial real estate Concentrations.* FDIC Supervisory Insights.

Keys, B., Mukherjee, T., Seru, A., & Vig, V. (2010). Did securitization lead to lax screening? Evidence from subprime loans. *The Quarterly Journal of Economics*, 125(1), 307–362. DOI: 10.1162/qjec.2010.125.1.307

Keys, B., Seru, A., & Vig, V. (2012). Lender screening and the role of securitization: Evidence from prime and subprime mortgage markets. *Review of Financial Studies*, 25(7), 2071–2108. DOI: 10.1093/rfs/hhs059

Kindleberger, C. P., & Aliber, R. Z. (2015). Manias, Panics, and Crashes: A History of Financial Crises. Publishing house John Wiley & son. DOI: 355. ISBN: 978-1-137-52575-8DOI: 10.1007/978-1-137-52574-1.pages

www.nsi.bg– Macroeconomic data, 2016-2024

Mera, K., & Renaud, B. (2000). Asia's Financial Crisis and the Role of Real Estate. eBook Published. First edition. New York, DOI: , Pages 312. ISBN9781315500010DOI: 10.4324/9781315500010

Müller, M., & Lausberg, C. (2010). "Why Volatility is an Inappropriate Measure for Real Estate." *ERES Conference 2010, Milan, June 23-26, 2010.*DOI: DOI: 10.15396/eres2010_272

Philippon, T. (2016). "The FinTech Opportunity". *Working Paper N 22476*, National Bureau of Economic Research.

Quigley, J. M., & Raphael, S. (2001). THE ECONOMICS OF HOMELESSNESS: THE EVIDENCE FROM NORTH AMERICA. *European Journal of Housing Policy*, 1(3), 323–336. DOI: 10.1080/14616710110091525

Renaud, B. (1995). The 1985-94 global real estate cycle: its causes and consequences, World Bank, Policy Research. Working paper N 1452.

www.bnb.bg- Statistics,2005-2024

Syverson, C. (2011). What Determines Productivity? *Journal of Economic Literature*, 49(2), 326–365. DOI: 10.1257/jel.49.2.326

Chapter 12
Intellectual Structure of Unemployment Studies: A Bibliometric Analysis

Enes Cengiz Oguz
https://orcid.org/0009-0007-0337-9844
Anglia Ruskin University, UK

Yusuf Elkoca
https://orcid.org/0000-0003-3811-7610
Royal Holloway, University of London, UK

Sibel Aybar
https://orcid.org/0000-0003-4725-9653
Istanbul Gelisim University, Turkey

Evans Akwasi Gyasi
https://orcid.org/0000-0002-1104-8515
Anglia Ruskin University, UK

ABSTRACT

Unemployment remains a critical issue for policymakers and economists, shaped by dynamic and interconnected factors. This study uses bibliometric analysis of 2,504 papers to explore unemployment determinants, highlighting an overlooked link between technological advancements and unemployment. While prior research emphasizes macroeconomic factors and labor market institutions, it underestimates the disruptive impact of technologies like automation, AI, and ICT. These innovations, while boosting productivity and economic growth, also contribute to job displacement, reshaping global labor markets. To mitigate these effects, a balanced approach is needed, including investment in high-skill jobs, retraining programs, and

DOI: 10.4018/979-8-3373-2523-1.ch012

regulatory frameworks. Strategic policy interventions are crucial to ensure inclusive economic growth amid technological disruption. This paper offers valuable insights for policymakers and business leaders on addressing unemployment's multifaceted nature and fostering sustainable development.

1. INTRODUCTION

The unemployment rate is one of the most crucial economic indicators depicting the countries' labour market (OECD, 2022). For instance, a declining unemployment rate indicates a robust economy with rising economic growth. In contrast, a rising unemployment rate is viewed as an indication of a feeble economy with sluggish economic growth. The factors influencing unemployment rates are multifaceted and interconnected. Extant studies have examined macroeconomic factors such as inflation, business cycles, and labour market institutions, including laws, policies, and practices influencing unemployment (Stockhammer & Klar, 2011; Heimberger, 2021).

However, there remains a need for a more integrated understanding of the other factors contributing to unemployment regarding technological changes. One of the most significant economic issues today is the persistently high unemployment rate, exacerbated by integrating technology into nearly every sector of the economy. The labour market is sensitive to imbalances brought about by rapid changes in economic and technological environments. In this sense, purely economic factors are insufficient to explain labour market shifts; technological change must also be considered. The rapid technological advancements have not only expanded global connectivity but also transformed how economic activities are conducted. Whether a business operates internationally or domestically, the global influence of technological developments has become an inescapable reality, profoundly impacting labour markets.

This study contributed to understanding the determinants of unemployment for several reasons. First, unemployment directly impacts economic productivity and growth. Thus, it is a key challenge in developed and developing economies. Based on implied bibliometric analysis, we find that the geographic distribution of publications shows that research on unemployment is concentrated in developed economies, such as the United States, the United Kingdom, and the European Union. Canada and Japan also contribute significantly, reflecting their status as economies that closely monitor labour market trends. This finding indicates comparatively less research on unemployment in underdeveloped and developing countries, despite these regions often experiencing higher unemployment rates and more severe economic consequences.

Second, unemployment is linked to increased levels of poverty, inequality, and social exclusion, as well as adverse effects on mental health and well-being. The longer individuals remain unemployed, the more their employability declines, further complicating the issue of reemployment. Politically, high unemployment can lead to social unrest and instability, particularly in regions with high youth unemployment. For example, in underdeveloped and developing economies, the impact of technological unemployment is even more pronounced due to the prevalence of young populations and insufficient vocational training systems. High youth unemployment rates in these regions pose significant long-term risks, as young people unable to enter the labour market may face lifelong economic and social disadvantages. This highlights the importance of targeted employment policies, particularly those aimed at vocational training, entrepreneurship, and employment counselling (Bozdağlıoğlu, 2008). From a policy perspective, addressing unemployment is essential for maintaining social cohesion and promoting economic resilience. We suggest policymakers understand unemployment's root causes to develop effective solutions. This includes addressing the immediate factors, such as fluctuations in the business cycle, and considering the structural elements, such as mismatches between worker skills and job requirements, technological advancements, and labour market institutions. Therefore, understanding the determinants of unemployment is crucial for crafting policies that can reduce unemployment rates and mitigate their social and economic consequences (OECD, 2022).

Third, adopting advanced technologies like AI and automation, particularly under the Industry 4.0 paradigm, has raised concerns about job displacement. The increasing use of robotics, particularly in manufacturing and logistics, improves efficiency while also displacing jobs traditionally held by humans. The COVID-19 pandemic has accelerated the emergence of technological implications. Businesses that quickly adopted digital transformation during the pandemic managed to survive or thrive, while sectors reliant on physical labour experienced significant job losses (OECD, 2022). However, the full extent of this impact is still debated, with some studies suggesting that technological advancements might not lead to mass unemployment but rather transform job types and skills requirements (İşcan, 2021). AI can also create new job opportunities in areas that require human creativity and advanced skills (Jefrine, 2023). As technology evolves, its impact on unemployment remains critical for policymakers, economists, and businesses alike.

This paper is structured as follows: first, research methodology, including research questions, design, and bibliometric method. Then, the results of the bibliometric analysis are presented, detailing key trends in unemployment research. Next, the literature identifies major themes and contributions to the field. Finally, the paper discusses the implications of government policy and offers recommendations for business directors to address the unemployment issue in a global business. The paper concludes by identifying future research areas, especially the need for more studies on the impact of technological advancements and labour market institutions on unemployment.

2. RESEARCH METHODOLOGY

We employed a bibliometric analysis to explore the unemployment research in the literature.

2.1. Research Questions

In this study, research design was based on identifying topics relevant to the research objective, and the following research questions were formulated:

R_1: What are the most cited authors and publication countries in the unemployment literature?
R_2: What are the factors and subtopics studied in the unemployment literature?
R_3: What are emerging themes in the unemployment literature?

2.2. Aim of the Research

This paper aims to explore the factors driving unemployment, the current state of unemployment across various sectors, and the policy interventions necessary to address these challenges.

2.3. Design of the Research

The search was conducted using the Web of Science (WOS) engines. The literature review establishes inclusion and exclusion criteria to limit the research to a set of studies for comprehensive analysis. Utilizing each criterion enhanced the quality of our literature review. The inclusion and exclusion criteria are given as follows:

The inclusion criteria:

1. The unemployment issue has been studied since the great depression in 1929; thus, we don't have a period limit.
2. Journals with peer review as empirical articles.
3. The paper language is English.
4. Paper published based on the Social Science Citation Index (SSCI)

5. A paper published in economics research and business economics categories was selected.
6. Paper subtopics focus on monetary, economic growth and unemployment.

The exclusionary criteria:

1. Exclude duplicated research.
2. Excluding non-peer-reviewed studies.
3. Exclude studies not in English.
4. Exclude theoretical and conceptual research.
5. This study did not consider unemployment studies on the sociological consequences of individual (e.g., mental and physical affect) and psychological consequences (e.g., poverty, crime, and life satisfaction).

2.4. Method: Bibliometric Study

Unemployment, as defined by Putri and Devi (2019), refers to individuals who are capable of working and actively seeking employment but cannot find work. This study applies bibliometric analysis to unemployment research to provide a comprehensive overview of scholarly work. Bibliometric analysis quantitatively assesses trends, patterns, and impact of academic publications, offering insights into how the field has evolved. Bibliometric analysis is a rigorous technique for investigating and analyzing vast scientific data. It enables researchers to deconstruct the evolutionary nuances of a particular field, such as unemployment, while casting light on the emerging areas of that field (Donthu et al., 2021). Comparatively, systematic literature reviews employing traditional methods necessitate a limited study scope and, consequently, review fewer papers. This way, systematic literature reviews are better adapted for specialized or niche research fields (Donthu et al., 2010). In contrast to systematic literature reviews, which typically rely on qualitative methods, bibliometric analysis employs quantitative methods. The Bibliometric analysis search used only one keyword, "unemployment rate' through a Web of Science (WoS).

The 2,504 research papers in Table 1, such as peer-reviewed articles, conference papers, and book chapters, were discovered to contain pertinent keywords. The initial phase of this study involves conducting a bibliometric analysis, as several works are directly related to unemployment and indirectly related to subtopics of unemployment.

Table 1. Descriptive result

Timespan	**1979:2023**
Sources (Journals, Books, etc)	255
DOCUMENT TYPES	**2504**
Article	2345
article; early access	24
article; proceedings paper	135

3. BIBLIOMETRIC FINDINGS

This study involves conducting a bibliometric analysis to find 2504 papers. The topic of unemployment has been interesting over the years. Unemployment directly impacts economic productivity and growth. When individuals are unemployed, they are not contributing to the economy, resulting in a loss of potential output. This loss is particularly damaging during periods of economic downturn, as unemployment tends to rise sharply, further reducing economic activity. Unemployment's consequences go beyond the immediate loss of income. Therefore, the topic of unemployment has been studied since the early 1980s. The bibliometric analysis shows that papers were published between 1979 and 2023. As illustrated in Figure 1, each year thereafter shows a steady increase over the previous year for an average of 50 publications from 1973 to 2005, respectively. This upward trend, which is likely to continue, clearly highlights a growing interest in and the attention of researchers on unemployment.

Figure 1. Unemployment publications over the years

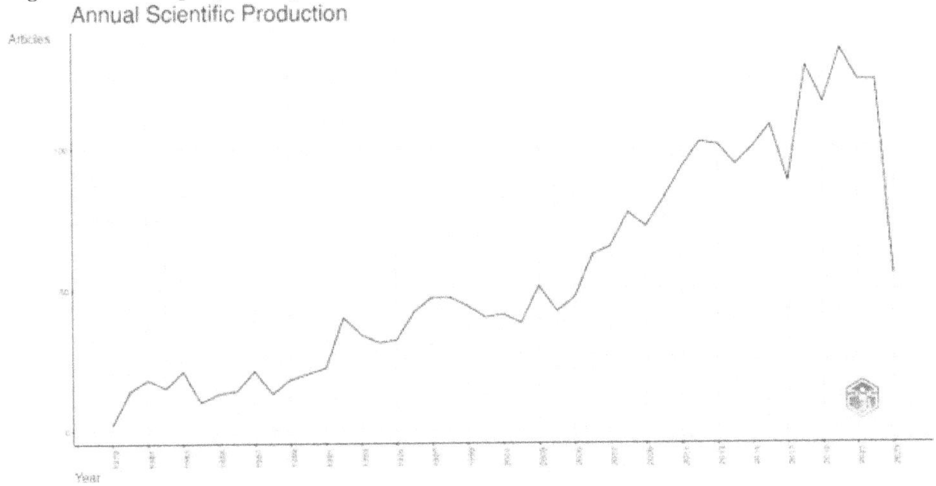

(Source: Own elaboration)

The most unemployment research is represented by 20 significant authors in Figure 2. The level of economic dependence of nations on the sector and their contribution to unemployment research are presented in Figure 2, where the first author's affiliation is used to identify the source of the item. The analysis of the geographical distribution of publications based on authors reveals that most publications originate from the United States, the United Kingdom, and the European Union. Canada and Japan are notable contributors to the other industrialized economies that rely heavily on unemployment. Taken together, the publications by geography and year reveal that most studies focus on unemployment, partly due to the primary issue of countries. The USA and EU governments have been actively promoting research and dealing with unemployment issues; thus, monetary policy, fiscal policy, inflation, business cycle, hysteresis and labour market have been accelerated with unemployment. Although full employment would be the norm in an ideal economic system with job opportunities available for everyone willing and able to work, the reality is far more complex, with unemployment persisting as a key challenge in developed and developing economies. At the macroeconomic level, high unemployment reduces consumer spending, lowers tax revenues, and increases demand for social welfare programs, all of which strain government finances. Over time, this leads to higher public debt and limits governments' ability to invest in critical areas such as education, healthcare, and infrastructure (Heimberger, 2021).

Figure 2. Bibliometric analysis of unemployment output: Country, authors, topics

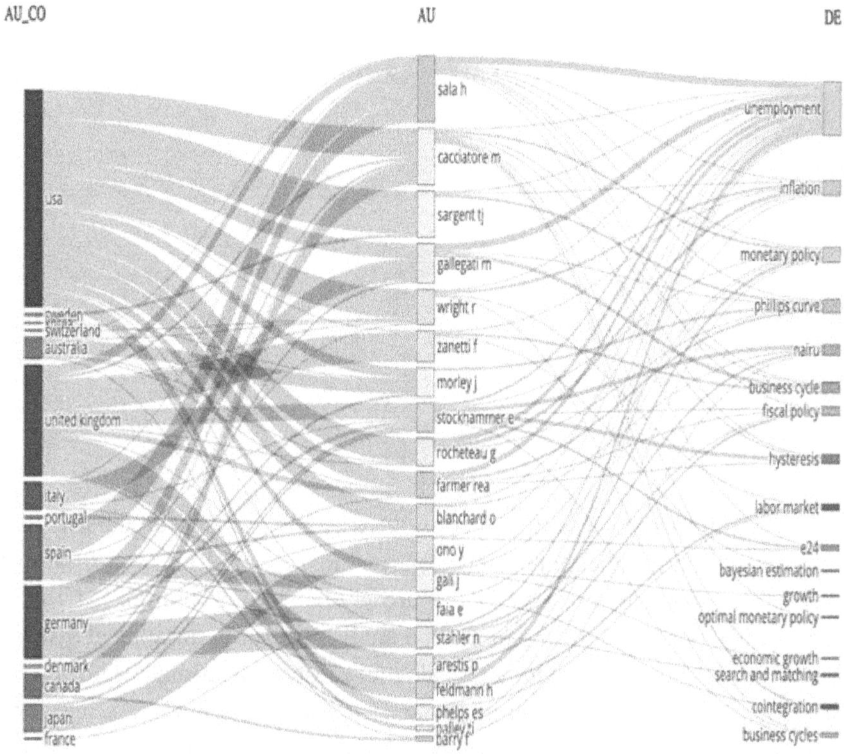

(Source: Own elaboration)

The analysis of the subtopics distribution of unemployment has been illustrated in Figure 2 and, more specifically, 3. This indicates that more than half of the publications originate from combined monetary and fiscal policies. The labour market, fluctuation, and the business cycle are other noteworthy contributors to unemployment. The factors influencing unemployment rates are multifaceted and interconnected. Extant studies have examined macroeconomic factors such as inflation, business cycles, and labour market institutions, including laws, policies, and practices influencing unemployment (Stockhammer & Klar, 2011; Heimberger, 2021). Traditional economic theories often emphasize macroeconomic variables such as inflation, monetary policy, and fiscal policy as key determinants of unemployment. For instance, high inflation rates can erode purchasing power, reduce consumer demand, and lead to lower production levels and subsequent job losses. Similarly, fiscal policies focusing on government spending and taxation can either stimulate or dampen economic activity, influencing employment levels (Stockhammer & Klar, 2011).

In contrast, labour market research has increasingly focused on structural factors. Labour market institutions—such as employment protection laws, collective bargaining practices, and unemployment benefit systems—significantly influence how unemployment rates respond to economic shocks. Rigid employment protection laws may discourage firms from hiring, as the cost of laying off workers becomes prohibitive during downturns. On the other hand, active labour market policies focused on retraining and job placement can help mitigate unemployment by improving worker mobility and matching job seekers with available opportunities (Heimberger, 2021).

Figure 3. Unemployment subtopics cluster

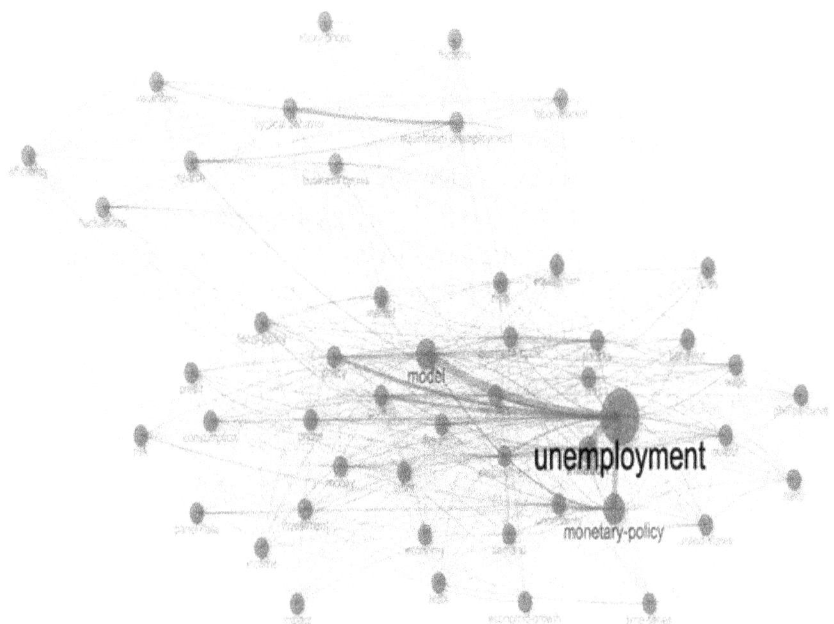

3.1. Summary of Bibliometric Findings and Discussion

Although extant unemployment research has been studied on macroeconomic and labour market issues, there remains a need for more factors in understanding the unemployment phenomenon. One of the most significant economic issues today is the persistently high unemployment rate, exacerbated by integrating technology into nearly every sector of the economy. The labour market is sensitive to imbalances brought about by rapid changes in economic and technological environments. In this sense, purely economic factors are insufficient to explain labour market shifts; technological change must also be considered. Technological unemployment, first recognized by Ataman (1998), refers to job losses caused by technological advancements replacing human labour with machines. The automation of production processes, the rise of artificial intelligence (AI), and the digitalization of services have all reduced labour demand, particularly in sectors that rely heavily on routine and manual work. This form of unemployment is not merely a temporary phase but a structural shift in the labour market, where certain jobs may be permanently eliminated.

As technology evolves, its impact on unemployment remains critical for policymakers, economists, and businesses alike. This trend, known as technological unemployment, has been accelerated by the COVID-19 pandemic. Businesses that quickly adopted digital transformation during the pandemic managed to survive or thrive, while sectors reliant on physical labour experienced significant job losses (OECD, 2022). Adopting advanced technologies like AI and automation, particularly under the Industry 4.0 paradigm, has raised concerns about job displacement. However, the full extent of this impact is still debated, with some studies suggesting that technological advancements might not lead to mass unemployment but rather transform job types and skills requirements (İşcan, 2021).

Zhu, Qiu, and Liu (2021) emphasize the dual impact of such technologies: while they can boost productivity and create high-skill jobs, they also reduce the need for low-skill labour, exacerbating unemployment among workers who lack the necessary skills for emerging roles in the digital economy. Technological advancements, such as automation and artificial intelligence (AI), are critical factors affecting unemployment. These technologies displace workers in routine jobs, particularly in industries dependent on manual labour, while simultaneously creating new opportunities in high-tech sectors. The rise of automation and AI has introduced a new wave of technological unemployment, particularly in industries that are highly susceptible to automation. Jobs that require repetitive tasks, such as manufacturing, customer service, and logistics, are increasingly being replaced by machines capable of performing these tasks with greater efficiency and precision. Automation, particularly the use of AI in various industries, has been identified as a key driver of technological unemployment. Automating routine and repetitive tasks can lead to job displacement, particularly in sectors that rely heavily on manual labour. Studies suggest that while automation boosts productivity, it also leads to short-term job losses due to the replacement of human workers by machines.

However, AI can also create new job opportunities in areas that require human creativity and advanced skills (Jefrine, 2023). The increasing use of robotics, particularly in manufacturing and logistics, is a major contributor to technological unemployment. While robots improve efficiency, they also displace jobs traditionally held by humans. For instance, in China, the adoption of robotics has been identified as a significant driver of unemployment in the short term. However, this effect reverses over a longer period, suggesting an adjustment phase where new job opportunities might emerge (Du & Wei, 2021). Digital automation, a key component of the Fourth Industrial Revolution, affects unemployment by transforming traditional job roles. Sectors that adopt digital technologies, such as e-commerce, digital marketing, and fintech, may experience employment growth. However, traditional sectors, such as retail and banking, might face job losses due to digitalization (İşcan, 2021).

While automation has historically driven economic progress, Lima et al. (2021) argue that contemporary technological unemployment is not solely a product of innovation but is shaped by deeper structural, economic, and policy factors. These include the corporate concentration on AI development, fiscal policies incentivizing automation over human labour, and global technological and skills training inequalities. Consequently, the challenge is not just how many jobs AI will replace, but who will benefit from AI-driven economic gains and who will bear the costs of workforce disruption. Lima et al. (2021) identify three primary drivers of technological unemployment: First, technological monopolization and corporate control. AI development is highly concentrated among a few multinational corporations, such as Google, Amazon, and Alibaba, which prioritize efficiency and profit maximization over workforce sustainability. These companies dictate the pace and scope of AI integration, often favouring automation over human labour when cost reductions and productivity gains outweigh the social consequences. This has led to a global divide, where countries and firms that control AI technologies extract disproportionate economic benefits while regions without AI development capabilities face outsourced unemployment. Second, skills mismatch and employment polarization: Automation has accelerated the divergence between low-skill and high-skill workers, leaving many middle-skill jobs obsolete. AI increasingly automates routine cognitive tasks, while workers who lack digital literacy or specialized expertise are excluded from emerging job markets. This trend will deepen labour market polarization without intervention, reinforcing income disparities (Lima et al., 2021). Third, economic incentives favour automation over human labour: Many tax structures currently penalize human employment through payroll taxes while allowing corporations to automate without equivalent financial obligations. Lima et al. (2021) argue that such fiscal policies artificially incentivize AI-driven job replacement, making labour displacement a technological inevitability and policy-induced outcome.

Shen (2024) highlights three primary mechanisms through which AI contributes to net job creation: enhanced labour productivity, division of labour refinement, and virtual agglomeration (VA). These mechanisms demonstrate that AI technologies not only displace jobs in some areas but also create new opportunities for employment growth. First, AI improves labour productivity by optimizing repetitive and routine tasks, allowing firms to expand operations and scale production. This productivity increase leads to higher labour demand, particularly in industries with the potential for large-scale expansion, such as labour-intensive manufacturing. Shen (2024) finds that these effects are particularly pronounced in labour-intensive industries where automation enhances efficiency without reducing workforce requirements, creating complementary roles such as AI maintenance specialists and robotics engineers. Second, division of labour refinement enables workers to shift their focus from low-value, repetitive tasks to higher-value activities requiring cognitive skills, creativity, and problem-solving abilities. For example, AI-powered systems in customer service manage routine queries, allowing human employees to specialize in resolving complex issues and improving client relationships. Similarly, AI systems streamline risk assessment and fraud detection in the finance sector, creating demand for specialized roles such as AI auditors and data analysts (Shen, 2024). This shift supports the evolution of job roles rather than their outright elimination. Third, the virtual agglomeration (VA) introduced by Shen (2024) is particularly significant in the digital era. Traditional employment clusters, such as industrial hubs, were historically tied to geographic proximity. However, AI-enabled digital platforms foster virtual labour clustering, allowing workers from geographically dispersed regions to contribute to centralized projects. This phenomenon is evident in the rise of remote work, gig-based employment, and crowdsourcing platforms like Upwork and Fiverr. Virtual agglomeration mitigates geographic disparities in job opportunities, enabling workers in underdeveloped regions to access global job markets (Shen, 2024).

Despite these benefits, the impacts of AI are unevenly distributed. Shen (2024) emphasizes that AI disproportionately benefits female workers, a surprising finding challenges earlier concerns about automation reinforcing gender disparities. Automation reduces physical labour demands and increases job flexibility, enabling women to participate in previously male-dominated sectors. Additionally, regions with strong digital infrastructure are better positioned to leverage AI for employment growth, as connectivity facilitates the integration of AI into local economies and enhances workforce adaptability. AI's sectoral impacts further illustrate its nuanced role in shaping employment patterns. While capital-intensive industries use AI to optimize manufacturing processes, technology-intensive industries experience rapid workforce expansion due to the growing demand for specialized AI skills. Paradoxically, labour-intensive industries—once considered highly vulnerable to automation—show the highest rates of job creation, as AI enhances productivity and scalability rather than replacing workers outright (Shen, 2024). Ultimately, the employment impact of AI depends on the interplay between displacement and job creation, with proactive measures playing a crucial role in shaping outcomes. As Shen (2024) argues, policymakers must invest in digital infrastructure, promote inclusive reskilling initiatives, and address regional disparities to ensure that AI-driven employment growth is equitable. By aligning workforce policies with technological advancements, governments can mitigate the risks of displacement while maximizing the job creation potential of AI.

Hammershøj (2019) argues that while AI can replicate many routines and even complex tasks, it lacks the capacity for creativity, intuition, and emotional intelligence—uniquely human qualities. Creativity, which involves connecting disparate domains, reimagining frameworks, and navigating ambiguity, cannot be encoded into machines because it relies on affective and intuitive processes. Machines, even advanced generative AI systems, can only operate within predefined parameters, producing outputs that require human oversight to assess their meaning and value. This highlights the critical role of human leadership in creative and innovative processes, where machines serve as tools to enhance rather than replace human ingenuity. The shifting division of labour between humans and machines has significant implications for the future workforce. As machines take over routine cognitive tasks and middle-skill jobs, human roles increasingly focus on high-value tasks requiring judgment, decision-making, and creativity. Hammershøj (2019) emphasizes that this shift will redefine the employment landscape, particularly in industries reliant on disruptive innovation and cross-disciplinary collaboration. For example, in smart manufacturing and digital design sectors, AI can handle repetitive functions like data analysis or pattern recognition, freeing workers to engage in creative problem-solving, strategic decision-making, and innovation leadership. These emerging hybrid roles underscore the importance of human-machine collaboration, where AI acts as a partner in augmenting human potential rather than as a substitute for human labour.

This evolving division of labour also highlights the challenges and limitations of machine creativity. While AI can optimize processes and generate novel outputs within its programmed parameters, it lacks the capacity for disruptive innovation, which requires stepping beyond established boundaries and creating entirely new paradigms. Effective human-machine collaboration will, therefore, depend on the ability of humans to lead and oversee creative processes, ensuring that machines enhance rather than constrain innovation (Hammershøj, 2019). This underscores the need for collaborative skills development, where humans are trained to leverage AI as partners in innovation while retaining ultimate responsibility for shaping creative outputs.

Information and communication technologies (ICT) have further accelerated this shift by automating clerical and administrative tasks, reducing the need for human workers in sectors traditionally providing significant employment. As Rao (2001) points out, while ICT has facilitated global business expansion and the creation of new job opportunities in high-tech sectors, it has also led to job losses in traditional industries that fail to adapt to digitalization. Feldmann's (2013) research demonstrates that technological advancements significantly increase unemployment in the short term across 21 industrial countries. However, this effect does not persist long term (Feldmann, 2013). A study examining 25 European countries found no significant long-term relationship between technological innovations and unemployment. The study suggested that while short-term effects might exist, technological advancements do not lead to sustained increases in unemployment (Matuzevičiūte et al., 2017). In Indonesia, technological developments have been linked to increased unemployment, especially in regions where human resources lag in adapting to technological changes. Conversely, other studies highlight that technology can reduce unemployment in regions with better-prepared workforces (Sumanto et al., 2020).

The labour displacement by AI and automation has wide-ranging socio-economic repercussions beyond immediate job losses. Lima et al. (2021) identify three key risks. First, widening Income Inequality: AI-driven automation disproportionately benefits high-skill workers and corporate owners, leaving low-skill workers with fewer employment opportunities. This has created a dual economy where those with AI-relevant skills experience wage growth while others face downward economic mobility. Second, fiscal Instability and the Automation Paradox: While automation increases productivity, it also reduces labor-based tax revenues by shrinking the number of taxable wage earners. At the same time, it increases government spending on unemployment benefits and social welfare, creating a paradox where economic efficiency does not translate into fiscal sustainability. Third, economic stagnation due to reduced consumer demand: AI enables businesses to cut labour costs, but when workers lose wages or employment, consumer purchasing power declines, reducing overall economic activity. This creates a scenario where increased efficiency leads to demand-side contraction, undermining long-term growth.

The rapid technological advancements have not only expanded global connectivity but also transformed how economic activities are conducted. Through technological breakthroughs, the world has shrunk in terms of both access to opportunities and how business decisions in one part of the world can affect enterprises and individuals elsewhere. Businesses, defined as units where economic activities are conducted, including producing, selling, and exchanging goods and services, are central to this interconnected landscape (Griffin & Ebert, 1996). Whether a business operates internationally or domestically, the global influence of technological developments has become an inescapable reality, profoundly impacting labour markets.

Furthermore, the effects of individual unemployment extend beyond simple economic metrics such as poverty, inequality, and social exclusion, as well as adverse effects on mental health and well-being. Addressing unemployment is not only an economic necessity but also crucial for maintaining social harmony and political stability (Stockhammer & Klar, 2011). A declining unemployment rate indicates a robust economy with rising economic growth, while a rising unemployment rate indicates a feeble economy with sluggish economic growth. High unemployment rates often lead to social unrest, increased poverty, and decreased public morale, making it a key focus for governments and institutions. Given its far-reaching impact on economic stability, social welfare, and individual livelihoods, unemployment remains a critical issue for policymakers and economists.

Long-term unemployment can lead to a loss of skills, making it more difficult for individuals to re-enter the workforce, a phenomenon known as hysteresis (Heimberger, 2021). The mental health effects of unemployment are also significant, with higher rates of depression, anxiety, and other psychological issues among those who are unemployed. As Rifkin (1996) suggests, reducing working hours due to automation can create a surplus of labour, leading to societal unrest and rising crime rates. Unemployment affects individuals economically and takes a toll on their psychological and physical well-being. Research indicates that unemployment is associated with higher levels of mental health problems, including depression, anxiety, and increased suicide rates (Rifkin, 1996). The longer individuals remain unemployed, the more their employability declines, further complicating the issue of reemployment.

Politically, high unemployment can lead to social unrest and instability, particularly in regions with high youth unemployment. For example, in less-developed and developing economies, the impact of technological unemployment is even more pronounced due to the prevalence of young populations and insufficient vocational training systems. High youth unemployment rates in these regions pose significant long-term risks, as young people unable to enter the labour market may face lifelong economic and social disadvantages. This highlights the importance of targeted employment policies, particularly those aimed at vocational training, entrepreneurship, and employment counselling (Bozdağlıoğlu, 2008). From a policy perspective, addressing unemployment is essential for maintaining social cohesion and promoting economic resilience. Policymakers need to understand the root causes of unemployment to develop effective solutions. This includes addressing the immediate factors, such as fluctuations in the business cycle, and considering the structural elements, such as mismatches between worker skills and job requirements, technological advancements, and labour market institutions. Therefore, understanding the determinants of unemployment is crucial for crafting policies that can reduce unemployment rates and mitigate their social and economic consequences (OECD, 2022).

The rise of artificial intelligence (AI) and digital-industrial technologies is reshaping labour markets at an unprecedented pace, demanding a fundamental shift in how societies approach skills development, education systems, and workforce adaptability. Annunziata and Bourgeois (2018) emphasize that the challenges posed by AI are not limited to job displacement but extend to the growing skills mismatch created by rapid technological advancements. As industries integrate AI to enhance productivity, the demand for routine and low-skilled labour continues to decline, while high-skilled roles in areas such as AI development, robotics engineering, and data science are expanding exponentially. This shift has made STEM education, digital fluency, and entrepreneurial agility indispensable components of future workforce strategies. Workers with these skills are better equipped to complement AI capabilities than compete with them. For instance, AI systems can process vast datasets and automate repetitive tasks, but human ingenuity remains essential for creative problem-solving, decision-making, and collaborative roles that require emotional intelligence (Annunziata & Bourgeois, 2018). Beyond technical skills, interpersonal adaptability and navigating complex, ambiguous work environments have become critical assets in an AI-driven world. Jobs combine human-AI collaboration, such as AI trainers, digital platform managers, and cybersecurity analysts, require workers to develop strong cognitive and relational skills alongside technical expertise (Annunziata & Bourgeois, 2018).

Additionally, entrepreneurial agility—the capacity to innovate and adapt within dynamic economic systems—is increasingly vital as workers shift away from traditional employment models toward platform-based work, gig economies, and hybrid roles. Annunziata and Bourgeois (2018) argue that these emerging skills clusters underscore the urgency of reforming education systems to prioritize lifelong learning, modular training programs, and continuous skill renewal. Policymakers must focus on creating flexible, adaptive education frameworks that prepare individuals for an ever-evolving job market while enabling them to pivot across industries throughout their careers.

The impacts of AI, however, are not evenly distributed, and sectoral and regional variations significantly shape how technological change manifests across the global workforce. Labor-intensive industries, such as manufacturing and agriculture, once considered the most vulnerable to automation, have paradoxically experienced significant job creation due to productivity scaling. For example, the integration of AI in agriculture has enhanced yield optimization and resource management, creating roles for technicians and engineers who oversee automated systems and precision agriculture technologies (Annunziata & Bourgeois, 2018). Similarly, smart manufacturing relies on AI-enhanced efficiency to create hybrid roles where human oversight complements machine capabilities. Conversely, technology-intensive industries, such as software development and AI research, continue to grow accelerated, driving demand for specialized professionals in data analytics, machine learning, and algorithmic development. Annunziata and Bourgeois (2018) highlight that while these industries offer opportunities for high-quality job growth, they also exacerbate inequality by concentrating benefits in regions with advanced digital infrastructure while leaving underdeveloped areas behind. This uneven distribution is compounded by systemic challenges such as gender disparities, regional inequities, and the accessibility of reskilling programs. Annunziata and Bourgeois (2018) emphasize that AI disproportionately benefits workers in regions with robust digital ecosystems, where the infrastructure needed to leverage digital-industrial technologies is already in place.

In contrast, regions with underdeveloped infrastructure, particularly in low- and middle-income countries, face significant barriers to workforce integration in AI-enabled industries. Similarly, while women have benefited from automation's ability to reduce physical labour intensity and increase job flexibility, systemic gender biases still limit their access to high-skill technical roles. Addressing these disparities requires targeted investments in digital infrastructure, inclusive education programs, and gender-sensitive workforce policies to ensure that the benefits of AI-driven growth are equitably distributed across demographics and geographies.

Policymakers have a critical role to play in mitigating the challenges of workforce displacement while maximizing the benefits of AI. Annunziata and Bourgeois (2018) propose a three-tiered strategy to manage this transition: (1) facilitate labour mobility by removing barriers to job transitions, (2) strengthen social safety nets to protect workers during periods of disruption, and (3) invest in reskilling programs that are tailored to the specific needs of displaced workers and regional economies. For example, adopting portable social security systems would enable workers to transition between industries without losing benefits, fostering greater economic flexibility. Moreover, creating accessible, AI-driven reskilling platforms would allow individuals to acquire new competencies in response to shifting labour market demands. By aligning policies with technological advancements, governments can address systemic inequalities, support workforce adaptability, and position their economies to thrive in an era of digital transformation. Ultimately, the narrative surrounding AI and employment must move beyond simplistic concerns about job loss to focus on the complex interplay between displacement, augmentation, and creation. As Annunziata and Bourgeois (2018) demonstrate, AI's transformative potential lies in its ability to reshape labour markets in ways that foster innovation, productivity, and new opportunities for human ingenuity. However, realizing these benefits requires a proactive, inclusive approach that combines education reform, policy innovation, and public-private collaboration to build an equitable, adaptable, and sustainable future of work.

Naastepad and Houghton Budd (2019) argue that the universal basic income (UBI) and reskilling programs are fundamentally incomplete because they fail to address the deeper structural and philosophical dimensions of the relationship between capital, technological progress, and human well-being. Rather than viewing technological unemployment as an inevitable consequence of automation, the authors emphasize that the true challenge lies in how societies allocate capital freed by AI-driven efficiencies. Suppose capital accumulation continues to be guided by profit maximization alone. In that case, the benefits of AI will disproportionately flow toward corporate entities and investors, exacerbating income inequality, social exclusion, and workforce displacement. Conversely, if capital is strategically redirected toward human-centred economic models, AI can serve as a force for inclusive growth, workforce empowerment, and broader societal progress (Naastepad & Houghton Budd, 2019). This requires rethinking economic priorities, shifting from a model prioritizing material efficiency to integrating social, educational, and ethical considerations into technological development.

A critical limitation of mainstream economic approaches to automation is their over-reliance on labour-saving technology, which treats workers as cost factors to be minimized rather than as contributors to innovation and productivity. Naastepad and Houghton Budd (2019) argue that AI and automation should not be solely optimized for cost-cutting but designed as labour-enhancing technologies that augment human capabilities rather than replace them. This approach necessitates a paradigm shift where AI deployment prioritizes skills enhancement, human-machine collaboration, and the creation of new forms of meaningful work. For instance, organizations could use AI to handle routine inquiries instead of replacing administrative staff with AI-powered chatbots while allowing human employees to focus on high-value interpersonal interactions, strategic planning, and problem-solving. Similarly, in smart manufacturing, rather than fully automated production lines, AI could be leveraged to assist workers in optimizing processes, reducing workplace hazards, and enhancing creative problem-solving in design and engineering (Naastepad & Houghton Budd, 2019). These applications demonstrate that technological unemployment is not a deterministic outcome of automation but rather a function of how AI is integrated into economic and social systems.

One of the most thought-provoking arguments by Naastepad and Houghton Budd (2019) is their critique of capital's current role in exacerbating labour-market polarization. They argue that the narrow, profit-driven conception of capital fails to recognize its dual purpose: (1) as an instrument for economic production and (2) as a resource for fostering human development. In traditional economic models, productivity gains from AI typically reduce labour demand, leading to capital accumulation within corporate reserves or speculative financial markets, where wealth concentration is intensified. However, the authors propose an alternative framework where freed capital is reinvested into human capabilities, particularly in education, lifelong learning, cultural industries, and social innovation. By redirecting AI-driven economic gains into adaptive education models, creative industries, and decentralized knowledge networks, societies can ensure that automation enriches, rather than diminishes, human potential (Naastepad & Houghton Budd, 2019). This aligns with broader debates on human-centric economic models, where technological progress is not merely a tool for increasing GDP but a mechanism for advancing societal well-being.

Another key insight from Naastepad and Houghton Budd (2019) is their critique of universal basic income (UBI) as a passive solution to automation-induced job losses. While UBI provides financial security for displaced workers, it does not address the deeper issue of human purpose and agency in the workforce. The authors argue that rather than merely compensating workers for job loss, capital should be strategically reinvested to create new forms of work that integrate AI into human-centred economic models. This means transitioning from traditional full-time employment models to more diverse, flexible, and cooperative labour arrangements that leverage AI's capabilities while preserving human creativity and social engagement. For example, platform economies could evolve beyond gig-based precarity by integrating worker-owned AI-driven cooperatives, where workers have greater autonomy and profit-sharing incentives. Governments could also explore public-private partnerships that leverage AI-driven economic surpluses to fund social enterprises, community-driven innovation labs, and interdisciplinary research hubs, ensuring displaced workers transition into meaningful, purpose-driven employment (Naastepad & Houghton Budd, 2019). These proposals challenge conventional automation narratives by shifting the discussion from how to compensate for lost jobs in the age of AI.

Furthermore, Naastepad and Houghton Budd (2019) warn that an AI-dominated economy governed purely by market forces could lead to an economic concentration where wealth and decision-making power become increasingly centralized among technological elites. The deployment of AI is not ethically neutral—its societal impact depends on who controls its development and implementation. If AI remains in the hands of large multinational corporations with minimal oversight, it risks exacerbating economic inequalities, wage stagnation, and systemic job insecurity. To counteract this, the authors call for greater democratic governance over AI deployment, ensuring that automation is aligned with the public interest, ethical labour practices, and inclusive economic development. This requires AI policy interventions to prioritize well-being over corporate profits, including stronger labour rights protections, inclusive AI governance frameworks, and strategic public investments in socially responsible automation (Naastepad & Houghton Budd, 2019). Such measures would help prevent AI from becoming an instrument of social division and instead position it as a catalyst for inclusive economic progress.

The question of technological unemployment is not simply a matter of automation replacing jobs but a broader issue of how societies choose to integrate AI within economic, social, and ethical frameworks. Naastepad and Houghton Budd (2019) argue that the future of work should not be dictated by short-term cost-efficiency strategies but rather by long-term investments in human capital, adaptive labour models, and ethical AI deployment. The authors challenge policymakers to redefine progress beyond GDP metrics, advocating for a holistic approach where automation is an instrument of human and societal flourishing. By embracing this perspective, governments and institutions can ensure that AI-driven transformations lead to greater economic inclusivity, sustainable labour markets, and meaningful workforce participation rather than perpetuating cycles of displacement and inequality.

The future division of labour between humans and machines will not be determined by technological capabilities alone but by how societies choose to integrate and govern these technologies. As Hammershøj (2019) emphasize, the goal of automation should not be to replace human labour but to augment human potential, enabling individuals to engage in higher-order tasks that foster creativity, innovation, and social progress. This requires a fundamental shift in how policymakers, educators, and industry leaders approach workforce development. By investing in creative education models, fostering human-machine collaboration, and prioritizing man-centric economic policies, societies can ensure that automation serves as a catalyst for inclusive growth and meaningful work rather than a force for displacement and inequality. Education systems must adapt to this new reality by emphasizing pose-oriented learning that cultivates human capacities that are resistant to automation. Hammershøj (2019) critiques traditional skills-based education models, arguing that they are ill-suited to prepare students for the creative economy. Instead, he advocates for curricula prioritizing creativity, emotional intelligence, and the ability to manage and create change. This includes teaching students to work collaboratively with machines and equipping them with the tools to lead innovation processes. For example, students should learn how to use AI tools and integrate them into workflows that require critical thinking and adaptive decision-making. As routine work becomes increasingly automated, the ability to reimagine existing systems, challenge conventional thinking, and lead change will define the future workforce.

Lima et al. (2021) propose a range of policy interventions that could mitigate the risks associated with automation while ensuring an equitable distribution of AI-driven benefits. These include corporate investment in workforce reskilling. Instead of leaving reskilling entirely to governments, firms that adopt AI should be required to invest in retraining their displaced workers. Lima et al. (2021) argue that corporate responsibility should be embedded into AI integration strategies, ensuring that automation does not result in mass layoffs without transition plans. Targeted reskilling and lifelong learning programs. Governments must prioritize continuous workforce development, including AI literacy programs, vocational retraining, and upskilling initiatives. These should be tailored to displaced workers, ensuring they have access to emerging job markets rather than being permanently excluded.

4. CONCLUSION

This paper explores the factors driving unemployment based on bibliometric analysis and provides a comprehensive overview of the factors influencing unemployment. The bibliometric analysis shows that the unemployment studies mainly focused on the subtopics of unemployment such as monetary policy, fiscal policy, inflation, business cycle, hysteresis and labour market. Upon analyzing the geographic distribution of publications, it becomes evident that most articles originate from the United States, the United Kingdom, and the European Union. This study also reveals that the role of technological advancements is underestimated. The rapid incorporation of technological advancements into the production process has undeniably transformed the labour market, leading to positive and negative outcomes. While technological innovations have the potential to drive economic growth and create new job opportunities, they also contribute to rising unemployment in sectors that are less adaptable to technological change. This study offers a comprehensive view of how governments and businesses can better manage the transition toward a technology-driven economy while minimizing adverse effects on employment.

4.1. Future Research Directions

Despite extensive research on unemployment, several gaps remain. First, there is a need for more research on unemployment in developing countries, where labour markets are more volatile and subject to external shocks. Second, future studies should focus on the long-term effects of technological unemployment, particularly given the rise of automation and artificial intelligence. Understanding how these technologies affect job creation and destruction will be crucial for policymakers. Finally, more empirical research is needed to assess the effectiveness of government and business policy interventions, such as retraining programs and social safety nets, in addressing unemployment.

Future Studies on Developing/Emerging Markets: Recent unemployment literature has shifted toward a global and comparative perspective, driven by globalization, technological advancements, and the interconnectedness of labour markets.

Studies increasingly focus on cross-country or regional analyses to better understand how different institutional settings, such as labour policies and welfare systems, influence unemployment across nations. The key reasons for this shift include the growing interdependence of national economies, the widespread impact of technological advancements like automation and digital platforms, and the importance of international labour mobility in shaping unemployment trends. There is a lack of detailed studies exploring how Compensation Theory applies specifically to emerging markets' economic and labour conditions. These economies often have distinct characteristics, such as higher levels of informal employment, different sectoral compositions (e.g., a larger agricultural sector), and varying levels of technological infrastructure. Emerging markets often have a larger pool of low-skilled labour, and introducing technology can initially lead to job displacement. However, according to Compensation Theory, as these economies develop, there is potential for new industries to emerge that can absorb this labour, particularly through sectors like digital services, renewable energy, and technology-based entrepreneurship.

Short-Term vs. Long-Term Effects: Recent advances in new technological machine learning and robotics have hurt human employment opportunities. Numerous studies report an alarming decline in employment resulting from replacing the workforce with machines. A pioneering study by Frey and Osborne in 2013 predicted that 47% of 702 occupations surveyed in the US are at risk of experiencing employment rate declines over the next 10-25 years due to computerization wholesale replacement of the labour force with machines could destroy the creativity many occupations require. Despite these obstacles, it is likely that computerization will significantly impact the current market. The extent to which technological change has affected, and may continue to affect, the economic landscape of the developed world is not foreseeable. While neglect of technological change may be detrimental to many lines of business, appropriate government interventions and modified curricular programmes may bring more radical career opportunities to an increasingly globalized computerized economy. Technology has spread rapidly in our lives, affecting companies on a micro basis and countries on a macro basis. From the past to the present, technological advances have paved the way for industrial revolutions. As a result of the industrial revolutions, how technology will affect unemployment has always been discussed, which is an important issue worldwide with using machines instead of armed labour. Unemployment resulting from capital-intensive technologies instead of labour-intensive technologies in production is called technological unemployment (Postel-Vinay, F., 2002). While production increases in the sectors where the new technology is introduced, those working in this sector become unemployed, and labour flows from this sector to other sectors begin. While Compensation Theory suggests that technological advancements will eventually lead to job creation, there is limited research on the time lag between job displacement and new job creation in emerging markets. Understanding this time lag is crucial for policymakers who must mitigate short-term unemployment while awaiting the long-term benefits of technology-driven growth. Long-Term Development: Emerging markets often have a larger pool of low-skilled labour, and introducing technology can initially lead to job displacement. However, according to Compensation Theory, as these economies develop, there is potential for new industries to emerge that can absorb this labour, particularly through sectors like digital services, renewable energy, and technology-based entrepreneurship.

Economic Growth and Dual Effect on Technology: Technological advancements in developing and emerging markets can lead to significant productivity gains, which are crucial for economic growth. Compensation Theory suggests that while technology may initially displace some jobs, the overall increase in productivity and economic expansion can lead to the creation of new industries and jobs, especially in sectors that leverage these advancements. Technological advances affect unemployment in two aspects. The first is unemployment, which results from substituting capital for labour, a negative situation. The second, which reflects the positive situation, is the creation of new jobs with the increase in demand for new products and services and the shift of employment towards new business areas in this direction (Schwab, 2017, p. 44). When machines started to be used instead of muscle power, there were changes in professions and business lines from unskilled labour to skilled labour. Unemployment caused by technological advances is unemployment, and various views exist on this issue (Carvalho et al., 2020). According to the first view, which is the optimistic view, new technologies have a positive effect on employment, and information technology that improves the quality of working life creates employment. According to optimists, unemployment occurs not when new technologies are used but when they are not. Even if new technologies cause unemployment, the productivity resulting from these technologies will increase welfare. They believe that new products, markets, and industries will provide new employment opportunities and positively affect price or demand. This view supports Schumpeter's view of creative destruction. According to another pessimistic view, substituting machinery for labour and using new technologies increase unemployment. According to the balancing view, which tries to keep both views in balance, the effect of technological advances depends on the way, purpose and shape of the people who benefit from technology (Orhan & Savuk, 2014, p. 16).

Sectoral Analysis: In many emerging markets, traditional sectors like agriculture and manufacturing are gradually being complemented or replaced by technology-driven sectors. Compensation Theory explains how these structural shifts can lead to the emergence of new employment opportunities as economies modernize and diversify. There is a need for sector-specific research to identify which industries in emerging markets are most likely to benefit from technological advancements and create new jobs and which are most vulnerable to job losses. Such analysis is often underexplored in current literature. There is also a gap in research evaluating the effectiveness of policies aimed at leveraging technological advancements for job creation in emerging markets. This includes understanding the role of education, training, and industrial policy in facilitating the transition of displaced workers into new, technology-driven sectors. A prominent trend in the literature is the exploration of structural unemployment, particularly how technology and automation contribute to labour market mismatches. Autor and Dorn (2013) documented the popularization of labour markets, with a rise in low-wage service jobs and a decline in middle-skill manufacturing positions. Another significant focus is on the relationship between unemployment and income inequality, with studies showing that prolonged unemployment widens inequality and reduces social mobility. Ostry et al. (2014) emphasized the effects, particularly in the aftermath of financial crises and the COVID-19 pandemic. The pandemic has further shaped unemployment research, with studies examining its long-term impact on job displacement, skill obsolescence, and youth unemployment. Bell and Blanchflower (2020) argued that young workers have been disproportionately affected, with lasting consequences for the future of work.

Policy Implications: The findings have important implications for policymakers and business directors. Governments must take a proactive approach to managing unemployment by investing in education and retraining programs that equip workers with the skills needed for the jobs of the future. Strengthening labour market institutions to provide greater flexibility and support for workers during economic transitions is also necessary. Lima et al. (2021) ultimately argue that technological unemployment is not an inevitability but a policy choice. If left unregulated, AI and automation will likely concentrate economic gains among a small elite while exacerbating social inequalities and fiscal burdens. However, with well-designed policies—such as robot taxation, mandated corporate reskilling initiatives, and progressive workforce training programs—it is possible to align AI development with inclusive economic progress.

Furthermore, the debate over UBI vs. employment-centered reforms underscores the importance of balancing income security with workforce participation. Governments must avoid treating displaced workers as passive welfare recipients and instead design policies that actively reintegrate them into emerging AI-driven industries. By doing so, societies can harness AI's potential for innovation and growth without sacrificing social stability. Additionally, social safety nets must be enhanced to protect vulnerable workers from the adverse effects of job displacement. For developing countries, the emphasis on policies that support new industry creation, education, and skills development aligns with Compensation Theory. It highlights the need for strategies that address immediate job losses and foster long-term economic transformation and employment growth.

Technological impact on unemployment can also be closely linked with strategic management in business organizations. Businesses integrate technology into their strategies; they must navigate the potential for technological unemployment both internally (within their workforce) and externally (in the labour market) in various ways. First, investing in technological innovation is crucial for maintaining competitive advantage. However, these investments often lead to efficiencies that reduce the demand for certain job roles, contributing to technological unemployment. Strategic decisions on balancing innovation and human capital are essential for maintaining morale and productivity. For example, retail companies like Amazon use AI and robotics in warehouses to streamline operations, reducing the need for warehouse workers. Second, strategic management requires forecasting and aligning workforce needs with the company's goals. Companies adopting automation, AI, and other advanced technologies may reduce the need for certain jobs. Managers must strategically plan how to handle workforce reductions or reallocations to avoid negative impacts like layoffs or to redeploy employees into new roles requiring upskilling or reskilling. For example, automation and robotics have reduced the need for manual labour in manufacturing. Strategic management would involve transitioning employees to more technical or supervisory roles, mitigating the effects of job displacement. Third, introducing new technology requires strategic change management to help the organization. This often includes addressing potential resistance from employees who fear job loss due to automation. Strategic management involves not only the adoption of new technology but also guiding the organization through this transition by managing technological unemployment's impact on the corporate culture. For example, companies in the financial services sector adopting blockchain and AI for fraud detection need strategic frameworks to help employees transition from traditional to tech-based roles, thereby minimizing technological unemployment. Fourth, technological unemployment does not just affect the internal workforce—it also shapes the broader market in which a company operates. As other firms adopt technology, job markets shift. Strategic management must account for how these changes affect customer bases, competitors, and suppliers. If technological unemployment leads to significant societal shifts, companies might need to adjust their business models to align with new consumer behaviours or economic conditions. For example, ride-sharing apps and autonomous vehicles may lead to technological unemployment among drivers in the transportation industry. Strategic managers must anticipate how these shifts will impact market demand, competition, and regulation, potentially developing new revenue streams or business models. Finally, strategic leaders can capitalize on these advantages while addressing the unemployment challenges through careful workforce planning. Companies like Tesla and Apple leverage automation and AI in production, gaining strategic advantages by operating more efficiently. However, they balance this by offering roles in more skilled areas like research, engineering, and software development, showing a strategic response to manage the fallout of technological unemployment.

REFERENCES

Annunziata, M., & Bourgeois, H. (2018). The future of work: How G20 countries can leverage digital-industrial innovations into stronger high-quality jobs growth. *Economics, 12*(1), 20180042. DOI: 10.5018/economics-ejournal.ja.2018-42

Ataman, B. C. (1998). New approaches to the unemployment problem. *Ankara University SBF Journal, 53*(1), 59–72.

Autor, D. H., & Dorn, D. (2013). The growth of low-skill service jobs and the popularization of the US labour market. *The American Economic Review, 103*(5), 1553–1597. DOI: 10.1257/aer.103.5.1553

Bell, D. N., & Blanchflower, D. G. (2020). US and UK labour markets before and during the Covid-19 crash. *National Institute Economic Review, 252*, R52–R69. DOI: 10.1017/nie.2020.14

Bozdağlıoğlu, U. Y. (2008). Characteristics of unemployment in Turkey and policies to combat unemployment. *Journal of Social Sciences, 20*, 47.

Carvalho, L., & Di Guilmi, C. (2020). Technological unemployment and income inequality: A stock-flow consistent agent-based approach. *Journal of Evolutionary Economics, 30*(1), 39–73. DOI: 10.1007/s00191-019-00628-9

Donthu, N., Kumar, S., Mukherjee, D., Pandey, N., & Lim, W. M. (2021). How to conduct a bibliometric analysis: An overview and guidelines. *Journal of Business Research, 133*, 285–296. DOI: 10.1016/j.jbusres.2021.04.070

Du, Y., & Wei, L. (2021). The impact of robotics adoption on labour markets: Evidence from China. *Journal of Economic Studies (Glasgow, Scotland), 48*(1), 45–60. DOI: 10.1108/JES-04-2020-0197

Erol, H. (2010). The role of the Unemployment Insurance Law No. 4447 in addressing the negative consequences of unemployment in Turkey. *TISK Academy, 5*(10), 8.

Feldmann, H. (2013). Technological unemployment in industrial countries: Causes and policy recommendations. *Revista de Economia Institucional, 4*(1), 1–20. DOI: 10.5202/rei.v4i1.90

Frey, C. B., & Osborne, M. A. (2017). The future of employment: How susceptible are jobs to computeri*zation technological Forecasting and Social Change, 114*, 254–280. https://doi.org/DOI: 10.1016/j.techfore.2016.08.019

Griffin, R., & Ebert, R. J. (1996). *Business: Book one* (4th ed.). Prentice Hall.

Hammershøj, L. G. (2019). The new division of labour between humans and machines and its educational implications. *Technology in Society, 59*, 101142. DOI: 10.1016/j.techsoc.2019.05.006

Heimberger, P. (2021). Does economic globalization affect unemployment? A meta-analysis. *Review of World Economics, 157*(2), 1–33. DOI: 10.1007/s10290-021-00427-w

İşcan, E. (2021). An old problem in the new era: Effects of artificial intelligence on unemployment on the way to industry 5.0. *Yaşar Üniversitesi E-Dergisi, 16*(61), 77–94.

Jefrine, G. (2023). The role of AI in technological unemployment and job displacement. *Journal of Future Technologies, 35*(1), 100–120. DOI: 10.1080/10438599.2023.125463

Lima, Y., Barbosa, C. E., dos Santos, H. S., & de Souza, J. M. (2021). Understanding technological unemployment: A review of causes, consequences, and solutions. *Societies (Basel, Switzerland), 11*(2), 50. DOI: 10.3390/soc11020050

Lindsay, A., Downs, D., & Lunn, K. (2003). Business processes: Attempts to find a definition. *Information and Software Technology, 45*(15), 1015–1019. DOI: 10.1016/S0950-5849(03)00129-0

Matuzevičiūte, K., Zuperkiene, E., & Simanavičiene, Ž. (2017). The long-term impact of technological innovations on unemployment in European countries. *Baltic Journal of Economic Studies, 3*(2), 145–153. DOI: 10.30525/2256-0742/2017-3-2-145-153

Naastepad, C. W. M., & Houghton Budd, C. (2019). Preventing technological unemployment by widening our understanding of capital and Progress: Making robots work for us. *Ethics & Social Welfare, 13*(2), 115–132. DOI: 10.1080/17496535.2018.1512641

Nickell, S., Nunziata, L., & Ochel, W. (2005). Unemployment in the OECD since the 1960s: What do we know? *Economic Journal (London), 115*(500), 1–27. DOI: 10.1111/j.1468-0297.2004.00958.x

OECD. (2022). [*Analysis of unemployment trends.* OrgOrganizationr Economic Co-operation and Development.]. *Economic Outlook*, •••, 2022.

Orhan, S., & Savuk, F. (2014). Emek-teknoloji-işsizlik ilişkisi. *Çalışma ve Sosyal Güvenlik Bakanlığı Çalışma Dünyası Dergisi, 2*(2), 9-24.

Ostry, J. D., Berg, A., & Tsangarides, C. G. (2014). *Redistribution, inequality, and growth.* IMF Staff Discussion Note., DOI: 10.5089/9781484352076.006

Postel-Vinay, F. (2002). The dynamics of technological unemployment. *International Economic Review, 43*(3), 737–760. DOI: 10.1111/1468-2354.t01-1-00033

Putri, M. D., & Devi, R. N. (2019). Impact of unemployment on well-being: A socio-psychological perspective. *IOP Conference Series. Materials Science and Engineering, 508*, 1–8. DOI: 10.1088/1757-899X/508/1/012017

Rao, P. M. (2001). The ICT revolution, int internationalization technological activity, and the emerging economies: Implications for global marketing. *International Business Review, 10*(5), 571–596. DOI: 10.1016/S0969-5931(01)00033-6

Rifkin, J. (1996). *The end of work* (Rouve, P., Trans.). La Decouverte.

Schwab, K. (2017). *Dördüncü sanayi devrimi* (Dicleli, Z., Trans.). Optimist Yayınları.

Shen, Y. (2024). Future jobs: An analysis of the impact of artificial intelligence on employment and its mechanisms. *Economic Change and Restructuring, 57*(2), 34. DOI: 10.1007/s10644-024-09629-6

Stockhammer, E., & Klar, M. (2011). Capital accumulation, labour market institutions, and unemployment in Europe. *Cambridge Journal of Economics, 35*(2), 437–457. DOI: 10.1093/cje/beq020

Sumanto, B., Rachmawati, R., & Suryani, D. (2020). The impact of technological development on unemployment in Indonesia. *Indonesian Journal of Economics and Development, 30*(4), 302–311. DOI: 10.20885/ejem.vol30.iss4.art7

Zhu, C., Qiu, Z., & Liu, F. (2021). Does innovation stimulate employment? Evidence from China. *Economic Modelling, 94*, 1007–1017. DOI: 10.1016/j.econmod.2020.02.041

Compilation of References

Abbu, H., Mugge, P., Gudergan, G., Hoeborn, G., & Kwiatkowski, A. (2022). Measuring the Human Dimensions of Digital Leadership for Successful Digital Transformation: Digital leaders can use the authors' Digital Leadership Scale to assess their own readiness and ability to accelerate digital transformation. *Research Technology Management*, 65(3), 39–49. DOI: 10.1080/08956308.2022.2048588

Abdallah, Y. O., Shehab, E., & Al-Ashaab, A. (2021). Digital Transformation Challenges in the Manufacturing Industry. In Shafik, M., & Case, K. (Eds.), *Advances in Transdisciplinary Engineering*. IOS Press., DOI: 10.3233/ATDE210004

Adnan, A. T. M. (2023). Asian perspective of capital market performance amin the Covid-19 pandemic. *Asian Journal of Accounting Research*, 8(3), 210–235. DOI: 10.1108/AJAR-10-2021-0223

Agency, E. U., & the Space Programme. (2023). EU Space for Green Transformation: A new tool for companies to monitor their sustainability targets. Retrieved from https://www.euspa.europa.eu/sites/default/files/eu_space_for_green_transformation_a_new_tool_for_companies_to_monitor_their_sustainability_targets_2023_issue_1.pdf

Aggity. (2018). Industria 4.0 en el sector madera y mueble. *Industria y Producción*. https://aggity.com/industria-4-0-en-el-sector-madera-y-mueble/

Agustian, K., Mubarok, E. S., Zen, A., Wiwin, W., & Malik, A. J. (2023). The Impact of Digital Transformation on Business Models and Competitive Advantage. [TACIT]. *Technology and Society Perspectives*, 1(2), 79–93. DOI: 10.61100/tacit.v1i2.55

Agyabeng-Mensah, Y., Afum, E., & Ahenkorah, E. (2020). Exploring financial performance and green logistics management practices: Examining the mediating influences of market, environmental and social performances. *Journal of Cleaner Production*, 258, XX–XX. DOI: 10.1016/j.jclepro.2020.120613

Ahlers, J., Hemkhaus, M., Hibler, S., & Hannak, J. (2021, junio). *Analysis of Extended Producer Responsibility Schemes*. adelphi consult GmbH. https://erp-recycling.org/wp-content/uploads/2021/07/adelphi_study_Analysis_of_EPR_Schemes_July_2021.pdf

Ahmad, F., Widén, G., & Huvila, I. (2020). The impact of workplace information literacy on organizational innovation: An empirical study. *International Journal of Information Management*, 51, 51. DOI: 10.1016/j.ijinfomgt.2019.102041

Ahmed, W., Hizam, S. M., & Sentosa, I. (2022). Digital dexterity: Employee as consumer approach towards organizational success. *Human Resource Development International*, 25(5), 631–641. DOI: 10.1080/13678868.2020.1835107

AIDIMME. AMUEBLA, CENFIM, & CETEM. (2018). *Análisis de la viabilidad para la implantación de la Industria 4.0 en el sector del hábitat* (AEI-010600-2017-141, p. 99). HABITAT 4.0. https://www.cenfim.org/images/Noticias/Documents/PUBLICACION-HABITAT-4-0-REV-08.pdf

Ailawadi, K. L., Lehmann, D. R., & Neslin, S. A. (2003). Revenue premium as an outcome measure of brand equity. *Journal of Marketing*, 67(4), 1–17. DOI: 10.1509/jmkg.67.4.1.18688

Ailawadi, K. L., Neslin, S. A., & Gedenk, K. (2001). Pursuing the value-conscious consumer: Store brands versus national brand promotions. *Journal of Marketing*, 65(1), 71–89. DOI: 10.1509/jmkg.65.1.71.18132

Ailawadi, K. L., Pauwels, K., & Steenkamp, J. B. E. (2008). Private-label use and store loyalty. *Journal of Marketing*, 72(6), 19–30. DOI: 10.1509/jmkg.72.6.019

Ajmal, M. M., Khan, M., Hussain, M., & Helo, P. (2018). Conceptualizing and incorporating social sustainability in the business world. *International Journal of Sustainable Development and World Ecology*, 25(4), 327–339. DOI: 10.1080/13504509.2017.1408714

Ajzen, I. (1991). The theory at planned behavior. *Organizational Behavior and Human Decision Processes*, 50(2), 179–211. DOI: 10.1016/0749-5978(91)90020-T

Akgün, A. (2023). Otel faaliyetleri için yapay zekâ destekli uygulamalar. *Selçuk Turizm ve Bilişim Araştırmaları Dergisi*, (3), 1–21.

Akin, F., & Dinçer, S. (2024). "Endüstri 4.0 ve Çevresel Sürdürülebilirlik Arasındaki İlişki: Avrupa Birliği Ülkeleri Üzerine Ampirik Bir Analiz." Yönetim Bilimleri Dergisi/Journal of Administrative Sciences, 22(54), 2449-2469. DOI: DOI: 10.20460/JGSM.2011515820

Aksoy, M., & Yilmaz, M. K. (2024). Stock market response to natural disasters: Does corporate sustainability performance make difference? *Journal of Cleaner Production*, 454, 142294. DOI: 10.1016/j.jclepro.2024.142294

Alberola, E., Arslan, Y., Cheng, G., & Moessner, R. (2021). Fiscal response to the COVID-19 crisis in advanced and emerging market economies. *Pacific Economic Review*, 26(4), 459–468. DOI: 10.1111/1468-0106.12370

Albuquerque, R., Koskinen, Y., Yang, S., & Zhang, C. (2020, November). Resiliency of Environmental and Social Stocks: An Analysis of the Exogenous COVID-19 Market Crash. *The Review of Corporate Finance Studies*, 9(3), 593–621. DOI: 10.1093/rcfs/cfaa011

Aleksander, I. (2017). Partners of Humans: A Realistic Assessment of the Role of Robots in the Foreseeable Future. *Journal of Information Technology*, 32(1), 1–9. DOI: 10.1057/s41265-016-0032-4

Alexandro, R., & Basrowi, B. (2024). The influence of macroeconomic infrastructure on supply chain smoothness and national competitiveness and its implications on a country's economic growth: Evidence from BRICS countries. *Uncertain Supply Chain Management*, 12(1), 167–180. DOI: 10.5267/j.uscm.2023.10.007

Ali, M. N., Senthil, T. S., Ilakkiya, T., Hasan, D. S., Ganapathy, N. B. S., & Boopathi, S. (2024). IoT's Role in Smart Manufacturing Transformation for Enhanced Household Product Quality. In Revathy, G. (Ed.), (pp. 252–289). Advances in Systems Analysis, Software Engineering, and High Performance Computing. IGI Global., DOI: 10.4018/979-8-3693-1694-8.ch014

Allam, Z., Bibri, S. E., & Sharpe, S. A. (2022). The Rising Impacts of the COVID-19 Pandemic and the Russia–Ukraine War: Energy Transition, Climate Justice, Global Inequality, and Supply Chain Disruption. *Resources*, 11(11), 99. DOI: 10.3390/resources11110099

Alsheiabni, S., Cheung, Y., & Messom, C. (2018). Artificial intelligence adoption: AI-readiness at firm-level. In: PACIS 2018 Proceedings.

Al-Swidi, A. K., Hair, J. F., & Al-Hakimi, M. A. (2023). Sustainable development-oriented regulatory and competitive pressures to shift toward a circular economy: The role of environmental orientation and Industry 4.0 technologies. *Business Strategy and the Environment*, 32(7), 4782–4797. DOI: 10.1002/bse.3393

Amalia, A., & Suprayogi, M. (2019, October). Engaging millennials on using chatbot messenger for eco-tourism. *Third International Conference on Sustainable Innovation 2019–Humanity, Education and Social Sciences (IcoSIHESS 2019)* (pp. 484-487). Atlantis Press. DOI: 10.2991/icosihess-19.2019.84

AMBIT. (2024, junio 28). AMBIT presenta a sus asociados la nueva legislación sobre final de vida de muebles y enseres. *Ambit actualidad.* https://ambitcluster.org/es/actualidad/noticias/3097-ambit-presenta-a-sus-asociados-la-nueva-legislacion-sobre-final-de-vida-de-muebles-y-enseres

Amihud, Y., & Lev, B. (1999). Risk reduction as a managerial motive for conglomerate mergers. *The Bell Journal of Economics*, 12(2), 605–617. DOI: 10.2307/3003575

Anderson, B. (2016). "Banks Pick Up Greater Share of Multifamily Lending Business". *National Real Estate Investor.*https://newslink.mba.org/mba-newslinks/2016/october/mba-newslink-wednesday-10-19-16/banks-pick-up-greater-share-of-multifamily-lending-business/

Anderson, E. W., Fornell, C., & Lehmann, D. R. (1994). Customer satisfaction, market share, and profitability: Findings from Sweden. *Journal of Marketing*, 58(3), 53–66. DOI: 10.1177/002224299405800304

Annunziata, M., & Bourgeois, H. (2018). The future of work: How G20 countries can leverage digital-industrial innovations into stronger high-quality jobs growth. *Economics*, 12(1), 20180042. DOI: 10.5018/economics-ejournal.ja.2018-42

ANSES & Bureau REACH. (2019, junio 7). *SUBSTANCE EVALUATION CONCLUSION as required by REACH Article 48 and EVALUATION REPORT for Formaldehyde EC No 200-001-8 CAS No 50-00-0.* https://echa.europa.eu/documents/10162/cc0acabf-6e82-f2ed-5dbe-8058f48ce6c4

Antoniades, A. (2015). "Commercial Bank Failures During the Great Recession: The Real (Estate) Story." *European Central Bank Macroprudential Research Network, No. 1779.*https://www.ecb.europa.eu › ecbwp1779.en.pdf

Antoniadis, I., Spinthiropoulos, K., & Kontsas, S. (2020). Blockchain applications in tourism and tourism marketing: A short review. *Strategic innovative marketing and tourism*, 375-384.

Appolloni, A., D'Adamo, I., Gastaldi, M., Santibanez-Gonzalez, E. D. R., & Settembre-Blundo, D. (2021). Growing e-waste management risk awareness points towards new recycling scenarios: The view of the Big Four's youngest consultants. *Environmental Technology & Innovation*, 23, 101716. DOI: 10.1016/j.eti.2021.101716

Arangiaro, V., Vishkaei, B. M., & De Giovanni, P. (2022). Blockchain for Circular Economy in the Furniture Sector: The Case of Cubo Design S.r.l. In De Giovanni, P. (Ed.), *Cases on Circular Economy in Practice* (pp. 238–275). IGI Global., DOI: 10.4018/978-1-6684-5001-7.ch011

AREMA. (2019). *Informe de tendencias en el comercio internacional de muebles.* AREMA.

Armenakis, A., Harris, S., & Mossholder, K. (1993). Creating readiness for organizational change. *Human Relations*, 46(6), 681–703. DOI: 10.1177/001872679304600601

Assante, D., Flamini, M., & Trinca, E. (2023). Towards Industry 5.0: Fostering a Circular Human Resources Management in the Foundry Sector. *2023 6th Experiment@ International Conference (exp.at'23)*, 232–236. DOI: 10.1109/exp.at2358782.2023.10545670

Assent. (s. f.). *What Is the ECHA?* Recuperado 8 de septiembre de 2024, de https://www.assent.com/resources/knowledge-article/what-is-the-echa/

Ataman, B. C. (1998). New approaches to the unemployment problem. *Ankara University SBF Journal*, 53(1), 59–72.

Atif, S. (2023). Analysing the alignment between circular economy and industry 4.0 nexus with industry 5.0 era: An integrative systematic literature review. *Sustainable Development (Bradford)*, 31(4), 2155–2175. DOI: 10.1002/sd.2542

Attaran, M., & Celik, B. G. (2023). Digital Twin: Benefits, use cases, challenges, and opportunities. *Decision Analytics Journal*, 6, 100165. DOI: 10.1016/j.dajour.2023.100165

Autor, D. H., & Dorn, D. (2013). The growth of low-skill service jobs and the popularization of the US labour market. *The American Economic Review*, 103(5), 1553–1597. DOI: 10.1257/aer.103.5.1553

Awan, U., Sroufe, R., Godinho Filho, M., & Shahbaz, M. (2021). Industry 4.0 and the circular economy: A literature review and recommendations for future research. *Business Strategy and the Environment*, 30(1), 2038–2060. DOI: 10.1002/bse.2731

Badi, S. (2024). IoT and Big Data Analytics: Revolutionizing Business and Society with Advanced Insights. *International Journal of Applied Mathematics and Computer Science*, •••, 42–56.

Bag, S., & Pretorius, J. H. C. (2022). Relationships between Industry 4.0, sustainable manufacturing and circular economy: Proposal of a research framework. *The International Journal of Organizational Analysis*, 30(4), 864-898.

Baker, W. E., & Lutz, R. J. (2000). An empirical test of an updated relevance accessibility model of advertising effectiveness. *Journal of Advertising*, 29(1), 1–14. DOI: 10.1080/00913367.2000.10673599

Baltagi, B. H. (2008). Econometric analysis of panel data. *Econometric Theory*, 13(05), 351.

Balwada, J., Samaiya, S., & Mishra, R. P. (2021). Packaging Plastic Waste Management for a Circular Economy and Identifying a better Waste Collection System using Analytical Hierarchy Process (AHP). *Procedia CIRP*, 98, 270–275. DOI: 10.1016/j.procir.2021.01.102

Banjanović-Mehmedović, L., & Mehmedović, F. (2020). Intelligent manufacturing systems are driven by artificial intelligence in Industry 4.0. In *Handbook of Research on Integrating Industry 4.0 in Business and Manufacturing* (pp. 31–52). IGI Global. DOI: 10.4018/978-1-7998-2725-2.ch002

Banjanovi-Mehmedovic, L., & Dželilović, N. (2024). Towards a Greener Future: Sensor-Based Material Characterization in Waste Sorting for a Sustainable Recycling Model. Em I. Karabegovic, A. Kovačević, & S. Mandzuka (Orgs.), *New Technologies, Development and Application VII* (Vol. 1070, p. 3–11). Springer Nature Switzerland. DOI: 10.1007/978-3-031-66271-3_1

Baptista, J., Stein, M.-K., Klein, S., Watson-Manheim, M., & Lee, J. (2020). Digital work and organisational transformation: Emergent digital/human work configurations in modern organisations. *The Journal of Strategic Information Systems*, 29(2), 101618. DOI: 10.1016/j.jsis.2020.101618

Barbier, E. B., & Burgess, J. C. (2020). Sustainability and development after COVID-19. *World Development*, 135, 105082. DOI: 10.1016/j.worlddev.2020.105082 PMID: 32834381

Barrett, A., & Baum, S. (2016). A Model of Pathways to Artificial Superintelligence Catastrophe for Risk and Decision Analysis. *Journal of Experimental & Theoretical Artificial Intelligence*, 29(2), 1–18.

Batty, M. (2018). Digital twins. *Environment and Planning. B, Urban Analytics and City Science*, 45(5), 817–820. DOI: 10.1177/2399808318796416

Bayindir, A. B., & Aksoy, M. (2024). The Relationship Between Corporate Sustainability Performance And Financial Performance During The Covid-19 Pandemic Period. *Anadolu University Journal of Economics and Administrative Sciences*, 25(1), 453–478.

Bebbington, J., Larrinaga, C., & Moneva, J. M. (2008). Corporate social reporting and reputation risk management. *Accounting, Auditing & Accountability Journal*, 21(3), 337–361. DOI: 10.1108/09513570810863932

Behl, A., Singh, R., Pereira, V., & Laker, B. (2023). Analysis of Industry 4.0 and circular economy enablers: A step towards resilient sustainable operations management. *Technological Forecasting and Social Change*, 189. DOI: 10.1016/j.techfore.2023.122363

Bekele, H., & Raj, S. (2024). Digitalization and digital transformation in the tourism industry: a bibliometric review and research agenda. *Tourism Review*, (ahead-of-print).

Bell, D. N., & Blanchflower, D. G. (2020). US and UK labour markets before and during the Covid-19 crash. *National Institute Economic Review*, 252, R52–R69. DOI: 10.1017/nie.2020.14

Benešová, A., Baslb, J., Tupa, J., & Steiner, F. (2021). Design of a business readiness model to realise a green Industry 4.0 company. *International Journal of Computer Integrated Manufacturing*, 34(9), 920–932. DOI: 10.1080/0951192X.2021.1946858

Benítez-Márquez, M. D., Sánchez-Teba, E. M., & Coronado-Maldonado, I. (2022). An alternative index to the global competitiveness index. *PLoS One*, 17(3), XX–XX. DOI: 10.1371/journal.pone.0265045 PMID: 35312691

Benito, N. (2019). El papel de las empresas en la transición ecológica. *El Periódico-Valores*. https://www.elperiodico.com/es/activos/valores/20190118/empresas-transicion-ecologica-7253078

Benlemlih, M., Shaukat, A., Qiu, Y., & Trojanowski, G. (2016). Environmental and social disclosures and firm risk. *Journal of Business Ethics*, 152(3), 613–626. DOI: 10.1007/s10551-016-3285-5

Berkhout, T., Kil, J., Post, J., & Schrader, J. (2014). *Identifying Risk Perceptions by Real Estate Investors and Banks*. ING Real Estate Finance.

Berson, Y., & Avolio, B. (2004). Transformational leadership and the dissemination of organizational goals: A case study of a telecommunication firm. *The Leadership Quarterly*, 15(5), 625–646. DOI: 10.1016/j.leaqua.2004.07.003

Blanka, C., Krumay, B., & Rueckel, D. (2022). The interplay of digital transformation and employee competency: A design science approach. *Technological Forecasting and Social Change*, 178, 121575. DOI: 10.1016/j.techfore.2022.121575

Bolden-Barrett, V. (2018, February 20). Employees think AI is good, but employers' silence creates fear. Retrieved April 2, 2020, from HRDive: https://www.hrdive.com/news/employees-think-ai-is-good-but-employers-silence-creates-fear/517361/

Bommer, W., Rich, G., & Rubin, R. (2005). Changing attitudes about change: Longitudinal effects of transformational leader behavior on employee cynicism about organizational change. *Journal of Organizational Behavior*, 26(7), 733–753. DOI: 10.1002/job.342

Borges, A., Laurindo, F., Spínola, M., Gonçalves, R., & Mattos, C. (2020). The strategic use of artificial intelligence in the digital era: Systematic literature review and future research directions. *International Journal of Information Management*.

Bose, S., Shams, S., Ali, M. J., & Mihret, D. (2022). COVID-19 impact, sustainability performance and firm value: International evidence. *Accounting and Finance*, 62(1), 597–643. DOI: 10.1111/acfi.12801

Bostrom, N. (2016). *Superintelligence: Paths, Dangers, Strategies*. Oxford University.

Bowen, J., & Whalen, E. (2017). Trends that are changing travel and tourism. *Worldwide Hospitality and Tourism Themes*, 9(6), 592–602. DOI: 10.1108/WHATT-09-2017-0045

Bozdağlıoğlu, U. Y. (2008). Characteristics of unemployment in Turkey and policies to combat unemployment. *Journal of Social Sciences*, 20, 47.

Bradić-Martinović, A., & Banović, J. (2018). Assessment of digital skills in Serbia with focus on gender gap. *JWEE*, (1-2), 54–67. DOI: 10.28934/jwee18.12.pp54-67

Brains, E. (2024, junio 13). Robotics in Manufacturing: Increasing Productivity and Safety. *Medium*. https://medium.com/@emperorbrains/robotics-in-manufacturing-increasing-productivity-and-safety-c44fd62916d7

Bretzfield, M. (2024, abril 4). Harnessing Data Analytics for Enhanced Customer Insight and Personalized Marketing. *Linkedin*. https://www.linkedin.com/pulse/harnessing-data-analytics-enhanced-customer-insight-bretzfield-lhsqc/

Broadstock, D. C., Chan, K., Cheng, L. T., & Wang, X. (2021). The role of ESG performance during times of financial crisis: Evidence from COVID-19 in China. *Finance Research Letters*, 38, 101716. DOI: 10.1016/j.frl.2020.101716 PMID: 32837385

Brock, J. K.-U., & Von Wangenheim, F. (2019). Demystifying AI: What Digital Transformation Leaders Can Teach You about Realistic Artificial Intelligence. *California Management Review*, 61(4), 110–134. DOI: 10.1177/1536504219865226

Brynjolfsson, E., & McAfee, A. (2017). The Business of Artificial Intelligence: What it can — and cannot — do for your organization.

Bughin, J., Seong, J., Manyika, J., Chui, M., & Joshi, R. (2018). *Notes from the AI frontier: Modeling the impact of AI on the world economy*. McKinsey Global Institute.

Bułkowska, K., Zielińska, M., & Bułkowski, M. (2023). Implementation of Blockchain Technology in Waste Management. *Energies*, 16(23), 7742. DOI: 10.3390/en16237742

Buonocore, F., Agrifoglio, R., & De Gennaro, D. 2021. "The role of digital competencies and creativity for job crafting in public administration". Digital Transformation and Human Behavior: Innovation for People and Organisations. Editörler: Metallo, C., Ferrara, M., Lazazzara, A., Za, S. Springer International Publishing. DOI: 10.1007/978-3-030-47539-0_7

Buonocore, F., Annosi, M. C., de Gennaro, D., & Riemma, F. (2024). Digital transformation and social change: Leadership strategies for responsible innovation. *Journal of Engineering and Technology Management*, 74, 101843. DOI: 10.1016/j.jengtecman.2024.101843

Butschan, J., Heidenreich, S., Weber, B., & Kraemer, T. (2019). Tackling hurdles to digital transformation—The role of competencies for successful industrial internet of things (IIoT) implementation. *International Journal of Innovation Management*, 23(04), 1950036. DOI: 10.1142/S1363919619500361

Çakır, V. (2007). Tüketici ilgilenimini ölçmek. *Selçuk Üniversitesi İletişim Fakültesi Dergisi*, 4(4), 167–180.

Canals, J., & Heukamp, F. (2020). *The Future of Management in an AI World: Redefining Purpose and Strategy in the Forth Industrial Revolution*. IESE Business Collection. DOI: 10.1007/978-3-030-20680-2

Cannas, V. G., Ciano, M. P., Saltalamacchia, M., & Secchi, R. (2024). Artificial intelligence in supply chain and operations management: A multiple case study research. *International Journal of Production Research*, 62(9), 3333–3360. DOI: 10.1080/00207543.2023.2232050

Carriço, G. (2018). The EU and artificial intelligence: A human-centred perspective. *European View*, 17(1), 29–36. DOI: 10.1177/1781685818764821

Carrillo González, G., Vázquez García, Á. W., & Solís Tepexpa, S. (2020). Ecodiseño: Estrategia Clave para la economía circular empresas del sector mueblero. En *Economía circular y ecodiseño en la industria del mueble* (1.ª ed., Vol. 4, p. 134). Universidad Autónoma de Querétano, México.

Carvalho, L., & Di Guilmi, C. (2020). Technological unemployment and income inequality: A stock-flow consistent agent-based approach. *Journal of Evolutionary Economics*, 30(1), 39–73. DOI: 10.1007/s00191-019-00628-9

Cathles, A., Cardenas, G., & Henriquez Leblanc, P. (2023). *Opportunities and Challenges for the Twin Transition in Latin America and the Caribbean*. Inter-American Development Bank, Washington, D.C. USA. https://sdgs.un.org/sites/default/files/2023-05/A15%20-%20Cathles%20-%20Twin%20Transition%20in%20Latin%20America%20and%20the%20Caribbean.pdf

Çetindamar-Kozanoğlu, D., & Abedin, B. (2021). Understanding the role of employees in digital transformation: Conceptualization of digital literacy of employees as a multi-dimensional organizational affordance. *Journal of Enterprise Information Management*, 34(6), 1649–1672. DOI: 10.1108/JEIM-01-2020-0010

CGIFURNITURE. (2023, junio 1). *Digital Twins in Product Development:*https://cgifurniture.com/digital-twins-in-product-development-a-short-guide/ COM/2019/640 final. (2019). *The European Green Deal*. European Commission. https://eur-lex.europa.eu/legal-content/EN/TXT/?uri=COM%3A2019%3A640%3AFIN COM/2020/98 final. (2020). *A new Circular Economy Action Plan For a cleaner and more competitive Europe*. European Commission. https://eur-lex.europa.eu/legal-content/EN/TXT/?qid=1583933814386&uri=COM:2020:98:FIN

Chandon, P., Wansink, B., & Laurent, G. (2000). A benefit congruency framework of sales promotion effectiveness. *Journal of Marketing*, 64(4), 65–81. DOI: 10.1509/jmkg.64.4.65.18071

Chatterjee, S., Chaudhuri, R., Vrontis, D., & Giovando, G. (2023). Digital workplace and organization performance: Moderating role of digital leadership capability. *Journal of Innovation & Knowledge*, 8(1), 100334. DOI: 10.1016/j.jik.2023.100334

Cheema-Fox, A., LaPerla, B. R., & Serafeim, G. (2021). Corporate Resilience and Response to COVID-19. *The Bank of America Journal of Applied Corporate Finance*, 33(2), 24–40. DOI: 10.1111/jacf.12457

Chin, W. W. (1998). Issues and opinion on structural equation modeling management. *Management Information Systems Quarterly*, 22(1), 19–24.

Chin, W. W., & Newsted, P. R. (1999). Structural equation modeling analysis with small samples using partial least squares. *Statistical Strategies for Small Sample Research*, 1(1), 307–341.

Chin, W. W., & Todd, P. A. (1995). On the use, usefulness, and ease of use of structural equation modeling in mis research: A note of caution. *Management Information Systems Quarterly*, 19(2), 237–246. DOI: 10.2307/249690

Chowdhury, G., & Hu, S. (2022). Employee Perceptions of AI Integration in Workplaces. *Journal of Organizational Behavior*, 43(5), 987–1002.

Chwelos, P., Benbasat, I., & Dexter, A. (2001). Research Report: Empirical Test of an EDI Adoption Model. *Information Systems Research*, 12(3), 304–321. DOI: 10.1287/isre.12.3.304.9708

Cichosz, M., Wallenburg, C. M., & Knemeyer, A. M. (2020). Digital transformation at logistics service providers: Barriers, success factors and leading practices. *International Journal of Logistics Management*, 31(2), 209–238. DOI: 10.1108/IJLM-08-2019-0229

Ciliberti, E. C., Fiore, M., & Mongiello, M. (2023, June). Development of a metaverse platform for tourism promotion in Apulia. In *2023 IEEE International Conference on Metaverse Computing, Networking and Applications (MetaCom)* (pp. 680-681). IEEE. DOI: 10.1109/MetaCom57706.2023.00123

Collard-Wexler, A., & De Loecker, J. (2015). Reallocation and Technology: Evidence from the US Steel Industry. *The American Economic Review*, 105(1), 131–171. DOI: 10.1257/aer.20130090

Conger, D. S. (2002). "Social inventions". *The Innovation Journal*. http: //www.innovation.cc/books/social-inventions-isbn

Cong, J., Zheng, P., Bian, Y., Chen, C.-H., Li, J., & Li, X. (2022). A machine learning-based iterative design approach to automate user satisfaction degree prediction in smart product-service system. *Computers & Industrial Engineering*, 165, 107939. DOI: 10.1016/j.cie.2022.107939

Cortellazzo, L., Bruni, E., & Zampieri, R. (2019). The role of leadership in a digitalized world: A review. *Frontiers in Psychology*, 10, 1938. DOI: 10.3389/fpsyg.2019.01938 PMID: 31507494

Council on Foreign Relations. (2023, julio 25). How Do Governments Combat Climate Change? *Climate & Change*. https://education.cfr.org/learn/reading/how-do-governments-combat-climate-change

Cousins, P. D., Lawson, B., Petersen, K. J., & Fugate, B. (2019). Investigating green supply chain management practices and performance: The moderating roles of supply chain ecocentricity and traceability. *International Journal of Operations & Production Management*, 39(5), 767–786. DOI: 10.1108/IJOPM-11-2018-0676

Culot, G., Nassimbeni, G., Orzes, G., & Sartor, M. (2020). Behind the definition of Industry 4.0: Analysis and open questions. *International Journal of Production Economics*, 226(107617), 107617. DOI: 10.1016/j.ijpe.2020.107617

Dabo, A.-A. A., & Hosseinian-Far, A. (2023). An Integrated Methodology for Enhancing Reverse Logistics Flows and Networks in Industry 5.0. *Logistics (Basel)*, 7(4), 97. DOI: 10.3390/logistics7040097

Dalenogare, L. S., Benitez, G. B., Ayala, N. F., & Frank, A. G. (2018). The expected contribution of Industry 4.0 technologies for industrial performance. *International Journal of Production Economics*, 204, 383–394. DOI: 10.1016/j.ijpe.2018.08.019

Damanpour, F., & Schneider, M. (2006). Phases of the Adoption of Innovation in Organizations: Effects of Environment, Organization and Top Managers. *British Journal of Management*, 17(3), 215–236. DOI: 10.1111/j.1467-8551.2006.00498.x

Darke, P. R., & Dahl, D. W. (2003). Fairness and discounts: The subjective value of a bargain. *Journal of Consumer Psychology*, 13(3), 328–338. DOI: 10.1207/S15327663JCP1303_13

Daugherty, P., & Wilson, H. (2018). *Human + Machine: Reimagining Work in the Age of AI*. Harvard Business Review Press.

Davenport, T. (2020). The State of AI in Businesses. In T. Davenport, E. Brynjolfsson, A. McAfee, & H. Wilson, Artificial Intelligence: The Insights You Need from Harvard Business Review.

Davenport, T. (2019). Can We Solve AI's′ Trust Problem'? *MIT Sloan Management Review*, 60(3), 1–5.

Davidson, L. (2019, August 12). Narrow vs. General AI: What's Next for Artificial Intelligence? Retrieved from Springboard: https://www.springboard.com/blog/narrow-vs-general-ai/

de Jesus Pacheco, D. A., & Schougaard, T. (2024). Operational performance improvement in manual assembly lines: A case study in Denmark and conceptual model for quick and long-term wins. *International Journal of Productivity and Performance Management*, 73(6), 1689–1718. DOI: 10.1108/IJPPM-11-2022-0566

de Mattos Nascimento, D. L., de Oliveira-Dias, D., Moyano-Fuentes, J., Maqueira Marín, J. M., & Garza-Reyes, J. A. (2024). Interrelationships between circular economy and Industry 4.0: A research agenda for sustainable supply chains. *Business Strategy and the Environment*, 33(2), 575–596. DOI: 10.1002/bse.3502 de Witte, L., & Hagen, R. (2022, julio 13). The urgent need for fire safe upholstered furniture and mattresses in homes. *EURACTIV.* https://www.europeanfiresafetyalliance.org/news/need-for-fire-safe-upholstered-furniture-and-mattresses/

Delbari, S. A., & Hof, L. A. (2024). Glass waste circular economy—Advancing to high-value glass sheets recovery using industry 4.0 and 5.0 technologies. *Journal of Cleaner Production*, 462, 142629. DOI: 10.1016/j.jclepro.2024.142629

DeLisle, J. R. (2010). "Chapter 4. Real Estate Risk Management." Fundamentals of Real Estate: A Behavioral Approach. 97-124.

Deloitte. (2022). State of AI in the Enterprise, 4th Edition. Deloitte Insights. https://www2.deloitte.com/us/en/insights/focus/cognitive-technologies/enterprise-artificial-intelligence-4th-edition.html

Deloitte. (s. f.-a). *Making blockchain real for customer loyalty rewards programs.* Recuperado 8 de agosto de 2024, de https://www2.deloitte.com/us/en/pages/financial-services/articles/making-blockchain-real-customer-loyalty-rewards-programs.html

Deloitte. (s. f.-b). *Using blockchain to drive supply chain transparency.* Recuperado 8 de agosto de 2024, de https://www2.deloitte.com/us/en/pages/operations/articles/blockchain-supply-chain-innovation.html

Demirel (2023), İş dünyasını değiştirecek 2030 yetkinlikleri, Harvard Business Review Türkiye, https://hbrturkiye.com/sponsorlu-icerik/is-dunyasini-degistirecek-2030-yetkinlikleri

Denyer, K.L.R (2023), A Just Transition for UK oil and gas workers? Re-employment after job lossDOI: 10.1080/21582041.2024.2316656

Dhaliwal, D. S., Li, O. Z., Tsang, A., & Yang, Y. G. (2011). Voluntary nonfinancial disclosure and the cost of equity capital: The initiation of corporate social responsibility reporting. *The Accounting Review*, 86(1), 59–100. DOI: 10.2308/accr.00000005

Dhayal, K. S., Giri, A. K., Kumar, A., Samadhiya, A., Agrawal, S., & Agrawal, R. (2023). Can green finance facilitate Industry 5.0 transition to achieve sustainability? A systematic review with future research directions. *Environmental Science and Pollution Research International*, 30(46), 102158–102180. DOI: 10.1007/s11356-023-29539-w PMID: 37695480

Diallo, M. F. (2012). Effects of store image and store brand price-image on store brand purchase intention: Application to an emerging market. *Journal of Retailing and Consumer Services*, 19(3), 360–367. DOI: 10.1016/j.jretconser.2012.03.010

DiCicco-Bloom, B., & Crabtree, B. F. (2006). The qualitative research interview. *Medical Education*, 40(4), 314–321. DOI: 10.1111/j.1365-2929.2006.02418.x PMID: 16573666

Ding, W., Levine, R., Lin, C., & Xie, W. (2021). Corporate immunity to the COVID-19 pandemic. *Journal of Financial Economics*, 141(2), 802–830. DOI: 10.1016/j.jfineco.2021.03.005 PMID: 34580557

Dini, M., Gligo, N., & Patiño, A. (2021). *Transformación digital de las mipymes. Elementos para el diseño de políticas*. División de Desarrollo Productivo y Empresarial de la Comisión Económica para América Latina y el Caribe.

Dizman, C., & Kaçakgi, L. E. C. (2023). Alkyd resins produced from bio-based resources for more sustainable and environmentally friendly coating applications. *Turkish Journal of Chemistry*, 47(1), 1–23. DOI: 10.55730/1300-0527.3511 PMID: 37731964

Dogangun, I., Oral, E., Akkartal, E., & Turegun, N. (2023). Exploring the multifractality in the precious metal market. *Fluctuation and Noise Letters*, 22(4), XX–XX. DOI: 10.1142/S0219477523400096

Donthu, N., Kumar, S., Mukherjee, D., Pandey, N., & Lim, W. M. (2021). How to conduct a bibliometric analysis: An overview and guidelines. *Journal of Business Research*, 133, 285–296. DOI: 10.1016/j.jbusres.2021.04.070

Duan, Y., Yang, F., & Xiong, L. (2023). Environmental, Social, and Governance (ESG) Performance and Firm Value: Evidence from Chinese Manufacturing Firms. *Sustainability (Basel)*, 15(17), 12858. DOI: 10.3390/su151712858

Du, X., & Jiang, K. (2022). Promoting enterprise productivity: The role of digital transformation. *Borsa Istanbul Review*, 22(6), 1165–1181. DOI: 10.1016/j.bir.2022.08.005

Du, Y., & Wei, L. (2021). The impact of robotics adoption on labour markets: Evidence from China. *Journal of Economic Studies (Glasgow, Scotland)*, 48(1), 45–60. DOI: 10.1108/JES-04-2020-0197

Dwivedi, A., Agrawal, D., Jha, A., & Mathiyazhagan, K. (2023). Studying the interactions among Industry 5.0 and circular supply chain: Towards attaining sustainable development. *Computers & Industrial Engineering*, 176, 108927. DOI: 10.1016/j.cie.2022.108927

Ebert, C., & Duarte, C. H. C. (2018). Digital transformation. *IEEE Software*, 35(4), 16–21. DOI: 10.1109/MS.2018.2801537

Eccles, R. G., Ioannou, I., & Serafeim, G. (2014). The Impact of Corporate Sustainability on Organizational Processes and Performance. *Management Science*, 60(11), 2835–2857. DOI: 10.1287/mnsc.2014.1984

Eco, R. A. E. E. (2019, marzo 12). *El Ministerio para la Transición Ecológica publica los objetivos de recogida selectiva de RAEE para 2019*. https://www.eco-raee.com/resolucion-y-objetivos-minimos-recogida-de-raee-estatales-y-autonomicos-2019/

EcoMaison. (s. f.). *Furniture industry- A reuse and recycling network to give objects a second life*. Recuperado 6 de septiembre de 2024, de https://ecomaison.com/en/filiere-ameublement/

Edmans, A. (2020). *Grow the pie: How great companies deliver both purpose and profit*. Cambridge University Press. DOI: 10.1017/9781108860093

Edwards-Schachter, M. E., Matti, C. E., & Alcántara, E.Edwards--Schachter. (2012). Fostering quality of life through social innovation: A living lab methodology study case. *The Review of Policy Research*, 29(6), 672–692. DOI: 10.1111/j.1541-1338.2012.00588.x

Eisenbach, R., Watson, K., & Pillai, R. (1999). Transformational leadership in the context of organizational change. *Journal of Organizational Change Management*, 12(2), 80–88. DOI: 10.1108/09534819910263631

El Naqa, I., & Murphy, M. (2015). What is Machine Learning? In I. El Naqa, R. Li, & M. Murphy,Machine Learning in Radiation Oncology (pp. 3-11). Springer. DOI: 10.1007/978-3-319-18305-3_1

Elçi, Ş. (2006). *İnovasyon Kalkınmanın ve Rekabetin Anahtarı*. Pelin Ofset.

Ellefsen, A., Oleśków-Szłapka, J., Pawłowski, G., & Tobola, A. (2019). Striving for Excellence in AI Implementation: AI Maturity Model Framework and Preliminary Research Results. *Scientific Journal of Logistics*, 15(3), 363–376.

Eller, R., Alford, P., Kallmünzer, A., & Peters, M. (2020). Antecedents, consequences, and challenges of small and medium-sized enterprise digitalization. *Journal of Business Research*, 112, 119–127. DOI: 10.1016/j.jbusres.2020.03.004

Ellström, D., Holtström, J., Berg, E., & Josefsson, C. (2021). Dynamic capabilities for digital transformation. *Journal of Strategy and Management*, 15(2), 272–286. DOI: 10.1108/JSMA-04-2021-0089

Emam, A. (2023). Robot-aided manufacturing and its impact on the future of the furniture industry in Egypt. *International Design Journal*, 13(2), 389–406. DOI: 10.21608/idj.2023.288432

Envira. (2023, diciembre 19). Puntos clave de la Ley de Residuos y Suelos contaminados para una Economía Circular. *Envira.* https://envira.es/es/ley-de-residuos-y-suelos-contaminados/

EPA. (s. f.). *End of Waste (Art. 28).* Recuperado 8 de septiembre de 2024, de https://www.epa.ie/our-services/licensing/waste/end-of-waste-art-28/

ERA. (s. f.). *End-of-Waste Criteria.* Recuperado 8 de septiembre de 2024, de https://era.org.mt/topic/end-of-waste-criteria/

Erdem, A., & Şeker, F. (2022). Tourist Experience and Digital Transformation. In *Handbook of Research on Digital Communications, Internet of Things, and the Future of Cultural Tourism* (pp. 103–120). IGI Global. DOI: 10.4018/978-1-7998-8528-3.ch006

Eren, H. (2010). *Üniversite Öğrencilerinin Sosyal Yenilikçilik Kapasitelerinin Teknolojik Yenilikçilik Eğilimlerine Etkisini Ölçmeye Yönelik Bir Model Önerisi* (Vol. 37). KHO Savunma Bilimleri Enstitüsü.

Erol, H. (2010). The role of the Unemployment Insurance Law No. 4447 in addressing the negative consequences of unemployment in Turkey. *TISK Academy*, 5(10), 8.

European Commission. (2019), The European Green Deal. Retrieved from https://eur-lex.europa.eu/legal-content/EN/TXT/?uri=CELEX:52019DC0640

European Commission. (2023), Carbon Border Adjustment Mechanism, https://trade.ec.europa.eu/access-to-markets/en/news/carbon-border-adjustment-mechanism-cbam

European Commission. (2023, julio 5). *Circular economy for textiles: Taking responsibility to reduce, reuse and recycle textile waste and boosting markets for used textiles.* https://ec.europa.eu/commission/presscorner/detail/en/ip_23_3635

European Commission. (2024a), The green transition: What implications for employment? Retrieved from https://ec.europa.eu/regional_policy/whats-new/panorama/2024/06/06-12-2024-the-green-transition-what-implications-for-employment_en

European Commission. (2024b), Digital skills and knowledge concepts. ESCO. https://esco.ec.europa.eu/cs/node/427#:~:text=It%20includes%20information%20and%20data,problem%20solving%20and%20critical%20thinking

European Commission. (s. f.-a). Renewable Energy Directive. *European Commission.* Recuperado 8 de septiembre de 2024, de https://energy.ec.europa.eu/topics/renewable-energy/renewable-energy-directive-targets-and-rules/renewable-energy-directive_en#:~:text=The%20revised%20Directive,-%C2%A9AdobeStock%20Rafa&text=Given%20the%20need%20to%20speed,force%20on%2020%20November%202023

European Commission. (s. f.-b). *Restriction of Hazardous Substances in Electrical and Electronic Equipment (RoHS).* Recuperado 6 de agosto de 2024, de https://environment.ec.europa.eu/topics/waste-and-recycling/rohs-directive_en

European Commission. (s. f.-c). *Waste from Electrical and Electronic Equipment (WEEE).* Recuperado 6 de agosto de 2024, de https://environment.ec.europa.eu/topics/waste-and-recycling/waste-electrical-and-electronic-equipment-weee_en

European Commission. Directorate General for Communication. (2020). *A European industrial strategy: Unleashing the full potential of European SMEs.* Publications Office. https://data.europa.eu/doi/10.2775/296379

European Commission. Directorate General for Research and Innovation. (2021). *Industry 5.0: Towards a sustainable, human centric and resilient European industry.* Publications Office. https://data.europa.eu/doi/10.2777/308407

European Environment Agency. (2024, marzo 25). Climate change mitigation: Reducing emissions. *In-Depth Topics.* https://www.eea.europa.eu/en/topics/in-depth/climate-change-mitigation-reducing-emissions

European Panel Federation. (2019, mayo 8). EPF strongly supports the Single Market. *European Panel Federation News Archive.* https://europanels.org/epf-strongly-supports-the-single-market/

European Subcontracting Network. (s. f.). *How the Internet of Things is Driving Growth in Furniture Manufacturing?* Recuperado 8 de agosto de 2024, de https://subcontracteu.com/en/blog/internet-of-things-driving-growth-furniture-manufacturing

EY (Ernst and Young). (2020). *COVID-19: Impact on Malaysian businesses.* EY Malaysia. https://www.ey.com/en_my/take-5-business-alert/covid-19-impact-on-malaysian-businesses

Fadal, K., & Brown, S. (2010). Information Systems Appraisal and Coping: The Role of User Perceptions. *Communications of the Association for Information Systems,* 26(1). Advance online publication. DOI: 10.17705/1CAIS.02606

Falkenberg, K. (2012, junio). *Guidance on the interpretation of key provisions of Directive 2008/98/EC on waste.* https://ens.dk/sites/ens.dk/files/Affald/guidance_on_the_interpretation_of_key_provisions_on_waste.pdf

Fama living. (2022). Fama obtiene la certificación de Residuo Cero. *Noticias Fama*. https://www.fama.es/noticias/fama-obtiene-la-certificacion-de-residuo-cero

Fatemi, A., Glaum, M., & Kaiser, S. (2018). ESG performance and firm value: The moderating role of disclosure. *Global Finance Journal*, 38, 45–64. DOI: 10.1016/j.gfj.2017.03.001

Feldmann, H. (2013). Technological unemployment in industrial countries: Causes and policy recommendations. *Revista de Economia Institucional*, 4(1), 1–20. DOI: 10.5202/rei.v4i1.90

Festinger, L. (1957). *A theory of cognitive dissonance*. Stanford University Press. DOI: 10.1515/9781503620766

Filipiak, B.. (2020). Economic development trends in the EU tourism industry. Towards the digitalization process and sustainability. *Quality & Quantity*. Advance online publication. DOI: 10.1007/s11135-020-01056-9 PMID: 33132445

Fiol, C., Harris, D., & House, R. (1999). Charismatic leadership: Strategies for effecting social change. *The Leadership Quarterly*, 10(3), 449–482. DOI: 10.1016/S1048-9843(99)00021-1

Fishbeın, M., & Ajzen, I. (1975). *Bellefatlitude, Intention And Behavior: An Inlrod. Uc.Lion Theory And Research*. Addison-Wesley.

Flacandji, M., & Vlad, M. (2022). The relationship between retailer app use, perceived shopping value and loyalty: The moderating role of deal proneness. *International Journal of Retail & Distribution Management*, 50(8/9), 981–995. DOI: 10.1108/IJRDM-10-2021-0484

Foerster-Metz, U. S. F. P., & Golowko, N. (2018). The need for digital and soft skills in the Romanian business service industry. *Management & Marketing*, 13(1), 831–847. DOI: 10.2478/mmcks-2018-0008

Fonseca, P., & Picoto, W. N. (2020). The competencies needed for digital transformation. [OJAKM]. *Online Journal of Applied Knowledge Management*, 8(2), 53–70. DOI: 10.36965/OJAKM.2020.8(2)53-70

Fornell, C. (1992). A national customer satisfaction barometer: The Swedish experience. *Journal of Marketing*, 56(1), 6–21. DOI: 10.1177/002224299205600103

Forrest, A., Hilton, M., Ballinger, A., & Whittaker, D. (2017, septiembre). *CIRCULAR ECONOMY OPPORTUNITIES IN THE FURNITURE SECTOR*. European Environmental Bureau (EEB). https://eeb.org/wp-content/uploads/2019/05/Report-on-the-Circular-Economy-in-the-Furniture-Sector.pdf

Fraga-Lamas, P., Lopes, S. I., & Fernández-Caramés, T. M. (2021). Green IoT and Edge AI as Key Technological Enablers for a Sustainable Digital Transition towards a Smart Circular Economy: An Industry 5.0 Use Case. *Sensors (Basel)*, 21(17), 5745. DOI: 10.3390/s21175745 PMID: 34502637

Franke, A. (2023, octubre 9). EU adopts renewable energy directive targeting 42.5% share in 2030. *S&P Global*. https://www.spglobal.com/commodityinsights/en/market-insights/latest-news/electric-power/100923-eu-adopts-renewable-energy-directive-targeting-425-share-in-2030

Freeman, R. E. (1984). *Strategic Management: A Stakeholder Perspective*. Pitman.

Frey, C. B., & Osborne, M. A. (2017). The future of employment: How susceptible are jobs to computeri*zation technological Forecasting and Social Change, 114*, 254–280. https://doi.org/DOI: 10.1016/j.techfore.2016.08.019

Frick, N., Mirbabaie, M., Stieglitz, S., & Salomon, J. (2021). Maneuvering through the stormy seas of digital transformation: The impact of empowering leadership on the AI readiness of enterprises. *Journal of Decision Systems*, 30(2-3), 235–258. DOI: 10.1080/12460125.2020.1870065

Friede, G., Busch, T., & Bassen, A. (2015). ESG and financial performance: Aggregated evidence from more than 2000 empirical studies. *Journal of Sustainable Finance & Investment*, 5(4), 210–233. DOI: 10.1080/20430795.2015.1118917

Future, B. B. C. (2024). Visualizing the Great Pacific Garbage Patch. Retrieved from https://www.bbc.com/future/article/20240115-visualising-the-great-pacific-garbage-patch

Galanis, G., Napoletano, M., Popoyan, L., Sapio, A., & Vardakoulias, O. (2024). Defining just transition. *Ecological Economics*, 227, 108370. DOI: 10.1016/j.ecolecon.2024.108370

Galbraith, J. R. (2014). *Designing Organizations: Strategy, Structure, and Process at the Business Unit and Enterprise Levels*. Jossey-Bass.

Gallivan, M. (2001). Organizational adoption and assimilation of complex technological innovations: Development and application of a new framework. *The Data Base for Advances in Information Systems*, 32(3), 51–85. DOI: 10.1145/506724.506729

Galvin, J., LaBerge, L., & Williams, E. (2021, mayo 26). The new digital edge: Rethinking strategy for the postpandemic era. *MC Kinsey Digital*, 17.

Ganz, W., Dworschak, B., & Schnalzer, K. (2018, June). Competences and competence development in a digitalized world of work. In *International Conference on Applied Human Factors and Ergonomics* (pp. 312-320). Cham: Springer International Publishing.

Garrido, S., Muniz, J.Jr, & Batista Ribeiro, V. (2024). Operations Management, Sustainability & Industry 5.0: A critical analysis and future agenda. *Cleaner Logistics and Supply Chain*, 10, 100141. DOI: 10.1016/j.clscn.2024.100141

Gaskell, A. (2019). The Key To Solving Future Skills Challenges. Forbes. https://www.forbes.com/sites/adigaskell/2019/01/02/solving-future-skills-challenges/

Gaur, V., & Gaiha, A. (2020, junio). Building a Transparent Supply Chain. *Harvard Business Review*. https://hbr.org/2020/05/building-a-transparent-supply-chain

General de Estudios, S. Análisis y Planes de Actuación. (2024). *Índice de fichas sectoriales* (p. 46). Ministerio de Industria y Turismo. https://www.mintur.gob.es/es-es/IndicadoresyEstadisticas/Sectores/sectores%20industria.pdf

George, D., & Mallery, P. (2019). *IBM SPSS Statistics 26 Step by Step: A simple guide and reference*. Routledge. DOI: 10.4324/9780429056765

George, G., & Schillebeeckx, S. J. (2022). Digital transformation, sustainability, and purpose in the multinational enterprise. *Journal of World Business*, 57(3), 101326. DOI: 10.1016/j.jwb.2022.101326

Ghaithan, A. M., Alshammakhi, Y., Mohammed, A., & Mazher, K. M. (2023). Integrated impact of circular economy, Industry 4.0, and lean manufacturing on sustainability performance of manufacturing firms. *International Journal of Environmental Research and Public Health*, 20(6), XX–XX. DOI: 10.3390/ijerph20065119 PMID: 36982026

Ghobakhloo, M., & Iranmanesh, M. (2021). Digital transformation success under Industry 4.0: A strategic guideline for manufacturing SMEs. *Journal of Manufacturing Technology Management*, 32(8), 1533–1556. DOI: 10.1108/JMTM-11-2020-0455

Ghobakhloo, M., Iranmanesh, M., Foroughi, B., Babaee Tirkolaee, E., Asadi, S., & Amran, A. (2023). Industry 5.0 implications for inclusive sustainable manufacturing: An evidence-knowledge-based strategic roadmap. *Journal of Cleaner Production*, 417, 138023. DOI: 10.1016/j.jclepro.2023.138023

Ghobakhloo, M., Iranmanesh, M., Vilkas, M., Grybauskas, A., & Amran, A. (2022). Drivers and barriers of Industry 4.0 technology adoption among manufacturing SMEs: A systematic review and transformation roadmap. *Journal of Manufacturing Technology Management*, 33(6), 1029–1058. DOI: 10.1108/JMTM-12-2021-0505

Giannopoulos, G., Kihle Fagernes, R. V., Elmarzouky, M., & Afzal Hossain, K. A. B. M. (2022). The ESG Disclosure and the Financial Performance of Norwegian Listed Firms. *Journal of Risk and Financial Management*, 15(6), 237. DOI: 10.3390/jrfm15060237

Gibbin, R. V., Sigahi, T. F. A. C., Pinto, J. D. S., Rampasso, I. S., & Anholon, R. (2023). Thematic evolution and trends linking sustainability and project management: Scientific mapping using SciMAT. *Journal of Cleaner Production*, 414, 137753. DOI: 10.1016/j.jclepro.2023.137753

Gibson, R., Krueger, P., & Schmidt, P. S. (2021). ESG Rating Disagreement and Stock Returns. *Financial Analysts Journal*, 77(4), 104–127. DOI: 10.1080/0015198X.2021.1963186

Giese, G., Lee, L.-E., Melas, D., Nagy, Z., & Nishikawa, L. (2019). Foundations of ESG Investing: How ESG Affects Equity Valuation, Risk, and Performance. *Journal of Portfolio Management*, 45(5), 69–83. DOI: 10.3905/jpm.2019.45.5.069

Global Regulation. (s. f.). *Royal Decree 187/2011,18February, Concerning The Establishment Of Eco-Design Requirements For Energy-Related Products*. Recuperado 6 de septiembre de 2024, de https://www.global-regulation.com/translation/spain/1437999/royal-decree-187-2011%252c-18-february%252c-concerning-the-establishment-of-eco-design-requirements-for-energy-related-products.html

Gögus, C. G., & Özer, G. (2014). The roles of technology acceptance model antecedents and switching cost on accounting software use. *Academy of Information and Management Sciences Journal*, 17(1), 1–24.

Goldenberg, M. (2004a), *Social Innovation in Canada How the Non-profit Sector Serves Canadians and How It Can Serve Them Beter*. Ottowa: Canadian Policy Research Networks Inc. Project (CPRN) Research Report W/25.

Goldenberg, M. (2004b), *The Future of Social Innovation in Canada*. Ottowa: Canadian Policy Research Networks Inc. Project (CPRN), Research Report W/26.

Gomes, J. G. C., Okano, M. T., Simões, E. A., & Otola, I. (2019). Management strategy and business models in the era of digital transformation. *South American Development Society Journal*, 5(14), 252. DOI: 10.24325/issn.2446-5763.v5i14p252-270

Gompers, P., Ishii, J., & Metrick, A. (2003). Corporate governance and equity prices. *The Quarterly Journal of Economics*, 118(1), 107–155. DOI: 10.1162/00335530360535162

Goodman, W.(2016). The promises and pitfalls of Benford's law. *Significance journal*, 13(3), 38-41. DOI:DOI: 10.1111/j.1740-9713.2016.00919.x

Gordon, B. R., Goldfarb, A., & Li, Y. (2013). Does price elasticity vary with economic growth? A cross-category analysis. *JMR, Journal of Marketing Research*, 50(1), 4–23. DOI: 10.1509/jmr.11.0162

Götz, M. (2020). Cluster role in Industry 4.0 – a pilot study from Germany. *Competitiveness Review*, 31(1), 54–82. DOI: 10.1108/CR-10-2019-0091

Greene, J. A., Seung, B. Y., & Copeland, D. Z. (2014). Measuring critical components of digital literacy and their relationships with learning. *Computers & Education*, 76, 55–69. DOI: 10.1016/j.compedu.2014.03.008

Greenhoot, A. F., & Dowsett, C. J. (2012). Secondary Data Analysis: An Important Tool for Addressing Developmental Questions. *Journal of Cognition and Development*, 13(1), 2–18. DOI: 10.1080/15248372.2012.646613

Grewal, D., Monroe, K. B., & Krishnan, R. (1998). The effects of price-comparison advertising on buyers' perceptions of acquisition value, transaction value, and behavioral intentions. *Journal of Marketing*, 62(2), 46–59. DOI: 10.2307/1252160

Griffin, R., & Ebert, R. J. (1996). *Business: Book one* (4th ed.). Prentice Hall.

Griggs, T., Griffiths, M., & Fletcher, G. (2019). Managing the digital transformation of an organisation. In *Strategic Digital Transformation* (pp. 48–54). Routledge. DOI: 10.4324/9780429020469-5

Groopman, J. (2018). *AI Readiness; Five Areas Businesses Must Prepare for Success in Artificial Intelligence*. Kaleido Insights.

Guba, E. G., & Lincoln, Y. S. (1982). Epistemological and methodological bases of naturalistic inquiry. *Educational Communication and Technology*, 30(4), 233252. DOI: 10.1007/BF02765185

Güven, T., Çam, F. B., Bilgili, B., & Ercîş, A. (2024). The impact of social innovation on environmentally friendly product involvement. *Innovation & Management Review*, 21(2), 94–109. DOI: 10.1108/INMR-10-2021-0191

Guzman, A. C., Francisco, M., & Rodrıguez, S. (2021). Do consumers value environmental innovation in product? *Administrative Sciences*, 11(33), 33. DOI: 10.3390/admsci11010033

Hadi, A., Cheung, F., Adjei, S., & Dulaimi, A. (2023). Evaluation of Lean Off-Site Construction Literature through the Lens of Industry 4.0 and 5.0. *Journal of Construction Engineering and Management*, 149(12), 03123007. DOI: 10.1061/JCEMD4.COENG-13622

Hague, B., Kozáková, J., & Veselá, A. (2023, julio). *Closing the loop on wood: Circular Bioeconomy Opportunities in the Value Chain for Forest Products and Wood in Czechia*. Institute of Circular Economy (INCIEN). https://circulareconomy.europa.eu/platform/sites/default/files/2023-07/Closing-the-loop-on-wood.pdf

Hair, J. F., Black, B., Babin, B., Anderson, R. E., & Tatham, R. L. (2006). *Multivariate Data Analysis* (6th ed.). Prentice Hall.

Hair, J. F.Jr. (2021). Next-generation prediction metrics for composite-based PLS-SEM. *Industrial Management & Data Systems*, 121(1), 5–11. DOI: 10.1108/IMDS-08-2020-0505

Hair, J. F.Jr, Black, W. C., Babin, B. J., & Anderson, R. E. (2014). *Multivariate data analysis (Pearson new internat* (Jersey, N., Ed.). Pearson.

Hair, J. F.Jr, Ringle, C. M., & Sarstedt, M. (2011). PLS-SEM: Indeed a silver bullet. *Journal of Marketing Theory and Practice*, 19(2), 139–151. DOI: 10.2753/MTP1069-6679190202

Hair, J. F.Jr, Sarstedt, M., Hopkins, L., & Kuppelwieser, V. G. (2014). Partial least squares structural equation modeling (PLS-SEM). *European Business Review*, 26(2), 106–121. DOI: 10.1108/EBR-10-2013-0128

Hair, J. F., Risher, J. J., Sarstedt, M., & Ringle, C. M. (2019). When to use and how to report the results of PLS-SEM. *European Business Review*, 31(1), 2–24. DOI: 10.1108/EBR-11-2018-0203

Halaç, D. S., Eren, H., & Bulut, Ç. (2014). Sosyal yenilikçilik: Bir ölçek geliştirme çalışması. *Hacettepe Üniversitesi İktisadi ve İdari Bilimler Fakültesi Dergisi*, 32(1), 165–190.

Haleem, A., Javaid, M., Rab, S., Singh, R. P., Suman, R., & Kumar, L. (2023). Significant potential and materials used in additive manufacturing technologies towards sustainability. *Sustainable Operations and Computers*, 4, 172–182. DOI: 10.1016/j.susoc.2023.11.004

Hammershøj, L. G. (2019). The new division of labour between humans and machines and its educational implications. *Technology in Society*, 59, 101142. DOI: 10.1016/j.techsoc.2019.05.006

Handarkho, Y. D., & Harjoseputro, Y. (2019). Intention to adopt mobile payment in physical stores. *Journal of Enterprise Information Management*, 33(1), 53–67. DOI: 10.1108/JEIM-06-2019-0179

Hanelt, A., Bohnsack, R., Marz, D., & Antunes Marante, C. (2021). A systematic review of the literature on digital transformation: Insights and implications for strategy and organizational change. *Journal of Management Studies*, 58(5), 1159–1197. DOI: 10.1111/joms.12639

Hang, N. T. (2021). Universal education development to enhance the quality of human resources in the context of digital transformation and industrial revolution 4.0. *The USV Annals of Economics and Public Administration*, 21(1 (33)), 88–95.

Hanna, D., & Huang, Y. (2004). The impact of SARS on Asian economies. *Asian Economic Papers*, 3(1), 102–112. DOI: 10.1162/1535351041747978

Hariyani, D., Hariyani, P., Mishra, S., & Kumar Sharma, M. (2024). Leveraging digital technologies for advancing circular economy practices and enhancing life cycle analysis: A systematic literature review. *Waste Management Bulletin*, 2(3), 69–83. DOI: 10.1016/j.wmb.2024.06.007

Harymawan, I., Putra, F. K. G., Fianto, B. A., & Wan Ismail, W. A. (2021). Financially Distressed Firms: Environmental, Social, and Governance Reporting in Indonesia. *Sustainability (Basel)*, 13(18), 10156. DOI: 10.3390/su131810156

Health Spanish Ministry. (s. f.). Normativa relativa a los Reglamentos REACH y CLP. *Ministerio de Sanidad*. Recuperado 8 de septiembre de 2024, de https://www.sanidad.gob.es/ciudadanos/saludAmbLaboral/prodQuimicos/sustPreparatorias/reach/normativa.htm

Heavin, C., & Power, D. (2018). Challenges for digital transformation – Towards a conceptual decision support guide for managers. *Journal of Decision Systems*, 27(1), 38–45. DOI: 10.1080/12460125.2018.1468697

Heimberger, P. (2021). Does economic globalization affect unemployment? A meta-analysis. *Review of World Economics*, 157(2), 1–33. DOI: 10.1007/s10290-021-00427-w

Henseler, J., Ringle, C. M., & Sarstedt, M. (2015). A new criterion for assessing discriminant validity in variance-based structural equation modeling. *Journal of the Academy of Marketing Science*, 43(1), 115–135. DOI: 10.1007/s11747-014-0403-8

Hensellek, S. (2020). Digital leadership: A framework for successful leadership in the digital age [JMME]. *Journal of Media Management and Entrepreneurship*, 2(1), 1–15. DOI: 10.4018/JMME.2020010104

Heo, J., & Muralidharan, S. (2019). What triggers young Millennials to purchase eco-friendly products?: The interrelationships among knowledge, perceived consumer effectiveness, and environmental concern. *Journal of Marketing Communications*, 25(4), 421–437. DOI: 10.1080/13527266.2017.1303623

Herring, R. J., & Wachter, S. M. (1999). Real Estate Booms and Banking Busts: An International Perspective. *The Wharton School Research Paper No. 99-27*. https://ssrn.com/abstract=2546407

Herrmann, M., Boehme, P., Mondritzki, T., Ehlers, J. P., Kavadias, S., & Truebel, H. (2018). Digital transformation and disruption of the health care sector: Internet-based observational study. *Journal of Medical Internet Research*, 20(3), e9498. DOI: 10.2196/jmir.9498 PMID: 29588274

Hestya. (2024, enero 25). *AI-Driven Furniture and Appliance Design: Shaping the Future of Home Interiors*. https://www.hestyadesign.com/post/ai-driven-furniture-and-appliance-design-shaping-the-future-of-home-interiors

Hetmanczyk, M. P. (2024a). A Method for Evaluating the Maturity Level of Production Process Automation in the Context of Digital Transformation—Polish Case Study. *Applied Sciences (Basel, Switzerland)*, 14(11), 4380. DOI: 10.3390/app14114380

Hetmanczyk, M. P. (2024b). A Method to Evaluate the Maturity Level of Robotization of Production Processes in the Context of Digital Transformation—Polish Case Study. *Applied Sciences (Basel, Switzerland)*, 14(13), 5401. DOI: 10.3390/app14135401

Higgs, M., & Rowland, D. (2000). Building change leadership capability: 'The quest for change competence'. *Journal of Change Management*, 1(2), 116–130. DOI: 10.1080/714042459

Higgs, M., & Rowland, D. (2005). All changes great and small: Exploring approaches to change and its leadership. *Journal of Change Management*, 5(2), 121–151. DOI: 10.1080/14697010500082902

Ho, K. (2023, septiembre 21). Understanding RoHS Compliance: A Comprehensive Guide. *Nemko*. https://www.nemko.com/blog/rohs-explained-a-comprehensive-guide-to-hazardous-substance-restrictions#:~:text=Requirements%3A%20RoHS%20restricts%20the%20presence,comply%20with%20these%20substance%20restrictions

Holberton, R., Hallissey, A., Chang, D., & Chirgwin, B. (2012). *Risk Management in Corporate Real Estate within the Global Banking and Finance Sector*. CBRE Global Viewpoint.

Holmström, J. (2022). From AI to digital transformation: The AI readiness framework. *Business Horizons*, 65(3), 329–339. DOI: 10.1016/j.bushor.2021.03.006

Holuša, V., Vaněk, M., Beneš, F., Švub, J., & Staša, P. (2023). Virtual Reality as a Tool for Sustainable Training and Education of Employees in Industrial Enterprises. *Sustainability (Basel)*, 15(17), 12886. DOI: 10.3390/su151712886

Horváth, D., & Szabó, R. Z. (2019). Driving forces and barriers of Industry 4.0: Do multinational and small and medium-sized companies have equal opportunities? *Technological Forecasting and Social Change*, 146, 119–132. DOI: 10.1016/j.techfore.2019.05.021

House, R., Spangler, W., & Woycke, J. (1991). (1991). Personality and charisma in the US presidency: A psychological theory of leader effectiveness. *Administrative Science Quarterly*, 36(3), 364–396. DOI: 10.2307/2393201

Housing Wire. (2015): "Guaranteed Rate Purchases Remains of Discover Home Loans". https://www.housingwire.com/articles/34986-guaranteed-rate-purchases-remains-of-discover-home-loans/

Howell, J., & Higgins, C. (1990). Champions of technological innovation. *Administrative Science Quarterly*, 35(2), 317–341. DOI: 10.2307/2393393

Hristova, T. (2024). Tracking mining company electric vehicles for sustainable development optimization using Distributed Ledger Technologies. *Journal of Sustainable Mining*, 23(3), 299–314. DOI: 10.46873/2300-3960.1425

Hunter, I. (2018). Digital literacy in the workplace: A view from the legal sector. *Business Information Review*, 35(2), 56–59. DOI: 10.1177/0266382118772675

Hussin, M. H., Abd Latif, N. H., Hamidon, T. S., Idris, N. N., Hashim, R., Appaturi, J. N., Brosse, N., Ziegler-Devin, I., Chrusiel, L., Fatriasari, W., Syamani, F. A., Iswanto, A. H., Hua, L. S., Al Edrus, S. S. A. O., Lum, W. C., Antov, P., Savov, V., Rahandi Lubis, M. A., Kristak, L., & Sedliačik, J. (2022). Latest advancements in high-performance bio-based wood adhesives: A critical review. *Journal of Materials Research and Technology*, 21, 3909–3946. DOI: 10.1016/j.jmrt.2022.10.156

Iacovou, C., Benbasat, I., & Dexter, A. (1995). Electronic Data Interchange and Small Organizations: Adoption and Impact of Technology. *Management Information Systems Quarterly*, 19(4), 465–485. DOI: 10.2307/249629

ICCT. (2018, julio). *FINAL RECAST RENEWABLE ENERGY DIRECTIVE FOR 2021-2030 IN THE EUROPEAN UNION*. ICCT. https://theicct.org/wp-content/uploads/2021/06/EU_Fuels_Policy_Update_20180719.pdf

ICCT. (2023), International Council on Clean Transportation (ICCT). (2023). European Vehicle Market Statistics 2023/24 Pocketbook. https://theicct.org/publication/european-vehicle-market-statistics-2023-24/

IEA, 2024, International Energy Agency-World Energy Outlook 2024.

ILO (2015), International Labour Organization, Guidelines for a just transition towards environmentally sustainable economies and societies for all

ILO. (2013), ILO Report V: Sustainable development, decent work and green jobs. International Labour Conference, 102nd Session.

ILO. (2024), Green jobs: Just transition towards environmentally sustainable economies and societies, https://www.ilo.org/topics-and-sectors/just-transition-towards-environmentally-sustainable-economies-and-societies#:~:text=ILO%20studies%20show%20that%20implementing,18%20million%20jobs%20by%202030

Ilomäki, L., Paavola, S., Lakkala, M., & Kantosalo, A. (2016). Digital competence–an emergent boundary concept for policy and educational research. *Education and Information Technologies*, 21(3), 655–679. DOI: 10.1007/s10639-014-9346-4

IMQ. (s. f.). *Directive2009/125/EC, Energy-Related Products (Ecodesign—ErP): Third-party verification of energy efficiency and performance, as a guarantee of transparency on the market.* Recuperado 6 de septiembre de 2024, de https://www.imq.it/en/eu-directives/ecodesign-directive-2009-125-ec

Imran, F., Shahzad, K., Butt, A., & Kantola, J. (2021). Digital transformation of industrial organizations: Toward an integrated framework. *Journal of Change Management*, 21(4), 451–479. DOI: 10.1080/14697017.2021.1929406

INSHT. (2016, diciembre). *Formaldehído en la industria de fabricación de tableros.* Instituto Nacional de Seguridad e Higiene en el Trabajo (INSH. https://www.insst.es/documents/94886/96076/Formaldehido.pdf/9d0297a4-8e99-4362-870a-ce15a92c18af?t=1527163280572

InStyle. (2024, enero 16). *The Impact of AI in the Furniture Industry and Home Decor.* https://www.instyledirect.com/blog/news/ai-in-furniture-industry/#:~:text=AI%20in%20Furniture%20Design%20Industry&text=AI%20algorithms%20can%20analyse%20vast,pleasing%20but%20also%20highly%20functional

Intertek. (s. f.). *Energy-related Products (ErP) Directive2009/125/EC (Formerly EuP).* Recuperado 6 de septiembre de 2024, de https://www.intertek.com/electrical/erp-directive/

İşcan, E. (2021). An old problem in the new era: Effects of artificial intelligence on unemployment on the way to industry 5.0. *Yaşar Üniversitesi E-Dergisi*, 16(61), 77–94.

İŞKUR (2023), Institution of Providing Jobs and Employees' Labor Market Research Report for Türkiye

Jackie Hsu, W.-C., Lin, K.-Y., Lo, H.-W., & Yang, J.-J. (2024). Assessing corporation sustainability performance towards achieving sustainable development goals using a novel trapezoidal fuzzy ITARA-RIM approach. *Annals of Operations Research.* Advance online publication. DOI: 10.1007/s10479-024-05987-6

Jain, N. K., Panda, A., & Choudhary, P. (2020). Institutional pressures and circular economy performance: The role of environmental management system and organizational flexibility in oil and gas sector. *Business Strategy and the Environment*, 29(8), 3509–3525. DOI: 10.1002/bse.2593

Javaid, M., Haleem, A., Singh, R. P., & Suman, R. (2021). Substantial capabilities of robotics in enhancing industry 4.0 implementation. *Cognitive Robotics*, 1, 58–75. DOI: 10.1016/j.cogr.2021.06.001

Javaid, M., Haleem, A., Singh, R. P., Suman, R., & Rab, S. (2021). Role of additive manufacturing applications towards environmental sustainability. *Advanced Industrial and Engineering Polymer Research*, 4(4), 312–322. DOI: 10.1016/j.aiepr.2021.07.005

Jefrine, G. (2023). The role of AI in technological unemployment and job displacement. *Journal of Future Technologies*, 35(1), 100–120. DOI: 10.1080/10438599.2023.125463

Jensen, B. C. (2024, febrero 7). The Role of Augmented Reality in Enhancing Customer Experience. *Medium.* https://medium.com/@briancjensen1/the-role-of-augmented-reality-in-enhancing-customer-experience-4abb786fd38e

Jhanji, A., & Connor, Y. (2021). ESG resilience: A true measure of success Activating ESG through the risk lens in GrantThornton. Availabe on: https://www.grantthornton.com/content/dam/grantthornton/website/assets/content-page-files/advisory/pdfs/2021/esg-resilience-true-measure-success/esg-resilience-true-measure-success.pdf.coredownload.pdf

Jöhnk, J., Weißert, M., & Wyrtki, K. (2020). *Ready or Not.* AI Comes— An Interview Study of Organizational AI Readiness Factors.

Johnson, D., & Verdicchio, M. (2017). AI Anxiety. *Journal of the Association for Information Science and Technology*, 68(9), 2267–2270. DOI: 10.1002/asi.23867

Johnson, S., Sheely, M., Fitzgerald, T., & Foster, C. (2007). *Managing commercial real estate Concentrations*. FDIC Supervisory Insights.

Johnston, M. P. (2014). *Secondary Data Analysis: A Method of which the Time Has Come. Qualitative and Quantitative Methods in Libraries, 3(3).* Issue.

Jones, M. D., Hutcheson, S., & Camba, J. D. (2021). Past, present, and future barriers to digital transformation in manufacturing: A review. *Journal of Manufacturing Systems*, 60, 936–948. DOI: 10.1016/j.jmsy.2021.03.006

Joshi, N. (2024, julio 14). The Role of Digital Transformation in Achieving Sustainable Manufacturing Operations. *Snic Solutions*. https://snicsolutions.com/blog/the-role-of-digital-transformation-in-achieving-sustainable-manufacturing-operations#:~:text=Digital%20transformation%20plays%20a%20crucial,waste%2C%20and%20improve%20resource%20efficiency

Jovevski, D., Drakulevski, L., & Firfov, O. (2023). DIGITAL TRANSFORMATION AND PRODUCTIVITY. *KNOWLEDGE -. International Journal (Toronto, Ont.)*, 59(1), 15–21.

Jung, T., Chung, N., & Leue, M. C. (2015). The determinants of recommendations to use augmented reality technologies: The case of a Koreanthemepark. *Tourism Management*, 49, 75–86. DOI: 10.1016/j.tourman.2015.02.013

Kamalaldin, A., Linde, L., Sjödin, D., & Parida, V. (2020). Transforming Provider-Customer Relationships in Digital Servitization: A Relational View on Digitalization. *Industrial Marketing Management*, 89, 306–325. DOI: 10.1016/j.indmarman.2020.02.004

Kane, G. (2019). The technology fallacy: People are the real key to digital transformation. *Research Technology Management*, 62(6), 44–49. DOI: 10.1080/08956308.2019.1661079

Kannan, R. (s. f.). The future of manufacturing: Self-optimizing factories powered by IIoT and digital twins. *UST*. Recuperado 2 de septiembre de 2024, de https://www.ust.com/en/insights/the-future-of-manufacturing-self-optimizing-factories-powered-by-iiot-and-digital-twins

Kaplan, S. (s. f.-a). Driving Innovation: Mass Customization in Manufacturing Unleashed. *Praxie*. Recuperado 2 de septiembre de 2024, de https://praxie.com/mass-customization-in-manufacturing/

Kaplan, S. (s. f.-b). Revolutionizing Home Furnishings: The Power of Robotics in Manufacturing. *Praxie*. Recuperado 2 de septiembre de 2024, de https://praxie.com/robotics-in-home-furnishings-manufacturing/

Kaplan, S. (s. f.-c). Transforming the Furniture Industry: The Impact of Data Analytics. *Praxie*. Recuperado 2 de septiembre de 2024, de https://praxie.com/data-analytics-in-furniture-industry/

Karaçay, G., & Alpkan, L. (2019). Dijital dönüşümün işgücü piyasalarına etkileri: türkiye işgücü piyasası için sosyal politika önerileri (Effects of digital transformation on labor markets: social policy recommendations for the Turkish labor market). *Türk İdare Dergisi*, 91(488), 345–373.

Karakadilar, I. S. (2023). A scale development study for Turkish exporting industries oriented to the Industry 4.0 and circular economy implementations. *Journal of Economics Business and Political Researches*, 21(8), 403–420.

Kawaguchi, K. (2021). Enhancing Decision-Making Processes with Artificial Intelligence: A Comprehensive Overview. *Journal of Decision Systems*, 30(4), 321–334.

Kensbock, J. M., & Stöckmann, C. (2021). "Big brother is watching you": Surveillance via technology undermines employees' learning and voice behavior during digital transformation. *Journal of Business Economics*, 91(4), 565–594. DOI: 10.1007/s11573-020-01012-x

Keogh-Brown, M. C., & Smith, R. D. (2008). The Economic Impact of SARS: How Does the reality match the predictions? *Health Policy (Amsterdam)*, 88(1), 110–120. DOI: 10.1016/j.healthpol.2008.03.003 PMID: 18436332

Keys, B., Mukherjee, T., Seru, A., & Vig, V. (2010). Did securitization lead to lax screening? Evidence from subprime loans. *The Quarterly Journal of Economics*, 125(1), 307–362. DOI: 10.1162/qjec.2010.125.1.307

Keys, B., Seru, A., & Vig, V. (2012). Lender screening and the role of securitization: Evidence from prime and subprime mortgage markets. *Review of Financial Studies*, 25(7), 2071–2108. DOI: 10.1093/rfs/hhs059

Khan, A. A., & Abonyi, J. (2022). Information sharing in supply chains – Interoperability in an era of circular economy. *Cleaner Logistics and Supply Chain*, 5, 100074. DOI: 10.1016/j.clscn.2022.100074

Khandelwal, V., Sharma, P., & Chotia, V. (2023). ESG Disclosure and Firm Performance: An Asset-Pricing Approach. *Risks*, 11(6), 112. DOI: 10.3390/risks11060112

Khan, M., Serafeim, G., & Yoon, A. (2016). Corporate Sustainability: First Evidence on Materiality. *The Accounting Review*, 91(6), 1697–1724. DOI: 10.2308/accr-51383

Khan, S. A. R., Razzaq, A., Yu, Z., & Miller, S. (2021). Industry 4.0 and circular economy practices: A new era business strategies for environmental sustainability. *Business Strategy and the Environment*, 30(8), 4001–4014. DOI: 10.1002/bse.2853

Kim, J., Choi, D., Cho, E., Okafor, C. E., & Park, B. I. (2022). Corporate Sustainability in the Wake of the COVID-19 Global Pandemic: Does CSR Enhance Corporate Survival during a Market Crisis? *Sustainability (Basel)*, 14(21), 14438. DOI: 10.3390/su142114438

Kim, T.-G., Hornung, S., & Rousseau, D. (2011). Change-supportive behavior: Antecedents and the moderating role of time. *Journal of Management*, 37(6), 1664–1693. DOI: 10.1177/0149206310364243

Kindleberger, C. P., & Aliber, R. Z. (2015). Manias, Panics, and Crashes: A History of Financial Crises. Publishing house John Wiley & son. DOI: 355. ISBN: 978-1-137-52575-8DOI: 10.1007/978-1-137-52574-1.pages

Kirchherr, J., Reike, D., & Hekkert, M. (2017). Conceptualizing the circular economy: An analysis of 114 definitions. *Resources, Conservation and Recycling*, 127, 221–232. DOI: 10.1016/j.resconrec.2017.09.005

Klubnikin, A. (2023, febrero 14). The Surprising Benefits of Data Analytics for Furniture Stores. *Smart Data Collective*. https://www.smartdatacollective.com/benefits-data-analytics-for-furniture-stores/

Knickrehm, M. (2018). *How will AI Change the Work*. Harvard Business Review Press.

Ko, A., Fehér, P., Kovacs, T., Mitev, A., & Szabó, Z. (2022). Influencing factors of digital transformation: Management or IT is the driving force? *International Journal of Innovation Science*, 14(1), 1–20. DOI: 10.1108/IJIS-01-2021-0007

Koç, E. (2007). *Tüketici Davranısları ve Pazarlama Stratejileri: Global ve Yerel Yaklaşım*. Seçkin Yayınları.

Kopeinig, J., Woschank, M., & Olipp, N. (2024). Industry 4.0 Technologies and their Implications for Environmental Sustainability in the Manufacturing Industry. *Procedia Computer Science*, 232, 2777–2789. DOI: 10.1016/j.procs.2024.02.095

Kotler, P., & Armstrong, G. (2008). *Principles of Marketing* (Vol. 12). Pearson Prentice Hall.

Kotter, J., & Schlesinger, L. (2008). Choosing Strategies for Change. *Harvard Business Review*, •••, 106–114. PMID: 10240501

Kraus, S., Jones, P., Kailer, N., Weinmann, A., Chaparro-Banegas, N., & Roig-Tierno, N. (2021). Digital Transformation: An Overview of the Current State of the Art of Research. *SAGE Open*, 11(3), 215824402110475. DOI: 10.1177/21582440211047576

Krishna, A., Briesch, R., Lehmann, D. R., & Yuan, H. (2002). A meta-analysis of the impact of price presentation on perceived savings. *Journal of Retailing*, 78(2), 101–118. DOI: 10.1016/S0022-4359(02)00072-6

Kristjánsdóttir, H. (2017). National and regional competitiveness: Country competitiveness an empirical study. *Baltic Region*, 9(2), 31–44. DOI: 10.5922/2079-8555-2017-2-3

Krugman, H. E. (1965). The impact of television advertising: Learning without involvement. *Public Opinion Quarterly*, 29(3), 349–356. DOI: 10.1086/267335

Kumar, R., Kariminejad, A., Antonov, M., Goljandin, D., Klimczyk, P., & Hussainova, I. (2023). Progress in Sustainable Recycling and Circular Economy of Tungsten Carbide Hard Metal Scraps for Industry 5.0 and Onwards. *Sustainability (Basel)*, 15(16), 12249. DOI: 10.3390/su151612249

Kurt, A. S. (2020). Dijital dönüşümün ekonomiye etkileri: Türkiye Ekonomisi'ne yansımaları. *OPUS Uluslararası Toplum Araştırmaları Dergisi*, 16(30), 3083–3109. DOI: 10.26466/opus.714393

Kurtuluş, K. (2004). *Pazarlama Araştırmaları*. Literatür Yayıncılık.

Lamey, L., Deleersnyder, B., Dekimpe, M. G., & Steenkamp, J. B. E. (2007). How business cycles contribute to private-label success: Evidence from the United States and Europe. *Journal of Marketing*, 71(1), 1–15. DOI: 10.1509/jmkg.71.1.001

Lamey, L., Deleersnyder, B., Steenkamp, J. B. E., & Dekimpe, M. G. (2012). The effect of business-cycle fluctuations on private-label share: What has marketing conduct got to do with it? *Journal of Marketing*, 76(1), 1–19. DOI: 10.1509/jm.09.0320

Landbell Group. (2022, mayo 9). *A step forward for EPR in Spain*. https://landbell-group.com/news/a-step-forward-for-epr-in-spain/

Lasi, H., Fettke, P., Kemper, H.-G., Feld, T., & Hoffman, M. (2014). Industry 4.0. *Business & Information Systems Engineering*, 4(4), 239–242. DOI: 10.1007/s12599-014-0334-4

Laurent, G., & Kapferer, J. N. (1985a). Measuring consumer involvement profiles. *JMR, Journal of Marketing Research*, 22(1), 41–53. DOI: 10.1177/002224378502200104

Lavrynenko, A., Shmatko, N., & Meissner, D. (2018). Managing skills for open innovation: The case of biotechnology. *Management Decision*, 56(6), 1336–1347. DOI: 10.1108/MD-04-2017-0301

Lazarus, R., & Folkman, S. (1984). *Stress, Appraisal and Coping*. Springer.

Le Moigne, R. (2021). The power of digital technologies to enable the circular economy. *Medium*. h

Lei, Z., Cai, S., Cui, L., Wu, L., & Liu, Y. (2023). How do different Industry 4.0 technologies support certain circular economy practices? *Industrial Management & Data Systems*, 123(4), 1220–1251. DOI: 10.1108/IMDS-05-2022-0270

Lele, A. (2019). Industry 4.0. In A. Lele, Disruptive Technologies for the Militaries and Security (pp.205-215). Springer.

Leng, J., Sha, W., Wang, B., Zheng, P., Zhuang, C., Liu, Q., Wuest, T., Mourtzis, D., & Wang, L. (2022) Industry 5.0: Prospect and retrospect, Journal of Manufacturing Systems, 65, 279-295, ISSN 0278-6125, DOI: 10.1016/j.jmsy.2022.09.017

Libert, B., Beck, M., & Wind, Y. (2016). How to navigate a digital transformation. *Harvard Business Review*, •••, 4.

Lichtenstein, D. R., Netemeyer, R. G., & Burton, S. (1990). Distinguishing coupon proneness from value consciousness: An acquisition-transaction utility theory perspective. *Journal of Marketing*, 54(3), 54–67. DOI: 10.1177/002224299005400305

Lichtenstein, D. R., Ridgway, N. M., & Netemeyer, R. G. (1993). Price perceptions and consumer shopping behavior: A field study. *JMR, Journal of Marketing Research*, 30(2), 234–245. DOI: 10.1177/002224379303000208

Lichtenthaler, U. (2020). Beyond artificial intelligence: Why companies need to go the extra step. Journal of Business Strategy. *The Journal of Business Strategy*, 41(1), 19–26. DOI: 10.1108/JBS-05-2018-0086

Lima, Y., Barbosa, C. E., dos Santos, H. S., & de Souza, J. M. (2021). Understanding technological unemployment: A review of causes, consequences, and solutions. *Societies (Basel, Switzerland)*, 11(2), 50. DOI: 10.3390/soc11020050

Lindenmeier, J., & Tscheulin, D. K. (2008). The effects of inventory control and denied boarding on customer satisfaction: The case of capacity-based airline revenue management. *Tourism Management*, 29(1), 32–43. DOI: 10.1016/j.tourman.2007.04.004

Lindsay, A., Downs, D., & Lunn, K. (2003). Business processes: Attempts to find a definition. *Information and Software Technology*, 45(15), 1015–1019. DOI: 10.1016/S0950-5849(03)00129-0

Lins, K. V., Servaes, H., & Tamayo, A. (2017). Social Capital, Trust, and Firm Performance: The Value of Corporate Social Responsibility during the Financial Crisis. *The Journal of Finance*, 72(4), 1785–1824. DOI: 10.1111/jofi.12505

Liu, J., Liu, Z., Yang, Q., Osmani, M., & Demian, P. (2022). A Conceptual Blockchain Enhanced Information Model of Product Service Systems Framework for Sustainable Furniture. *Buildings (Basel, Switzerland)*, 13(1), 85. DOI: 10.3390/buildings13010085

Liu, L., Song, W., & Liu, Y. (2023). Leveraging digital capabilities toward a circular economy: Reinforcing sustainable supply chain management with Industry 4.0 technologies. *Computers & Industrial Engineering*, 178, XX–XX. DOI: 10.1016/j.cie.2023.109113

Liu-Thompkins, Y., Khoshghadam, L., Shoushtari, A. A., & Zal, S. (2022). What drives retailer loyalty? A meta-analysis of the role of cognitive, affective, and social factors across five decades. *Journal of Retailing*, 98(1), 92–110. DOI: 10.1016/j.jretai.2022.02.005

Lokuge, S., Sedera, D., Grover, V., & Dongming, X. (2019). Organizational readiness for digital innovation: Development and empirical calibration of a construct. *Information & Management*, 56(3), 445–461. DOI: 10.1016/j.im.2018.09.001

Lola, I., & Bakeev, M. (2020). Digital Transformation In Manufacturing: Drivers, Barriers, And Benefits. SSRN *Electronic Journal*. DOI: 10.2139/ssrn.3570342

Lopes de Sousa Jabbour, A. B., Jabbour, C. J. C., Godinho Filho, M., & Roubaud, D. (2018). Industry 4.0 and the circular economy: A proposed research agenda and original roadmap for sustainable operations. *Annals of Operations Research*, 270(1), 273–286. DOI: 10.1007/s10479-018-2772-8

Lučić, S. (2022). Digitalization And Artificial Intelligence: New Dimensions In Tourism. *Tourism and Hospitality Management Conference Proceedings*. DOI: DOI: 10.52370/TISC22564SL

Luo, X., Cheah, J. H., Hollebeek, L. D., & Lim, X. J. (2024). Boosting customers' impulsive buying tendency in live-streaming commerce: The role of customer engagement and deal proneness. *Journal of Retailing and Consumer Services*, 77, 103644. DOI: 10.1016/j.jretconser.2023.103644

Lu, Y. (2017). Industry 4.0: A survey on technologies, applications, and open research issues. *Journal of Industrial Information Integration*, 6, 1–10. DOI: 10.1016/j.jii.2017.04.005

Lv, H., Shi, S., & Gursoy, D. (2022). A look back and a leap forward: Are view and synthesis of big data and artificial intelligence literature in hospitality and tourism. *Journal of Hospitality Marketing & Management*, 31(2), 145–175. DOI: 10.1080/19368623.2021.1937434

Lyons, B., & Henderson, K. (2005). Opinion leadership in a computer-mediated environment. *Journal of Consumer Behaviour*, 4(5), 319–329. DOI: 10.1002/cb.22

Ma, D., Fan, X., Gausemeier, J., & Grafe, M. (Eds.). (2011). *Virtual Reality & Augmented Reality in Industry*. Springer Berlin Heidelberg., DOI: 10.1007/978-3-642-17376-9

Madrid-Guijarro, A., Garcia, D., & Van Auken, H. (2009). Barriers to Innovation among Spanish Manufacturing SMEs. *Journal of Small Business Management*, 47(4), 465–488. DOI: 10.1111/j.1540-627X.2009.00279.x

Magesa, M. M., & Jonathan, J. (2022). Conceptualizing digital leadership characteristics for successful digital transformation: The case of Tanzania. *Information Technology for Development*, 28(4), 777–796. DOI: 10.1080/02681102.2021.1991872

Maji, S. G., & Lohia, P. (2023). Environmental, social and governance (ESG) performance and firm performance in India. *Society and Business Review*, 18(1), 175–194. DOI: 10.1108/SBR-06-2022-0162

Malik, A., & Nguyen, N. (2022). The Impact of AI-Powered Digital Assistants on Workplace Productivity. *Journal of Artificial Intelligence Research*, 45(3), 123–145.

Mammonas, D. (2023, octubre 9). Renewable energy: Council adopts new rules. *Council of the EU*. https://www.consilium.europa.eu/en/press/press-releases/2023/10/09/renewable-energy-council-adopts-new-rules/#:~:text=The%20Council%20today%20adopted%20the,contribute%20to%20this%20common%20target

Manickam, P. (s. f.). WEEE Directives: Managing E-Waste in the EU. *Talema Group*. Recuperado 8 de septiembre de 2024, de https://talema.com/weee-directives-managing-e-waste-in-the-eu/# MAPA. (2017). *Plan estatal marco de gestión de residuos (PEMAR) 2016-2022* (p. 192). MAPA. https://www.miteco.gob.es/content/dam/miteco/es/calidad-y-evaluacion-ambiental/planes-y-estrategias/pemaraprobado6noviembrecondae_tcm30-170428.pdf

Mao, S., Wang, B., Tang, Y., & Qian, F. (2019). Opportunities and Challenges of Artificial Intelligence for Green Manufacturing in the Process Industry. *Engineering (Beijing)*, 6(6), 995–1002. DOI: 10.1016/j.eng.2019.08.013

Marić, J., Opazo-Basáez, M., Vlačić, B., & Dabić, M. (2023). Innovation management of three-dimensional printing (3DP) technology: Disclosing insights from existing literature and determining future research streams. *Technological Forecasting and Social Change*, 193, 122605. DOI: 10.1016/j.techfore.2023.122605

Marikyan, D., Papagiannidis, S., & Alamanos, E. (2022). The Role of Digital Assistants in Enhancing Employee Productivity: An Empirical Study. *Journal of Business Research*, 144, 106–121.

Marklund, M. J. (2023), At the heart of the transition? Making sense of agency, policy, and post-politics within just transition in Scotland

Marr (2024), https://www.euronews.com/next/2024/09/28

Martin, C., & Leurent, H. (2017, March 31). White Paper: Technology and Innovation for the Future of Production: Accelerating Value Creation. Retrieved April 1, 2021, from World Economic Forum: https://www.weforum.org/whitepapers/technology -and-innovation-for-the-future-of- production-accelerating-value-creation

Martínez, E., & Montaner, T. (2006). The effect of consumer's psychographic variables upon deal-proneness. *Journal of Retailing and Consumer Services*, 13(3), 157–168. DOI: 10.1016/j.jretconser.2005.08.001

Martínez-Peláez, R., Ochoa-Brust, A., Rivera, S., Félix, V. G., Ostos, R., Brito, H., Félix, R. A., & Mena, L. J. (2023). Role of Digital Transformation for Achieving Sustainability: Mediated Role of Stakeholders, Key Capabilities, and Technology. *Sustainability (Basel)*, 15(14), 11221. DOI: 10.3390/su151411221

Martini, B., Bellisario, D., & Coletti, P. (2024). Human-Centered and Sustainable Artificial Intelligence in Industry 5.0: Challenges and Perspectives. *Sustainability (Basel)*, 16(13), 5448. DOI: 10.3390/su16135448

Ma, S., Ding, W., Liu, Y., Zhang, Y., Ren, S., Kong, X., & Leng, J. (2024). Industry 4.0 and cleaner production: A comprehensive review of sustainable and intelligent manufacturing for energy-intensive manufacturing industries. *Journal of Cleaner Production*, 467, 142879. DOI: 10.1016/j.jclepro.2024.142879

Masood, T., & Sonntag, P. (2020). Industry 4.0: Adoption challenges and benefits for SMEs. *Computers in Industry*, 121, 103261. DOI: 10.1016/j.compind.2020.103261

Matuzevičiūte, K., Zuperkiene, E., & Simanavičiene, Ž. (2017). The long-term impact of technological innovations on unemployment in European countries. *Baltic Journal of Economic Studies*, 3(2), 145–153. DOI: 10.30525/2256-0742/2017-3-2-145-153

May, G., & Psarommatis, F. (2023). Maximizing Energy Efficiency in Additive Manufacturing: A Review and Framework for Future Research. *Energies*, 16(10), 4179. DOI: 10.3390/en16104179

McCabe, S., Clement, S., & Ochoa, A. (2009). *Sustainable Procurement Guidelines for Office Furniture. Background report.* Local Goverment for Sustainability., https://sustainableprocurement.eu.com/documents/Category_Mangt/Furniture/United_Nations/UN_tech_report_furniture.pdf

McCabe, S., & Illodo, I. B. (2018). Thrilled to have "bagged a bargain" or "bitter" and "very frustrating"? Exploring consumer attitudes to value and deals in tourism. *Journal of Travel Research*, 58(4), 575–593. DOI: 10.1177/0047287518790403

McCarthy, P., Sammon, D., & Alhassan, I. (2022). Digital transformation leadership characteristics: A literature analysis. *Journal of Decision Systems*, 32(1), 1–31. DOI: 10.1080/12460125.2021.1908934

McKinsey & Company. (2020). Future of Work: Turkey's Talent Transformation in the Digital Era.

McWilliams, A., & Siegel, D. S. (2001). Corporate social responsibility: A theory of the firm perspective. *Academy of Management Review*, 26(1), 117–127. DOI: 10.2307/259398

Meijer, A., Conradie, P., & Choenni, S. (2021). Improving Decision-Making through Data-Driven Policing: A Case Study of the Rotterdam Police Force. *Government Information Quarterly*, 38(1), 101534.

Menner, M., Reichert, G., Voßwinkel, J. S., & Wolf, A. (2024). Towards decarbonised road transport driven by a globally competitive EU automotive industry: Further development of a resilient EU regulatory framework to safeguard the transformation.

Mera, K., & Renaud, B. (2000). Asia's Financial Crisis and the Role of Real Estate. eBook Published. First edition. New York, DOI: , Pages 312. ISBN9781315500010DOI: 10.4324/9781315500010

Mesjasz-Lech, A., Kemendi, Á., & Michelberger, P. (2024). Circular manufacturing and Industry 5.0. Assessing material flows in the manufacturing process in relation to e-waste streams. *Engineering Management in Production and Services*, 16(1), 114–133. DOI: 10.2478/emj-2024-0009

Meyer, B. (2023, julio 20). EU-wide regulation of formaldehyde limits from August 6, 2026: Fraunhofer WKI offers "REAC-H-CHO" certification. *Fraunhofer WKI*. https://www.wki.fraunhofer.de/en/departments/qa/profile/news/certification-reach.html

Miles ve Huberman. M. B. (2015). Nitel Veri Analizi. Ankara: Pegem Akademi Yayıncılık.

Miller, V., Johnson, J., & Grau, J. (1994). Antecedents to willingness to participate in a planned organizational change. *Journal of Applied Communication Research*, 22(1), 59–80. DOI: 10.1080/00909889409365387

Ministerio de Industria y Turismo. (s. f.). Aparatos eléctricos y electrónicos y la gestión de sus residuos. *Ministerio de Industria y Turismo*. Recuperado 8 de septiembre de 2024, de https://industria.gob.es/Calidad-Industrial/legislaciongeneral/Paginas/aparatos-electricos-gestion-residuos-rd-110-2015.aspx

Mintzberg, H. (1979). *The Structuring of Organizations: A Synthesis of the Research*. Prentice-Hall.

Mishra, R., Singh, R. K., & Govindan, K. (2022). Barriers to the adoption of circular economy practices in micro, small and medium enterprises: Instrument development, measurement and validation. *Journal of Cleaner Production*, 351, XX–XX. DOI: 10.1016/j.jclepro.2022.131389

MITECO. (2020a). *España Circular 2030. Estrategia Española de Economía Circular* (p. 65). MITECO. https://www.miteco.gob.es/es/calidad-y-evaluacion-ambiental/temas/economia-circular/espanacircular2030_def1_tcm30-509532.PDF

MITECO. (2020b, enero 20). *Plan Nacional integrado de energía y clima 2021-2030*. MITECO. https://www.miteco.gob.es/content/dam/miteco/es/ministerio/planes-estrategias/plan-nacional-integrado-energia-clima/plannacionalintegradodeenergiayclima2021-2030_tcm30-546623.pdf

Mithas, S., Tafti, A., & Mitchell, W. (2013). How a firm's competitive environment and digital strategic posture influence digital business strategy. *Management Information Systems Quarterly*, 37(2), 511–536. DOI: 10.25300/MISQ/2013/37.2.09

Miura, T., & Okabe, H. (2024, julio 16). Leveraging the Industrial Metaverse for Digital Transformation in Manufacturing. *EY*. https://www.ey.com/en_jp/technology/industrial-metaverse-unlocks-the-future-realizing-next-generation-factories-through-digital-transformation

Mochón Morcillo, F., & Cardona, P. (2021). *Transformación digital de la empresa: Casos de éxito*. Marcombo.

Modigliani, F., & Miller, M. H. (1958). The cost of capital, corporation finance and the theory of investment. *The American Economic Review*, 48(3), 261–297.

Moghrabi, I. A. R., Bhat, S. A., Szczuko, P., AlKhaled, R. A., & Dar, M. A. (2023). Digital Transformation and Its Influence on Sustainable Manufacturing and Business Practices. *Sustainability (Basel)*, 15(4), 3010. DOI: 10.3390/su15043010

Mohiuddin, M., Al Mamun, A., Syed, F. A., Mehedi Masud, M., & Su, Z. (2018). Environmental knowledge, awareness, and business school students' intentions to purchase green vehicles in emerging countries. *Sustainability (Basel)*, 10(5), 1534. DOI: 10.3390/su10051534

Moktadir, M. A., Ali, S. M., Kusi-Sarpong, S., & Shaikh, M. A. A. (2018). Assessing challenges for implementing Industry 4.0: Implications for process safety and environmental protection. *Process Safety and Environmental Protection*, 117, 730–741. DOI: 10.1016/j.psep.2018.04.020

MoldStud. (2024, febrero 2). Applying Virtual Reality in Prototype Development for Product Engineers. *MoldStud*. https://moldstud.com/articles/p-applying-virtual-reality-in-prototype-development-for-product-engineers

Moller, D. P. F., Vakilzadian, H., & Haas, R. E. (2022). From Industry 4.0 towards Industry 5.0. *2022 IEEE International Conference on Electro Information Technology (eIT)*, 61–68. DOI: 10.1109/eIT53891.2022.9813831

Momani, S. (2024, enero 23). Cost Savings Through Automation: Unlocking Efficiency with AI Technologies Across Business Departments. *Linkedin*. https://www.linkedin.com/pulse/cost-savings-through-automation-unlocking-efficiency-ai-sam-momani-zxb3c/

Monitor, E. U. (s. f.). *Directive2009/125—Framework for the setting of ecodesign requirements for energy-related products (recast)*. Recuperado 6 de septiembre de 2024, de https://www.eumonitor.eu/9353000/1/j9vvik7m1c3gyxp/vitgbgiu1owm

Moran, K. (s. f.). Benefits of Industry 4.0. *SL Controls*. Recuperado 25 de enero de 2022, de https://slcontrols.com/benefits-of-industry-4-0/

Morgan, G. (2006). *Images of Organization. Updated Edition*. SAGE Publications.

Morgon, J. (2016, February 19). What is the Forth Industrial Revolution? Retrieved April 1, 2021, from Forbes: https://www.forbes.com/sites/jacobmorgan/2016/02/19/what-is-the-4th- industrial-revolution/?sh=3dad0a72f392

Moroz, M. (2018). Acceleration of digital transformation as a result of launching programs financed from public funds: Assessment of the implementation of the operational program digital Poland. *Foundations of Management*, 10(1), 59–74. DOI: 10.2478/fman-2018-0006

Mulgan, G. (2006). *Social Silicon Valleys-A Manifesto for Social Innovation*. The Young Foundation.

Müller, M., & Lausberg, C. (2010). "Why Volatility is an Inappropriate Measure for Real Estate." *ERES Conference 2010, Milan, June 23-26, 2010*.DOI: DOI: 10.15396/eres2010_272

Murugan, T. (2024, marzo 17). *Enhancing Sustainability in the Manufacturing Industry through IoT* [LinkedIN]. https://www.linkedin.com/pulse/enhancing-sustainability-manufacturing-industry-through-murugan-h1lac/

Myers, S. C. (1977). Determinants of corporate borrowing. *Journal of Financial Economics*, 5(2), 147–175. DOI: 10.1016/0304-405X(77)90015-0

Naastepad, C. W. M., & Houghton Budd, C. (2019). Preventing technological unemployment by widening our understanding of capital and Progress: Making robots work for us. *Ethics & Social Welfare*, 13(2), 115–132. DOI: 10.1080/17496535.2018.1512641

Nadkarni, S., & Prügl, R. (2021). Digital transformation: A review, synthesis and opportunities for future research. *Management Review Quarterly*, 71(2), 233–341. DOI: 10.1007/s11301-020-00185-7

Naik, S., Sony, M., Antony, J., McDermott, O., Tortorella, G. L., & Jayaraman, R. (2024). Operational excellence framework for sustainability in the organisation: A design science approach. *Production Planning and Control*, 35(11), 1215–1231. DOI: 10.1080/09537287.2023.2165188

Nareswari, N., Tarczyńska-Łuniewska, M., & Hashfi, R. U. A. (2023). Analysis of Environmental, Social, and Governance Performance in Indonesia: Role of ESG on Corporate Performance, *Procedia Computer Science*, Nippani, S., & Washer, K. M. (2004). SARS: a non-event for affected countries' stock markets? *Applied Financial Economics*, 14(15), 1105–1110.

Narula, S., Tamvada, J. P., Kumar, A., Puppala, H., & Gupta, N. (2024). Putting Digital Technologies at the Forefront of Industry 5.0 for the Implementation of a Circular Economy in Manufacturing Industries. *IEEE Transactions on Engineering Management*, 71, 3363–3374. DOI: 10.1109/TEM.2023.3344373

Na, S., Heo, S., Han, S., Shin, Y., & Roh, Y. (2022). Acceptance Model of Artificial Intelligence (AI)-Based Technologies in Construction Firms: Applying the Technology Acceptance Model (TAM) in Combination with the Technology–Organisation–Environment (TOE) Framework. *Buildings (Basel, Switzerland)*, 12(2), 90. DOI: 10.3390/buildings12020090

Nascimento, D. L. M., Alencastro, V., Quelhas, O. L. G., Caiado, R. G. G., Garza-Reyes, J. A., Rocha-Lona, L., & Tortorella, G. (2019). Exploring Industry 4.0 technologies to enable circular economy practices in a manufacturing context: A business model proposal. *Journal of Manufacturing Technology Management*, 30(3), 607–627. DOI: 10.1108/JMTM-03-2018-0071

Neamtan, N. (2003), *Non-profit Sector and Evaluation: The State of Play in Quebec (OEDC ed.). The Non-Profit Sector in a Changing Economy*, 221-238.

Ng, A. (2019). *How to Choose Your First AI Project.* Harvard Business Review Press.

Nguyen, N., & Malik, A. (2022a). Job Satisfaction and Artificial Intelligence: A Study. *International Journal of Human-Computer Studies*, 68(2), 98–115.

Nguyen, X. T., & Luu, Q. K. (2020). Factors affecting adoption of Industry 4.0 by small and medium-sized enterprises: A case in Ho Chi Minh City, Vietnam. *The Journal of Asian Finance, Economics and Business*, 7(6), 255–264. DOI: 10.13106/jafeb.2020.vol7.no6.255

Nickel, L. (2024). *Ecodesign for Sustainable Products Regulation (ESPR) – 2024 Overview*. https://ecochain.com/blog/espr-2024-overview/

Nickell, S., Nunziata, L., & Ochel, W. (2005). Unemployment in the OECD since the 1960s: What do we know? *Economic Journal (London)*, 115(500), 1–27. DOI: 10.1111/j.1468-0297.2004.00958.x

Nohria, N., & Beer, M. (2000). Cracking the Code of Change. *Harvard Business Review*. PMID: 11183975

Nunez, C. (2019). Carbon dioxide levels are at a record high. National Geographic. Retrieved from https://www.nationalgeographic.com/environment/article/greenhouse-gases

Nunkoo, R., & Ramkissoon, H. (2010). Gendered theory of planned behaviour and residents' support for tourism. *Current Issues in Tourism*, 13(6), 525–540. DOI: 10.1080/13683500903173967

Nuryanto, U. W., Basrowi, , Quraysin, I., & Pratiwi, I. (2024). Environmental management control system, blockchain adoption, cleaner production, and product efficiency on environmental reputation and performance: Empirical evidence from Indonesia. *Sustainable Futures : An Applied Journal of Technology, Environment and Society*, 7, 100190. DOI: 10.1016/j.sftr.2024.100190

Oberländer, M., Beinicke, A., & Bipp, T. (2020). Digital competencies: A review of the literature and applications in the workplace. *Computers & Education*, 146, 103752. DOI: 10.1016/j.compedu.2019.103752

O'Carroll, B. (2017). What are the 3 types of AI? A guide to narrow, general, and super artificial intelligence.

OECD (2019), OECD Future of Education and Skills 2030, OECD Learning Compass 2030, A Series of Concept Notes

OECD. (2016). Skills for a Digital World. In *Policy Brief on The Future of Work*. OECD Publishing.

OECD. (2021). Indonesia: Public deficit and effects of Covid indicators. *OECD Economic Outlook.*: Vol. 2021. *Issue 2*. OECD Publishing.

OECD. (2022). [*Analysis of unemployment trends*. OrgOrganizationr Economic Co-operation and Development.]. *Economic Outlook*, •••, 2022.

OECD. (2024), Fertility rates, Retrieved from https://www.oecd.org/en/data/indicators/fertility-rates.html

OECD. (2024, abril 17). Extended Producer Responsibility: Basic facts and key principles. *OECD Publishing Paris, 41*. https://www.oecd.org/content/dam/oecd/en/publications/reports/2024/04/extended-producer-responsibility_4274765d/67587b0b-en.pdf

Öhgren, M., Milios, L., Dalhammar, C., & Lindahl, M. (2019). Public Procurement of reconditioned furniture and the potential transition to product service systems solutions. *Procedia CIRP*, 83, 151–156. https://www.diva-portal.org/smash/get/diva2:1465151/FULLTEXT01.pdf. DOI: 10.1016/j.procir.2019.02.134

OJK. (Indonesian Financial Service Authority (2014). *The Indonesia Corporate Governance Manual. OJK and IFC advisory service in Indonesia*. Jakarta. https://www.ojk.go.id/Files/box/The-Indonesia-Corporate-Governance-Manual-First-Edition.pdf

Oliveira, O., Gamboa, D., & Fernandes, P. (2016). An Information System for the Furniture Industry to Optimize the Cutting Process and the Waste Generated. *Procedia Computer Science*, 100, 711–716. DOI: 10.1016/j.procs.2016.09.215

Oliver, R. L. (1980). A cognitive model of the antecedents and consequences of satisfaction decisions. *JMR, Journal of Marketing Research*, 17(4), 460–469. DOI: 10.1177/002224378001700405

Oliver, R. L., Rust, R. T., & Varki, S. (1997). Customer delight: Foundations, findings, and managerial insight. *Journal of Retailing*, 73(3), 311–336. DOI: 10.1016/S0022-4359(97)90021-X

Onyeneke, G. B., & Abe, T. (2021). The effect of change leadership on employee attitudinal support for planned organizational change. *Journal of Organizational Change Management*, 34(2), 403–415. DOI: 10.1108/JOCM-08-2020-0244

Orhan, S., & Savuk, F. (2014). Emek-teknoloji-işsizlik ilişkisi. *Çalışma ve Sosyal Güvenlik Bakanlığı Çalışma Dünyası Dergisi, 2*(2), 9-24.

Ortega-Gras, J.-J., Bueno-Delgado, M.-V., Cañavate-Cruzado, G., & Garrido-Lova, J. (2021). Twin Transition through the Implementation of Industry 4.0 Technologies: Desk-Research Analysis and Practical Use Cases in Europe. *Sustainability (Basel)*, 13(24), 13601. DOI: 10.3390/su132413601

Ostmeier, E., & Strobel, M. (2022). Building skills in the context of digital transformation: How industry digital maturity drives proactive skill development. *Journal of Business Research*, 139, 718–730. DOI: 10.1016/j.jbusres.2021.09.020

Ostry, J. D., Berg, A., & Tsangarides, C. G. (2014). *Redistribution, inequality, and growth.* IMF Staff Discussion Note., DOI: 10.5089/9781484352076.006

Ozdemir, A. I., Ar, I. M., & Erol, I. (2020). Assessment of blockchain applications in the travel and tourism industry. *Quality & Quantity*, 54(5), 1549–1563. DOI: 10.1007/s11135-019-00901-w

Panza, L., Bruno, G., & Lombardi, F. (2023). Integrating Absolute Sustainability and Social Sustainability in the Digital Product Passport to Promote Industry 5.0. *Sustainability (Basel)*, 15(16), 12552. DOI: 10.3390/su151612552

Pasupuleti, V., Thuraka, B., Kodete, C. S., & Malisetty, S. (2024). Enhancing supply chain agility and sustainability through machine learning: Optimization techniques for logistics and inventory management. *Logistics (Basel)*, 8(3), XX–XX. DOI: 10.3390/logistics8030073

Patton, M. Q. (2002). *Qualitative research and evaluation methods. Thousand Oaks*. Sage Publications.

Pavlov, D. (2023, septiembre 22). Augmented Reality in Furniture Industry: How Can Brands Use It? *SmarTek*. https://smarttek.solutions/blog/augmented-reality-in-furniture-industry

Payer, R. C., Quelhas, O. L. G., & Bergiante, N. C. R. (2024). Framework to supporting monitoring the circular economy in the context of industry 5.0: A proposal considering circularity indicators, digital transformation, and sustainability. *Journal of Cleaner Production*, 466, 142850. DOI: 10.1016/j.jclepro.2024.142850

Pedhazur, E. J. (1997). *Multiple regression in behavioral research.* Retrieved from https://www.amazon.com/J-Pedhazur-Multiple-Regression-Behavioral/dp/B008VR4WMG

Pencarelli, T. (2020). The digital revolution in the travel and tourism industry. *Information Technology & Tourism*, 22(3), 455–476. DOI: 10.1007/s40558-019-00160-3

Peres, R. S., Jia, X., Lee, J., Sun, K., Colombo, A. W., & Barata, J. (2020). Industrial artificial intelligence in Industry 4.0-systematic review, challenges and outlook. *IEEE Access : Practical Innovations, Open Solutions*, 8, 220121–220139. DOI: 10.1109/ACCESS.2020.3042874

Pérez, A. (2023, julio 5). El Gobierno saca a información pública el Plan de Residuos para 2035. *El Economista*. https://www.eleconomista.es/energia/noticias/12354348/07/23/el-gobierno-saca-a-informacion-publica-el-plan-de-residuos-para-2035.html

Pharoah, M. (2018). Preparing for the inevitable resistance to Artificial Intelligence

Philippon, T. (2016). "The FinTech Opportunity". *Working Paper N 22476*, National Bureau of Economic Research.

Pihlajamaa, M., Malmelin, N., & Wallin, A. (2023). Competence combination for digital transformation: A study of manufacturing companies in Finlan. *Technology Analysis and Strategic Management*, 35(10), 1355–1368. DOI: 10.1080/09537325.2021.2004111

Pongcharoensuk, P., Adisasmito, W., Sat, L. M., Silkavute, P., Muchlisoh, L., Cong Hoat, P., & Coker, R. (2012, August). Adisasmito, w., Sat, L, M., Silkavute, P., Muchlisoh, L., Hoat, P, C., Coker, R., Avian and pandemic human influenza policy in South-East Asia: The interface between economic and public health imperatives. *Health Policy and Planning*, 27(5), 374–383. DOI: 10.1093/heapol/czr056 PMID: 21859775

Postel-Vinay, F. (2002). The dynamics of technological unemployment. *International Economic Review*, 43(3), 737–760. DOI: 10.1111/1468-2354.t01-1-00033

Prakosa, R. M. (2023). Information Technology Implementation (Digitalization) on Booking and Payment Online System to Village's Tourism Product in Bali. *Journal of Tourism and Cultural Change*. Advance online publication. DOI: 10.19184/etc.v7i1.37868

Praxie. (s. f.-a). Breaking Boundaries: How Digital Transformation is Revolutionizing Manufacturing. *Praxie*. https://praxie.com/manufacturing-industry-digital-transformation/#:~:text=In%20the%20context%20of%20the,and%20improve%20overall%20operational%20efficiency

Praxie. (s. f.-b). *From Traditional to Technological: AI in Furniture Manufacturing*. Recuperado 8 de agosto de 2024, de https://praxie.com/ai-in-furniture-manufacturing/

Praxie. (s. f.-c). *Streamlining the Future: How IoT Transforms Furniture Manufacturing*. Recuperado 8 de agosto de 2024, de https://praxie.com/iot-in-furniture-manufacturing/

Prince, K. (2017). Industrie 4.0 and Leadership. In: *International Conference on Electronic Business* (pp. 132-139). Association for Information System.

Pringle, T., & Zoller, E. (2018). *How to Achieve AI Maturity and Why It Matters*. Ovum.

Pronost, G., Mayer, F., Camargo, M., & Dupont, L. (2024). Digital Twins along the product lifecycle: A systematic literature review of applications in manufacturing. *Digital Twin*, 3, 3. DOI: 10.12688/digitaltwin.17807.2

Prosci. (2018). Best Practices in Change Management (11 ed.). Prosci Inc. Prosci. (n.d.). Definition of Change Management. Retrieved March 31, 2021, from Prosci: https://www.prosci.com/resources/articles/definition-of-change-management

Putri, M. D., & Devi, R. N. (2019). Impact of unemployment on well-being: A socio-psychological perspective. *IOP Conference Series. Materials Science and Engineering*, 508, 1–8. DOI: 10.1088/1757-899X/508/1/012017

Qiu, X., & Zhang, Y. (2022). Reducing Mental and Physical Fatigue of Workers with AI: A Comprehensive Study. *Journal of Human-Computer Interaction*, 38(4), 567–580.

Quigley, J. M., & Raphael, S. (2001). THE ECONOMICS OF HOMELESSNESS: THE EVIDENCE FROM NORTH AMERICA. *European Journal of Housing Policy*, 1(3), 323–336. DOI: 10.1080/14616710110091525

Rafferty, A., Jimmieson, N., & Armenakis, A. (2012). Change Readiness: A Multilevel Review. *Journal of Management*, 39(1), 110–135. DOI: 10.1177/0149206312457417

Rahman, S. (2024, febrero 19). How Robotics and AI Will Transform Furniture Manufacturing: HATIL Case Study. *Linkedin*. https://www.linkedin.com/pulse/how-robotics-ai-transform-furniture-manufacturing-hatil-rahman-rxz3c/

Raman (2024), 6 Critical Human Skills for the Age of AI, https://www.linkedin.com/business/talent/blog/learning-and-development/human-skills-age-of-ai

Rame, R., Purwanto, P., & Sudarno, S. (2023). Transforming The Furniture Industry in The Digital Age. *Jurnal Riset Teknologi Pencegahan Pencemaran Industri, 14*(3), 53-69. Real Decreto 219/2013, de 22 de marzo, sobre restricciones a la utilización de determinadas sustancias peligrosas en aparatos eléctricos y electrónicos., BOE-A-2013-3210, Ministerio de la Presidencia 22935-11, BOE-A-2013-3210 (2213). 06/08/2024DOI: 10.21771/jrtppi.2023.v14.no3.p53-69

Ramírez-Correa, P., Rond'an-Catalu˜na, F. J., Arenas-Gait'an, J., & Martín-Velicia, F. (2019). Analysing the acceptation of online games in mobile devices: An application of UTAUT2. *Journal of Retailing and Consumer Services*, 50(May), 85–93. DOI: 10.1016/j.jretconser.2019.04.018

Ramírez-Peña, M., Cerezo-Narváez, A., Pastor-Fernández, A., Otero-Mateo, M., & Ballesteros-Pérez, P. (2023). Determination of Requirements for the Improvement of Occupational Safety in the Cleaning of Vertical Tanks of Petroleum Products. *Safety (Basel, Switzerland)*, 9(1), 6. DOI: 10.3390/safety9010006

Ramsarup, P., McGrath, S., & Lotz-Sisitka, H. (2023). Reframing skills ecosystems for sustainable and just futures. *International Journal of Educational Development*, 101, 102836. DOI: 10.1016/j.ijedudev.2023.102836

Rani, P. (2014). Factors influencing consumer behaviour. *International Journal of Current Research and Academic Review*, 2(9), 52–61.

Ransbotham, S., Kiron, D., Gerpert, P., & Reeves, M. (2017). Reshaping Business with Artificial Intelligence: Closing the Gap Between Ambition and Action. *MIT Sloan Management Review*.

Rao, P. M. (2001). The ICT revolution, int internationalization technological activity, and the emerging economies: Implications for global marketing. *International Business Review*, 10(5), 571–596. DOI: 10.1016/S0969-5931(01)00033-6

Rawal, Y. S., Soni, H., Dani, R., & Bagchi, P. (2023). A Review on Service Delivery in Tourism and Hospitality Industry Through Artificial Intelligence. In *Proceedings ofThird InternationalConferenceonComputing, Communications, and Cyber-Security* (pp. 427–436). Springer. DOI: 10.1007/978-981-19-1142-2_34

Rehman, S., Hamdan, Y. H., & Sindhu, M. (2024). Impact of Industry 4.0 on firms' sustainable development in the GCC economies: A mediation and moderation approach. *Brazilian Journal of Operations & Production Management*, 21(4), XX–XX. DOI: 10.14488/BJOPM.2166.2024

Rejeb, A., & Karim, R. (2019). Blockchain technology in tourism: Applications and possibilities. *World Scientific News*, 137, 119–144.

Rejeb, A., Suhaiza, Z., Rejeb, K., Seuring, S., & Treiblmaier, H. (2022). The Internet of Things and the circular economy: A systematic literature review and research agenda. *Journal of Cleaner Production*, 350, 131439. DOI: 10.1016/j.jclepro.2022.131439

Renaud, B. (1995). The 1985-94 global real estate cycle: its causes and consequences, World Bank, Policy Research. Working paper N 1452.

Riberio, J. (2021, February 2). A (very) Brief Introduction to AI in the Industry 4.0. Retrieved April 1, 2021, from Towards Data Science: https://towardsdatascience.com/a-very-brief-introduction-to-ai-in-the-industry-4-0-14e6f4b46cd1

Rifkin, J. (1996). *The end of work* (Rouve, P., Trans.). La Decouverte.

Rishabh Software. (2023, noviembre 17). How Digital Transformation in Manufacturing is A Game-Changer for Industry 4.0. *Rishabh Software*. https://www.rishabhsoft.com/blog/digital-transformation-in-manufacturing-industry

Roberts, J. A. (1996). Green consumers in the 1990s: Profile and implications for advertising. *Journal of Business Research*, 36(3), 217–231. DOI: 10.1016/0148-2963(95)00150-6

Robey, D., Ghiyoung, I., & Wareham, J. (2008). Theoretical Foundations of Empirical Research on Interorganizational Systems: Assessing Past Contributions and Guiding Future Directions. *Journal of the Association for Information Systems*, 9(9), 497–518. DOI: 10.17705/1jais.00171

Rodrigues, J. C. (2022). Business models for the digital transformation of audiovisual archives. *International Journal of Entrepreneurial Behaviour & Research*, 28(8), 1975–1999. DOI: 10.1108/IJEBR-01-2021-0073

Rogers, E. M. (1983). *Diffusion of Innovations* (3rd ed.). The Free Press.

Rommel, S., & Fischer, A. (2013). Additive Manufacturing – A Growing Possibility to Lighten the Burden of Spare Parts Supply. In Kovács, G. L., & Kochan, D. (Eds.), *Digital Product and Process Development Systems* (Vol. 411, pp. 112–123). Springer Berlin Heidelberg., DOI: 10.1007/978-3-642-41329-2_13

RTS labs. (2024, marzo 15). *The Environmental Imperative: How AI is Reshaping Sustainable Logistics*. https://rtslabs.com/green-logistics-ai

Ruiz-de-la-Torre-Acha, A., Guevara-Ramirez, W., Río-Belver, R. M., & Borregan-Alvarado, J. (2023). Industry 5.0. The Road to Sustainability. Em Y. Borgianni, D. T. Matt, M. Molinaro, & G. Orzes (Orgs.), *Towards a Smart, Resilient and Sustainable Industry* (Vol. 745, p. 247–257). Springer Nature Switzerland. DOI: 10.1007/978-3-031-38274-1_21

Russell, S., & Norvig, P. (2016). Artificial Intelligence: A Modern Approach (3 ed.). Pearson.

Saaty, R. W. (1987). The analytic hierarchy process—What it is and how it is used. *Mathematical Modelling*, 9(3–5), 161–176. DOI: 10.1016/0270-0255(87)90473-8

Sabato, S., & Mandelli, M. (2024). Towards an EU framework for a just transition: Welfare policies and politics for the socio-ecological transition. *European Political Science*, 23(1), 14–26. DOI: 10.1057/s41304-023-00458-1

Sakkthivel, A. M., & Ramu, N. J. (2018). Investigating the gender influence on technology adoption model towards smart phones-evidences from emerging economies. *International Journal of Business Excellence*, 16(1), 35–46. DOI: 10.1504/IJBEX.2018.094570

Salvato, C., & Rerup, C. (2011). Beyond collective entities: Multilevel research on organizational routines and capabilities. *Journal of Management*, 37(2), 468–490. DOI: 10.1177/0149206310371691

Sánchez-García, E., Martínez-Falcó, J., Marco-Lajara, B., & Manresa-Marhuenda, E. (2024). Revolutionizing the circular economy through new technologies: A new era of sustainable progress. *Environmental Technology & Innovation*, 33, 103509. DOI: 10.1016/j.eti.2023.103509

Sanga, B. (2023), Top 10 green skills shaping the future, LinkedIn, https://www.linkedin.com/pulse/top-10-green-skills-shaping-future-beuuy-sanga-cfowf

Santolaya, C., & Blanxart, A. F. (2001). *NTP 590: Prevención de la exposición a formaldehído*. INSST. https://www.insst.es/documents/94886/327064/ntp_590.pdf/0d2e6ea7-16a1-4bd7-9100-2db6c9c197a6

Satav, A. G., Kubade, S., Amrutkar, C., Arya, G., & Pawar, A. (2023). A state-of-the-art review on robotics in waste sorting: Scope and challenges. [IJIDeM]. *International Journal on Interactive Design and Manufacturing*, 17(6), 2789–2806. DOI: 10.1007/s12008-023-01320-w

Schallmo, D., Williams, C. A., & Boardman, L. (2020). Digital transformation of business models—best practice, enablers, and roadmap. In *Digital Disruptive Innovation* (pp. 119- 138).

Schiuma, G., Santarsiero, F., Carlucci, D., & Jarrar, Y. (2024). Transformative leadership competencies for organizational digital transformation. *Business Horizons*, 67(4), 425–437. DOI: 10.1016/j.bushor.2024.04.004

Schiuma, G., Schettini, E., Santarsiero, F., & Carlucci, D. (2022). The transformative leadership compass: Six competencies for digital transformation entrepreneurship. *International Journal of Entrepreneurial Behaviour & Research*, 28(5), 1273–1291. DOI: 10.1108/IJEBR-01-2021-0087

Schwab, K. (2016). The Fourth Industrial Revolution: What it means and how to respond. *World Economic Forum*. The Fourth Industrial Revolution: what it means and how to respond

Schwab, K. (2017). *Dördüncü sanayi devrimi* (Dicleli, Z., Trans.). Optimist Yayınları.

Schwartz, S. H., & Bilsky, W. (1990). Toward a theory of universal content and structure of values: Extensions and cross-cultural replications. *Journal of Personality and Social Psychology*, 58(5), 878–891. DOI: 10.1037/0022-3514.58.5.878

Seseni, L., & Mbohwa, C. (2018). The effects of using Big Data in Furniture Manufacturing SMEs. *Proceedings of the International Conference on Industrial Engineering and Operations Management, September 27-29*, 9. https://ieomsociety.org/dc2018/papers/385.pdf

Sgaravatti, G. (2021, junio 22). The Twin Transition Challenges [Web]. *Jeune Europe*. https://jeuneurope.com/the-twin-transition-challenges/

Shang, Y., Raza, S. A., Huo, Z., Shahzad, U., & Zhao, X. (2023). Does enterprise digital transformation contribute to the carbon emission reduction? Micro-level evidence from China. *International Review of Economics & Finance*, 86, 1–13. DOI: 10.1016/j.iref.2023.02.019

Shao, Z., Li, X., & Wang, Q. (2022). From ambidextrous learning to digital creativity: An integrative theoretical framework. *Information Systems Journal*, 32(3), 544–572. DOI: 10.1111/isj.12361

Shaukat, K., Iqbal, F., Alam, T. M., Aujla, G. K., Devnath, L., Khan, A. G., Iqbal, R., Shahzadi, I., Rubab, A. (2024). The impact of artificial intelligence and robotics on the future employment opportunities.

Sheng, H., Feng, T., & Liu, L. (2023). The influence of digital transformation on low-carbon operations management practices and performance: Does CEO ambivalence matter? *International Journal of Production Research*, 61(18), 6215–6229. DOI: 10.1080/00207543.2022.2088426

Shen, Y. (2024). Future jobs: An analysis of the impact of artificial intelligence on employment and its mechanisms. *Economic Change and Restructuring*, 57(2), 34. DOI: 10.1007/s10644-024-09629-6

Shirer, M. (2022, octubre 26). IDC Spending Guide Sees Worldwide Digital Transformation Investments Reaching $3.4 Trillion in 2026. *IDC Media Center*. https://www.idc.com/getdoc.jsp?containerId=prUS49797222

Shmueli, G., Ray, S., Manuel, J., Estrada, V., & Chatla, S. B. (2016). The elephant in the room: Predictive performance of PLS models. *Journal of Business Research*, 69(10), 4552–4564. DOI: 10.1016/j.jbusres.2016.03.049

Shoplogix. (2024, abril 30). 6 Key Challenges of Digital Transformation in Manufacturing. *Shoplogix*. https://shoplogix.com/challenges-of-digital-transformation/#:~:text=One%20of%20the%20major%20challenges,requires%20a%20significant%20financial%20investment

Shrivastava, S. (2017). Digital disruption is redefining the customer experience: The digital transformation approach of the communications service providers. *Telecom Business Review*, 10(1), 41.

Shui, X., Zhang, M., Wang, Y., & Smart, P. (2024). Do Climate Change Regulatory Pressures Increase Corporate Environmental Sustainability Performance? The Moderating Roles of Foreign Market Exposure and Industry Carbon Intensity. *British Journal of Management*, 1467-8551.12841. DOI: 10.1111/1467-8551.12841

Siakas, D., Lampropoulos, G., Rahanu, H., Georgiadou, E., & Siakas, K. (2023). Emerging Technologies Enabling the Transition Toward a Sustainable and Circular Economy: The 4R Sustainability Framework. Em M. Yilmaz, P. Clarke, A. Riel, & R. Messnarz (Orgs.), *Systems, Software and Services Process Improvement* (Vol. 1891, p. 166–181). Springer Nature Switzerland. DOI: 10.1007/978-3-031-42310-9_12

Siam. (s. f.). *Everything you need to know about the Regulation (EC) No1907/2006—REACH*. Recuperado 8 de septiembre de 2024, de https://www.siam-it.com/en/legislation/reach

Sichinsambwe, C., Simasiku, P. L., Sikombe, S., & Nyimbili, H. (2023). Kaizen practices and performance improvement in Zambian manufacturing companies. *Cogent Engineering*, 10(1), XX–XX. DOI: 10.1080/23311916.2023.2183590

Siddi, M. (2020). *The European Green Deal. Assessing its current state and future implementation* (114; FIIA Working Paper, p. 15). Finnish Institute of International Affairs.

Şimşek, H., & Yıldırım, A. (2011). Sosyal bilimlerde nitel araştırma yöntemleri. *Ankara. Seçkin Yayıncılık*, 432, 113–118.

Singh, S. (2003). Simple Random Sampling. In *Advanced Sampling Theory with Applications*. Springer. DOI: 10.1007/978-94-007-0789-4_2

Snyder-Halpern, R. (2021). Indicators of Organizational Readiness for Clinical Information Technology/Systems Innovation: A Delphi Study. *International Journal of Medical Informatics*, 63(3), 179–204. DOI: 10.1016/S1386-5056(01)00179-4 PMID: 11502432

Sohailkhan2k22. (2024, febrero 18). The Role of Robotics in Waste Sorting and Recycling. *Green.Org*. https://green.org/2024/01/30/the-role-of-robotics-in-waste-sorting-and-recycling/

Solomon, M., Bamossy, G., & Askegaard, S. (2006). *Consumer Behaviour: A European Perspective* (3rd ed.). Pearson Education.

Soori, M., Arezoo, B., & Dastres, R. (2023). Internet of things for smart factories in industry 4.0, a review. *Internet of Things and Cyber-Physical Systems*, 3, 192–204. DOI: 10.1016/j.iotcps.2023.04.006

Sowa, J. F., Hu, S., & Shapiro, R. (2021). The Impact of AI on Repetitive Task Management. *Journal of Organizational Behavior*, 42(5), 1025–1040.

Sowa, J. F., & Przegalinska, A. (2020). Enhancing Employee Productivity with AI: Case Studies and Insights. *Journal of Artificial Intelligence Research*, 44(3), 150–165.

Sow, M., & Aborbie, S. (2018). Impact of leadership on digital transformation. *Business and Economic Review*, 8(3), 139–148.

SpencerStuart (2024) 5 Essential Elements of an AI-Ready Corporate Culture

Stankov, U., & Gretzel, U. (2020). Tourism 4.0 technologies and tourist experiences: A human-centered design perspective. *Information Technology & Tourism*, 22(3), 477–488. DOI: 10.1007/s40558-020-00186-y

Stanley, A. (2023), African Century, IMF, https://www.imf.org/en/Publications/fandd/issues/2023/09/PT-african-century

Stasiškienė, Ž. (2008). Corporate Decision-Making in Furniture Industry: Weight of EMA and a Sustainability Balanced Scoreboard. *Environmental Research, Engineering and Management*, 1(43), 69–79.

Stefanou, C. (2001). Organizational key success factors for implementing SCM/ERP systems to support decision making. *Journal of Decision Systems*, 10(1), 49–64. DOI: 10.3166/jds.10.49-64

Stocker, F., Sajjad, A., Raziq, M. M., & Pacheco, L. M. (2022). Editorial: Innovation and business strategy for sustainability. *Innovation & Management Review*, 19(3), 174–179. DOI: 10.1108/INMR-07-2022-183

Stockhammer, E., & Klar, M. (2011). Capital accumulation, labour market institutions, and unemployment in Europe. *Cambridge Journal of Economics*, 35(2), 437–457. DOI: 10.1093/cje/beq020

Store, J. (2022, noviembre 24). EU to speed up permitting process for renewable energy projects. *Council of the EU*. https://www.consilium.europa.eu/en/press/press-releases/2022/11/24/eu-to-speed-up-permitting-process-for-renewable-energy-projects/

Straughan, R. D., & Roberts, J. A. (1999). Environmental segmentation alternatives: A look at green consumer behavior in the New Millennium. *Journal of Consumer Marketing*, 16(6), 558–575. DOI: 10.1108/07363769910297506

Strauss, A., & Corbin, J. (1990). *Basics of Qualitative Research: Grounded Theory Procedures and Techniques*. SAGE Publications.

Struckman, C., & Yammarino, F. (2003). Managing through multiple change activities: A solution to the enigma of the 21st century. *Organizational Dynamics*, 32(3), 234–246. DOI: 10.1016/S0090-2616(03)00033-0

Suarez-Fernandez De Miranda, S., Aguayo-González, F., Ávila-Gutiérrez, M. J., & Córdoba-Roldán, A. (2021). Neuro-Competence Approach for Sustainable Engineering. *Sustainability (Basel)*, 13(8), 4389. DOI: 10.3390/su13084389

Suchman, M. C. (1995). Managing legitimacy: Strategic and institutional approaches. *Academy of Management Journal*, 20(3), 571–610.

Sui, X., Jiao, S., Wang, Y., & Wang, H. (2024). Digital transformation and manufacturing company competitiveness. *Finance Research Letters*, 59, 104683. DOI: 10.1016/j.frl.2023.104683

Sulich, A. (2024). Model of Relationship Between Circular Economy and Industry 5.0. Em E. Mercier-Laurent, G. Kayakutlu, M. L. Owoc, A. Wahid, & K. Mason (Orgs.), *Artificial Intelligence for Knowledge Management, Energy and Sustainability* (Vol. 693, p. 220–236). Springer Nature Switzerland. DOI: 10.1007/978-3-031-61069-1_16

Sumanto, B., Rachmawati, R., & Suryani, D. (2020). The impact of technological development on unemployment in Indonesia. *Indonesian Journal of Economics and Development*, 30(4), 302–311. DOI: 10.20885/ejem.vol30.iss4.art7

Sunny, J., Undralla, N., & Madhusudanan Pillai, V. (2020). Supply chain transparency through blockchain-based traceability: An overview with demonstration. *Computers & Industrial Engineering*, 150, 106895. DOI: 10.1016/j.cie.2020.106895

Sun, X., & Wang, X. (2022). Modeling and analyzing the impact of the internet of things-based Industry 4.0 on circular economy practices for sustainable development: Evidence from the food processing industry of China. *Frontiers in Psychology*, 13, XX–XX. DOI: 10.3389/fpsyg.2022.866361 PMID: 35548486

Sun, Y., & Wang, S. (2020). Understanding consumers' intentions to purchase green products in the social media marketing context. *Asia Pacific Journal of Marketing and Logistics*, 32(4), 860–878. DOI: 10.1108/APJML-03-2019-0178

Suzan, S., & Smailagic, B. (2024, julio). *The advanced and waste biofuels paradox: Availability and sustainability of advanced and waste biofuels*. T&E. https://www.transportenvironment.org/uploads/files/202407_TE_advanced_biofuels_report-1.pdf

Syverson, C. (2011). What Determines Productivity? *Journal of Economic Literature*, 49(2), 326–365. DOI: 10.1257/jel.49.2.326

T4 Education. (2023). Sustainable education for a sustainable future. Retrieved October 10, 2024, from https://t4.education/blog/sustainable-education-for-a-sustainable-future/

Tandelilin, E., & Usman, B. (2023). Toward a better understanding of social impact, CSR reporting and firm performance: A look at the ASEAN banking industry. *Social Responsibility Journal*, 19(3), 579–600. DOI: 10.1108/SRJ-04-2021-0167

Tangi, L., Janssen, M., Benedetti, M., & Noci, G. (2020). Barriers and drivers of digital transformation in public organizations: Results from a survey in the Netherlands. In Electronic Government: 19th IFIP WG 8.5 International Conference, EGOV 2020, Linköping, Sweden, August 31–September 2, 2020 [Springer International Publishing.]. *Proceedings*, 19, 42–56.

Tanimoto, K., & Doi, M. (2007). Social innovation cluster in action: A case study of the San Francisco Bay Area. *Hitotsubashi Journal of Commerce and Management*, 41(1), 1–17.

Tatar, Ş. B., & Arslan, M. (2017). Sosyal inovasyon kavramı: Bir literatür taraması. *International Journal of Academic Value Studies*, 3(12), 321–338.

Tellius, I. (2024, enero 18). Leveraging the Power of Inventory Management Predictive Analytics. *Medium*. https://medium.com/@telliusua12/leveraging-the-power-of-inventory-management-predictive-analytics-c9d89f55117b

The Alliance for Flame Retardants Free Furniture. (2019). *Policy paper Safe fire safety for everyone Avoid toxic flame retardants in our furniture*. https://zerowasteeurope.eu/wp-content/uploads/2019/11/FRFFalliance_policy_paper_en.pdf

Thees, H., Erschbamer, G., & Pechlaner, H. (2020). The application of blockchain in tourism: Use cases in the tourism value system. *European Journal of Tourism Research*, 26, 26. DOI: 10.54055/ejtr.v26i.1933

Thomas, A., Chawla, Y., Varma, A., & Szleter, P. (2024). The Role of Business Leaders in Industry 5.0. Em A. Visvizi, O. Troisi, & V. Corvello (Orgs.), *Research and Innovation Forum 2023* (p. 629–640). Springer International Publishing. DOI: 10.1007/978-3-031-44721-1_47

Tickner, J., & Jacobs, M. (2016, agosto). *Improving the Identification, Evaluation, Adoption and Development of Safer Alternatives: Needs and Opportunities to Enhance Substitution Efforts within the Context of REACH*. https://www.actu-environnement.com/media/pdf/news-27483-substitution-chimique.pdf

Tigre, F. B., Curado, C., & Henriques, P. L. (2023). Digital leadership: A bibliometric analysis. *Journal of Leadership & Organizational Studies*, 30(1), 40–70. DOI: 10.1177/15480518221123132

Tiwana, A., Konsynski, B., & Bush, A. A. (2010). Research commentary—Platform evolution: Coevolution of platform architecture, governance, and environmental dynamics. *Information Systems Research*, 21(4), 675–687. DOI: 10.1287/isre.1100.0323

Tóxicos, H. S. (s. f.). Retardantes de llama. *Hogar Sin Tóxicos*. Recuperado 8 de septiembre de 2024, de https://www.hogarsintoxicos.org/es/riesgos/retardantes-llama/

Töytäri, P., Turunen, T., Klein, M., Eloranta, V., Biehl, S., Rajala, R., & Hakanen, E. (2017), "Overcoming institutional and capability barriers to smart services", Proceedings of the 5oth Hawaii International Conference on System Sciences, pp. 1642-1651.

Tr n, N. T., Tri u, H. T., Tr n, V. T., Ngô, H. H., & Đào, Q. K. (2021). An overview of the application of machine learning in predictive maintenance. *Petrovietnam Journal*, 10, 47–61. DOI: 10.47800/PVJ.2021.10-05

Trenerry, B., Chng, S., Wang, Y., Suhaila, Z. S., Lim, S. S., Lu, H. Y., & Oh, P. H. (2021). Preparing workplaces for digital transformation: An integrative review and framework of multi-level factors. *Frontiers in Psychology*, 12, 620766. DOI: 10.3389/fpsyg.2021.620766 PMID: 33833714

Tsang, H. (2019, julio 3). EU Publishes POPs Recast Regulation. *SGS*. https://www.sgs.com/en/news/2019/07/safeguards-09519-eu-publishes-pops-recast-regulation

Tsang, Y. P., Wu, C. H., Lin, K.-Y., Tse, Y. K., Ho, G. T. S., & Lee, C. K. M. (2022). Unlocking the power of big data analytics in new product development: An intelligent product design framework in the furniture industry. *Journal of Manufacturing Systems*, 62, 777–791. DOI: 10.1016/j.jmsy.2021.02.003

Turner, C., & Oyekan, J. (2023a). Manufacturing in the Age of Human-Centric and Sustainable Industry 5.0: Application to Holonic, Flexible, Reconfigurable and Smart Manufacturing Systems. *Sustainability (Basel)*, 15(13), 10169. DOI: 10.3390/su151310169

Turner, C., & Oyekan, J. (2023b). Personalised Production in the Age of Circular Additive Manufacturing. *Applied Sciences (Basel, Switzerland)*, 13(8), 4912. DOI: 10.3390/app13084912

Turner, C., Oyekan, J., Garn, W., Duggan, C., & Abdou, K. (2022). Industry 5.0 and the Circular Economy: Utilizing LCA with Intelligent Products. *Sustainability (Basel)*, 14(22), 14847. DOI: 10.3390/su142214847

Uchiyama, S., Matsushima, E., Kitao, N., Tokunaga, H., Ando, M., & Otsubo, Y. (2007). Effect of natural compounds on reducing formaldehyde emission from plywood. *Atmospheric Environment*, 41(38), 8825–8830. DOI: 10.1016/j.atmosenv.2007.09.046

UNDP. (2021). *The Changing Nature of Work, 30 signals to consider for a sustainable future*. UNDP Accelerator Labs.

UNEP(2024), United Nations Environment Programme, Food Waste Index Report 2024

United Nations. (2024), Global issues: Ageing. Retrieved from https://www.un.org/en/global-issues/ageing

Usman, B. (2019). Ownership structures, control mechanism and related party transaction: An empirical study of the Indonesian public listed companies. *International Journal of Economics and Management*, 13(1), 1–20.

Usman, B., Bernardes, O. T. F., & Kananlua, P. S. (2020). On the nexus between CSR practices, ESG performance, and asymmetric information. *Gadjah Mada International Journal of Business*, 22(2), 151–177. DOI: 10.22146/gamaijb.54053

Ustundag, A., & Cevikcan, E. (2017). *Industry 4.0: managing the digital transformation*. Springer.

Ustun, K., & Akkartal, E. (2024). The Role of Logistics in Decent Work and Economic Growth. In *Effective Logistics for Sustainable Development Goals* (pp. 48–78). IGI Global. DOI: 10.4018/979-8-3693-7071-1.ch003

Van Erp, T., Carvalho, N. G. P., Gerolamo, M. C., Gonçalves, R., Rytter, N. G. M., & Gladysz, B. (2024). Industry 5.0: A new strategy framework for sustainability management and beyond. *Journal of Cleaner Production*, 461, 142271. DOI: 10.1016/j.jclepro.2024.142271

Van Heerde, H. J., Gijsenberg, M. J., Dekimpe, M. G., & Steenkamp, J. B. E. (2013). Price and advertising effectiveness over the business cycle. *JMR, Journal of Marketing Research*, 50(2), 177–193. DOI: 10.1509/jmr.10.0414

Van Laar, E., van Deursen, A. J., Van Dijk, J. A., & de Haan, J. (2019). Twenty-first century digital skills for the creative industries workforce: Perspectives from industry experts. *First Monday*. Advance online publication. DOI: 10.5210/fm.v24i1.9476

Vatan, A., & Dogan, S. (2021). What do hotel employees think about service robots? A qualitative study in Turkey. *Tourism Management Perspectives*, 37, 100775. DOI: 10.1016/j.tmp.2020.100775

VDA. (2024), German Association of the Automotive Industry (VDA). (2024). August 2024 production and registration figures for the German automotive market. https://www.vda.de/en/press/press-releases/2024/240904_PM_National_PM_Production_and_market_in_August_2024

Venturi, F., Tonacci, A., Ascrizzi, R., Sansone, F., Conte, R., Pala, A. P., Tarabella, A., Sanmartin, C., Taglieri, I., Marangoni, R., Bietresato, M., Comuzzo, P., Zironi, R., Zironi, A., Ciotti, G., & Gubiani, R. (2024). "CANTINA 5.0"—A Novel, Industry 5.0-Based Paradigm Applied to the Winemaking Industry in Italy. *Applied Sciences (Basel, Switzerland)*, 14(11), 4777. DOI: 10.3390/app14114777

Verhoef, P. C., Broekhuizen, T., Bart, Y., Bhattacharya, A., Dong, J. Q., Fabian, N., & Haenlein, M. (2021). Digital transformation: A multidisciplinary reflection and research agenda. *Journal of Business Research*, 122, 889–901. DOI: 10.1016/j.jbusres.2019.09.022

Verma, R., & Singh, P. (2022). Organizational Strategies for AI Adoption: Mitigating Displacement Fears and Enhancing Productivity. *Journal of Organizational Behavior*, 43(7), 789–810.

Vial, G. (2019). Understanding digital transformation: A review and a research agenda. *The Journal of Strategic Information Systems*, 28(2), 118–144. DOI: 10.1016/j.jsis.2019.01.003

Vicente-Molina, M. A., Fernández-Sainz, A., & Izagirre-Olaizola, J. (2018). Does gender make a difference in pro-environmental behavior? The case of the Basque Country University students. *Journal of Cleaner Production*, 176, 89–98. DOI: 10.1016/j.jclepro.2017.12.079

Vidwans, A. (2024, julio 29). *IoT and Quality Control: Ensuring Precision and Reducing Defects* [LinkedIN]. https://www.linkedin.com/pulse/iot-quality-control-ensuring-precision-reducing-defects-amol-vidwans-dj2yf/

Voulgaridis, K., Lagkas, T., & Sarigiannidis, P. (2022). Towards Industry 5.0 and Digital Circular Economy: Current Research and Application Trends. *2022 18th International Conference on Distributed Computing in Sensor Systems (DCOSS)*, 153–158. DOI: 10.1109/DCOSS54816.2022.00037

Voulgaridis, K., Lagkas, T., Karampatzakis, D., Argyriou, V., & Sarigiannidis, P. (2023). Realizing Digital Product Passports with Crowdsourcing Principles: The Case of Sustainable Smart Grids. *2023 19th International Conference on Distributed Computing in Smart Systems and the Internet of Things (DCOSS-IoT)*, 381–388. DOI: 10.1109/DCOSS-IoT58021.2023.00068

Voulgaridis, K., Lagkas, T., Angelopoulos, C. M., Boulogeorgos, A.-A. A., Argyriou, V., & Sarigiannidis, P. (2024). Digital product passports as enablers of digital circular economy: A framework based on technological perspective. *Telecommunication Systems*, 85(4), 699–715. DOI: 10.1007/s11235-024-01104-x

Voulgaridis, K., Lagkas, T., Angelopoulos, C. M., & Nikoletseas, S. E. (2022). IoT and digital circular economy: Principles, applications, and challenges. *Computer Networks*, 219, 109456. DOI: 10.1016/j.comnet.2022.109456

Waldman, D., Javidan, M., & Varella, P. (2004). (2004). Charismatic leadership at the strategic level: A new application of upper echelons theory. *The Leadership Quarterly*, 15(3), 355–380. DOI: 10.1016/j.leaqua.2004.02.013

Wang, K. (2006). M., & Thi, T.-B. N. (2006). Does Contagion Effect Exist Between Stock Markets of Thailand and Chinese Economic Area (CEA) during the "Asian Flu?". *Asian Journal of Management and Humanity Sciences*, 1(1), 16–36.

Warner, K. S., & Wäger, M. (2019). Building dynamic capabilities for digital transformation: An ongoing process of strategic renewal. *Long Range Planning*, 52(3), 326–349. DOI: 10.1016/j.lrp.2018.12.001

WCED. 1987, Our Common Future, Oxford University Press, 1987, https://sustainabledevelopment.un.org/content/documents/5987our-common-future.pdf

Web Magazine, W. O. W. (2021). SUSTAINABILITY IS CHANGING THE FURNITURE INDUSTRY, LET'S FIND OUT HOW. *Ways of Working WOW!*https://wow-webmagazine.com/sustainability-is-changing-the-furniture-industry-lets-find-out-how

Weber, E., Büttgen, M., & Bartsch, S. (2022). How to take employees on the digital transformation journey: An experimental study on complementary leadership behaviors in managing organizational change. *Journal of Business Research*, 143, 225–238. DOI: 10.1016/j.jbusres.2022.01.036

Weber, E., Krehl, E. H., & Büttgen, M. (2022). The digital transformation leadership framework: Conceptual and empirical insights into leadership roles in technology-driven business environments. *Journal of Leadership Studies*, 16(1), 6–22. DOI: 10.1002/jls.21810

Weiner, B. (2009). A theory of organizational readiness to change. *Implementation Science : IS*, 4(1), 1–9. DOI: 10.1186/1748-5908-4-67 PMID: 19840381

Wei, S., Ang, T., & Jancenelle, V. E. (2018). Willingness to pay more for green products: The interplay of consumer characteristics and customer participation. *Journal of Retailing and Consumer Services*, 45, 230–238. DOI: 10.1016/j.jretconser.2018.08.015

Wells, W. D. ve Prensky, D. (1996). *Consumer Behavior*. Kanada: John Wiley & Sons, Inc

Whelan, T., & Fink, C. (2016). The Comprehensive Business Case for Sustainability. *Harvard Business Review*. Retrieved from https://hbr.org/2016/10/the-comprehensive-business-case-for-sustainability

White, K., Hardisty, D. J., & Habib, R. (2019, julio). The Elusive Green Consumer. *Harvard Business Review*. https://hbr.org/2019/07/the-elusive-green-consumer

Wong, L. W., Tan, G. W. H., Ooi, K. B., Lin, B., & Dwivedi, Y. K. (2024). Artificial intelligence-driven risk management for enhancing supply chain agility: A deep-learning based dual-stage PLS-SEM-ANN analysis. *International Journal of Production Research*, 62(15), 5535–5555. DOI: 10.1080/00207543.2022.2063089

World Bank. (2020). COVID-19 to plunge global economy into worst recession since World War II. Available at: https://www.worldbank.org/en/news/press-release/2020/06/08/covid-19-to-plunge-global-economy-into-worst-recession-since-world-war-ii

World Bank. (2020). *Indonesia economic prospects: Towards a secure and fast recovery*. World Bank.

World Economic Forum. (2020), The Future of Jobs Report 2020

World Furniture online. (2024, octubre). Priorities and Perspectives of Digital Solutions in the Furniture Industry. *World Furniture Online*. https://www.worldfurnitureonline.com/trends/priorities-and-perspectives-of-digital-solutions-in-the-furniture-industry/

Worldometers (2024), World population by year. Retrieved from https://www.worldometers.info/world-population/world-population-by-year/

Wright, P. M., & Schultz, L. (2018). Organizational Readiness for Change: Integrating Employee and Management Perspectives. *Journal of Organizational Change Management*, 31(3), 523–538.

www.bnb.bg- Statistics,2005-2024

www.nsi.bg– Macroeconomic data, 2016-2024

Xie, D., & He, Y. (2022). Marketing Strategy of Rural Tourism Based on Big Data and Artificial Intelligence. *Mobile Information Systems*, 2022, 2022. DOI: 10.1155/2022/9154351

Yang, S., & Du, P. (2022). The Application of 3D Printing Technology in Furniture Design. *Scientific Programming*, 2022, 1–7. DOI: 10.1155/2022/1960038

Yao, Q., Tang, H., Liu, Y., & Boadu, F. (2024). The penetration effect of digital leadership on digital transformation: The role of digital strategy consensus and diversity types. *Journal of Enterprise Information Management*, 37(3), 903–927. DOI: 10.1108/JEIM-09-2022-0350

Yazdanparast, A., & Kukar-Kinney, M. (2023). The effect of product touch information and sale proneness on consumers' responses to price discounts. *Psychology and Marketing*, 40(1), 146–168. DOI: 10.1002/mar.21755

Yilmaz, M. K., Hacioglu, U., Tatoglu, E., Aksoy, M., & Duran, S. (2023). Measuring the impact of board gender and cultural diversity on corporate governance and social performance: Evidence from emerging markets. *Economic research-. Ekonomska Istrazivanja*, 36(2), 2106503. DOI: 10.1080/1331677X.2022.2106503

Yüksel, C. A., & Okumuş, A. (2001). Çevre Dostu Ürün Satınalma İle İlgisi Bulunan Değişkenlerin Belirlenmesine Yönelik Araştırma. *Yönetim Dergisi:İstanbulÜniversitesi İşletme Fakültesi İşletme İktisadi Enstitüsü*, 12(40), 29–38.

Yung, R., & Khoo-Lattimore, C. (2019). New realities: A systematic literature review on virtual reality and augmented reality in tourism research. *Current Issues in Tourism*, 22(17), 2056–2081. DOI: 10.1080/13683500.2017.1417359

Zahra, N. (2023). Role of artificial intelligence technology in the development of furniture design Process. *International Design Journal*, 13(6), 503–520. DOI: 10.21608/idj.2023.320147

Zaichkowsky, J. L. (1985). Measuring the Involvement Construct. *The Journal of Consumer Research*, 12(3), 341–352. DOI: 10.1086/208520

Zaki, M. (2019). Digital transformation: Harnessing digital technologies for the next generation of services. *Journal of Services Marketing*, 33(4), 429–435. DOI: 10.1108/JSM-01-2019-0034

Zhao, W., Yin, C., Hua, T., Meadows, M. E., Li, Y., Liu, Y., Liu, Y., Cherubini, F., Pereira, P., & Fu, B. (2022). Achieving the Sustainable Development Goals in the post-pandemic era. *Humanities & Social Sciences Communications*, 9(1), 1–7. DOI: 10.1057/s41599-022-01283-5 PMID: 35967482

Zhao, Y. (2024). Internet of Things Technology in Smart Furniture: An Overview. *Journal of Electrotechnology. Electrical Engineering and Management*, 7(1). Advance online publication. DOI: 10.23977/jeeem.2024.070114

Zhen, M., & Ding, W. (2024). Empowering employees for digital transformation in manufacturing enterprises: A case study. *South African Journal of Business Management*, 55(1), 4207. DOI: 10.4102/sajbm.v55i1.4207

Zhou, Y., Yan, S., Li, G., Xiong, Y., & Lin, Z. (2023). The impact of consumer skepticism on blockchain-enabled sustainability disclosure in a supply chain. *Transportation Research Part E, Logistics and Transportation Review*, 179, 103323. DOI: 10.1016/j.tre.2023.103323

Zhu, C., Qiu, Z., & Liu, F. (2021). Does innovation stimulate employment? Evidence from China. *Economic Modelling*, 94, 1007–1017. DOI: 10.1016/j.econmod.2020.02.041

Zhu, J., Zhang, B., Xie, M., & Cao, Q. (2022). Digital leadership and employee creativity: The role of employee job crafting and person-organization fit. *Frontiers in Psychology*, 13, 827057. DOI: 10.3389/fpsyg.2022.827057 PMID: 35615170

Zhu, Y.-Q., Corbett, J., & Chiu, Y.-T. (2020). Understanding employees' responses to artificial intelligence. *Organizational Dynamics*, •••, 1–10.

Zimmer, M. R., Stafford, T. F., & Stafford, M. R. (1994). Green issues: Dimensions ofenvironmental concern. *Journal of Business Research*, 30(1), 63–74. DOI: 10.1016/0148-2963(94)90069-8

Zurich Insurance Group. (2021), 5 green jobs of the future. Retrieved from https://www.zurich.com/media/magazine/2021/5-green-jobs-of-the-future

About the Contributors

Mehtap Özşahin received her BA degree from Bogaziçi University, Faculty of Economics and Administrative Sciences in 2001. She had her masters and Ph.D. degrees in the field of Management from Gebze Institute of Technology, in 2005 and 2011 respectively. She has taught courses and conducted research in the fields of strategic management, leadership, digital transformation, business ethics, international business and organizational behavior. She has held the co-chair (between the years of 2014-2021) and chair (since 2022) positions at International Strategic Management Conference, which is held annually for last 19 years. She also serves as a member of the organizing committee for two international conferences-International Strategic Management Conference and International Conference on Leadership, Technology, Innovation and Business Management since their inceptions in 2005 and 2011 respectively.

Vladimir Simović is the Head of Digital Economics Department at the Institute of Economic Sciences (IES) in Belgrade, Serbia and Associate Professor at the Australian University, Kuwait (AU). The areas of his professional interests are digital marketing, digital entrepreneurship, digital competencies, and information systems in business. He is a project manager of the European ESF+ project on digital marketing competencies and the participant of European COST Action on Artificial intelligence in business with 15+ years of experience in research and teaching. He is the founder of several digital start ups in Serbia as well as a think tank dedicated to innovative learning practices.

Alper Erturk obtained his B.Sc. in Industrial Engineering from Turkish Naval Academy, received his M.Sc. in Information Technology Management (with distinction) from Naval Postgraduate School, CA, USA in 2000. He got his Ph.D. in Management Science from Gebze Technical University, Turkey in 2003. Very recently, he obtained his Post Graduate Diploma in Data Science and Business Analytics from Texas University McCombs Business School, USA in 2023. Prof.

Erturk has been an active academician and researcher in Business Management & Analytics field for more than 15 years of experience in Turkey, the U.S., Belgium, Germany, Morocco, and Kuwait. Throughout his academic studies, he published 3 books, more than 30 articles, more than 10 book chapters and presented more than 30 papers in international academic conferences. He is an internationally recognized researcher with an h-index of 20 and i-index of 28. During his career, Prof.Ertürk achieved to receive many awards including "Most Cited Researcher of the year", "Outstanding Teaching Award", "Best Paper Award", as well as he was also a recipient of Fulbright Scholarship in 2019 and studied at Portland State University, OR, USA. Prof.Ertürk is currently working as a Full Professor and Chair of Management Department at Australian University – Kuwait since February 2022.

***

Mine Aksoy is a distinguished full professor in the Department of Business Administration, specializing in Accounting and Finance. With a rich academic career, she is actively involved in teaching both undergraduate and postgraduate courses, where she brings her extensive knowledge and research expertise to her students. Prof. Aksoy is also a dedicated reviewer for several high-ranking academic journals, contributing to the advancement of knowledge in her field. Her research is widely recognized, with numerous publications in prestigious international journals indexed by Web of Science (SSCI) and Scopus. Her commitment to academia and impactful research has established her as a respected figure in the field of accounting and finance.

Bilsen Bilgili is Associated Professor at Tourism Faculty, Kocaeli University, Turkey. Her research primarily focuses on marketing (brand equity, brand management, consumer behaviour, environmental marketing, tourism marketing).

Burcu Çam is Professor at Faculty of Economics and Administrative Sciences, Kocaeli University, Turkey. Her research primarily focuses on marketing (retail, social marketing, environmental marketing, service marketing, consumer behaviour).

Aysel Erciş is Professor at Faculty of Economics and Administrative Sciences, Ataturk University, Turkey. Her research primarily focuses on marketing (social marketing, environmental marketing, product management, consumer behaviour).

Tayfun Güven is Assistant Professor at Faculty of Economics Administrative Social Sciences, İstanbul Ayvansaray University, Turkey. His research primarily focuses on marketing (social marketing, product management, environmental marketing, service marketing, consumer behaviour).

Ana JIménez-Zarco is an Associate Professor of Innovation and Marketing. Economics and Business Department, Universitat Oberta de Catalunya (UOC). A part-time professor at ICADE. Pontificia of Comillas University Ph.D. in Economics and Business Sciences from the University of Castilla-la Mancha, Spain. Postdegre in Building Models in Ecology and Natural Resources Management from Politecnica University of Catalonia. Until 2002, She carried out her teaching and research activities in the Marketing Area of the University of Castilla la Mancha, and during short periods in East Anglia University, Brighton University (U.K) and Chapingo University (Mexic). From 2003 to 2006 she has been a co-director of the Master's Degree Programme in Marketing and Communication Management, and from 2006 to 2012 she was served as Programme Director of the Bachelor's Degree in Business Administration at UOC. As a researcher, her main areas of research interest concern product innovation, brand image and identity and marketing/e-learning interface. She is the author of several books and articles on these areas, and serve as a reviewer and associate editor of several international journals in the marketing area.

Ibrahim Sarper Karakadilar is a scholar member of Kahramanmaras Istiklal University. In 2011, Ibrahim Sarper Karakadilar earned his PhD in Business Management from the Gebze Institute of Technology (GYTE). He has been employed as a lecturer since 2012 and is currently teaching Transportation Systems, Freight Legislation, Customs Regulations, Lean Management, Project Management, System Analysis and Design. He has co-authored manuscripts with his colleagues published in 'Journal of Production Research', 'Expert Systems with Applications (ESWA)', and 'Total Quality Management Business Excellence'. His principal areas of research are logistics and supply chain management, marketing, lean operations, and other current issues in business and operation management.

Almudena Muñoz Puche is a Graduate in Chemistry from the University of Valencia, MBA from the Barcelona Business School and Master in Innovation and Digital Transformation from the UOC. Currently pursuing a PhD in the Inter-University Programme in Business Administration and Management at the Universitat Oberta de Catalunya. R&D project manager in the International Projects Department at CETEM. She has extensive experience in the preparation, management and justification of national and international R&D projects related to innovation, disruptive technologies, as well as Circular Economy and Industrial Symbiosis. She has more than 10 articles published thanks to her research and the results obtained in different projects. In addition, she is currently a collaborating professor at the Universitat Oberta de Catalunya.

Osvaldo Quelhas is a Doctor in Production Engineering (1994),on decision-making for supplier choices in the production chain, by Federal University of Rio de Janeiro, COPPE. With 22 years of professional experience: oil and gas industry and in engineering design and execution companies. I have international experience in training in Spain and Italy; Full Professor at the Fluminense Federal University at the School of Engineering, UFF. Participates as a professor and supervisor of the Master's and Doctoral Program of the Postgraduate Program in Production Engineering, Coordinator of the Doctorate in Sustainable Management Systems, Vice Coordinator of the Professional Master's Degree in Management Systems at the Department of Production Engineering, UFF. Ad Hoc Consultant. Vice Editor of BJO&PM Magazine - Brazilian Journal of Operations and Production Management (ISSN: 2237-8960) / president of ABEPRO (Association of Production Engineering) 2006-2007 and 2008-2009. Works in Production Management, Sustainable Production and Organizational Social Responsibility.

Tolga Tacettin Tuncer serves as a board member and the General Manager of One Dose Health, where he leads pioneering efforts in the fields of Healthcare Digital Transformation, AI-powered diagnostic support applications, and remote health management. His work focuses on integrating advanced technologies with healthcare practices, utilizing devices that monitor vital signs to ensure comprehensive, accessible, and data-driven health management solutions. Mr. Tuncer has a robust academic and professional foundation. With a bachelor's degree in computer engineering and a master's degree in information law, he combines technical expertise with a nuanced understanding of the legal frameworks that govern digital and health-related information. Currently, he is further advancing his academic credentials by pursuing a Ph.D. in Business Administration at Başkent University, where his research interests lie at the intersection of healthcare innovation, technology management, and organizational development. Prior to his current role, Mr. Tuncer amassed considerable experience in leading global organizations, including Microsoft, GE Healthcare, and UiPath. In these roles, he gained extensive expertise in technology management, strategic planning, and international business operations. Inspired by a commitment to contribute meaningfully to his home country, he transitioned to a role that would allow him to foster local and national growth in the healthcare informatics sector. This endeavor led to the establishment of an R&D initiative focused on creating innovative, locally-driven healthcare solutions. Today, he actively collaborates with a range of partners—including domestic and international companies, hospitals, universities, and research institutes—to develop and implement technology solutions that meet both local and global healthcare challenges. In addition to his responsibilities at One Dose Health, Mr. Tuncer holds the position of Executive Chair of the Turkish

Informatics Association, where he plays a key role in advancing Turkey's digital transformation agenda. Through this role, he advocates for policies and initiatives that support innovation, digital literacy, and data sovereignty, striving to empower Turkey's position in the global information and technology economy.

Berto Usman is an Assistant Professor of finance at the Department of Management, University of Bengkulu – Indonesia. He obtained his Ph.D (2020) from the Department of Economics and Management, University of Padua – Italy. Has was also a research associate (2018) at the Department of Accounting, University of Exeter – England. Prior to his Ph.D., he participated in several short-course programs (2015) at Marmara University, Istanbul. While, his M.Sc was obtained from Universitas Gadjah Mada (2012), and his bachelor was from the University of Bengkulu (2010). Currently, Berto is responsible for teaching at the undergraduate and postgraduate programs at the University of Bengkulu and Open University of Indonesia. His research interests lie at the intersection between the fields of accounting and finance; voluntary disclosure, corporate social responsibility (CSR), corporate governance, corporate finance, and capital markets, and digital business.

Pelin Vardarlıer is a Professor in Management and Organization at Balıkesir University in Balıkesir (Turkey). She worked as an Associate Professor in Management and Strategy at Istanbul Medipol University in Istanbul (Turkey). She received a Ph.D. in Business Administration at Beykent University, Turkey. She has worked in managerial and management positions in total quality and human resources departments in various sectors for more than 10 years. She has Innovative Entrepreneurs Empowering and Making Difference Mentoring and ICF Certified Professional Coaching training certificates. Her research interests cover topics in strategy and human resource management, such as leadership, mentoring, and coaching. She also focuses on digital transformation, digital HRM, gamification, and social media management. She performed research projects at the national and international levels. She has many articles and book chapters published on these subjects in the most indexed Springer, Scopus, SCI-Expanded, and SSCI journals. She worked as the head of the human resources management department at Istanbul Medipol University.

Abdül Kadir Varoğlu graduated from the Turkish Military Academy in 1979 as an Artillery officer with a Bachelor's degree in Business Administration. He later completed his Master's in Business Administration at Middle East Technical University in 1985 and earned his Ph.D. in Management from the Faculty of Political Science at Ankara University in 1992. Between 1984 and 2004, he served as a faculty member at the Turkish Military Academy, holding various roles including Head of the Management-Leadership Laboratory, Chair of the Department of Systems Management Sciences, Head of the Academic Advisory and Training Center, and founding Director of the Defense Sciences Institute. He also worked as a Human Resources Specialist at the Canadian Department of National Defence for one and a half years. In addition to his full-time roles, Prof. Varoğlu has lectured part-time in the Business Administration departments of Middle East Technical University, Ankara University's Faculty of Political Science, and Yeditepe University, as well as at TODAİE, the National Security Academy, the Ministry of National Defense SATEM, the War Academies (Land, Naval, and Air Forces), the National Defense University, the Center of Excellence for Counterterrorism, and the NATO School in Germany. He has also served as a delegate and chair in NATO's Individual Training Working Group. In late 2004, he retired from the Armed Forces with the rank of Colonel and an Associate Professorship. Currently, Prof. Varoğlu is a faculty member at Başkent University's Faculty of Economics and Administrative Sciences, where he has held various roles including Head of the Department of Business Administration, Dean of the Faculty of Economics and Administrative Sciences, Deputy Director of the Institute of Social Sciences, Coordinator of International Relations and Academic Assessment, and Director of the Strategic Research Center. For the past seven years, he has been serving as Vice Rector of the University. Prof. Varoğlu has published numerous national and international articles and books in areas such as Strategic Management, Leadership, Negotiation, International Management, the Management of International Military Operations, and Military Sociology.

Index

A

B

C

D

E

F

G

I

L

M

O

P

R

S

T

U

V

W

www.ingramcontent.com/pod-product-compliance
Lightning Source LLC
LaVergne TN
LVHW080610300926
849162LV00005B/1100
* 9 7 9 8 3 3 7 3 2 5 2 3 1 *